Introduction to C Programming: A Modular Approach

Second Edition

DAVID M. COLLOPY
Ohio University

Upper Saddle River, New Jersey
Columbus, Ohio

Library of Congress Cataloging-in-Publication Data

Collopy, David M.
    Introduction to C programming: a modular approach / David M. Collopy. -- 2nd ed.
        p. cm.
    ISBN 0-13-060855-6
    1. C (Computer program language)   I. Title.
    QA76.73.C15 C65 2003
    005.13'3--dc21   2002070426

Editor in Chief: Stephen Helba
Assistant Vice President and Publisher: Charles E. Stewart, Jr.
Production Editor: Alexandrina Benedicto Wolf
Production Coordination: Custom Editorial Productions, Inc.
Design Coordinator: Diane Ernsberger
Cover Designer: Linda Sorrells-Smith
Cover Image: Corbis Stock Market
Production Manager: Matthew Ottenweller

This book was set in Times Roman by Custom Editorial Productions, Inc., and was printed and bound by R. R. Donnelley & Sons Company. The cover was printed by The Lehigh Press, Inc.

Pearson Education Ltd.
Pearson Education Australia Pty. Limited
Pearson Education Singapore Pte. Ltd.
Pearson Education North Asia Ltd.
Pearson Education Canada, Ltd.
Pearson Educación de Mexico, S.A. de C.V.
Pearson Education—Japan
Pearson Education Malaysia Pte. Ltd.
Pearson Education, *Upper Saddle River, New Jersey*

10 9 8 7 6 5 4 3 2 1
ISBN: 0-13-060855-6

Dedicated to the memory of my father

Eugene R. Collopy

He taught me the value of hard work.

Also dedicated to my mother

Mickey

She has always been an inspiration to me.

And to my family for their support

Cindy, Ryan, and Suzie Q

Preface

This book is designed as an introduction to computer programming using the C programming language. It is written for anyone who wants to learn to program in C but who has little or no previous programming background or mathematics beyond high school algebra. Its simplified approach stresses top-down logic design and modular structured programming with business applications.

The text presents the C language at a level that new students or programmers can understand. It may be used as a one-semester or two-quarter introduction to computer programming for technology, computer science, business, social science, or physical science students.

This exciting new edition makes C interesting and fun for students to learn and easy for the instructor to teach.

Special Features

Teaching by Example

The text takes a "teach by example" approach that both simplifies and reinforces the learning process by showing examples of how the programming elements work. Each chapter introduces two or more complete sample programs that illustrate how the textbook material can be applied to actual programming applications.

Furthermore, each sample program illustrates the program development process from start to finish. This process includes defining the format of the input and output, identifying the processing requirements, developing the logic, and coding the program. The output of each sample program is shown after the program code.

Incorporation of the Program Development Process

The program development process is emphasized throughout the textbook. More than forty complete sample programs are illustrated. (These are not short segment programs, but comprehensive programming applications.) The reader is introduced early to the importance of using top-down logic design and modular structured programming to construct high-quality, easy-to-read programs. For each sample program, the complete logic design is shown—hierarchy charts, pseudocode, and program flowcharts—as well as the other steps in the program development process.

Conversational Tone

The text's conversational tone makes it easy to read for new programmers. Many programming C textbooks are written at a technical level, but care has been taken here to simplify complex topics and present them at a level students can understand.

Program Dissections

Each sample program is dissected, taking the reader through the code step by step and explaining how the program statements work together to produce the output. The program dissections help students understand the code and the programming process.

Notes and Tips

Notes and tips are found at the end of each sample program. They provide additional information about the statements and functions presented in the sample program, as well as things to remember, things to look out for, coding tips, and traps to avoid.

Self-Paced Tutorials

The self-paced tutorials give students the opportunity to analyze a problem, study the logic, enter the source code, and test and debug the sample programs; this process gives students a chance to see how everything fits together. Since many students "learn by doing," the tutorial approach provides the hands-on skills they need to be successful. The tutorials also help prepare them for the end-of-chapter programming projects.

Checkpoint Exercises

Checkpoint exercises, which appear throughout the textbook, reinforce the main topics covered in the chapters. The exercises include self-directed questions and activities that provide feedback to students on how well they understand the material covered since the last checkpoint. Answers to the checkpoint exercises appear in the Instructor's Manual.

Chapter Summaries

The chapter summaries highlight important concepts, define key terms, and describe major programming elements. The summaries provide a comprehensive review that helps reinforce the chapter material.

Programming Projects

Every chapter contains programming projects that give students the opportunity to apply the material. Different programming projects may be assigned or the same project may be expanded, using a spiral approach, as new material is covered.

Menu-Driven Programming

Menu-driven programs are introduced in Chapter 6. This chapter includes topics on data validation, guidelines for creating effective menu systems, and techniques for menu selection processing. This topic is presented in an easy-to-follow manner.

Comprehensive Coverage of Files

Comprehensive coverage of sequential files, random access files, and indexed files is presented. These important topics are covered (including file-update processing) from top to bottom in a nontechnical manner that the reader can understand.

C/C++ Compiler

A special edition of Microsoft Visual C++ compiler is packaged with the textbook. The compiler allows users to write, test, and execute C programs on their microcomputers.

Teaching Strategy

This book takes a unique approach to presenting pointers and local/global variables. Pointers are introduced in the text as needed; the use of local/global variables is presented from a business programming perspective.

Pointers

Students normally have difficulty grasping the concept of pointers. Instead of presenting pointers all at once in one chapter, when a situation calls for a pointer, it is explained and illustrated. This approach makes it easier for the reader to understand when and why pointers are necessary, as well as how to use them.

Global and Local Variables

This text departs from "traditional" C in its approach to global and local variables. Although it is reasonable to argue that local variables protect the variables in one function from errors made in another, this isn't necessarily the best way to develop a program to meet the needs of a business. Corporate applications differ from retail applications and require a different design strategy.

Essentially, local variables are used to build applications that require a series of features commonly found in software packages developed for retail sales. Global variables, on the other hand, are often used to construct corporate applications that are developed and maintained by in-house programmers.

Although local variables are used in this text, their use is not extreme. If a variable can better serve the application by being declared as local, it is. On the other hand, if a variable can better serve the application by being declared as global, it is.

Instructor's Manual

The Instructor's Manual provides planning guidelines and teaching tips. It includes the following materials for each chapter: learning objectives; study guides; lecture outlines; answers to checkpoint exercises; test bank (multiple choice and true/false questions); and solutions to the test bank. The test bank comes with Test Manager software that allows the instructor to generate a variety of unique exams and quizzes.

Acknowledgments

First and foremost, I would like to express my sincere gratitude and thanks to all the people who contributed helpful comments and suggestions for improving this text, including the following: Ann Burroughs, Humbolt State University; John Corwin, University of Austin; Carl C. Hommer, Purdue University North Central; Usha R. Jindal, Washtenaw Community College; Bill Martin, Oklahoma State University; Philip Regalbuto, Trident Technical College; and Edwin C. Sheffield, Jr., Northeast State Technical Community College.

A special thanks goes to my family—Cindy, Ryan, and Suzie Q (the family pet)—for giving me the support and quiet time that I needed to make this book a success. A big thank you goes out to my former student, Cathy Young, who spent a great deal of time proofreading the material and offering constructive suggestions.

I would also like to thank the editorial staff at Prentice Hall for their dedication, leadership, and effort in turning this manuscript into a unique introduction to C programming.

David M. Collopy

Contents

7 TEXT FILES 227

8 PAGE AND CONTROL BREAKS 267

9 MULTILEVEL CONTROL BREAKS 305

10 ARRAYS AND SORTING 353

11 MULTIDIMENSIONAL ARRAYS 407

12 SEQUENTIAL FILES 451

13 UPDATING SEQUENTIAL FILES 485

14 STRUCTURES AND RANDOM FILES 551

15 INDEXED FILES 611

1   Basic Concepts

Overview

Learning Objectives

After you have read this chapter and completed the exercises, you should be able to

- define the term *computer* and discuss the hardware and software components associated with computers
- discuss the hierarchical organization of data
- understand the program development process
- distinguish between syntax and logical errors
- describe the process that C goes through to convert source statements into an executable program
- design and write simple programming applications in C

What Is a Computer?

A **computer** is an electronic device that accepts input, processes it according to a given set of instructions, and provides the results of the processing. This process is shown schematically in Figure 1.1. **Input** is a term used to define the **data**, or unprocessed facts, manipulated by the computer. **Output** refers to the processed information, or results, produced by the computer. Output takes many forms. Some examples of output are a list of names or values, a payroll check, a ticket to a baseball game, a printed report, and an updated file.

Essentially, a computer converts data into meaningful information. It is an electronic data processing device with internal storage for holding data and program instructions. Although a computer can perform complex computations with extraordinary speed and accuracy, it cannot do anything on its own. It must be told what to do every step of the way. The instructions that the computer follows are called a **program**, and the individual responsible for writing computer programs is called a **programmer**.

A **computer system** consists of software (the instructions for processing the data) and hardware (the physical equipment used to process the data). **Software** includes application programs and the operating system. **Hardware** consists of input/output devices and the central processing or system unit. We shall discuss these components in the sections that follow.

FIGURE 1.1   Basic Functions Performed by the Computer

The Computer System

Software Concepts

Software tells the computer what to do. It issues commands and directs the hardware in performing its work. There are two major types of software: applications and systems software.

Written for end-users, **applications software** is designed to perform a specific task, such as billing customers, administering payroll, taking inventory, or collecting accounts receivables. An **end-user** is anyone who uses a computer system to perform a task related to data processing. Application software may be acquired by purchasing off-the-shelf packages or by designing and creating them for one's own purpose (custom made).

Packaged, or **off-the-shelf**, programs are prewritten and ready to use. They are available from many retail outlets and software firms. There are thousands of packaged programs on the market today designed for many different applications.

Custom-made programs are usually written by in-house trained professionals employed as programmers or by outside consulting firms specializing in custom programming. In business, applications software has one main objective—to provide management with accurate, up-to-date, and timely information about the operations of the company.

Systems software is normally supplied by the manufacturer of the computer system and consists of utility programs and operating aids that facilitate the use and performance of the computer. It includes the computer's operating system and related software that manages the system's resources and controls the operations of the hardware.

The **operating system** acts as an interface between the applications software and the computer itself. It allows the user to enter and run application programs. Other functions performed by the operating system include managing internal resources, controlling input/output operations, translating program statements into machine code, scheduling and running jobs, and organizing and manipulating files.

Hardware Concepts

Hardware is the physical components of the computer system. It includes input/output devices, the central processing unit, and secondary storage devices. The term **hardware** refers to the actual equipment used to process the input data.

Input devices, such as the keyboard and mouse, are used to enter data and programs into the computer. They translate input that people understand into electronic signals that the computer understands.

Output devices, such as printers and monitors, on the other hand, are used to display the results processed by the computer. They translate the electronic signals that the computer understands into a form that people understand.

The **central processing unit** (CPU) is considered to be the heart of the computer. It is responsible for processing the data and producing the output. The CPU is composed of the control unit, the arithmetic/logic unit, and the storage unit, as shown in Figure 1.2.

The **control unit** supervises and monitors the activities performed by the computer system. It does not process the data itself, but directs the processing operations and coordinates the flow of data to the arithmetic/logic and storage units.

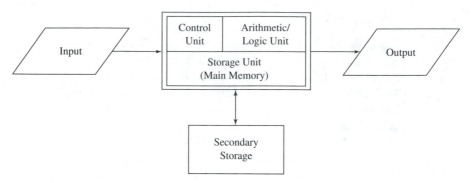

FIGURE 1.2   The Computer System

After the control unit instructs the input device to load the program and data, it interprets the program statements one at a time and tells the arithmetic/logic unit to carry out the instructions. It also tells the input device when to read more data and the output device when to write the results.

As the name implies, the **arithmetic/logic unit** (ALU) performs the arithmetic and logical operations required by the program. Arithmetic computations include addition, subtraction, multiplication, and division. Logical operations involve comparing the values of two data items to determine if one value is equal to, less than, or greater than the other. Hence, the major function of the ALU is to do the work, that is, to carry out the processing activities specified by the program.

The **primary storage unit**, or main memory, accepts input data, program instructions, intermediate results and values, and processed information and temporarily stores them for subsequent processing. Before the computer can execute a program, the instructions and data must reside within the computer's memory.

There are two important facts to know about the storage unit. First, the amount of storage space is limited; only a finite number of characters can be held at any one time. Second, the contents of storage are nonpermanent and are only temporarily maintained while the computer's power is on. Once the computer is turned off, the contents of main memory are lost and cannot be recovered unless they were previously saved to a secondary storage device.

Secondary storage media, such as magnetic tape or disks, permanently store data, programs, and processed information so that they are available to the computer on a per-need basis. That is, programs and data may be accessed by and transferred to the computer when they are called by the CPU. The contents of secondary storage remain intact until they are physically removed or deleted by the programmer.

Data Organization

Data is organized in a special way to facilitate processing by the computer. Individual characters entered at the keyboard can be organized into hierarchical structures ranging from simple data fields to complex networks of integrated databases.

```
                  (field 1)     (field 2)     (field 3)     (field 4)

                  Account       Customer      Credit        Balance
                  Number        Name          Limit         Due

(record 1)        12345         Brad Anders   5000.00       2500.00
(record 2)        16789         Tara Atkins   7000.00       5748.00
(record 3)        20161         Karen Baker   5000.00       0000.00
    :               :             :             :             :

    :               :             :             :             :

    :               :             :             :             :
(record n)        97865         Dave Zetler   3000.00       0125.00

                                 (character)
```

FIGURE 1.3   Customer File

As shown in Figure 1.3, fields can be grouped to form a record and records can be grouped to form a file. Note also that a field is simply a collection of characters.

The following list contains data organization terms and their definitions.

Character: A letter, numeric digit, punctuation mark, or special symbol such as %, @, &, and so on.

Field: A set of characters grouped together to form a single unit of data. For example, in Figure 1.3, five characters have been grouped together to form the customer's account number and eleven characters have been assigned to hold the customer's name.

Record: A set of logically related fields. In Figure 1.3, a record consists of the following fields: account number, customer name, credit limit, and balance due.

File: A finite set of logically related records. When records for a specific application are grouped together, they are called a file. For example, if an accounts receivable application services 2,453 customers, then the customer file would consist of 2,453 records.

Database: A set of integrated records or files. A database consists of a pool of centrally located files that may be accessed and processed by multiple applications. For example, a customer database could be set up to store the customer account files for the home office as well as the customer account files for all the branch offices.

Checkpoint 1A

1. Define the term *computer*.
2. Distinguish between applications software and systems software.
3. Explain the purpose of the input/output devices. Give examples of each.

4. Define the term *central processing unit* (CPU). Identify and explain the three components of the CPU.

5. Explain the difference between primary storage and secondary storage.

6. Explain how data is organized.

Planning the Program

Programs should be planned. Trial-and-error guesswork has no place in the programming profession. Designing a program can be compared to building an expressway. The engineer would lay out detailed plans before going through the time, trouble, and expense of building a complex network of highways. Construction would not begin until the completed plan had been carefully laid out in writing. Similarly, the programmer should plan carefully and write out the design for a program before sitting down at the computer. A good plan can save hours of frustration at the keyboard and produce successful results within a short period of time.

Structured program development not only saves time, it also increases programmer productivity. Programming can be a complex process involving a multitude of interrelated operations and computations. However, when the processing activities are planned carefully, even the most difficult application can be effectively and efficiently managed. When used properly, the seven-step program development process presented below will help to produce a more reliable program in less time and one that can be maintained more easily throughout its use.

The Program Development Process

Step 1: Define the problem

- Determine the objectives of the program. Write a brief statement or paragraph describing the purpose of the program.

Step 2: Analyze the problem

- Determine what the output should look like. Sketch a rough draft of the output. Use paper and pencil to lay out the fields, records, and files. Design and erase as you go.
- Determine the input. Use the output to determine the input data. Focus on identifying the input required by the program to produce the output.
- Define the processing tasks required by the program. Identify the steps, activities, or calculations required to manipulate the input data and produce the output.
- List the processing tasks on paper. Don't pay attention to their order; simply write them down as they are identified. Once all of the tasks have been listed, arrange them in processing order. If possible, group related tasks together, but only when it is obvious they belong together.

Step 3: Design the logic

- Use the ordered list of tasks identified in Step 2 to design the program logic. There are three basic design tools that may be used to develop the program logic—hierarchy charts, pseudocode, and program flowcharts. Pseudocode and flowcharting will be illustrated later in this chapter. Hierarchy charts will be introduced in Chapter 3.

- Desk check the program logic, and make corrections as needed. When the logic is complete, the programmer checks it over manually by tracing the flow of data through the logic. This process of verifying the logic is called **desk checking**. Of course, corrections are made until the logic produces the desired output.

Step 4: Code the program

- The hierarchy chart, pseudocode, or flowchart is used to translate the program logic into C statements. That is, the program is coded from the logic design. For the student programmer, this can be accomplished by writing out the program code on paper.
- Desk check the C statements, and make corrections as needed.

Step 5: Key in the program

- Using the C editor, enter the program code into the computer by keying in the statements.

Step 6: Test and debug the program

- Test the code by running the program. If errors are found during the run, it is the programmer's responsibility to fix those parts of the program that did not work. In programming, an error is called a **bug** and **debugging** refers to the process of eliminating errors. In short, a bug is any code that prevents a program from producing the correct output.

Step 7: Gather the program documentation

- Gather the documentation that you have created throughout the programming process. Documentation provides information about the program and is used as a reference when updating or maintaining the program. Documentation includes a statement of the problem, input/output definitions, a list of the processing functions, the logic design, a program listing, and samples of the output.

Designing Reports

For the most part, business application programs are written to provide management with meaningful information. Management uses this information to monitor the operations of the company and to assist its employees in making profitable decisions about the business.

But before any information can be produced by the computer, it must first be carefully planned. The data processing results should be organized so that they provide the information management needs. The output should provide meaningful, relevant, and timely information about the business enterprise.

Take a look at the computer-generated report shown in Figure 1.4. As simple as it may seem, it provides management with relevant information about the company's customers. It consists of column headings that form a four-column report with each customer's name, balance due, monthly payment made, and new balance.

The body of the report is made up of **detail lines**. The first detail line of the report gives information about the account belonging to a customer named Ayers. At the time the

```
CUSTOMER        BALANCE        MONTHLY          NEW
  NAME            DUE          PAYMENT        BALANCE

Ayers          500.00         200.00         300.00
Fontaine       750.00         600.00         150.00
Howard         400.00         300.00         100.00
Ryan           300.00         175.00         125.00
Walker         563.00         563.00         000.00

TOTALS        2513.00        1838.00         675.00
```

FIGURE 1.4   Accounts Receivable

report was generated, Ayers had a previous balance of $500, made a $200 payment, and currently owes $300. The customer named Walker, on the other hand, has paid in full.

This particular report shows the current status of the accounts receivable system. When customers call to ask their current balance due, management can retrieve this information readily. Similarly, management can use the information in the report to monitor overdue accounts.

The last line in Figure 1.4 shows report totals for balances due, monthly payments, and new balances.

Reports may vary significantly in design, size, and layout. Usually, clients have a rough idea of what they want the report to look like as well as the information it should contain. However, it may be necessary for the programmer to sit down and work with a client to design the layout of the report.

Forms and reports are designed to fit the horizontal and vertical spacing given for the printer being used. Common printer specifications for the micro- and mainframe computers are shown in Table 1.1. Spacing across the page is measured in **characters per inch** (CPI); spacing down the page is given as **lines per inch** (LPI). From the table, we see that the 80-character line printer for the microcomputer has a horizontal spacing of 10 CPI and a vertical spacing of 6 LPI.

The report shown in Figure 1.5, for Tamarack Automotive Services, was designed with the help of a **printer spacing chart** (see Figure 1.6). The printer spacing chart in Figure 1.6 is made up of rows and columns corresponding to the horizontal and vertical print positions of the printer. A programmer uses the print chart to design and lay out reports. Once the design is complete, the programmer codes C statements to set up page

TABLE 1.1   Printer Specifications

	Horizontal	**Vertical**
Micro	80-character line with 10 CPI	6 LPI
Mainframe	132-character line with 10–12 CPI	6–8 LPI

```
                    TAMARACK AUTOMOTIVE SERVICES
                         Accounts Receivable
                              mm/dd/yy


      CUSTOMER        BALANCE        MONTHLY         NEW
        NAME            DUE          PAYMENT       BALANCE


      Ayers           500.00        200.00        300.00
      Fontaine        750.00        600.00        150.00
      Howard          400.00        300.00        100.00
      Ryan            300.00        175.00        125.00
      Walker          563.00        563.00        000.00


      TOTALS:        2513.00       1838.00        675.00


      LARGEST NEW BALANCE   $ 300.00
      LARGEST PAYMENT MADE  $ 600.00
```

FIGURE 1.5   Output Report

titles, column headings, detail lines, and so on. The abbreviations PT, HL, DL, TL, and SL shown on the left side of the printer spacing chart stand for Page Title, Heading Line, Detail Line, Total Line, and Summary Line, respectively. They are notations that remind the programmer to define and assign names to the appropriate print lines at coding time. We shall discuss this topic further in the section that follows, entitled Report Planning Guidelines. Also note the use of the Xs and the 9s. They specify the maximum field size (print positions) reserved for printing character (X) and numeric (9) data.

Report Planning Guidelines

There are guidelines the programmer should follow when designing printer output for the user. The purpose of the guidelines is to provide a set of standards or procedures that help produce reports that are easier to read and understand. It can be extremely frustrating for the user to thumb through a stack of computer reports that are difficult to read or understand.

The following guidelines were used to design the report shown in Figure 1.5.

Step 1: Start on a new page
Start the report at the top of the page. Skip five or six lines before printing the page titles.

Step 2: Page titles
Center the page title *(PT)* by subtracting the number of characters in the line from 80. Then compute the starting position of the left margin by dividing the difference by 2. Code the line on the printer spacing chart beginning at the left margin. Single-space multiple page titles, and use *PT1, PT2, PT3,* and so on, to identify them.

PRINTER SPACING CHART

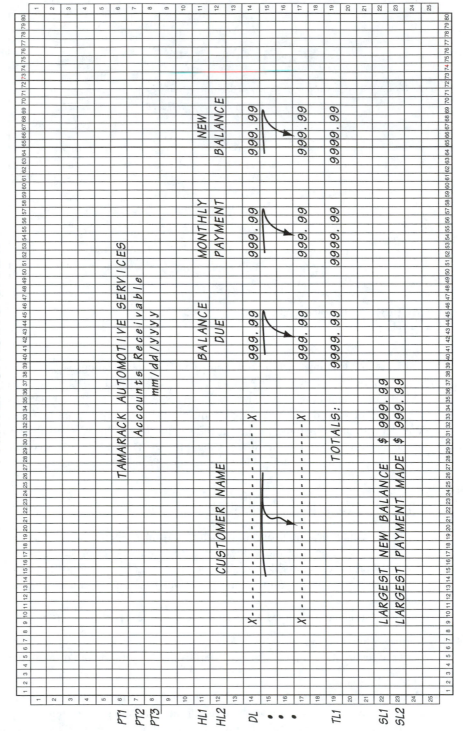

FIGURE 1.6 Printer Spacing Chart

10

Step 3: Heading lines

Skip two lines, and center the heading line *(HL)*. Unless instructed otherwise by the user, leave two blank lines between the last page title and the first heading line. Column headings are normally centered above the data to which they refer. Single-space multiple headings, and use *HL1, HL2, HL3,* and so on, to identify them.

> *Note:* Print the page titles, column headings, and page number at the top of each page.

Step 4: Detail lines

Skip a line, and print the first detail line *(DL)*. Detail lines represent the body of the report and are normally single spaced. They should be centered on the printer spacing chart before coding the column headings. Use the following method to center the detail lines. First, print one detail line on a piece of scrap paper. Second, decide how many spaces you want between the data items; usually, three to five blank spaces will do. Third, use the method described in step 2 to center the line. Center each column heading above the data to which it refers.

Step 5: Total lines

Use one or two blank lines to separate the last detail line from the first total line *(TL)*. Single-space multiple total lines, and use *TL1, TL2, TL3,* and so on, to identify them.

Step 6: Summary lines

Skip two lines, and print the summary line *(SL)*. Single-space multiple summary lines and use *SL1, SL2, SL3,* and so on, to identify them.

Compiling a Program

The compilation process that follows has been simplified to provide a basic understanding of how programs are executed by the computer. The exact details of this process are involved and complex and, therefore, are beyond the scope of this text.

Programmers write instructions in a programming language for the computer to follow. These English-like commands, called the **source program**, are read by the computer and stored in memory for subsequent processing. Since the computer cannot execute the source program in this form, each statement must undergo a series of transformations before it can be processed by the computer.

As Figure 1.7 shows, the source program is created by entering the C statements into the **text editor**. Next, the **compiler** translates the source program into an intermediate form called the object program. The **object program** represents the machine code equivalent of the source program. Each statement in the source program is read and scanned by the compiler. During the scanning process, the compiler translates the source statements into **machine code** (binary code that the computer understands) and checks for syntax errors.

If errors are detected, the compiler flags the erroneous statements and prints a list of **diagnostic error messages** that briefly describe any **syntax errors** (code that violates the rules for writing valid C statements). At this point, it is up to the programmer to fix the errors and recompile the program. This process of locating and fixing errors, called **debugging**, continues until the compiler indicates that no errors were found during the compilation.

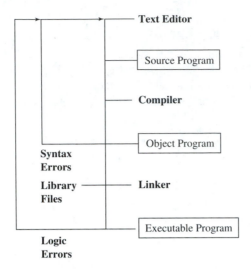

FIGURE 1.7   Compiler and Linker

Even though the object module (program) exists in machine code form, it cannot be executed directly by the computer. It must first undergo further transformation by the linker before the program is ready for execution. C programs normally contain references to precoded functions that are stored in libraries called header files. The primary objective of the **linker** is to include and insert the precompiled library code into the object program and to create an **executable program**.

The final step results in execution of the program. It is during the final step that the program produces the output.

Errors and Debugging

During program execution, one of three things may occur:

1. The computer detects one or more syntax errors.
2. The computer detects no syntax errors, but the output contains one or more logic errors.
3. The computer detects no syntax errors, and the program results in a clean run.

Case 1: Syntax Errors
If an error was detected during the run, then the program contains one or more syntax errors. A **syntax error** is an error that violates the rules of the programming language. In other words, a statement was incorrectly coded and has been rejected as erroneous. Often syntax errors are the result of misspelling or miskeying. Whatever the cause, syntax errors must be corrected and the source code recompiled before the program will run successfully.

Case 2: Logic Errors
A **logic error** is an error either in the design of the program or in the implementation of the design. At times, logic errors can be extremely difficult to locate. Unlike syntax errors, the computer has no way of detecting logic errors. Logic errors are usually the result of poor

program planning or faulty reasoning. Even though the statements coded are syntactically correct, the program produces incorrect output.

For example, if the programmer assigns the numeric value 4 to hours worked when 40 should have been assigned, the program will run but produce output different from what was expected. Also, if pay rate and hours worked were added instead of multiplied, the program would run but produce incorrect results.

Case 3: Clean Run

A **clean run** occurs when the program produces the correct output. It is often a surprise to the student programmer to discover that programs normally do not run cleanly on the first try. Programming involves managing a multitude of details and complex logic. Once this is understood, it is no longer a surprise to the student to see errors during a run. The major purpose of the program development process is to reduce the number and complexity of errors by applying a structured approach to managing the programming application.

Checkpoint 1B

1. What is the purpose of the program development process?
2. Identify and explain the seven steps in the program development process.
3. What is the purpose of the report planning guidelines?
4. Differentiate between a source program and an object program.
5. Explain the difference between a syntax error and a logic error.

Developing Our First Program

This section introduces our first C program. The program logic and code were developed using the program development process. Although the program is a relatively simple one, it is important to realize that the planning process can be applied to any application, simple or complex. Once you are familiar with the steps, you will be able to design the program logic and construct the code in less time.

Walk through the steps. Try to get a feel for how the planning process works.

Sample Program CHAP1A

Write a program to compute the course grade for Tara Nelson. Assume that Tara earned 45 out of 50 points on the midterm and 42 out of 50 points on the final exam. Compute the course grade by adding the points for the midterm and final exam.

Step 1: Define the problem

Write a program to compute the course grade for Tara Nelson.

Step 2: Analyze the problem

    Input: Midterm and final scores
    Processing: Course grade = midterm + final
    Output: Print the course grade

Step 3: Design the logic

Pseudocode: Pseudocode uses English-like statements to outline or describe the processing tasks performed by the program. The pseudocode for sample program CHAP1A is shown below.

```
START: Main
Initialize midterm to 45
Initialize final to 42
Calculate course grade
     midterm + final
Print course grade
END
```

Program Flowchart: A flowchart is a pictorial diagram that shows detailed processing steps and the order they are performed by the computer. Figure 1.8 shows the flowchart version of the program logic.

Figure 1.9 shows the major standard flowcharting symbols. The shape of each symbol indicates a particular type of activity. For example, a rectangle specifies a processing activity and a parallelogram specifies an input/output operation.

Step 4: Code the program

Use the logic design (hierarchy chart, pseudocode, or flowchart) to code the program on paper. Afterwards, walk through the code and make corrections as needed.

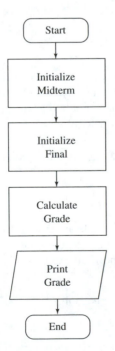

FIGURE 1.8   Program Flowchart for CHAP1A

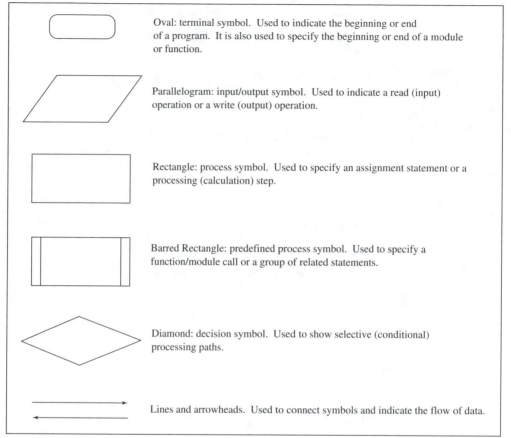

FIGURE 1.9   Standard Program Flowchart Symbols

Step 5: Key in the program
Use the program editor to enter the statements developed in step 4. The program code and output are shown in Figures 1.10 and 1.11, respectively.

Step 6: Test and debug the program
Test the code by executing the program. If errors are detected by the compiler, correct them and rerun the program.

Dissection of Sample Program CHAP1A

This is where we dissect and analyze the program code. Our purpose is to look at one statement or block of code at a time and explain what it does. As we go through the code, focus on understanding how the different parts of the program work together to produce the output.

```
/* COURSE GRADE: Compute the course grade for Tara Nelson. */
/* Author:    David M. Collopy                             */
```

```
/* COURSE GRADE: Compute the course grade for Tara Nelson. */
/* Author:    David M. Collopy                           */

#include <stdio.h>

main()
{
    /* declare variables */
    int iMidterm;                /* midterm grade */
    int iFinal;                  /* final grade   */
    int iGrade;                  /* course grade  */

    /* initialize variables */
    iMidterm = 45;
    iFinal = 42;

    /* calculate course grade */
    iGrade = iMidterm + iFinal;

    /* display the ouput on the screen */
    printf("Course grade is: %d", iGrade);

    return 0;
}
```

FIGURE 1.10   Program Code for CHAP1A

```
Course grade is: 87
```

FIGURE 1.11   Program Output for CHAP1A

A **comment** begins with /* and ends with */. Comments are used by the programmer to document the purpose of the program and to explain what the code does. The first **line comment** gives the title of the program and tells what the program does. The second line shows the programmer's name.

```
#include <stdio.h>
```

The **include statement** directs the computer to include the *stdio.h* header file in the program. In brief, this file contains precompiled code that enables the program to print the output. Since we intend to display Tara Nelson's course grade on the screen, the *#include* is required. This statement is covered in more detail in Chapter 2.

```
main()
{
```

All C programs begin with the **main function**. The opening and closing parentheses are required. This function signals the start of the program. The opening or **left brace** shown on the second line marks the beginning of the statement body of the *main* function. A C program normally consists of one or more functions. In general, a **function** represents a series of statements that perform a specific task.

```
/* declare variables */
```

The above line comment is used to describe the purpose of the block of code that follows. It indicates that this is where the program variables are declared. Note that this line is indented. For readability purposes, we will indent all statements coded in the body of a function four spaces.

```
int iMidterm;          /* midterm grade */
int iFinal;            /* final grade   */
int iGrade;            /* course grade  */
```

The above statements are declarations. **Declarations** are used to define the program variables. A **variable** is a data item that may assume different values. The variables *iMidterm*, *iFinal*, and *iGrade* are declared as integers (*int*). **Integers variables** hold whole numbers, which are numbers without decimal points—59, 71, 655, 1458, and so on. As a rule, we will append the prefix *i* to variable names that represent integer data items.

Note that declarations end with a **semicolon**; it marks the end of the statement. Also note the statement comments coded next to the declarations. Although optional, we will normally use **statement comments** to document the purpose of the program variables.

```
/* initialize variables */
iMidterm = 45;
iFinal = 42;
```

The first line states the purpose of the block of code. The next two lines initialize the variables *iMidterm* to 45 and *iFinal* to 42. Both statements assign the integer coded on the right side of the equal sign to the variable shown on the left side. Each statement terminates with a semicolon.

```
/* calculate course grade */
iGrade = iMidterm + iFinal;
```

The above **assignment statement** adds the value stored at *iFinal* to the value stored at *iMidterm* and assigns the sum to *iGrade*. The trailing semicolon is required. Addition, subtraction, multiplication, and division are specified by using the **arithmetic operators** +, -, *, and /, respectively. The arithmetic operators tell the computer what actions to perform on the data stored at the variables.

```
/* display output on the screen */
printf("Course grade is: %d", iGrade);
```

The **print statement** displays a message and the grade on the screen. It consists of a control string and the variable *iGrade*. The **control string** is enclosed within quotation marks (double quotes); it contains an output message and a format specifier. The *%d* is called a **format** or **conversion specifier**. It tells the computer to format *grade* as a decimal (*d*) integer field and to replace the specifier with the result. A semicolon marks the end of the statement.

When executed, the print statement displays `Course grade is: 87` on the screen. Notice how the formatted result replaced the conversion specifier in the control string.

```
return 0;
```

The above **return statement** returns a 0 to the operating system. A return value of 0 is commonly used to indicate a successful run.

```
}
```

All functions terminate with a right brace. The closing or **right brace** signals the end of the function. In this case, the right brace marks the end of the body of the main function and the end of the program.

Notes and Tips

1. Write a brief comment to explain what the program does, and put your name at the top of the program. Be sure to open a comment with /* and end it with */.
2. Don't forget to include the *stdio.h* file above the *main* function. Remember, include directives do not end with a semicolon.
3. Append the prefix *i* to all integer data items. This can save time since the variable name itself includes the data type—there is no need to look it up to see how it was declared. This will be particularly helpful when coding, debugging, or maintaining larger programs.
4. For readability purposes, make it a habit to indent (four spaces to the right) the statements coded in the body of the main function.
5. It may be a good idea (at least for now) to use blank lines to highlight and group certain sections of the code. (Note how they are used in the *main* function to block the code.) Grouping similar statements into logically related sections makes the program easier to read and understand.
6. Always terminate declarations and statements with a semicolon.

Tutorial CHAP1A

1. The objectives of this tutorial are to
   - practice entering and executing a C program
   - become familiar with your C editor/compiler system
   - identify and correct syntax and logic errors
2. Open your text editor, and insert your work disk in the appropriate drive. Your instructor will provide specific details for using the text editor and compiler system installed at your lab site.
3. Enter the comment lines and program statements exactly as shown in Figure 1.10. Pay close attention to spelling; indentation; and placement of double quotes, semicolons, parentheses, and braces.

4. Save the program on your work disk as CHAP1A.

5. Execute (compile and run) your program. If syntax or logic errors are found, debug the code. In other words, check for keyboarding errors—compare your code with the statements shown in the sample program. Correct the errors, save, and execute the program again.

6. Once the program produces the correct output (see Figure 1.11), show the results to your instructor.

Quick Quiz

Answer the following questions.

1. What is the purpose of the *#include* statement?

2. Are the opening and closing braces shown in the *main* function really necessary?

3. Discuss the purpose of the *declaration* statements.

4. Define the term *integer variable*.

5. Why do you append the prefix *i* to the variable names?

6. Why do you indent the statements in the body of the *main* function?

7. Explain what the *%d* conversion specifier does.

8. Did you have any problems or errors when you ran the sample program? If so, what were they and what did you do to correct them?

Sample Program CHAP1B

Sample program CHAP1B computes the total pay earned by an employee who is paid $25.10 per hour and has worked 38 hours during the week. The flowchart is shown in Figure 1.12, and the program code is shown in Figure 1.13. the output is shown in Figure 1.14.

The following specifications apply:

Input (internal):

Define and initialize the program variables. Use the variable names and values shown below.

    payrate = 25.10
    hours = 38

Output (screen):

Use the variable name *totalPay* for the output, and print the following information on the screen.

```
Author          Payroll Program          mm/dd/yy

Total pay is $ 999.99
```

Note: 9s are used to specify the maximum field size reserved for printing numeric data.

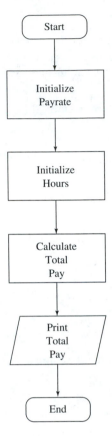

FIGURE 1.12   Program Flowchart for CHAP1B

Processing Requirements:

- Define and initialize the program variables.
- Compute the total pay:
  payrate × hours.
- Print the output on the screen.

Pseudocode:

        START: Main
        Initialize payrate to 25.10
        Initialize hours to 38
        Calculate total pay:
            payrate x hours
        Print title line
        Print total pay
        END

Program Flowchart: See Figure 1.12.

```
/*--------------------------------------------------------
TOTAL PAY: Compute total pay given the payrate and hours
worked.

Program:    CHAP1B.C
Author:     David M. Collopy
Date:       mm/dd/yy
Project:    Sample program
************************************************************/

#include <stdio.h>

main()
{
    /* declare variables */
    float fPayrate;              /* hourly pay rate */
    int   iHours;                /* hours worked    */
    float fTotPay;               /* total pay       */

    /* initialize variables */
    fPayrate = 25.10;
    iHours = 38;

    /* calculate total pay */
    fTotPay = fPayrate * iHours;

    /* display output on the screen */
    printf("DCollopy    Payroll Program    mm/dd/yy\n\n");
    printf("Total pay is $ %6.2f", fTotPay);

    return 0;
}
```

FIGURE 1.13   Program Code for CHAP1B

```
DCollopy      Payroll Program        mm/dd/yy

Total pay is $ 953.80
```

FIGURE 1.14   Program Output for CHAP1B

Dissection of Sample Program CHAP1B

```
/*----------------------------------------------------------------
TOTAL PAY: Compute total pay given payrate and hours worked.

Program:     CHAP1B.C
Author:      David M. Collopy
Date:        mm/dd/yy
Project:     Sample program
***************************************************************/
```

The above lines are comments. Recall that comments are enclosed between /* and */. For the remainder of this text, we will use this method to document the purpose of the program and to identify the program name, author, current date, and information about the project (lab number, page number, project number, and so on).

```
#include <stdio.h>
```

The above statement enables the program to display output on the screen. It tells the computer to include the *stdio.h* header file in the program.

```
main()
{
```

The first statement defines the main function. The second statement (left brace) marks the beginning of the body of the main function.

```
    /* declare variables */
    float fPayrate;
    int   iHours;
    float fTotPay;
```

The above statements declare the program variables. The variables *fPayrate* and *fTotPay* are declared as *float*, and *iHours* is declared as an integer. **Float variables** hold floating-point numbers, which are numbers with decimal points—7.0, 59.14, 213.45, 925.615, and so on. As a standard, we will append the prefix *f* to variable names that represent floating-point data items.

```
    /* initialize variables */
    fPayrate = 25.10;
    iHours = 38;
```

The above statements assign the constant or value on the right side of the equal sign to the variable on the left. Hence, *fPayrate* equals 25.10 and *iHours* equals 38. Note that a floating-point value is assigned to a float variable and an integer value is assigned to an integer variable. In general, you should match the data type of the constant to the data type of the variable.

```
    /* calculate total pay */
    fTotPay = fPayrate * iHours;
```

In this statement, the program multiplies the value stored at *fPayrate* times the value stored at *iHours* and assigns the product to *fTotPay*.

```
/* display output on the screen */
printf("DCollopy     Payroll Program     mm/dd/yy\n\n");
```

The print statement displays the message string enclosed within double quotes on the screen. When executed, this statement displays the programmer's name, the report title, and the date on the screen. The \n is called a **newline character**. One \n forces a single space down the screen; two force a double space. Since the newline characters are placed at the end of the message string, the print statement executes a double space after printing the line. The \n\n is not part of the printed message. It is, however, used to control the spacing of the output.

```
printf("Total pay is $ %6.2f", fTotPay);
```

The above statement displays a message string and total pay on the screen. The conversion specifier (%6.2f) formats total pay as a fixed-length floating-point (f) field and replaces the specifier with the result. In other words, total pay is formatted and placed in a field that is six positions wide (6.2) with two positions to the left of the decimal point. The decimal point counts as part of the field width (999.99).

When executed, the print statement displays `Total pay is $ 953.80` on the screen. Notice how the formatted result replaced the conversion specifier in the control string.

```
    return 0;
}
```

The above statement returns a 0 to the operating system, and the closing brace signals the end of the main function.

Notes and Tips

1. If you forget or misplace parts of a statement, the compiler may produce an error message that seems cryptic and totally unrelated to the cause of the problem. In time, you will be able to decipher these strange error messages and figure out the problem.

2. Always enclose the statement body of the main function with left and right braces, respectively.

3. Once again, be sure to terminate all declaration, assignment, print, and return statements with a semicolon. However, do not code a semicolon after the *main()* function; function names do not require ending punctuation.

4. Since print statements can be tricky, be sure to enclose the control string within a pair of double quotes and separate the variable name from the control string with a comma. In turn, enclose the entire print statement within a pair of parentheses.

5. Watch out for those conversion specifiers too. At this point, they should begin with a % and end with either a *d* (integer) or an *f* (float).

6. Float conversion specifiers should specify a field width and decimal positions. Make the conversion specifier big enough to hold the largest (or in some cases, the smallest) possible value.

Tutorial CHAP1B

1. The objectives of this tutorial are to
   - use integer and floating-point variables
   - print the output in report format
   - get more practice working with errors

2. If necessary, open your text editor and enter the sample program shown in Figure 1.13.

3. Save the program on your work disk as CHAP1B.

4. Execute the program, and correct any errors detected by the compiler. Compare your screen output with the results shown in Figure 1.14. If the output is not the same, check your code for errors and execute the program again. *Warning:* Always save your program after making corrections to it.

5. Once your output is correct, show the results to your instructor.

Quick Quiz

Answer the following questions:

1. Differentiate between a floating-point number and an integer.

2. What is the \n called? Describe what \n\n does.

3. Why do you append the prefix *f* to a floating-point variable?

4. In your own words, describe what happens when computer processes the following statement:

   ```
   fTotPay = fPayrate * iHours;
   ```

5. When executed, what exactly does the conversion specifier *%8.3f* do? How many digits are there to the left of the decimal point?

6. Did you have any problems or errors when you ran the sample program? If so, what were they and what did you do to correct them?

Creating Identifier Names

C has a set of rules for creating identifier names. **Identifiers** are programmer-defined names. Identifiers are used to describe variables, constants, modules, and functions, as well as other elements in the program. The rules for creating identifiers are as follows:

1. A name may contain up to 32 characters.

2. A name may consist of letters (uppercase and lowercase), numeric digits, and the underscore.

3. A name may *not* begin with a numeric digit.

4. A name may *not* include blanks or special characters.

5. A name may *not* be a **keyword** (words reserved by C that have special meaning).

Each name should be meaningful and self-documenting. Examples of valid identifiers are *InputData, quantity, date_of_birth, payrate, _netPay,* and *item_cost_.* Examples of invalid identifiers are *1st_name, total count, $VALUE, ID-NUMBER, *TaxTotal,* and *%increase.*

Case Sensitivity

C is case-sensitive. For example, C interprets *taxrate, TaxRate,* and *TAXRATE* as three different identifier names. It is important to keep case sensitivity in mind when coding statements in C.

Although identifiers may be written in upper- and/or lowercase letters, there are situations that stipulate that certain elements be coded in upper- or lowercase. We will discuss these cases as they occur.

Keywords

An identifier is a programmer-defined name that describes various elements in the program, whereas a keyword is a predefined name that indicates a specific action or operation. Essentially, a **keyword** is a reserved word that has special meaning to the compiler. As such, keywords may not be redefined or used in the program as identifiers. Although they may vary from one system to another, the standard keywords are as follows:

auto	double	int	struct
break	else	long	switch
case	enum	register	typedef
char	extern	return	union
const	float	short	unsigned
continue	for	signed	void
default	goto	sizeof	volatile
do	if	static	while

Checkpoint 1C

1. Identify two methods used to design program logic.
2. For the identifier names given below, indicate whether they are valid or invalid.
    a. _answer_
    b. 2nd_chance
    c. street number
    d. balanceDue
    e. total_expense$
    f. discount%
    g. sum.total
    h. xYz
    i. payment-code
    j. _result
3. Distinguish between identifiers and keywords.
4. Explain what is meant by the statement "C is case-sensitive."

Summary

1. A computer is an electronic device that accepts input, processes it according to a given set of instructions, and provides the results in the form of output.

2. Instructions written for the computer to follow are called a program, and the individual responsible for writing computer programs is called a programmer.

3. Applications software is designed to perform a specific task, such as billing customers, administering payroll, taking inventory, or collecting accounts receivable.

4. Systems software is normally supplied by the manufacturer of the computer system and consists of utility programs and operating aids that facilitate the use and performance of the computer.

5. Hardware is the physical components of the computer and includes input/output devices, the central processing unit, and secondary storage devices.

6. Data is organized into fields, records, files, and databases to facilitate processing by the computer.

7. The program development process represents a structured approach to constructing programs that are more reliable and easier to understand and maintain. The seven-step procedure includes defining the problem, analyzing the problem, designing the logic, coding the program, keying in the program, testing and debugging the program, and gathering the program documentation.

8. Programmers use hierarchy charts, pseudocode, and program flowcharts to design program logic.

9. A printer spacing chart is used to plan printer-generated output. It consists of a grid of rows and columns that are used to design the format of the report.

10. A program is compiled and translated into machine code before it can be executed by the computer. Since the computer cannot execute the source program in its current form, each statement must undergo a series of transformations before it can be processed by the computer.

11. Errors can be made in either syntax or logic. A syntax error occurs when the rules for constructing a valid statement are violated. A logic error occurs when the program produces incorrect results.

12. In general, identifiers are programmer-defined names that describe the variables, constants, modules, and functions required by the program.

13. An identifier name may include letters, digits, and the underscore. An identifier may not include a blank space, be the same as a keyword, or begin with a digit.

14. C is case-sensitive and treats the identifiers *miles* and *Miles* as two completely different variable names.

15. A keyword is a reserved word that has special meaning to the compiler. Keywords may not be used as programmer-defined identifiers.

Programming Projects

For each project, design the logic and write the program to produce the output. Code your name as the author, and include the current date on the output. Model your program after the sample programs presented in the chapter. Verify your output.

Note: 9s are used to specify the maximum field size reserved for printing numeric data.

Project 1–1   **Charge Account**

Write a program to compute and print the monthly finance charge. Assume a monthly finance rate of 1.5% on the unpaid balance.

Input (internal):
Create variables names for the following data items, and initialize them to the values shown below.

> previous balance = 3400.00
> payments = 400.00
> charges = 100.00

Output (screen):
Print the following billing information:

```
Author     CHARGE ACCOUNT     mm/dd/yy


Monthly finance charge $ 99.99
```

Processing Requirements:

- Define and initialize the program variables.
- Compute the new balance:
  previous balance – payments + charges.
- Compute the monthly finance charge:
  new balance × 0.015.
- Print the output on the screen.

Project 1–2   **Payroll**

Write a program to compute and print the net pay. Assume deductions amount to 9% of the gross pay.

Input (internal):
Create variables names for the following data items, and initialize them to the values shown below.

> payrate = 7.76
> hours = 40

Output (screen):
Print the following payroll information:

```
Author      PAYROLL REPORT      mm/dd/yy

Net pay: $ 999.99
```

Processing Requirements:

- Define and initialize the program variables.
- Compute the gross pay:
  payrate × hours.
- Compute the deductions:
  gross pay × 0.09.
- Compute the net pay:
  gross pay – deductions.
- Print the output on the screen.

Project 1–3   Sales

Write a program to calculate and print the net profit.

Input (internal):
Create variables names for the following data items, and initialize them to the values shown below.

> total sales = 12710.14
> cost of sales = 6235.38

Output (screen):
Print the following sales information:

```
Author      SALES REPORT      mm/dd/yy

Net profit is $ 9999.99
```

Processing Requirements:

- Define and initialize the program variables.
- Compute the net profit:
  total sales – cost of sales.
- Print the output on the screen.

Project 1–4   Inventory

Write a program to compute and print the item profit.

Input (internal):
Create variables names for the following data items, and initialize them to the values shown below.

> quantity = 48
> cost per unit = 4.49
> selling price = 9.95

Output (screen):

Print the following inventory information:

```
Author    INVENTORY REPORT    mm/dd/yy

Item profit is $ 999.99
```

Processing Requirements:

- Define and initialize the program variables.
- Compute the unit profit:
  selling price – cost per unit.
- Compute the item profit:
  quantity × unit profit.
- Print the output on the screen.

Project 1–5   **Personnel**

Write a program to calculate and print the new salary. Assume the employee receives a 6% increase in pay.

Input (internal):

Create variables names for the following data items, and initialize them to the values shown below.

old salary = 40126.00
percent increase = 0.06

Output (screen):

Print the following personnel information:

```
Author    PERSONNEL REPORT    mm/dd/yy

New salary: $ 99999.99
```

Processing Requirements:

- Define and initialize the program variables.
- Compute the raise amount:
  old salary × percent increase.
- Compute the new salary:
  old salary + raise amount.
- Print the output on the screen.

Project 1–6   **Accounts Payable**

Write a program to compute and print the amount due.

Input (internal):

Create variables names for the following data items, and initialize them to the values shown below.

invoice amount = 4563.78
discount rate = 0.06

Output (screen):
Print the following accounts payable information:

```
Author      ACCOUNTS PAYABLE      mm/dd/yy

Amount due: $ 9999.99
```

Processing Requirements:

- Define and initialize the program variables.
- Compute the discount amount:
  invoice amount × discount rate.
- Compute the amount due:
  invoice amount – discount amount.
- Print the output on the screen.

Project 1–7   Production Cost

Write a program to compute and print the item production cost.

Input (internal):
Create variables names for the following data items, and initialize them to the values shown below.

> units made = 72
> cost per unit = 4.25

Output (screen):
Print the following production information:

```
Author      PRODUCTION COST      mm/dd/yy

Item production cost: $ 999.99
```

Processing Requirements:

- Define and initialize the program variables.
- Compute the item production cost:
  units made × cost per unit.
- Print the output on the screen.

2   Taking a Closer Look

Overview

Learning Objectives

After you have read this chapter and completed the exercises, you should be able to

- discuss the basic structure of a C program and the purpose of the main() function
- define constants and variables
- declare and assign data to integer and floating-point data types
- declare and assign data to character and string data types
- code standard input and output operations using scanf() and printf() functions
- write programs to accept input from the keyboard

Functions: The Basic Structure

C uses functions as its basic building block. Essentially, a C program consists of a series of **programmer-defined functions** that interact with one another to perform the processing task. In this book, we will use the term *module* to describe a programmer-defined function.

Basically, a **module** is a self-contained, logical unit of a program that performs either a particular procedure or a major processing task. Consider, for instance, a program that reads data, performs calculations, and prints output. Since each of these activities represents a distinct processing task, they are coded as separate modules—one for reading the input, one for performing the calculations, and one for printing the output.

Modules may call other modules. A module that invokes another is referred to as the **calling module**, and the module that is invoked is referred to as the **called module**. Furthermore, a module may accept data and/or return a value. After all the modules have been developed, they are assembled to form the completed program.

Functions may be either precoded or created by the programmer. As you may recall, C comes with a **standard library** of precompiled functions that may be used to assist the program in performing its processing activities. The library includes functions that perform standard input/output, mathematical, and character string operations, to mention a few. Later in the chapter, you will learn how the **preprocessor** includes the standard library in your source code.

Comments

Comments are text statements that document and describe the program. Comments are optional, nonexecutable statements that are placed in the program to explain what the program does and how the code works. (**Nonexecutable statements** are not processed by the computer.) A comment begins with /* and ends with */.

Examples:

Examples 1–5 demonstrate how to code a comment. Look at the last example. It shows an invalid comment. Comments may not be nested, that is, one comment cannot be enclosed within another.

```
1. /*  A comment may be coded like this  */
2. /*  A comment

       may be

       coded like this  */
3. /*

    *  A comment

    *  may be coded

    *  like this

    */
4. /*  First Comment  */    /******  Second Comment  ******/
5. /*******************************************

    *                                          *

    *            Comments may be boxed          *

    *                                          *

    *******************************************/
6. /*  A comment may /* not be coded */ like this!  */
```

The #include Directive

Format:

```
#include <filename>
```

Purpose: To merge a file with the source program. The *#include* preprocessing directive tells the preprocessor to replace the directive with a copy of the file specified by the *filename* argument enclosed within angle brackets <>. Preprocessing directives are coded before the main() function.

The **preprocessor** is a utility program that performs various modifications to the source program. A **preprocessing directive** instructs the preprocessor to modify the source code before the compiler executes the program. The # symbol indicates that the *include* represents an instruction to the preprocessor. Directives do not end with a semicolon.

Unlike other programming languages, C does not have the input/output functions built in. For applications that do not require these functions, they are not included with the program. This, of course, streamlines the compilation process and provides a more efficient programming environment.

Example:

```
#include <stdio.h>
```

According to the example, a copy of the **standard input/output header file** replaces the directive in the source code. The *stdio.h* header file enables the program to perform basic input and output operations. That is, the *stdio.h* header file contains information about the functions that allows the program to accept input from the keyboard and display output on the screen.

The main() Function

Format:

```
main()
{
    statements
}
```

Purpose: To define the main() function. All C programs begin with the main() function. It signals the start of the program. The opening and closing parentheses () indicate that the identifier is a function. The opening and closing braces {} define the body of the function.

Normally, the body consists of a sequence of statements that end with a semicolon. Statements tell the computer what to do—what operations to perform. A semicolon specifies the end of each statement. The statement body may include functions and calls to other modules.

Perhaps we should pause here to mention that C is a "free-form" language. This means that we may code a statement on the line anywhere we wish. However, for the sake of clarity, we will adopt the practice of indenting the body of a function or module four spaces to the right. We will also code one statement per line. This makes the code easier to read and understand.

Common Data Types

Data types stipulate how and in what format the data is stored in memory. The most basic or common data types are integer, long, float, double, void, and character. Although C allows for other data types, these are the ones we will normally use to design and implement our programs.

Integer: An integer is a whole number. Examples of integer values are 5, 16, and 8724. An integer variable is declared by specifying *int* as the data type. Typically, integer variables hold data in the range −32768 to 32767. The actual range of values may vary from one compiler to another.

If larger integers are required, then specify *long* as the data type. A long integer holds data well beyond the range –32768 to 32767. Long integers are declared by specifying *long*.

Float: Real or floating-point numbers have decimal points. Examples of floating-point values are 2.651, 74.8, and 653.49. A floating-point variable is declared by specifying *float* as the data type.

If larger floating-point values are required, then specify *double* as the data type. A double-precision variable holds extremely small or large data values. Double-precision variables are declared by specifying *double*.

Void: Type *void* indicates that a module does not receive arguments or data. It also specifies that a module does not return a value to the calling environment. We will discuss the *void* data type and module calls in Chapter 3.

Character: A character is any single letter, numeric digit, punctuation mark, or special symbol. A character is declared by specifying *char* for the data type.

If we need more than one character, then we may define a string. A **string** is a group of two or more characters. A string variable is declared by specifying *char* for the data type.

Numeric Constants

A **numeric constant** is the actual value assigned to a numeric variable. Numeric constants include integer and floating-point values. In either case, the data type of the constant should be compatible with the type specified for the variable. That is, assign integer constants to integer variables and float constants to float variables.

Integer Constants: An integer constant is a whole number. Integer constants consist of digits and a unary sign (+ or –). The sign is written in front of the number and may be omitted for positive values. Examples of integer constants are as follows:

0	–34	245
14	900	+48
78	1234	–73503

Floating-Point Constants: A floating-point constant is a real number, a numeric value with a decimal point. Floating-point constants consist of digits, a decimal point, and a unary sign. Positive values may have their signs omitted. Examples of floating-point constants are as follows:

9.1	10.0	45.127
–0.75	0.1234	123.987
87.004	5672.3	+8734.0071

Dollar signs, percent signs, commas, and other special symbols are not permitted. Any illegal character coded in the constant will cause an error.

Numeric Variables

A **numeric variable** reserves a location in memory for storing numeric data. Numeric variables define integer and floating-point data. All variable declarations end with a semicolon.

Integer Variables: An integer variable allocates storage space in memory for integer data. Examples of integer variables are as follows:

```
int   iLineCount;
long  lBigNum;
int   iItem_num, iQuantity, iReorder_point;
int   iEmployee_num, iGrossPay, iDeductions, iNetPay;
```

We can define one variable to a line or several on the same line. Note that commas separate multiple declarations. Here the commas serve as **delimiters**; they indicate where one name begins and another ends. However, it may be wise to declare only one variable per line. This makes them easier to find, especially if the names are arranged alphabetically. This may also help eliminate errors. For example, it's easy to unintentionally use a semicolon for a delimiter rather than a comma. Hence, any name declared after the semicolon will be unknown to the program.

Floating-Point Variables: A floating-point variable reserves storage space in memory for floating-point data. Examples of floating-point variables are as follows:

```
float fAmount_due;
float fScore, fVariance;
double dDistance;
double dDividend, dDivisor, dQuotient;
```

Note: It is important to understand that the contents of a variable may change several times before a program completes its processing task.

Assigning Data to Numeric Variables

Numeric assignment statements assign either integer or floating-point data to the storage areas reserved for the variables. The value assigned to a variable may be in the form of a constant, a variable, or an arithmetic expression. Data previously stored at a variable is overwritten by the assignment statement.

Examples of assignment statements are as follows:

```
/*--- Variable Declarations ---*/

    int     iFactor, iCount, iProduct, iOnOrder = 2;
    float   fCost = 14.58, fAmount_due;
    double  dTotal;

/*--- Numeric Assignment Statements ---*/

    iFactor = 76;
    fAmount_due = 5.98;

    iCount = iOnOrder;
    dTotal = fCost;

    iProduct = iFactor * iCount;
```

The first pair assigns the integer constant 76 to *iFactor* and the floating-point constant 5.98 to *fAmount_due*. The second pair assigns the contents of *iOnOrder* to *iCount* and the value stored at *fCost* to *dTotal*.

Note that *dTotal* is a double. This means that the floating-point value stored at *fCost* is **promoted** (converted) to a double and then assigned to *dTotal*. The declaration of *fCost* not only defines the variable, it also initializes it to 14.58. Similarly, *iOnOrder* is initialized to 2.

The last statement assigns the integer expression *iFactor * iCount* to *iProduct*.

Since C is data type sensitive, we must be careful to assign integer constants to integer variables, float constants to float variables, and so on. We can, however, promote compatible types as we did when 14.58 was promoted to a double.

Symbolic Constants: The #define Directive

Format:

```
#define IDENTIFIER constant
```

Purpose: To define symbolic constants. The *#define* directive tells the preprocessor to substitute all occurrences of the *IDENTIFIER* with the *constant*. A defined constant retains its value during the program run. To make them stand out, symbolic constants are coded in uppercase letters. Normally, the *#define* directives are placed at the beginning of the program, that is, after the *#include* directives. Once again note that directives do not end with a semicolon.

Example:

```
#define FRATE 0.08
   .....

fInterest = fDeposit * FRATE;
```

According to the example, the *#define* directive instructs the preprocessor to substitute all occurrences of *FRATE* with the constant `0.08` before the program is executed.

Screen Output: The printf() Function

Format:

```
printf("control string", variable/s);
```

Header File: stdio.h

Purpose: To print output on the screen. Normally, the printf() function consists of two arguments, a control string and a variable list. The **control string** is enclosed within double quotes and may include screen messages and conversion specifiers. A **conversion specifier** formats the output and prints the result in place of the specifier.

The second argument refers to the data that is printed on the screen. Multiple variables are separated by commas. A semicolon marks the end of the print statement. Be sure to include the standard input/output header file in the program. It contains the precompiled code for the printf() function.

Examples:

For each example, assume the variables contain the following data: *iGrade* = 87, *iHours* = 3, *iMinutes* = 45, *fNum1* = 5.0, and *fNum2* = 34.5678.

```
printf("This is my first course in C.");
OUTPUT:  This is my first course in C.
```

The print statement displays the message enclosed within double quotes on the screen. Observe that there are no variable arguments.

```
printf("%d", iGrade);
OUTPUT:  87
```

The print statement displays grade in decimal form. The conversion specifier begins with a **%**, and the d tells the computer to format *iGrade* as a decimal integer.

```
printf("\nCourse grade is: %d", iGrade);
OUTPUT:  [advance to new line]
         Course grade is: 87
```

The print statement advances to a new line and displays *iGrade* as a decimal integer. The \n (backslash n), the **newline character**, forces the cursor to the beginning of a new line. When coded at the beginning of the control string, the cursor advances to a new line before the program prints the output.

```
printf("Course grade is: %d\n", iGrade);
OUTPUT:  Course grade is: 87
         [advance to new line]
```

The print statement displays *iGrade* as a decimal integer and advances to a new line. When the newline character is coded at the end of the control string, the cursor advances to a new line after the program prints the output.

```
printf("Time spent on project: %d hours and %d minutes\n",
       iHours, iMinutes)
OUTPUT:  Time spent on project: 3 hours and 45 minutes
         [advance to new line]
```

The print statement displays the output on the screen and advances to a new line. Notice that data replaces the conversion specifiers in the control string.

```
printf("%.1f %.2f   %.3f    %.4f", fNum1, fNum1, fNum1, fNum1);
OUTPUT:  5.0 5.00   5.000    5.0000
```

The print statement displays the output in fixed decimal format. For example, `%.1f` indicates that the output is rounded to the nearest tenth. Observe the spacing between the values. The output corresponds to the spacing specified by the control string.

```
printf("%4.1f %5.2f %6.3f", fNum2, fNum2, fNum2);
OUTPUT:  34.6 34.57 34.568
```

The conversion specifier `%4.1f` indicates that the output field is 4 positions wide, with 1 position to the right of the decimal point (99.9). The decimal point is included in the width. Similarly, `%5.2f` specifies a field width of 5 with 2 decimal places (99.99) and `%6.3f` specifies a field width of 6 with 3 decimal places (99.999).

Escape Sequences

An **escape sequence** is a sequence of characters that begins with a backslash \; the compiler treats the sequence as a single character. Some common escape sequences are shown in Table 2.1. For example, the \ f escape sequence tells the compiler to "escape" the normal meaning of the character f and to advance to the top of the next page.

Examples of escape sequences are as follows:

1. `printf("Saved by the bell!\a");`

   OUTPUT: Saved by the bell! <sound the bell>

2. `printf("My name is Shawn O\'Brien.");`

   OUTPUT: My name is Shawn O'Brien.

3. `printf("The coach said, \"Practice two hours a day.\" ");`

   OUTPUT: The coach said, "Practice two hours a day."

4. `printf("Student Name:\tExam1\tExam2\tExam3");`

   OUTPUT: Student Name: Exam1   Exam2   Exam3

TABLE 2.1   Escape Sequences

Escape Sequence	Meaning
\a	alert—sound the bell
\f	form feed—advance to top of next page
\r	carriage return—return to beginning of line
\n	newline—advance to next line
\b	backspace—move back one space
\t	tab—move to next tab setting
\\	backslash—print a backslash
\'	single quote—print a single quote
\"	double quote—print a double quote
\0	zero—null character

Note: The single quote and double quote have special meaning to the compiler. We may, however, use them for other purposes by coding them as escape sequences (see Examples 2 and 3 above).

In Example 4 above, the actual number of spaces inserted by the tab *t* escape sequence depends on the number of spaces assigned to the tab.

Keyboard Input: The scanf() Function

Format:

```
scanf(" control string", &variable/s);
```

Header File: stdio.h

Purpose: To read data from the keyboard. This function has two arguments, a control string and a variable list. The **control string** is enclosed within double quotes and consists of one or more conversion specifiers. The scanf() waits for the input and the enter keypress. Once a value is entered, it is converted to the type specified by the control string and the result is stored at the address of the **variable**.

Note the leading space in the control string. The leading space can, in certain situations, improve the performance of the input process. Make it a habit to put the space in front of the conversion specifier.

The &, or **address operator**, specifies the address of the variable and is required for numeric data. An **address** is a location in memory. The computer uses addresses to track the data stored at the program variables. Multiple variables are separated by commas. A semicolon marks the end of the statement.

It is important to understand that C treats keyboard input (letters, digits, and special characters) as a continuous stream of characters. Hence, scanf() uses the conversion specifiers to convert the input to the types specified by the programmer.

Examples:

For each example, assume the variables are defined as *int iGrade, int iHours, int iMinutes, int iNum1, int iNum2, int iNum, long lNum, float fNum3, float fNum4, float fNum,* and *double dNum.*

```
INPUT:  87
scanf(" %d", &iGrade);
STORAGE:  iGrade = 87
```

The string 87 is entered at the keyboard. After the enter keypress, the control string converts the 87 to a decimal integer and assigns the result to *grade*.

```
INPUT:  3 45
scanf(" %d%d", &iHours, &iMinutes);
STORAGE:  iHours = 3
          iMinutes = 45
```

The data is entered at the keyboard. After the enter keypress, the control string converts the 3 and the 45 to decimal integers and assigns the results to *iHours* and *iMinutes*, respectively.

The space between the 3 and 45 serves as a delimiter. It tells scanf() that the input stream consists of two substrings.

```
INPUT:  19 245  38.6     4.812
scanf(" %d%d%f%f", &iNum1, &iNum2, &fNum3, &fNum4);
STORAGE:  iNum1 = 19
          iNum2 = 245
          fNum3 = 38.6
          fNum4 = 4.812
```

Four substrings are entered at the keyboard. After the enter keypress, the control string converts the first two substrings to decimal integers and the last two to floating-point numbers. The results are assigned to the variables. Notice that the spaces separating the data may vary.

```
INPUT:  27 453935 899.95 3.141593
scanf(" %d %l %f %lf", &iNum, &lNum, &fNum, &dNum);
STORAGE:  iNum = 27
          lNum = 453935
          fNum = 899.95
          dNum = 3.141593
```

The scanf() reads the input stream and identifies the substrings. According to the control string, the first substring is converted to an *integer,* the second to *long,* the third to *float,* and the fourth to *double.*

Caution: Be careful when using type doubles. For example, scanf() requires %f to read a floating-point value and %lf to read a double. However, printf() uses %f to print either a float or a double.

Arithmetic Operations

Arithmetic operations represent the standard mathematical operations of addition, subtraction, multiplication, division, and modulus. The symbols used to express the arithmetic operations are shown in Table 2.2.

Modulus is the only operation that requires integer variables. When executed, **modulus** computes the remainder by dividing the first integer by the value of the second. For example, the expression $a = b \% c$, where $b = 11$ and $c = 3$, results in a modulus of 2. In other words, the remainder 2 is assigned to a.

TABLE 2.2 Arithmetic Operators

Operator	Operation	Example
+	addition	b + c
−	subtraction	b − c
*	multiplication	b * c
/	division	b / c
%	modulus	b % c

This section also introduces three frequently used math functions that manipulate numeric data—fabs(), pow(), and sqrt(). Since these functions require the *math.h* header file, we must include it with the *stdio.h* header file. The argument types and return types are doubles.

Absolute Value: The fabs() function returns the absolute value of a number. The absolute value of a positive or negative number is the number itself, without reference to its sign. Examples of absolute values are as follows:

```
fabs(1.5)      returns  1.5          fabs(-1.5)    returns 1.5
fabs(27.0)     returns 27.0          fabs(-0.9)    returns 0.9
```

Exponentiation: The pow() function returns the power of a number. Exponentiation raises a number to a given power. The first argument inside the parentheses is the base, and the second is the power. Examples of exponentiations are as follows:

```
pow(5.0, 2.0)  returns  25.0         pow(2.0, 7.0)   returns  128.0
pow(4.0, 4.0)  returns 256.0         pow(10.0, 3.0)  returns 1000.0
```

Square Root: The sqrt() function returns the square root of a positive number. Negative arguments produce errors. The square root of a number represents a factor that when multiplied by itself, gives the number. Examples of square roots are as follows:

```
sqrt(25.0)     returns 5.0       sqrt(9.0)      returns 3.0
sqrt(81.0)     returns 9.0       sqrt(100.0)    returns 10.0
```

Note: See Appendix D for a summary reference of math and related functions.

Arithmetic Expressions

An **arithmetic expression** is a statement that combines numeric constants and/or variables with one or more arithmetic operators. For example, the following arithmetic expression

```
fPay = fHours * fPayrate + fBonus;
```

computes take-home pay. The statement consists of three variables (*fHours, fPayrate,* and *fBonus*) and two operators (* and +). The expression is evaluated according to the **order of precedence**. The result is assigned to *fPay*.

The order of precedence is also known as the **hierarchy of operations**. When an expression contains two or more arithmetic operators, the computer determines the order in which to perform the operations. The hierarchy of operations is shown in Table 2.3 (high to low order).

TABLE 2.3   Hierarchy of Operations

Order	Hierarchy of Operations
1	exponentiation
2	multiplication, division, modulus
3	addition, subtraction

For example, let *fHours* = 20.0, *fPayrate* = 8.00, and *fBonus* = 15.00. Then by substitution,

```
fPay = 20.0 * 8.00 + 15.00;
```

According to the hierarchy of operations, multiplication is performed first (20.0 * 8.00 = 160.00), then the addition (160.00 + 15.00 = 175.00).

By using parentheses, we can change the order in which the computer performs the operations. For example, if we insert

```
fPay = 20.0 * (8.00 + 15.00);
```

with parentheses as shown, we can change the resulting value of the expression. In this particular case, the expression will produce an incorrect result (20.0 * 23.00 = 460.00). However, there will be situations when parentheses are required in order to produce the correct result.

Checkpoint 2A

1. Describe the basic structure of a C program, and define the term *programmer-defined functions*.

2. Explain the purpose of the *#define* preprocessing directive.

3. Explain the purpose of the standard input/output header file.

4. Explain the purpose of the main() function. Is it necessary for each program to contain this function?

5. For the following statements, locate and correct any syntax errors.
   ```
   a. /*  Account Receivable System   /*
   b. #include <stdio.h>
   c. main();
      {
           /*  This is a C program  */
      }
   d. float fTotalAmt            /*   total amount due   */
   e. int iAge;                  /*   age in months      */
   f. int iDept, iEmplNum, iWages:   /*   data fields     */
   g. scanf(" %f", &fGPA);
   h. print("%d ", &iResult);
   i. printf("*** %d", iTotalCount);
   j. scanf(" %d%d%f", iNum1, iNum2, iNum3);
   ```

6. The sample program below computes the product of two integers by multiplying the value of the first integer by the value of the second. Locate and correct any logic errors. Desk check the code by tracing the flow of data through the program line by line.

   ```
   #include <stdio.h>

   main()
   {
        int iNum1, iNum2, iResult;
   ```

```
            iNum1 = 30;
            iNum2 = 40;
            printf("\nThe product is: %d", iResult);
            iResult = iNum1 * iNum2;
            return0
    }
```

7. What value (if any) do the following functions return?
    a. `fabs(-2.7);`
    b. `pow(4.0, 2.0);`
    c. `sqrt(81.0);`
    d. `fabs(16.8);`
    e. `sqrt(-4.0);`
    f. `pow(5.0, 3.0);`

Sample Program CHAP2A

Sample program CHAP2A is an interactive program that accepts data from the keyboard, computes the earned pay, and prints the output on the screen. (The flowchart for the application is shown in Figure 2.1; the program code is in Figure 2.2.) An **interactive program** involves a dialog between the user and the computer—the user and the computer interact to produce the output. For example, the payroll program prompts (displays a message on the screen) the user when to enter pay rate and hours worked. Figure 2.3 shows the input and output.

The following specifications apply:

Input (keyboard):
Prompt for and enter the following data:

Pay Rate	Hours Worked
25.10	38.5

Output (screen):
Print the following payroll information:

```
D Collopy      Total Pay      mm/dd/yy

Total pay is $999.99
```

Processing Requirements:

- Define the program variables.
- Compute the total pay:
  pay rate × hours worked.
- Print the output on the screen.

Pseudocode:

```
START: Main
Prompt and enter payrate
Prompt and enter hours worked
Calculate total pay:
```

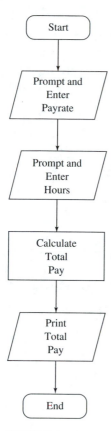

FIGURE 2.1   Program Flowchart for CHAP2A

        payrate × hours
   Print title line
   Print total pay
   END

Program Flowchart: See Figure 2.1.

From Chapter 1, you know that the parallelogram is used for input and output operations. Technically, a "prompt-and-enter" activity consists of two operations—one for displaying the prompt (output) and one for entering the data (input). However, this particular combination is so common that it can be shown as one operation.

     In the program flowchart, notice how the parallelograms are used to specify the "prompt-and-enter" activities.

Dissection of Sample Program CHAP2A

The first nine lines of the program are comments. Comments, as we know, are not processed by the computer. They are placed in the source code to document the purpose of the program and to explain various parts of the code.

```
/*------------------------------------------------------------
TOTAL PAY: Input the data from the keyboard, compute, and print
total pay.

Program:    CHAP2A.C
Author:     David M. Collopy
Date:       mm/dd/yy
Project:    Sample program
*************************************************************/

#include <stdio.h>

main()
{
    /* declare variables */
    float fPayrate;             /* hourly pay rate */
    float fHours;               /* hours worked    */
    float fTotPay;              /* total pay       */

    /* input the data */
    printf("Enter pay rate: $ ");
    scanf(" %f", &fPayrate);
    printf("Enter hours worked: ");
    scanf(" %f", &fHours);

    /* calculate total pay */
    fTotPay = fPayrate * fHours;

    /* display output on the screen */
    printf("\n\nDCollopy     Total Pay      mm/dd/yy\n\n");
    printf("Total pay is $ %6.2f", fTotPay);

    return 0;
}
```

FIGURE 2.2   Program Code for CHAP2A

```
Enter pay rate: $ 25.10
Enter hours worked: 38.5

DCollopy         Total Pay         mm/dd/yy

Total pay is $ 966.35
```

FIGURE 2.3   Screen Input and Output for CHAP2A

```
#include <stdio.h>
```

This statement includes the standard input/output header file in the source code. The *stdio.h* header file contains precompiled code for the *scanf()* and *printf()* functions. Since we intend to input data from the keyboard and output information to the screen, we must include these functions in the source program. The include directive tells the computer to insert the standard input/output library functions into the source program.

```
main()
{
    /* declare variables */
    float fPayrate;          /* hourly pay rate */
    int   iHours;            /* hours worked    */
    float fTotPay;           /* total pay       */
```

The above statements declare the program variables. Note that *fPayrate*, *iHours*, and *fTotPay* represent **local variables**. Since they are declared inside the main function, they are local to or known by only the main function. However, in a one-module program such as the main(), it really does matter if the variables are declared inside or outside the function.

```
    /* input the data */
    printf("Enter pay rate: $ ");
```

The above print statement displays the message enclosed within double quotes on the screen. The message serves as a prompt that tells the user to enter the pay rate. A **prompt** represents a screen command or message that tells the user what to do.

```
    scanf(" %f", &fPayrate);
```

The above statement reads the input string, converts the string to a floating-point value, and stores the result at the address *&fPayrate*. In other words, a floating-point value is assigned to the variable *fPayrate*. For now, remember that the scanf() statement requires the address of the variable—so don't forget the address operator (&).

```
    printf("Enter hours worked: ");
    scanf(" %f", &fHours);
```

The above statements prompts for and reads hours worked, converts the input string to a floating-point value, and assigns the result to *fHours*.

```
    /* calculate total pay */
    fTotPay = fPayrate * fHours;
```

The above statement multiplies the pay rate by the number of hours worked and assigns the product to *fTotPay*.

```
    /* display output on the screen */
    printf("DCollopy     Total Pay     mm/dd/yy\n\n");
    printf("Total pay is $ %6.2f", fTotPay);
```

The first print statement displays the title line on the screen and then forces a double space (\n\n). The second displays the output message and total pay on the screen. Essentially, the conversion specifier (*%6.2f*) tells the computer to format total pay as a fixed-length floating-point field and to replace the specifier with the result.

```
        return 0;
}
```

The return statement sends a 0 to the operating system, and the closing brace marks the end of the function.

Notes and Tips

1. To avoid the possibility of error, declare only one variable per line.
2. When declaring symbolic constants, append the letter I to integer constants and F to float constants.
3. Remember to enclose the body of a scan statement within parentheses and to enclose the control string within double quotes.
4. The scan statement requires the address operator (&) for integer, float, and single-character variables. String variables do not use the address operator.
5. Although it is common for a print statement to include a field width in the control string, the scan usually does not.
6. For the scan, leave a blank space before the conversion specifier (" %f"). There are times when the leading space improves the input process.

Tutorial CHAP2A

1. The objectives of this tutorial are to
   • prompt the user to enter the data at the keyboard
   • use the scan statement to input the data
2. Open your text editor, and enter the code as shown in Figure 2.2.
3. Save your work as CHAP2A.
4. Execute the program. If errors are detected, compare your code with the sample program and make the necessary changes. Save and execute the program again. The output should produce three lines—a title line, a blank line, and a detail line that displays total pay (see Figure 2.3).
5. Once your output is correct, show the results to your instructor.

Quick Quiz

Answer the following questions.

1. Describe the relationship that exists between the scan and print functions and the *stdio.h* file.
2. Why are the print statements shown in the *input the data* section of the program called prompts?
3. What does the following statement do? Why is there an & in front of the variable name?
   ```
   scanf(" %f", &fPayrate);
   ```

4. In what way would the output results change if you forgot to code the address operator in the above scanf() statement?

5. The last printf() shown in the program has a $ in the control string. Is it part of the conversion specifier? Explain your answer.

6. Did you encounter any problems or errors when you ran your program? If so, what were they and what did you do to correct them?

Non-Numeric Constants

There are two types of **non-numeric constants**, character and string. A character constant is a single character assigned to a character variable; a string constant is a group of characters assigned to a string variable. Be sure to match the data types of the constants to those of the variables. A type mismatch can cause problems that may be difficult to find.

Character Constants: A **character constant** is any single letter (uppercase or lowercase), decimal digit, punctuation mark, or special symbol. Character constants are enclosed within *single quotes*. Examples of character constants are as follows:

```
'R'    'y'    'n'    '$'    '-'    '5'    '1'    ' '    '0'
```

String Constants: A **string constant** represents a group of two or more characters. String constants are enclosed within *double quotes* and are also called character arrays. An **array** is a collection of related items, and a **character array** is a collection of characters that make up the string. Examples of string constants are as follows:

```
"MAJESTIC MUSIC DISCOUNT"      "Accounts Receivable Report"
"Ohio University"              "February 14th"
"Tuesday"                      "C Programming I"
```

Non-Numeric Variables

Character and string variables are used to reserve storage space for non-numeric data. A character variable reserves storage for exactly one character, whereas a string variable or character array allocates enough space to hold the entire string.

Character Variables: A **character variable** reserves storage space in memory for one character of data. A character variable is defined by specifying type *char*. Examples of character variables are as follows (append *c* to character variable names):

```
char cSign;
char cFlag, cNo, cYes;
char cSetup, cMiddle_initial;
char cSymbol, cDollar;
```

String Variables: A **string variable** (also called a **character array**) reserves storage space in memory for string data. A string variable is defined by specifying type *char* and a length. The length is enclosed within brackets [ ] and must be long enough to hold the entire string and the string terminator. The **string terminator** or **null character** *0* marks the end of the string.

When defined, a character array represents an address to a location in memory where string data is stored. Examples of string variables are as follows (append *s* to string variable names):

```
char sDay[10];
char sLetter_head[24];
char sUniversity[28];
char sReportLine[27];
char sCourse[16];
char sCelebrate[14];
```

The lengths shown for the string variables include the null character. For example, the variable called *sDay* allocates storage space for ten characters. If the string *Tuesday* is stored at *sDay*, then the contents of *sDay* will look like this:

	0	1	2	3	4	5	6	7	8	9
sDay:	T	u	e	s	d	a	y	/0		

According to the example, *Tuesday* occupies storage positions 0–6 (storage positions are numbered from left to right starting with 0) and the null character \0 marks the end of the data. Hence, the variable *sDay* may hold a maximum of nine characters of data; the last position is reserved for the null character. C uses the null character to detect the end-of-the-string data.

Assigning Data to Non-Numeric Variables

Non-numeric assignment statements assign either character or string data to the storage areas reserved for the variables. Data assigned to a character or string variable can be in the form of either a constant or a variable.

Examples of character assignment statements are as follows:

```
/*--- Character Declarations ---*/

    char cSign;
    char cFlag, cNo = 'n', cYes = 'y';
    char cMiddle_initial;
    char cSymbol, cDollar = '$';

/*--- Character Assignment Statements ---*/

    cSign = '-';
    cMiddle_initial = 'M';
    cFlag = cYes;
    cSymbol = cDollar;
```

The first pair assigns the character '-' to *cSign* and the letter 'M' to *cMiddle_initial*. The second pair assigns the contents of the *cYes* to *cFlag* and the character stored at *cDollar* to *cSymbol*. The declarations of *cNo, cYes,* and *cDollar* not only define the variables, they also initialize them.

Examples of string assignment statements are as follows:

```
/*--- String Declarations ---*/

    char sLetter_head[24] = "MAJESTIC MUSIC DISCOUNT";
    char sMySchool[] = "Ohio University";
    char sDay[10];
    char sCelebrate[20], sBirthday[] = "November 18th";

/*--- String Assignment Statements ---*/

    strcpy(sDay, "Thursday");
    strcpy(sCelebrate, sBirthday);
```

Look at *sLetter_head*, *sMySchool*, and *sBirthday*. Notice that constants were assigned to them when they were declared. The length of *sLetter_head* is explicitly defined by the declaration, whereas the lengths of *sMySchool* and *sBirthday* are implicitly determined by the lengths of the strings assigned to the variables.

As odd as it may seem, we can only use the equal sign to assign data to a string variable when the variable is declared. For example, the assignment statement

```
sDay = "Thursday";
```

will cause an error. We can, however, accomplish the same thing by using the **string copy function** strcpy(). Before we can use strcpy(), we must include the **string header file** in our program by coding

```
#include<string.h>
```

Now look at the string copy functions. Thursday is assigned to *sDay*, and the contents of *sBirthday* are assigned to *sCelebrate*. We will discuss the details of strcpy() in Chapter 4.

Printing Non-Numeric Output

Until now, we have been using printf() to display numeric values on the screen. In this section, we will learn how to use the print function to format and print character and string data on the screen.

Examples:

For each example, assume the variables contain the following data: *cChar1* = `'N'`, *cChar2* = `'F'`, *cChar3* = `'L'`, and *sMessage[]* = `"Total points:"`.

```
    printf("%c%c%c", cChar1, cChar2, cChar3);
    OUTPUT:  NFL
```

The control string `"%c%c%c"` indicates that three characters are printed side by side.

```
    printf("%c %c   %c", cChar1, cChar2, cChar3);
    OUTPUT:  N F   L
```

The control string `"%c %c   %c"` separates the characters in the output. One space separates the *N* from the *F*, and three spaces separate the *F* from the *L*.

```
printf("%s %f", sMessage, 8.5);
```
OUTPUT: Total points: 8.500000

The control string `"%s %f"` displays a brief message and a floating-point constant on the screen. Notice that `%f` prints 8.5 as 8.500000. This represents the default setting for a floating-point value.

```
printf("%s%c", "C is fun", '!');
```
OUTPUT: C is fun!

The control string `"%s%c"` shows the output `"C is fun"` and `'!'` as a continuous string of characters.

```
printf("%12s%c", "C is fun", '!');
```
OUTPUT: C is fun!

The output appears to the right. The conversion specifier `%12s` tells the computer to right justify (shift right) the string in a 12-character field. Since the message (8 characters) is shorter than the output field, the compiler pads the first four positions with spaces.

```
printf("%-12s%c", "C is fun", '!');
```
OUTPUT: C is fun   !

The output appears to the left. The minus sign in the conversion specifier `%-12s` tells the computer to left-justify (shift left) the string. Since the message is shorter than the output field, the compiler pads the last four positions with spaces. Notice that the exclamation sign is printed at the end of the field.

Reading Non-Numeric Data

Thus far we have been using scanf() to read numeric data from the keyboard. In this section, we will learn how to use the scan function to input character and string data.

As you may recall, numeric variables are preceded with the address operator &; string variables are not. A string variable is a character array, and the identifier name associated with the array represents the address of the variable. Since the address of a string variable is already known, the address operator is not required.

Examples:

For each example, assume the variables are defined as follows: *char sName[16], char cGrade, int iStudentNum, char sFirstName[10],* and *char sLastName[15].*

INPUT: Maxwell B
```
scanf(" %s %c", sName, &sGrade);
```
STORAGE: sName = Maxwell
            sGrade = B

The space separating the data items tells scanf() that the input stream consists of two substrings. According to the conversion specifier `" %s %c"`, the first substring, `Maxwell`, is converted to a string and assigned to *sName* and the second substring, `B`, is converted to a character and assigned to *cGrade.*

```
INPUT:  1118 Ryan Adams
scanf(" %d %s %s", &iStudentNum, sFirstName, sLastName);
STORAGE:  iStudentNum = 1118
          sFirstName = Ryan
          sLastName = Adams
```

According to the conversion specifier " %d %s %s", the first substring, 1118, is converted to a decimal integer and assigned to *iStudentNum*; the second substring, Ryan, is converted to a string and assigned to *sFirstName*; and the third substring, Adams, is converted to a string and assigned to *sLastName*.

The return Statement

Format:

```
return value;
```

Purpose: To transfer control. The *return* statement sends control back to the calling environment (function, module, operating system, and so on). We will use this statement to exit a lower-level module and to return to the calling module.

The *value* argument is optional. If present, the value is returned to the calling environment. Return values can be in the form of a constant, a variable, or an arithmetic expression.

Examples:

1. `return;`
2. `return 0;`
3. `return (fResult);`
4. `return (ix + iy);`

Example 1 causes a return to the calling environment. Examples 2–4 not only send control back to their respective calling environments, they also return a value—a 0, the value stored at *fResult,* and the sum (*ix* + *iy*), respectively. Parentheses may be used to enclose the return expression.

Checkpoint 2B

1. What is a character array?
2. Explain the purpose of the *return* statement.
3. Determine if the following assignment statements are valid or invalid.
    a. `int       iNumber1 = 521;`
    b. `float     fNumber2 = 35.02;`
    c. `double    dNumber3 = 250000;`
    d. `char      sLast_name[7] = 'Wilson';`
    e. `char      sFirstName[7] = "Annette";`
    f. `int       iNumber4 = 326.89;`

```
g. long     lNumber5 = 64000
h. char     cMiddle_initial = "I";
i. char     sResponse[2] = 'Y';
j. float    fNumber6 = 2402;
```

4. Determine if the following *#define* directives are valid or invalid.
   ```
   a. #define  FTAX_RATE = 0.18
   b. #define  fPayrate 10.50
   c. define   FCOST 19.95
   d. #define  FINTEREST .08
   e. define   IZERO 0;
   ```

5. Evaluate the following arithmetic expressions.
   ```
   a. iCost = 25 + 18 * 2;
   b. fAmountDue = 3 * 4 / 6;
   c. fOutcome = 3.00 * 40 + 1.5 * 6.00 + 10;
   d. fResult = (3.00 * (40 + 1.5) * 6.00) + 10;
   ```

6. Code the *#define* directive to assign 7.85 to *FDISCOUNT*.

7. Code the variable declaration for a string variable called *sTitle* that will hold 20 characters.

8. Code the printf() function to print the value of *fAverage*. The output has a field width of 5 with 2 decimal places.

9. Code the scanf() function to read the input stream 35 394 847628 325.90 4.268975. Use the following variable names: *iNum1, iNum2, lNum, fNum, and dNum*.

Sample Program CHAP2B

Sample program CHAP2B accepts data from the keyboard, computes the volume of a storage carton, and displays the output on the screen. The flowchart is presented in Figure 2.4; the program code, in Figure 2.5. Figure 2.6 shows the output. The following specifications apply:

Input (keyboard):
Prompt for and enter the following data (length, width, and height are shown in feet):

Carton Type	Carton Number	Length	Width	Height
Desk	1180	3.5	2.3	4.1

Output (screen):
Print the carton volume report shown in Figure 2.6.

Processing Requirements:

- Define the program variables.
- Compute the volume:
  length × width × height.
- Print the output on the screen.

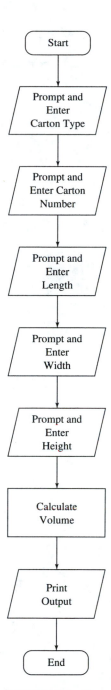

FIGURE 2.4 Program Flowchart for CHAP2B

```
/*-------------------------------------------------------------------
CARTON VOLUME: Input the data from the keyboard, compute, and print
the volume of a storage carton.

Program:   CHAP2B.C
Author:    David M. Collopy
Date:      mm/dd/yy
Project:   Sample program
*******************************************************************/

#include <stdio.h>

main()
{
    /* declare variables */
    char  sCartonType[10];      /* carton type    */
    int   iCartonNum;           /* carton number  */
    float fLength;              /* length of carton */
    float fWidth;               /* width of carton  */
    float fHeight;              /* height of carton */
    float fVolume;              /* volume of carton */

    /* input the data */
    printf("  Enter carton type: ");
    scanf(" %s", sCartonType);
    printf("Enter carton number: ");
    scanf(" %d", &iCartonNum);
    printf("Enter carton length: ");
    scanf(" %f", &fLength);
    printf(" Enter carton width: ");
    scanf(" %f", &fWidth);
    printf("Enter carton height: ");
    scanf(" %f", &fHeight);

    /* calculate volume */
    fVolume = fLength * fWidth * fHeight;

    /* display output on the screen*/
    printf("\n\nDCollopy      Carton Volume      mm/dd/yy\n");
    printf("\nCarton type: %-10s   Carton no: %d",
        sCartonType, iCartonNum);
    printf("\nLength:  %4.1f", fLength);
    printf("\nWidth:   %4.1f", fWidth);
    printf("\nHeight:  %4.1f", fHeight);
    printf("\nVolume:  %6.1f", fVolume);

    return 0;
}
```

FIGURE 2.5   Sample Program CHAP2B: Compute the Volume of a Storage Carton

```
   Enter carton type: Desk
Enter carton number: 1180
Enter carton length: 4.3
 Enter carton width: 2.3
Enter carton height: 4.1



DCollopy        Carton Volume        mm/dd/yy

Carton type: Desk            Carton no: 1180
Length:   3.5
Width:    2.3
Height:   4.1
Volume: 33.0
```

FIGURE 2.6   Screen Input and Output for CHAP2B

Pseudocode:

START: Main
Prompt and enter carton type
Prompt and enter carton number
Prompt and enter length
Prompt and enter width
Prompt and enter height
Calculate volume:
    length × width × height
Print output:
    title line
    carton type and carton number
    length
    width
    height
    volume
END

Program Flowchart: See Figure 2.4.

Dissection of Sample Program CHAP2B

```
#include <stdio.h>
```

The above statement includes the standard input/output header file in the source program.

```
main()
{
    /* declare variables */
    char  sCartonType[10];
```

The above declaration defines the string (*char*) variable *sCartonType* and reserves storage space in memory for ten characters *[10]* of data—nine for holding the carton type and one for the null character (\0).

```
int    iCartonNum;
float  fLength;
float  fWidth;
float  fHeight;
float  fVolume;
```

The above statements define the program variables. The *iCartonNum, fLength, fWidth,* and *fHeight* are input variables, whereas the *fVolume* represents the output produced by the program.

```
/* input the data */
printf("  Enter carton type ");
scanf(" %s", sCartonType);
```

The above statements prompt the user to enter the carton type. The blank spaces placed in front of the word *Enter* are used to align the input as the user keys it in.

The scan statement reads the input, converts it to a string (*%s*), and assigns the result to *sCartonType*. Notice that we did not code an address operator for the string variable. Recall that a string variable is a character array, and the identifier name associated with the array represents the address of the variable. Since the address is already know, the & is not required.

```
printf("Enter carton number: ");
scanf(" %d", &iCartonNum);
printf("   Enter the length: ");
scanf(" %f", &fLength);
printf("    Enter the width: ");
scanf(" %f", &fWidth);
printf("   Enter the height: ");
scanf(" %f", &fHeight);
```

The above statements prompt for the program data. The input is converted to data type shown and assigned to *iCartonNum, fLength, fWidth,* and *fHeight,* respectively

```
/* calculate volume */
fVolume = fLength * fWidth * fHeight;
```

The above statement computes the product and assigns the result to *fVolume*.

```
/* display output on the screen */
printf("\n\nDCollopy    Carton Volume    mm/dd/yy\n\n");
```

The above statement performs a double-space and then displays the author's name, the program title, and the date on the screen.

```
printf("\nCarton type: %-10s   Carton no: %d",
    sCartonType, iCartonNum);
```

The above statement performs a single space, replaces the output specifiers with the formatted results of carton type and carton number, and displays the line on the screen. The minus sign (-) in the format specifier tells the computer to left-justify the carton type in a ten-position field.

Look how the print statement was split into two lines. Long print statements should be coded on two lines by breaking the first line after the comma coded at the end of the control string.

```
printf("\nLength:    %4.1f", fLength);
printf("\nWidth:     %4.1f", fWidth);
printf("\nHeight:    %4.1f", fHeight);
printf("\nVolume:    %6.1f", fVolume);
```

Each of the above print statements executes a single space, replaces the output specifier with the formatted result, and displays the line on the screen.

```
    return 0;
}
```

The above statement returns a 0 to the operating system. The closing brace marks the end of the main function.

Notes and Tips

1. A character variable (type *char*) can hold exactly one character of data. Use single quotes to assign a constant to a character variable.

2. Like integer and float variables, character variables must have an address operator when used in a scan function.

3. A string variable, or character array (type *char*), can hold a specific number of characters. The length of the string, enclosed within brackets, must be large enough to hold the string and the null character. Double quotes are used to assign a constant to a string variable.

4. String variables do not have an address operator when used in a scan function.

5. Long print statements should be split across two or more lines. Break the statement after the control string at the comma. This convention makes the print statement easier to read. Make it a point never to code any statement beyond column 72.

6. In general, string output should be left-justified. Placing a minus sign in a format specifier will force the output to the left side of a fixed-length field. For example, the specifier *%-20s* will cause the output to shift to the left side of the 20-position field.

Tutorial CHAP2B

1. The objectives of this tutorial are to
   - declare a string variable
   - use the scan function to input numeric and non-numeric data
   - print and left-justify non-numeric data

2. If necessary, open your text editor and enter the sample program shown in Figure 2.5.

3. Save the program on your work disk as CHAP2B.

4. Execute the program. Your output should match the results shown in Figure 2.6. If it doesn't, compare your code with the sample program. Make corrections, save, and run the program again.

5. Once your output is correct, show the results to your instructor.

Quick Quiz

Answer the following questions.

1. Explain what the following declaration does. Why is there a number enclosed within brackets?

   ```
   char sCartonType[10];
   ```

2. In the following statement, what does the *%s* do? Why isn't there an address operator in front of the variable name?

   ```
   scanf(" %s", sCartonType);
   ```

3. Notice that each variable was declared on a separate line. Wouldn't it be easier to code two or more variables on the same line? Explain your answer.

4. Look at the print statement that is split across two lines. Why was this done?

5. Did you encounter any problems or errors when you ran your program? If so, what were they and what did you do to correct them?

Summary

1. A C program consists of a series of programmer-defined functions (modules) that interact wth one another to perform the processing task.

2. A module is a logical unit that performs either a particular procedure or a major processng task.

3. Comments are nonexecutable statements that are used to document the program.

4. The *#include* directive tells the compiler to insert a series of precoded functions in the source program.

5. All C programs have a main() function that signals the start of the program.

6. Data type stipulates how (in what format) the data is stored in memory. Numeric data types define integer and floating-point data. Non-numeric data types define character and string data.

7. A numeric constant represents the value assigned to a numeric variable. The constant may be either an integer or a floating-point number.

8. A numeric variable reserves a location in memory for integer or floating-point data. A variable may assume different values during the program run.

9. The value assigned to a numeric variable may be in the form of a constant, a variable, or an arithmetic expression.

10. The *#define* directive equates a constant to an identifier. Symbolic constants are written in uppercase and retain their values during the program run.

11. An arithmetic expression is a statement that may include numeric constants and variables connected by one or more arithmetic operators.

12. According to the hierarchy of operations, the computer performs exponentiation first; multiplication, division, and modulus second; and addition and subtraction last.

13. The printf() function formats the data stored at the program variables and displays the output on the screen.

14. An escape sequence represents a sequence of characters that begin with a backslash \; the compiler treats the sequence as a single character.

15. The scanf() function reads data from the keyboard and assigns the input to the program variables.

16. A character constant is any single letter, digit, punctuation mark, or special symbol enclosed within single quotes.

17. A string constant consists of two or more characters enclosed within double quotes.

18. A non-numeric variable reserves a location in memory for storing character data. There are two types of non-numeric variables—character and string.

19. The return statement is used to exit either a module or a function.

Programming Projects

For each project, design the logic and write the program to produce the output. Model your program after the samples presented in the chapter. Verify your output.

Note: Xs are used to specify where to print the string data.

Project 2–1   **Charge Account**

Write a program to compute and print the month-end balance. Assume an annual finance rate of 18% on the unpaid balance.

Input (keyboard):

For each customer, prompt for and enter the following data:

Last Name	Previous Balance	Payments	Charges
Allen	5000.00	0.00	200.00
Davis	2150.00	150.00	0.00
Fisher	3400.00	400.00	100.00
Navarez	625.00	125.00	74.00
Stiers	820.00	0.00	0.00
Wyatt	1070.00	200.00	45.00

Output (screen):

For each customer, print the following billing information:

```
Author              CHARGE ACCOUNT      mm/dd/yy

Customer:           X-------X
```

```
Finance charge:      $  99.99
Month-end balance:   $9999.99
```

Processing Requirements:

- Compute the new balance:
  previous balance – payments + charges.
- Compute the finance charge:
  new balance × (annual rate / 12).
- Compute the month-end balance:
  new balance + finance charge.

Project 2–2   Payroll

Write a program to calculate and print the net pay. Assume the current federal income tax (FIT) rate is 15%.

Input (keyboard):

For each employee, prompt for and enter the following data:

Employee	Hours Worked	Hourly Pay Rate
Bauer	40	7.50
Erickson	38	12.00
Howard	40	9.75
Miller	40	10.25
Rossi	35	8.00
York	36	11.00

Output (screen):

For each employee, print the following payroll information:

```
Author       PAYROLL REPORT    mm/dd/yy

Employee:  X--------X
Gross pay: $999.99
FIT:       $ 99.99
Net Pay:   $999.99
```

Processing Requirements:

- Compute the gross pay:
  hours × pay rate.
- Compute the federal income tax amount:
  gross pay × FIT rate.
- Compute the net pay:
  gross pay – FIT amount.

Project 2–3   Sales

Write a program to calculate and print the net profit.

Input (keyboard):

For each salesperson, prompt for and enter the following data:

Salesperson Name	Total Sales	Cost Of Sales
Conrad	8120.52	6450.71
Hickle	2245.78	1072.49
Perkins	12710.14	9735.38
Tian	4567.51	3119.22
Zimmerman	5793.59	4204.45

Output (screen):

For each salesperson, print the following sales information:

```
Author        SALES REPORT     mm/dd/yy


Salesperson:    X---------X
Total Sales:    $99999.99
Cost Of Sales:  $ 9999.99
Net Profit:     $ 9999.99
```

Processing Requirements:

- Compute the net profit:
  total sales – cost of sales.

Project 2–4   Inventory

Write a program to calculate and print the item profit.

Input (keyboard):

For each item, prompt for and enter the following data:

Item Number	Description	Quantity On Hand	Unit Cost	Selling Price
1000	Hammers	24	4.75	9.49
2000	Saws	14	7.50	14.99
3000	Drills	10	7.83	15.95
4000	Screwdrivers	36	2.27	4.98
5000	Pliers	12	2.65	5.49

Output (screen):

For each item, print the following inventory information:

```
Author            INVENTORY REPORT          mm/dd/yy


Item Number: 9999     Description: X--------X
Quantity:    99
Item Profit: $999.99
```

Processing Requirements:

- Compute the total cost:
  quantity × unit cost.

- Compute the total income:
  quantity × selling price.
- Compute the item profit:
  total income − total cost.

Project 2–5   Personnel

Write a program to compute and print the annual salary.

Input (keyboard):

For each employee, prompt for and enter the following data:

Employee Number	Employee Name	Dept Number	Annual Salary	Percent Increase
1926	Andrews	10	29000.00	0.10
2071	Cooper	14	30250.00	0.12
3550	Feldman	22	24175.00	0.07
4298	Palmer	35	33400.00	0.11
5409	Shields	47	27500.00	0.08
6552	Wolfe	31	31773.00	0.10

Output (screen):

For each employee, print the following personnel information:

```
Author              PERSONNEL REPORT           mm/dd/yy


Employee Number:    9999    Name: X--------X
Department Number: 99
Percent Increase:  0.99
New Salary:         $99999.99
```

Processing Requirements:

- Compute the raise amount:
  annual salary × percent increase.
- Compute the annual salary:
  annual salary + raise amount.

Project 2–6   Accounts Payable

Write a program to compute and print the amount due.

Input (keyboard):

For each vendor, prompt for and enter the following data:

Vendor Number	Vendor Name	Invoice Number	Invoice Amount	Discount Rate
217	Metacraft	A1239	2309.12	0.10
349	IntraTell	T9823	670.00	0.09
712	Reylock	F0176	4563.78	0.12
501	Universal	W0105	1200.00	0.09
196	Northland	X2781	3429.34	0.10

Output (screen):

For each vendor, print the following information:

```
Author            ACCOUNTS PAYABLE          mm/dd/yy


Invoice Number:   XXXXX
Vendor Number:    999
Vendor Name:      X--------X
Invoice Amount:   $ 9999.99
Discount Amount:  $  999.99
Amount Due:       $ 9999.99
```

Processing Requirements:

- Compute the discount amount:
  invoice amount × discount rate.
- Compute the amount due:
  invoice amount − discount amount.

Project 2–7   Production Cost

Write a program to compute and print the item production cost.

Input (keyboard):

For each item, prompt for and enter the following data:

Employee Name	Product Number	Units Produced	Unit Cost
Baum	A1234	24	5.50
Fitch	C4510	36	7.94
Hildebrand	R0934	18	6.75
Mullins	E3371	36	3.79
Renner	H9733	24	4.25
Tate	Z0182	27	8.10
West	A3235	30	2.95

Output (screen):

For each item, print the following production information:

```
Author            PRODUCTION COST           mm/dd/yy


Product Number:  XXXXX   Employee: X--------X
Units Produced:  99
Cost Per Unit:   $  9.99
Production Cost: $999.99
```

Processing Requirements:

- Compute the item production cost:
  units produced × unit cost.

3 Modular Programming

Overview

Learning Objectives

After you have read this chapter and completed the exercises, you should be able to

- discuss the concepts and benefits of modular structured programming
- divide a program into a series of self-contained modules
- explain the purpose of the logic structures—sequence, selection, and iteration
- explain why programming guidelines are necessary
- write C programs using top-down design and modular structured programming techniques

Modular Structured Programming

Modular structured programming is a design strategy that is used to manage, organize, and develop computer programs. It consists of a "divide and conquer" approach that breaks up the program into a series of logical units called modules.

Managing the Project

Real-world applications often involve pages upon pages of program logic and code. Even now, at our level, it is becoming clear that we need a better way to organize and manage the program logic.

The purpose of **modular structured programming** is to provide a methodology for managing the programming task. This method allows us to divide a large application into a finite number of self-contained modules. In this way, a large program becomes a series of smaller, logically related tasks that can be developed and tested independently. It is much easier to program one module at a time than to undertake an entire project all at once.

From Chapter 2, we know that a **module** is a self-contained, logical unit of a program that performs a major processing task. Once the modules have been coded and tested, they are assembled to form the completed program.

Once again, consider a program that reads input, performs calculations, and prints output. Obviously, these activities represent three different processing tasks. For logical purposes, it would be better to create three modules—one for reading the input, one for performing the calculations, and one for printing the results—than to combine the tasks into a single block of code.

Modular programming facilitates program management and error control. For example, if a payroll program produces an incorrect result for net pay, we can examine the calculations module directly and correct any errors. Similarly, we examine the output module to fix errors related to printing paychecks.

Modular programming simplifies the debugging process and saves time since errors can be traced more readily. Modular programs are also easier to design, read, and maintain.

Logic Structures

Any programming application, no matter how simple or complex, can be constructed using a combination of three basic logic structures: sequence, selection, and iteration.

Sequence: Sequence refers to the process of executing one statement after another in the order that it appears in the program (for example, input length, input width, input height, compute the volume, and print the output).

Selection: Selection refers to the process of choosing one of two processing options. Consider a payroll application. Compute regular pay. If hours worked exceed 40, compute overtime pay. Otherwise, skip the overtime routine.

A selection process that requires more than two options is called a **case** structure. For example, a bookstore may offer a 10% discount to customers purchasing 2–9 books, a 20% discount for 10–24 books, and a 30% discount for 25 or more books.

Iteration: Iteration refers to the process of repeating a series of statements a given number of times. Iteration is also called **looping**. Suppose we want to compute the paychecks for a department that has 20 employees. We would instruct the computer to compute gross pay, subtract deductions, and print the check and to repeat these steps 20 times—once for each employee.

Global and Local Variables

A variable may be declared either above *main* or inside a programmer-defined module. A variable declared above *main* is called a **global variable** and is available to all modules in the program. As a convention, we will declare global variables above the *main* in a section entitled *Program Variables*.

A **local variable**, on the other hand, is declared inside a specific module and is not available to any other module in the program. A local variable is declared only after the module is actually called by the program and is released upon a return to the calling environment. As a rule, we will declare local variables at the top of the statement body of their respective modules.

Strange as it may seem, local variable names do not have to be unique across modules. The same identifier name can be used in two or more modules. C treats each occurrence of the identifier as a separate variable. This means we can declare a variable called *iTotal* in Module1 to accumulate tickets sold and another variable also called *iTotal* in Module2 to track the number of employees. As far as C is concerned, the two variables are altogether different and it will not confuse one value with the other.

Programmer-Defined Modules

Format:

```
rtype Module(argument/s)
{
    declarations;

    statements;
    return rVariable;
}
```

Purpose: To create a programmer-defined module. The first line, known as the **module header**, specifies information about the module and any parameters required to perform its processing task. The module header does not end with a semicolon.

According to the header, **rtype** refers to the type of variable returned to the calling statement and **Module** refers to the name given to the block of code enclosed within braces. The **argument/s**, enclosed within parentheses, lists the types and names of the variables required by the module. If arguments are *not* passed during the call, then type *void* is coded inside the parentheses. Otherwise, the header identifies the local variables corresponding to the arguments passed to it.

The body of the module is enclosed within braces. Any other local variables required by the procedure are declared at the top of the module. The *return* marks the end of the processing statements and sends the computed result (**rVariable**) back to the calling statement. If coded, only one argument may be returned. The returned variable must match the *rtype* shown in the header.

Example 1:

```
float CalcTotPay(void);             /* module prototype  */
    . . . . .
fGrossPay = CalcTotPay();           /* calling statement */
    . . . . .


/*-------------------------------------------------------------
            CALCULATE TOTAL PAY
---------------------------------------------------------------*/
float CalcTotPay(void)
{
    float fTotPay;

    fTotPay = fHours * fPayrate;
    return fTotPay;
}
```

The prototype indicates that *CalcTotPay* returns a *float* argument, and type *void* says that arguments are not passed to it. Assume that *fHours* and *fPayrate* are global variables—that is, they are available to all modules of the progam—and that the calling statement is coded in the mainline.

When executed, the calling statement transfers control to *CalcTotPay*. The empty parentheses indicate that arguments are not passed. The module header specifies that a floating-point argument will be returned. From here, the module declares a local variable, computes total pay, and assigns the result to *fTotPay*. The last statement returns the result to the calling statement.

Upon returning to the calling statement, the value stored at *fTotPay* is assigned to *fGrossPay*. Basically, the return value replaces the module call shown on the right side of the equal sign. Notice that a boxed comment is used to identify the module. As a standard, we will capitalize the first letter of each word used to create the module name.

Example 2:

```
float CalcAvr(float, float);        /* module prototype  */
    . . . . .
float fAverage;
float fNum1;
```

```
float fNum2;

    .  .  .  .  .

fAverage = CalcAvr(fNum1, fNum2);   /* calling statement */

    .  .  .  .  .

/*-----------------------------------------------------------------
             CALCULATE AVERAGE
-------------------------------------------------------------------*/
float CalvAvr(float fNumX, float fNumY)
{
    float fAvr;

    fAvr = (fNumX + fNumY) / 2.0;
    return fAvr;
}
```

The prototype indicates that *CalcAvr* returns and receives *float* arguments. Assume that the variables declared above the boxed comment belong to the mainline. During the call, the floating-point arguments *fNum1* and *fNum2* are passed to *CalcAvr*. According to the module header, the return type is float and two local variables are declared—*fNumX* to hold *fNum1* and *fNumY* to hold *fNum2*. Next, the local variable *fAvr* is declared and the calculation statement computes the average. The last statement returns the average to the calling statement.

Function Prototypes

Format:

```
rtype Function(type list);
```

Purpose: To describe a function. A **function prototype** describes the characteristics of the function or module to the compiler. In particular, it gives information about the type of argument returned (*rtype*), the name of the module (*Function*), and the number and types of arguments passed (*type list*). It allows the compiler to check for errors—to assure that the types and number of arguments specified by the calling statement match those given by the prototype. All prototypes should be coded at the beginning of the program before *main*. Each function prototype ends with a semicolon.

Since programmer-defined modules are functions, they must be prototyped. Make it a habit to prototype all programmer-defined modules. Beginning with this chapter, we will code the function prototypes right after the preprocessing directives.

The *main* function is not prototyped. Since it is always the first module executed in the program and since no other modules call it, a prototype is not required. But it is the only module that falls into this category.

Examples:

```
1.  void GetInput(void);
2.  float CalcAverage(int, int);
3.  float ConvertMiles(float);
```

The first prototype tells the compiler that the module neither receives arguments nor returns a value. Look at the second example. It describes a module that receives two integer arguments and returns a floating-point value. The last example receives a floating-point argument and returns a floating-point value.

Checkpoint 3A

1. Explain the purpose of modular structured programming.
2. Identify and explain the three basic logic structures.
3. Differentiate between global and local variables.
4. Code the prototype to describe a programmer-defined module that receives an integer value and returns a floating-point value. Give it the name *ModOne*.
5. Code the prototype to describe a programmer-defined module that receives a character and returns no value. Give it the name *ModTwo*.
6. Code the prototype to describe a module that receives three float arguments and returns a float argument. Give it the name *ModThree*.

Sample Program CHAP3A

The one function program shown in Figure 3.1 was introduced in Chapter 2. Although the code is shown in its original form, the program will be modified to demonstrate the technique of modular structured programming.

Recall that the program computes the volume of a storage carton given the length, width, and height in feet. The input and output are shown in Figure 3.2; the specifications and logic design were given in Chapter 2. The hierarchy chart for the program is shown in Figure 3.3.

Sample program CHAP3A illustrates the modular version of the volume program. The modular version of the pseudocode is shown below. Note that in Figure 3.4, a *MAIN-LINE* has been added to the flowchart. This topic will be discussed further in the program dissection. The program code is shown in Figure 3.5.

Pseudocode:

Two new conventions introduced in the following pseudocode require explanation. First, any statement beginning with the word *Call* specifies a call to the named module. Second, a block of code beginning with *ENTER* and ending with *RETURN* represents a module.

```
START: Main
Call Input Data
Call Calculate Volume
Call Print Output
END

ENTER: Input Data
Prompt and enter carton type
Prompt and enter carton number
```

```
/*-----------------------------------------------------------------
CARTON VOLUME: Input the data from the keyboard, compute, and print
the volume of a storage carton.

Program:    CHAP2B.C
Author:     David M. Collopy
Date:       mm/dd/yy
Project:    Sample program from Chapter 2
*************************************************************************/

#include <stdio.h>

main()
{
    /* declare variables */
    char  sCartonType[10];      /* carton type      */
    int   iCartonNum;           /* carton number    */
    float fLength;              /* length of carton */
    float fWidth;               /* width of carton  */
    float fHeight;              /* height of carton */
    float fVolume;              /* volume of carton */

    /* input the data */
    printf("  Enter carton type: ");
    scanf(" %s", sCartonType);
    printf("Enter carton number: ");
    scanf(" %d", &iCartonNum);
    printf("Enter carton length: ");
    scanf(" %f", &fLength);
    printf(" Enter carton width: ");
    scanf(" %f", &fWidth);
    printf("Enter carton height: ");
    scanf(" %f", &fHeight);

    /* calculate volume */
    fVolume = fLength * fWidth * fHeight;

    /* display output on the screen*/
    printf("\n\nDCollopy      Carton Volume      mm/dd/yy\n");
    printf("\nCarton type: %-10s   Carton no: %d",
        sCartonType, iCartonNum);
    printf("\nLength:  %4.1f", fLength);
    printf("\nWidth:   %4.1f", fWidth);
    printf("\nHeight:  %4.1f", fHeight);
    printf("\nVolume:  %6.1f", fVolume);

    return 0;
}
```

FIGURE 3.1 Program Code to Compute the Volume of a Storage Carton

```
   Enter carton type: Desk
Enter carton number: 1180
Enter carton length: 3.5
 Enter carton width: 2.3
Enter carton height: 4.1


DCollopy        Carton Volume        mm/dd/yy

Carton type: Desk            Carton no: 1180
Length:   3.5
Width:    2.3
Height:   4.1
Volume: 33.0
```

FIGURE 3.2   Screen Input and Output

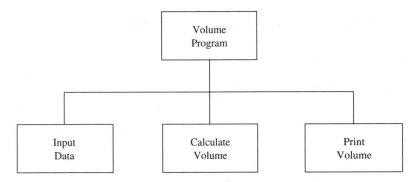

FIGURE 3.3   Hierarchy Chart for CHAP3A

Prompt and enter length
Prompt and enter width
Prompt and enter height
RETURN

ENTER: Calculate Volume
Compute volume:
    length × width × height
RETURN

ENTER: Print Output
Print output lines:
    title line
    carton type and carton number
    length

```
                    width
                    height
                    volume
            RETURN
```

Hierarchy Chart: A **hierarchy chart**, or block diagram, divides the program into levels of tasks (modules) and shows the relationship between them. Figure 3.3 shows the hierarchy chart for the sample program. The first level specifies the purpose of the program, whereas the second level shows the processing tasks performed by the program. In general, as we move down the chart, higher-level tasks requiring more detail are further subdivided into subordinate tasks.

Program Flowchart: See Figure 3.4.

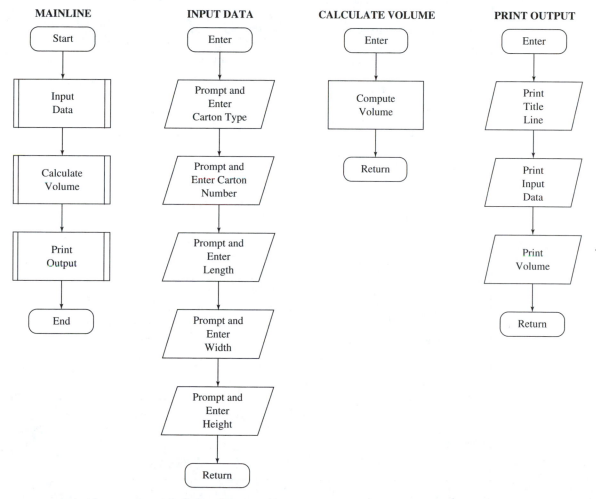

FIGURE 3.4   Program Flowchart for CHAP3A

```
/*----------------------------------------------------------------
CARTON VOLUME: Input the data from the keyboard, compute, and print
the volume of a storage carton.

Program:    CHAP3A.C
Author:     David M. Collopy
Date:       mm/dd/yy
Project:    Sample program - modular version
********************************************************************/

/*---- PREPROCESSING DIRECTIVES ----------------------------------*/

#include <stdio.h>

/*---- FUNCTION PROTOTYPES ---------------------------------------*/

void  InputData(void);          /* input data       */
float CalcVolume(void);         /* calculate volume */
void  PrnOutput(float);         /* print output     */

/*---- PROGRAM VARIABLES -----------------------------------------*/

char  sCartonType[10];          /* carton type      */
int   iCartonNum;               /* carton number    */
float fLength;                  /* length of carton */
float fWidth;                   /* width of carton  */
float fHeight;                  /* height of carton */

/*----------------------------------------------------------------
      MAINLINE CONTROL
----------------------------------------------------------------*/
main()
{
    float fVolume;              /* volume of carton      */

    InputData();               /* call input data       */
    fVolume = CalcVolume();    /* call calculate volume */
    PrnOutput(fVolume);        /* call print output     */
    return 0;
}

/*----------------------------------------------------------------
      INPUT DATA
----------------------------------------------------------------*/
void InputData(void)
{
```

FIGURE 3.5   Sample Program CHAP3A: Modular Version of the Volume Program

```
        printf("  Enter carton type: ");
        scanf(" %s", sCartonType);
        printf("Enter Carton number: ");
        scanf(" %d", &iCartonNum);
        printf("Enter carton length: ");
        scanf(" %f", &fLength);
        printf(" Enter carton width: ");
        scanf(" %f", &fWidth);
        printf("Enter carton height: ");
        scanf(" %f", &fHeight);
        return;
    }


    /*-------------------------------------------------------------
          CALCULATE VOLUME
    ----------------------------------------------------------------*/
    float CalcVolume(void)
    {
        float fVolume;                   /* return volume */

        fVolume = fLength * fWidth * fHeight;
        return fVolume;
    }


    /*-------------------------------------------------------------
          PRINT OUTPUT
    ----------------------------------------------------------------*/
    void PrnOutput(float fVolume)
    {
        printf("\n\nDCollopy      Carton Volume     mm/dd/yy\n");
        printf("\nCarton type: %-10s    Carton no: %d",
            sCartonType, iCartonNum);
        printf("\nLength:  %4.1f", fLength);
        printf("\nWidth:   %4.1f", fWidth);
        printf("\nHeight:  %4.1f", fHeight);
        printf("\nVolume:  %6.1f", fVolume);
        return;
    }
```

FIGURE 3.5   *Continued*

Dissection of Sample Program CHAP3A

The top-down modular version of the volume program consists of four modules: *MAIN-LINE CONTROL, INPUT DATA, CALCULATE VOLUME,* and *PRINT OUTPUT.* The first module, the *MAINLINE,* controls the sequence of calls to the other modules. In turn, the lower-level modules carry out the detailed processing tasks required by the program.

This arrangement of modules, from high-level control logic to low-level detail, is called top-down programming. **Top-down** refers to the strategy of developing the major program control logic first and the detailed processing steps last.

Notice how line comments are used to identify the different parts of the program and to highlight the processing modules. This makes the program code easier to read and understand.

```
/*---- PREPROCESSING DIRECTIVES -------------------------------*/

#include <stdio.h>
```

The line comment tells us that this is where the preprocessing directives are coded in the program. The *#include* directive instructs the compiler to insert the standard input/output header file in the source program.

```
/*---- FUNCTION PROTOTYPES ---------------------------------*/

void  InputData(void);
float CalcVolume(void);
void  PrnOutput(float);
```

Function prototypes describe the characteristics of the program modules to the compiler. Each prototype gives the name of the module, information about the number and type of arguments passed, and the type of return value.

Hence, the above prototypes tell the compiler that *InputData* neither receives arguments nor returns a value, *CalcVolume* returns a floating-point value, and *PrnOutput* receives a floating-point argument.

```
/*---- PROGRAM VARIABLES -----------------------------------*/

char    sCartonType[10];
int     iCartonNum;
float   fLength;
float   fWidth;
float   fHeight;
```

The above statement defines the global variables required by the program. Remember, global variables are visible (available) to all of the modules in the program. Since the input data items are usually required by several modules in the program, they will be declared as global variables.

```
/*---------------------------------------------------------
                MAINLINE CONTROL
-------------------------------------------------------*/
main()
{
```

The comment tells us that this is the *MAINLINE CONTROL* module. This is where the program controls the order in which the other modules are processed by the computer. We will normally use box-style comments to identify the modules.

```
    float fVolume();
```

The above statement declares volume as a local variable. A local variable is visible only to the module in which it is declared, that is, *fVolume* is local and visible only to the *main* function. Other modules do not have access to *fVolume* unless it is passed during a call.

```
    InputData();
```

The above statement issues a call and transfers processing control to the *InputData* module. The empty parentheses () tell the compiler that arguments are not passed to the module.

```
    fVolume = CalcVolume();
```

The above statement calls *CalcVolume* and performs the statements coded there. Upon completing its task, the called module returns an argument to the calling statement. The value of the return argument replaces the module call and is assigned to *fVolume*.

```
    PrnOutput(fVolume);
```

The above statement calls *PrnOutput* and passes the argument enclosed within parentheses to the module. This call gives the output module access to the data stored at *fVolume*.

```
    return 0;
}
```

For a successful run, the above statement returns a 0 to the operating system.

```
/*---------------------------------------------------------------
                INPUT DATA
-------------------------------------------------------------*/
void InputData(void)
{
```

The above comment identifies *InputData* as the second module. The opening brace marks the beginning of the statement body of the module.

```
    printf("  Enter carton type: ");
    scanf(" %s", sCartonType);
    printf("Enter carton number:   ");
    scanf(" %d", &iCartonNum);
    printf("Enter carton length:   ");
    scanf(" %f", &fLength);
    printf(" Enter carton width:   ");
    scanf(" %f", &fWidth);
    printf("Enter carton height: ");
    scanf(" %f", &fHeight);
    return;
}
```

The above statements prompt the user to input the type, number, length, width, and height of a storage carton. The *return* statement sends control back to the mainline, and the closing brace marks the end of the input module.

```
/*---------------------------------------------------------------
                CALCULATE VOLUME
-------------------------------------------------------------*/
```

```
float CalcVolume(void)
{
    float fVolume;

    fVolume = fLength * fWidth * fHeight;
    return fVolume;
}
```

The above module computes the volume of the storage carton and returns the result to the mainline. The first statement declares a local variable. The second computes the volume and assigns the result to *fVolume*. The third returns the volume to the calling statement in the mainline. Upon executing a return, all local variables defined by a module are released. In this case, *fVolume* is released from memory and is no longer available to the module.

```
/*-------------------------------------------------------------------
            PRINT OUTPUT
-------------------------------------------------------------------*/
void PrnOutput(float fVolume)
{
    printf("\n\nDCollopy      Carton Volume      mm/dd/yy\n);
    printf("\nCarton type: %-10s   Carton no: %d",
        sCartonType, iCartonNum);
    printf("\nLength:   %4.1f", fLength);
    printf("\nWidth:    %4.1f", fWidth);
    printf("\nHeight:   %4.1f", fHeight);
    printf("\nVolume:   %6.1f", fVolume);
    return;
}
```

The above statements print the output on the screen. Before the volume can be printed, the output module must have access to it. This is why *fVolume* is passed to *PrnOuput*. Since the other variables are global, there is no need to pass them to the output module.

Notes and Tips

1. Except for the *Mainline*, each module must have a prototype. Prototypes are placed in the program after the preprocessing directives.

2. If a module is not prototyped, the compiler will generate an error message.

3. The data types of the module header must match the data types shown for the prototype.

4. Do not terminate a module header with a semicolon. If you do, the compiler will produce an error message.

5. For debugging purposes, print off a hard copy of the source code. It is much easier to debug a program from a copy of the program than it is to scroll up and down the screen looking for errors.

6. In general, the input data items should be declared as global variables. Variables used to process the data should be declared as local.

7. For now, the structure of your programs consist of the following parts: Documentation Comments, Preprocessing Directives, Function Prototypes, Program Variables, Mainline Control, Input Data, Calculate Results, and Print Output.

Tutorial CHAP3A

1. The objectives of this tutorial are to
   - divide a program into a series of modules
   - use top-down design and modular structure programming techniques
   - call modules and pass and return arguments
2. Open the text editor, and retrieve the source file CHAP2B from your work disk. You completed this project in Tutorial CHAP2B. Use the changes shown in Figure 3.5 to modify your source code to include the modular structure shown in the sample program.
3. Desk check for keyboarding errors, and save your work as CHAP3A.
4. Compile, run, and debug your code until the program is running correctly. Figure 3.2 shows the output. Save your work after making changes to it.
5. Once the output is correct, show the results to your instructor.

Quick Quiz

Answer the following questions.

1. Why is it necessary to code prototypes for all of the programmer-defined modules?
2. Explain why type *void* is used in some of the prototypes.
3. What does the following prototype mean to you?

   float CalcVolume(void);
4. Explain how the *Mainline* controls the processing activities performed by the rest of the program.
5. What does the following call statement do?

   fVolume = CalcVolume();
6. Discuss the action(s) performed by the return statement shown below.

   return fVolume;
7. There seems to be a lot of work associated with the activity of dividing up a program into a series of tasked-based modules. So why bother?
8. Did you encounter any problems or errors when you ran your program? If so, what were they and what did you do to correct them?

Sample Program CHAP3B

To further illustrate the concepts of top-down design and modular programming, let's look at a second example. Sample program CHAP3B shows the code without modules, and

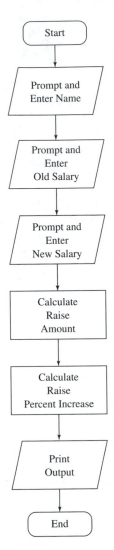

FIGURE 3.6   Program Flowchart for CHAP3B

sample program CHAP3C shows the code with modules. (The flowchart for CHAP3B is shown in Figure 3.6; the code, in Figure 3.7; and the output, in Figure 3.8.)

Both programs compute the new salary and percent increase for Mr. Wilson given his old salary and new salary. The following specifications apply:

Input (keyboard):
Prompt for and enter the following data:

Employee Name	Old Salary	New Salary
Wilson	25000.00	26450.00

```
/*-------------------------------------------------------------
RAISE INCREASE: Input the data from the keyboard, compute, and print
the raise amount and percent increase in pay for Mr. Wilson.

Program:    CHAP3B.C
Author:     David M. Collopy
Date:       mm/dd/yy
Project:    Sample program
*********************************************************************/

#include <stdio.h>

main()
{
    /* declare variables */
    char  sEmplName[12];               /* employee name           */
    float fOldSalary;                  /* old salary              */
    float fNewSalary;                  /* new salary              */
    float fRaiseAmt;                   /* raise amount increase   */
    float fRaisePerc;                  /* raise percent increase  */

    /* input the data */
    printf("Enter employee name: ");
    scanf(" %s", sEmplName);
    printf("   Enter old salary: ");
    scanf(" %f", &fOldSalary);
    printf("   Enter new salary: ");
    scanf(" %f", &fNewSalary);

    /* calculate results */
    fRaiseAmt = fNewSalary - fOldSalary;
    fRaisePerc = (fRaiseAmt / fOldSalary) * 100.00;

    /* display output on the screen */
    printf("\n\n%s received a %3.1f%% raise and",
        sEmplName, fRaisePerc);
    printf("\nnow earns $%7.2f more a year.",
        fRaiseAmt);

    return 0;
}
```

FIGURE 3.7   Sample Program CHAP3B: Compute Raise Amount and Percent Increase in Salary for Mr. Wilson

```
Enter employee name: Wilson
    Enter old salary: 25000.00
    Enter new salary: 26450.00

Wilson received a 5.8% raise and
now earns $1450.00 more a year.
```

FIGURE 3.8   Screen Input and Output for CHAP3B

Output (screen):
Print the following output on the screen:

```
Wilson received a 9.9% raise and
now earns $9999.99 more a year.
```

Processing Requirements:

- Define the program variables.
- Compute the raise amount:
  new salary – old salary.
- Compute the percent increase:
  (raise amount / old salary) × 100.
- Print the output on the screen.

Pseudocode:

START: Main
Prompt and enter the employee name
Prompt and enter old salary
Prompt and enter new salary
Calculate raise amount:
    new salary – old salary
Calculate raise percent:
    (raise amount / old salary) × 100
Print output lines:
    employee name and raise percent increase
    raise amount
END

Program Flowchart: See Figure 3.6.

Sample Program CHAP3C

Sample program CHAP3C shows the modular version of the raise program. The hierarchy chart is shown in Figure 3.9, and the program flowchart is shown in Figure 3.10. Sample program CHAP3C is presented in Figure 3.11.

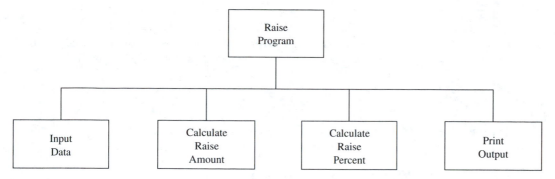

FIGURE 3.9   Hierarchy Chart for CHAP3C

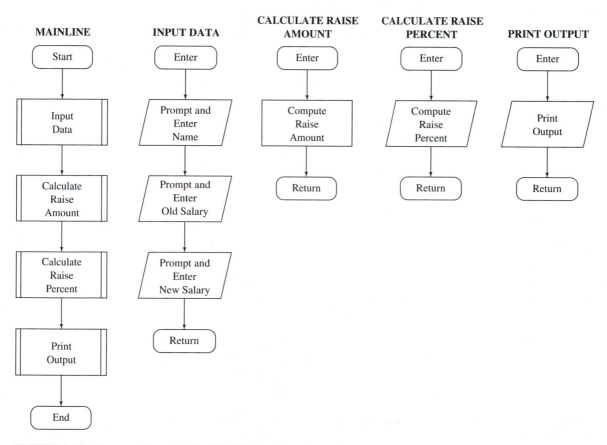

FIGURE 3.10   Program Flowchart for CHAP3C

```
/*------------------------------------------------------------
RAISE INCREASE: Input the data from the keyboard, compute, and print
the raise amount and percent increase in pay for Mr. Wilson.

Program:    CHAP3C.C
Author:     David M. Collopy
Date:       mm/dd/yy
Project:    Sample program - modular version
***************************************************************/


/*---- PREPROCESSING DIRECTIVE -----------------------------------*/

#include <stdio.h>


/*---- FUNCTION PROTOTYPES ---------------------------------------*/

void  InputData(void);          /* input data              */
float CalcRaiseAmt(void);       /* calculate raise amount  */
float CalcRaisePerc(float);     /* calculate raise percent */
void  PrnOutput(float, float);  /* print output            */


/*---- PROGRAM VARIABLES -----------------------------------------*/

char   sEmplName[12];           /* employee name */
float  fOldSalary;              /* old salary    */
float  fNewSalary;              /* new salary    */


/*------------------------------------------------------------
      MAINLINE CONTROL
------------------------------------------------------------*/
main()
{
    float fRaiseAmt;            /* raise dollar amount   */
    float fRaisePerc;          /* raise percent increase */

    InputData();
    fRaiseAmt = CalcRaiseAmt();
    fRaisePerc = CalcRaisePerc(fRaiseAmt);
    PrnOutput(fRaiseAmt, fRaisePerc);
    return 0;
}


/*------------------------------------------------------------
      INPUT DATA
------------------------------------------------------------*/
```

FIGURE 3.11   Sample Program CHAP3C: Modular Version of the Raise Program

```
void InputData(void)
{
    printf("Enter employee name: ");
    scanf(" %s", sEmplName);
    printf("   Enter old salary: ");
    scanf(" %f", &fOldSalary);
    printf("   Enter new salary: ");
    scanf(" %f", &fNewSalary);
    return;
}

/*----------------------------------------------------------------
      CALCULATE RAISE AMOUNT
----------------------------------------------------------------*/
float CalcRaiseAmt(void)
{
    float fRaiseAmt;              /* return raise amount */

    fRaiseAmt = fNewSalary - fOldSalary;
    return fRaiseAmt;
}

/*----------------------------------------------------------------
      CALCULATE RAISE PERCENT
----------------------------------------------------------------*/
float CalcRaisePerc(float fRaiseAmt)
{
    float fRaisePerc;            /* return raise percent */

    fRaisePerc = (fRaiseAmt / fOldSalary) * 100.00;
    return fRaisePerc;
}

/*----------------------------------------------------------------
      PRINT OUTPUT
----------------------------------------------------------------*/
void PrnOutput(float fRaiseAmt, float fRaisePerc)
{
    printf("\n\n%s received a %3.1f%% raise and",
        sEmplName, fRaisePerc);
    printf("\nnow earns $%7.2f more a year.",
        fRaiseAmt);
    return;
}
```

FIGURE 3.11 *Continued*

From the top down, the *MAINLINE* controls the order that the modules are called by the program. One by one the modules perform the detailed processing tasks required to produce the desired output.

Pseudocode:

```
START: Main
Call Input Data
Call Calculate Raise Amount
Call Calculate Raise Percent
Call Print Output
END

ENTER: Input Data
Prompt and enter employee name
Prompt and enter old salary
Prompt and enter new salary
RETURN

ENTER: Calculate Raise Amount
Compute raise amount:
     new salary – old salary
RETURN

ENTER: Calculate Raise Percent
Compute raise percent increase:
     (raise amount / old salary) × 100
RETURN

ENTER: Print output
Print output lines:
     employee name and raise percent increase
     raise amount
RETURN
```

Hierarchy Chart: See Figure 3.9.

Program Flowchart: See Figure 3.10.

Dissection of Sample Program CHAP3C

Let's pick up the dissection beginning with the function prototypes.

```
F U N C T I O N    P R O T O T Y P E S:
void   InputData(void);
float  CalcRaiseAmt(void);
float  CalcRaisePerc(float);
void   PrnOutput(float, float);
```

The above statements describe the processing modules to the compiler. The first prototype has no arguments. The second returns a floating-point argument. The third passes and returns a floating-point argument. The last prototype passes two floating-point arguments.

```
P R O G R A M   V A R I A B L E S:
char   sEmplName[12];
float  fOldSalary;
float  fNewSalary;
```

The above declarations identify and describe the input data items. Since they are declared above the *main*, the input variables are global and available to all modules in the program.

```
M A I N L I N E    C O N T R O L:

main()
{
    float  fRaiseAmt:
    float  fRaisePerc;

    InputData();
    fRaiseAmt = CalcRaiseAmt();
    fRaisePerc = CalcRaisePerc(fRaiseAmt);
    PrnOutput(fRaiseAmt, fRaisePerc);
    return 0;
}
```

The *main* declares two local variables and executes four calls to the processing modules in the order shown. The first call transfers control to *InputData*; the second calls *CalcRaiseAmt* and returns a value; the third calls *CalcRaisePerc*, passes an argument, and returns a value; and the fourth calls *PrnOutput* and passes two arguments. The last statement returns a 0 to the operating system.

```
I N P U T    D A T A:

void InputData(void)
{
    printf("Enter employee name: ");
    scanf(" %s", sEmplName);
```

This module neither receives arguments nor returns a value. The above statements prompt the user to enter the employee's name. The scan statement reads the input, converts it to a string, and assigns the result to *sEmplName*. There is no need to append the address operator (&) to the string variable. Since the identifier name, a character array, represents the address to the variable, the address is already known.

```
    printf("   Enter old salary: ");
    scanf(" %f", &fOldSalary);
    printf("   Enter new salary: ");
    scanf(" %f", &fNewSalary);
    return;
}
```

The above statements prompt the user to enter the old and new salaries. Essentially, the scan functions read the input, convert it to float, and assign the results to the variables *fOldSalary* and *fNewSalary*, respectively. Here you must append the address operator to the variable names. Since the identifier names associated with numeric variables do *not* represent addresses to the memory locations, the & must be coded.

C A L C U L A T E   R A I S E   A M O U N T:

```
float CalcRaiseAmt(void)
{
    float fRaiseAmt;
```

This module returns a floating-point argument to the calling statement. The declaration declares *fRaiseAmt* as a local variable. The local variable is used to store the return value.

```
    fRaiseAmt = fNewSalary - fOldSalary;
```

The above statement computes the dollar amount of the raise and assigns the result to *fRaiseAmt*.

```
    return fRaiseAmt;
}
```

The above statement returns the value stored at *fRaiseAmt* to the calling statement.

C A L C U L A T E   R A I S E   P E R C E N T:

```
float CalcRaisePerc(float fRaiseAmt)
{
    float fRaisePerc;
```

This module receives a floating-point argument that is assigned to the local variable *fRaiseAmt*. The declaration defines *fRaisePerc* as a local variable. The local variable is used to store the return value.

```
    fRaisePerc = (fRaiseAmt / fOldSalary) * 100.00;
```

The above statement divides the raise amount by the old salary. To show the result as a percentage, the expression enclosed within parentheses is multiplied by 100.

```
    return fRaisePerc;
}
```

The above statement returns the value stored at *fRaisePerc* to the calling statement.

P R I N T   O U T P U T:

```
void PrnOutput(float fRaiseAmt, float fRaisePerc)
{
    printf("\n\n%s received a %3.1f%% raise and",
        sEmplName, fRaisePerc);
```

The above module receives two arguments that are assigned to *fRaiseAmt* and *fRaisePerc*, respectively. The print statement performs a double space and displays the employee name and raise percentage on the screen. The %% in the control string tells the compiler that the second % sign is not part of the format specifier, but instead part of the output message.

```
        printf("\nnow earns $%7.2f more a year.",
            fRaiseAmt);
        return;
}
```

The above statement performs a single space and displays the raise amount on the screen.

Notes and Tips

Because it is important to understand how argument pass and return works, let's take another look at the following call coded in the *Mainline*:

```
        fRaisePerc = CalcRaisePerc(fRaiseAmt);
```

The above call (coded on the right side of the equal sign) passes the raise amount to *CalcRaisePerc*. Since *fRaiseAmt* is local to *main*, it must be passed to the called module. The called module, in turn, uses raise amount to compute the percent increase in salary. Once computed, the percent increase is returned to the calling statement and assigned to the variable (*fRaisePerc*) coded on the left side of the equal sign.

The interesting and confusing thing here is that when *fRaiseAmt* (a local variable known to *main*) is passed to the called module, it is assigned to a local variable (known only to *CalcRaisePerc*) with the same name. In other words, *fRaiseAmt* is assigned to *fRaiseAmt*. Now remember, this is not a problem in C. The compiler allows you to use the same identifier name in different modules. Even though the names are spelled the same, the address pointers to the variables are *not* the same. Hence, C is able to treat them as unique variables.

Tutorial CHAP3C

1. The objectives of this tutorial are to
   - divide a program into a series of modules
   - use top-down design and modular structure programming techniques
   - call modules and pass and return arguments
2. If necessary, open your text editor and enter the code as shown in Figure 3.11.
3. Save the source program on your work disk under the name CHAP3C.
4. Compile, run, and debug your program until the output matches the results shown in Figure 3.8. Develop the habit of saving your work frequently.
5. When completed, show your work to your instructor.

Quick Quiz

Answer the following questions.

1. What does the following prototype describe to the compiler?
   void PrnOutput(float, float);

2. Why are the input data items declared as global variables?

3. Describe what the following call statement does.

   fRaisePerc = CalcRaisePerc(fRaiseAmt);

4. Explain what the line below does. (Note that there is no semicolon coded at the end of the line.)

   void PrnOutput(float fRaiseAmt, float fRaisePerc)

5. Other than keyboarding errors, did you encounter any problems or errors when you ran your program? If so, what were they and what did you do to correct them?

Structured Programming

Structured programming represents the technique of writing programs that emphasizes top-down design and modular programming. This approach aids in the design and construction of high-quality programs that are easy to read, test, and debug.

Modular programming refers to the process of dividing up a program into smaller self-contained modules or functions. The basic idea behind this method is to group logically related statements that perform a single task.

Programming Guidelines

The purpose of **programming guidelines** is to provide standards that help design and construct programs that are reliable and easy to maintain over the life of the system.

The following guidelines apply to structured programming:

1. A module should have one entry point and one exit point. In sample program CHAP3C, control enters each module at the top and exits with the return at the bottom.

2. A module should perform one task. For example, reading data and computing totals represent two tasks. Therefore, they should be separate. Avoid putting unrelated tasks in the same module. Group only those statements that belong together.

3. A program should
   - be self-documenting (use identifier names that describe the variables, modules, and functions)
   - use comments to document the code and explain any unusual or complex processing
   - use simple coding structures
   - use comments to identify the modules and functions
   - consist of no more than 20 statements per module

It pays to develop good habits early. If you use the guidelines regularly, you should be able to write quality programs in less time. Not only that, you should be able to enjoy the benefits derived from structured programming as well.

1. Programs are easier to maintain—to update and modify.

2. Programs are easier to design and code—fewer errors are encountered during the development stages.

3. Programs are more reliable—fewer errors are encountered during production runs.

4. Programs are easier to read and understand, even by someone who is unfamiliar with them.

5. Programs are easier to test and debug.

6. Documentation is easier to write and maintain.

Checkpoint 3B

1. Describe top-down design and modular programming.

2. What three guidelines apply to structured programming? Why are they important?

3. Identify the six benefits associated with structured programming.

Summary

1. Modular structured programming is a design strategy that breaks up a program into a series of self-contained modules that are designed, programmed, and tested independently.

2. Logic structures—sequence, selection, and iteration—are used to construct a program.

3. Sequence refers to the process of executing one statement after another in the order that they appear in the program.

4. Selection refers to the process of choosing between two processing options. A selection process that requires more than two options is called a case structure.

5. Iteration refers to the process of repeating a series of statements a given number of times.

6. A global variable is declared outside the *main* function and is available to all modules of the program. A local variable is declared inside a specific module and is available only to that module.

7. A module is a logical segment of the program that performs a specific processing task. Modules can receive one or more arguments and return a value.

8. The first line of a programmer-defined module is called the module header. It specifies information about the module and any parameters required to perform its processing task.

9. A function prototype describes the parameters of the function to the compiler—function name, number and types of arguments, and the return type. Function prototypes are coded at the beginning of the program.

10. A hierarchy chart divides the program into levels of tasks and shows the relationship between them. As we move down the chart, higher-level tasks requiring more detail are further subdivided into subordinate tasks.

11. Top-down refers to the design strategy that focuses on coding the high-level control logic first and the detailed processing steps last.

12. The mainline, coded at the beginning of a program, controls the calls to the modules and the order in which they are processed.

13. Structured programming represents the technique of writing programs that emphasizes top-down design and modular programming.

14. The purpose of the programming guidelines is to provide standards that help design and construct quality programs that are easy to code, test, and debug.

Programming Projects

For each project, design the logic and write the modular structured program to produce the output. Model your program after the sample programs presented in the chapter. Verify your output.

Project 3–1   Charge Account

Write a program to compute and print the month-end balance. Assume an annual finance rate of 18% on the unpaid balance.

Input (keyboard):
For each customer, prompt for and enter the following data:

Last Name	Previous Balance	Payments	Charges
Allen	5000.00	0.00	200.00
Davis	2150.00	150.00	0.00
Fisher	3400.00	400.00	100.00
Navarez	625.00	125.00	74.00
Stiers	820.00	0.00	0.00
Wyatt	1070.00	200.00	45.00

Output (screen):
For each customer, print the following report:

```
Author       CHARGE ACCOUNT      mm/dd/yy

Customer:            X--------X
Finance charge:      $  99.99
Month-end balance: $9999.99
```

Processing Requirements:

- Compute the new balance:
  previous balance – payments + charges.
- Compute the finance charge:
  new balance × (annual rate / 12).
- Compute the month-end balance:
  new balance + finance charge.

Project 3–2   Payroll

Write a program to calculate and print the net pay. Assume the current federal income tax (FIT) rate is 15%.

Input (keyboard):

For each employee, prompt for and enter the following data:

Employee	Hours Worked	Hourly Pay Rate
Bauer	40	7.50
Erickson	38	12.00
Howard	40	9.75
Miller	40	10.25
Rossi	35	8.00
York	36	11.00

Output (screen):

For each employee, print the following report:

```
Author      PAYROLL REPORT    mm/dd/yy


Employee:  X--------X
Gross pay: $999.99
FIT:       $ 99.99
Net Pay:   $999.99
```

Processing Requirements:

- Compute the gross pay:
  hours × pay rate.
- Compute the federal income tax amount:
  gross pay × FIT rate.
- Compute the net pay:
  gross pay – FIT amount.

Project 3–3   Sales

Write a program to calculate and print the net profit.

Input (keyboard):

For each salesperson, prompt for and enter the following data:

Salesperson Name	Total Sales	Cost Of Sales
Conrad	8120.52	6450.71
Hickle	2245.78	1072.49
Perkins	12710.14	9735.38
Tian	4567.51	3119.22
Zimmerman	5793.59	4204.45

Output (screen):

For each salesperson, print the following report:

```
Author      SALES REPORT    mm/dd/yy


Salesperson:    X---------X
Total Sales:    $99999.99
Cost Of Sales:  $ 9999.99
Net Profit:     $ 9999.99
```

Processing Requirements:

- Compute the net profit:
  total sales – cost of sales.

Project 3–4   Inventory

Write a program to calculate and print the item profit.

Input (keyboard):
For each item, prompt for and enter the following data:

Item Number	Description	Quantity On Hand	Unit Cost	Selling Price
1000	Hammers	24	4.75	9.49
2000	Saws	14	7.50	14.99
3000	Drills	10	7.83	15.95
4000	Screwdrivers	36	2.27	4.98
5000	Pliers	12	2.65	5.49

Output (screen):
For each item, print the following report:

```
Author              INVENTORY REPORT              mm/dd/yy

Item Number: 9999    Description: X--------X
Quantity:    99
Item Profit: $999.99
```

Processing Requirements:

- Compute the total cost:
  quantity × unit cost.
- Compute the total income:
  quantity × selling price.
- Compute the item profit:
  total income – total cost.

Project 3–5   Personnel

Write a program to compute and print the annual salary.

Input (keyboard):
For each employee, prompt for and enter the following data:

Employee Number	Employee Name	Dept Number	Annual Salary	Percent Increase
1926	Andrews	10	29000.00	0.10
2071	Cooper	14	30250.00	0.12
3550	Feldman	22	24175.00	0.07
4298	Palmer	35	33400.00	0.11
5409	Shields	47	27500.00	0.08
6552	Wolfe	31	31773.00	0.10

Output (screen):

For each employee, print the following report:

```
Author            PERSONNEL REPORT           mm/dd/yy

Employee Number:    9999    Name: X--------X
Department Number: 99
Percent Increase:  0.99
New Salary:         $99999.99
```

Processing Requirements:

- Compute the raise amount:
  annual salary × percent increase.
- Compute the annual salary:
  annual salary + raise amount.

Project 3–6   Accounts Payable

Write a program to compute and print the amount due.

Input (keyboard):

For each vendor, prompt for and enter the following data:

Vendor Number	Vendor Name	Invoice Number	Invoice Amount	Discount Rate
217	Metacraft	A1239	2309.12	0.10
349	IntraTell	T9823	670.00	0.09
712	Reylock	F0176	4563.78	0.12
501	Universal	W0105	1200.00	0.09
196	Northland	X2781	3429.34	0.10

Output (screen):

For each vendor, print the following report:

```
Author            ACCOUNTS PAYABLE         mm/dd/yy

Invoice Number:    XXXX
Vendor Number:     999
Vendor Name:       X--------X
Invoice Amount:    $9999.99
Discount Amount:   $ 999.99
Amount Due:        $9999.99
```

Processing Requirements:

- Compute the discount amount:
  invoice amount × discount rate.
- Compute the amount due:
  invoice amount – discount amount.

Project 3–7   Production Cost

Write a program to compute and print the item production cost.

Input (keyboard):

For each item, prompt for and enter the following data:

Employee Name	Product Number	Units Produced	Unit Cost
Baum	A1234	24	5.50
Fitch	C4510	36	7.94
Hildebrand	R0934	18	6.75
Mullins	E3371	36	3.79
Renner	H9733	24	4.25
Tate	Z0182	27	8.10
West	A3235	30	2.95

Output (screen):

For each item, print the following report:

```
Author               PRODUCTION COST              mm/dd/yy

Product Number:  XXXXX    Employee: X--------X
Units Produced:  99
Cost Per Unit:   $  9.99
Production Cost: $999.99
```

Processing Requirements:

- Compute the item production cost:
  units produced × unit cost.

4 String Functions and Loops

Overview

Checkpoint 4D
Sample Program CHAP4B
Dissection of Sample Program CHAP4B
Notes and Tips
Tutorial CHAP4B
Printer Output: The fprintf() Function
Checkpoint 4E
Sample Program CHAP4C
Dissection of Sample Program CHAP4C
Notes and Tips
Tutorial CHAP4C
Summary
Programming Projects

Learning Objectives

After you have read this chapter and completed the exercises, you should be able to

- manipulate string data using the strcat(), strcpy(), strcmp(), and strlen() functions
- use the fflush() function to clear the keyboard buffer
- understand the concepts of iteration and loop processing
- use relational and logical operators to write conditional statements
- set up loops using the while, do/while, and for statements
- format printer output and accumulate report totals
- code nested loops

String Functions

Business-related programs are often required to input and process string data as well as numeric data. Items such as company names, customer telephone numbers, shipping addresses, job titles, item descriptions, and so on, represent strings.

Strings, like numbers, can be processed by the computer. For example, strings may be compared or concatenated (joined), one string may be assigned to another, or the number of characters in a string may be counted. In the sections that follow, we will learn how to manipulate strings, as well as how to set up a processing loop.

The strcat() Function

Format:

```
strcat(string1, string2);
```

Header File: string.h

Purpose: To concatenate strings. This function joins the second string to the first. Both arguments must be strings. The first string must be large enough to hold the combined string. The resulting string is placed in *string1*, while the contents of *string2* remain unchanged.

Example:

```
char sFullName[40] = "Myra ";
char sLastName[20] = "Kennedy";
   : :
   : :
strcat(sFullName, sLastName);
```

When processed, strcat() joins the contents of *sFullName* and *sLastName* into a single string and stores the result at *sFullName*. After execution, *sFullName* contains the string Myra Kennedy; *sLastName* still holds the string Kennedy.

Look at the space between the first name and last name. It is actually part of the string value assigned to *sFullName*. The strcat() function does not add spaces between strings.

The strcpy() Function

Format:

```
strcpy(string1, string2);
```

Header File: string.h

Purpose: To copy a string. This function copies the contents of the second string to the first. Both arguments must be strings. The first string must be large enough to hold the second. The original contents of *string1* are replaced by the contents of *string2;* the contents of *string2* remain unchanged.

Example:

```
char sPrevDept[20] = "Accounting";
char sCurrDept[20] = "Marketing";
   : :
   : :
strcpy(sPrevDept, sCurrDept);
```

At run time, the string stored at *sCurrDept* is copied to *sPrevDept*. The prior contents of *sPrevDept* are replaced, while the contents of *sCurrDept* remain unchanged. After performing the copy, both variables contain the string Marketing.

The strcmp() Function

Format:

```
strcmp(string1, string2);
```

Header File: string.h

Purpose: To compare strings. This function compares the contents of *string1* and *string2* and returns a 0 if they are equal. A return code less than 0 indicates that *string1* is less than *string2*, whereas a return code greater than 0 indicates that *string1* is greater than *string2*. The first argument specifies a string variable, whereas the second argument may be either a string variable or a literal. (A **literal** is a string enclosed within double quotes.)

Examples:

1.
```
char sName[21] = "Dan Corey";
   : :
   : :
strcmp(sName, "stop run");
```

2.
```
char sSalesRep[21] = "Stacy Adams";
char sPrevSalesRep[21] = "Stacy Adams";
   : :
   : :
strcmp(sSalesRep, sPrevSalesRep);
```

In Example 1, since `stop run` is greater (appears later in the alphabet) than `Dan Corey` (the string stored at *sName*), the compare function returns a value other than 0, indicating that the strings are not equal. In Example 2, the comparison returns a 0 since the contents of the string variables are equal—both contain the string `Stacy Adams`.

The strlen() Function

Format:

```
strlen(string);
```

Header File: string.h

Purpose: To determine the number of characters in a string. The strlen() function returns the number of characters found in the string argument. It does not include the null character in the count.

Example:

```
int  iCount;
char sLastName[20] = "Huffman";
       : :
       : :
count = strlen(sLastName);
```

During execution of the strlen() function, the total number of characters found in *sLast-Name* is assigned to the variable *iCount*. Hence, *iCount* is 7.

Checkpoint 4A

Use the following variable declarations to answer questions 1–4. For each question, assume the initial values given below.

```
char sFirstName[20] = "Molly";     char sProduct1[7] = "Pliers";
char sLastName[10] = "McPherson";  char sProduct2[10] = "Saw";
char sMessage[20] = "My name is "; int iCount;
```

1. Code the strcat() statement that will produce the desired results shown for *a* through *c*.
   a. Molly McPherson
   b. McPherson Molly
   c. My name is Molly

2. Code the strcpy() statement to copy the contents of *sLastName* to *sMessage*.

3. Evaluate the following strcmp() statements, and determine the function return code.
   a. `strcmp(sFirstName, "John");`
   b. `strcmp(sFirstName, "Molly");`
   c. `strcmp(sProduct1, sProduct2);`

4. Determine the value of *iCount* for the following strlen() statements.
   a. `iCount = strlen(sLastName);`
   b. `iCount = strlen(sProduct1);`
   c. `iCount = strlen(sProduct2);`
   d. `iCount = strlen("How long is this string?");`

5. Using the following variable declarations, indicate whether the following statements are valid or invalid.

   ```
   char sBrandName[20] = "Easton Electric";
   char sCompany[10] = "Dunn ";
   char sExtension[20] = "Tire Company";
   ```

   a. `strcat(sCompany, sBrandName);`
   b. `strcpy(sCompany, sExtension);`
   c. `strcpy(sExtension, sBrandName);`
   d. `strcat(sCompany, sExtension);`

String Input and the Scanset

We may specify a scanset for the scanf() function. A **scanset** is often used to input a specific set of characters from the input stream. Hence, the string specifier **%[scanset]** indicates that we wish to input a given set of characters. For example,

```
char sLetterGrades[21];
 .....

scanf(" %[ABCDF]", sLetterGrades);
```

The scanf() function scans the input stream for the scanset A, B, C, D, F. As long as a match is found, the input character is placed in the character array *sLetterGrades;* that is, up to a maximum of 20 characters. But for the first unmatched character, the scanning stops, and control skips to the next program statement.

This process is further illustrated below.

Examples:

1. ```
   char sLetterGrades[21];
    .....

   scanf(" %10[ABCDF]", sLetterGrades);
   ```
   ```

The scanf() function reads at most the first ten characters in the input stream and stores any matching characters in the character array.

As an example, assume the input stream `BADABCDEFDDA\n`. After executing the above scanf(), *sLetterGrades* will contain the string: `BADABCD`.

```
2. char sFullName[36];
   . . . . .
   scanf(" %35[^\n]", sFullName);
```

According to the scanset, scanf() reads the input stream up to the newline character (the enter keypress) and places the result in *sFullName*. The caret ^ tells the function to store everything except the enter keypress \n. At most, 35 characters are stored at *sFullName*; the last position is reserved for the null character \0.

For example, assume the input stream `Karen L. Moore\n`. Upon executing the scanf(), *sFullName* will contain the string `Karen L. Moore\0`.

Note: Appendix C shows a summary reference of input functions that read data.

The fflush() Function

Format:

`fflush(file);`

Header File: stdio.h

Purpose: To clear a file buffer. The fflush() removes any data left in the file buffer associated with the argument enclosed within parentheses. A **file buffer** is a temporary storage area reserved for the file stream. If the argument represents an input file, fflush() clears the input buffer. If the argument represents an output file, the function sends the unwritten data to the designated file.

So far, we have used the standard file buffer to input data from the keyboard and to write output to the screen. Since problems sometimes occur when reading data from the keyboard, we will show how to use the fflush() to clear the standard input buffer.

Example:

```
   . . . . .
printf("\nEnter the part number: ");
scanf(" %d", &iPartNum);
fflush(stdin);
printf("\nEnter the color code: ");
scanf(" %c", &cColorCode);
   . . . . .
```

This example clears the *stdin* (standard input) buffer after the part number is keyed in. But why is it necessary to clear the keyboard buffer in the first place? The problem is that the user must press the enter key after keying in the data. Although the input is assigned to *iPartNum,* the enter keypress remains in the buffer. Hence, the next scanf() picks up the enter keypress and assigns it to *cColorCode.* In other words, if the buffer is not cleared before the next scanf(), the program will not allow the user to enter the color code, and bad data will be assigned to it.

In general, if the next scanf() reads a single character or a string, then clear the buffer first. Or simply clear the buffer after each scanf() and not worry about when to do it.

Iteration and Loop Processing

Iteration is an important part of programming. A program can be set up to repeat a series of statements to process a group of related records. As an example, consider a program that computes the gross pay for Marie Osborne, given her pay rate and hours worked. But suppose we want to compute the gross pay for ten employees. Can we do this without running the program ten times?

We could prompt for pay rate and hours for ten employees (payrate1, payrate2,... payrate10 and hours1, hours2,...hours10) and code ten modules to compute and print the gross pay for each employee. Although this method would work, it isn't very efficient. What if there are 50 employees? We would have to code 50 modules. Fortunately, there is a better way.

What we want the computer to do is to execute the program once but repeat, or loop through, the instructions until all the data has been processed.

By definition, a **loop** is a logic structure that allows the program to process a set of statements until a given condition has been met. In other words, the condition tells the computer how many times to repeat the statements in the loop. In our example, the condition would tell the computer to repeat the payroll calculations until the program has computed gross pay for all ten employees.

Additionally, the **body of a loop** represents the set of instructions that is executed a specified number of times by the computer. The term **iteration** refers to the process of repeating a series of instructions a specific number of times.

Every loop has an entrance point and an exit point that encloses the body of the loop and controls the iteration process. In this chapter, we will see how to test for the occurrence of a specific condition to determine whether to repeat or exit the loop.

There are two types of loop structures: leading decision and trailing decision. A **leading decision** (*while* and *for*) performs the condition test at the beginning of the loop; a **trailing decision** (*do/while*) performs the decision test at the end of the loop.

Relational Operators

Relational operators are used to set up relational tests. A **relational test**, also called a **condition test**, compares the contents of two data items. The outcome of the test is either true or false. If the test is true, the condition statement evaluates to 1; otherwise, it evaluates to 0.

Be sure to compare data items of like types. That is, compare integers to integers, floats to floats, and so on.

A list of relational operators is shown in Table 4.1. The constant, variable, or expression on the right of the relational operator is compared to the constant, variable, or expression on the left.

TABLE 4.1   Relational Operators

Relational Operator	Description	Condition Test
==	equal to	(A == B)
!=	not equal to	(A != B)
<	less than	(A < B)
<=	less than or equal to	(A <= B)
>	greater than	(A > B)
>=	greater than or equal to	(A >= B)

Caution: Use a single equal sign (=) to assign a value to a variable and a double equal sign (= =) to compare two items.

Examples:

For each example, assume the variables contain the following data: *iQuantity* = 90, *fPrice* = 7.25, *iLineCount* = 46, *iMaxLines* = 45, *fPayrate* = 12.65, *fProfit* = 78.99, *fCost* = 41.00, and *iSales* = 3600.

Condition Test	Evaluates
(iQuantity == 144)	(0) false
(fPrice != 9.95)	(1) true
(iLineCount < iMaxLines)	(0) false
(fPayrate <= 15.50)	(1) true
(fProfit > 2.0 * fCost)	(0) false
(iSales >= 4500)	(0) false

Logical Operators

Logical operators are used to set up compound conditions or relational tests. A **compound condition** consists of two or more simple relational tests that are connected by logical operators. There are three logical operators: *&&* (and), *||* (or), and *!* (not).

Logical And Operator: The outcome of an *and &&* expression evaluates true when all conditions are true; otherwise, it is false.

condition1	and	condition2	evaluates
true	&&	true	true
true	&&	false	false
false	&&	true	false
false	&&	false	false

Logical Or Operator: The outcome of an *or ||* expression evaluates true when one or more of the conditions are true; otherwise, it is false.

condition1	or	condition2	evaluates
true	||	true	true
true	||	false	true
false	||	true	true
false	||	false	false

Logical Not Operator: The outcome of a *not !* expression is reversed. A true condition becomes false, and a false condition becomes true.

not	condition	evaluates
!	true	false
!	false	true

Examples:

For each example, assume the variables contain the following data: *iExam* = 75, *iChoice* = 8, *iResponse* = 0, *iSize* = 4, and *iColor* = 3.

Compound Conditions	Evaluates
(iExam >= 80 && iExam < 90)	false
(iChoice <= 1 || iChoice > 5)	true
(iResponse != 0 && iExam > 70)	false
(iResponse < iChoice || iExam > 80)	true
(iColor == 2 || iSize > 0 && iSize < 5)	true

Order of precedence: For compound conditions, the order of precedence is *and* before *or*. Look at the last example. The *and* condition is evaluated first. We may, however, use parentheses to clarify or change the order of precedence. For example, we may insert the parentheses as shown to indicate that the *or* is performed before the *and*.

```
((iColor == 2 || (iSize > 0) && iSize < 5)
```

Then, according to the order of precedence, the *or* condition is evaluated first and the *and* condition is evaluated second.

Checkpoint 4B

1. Briefly explain the concept of iteration and loop processing.

2. Evaluate (true or false) the following simple conditions using these variable values: *fGrossPay* = 1125.95, *iAmount* = 75, *fTotalBill* = 312.10, *iPageCount* = 3, *fTaxableAmount* = 1500.00.

   a. `(fGrossPay <= 1200.00)`

   b. `(iAmount != 80)`

   c. `(fTotalBill > 400.00)`

   d. `(iPageCount == 4)`

   e. `(fGrossPay > fTaxableAmount)`

3. Evaluate (true or false) the following compound conditions using these variable values: *iQtyOnHand* = 25, *iQtyOnOrder* = 30, *iAverage* = 79, *iScore1*= 90, *iScore2* = 85, *iScore3* = 70.

    a. `(iQtyOnOrder < 25 && iQtyOnHand <= 30)`
    b. `(iQtyOnHand <= 30 || iAverage >= 50)`
    c. `(iScore1 == 90 && iScore2 < iScore1)`
    d. `(iScore2 > iAverage && iScore3 < iAverage)`
    e. `(iScore1 < iAverage || iScore2 < iAverage || iScore3 < iAverage)`
    f. `(iQtyOnHand < 20 || iQtyOnOrder > 35)`

Increment and Decrement Operators

Formats:

    Increment: variable++;   **Decrement:** variable – –;
               ++variable;   – – variable;

Purpose: To modify the value of a counting variable. The increment operator ++ adds one to the value of the variable, whereas the decrement operator – – subtracts one. According to the format, the increment/decrement operators may be placed either before or after the variable name. The examples below show the increment/decrement statements and their equivalent expressions.

Examples:

Statement	Expression
1. ++iCount;	iCount = iCount + 1;
2. iCount++;	iCount = iCount + 1;
3. – –iQuantity;	iQuantity = iQuantity – 1;
4. iQuantity– –;	iQuantity = iQuantity – 1;

Although the statements *++iCount* and *iCount++* both increment the value of the variable (add 1 to *iCount*), they may have different effects. In Example 1, *++iCount* increments the current value of *iCount* and then assigns the new value to the expression. However, in the second example, *iCount++* assigns the current value of *iCount* to the expression and then increments *iCount*.

    In the last two examples, the statements – –*iQuantity* and *iQuantity*– – both decrement the value of the variable (subtract 1 from *iQuantity*), yet they may have different effects. In Example 3, – –*iQuantity* decrements the current value of *iQuantity* and then assigns the new value to the expression. In the fourth example, *iQuantity*– – assigns the current value of *iQuantity* to the expression and then decrements *iQuantity*.

The while Loop

Format:

```
while (condition)
{
    statements;
}
```

Purpose: To set up a conditional loop. The *while* statement performs the statements inside the loop as long as the condition is true. Since the condition test is made at the beginning of the loop, there may be situations where the statement body is not executed at all. A *while* loop should be used when the number of iterations is unknown.

Each time the *while* statement is encountered, the condition is evaluated to determine whether to continue or to exit the loop. As long as the condition is true, the program executes the statements inside the braces. At the end of the loop, control passes back to the *while* statement; the right brace marks the end of the loop. We may omit the braces when the body of the loop contains only one statement.

To terminate the loop, a statement or an operation inside the loop is used to modify the condition. Once the condition is false, control exits and continues with the first statement after the loop.

The *while* loop performs the following tasks:

- initializes the control variable (used to set up the condition test)
- evaluates the condition
- performs the statement body of the loop
- modifies the control variable

Examples:

1. Print the integers 1–8.
```
iCount = 1;
while (iCount < 9)
{
    printf("%4d", iCount);
    iCount++;
}
```
OUTPUT: 1   2   3   4   5   6   7   8

The control variable is initialized to 1 and compared to the ending value. As long as *iCount* is less than 9, the current value of the control variable is printed on the screen. On each pass through the loop, *iCount* is incremented by one.

2. Clear the screen.
```
iLine = 1;
while (iLine < 25)
{
    printf("\n");
    iLine++;
}
```
OUTPUT: a blank screen

As long as the control variable is less than 25, the cursor advances to a new line. This clears the screen by forcing 24 lines to scroll off the screen.

Note: You may be able to clear the screen with either *_clearscreen(0);* or *system("cls");*. The first command requires the **graph.h header file** (contains definitions and prototypes for the graphics functions), and the second is a *system call* that exits to the operating system and clears the screen. Since these may not work with your compiler, check your C reference manual or check with your instructor for the appropriate clear-screen function.

3. Example of an infinite (endless) loop.

```
iCount = 1;
while (iCount < 9)
{
    printf("%4d", iCount);
}
```

OUTPUT: 1   1   1   1   1   1   1   1 . . .

An endless string of ones fill the screen. Hold down the control key and press break to stop the loop. Since *iCount* is not incremented, it is always less than 9.

4. Example of dead code—code that does not execute.

```
iCount = 1;
while (iCount > 10)
{
       :   :
    iCount++;
}
```

OUTPUT: none

Each time this segment is executed, *iCount* is initialized to 1. Since *iCount* equals 1 when the *while* condition is evaluated, control never enters the loop.

Checkpoint 4C

1. What is the equivalent assignment statement for each of the following?
   a. `iSold--`
   b. `--iAmount`
   c. `++iAddOne`
   d. `iPage++`

2. What is the equivalent increment/decrement operator for each of the following?
   a. `iNumberStudents = iNumberStudents + 1;`
   b. `iEmployees = iEmployees - 1;`
   c. `iRow = iRow + 1;`
   d. `iQtyOnHand = iQtyOnHand - 1;`

3. List the tasks performed by the *while* loop.

4. What will print when the following statements are executed?
   a.
```
iCount = 1;
while (iCount <= 5)
{
    printf("%4d", iCount * 10);
    iCount++;
}
```

```
b. iCount = 1;
   while (iCount < 10)
   {
       print("%4d", iCount - 1);
       iCount++;
   }
c. iCount = 10;
   while (iCount > 0)
   {
       printf("%4d", iCount);
       iCount--;
   }
d. iCount = 1;
   while (iCount > 10)
   {
       printf("%4d", iCount + 3);
       iCount++;
   }
```

Sample Program CHAP4A

Sample program CHAP4A computes and displays the two-point field goal statistics earned by each player during a recent basketball game. (The program hierarchy chart is shown in Figure. 4.1; the flowchart, in Figure 4.2; and the code, in Figure 4.3.) Figure 4.4 shows the output for one player. The following specifications apply:

Input (keyboard):

Prompt for and enter the following record (enter "stop" to quit):

Player's Name	Field Goals Attempted	Field Goals Completed
Antoine Wilkes	23	15

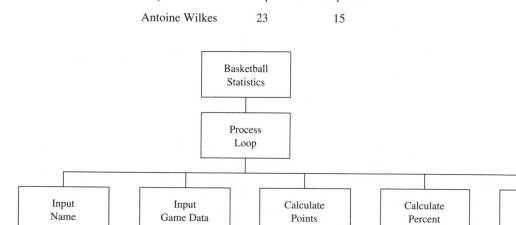

FIGURE 4.1 Hierarchy Chart for CHAP4A

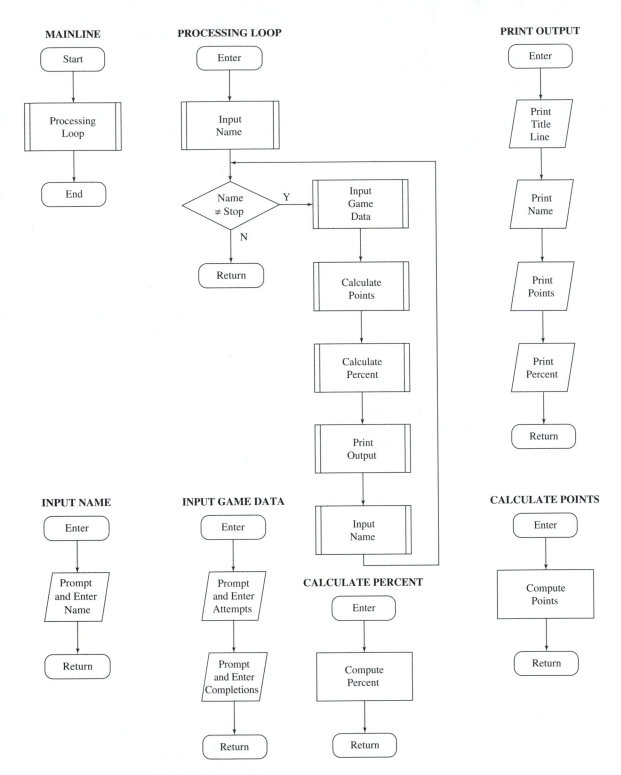

FIGURE 4.2 Program Flowchart for CHAP4A

```
/*------------------------------------------------------------
BASKETBALL STATISTICS: For each player, compute the two-point field
goal statistics scored during a recent game.

Program:    CHAP4A.C
Author:     David M. Collopy
Date:       mm/dd/yy
Project:    Sample program
*****************************************************************/

/*---- PREPROCESSING DIRECTIVES ----------------------------------*/

#include <stdio.h>            /* input-output functions */
#include <string.h>           /* string functions       */
#include <graph.h>            /* graphics functions      */

/*---- FUNCTION PROTOTYPES ---------------------------------------*/

void  ProcessLoop(void);      /* processing loop       */
void  InputName(void);        /* input player name     */
void  InputGameData(void);    /* input game data       */
float CalcPoints(void);       /* calculate points      */
float CalcPercent(void);      /* calculate percentage  */
void  PrnOutput(float, float); /* print output          */

/*---- PROGRAM VARIABLES -----------------------------------------*/

char  sName[21];              /* player name           */
float fAttempts;              /* shots attempted       */
float fCompletes;             /* shots made            */

/*------------------------------------------------------------
      MAINLINE CONTROL
-------------------------------------------------------------*/
main()
{
    _clearscreen(0);          /* clear screen          */
    ProcessLoop();            /* processing loop       */
    return 0;
}


/*------------------------------------------------------------
      PROCESSING LOOP
-------------------------------------------------------------*/
void ProcessLoop(void)
{
```

FIGURE 4.3   Sample Program CHAP4A: Compute Two-Point Field Goal Statistics per Player

```c
    float fPoints;              /* field goal points      */
    float fPercent;             /* field goal percentage */

    InputName();
    while (strcmp(sName, "stop") != 0)
    {
        InputGameData();
        fPoints  = CalcPoints();
        fPercent = CalcPercent();
        PrnOutput(fPoints, fPercent);
        InputName();
    }
    return;
}


/*-----------------------------------------------------------------
     INPUT NAME
-----------------------------------------------------------------*/
void InputName(void)
{
    printf("\n\nEnter name or 'stop' to quit: ");
    scanf(" %[^\n]", sName);
    fflush(stdin);
    return;
}


/*-----------------------------------------------------------------
     INPUT GAME DATA
-----------------------------------------------------------------*/
void InputGameData(void)
{
    printf("      Enter shots attempted: ");
    scanf(" %f", &fAttempts);
    fflush(stdin);
    printf("          Enter shots made: ");
    scanf(" %f", &fCompletes);
    fflush(stdin);
    return;
}


/*-----------------------------------------------------------------
     CALCULATE POINTS
-----------------------------------------------------------------*/
float CalcPoints(void)
{
```

FIGURE 4.3 *Continued*

```
    float fPoints;                 /* return points */

    fPoints = fCompletes * 2.0;
    return fPoints;
}


/*------------------------------------------------------------------
      CALCULATE PERCENTAGE
-----------------------------------------------------------------*/
float CalcPercent(void)
{
    float fPercent;                /* return percentage */

    fPercent = (fCompletes / fAttempts) * 100.0;
    return fPercent;
}


/*------------------------------------------------------------------
      PRINT OUTPUT
-----------------------------------------------------------------*/
void PrnOutput(float fPoints, float fPercent)
{
    printf("\n\nBasketball Two-Point Field Goal Statistics\n");
    printf("\n      Player: %-20s", sName);
    printf("\n      Points: %4.1f", fPoints);
    printf("\n  Percertage: %4.1f", fPercent);
    return;
}
```

FIGURE 4.3 *Continued*

```
Enter name or 'stop' to quit: Antoine Wilkes
      Enter shots attempted: 23
            Enter shots made: 15

Basketball Two-Point Field Goal Statistics

    Player: Antoine Wilkes
    Points: 30
Percentage: 65.2
```

FIGURE 4.4 Screen Input and Output for CHAP4A

Output (screen):
Print the following game statistics (see Figure 4.4):

```
Basketball Two-Point Field Goal Statistics
          Player:  X-------X
          Points:  99
      Percentage:  99.9
```

Processing Requirements:

- Compute the points scored:
  shots completed × 2.
- Compute the field goal percentage:
  (shots completed / shots attempted) × 100.

Pseudocode:

START: Main
Clear screen
Call Process Loop
END

ENTER: Process Loop
Call Input Name
LOOP while name not = stop
    Call Input Game Data
    Call Calculate Points
    Call Calculate Percentage
    Call Print Output
    Call Input Name
END LOOP
RETURN

ENTER: Input Name
Prompt and enter name
Clear keyboard buffer
RETURN

ENTER: Input Game Data
Prompt and enter shots attempted
Clear keyboard buffer
Prompt and enter shots made
Clear keyboard buffer
RETURN

ENTER: Calculate Point
Compute points:
    shots made × 2
RETURN

ENTER: Calculate Percentage

Compute percentage:
    (shots made / shots attempted) × 100
RETURN

ENTER: Print Output
Print output report:
    title line
    name
    points
    percentage
RETURN

Hierarchy Chart: See Figure 4.1.

Program Flowchart: See Figure 4.2.

Dissection of Sample Program CHAP4A

```
M A I N L I N E    C O N T R O L:
main()
{
    _clearscreen(0);
    ProcessLoop();
    return 0;
}
```

The above statements clear the screen, which removes any previous prompts or ouput left on the screen, and then transfer control to the *ProcessLoop* and execute the statements given there. When control returns to *main*, a 0 is passed to the operating system.

```
P R O C E S S I N G    L O O P:
void ProcessLoop(void)
{
    float fPoints;
    float fPercent;
```

The opening brace marks the beginning of the module. The above statements declare the local variables required by the module to complete its processing task.

```
    InputName();
    while (strcmp(sName, "stop") != 0)
    {
```

The first line sends control to *InputName* to get the player's name. Because the call is coded above the loop, it is referred to as the **priming input** call. This module gets the first player's name; it "primes" the condition and allows processing control to enter the loop.

    The condition shown on the second line consists of a string comparison function. It compares *sName* to the string literal *"stop"* and, based on the outcome, sets the function return code. In other words, as long as the input name is not equal to *"stop"*, control enters the loop. Otherwise, control exits and continues with the first statement after the loop.

Here is how it works. The `strcmp(sName, "stop")` sets the function return code to a nonzero value as long as *sName* is not equal to *"stop"*. The *while* condition is then evaluated as *(nonzero != 0)*, which is true; therefore, the statements in the loop are executed.

When the contents of *sName* equal *"stop"*, the function returns a 0 and the *while* condition *(0 != 0)* evaluates to false. Execution then continues with the first statement after the loop.

The opening brace marks the beginning of the *while* loop.

```
InputGameData();
fPoints  = CalcPoints();
fPercent = CalcPercent();
PrnOutput(fPoints, fPercent);
```

The above statements execute the modules in the order listed—*InputGameData*, *Calc-Points*, *CalcPercent*, and *PrnOutput*. The second and third module calls take return values and assign them to the variables *fPoints* and *fPercent*, respectively. The fourth call sends two floating-point arguments to the output module.

```
InputName();
```

The above statement transfers control to *InputPlayer*. Because this call is coded inside the loop, it is referred to as the **looping input** call. The priming input call gets the first player's name, and the looping input call gets all the other players' names.

```
    }
    return;
}
```

In the above lines, the first closing brace marks the end of the *while* loop, the *return* sends control back to *main*, and the second closing brace marks the end of the module.

```
I N P U T   N A M E:
void InputName(void)
{
    printf("\n\nEnter name or 'stop' to quit: ");
    scanf(" %[^\n]", sName);
    fflush(stdin);
    return;
}
```

The above statements perform a double space, display the prompt, and input the player's name. According to the scanset, the input stream is read up to (but not including) the enter-keypress and stored at the string variable *sName*. The fflush() clears the keyboard buffer (*stdin*), and the *return* sends control back to *ProcessLoop*.

```
I N P U T   G A M E   D A T A:
void InputGameData(void)
{
    printf("        Enter shots attempted: ");
    scanf(" %f", &fAttempts);
    fflush(stdin);
```

```
        printf("              Enter shots made: ");
        scanf(" %f", &fCompletes);
        fflush(stdin);
        return;
}
```

The above statements prompt the user to input the shots attempted and the shots completed and assign the data to the variables as shown. The fflush() clears the keyboard buffer before the program reads the name of the next player.

```
C A L C U L A T E    P O I N T S:
float CalcPoints(void)
{
        float fPoints;

        fPoints = fCompletes * 2.0;
        return fPoints;
}
```

The above statements declare a floating-point variable, compute points, and return the results (points) to the calling statement. Note that the return type shown in the module header is *float*. This corresponds to the data type shown for *fPoints*.

```
C A L C U L A T E    P E R C E N T A G E:
float CalcPercent(void)
{
        float fPercent;

        fPercent = (fCompletes / fAttempts) * 100.0;
        return fPercent;
}
```

The above statements declare a floating-point variable, compute the percentage, and return the results (percentage) to the calling statement. Again, the return type shown in the module header agrees with the data type given to the return variable.

The calculation statement divides the number of shots completed by the number attempted. The outcome is converted to a percentage by multiplying the result by 100.0.

```
P R I N T    O U T P U T:
void PrnOutput(float fPoints, float fPercent)
{
        printf("\n\nBasketball Two-Point Field Goal Statistics\n");
        printf("\n      Player: %-20s", sName);
        printf("\n      Points: %4.1f", fPoints);
        printf("\n  Percentage: %4.1f", fPercent);
        return;
}
```

The above module receives two arguments that are assigned to the local variables *fPoints* and *fPercent*, respectively. The body of the module prints the report title; formats the output; and displays the player's name, points, and percentage on the screen.

Notes and Tips

1. Terminate the string functions with a semicolon.

2. Use the *scanset* to input string data that contains multiple words—strings with spaces in them—such as your first and last names.

3. Form the habit of clearing the keyboard buffer after each scanf(). Then you won't have to worry about when you should or should not clear the buffer.

4. Note that the graphics header file was included in the sample progam. The *graph.h* header file contains the precompiled code for the *_clearscreen()* function. As you may recall, this function may or may not work with the compiler you are using. Check with your instructor for the appropriate statement to clear the screen.

5. For the *while* loop, do not place a semicolon after the *while* statement. Strange things may happen if you do!

6. For the *do/while* loop, be sure to terminate the *while* part with a semicolon.

7. Save your program before you compile and run. If something goes wrong and you lose the program, you can always retrieve a copy from your disk.

Tutorial CHAP4A

1. The objectives of this tutorial are to
   - code a scanset to input string data
   - use a while structure and a string condition to control the processing loop
   - utilize priming and looping input calls

2. Open the text editor, and enter the sample program as shown in Figure 4.3.

3. Save the source program on your work disk under the name CHAP4A. Double-check the code for keyboarding errors. Correct errors and save the program.

4. Compile, run, and debug your program until the output matches the results shown in Figure 4.4.

5. The program uses the fflush() function three times. Remove them from the code, but don't save the program. Compile and run the program, and see what happens.

6. When completed, show your work to your instructor.

Quick Quiz

Answer the following questions.

1. What happened when you ran the program without the fflush() functions?

2. Discuss the purpose of the *priming* input call.

3. Why does this program need the *string.h* file?

4. What does the following statement do?
   ```
   _clearscreen(0);
   ```

5. In your own words, explain how the following statement works.
   ```
   while (strcmp(sName, "stop") != 0)
   ```

6. What does the following statement do?

```
scanf(" %[^\n]", sName);
```

7. Did you encounter any problems or errors when you ran your program? If so, what were they and what did you do to correct them?

Accumulating Totals

Accumulating totals is a common task performed in programming. For example, it may be necessary to track totals for monthly sales, tickets sold, items received, and so on. The totaling process involves a numeric variable, called an **accumulator**, that is used to maintain a running sum. Normally, the accumulator is initialized to 0 and then incremented by a variable each time it is processed by the program.

Example:

```
fTotSales = 0.00;
InputSales();
while (fSalesAmt != 0.00)
{
      fTotSales = fTotSales + fSalesAmt;
      InputSales();
}
```

According to the example, total sales is set to 0 and the priming input call reads the sales data. As long as *fSalesAmt* is not equal to 0, control enters the loop and accumulates total sales. The looping input call reads the rest of the data.

The data below helps illustrate the accumulation process. Essentially, the value stored at *fSalesAmt* is added to the contents of *fTotSales* (right of equal sign) and then the sum is assigned to *fTotSales* (left of equal sign). The first time through the loop, the sales amount *10.00* is added to the initial value *0.00* and the result (*10.00*) is assigned to *fTot-Sales*; The second time, the sales amount *20.00* is added to the total *10.00*, and the result (*30.00*) is assigned to *fTotSales*; and so on. After the loop terminates, the total *85.00* is stored at *fTotSales*.

fTotSales	=	*fTotSales*	+	*fSalesAmt;*
10.00	=	0.00	+	10.00
30.00	=	10.00	+	20.00
55.00	=	30.00	+	25.00
85.00	=	55.00	+	30.00

The do/while Loop

Format:

```
do
{
      statements;
}
while (condition);
```

Purpose: To set up a conditional loop. The *do/while* statement performs the statements inside the loop before testing the condition. Hence, the body of the loop will always be executed at least once. A *do/while* loop should be used when the number of iterations is unknown and when the statement body of the loop must be performed at least once.

Each time the ending *while* decision is encountered, the condition is evaluated to determine whether to continue or to exit the loop. As long as the condition is true, control passes back to the *do* statement to repeat the loop. The braces are required when the loop contains more than one statement.

To terminate the loop, a statement or an operation inside the loop is used to modify the condition. Once the condition is false, control exits and continues with the first statement after the loop.

The *do/while* loop performs the following tasks:

- initializes the control variable
- performs the statements body of the loop
- modifies the control variable
- evaluates the condition

Examples:

1. Print the integers 1–8.

```
iCount = 1;
do
{
     printf("%4d", iCount);
     iCount++;
} while (iCount < 9);
```

   OUTPUT: 1   2   3   4   5   6   7   8

   Processing begins by setting *iCount* to 1. Look at the output. The test at the end of the loop compares the current value of *iCount* to the ending condition. While *iCount* is less than 9, control branches back to repeat the loop.

2. Set up a detail processing loop.

```
InputName();
do    {
     InputGameData();
     fPoints = CalcPoints();
     fPercent = CalcPercent();
     PrnOutput(fPoints, fPercent);
     InputName();
}
while (strcmp(sName, "stop") != 0);
```

   OUTPUT: none directly from this module

   We could substitute this section of code for the *while* loop shown in Sample Program CHAP4A; the output would be exactly the same.

   Note that the test at the end of the loop compares the player's name to the ending condition. While *sName* is not equal to *"stop"*, control branches back and repeats the loop.

The for Loop

Format:

```
for (initialize; test; modify)
{
    statements;
}
```

Purpose: To set up a counter-controlled loop. The *for* statement repeats the statements in the loop a given number of times; the statement body executes as long as the condition test is true. According to the format, the *for* loop consists of three arguments that initialize, test, and modify the control variable. A *for* loop should be used when the number of iterations is known.

On the first pass, the control variable is initialized and tested. If the outcome of the test is true, then the program performs the statements in the loop. On subsequent passes, the control variable is modified and tested. As long as the outcome is true, the loop continues. Control exits the *for* loop when the condition test is false.

We may omit the braces when the body of the loop contains only one statement.

The *for* loop performs the following tasks:

- initializes the control variable
- evaluates the condition
- performs the statement body of the loop
- modifies the control variable

Examples:

1. Print the integers 1–10.

```
for (iCount = 1; iCount <= 10; iCount++)

{
    printf("%4d", iCount);
}
```

OUTPUT: 1   2   3   4   5   6   7   8   9   10

The loop continues until *iCount* is greater than 10.

2. Print the odd numbers between 1 and 10.

```
for (iNum = 1; iNum < 10; iNum = iNum + 2)

{
    printf("%4d", iNum);
}
```

OUTPUT: 1   3   5   7   9

Only the odd numbers are printed. This is accomplished by setting the control variable to 1 and incrementing it thereafter in multiples of 2.

3. Compute and print the sum and square for the integers 1–5.

```
printf("  num      sum     square\n");
printf("----------------------\n");
for (iNum = 1; iNum <= 5; iNum++)
```

```
{
    iSquare = iNum * iNum;
    iSum = iSum + iNum;
    printf("%4d      %4d      %4d\n", iNum, iSum, iSquare);
}
```

OUTPUT: num   sum   square
              ----

num	sum	square
1	1	1
2	3	4
3	6	9
4	10	16
5	15	25

The output continues to print until the control variable *iNum* exceeds 5.

Nested Loops

A **nested loop** is a loop within a loop. Nested loops may go two, three, four, or more levels deep. The actual number of levels depends mostly on the application at hand. Rarely will you find it necessary to go beyond three levels.

It is important to realize that each **inner loop** must be completely enclosed within the preceding **outer loop.** For a two-level nested loop, the inner loop must be enclosed within the outer loop.

Examples:

  1. A two-level nested *while* loop

```
iOuter = 1;
while (iOuter <= 3)
{
    printf("\n Outside %d", iOuter);
    iInner = 1;
    while (iInner <= 2)
    {
        printf("\n    Inside %d", iInner);
        iInner++;
    }
    iOuter++;
}
```

  2. A two-level nested *do/while* loop

```
iOuter = 1;
do
{
    printf("\n Outside %d", iOuter);
    iInner = 1;
    do
    {
        printf("\n    Inside %d", iInner);
```

```
            iInner++;
        }
        while (iInner <= 2);
        iOuter++;
    }
    while (iOuter <= 3);
```

3. Two-level nested *for* loop

```
for (iOuter = 1; iOuter <= 3; iOuter++)
{
    printf("\n Outside %d", iOuter);
    for (iInner = 1; iInner <= 2; iInner++)
    {
        printf("\n    Inside %d", iInner);
    }
}
```

OUTPUT: `Outside 1`
              `Inside 1`
              `Inside 2`
          `Outside 2`
              `Inside 1`
              `Inside 2`
          `Outside 3`
              `Inside 1`
              `Inside 2`

Examples 1–3 produce the same output. Walk through the code. Pay close attention to the processing performed by inner loops and outer loops.

Checkpoint 4D

1. Differentiate between a *while* loop and a *do/while* loop.
2. Code a *for* loop to print the even numbers between 1 and 11; that is, 2, 4, 6, 8, and 10.
3. What will the following nested *for* loop print?

```
for (iX = 1; iX <= 2; iX++)
{
    for (iY = 1; iY <= 3; iY++)
    {
        printf("%4d", iX * iY);
    }
}
```

Sample Program CHAP4B

Sample program CHAP4B uses nested *for* loops to produce a sales summary report. The report shows annual sales for three branch office locations. (Figure 4.5 shows the hierarchy chart; Figure 4.6, the flowchart; and Figure 4.7, the code.) Figure 4.8 shows the output.

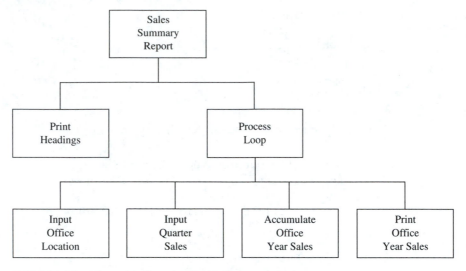

FIGURE 4.5   Hierarchy Chart for CHAP4B

The following specifications apply:

Input (keyboard):
Prompt for and enter the following data:

	Quarterly Sales			
Branch Office	1st	2nd	3rd	4th
North	30	35	36	30
South	40	40	42	43
East	35	30	40	45

Output (screen):
Print the sales summary report (see Figure 4.8).

Processing Requirements:

• Use nested *for* loops to control the processing activities.
• Compute annual sales:
  sum of quarterly sales.

Pseudocode:

```
START: Main
Clear screen
Call Print Heading Line
Call Process Loop
END

ENTER: Print Heading Line
Print heading line
RETURN
```

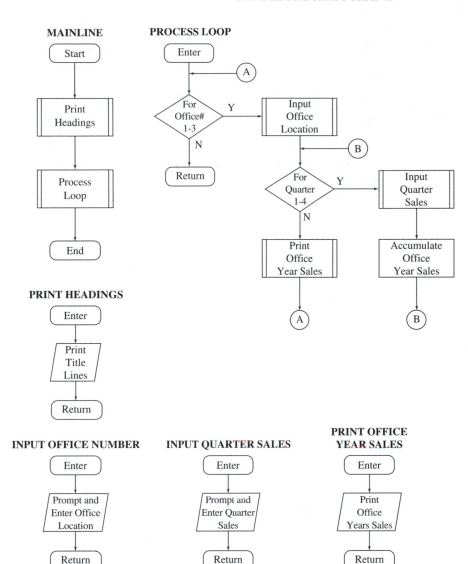

FIGURE 4.6   Program Flowchart for CHAP4B

```
ENTER: Process Loop
LOOP for office 1 to 3
     Let yearly sales = 0
     Call Input Office
     LOOP for quarter 1 to 4
          Call Input Sales
          Accumulate yearly sales:
                yearly sales + quarterly sales
     END LOOP
     Call Print Yearly Sales
```

```
END LOOP
RETURN

ENTER: Input Office
Prompt and enter office
Clear keyboard buffer
RETURN

ENTER: Input Sales
Prompt and enter quarterly sales
Clear keyboard buffer
RETURN

ENTER: Print Yearly Sales
Print sales line:
     office location
     yearly sales
RETURN
```

Hierarchy Chart: See Figure 4.5.

Program Flowchart: See Figure 4.6.

```
/*------------------------------------------------------------------
SALES SUMMARY: For each branch office, compute and print the yearly
sales figures.

Program:   CHAP4B.C
Author:    David M. Collopy
Date:      mm/dd/yy
Project:   Sample program
*****************************************************************/


/*---- PREPROCESSING DIRECTIVE --------------------------------*/

#include <stdio.h>
#include <graph.h>


/*---- FUNCTION PROTOTYPES -------------------------------------*/

void PrnHeadings(void);        /* print heading lines   */
void ProcessLoop(void);        /* processing loop       */
void InputOffice(void);        /* input office location */
void InputSales(void);         /* input quarterly sales */
void PrnYearSales(int);        /* print yearly sales    */
```

FIGURE 4.7   Sample Program CHAP4B: Compute and Print Yearly Sales Figures

```
/*---- PROGRAM VARIABLES ------------------------------------*/

char sOfficeLoc[6];                 /* office location    */
int  iQtrSales;                     /* quarterly sales    */


/*-------------------------------------------------------------
        MAINLINE CONTROL
-----------------------------------------------------------*/
main()
{
    _clearscreen(0);                /* clear screen        */
    PrnHeadings();                  /* print heading lines */
    ProcessLoop();                  /* processing loop     */
    return 0;
}


/*-------------------------------------------------------------
        PRINT HEADING LINES
-----------------------------------------------------------*/
void PrnHeadings(void)
{
    printf("\nQuarterly Sales Report");
    printf("\n      mm/dd/yy\n");
    return;
}


/*-------------------------------------------------------------
        PROCESSING LOOP
-----------------------------------------------------------*/
void ProcessLoop(void)
{
    int  iOfc;                      /* office loop control */
    int  iQtr;                      /* quarter loop control */
    int  iYearSales;                /* yearly sales        */

    for (iOfc = 1; iOfc <= 3; iOfc++)
    {
        iYearSales = 0;
        InputOffice();
        for (iQtr = 1; iQtr <= 4; iQtr++)
        {
            InputSales();
            iYearSales = iYearSales + iQtrSales;
        }
        PrnYearSales(iYearSales);
    }
```

FIGURE 4.7 *Continued*

```
        return;
    }

/*----------------------------------------------------------------
        INPUT OFFICE LOCATION
--------------------------------------------------------------*/
void InputOffice(void)
{
    printf("\n\tEnter office location: ");
    scanf(" %s", sOfficeLoc);
    fflush(stdin);
    return;
}


/*----------------------------------------------------------------
        INPUT QUARTERLY SALES
--------------------------------------------------------------*/
void InputSales(void)
{
    printf("\tEnter quarterly sales: $");
    scanf(" %d", &iQtrSales);
    fflush(stdin);
    return;
}


/*----------------------------------------------------------------
        PRINT YEARLY SALES
--------------------------------------------------------------*/
void PrnYearSales(int iYearSales)
{
    printf("\n %-5s      $%3d", sOfficeLoc, iYearSales);
    return;
}
```

FIGURE 4.7   *Continued*

```
Quarterly Sales Report
        mm/dd/yy

North       $131
South       $165
East        $150
```

FIGURE 4.8   Screen Output for CHAP4B

Dissection of Sample Program CHAP4B

Study the program code. Notice that the output, prompts, and input will intermix on the screen. Later you will learn how to correct this problem by using the *fprintf()* function to direct the output to the printer.

```
P R I N T   H E A D I N G   L I N E S:
void PrnHeadings(void)
{
    printf("\nQuarterly Sales Report");
    printf("\n        mm/dd/yy\n");
    return;
}
```

The above statements print the title lines and return to the *MAINLINE*.

```
P R O C E S S I N G   L O O P:

void ProcessLoop(void)
{
    int iOfc;
    int iQtr;
    int iYearSales;

    for (iOfc = 1; iOfc <= 3; iOfc++)
    {
```

The above statements declare the local variables and set up the parameters of the outer *for* loop. As long as *iOfc* is less than or equal to 3, control enters the loop. Otherwise, control skips the statement body of the outer loop.

```
        iYearSales = 0;
        InputOffice();
        for (iQtr = 1; iQtr <= 3; iQtr++)
        {
            InputSales();
            iYearSales = iYearSales + iQtrSales;
        }
```

The above statements initialize yearly sales to 0, call *InputOffice*, and set up the parameters of the inner *for* loop. As long as *iQtr* is less than or equal to 3, control enters the loop, calls *InputSales,* and accumulates yearly sales. Otherwise, control skips the statement body of the inner loop.

The opening and closing braces mark the statement body of the inner loop. When control exits the loop, processing continues with the first executable statement after the closing brace.

```
        PrnYearSales(iYearSales);
    }
```

The above statement transfers control to output module and prints the yearly sales for the given office. The closing brace marks the end of the outer loop. When control exits the loop, it jumps back to the top of the outer *for* statement.

```
        return;
}
```

The above statement returns control to the *MAINLINE*. The closing brace marks the end of the processing loop.

Notes and Tips

1. The *while* loop should be used when the number of iterations is unknown. For most applications, this loop structure works fine.

2. The *do/while* loop should be used when the number of iterations is unknown and when the statement body of the loop must be performed at least once.

3. The *for* loop should be used when the number of iterations is known.

4. As a rule, enclose the statement body of the loop within braces—even if the body contains only one statement.

5. A nested loop is used for applications that require a logical grouping of the output—similar to the output shown for sample program CHAP4B.

Tutorial CHAP4B

1. The objectives of this tutorial are to
   • set up a nested *for* loop
   • print a summary report for yearly sales

2. Enter the sample program into your text editor.

3. Save the source program on your work disk as CHAP4B. Check your code for keyboarding errors. Make corrections as needed, and save the program.

4. Compile, run, and debug your program until the output matches the results shown in Figure 4.8.

5. The *for* loop does not end with a semicolon. Put one after the first *for* statement, but don't save the program. Compile and run the program and see what happens.

6. When completed, show your work to your instructor.

Quick Quiz

Answer the following questions.

1. What happened during the program run when you put the semicolon after the first *for* statement?

2. In your own words, summarize how the nested *for* loop controls and performs the major processing activities required by the program.

3. Explain how the following statement works.
   ```
   for (iOfc = 1; iOfc <= 3; iOfc++)
   ```

4. Did you encounter any problems or errors when you ran the sample program? If so, what were they and what did you do to correct them?

Printer Output: The fprintf() Function

Format:

```
fprintf(file, "control string", variable/s);
```

Library: `stdio.h`

Purpose: To print output to a file. This function writes output to the designated file. The only difference between the printf() and fprintf() functions is that the latter requires a file argument. The *file* argument specifies where the output will be written. The conversion specifiers written in the control string are similar to those shown in Chapter 2 for the printf() function.

  The file argument may be either system- or programmer-defined. For now, we will use the system-defined file *stdprn* to direct the output stream to the printer. Later, in the chapters on file processing, we will learn how to use the fprintf() to write output to disk files. Refer to Appendix C for a summary reference of output functions that write data to a specific file.

Examples:

1. `fprintf(stdprn, "\f");`

  OUTPUT: [advance to the top of the next page]

2. `fprintf(stdprn, "P A Y R O L L    R E P O R T");`

  OUTPUT: P A Y R O L L R E P O R T

3. `char sCustName[20] = "Corrina Sanchez";`
  `float fBill = 1254.72;`

  `fprintf(stdprn, "\n %-20s   %7.2f", sCustName, fBill);`

  OUTPUT: Corrina Sanchez 1254.72

Examples 1–3 use the *stdprn* file. This predefined system file specifies that the output will be written to the printer. Check your system reference manual for the name of your printer file.

Checkpoint 4E

1. Differentiate between printf() and fprintf().

2. What will the following statement do?

  `fprintf(stdprn, "Welcome to C world!");`

3. Determine whether the following statements are valid or invalid.

  a. `fprintf("This is a valid statement.");`

  b. `printf(stdprn, "This is a valid statement.");`

  c. `fprintf(stdprn, "This is a valid statement.");`

Sample Program CHAP4C

Sample program CHAP4C computes and prints the daily billing log for Action Advertising. (The hierarchy chart is shown in Figure 4.9; the flowchart, in Figure 4.10; and the program code, in Figure 4.11.) Figure 4.12 shows the output for CHAP4C. The program specifications are shown below.

Input (keyboard):
Prompt for and enter the following data (enter "stop" to quit):

Client's Name	Time Spent on Account	Hourly Charge
Carson Pontiac	3.0	50.00
Bright Cleaners	5.1	75.00
Davis Delivery	1.6	35.00
Terrace TV	2.4	45.00
Zenkido Karate	2.9	35.00

Output (printer):
Print the daily billing log (see Figure 4.12).

Processing Requirements:
- Compute the bill:
  time × charge.
- Accumulate client count.
- Accumulate total for the daily bill.
- Compute the average daily bill:
  total bill / client count.

Pseudocode:

```
START: Main
Call Print Headings
Call Process Loop
END
```

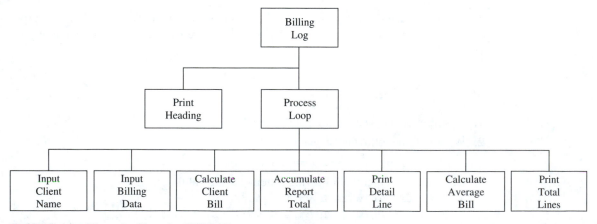

FIGURE 4.9   Hierarchy Chart for CHAP4C

MAINLINE

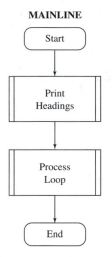

CALCULATE AVERAGE BILL

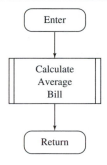

PROCESS LOOP

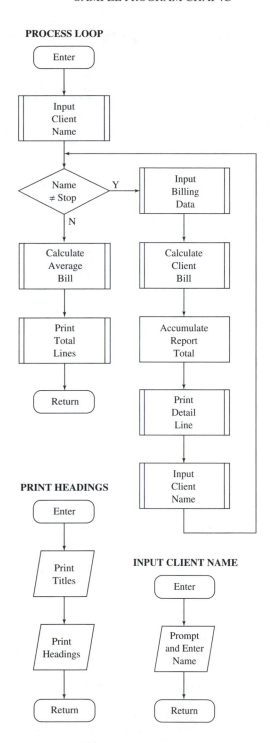

PRINT HEADINGS

INPUT CLIENT NAME

FIGURE 4.10   Program Flowchart for CHAP4C

INPUT BILLING DATA

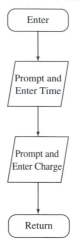

CALCULATE CLIENT BILL

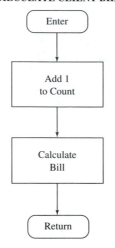

PRINT DETAIL LINE

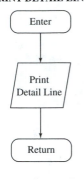

PRINT TOTAL LINES

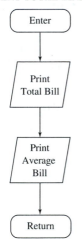

FIGURE 4.10   *Continued*

ENTER: Print Headings
Print 2 page title lines
Print 2 column heading lines
RETURN

ENTER: Process Loop
Clear screen
Call Input Client Name
LOOP while client name not = stop
    Call Input Billing Data

Call Calculate Bill
Accumulate Total Bill:
     total bill + bill
Call Print Detail Line
Clear screen
Call Input Client Name
END LOOP
Call Calculate Average Bill
Call Print Totals
RETURN

ENTER: Input Client Name
Prompt and enter client name (stop to quit)
Clear keyboard buffer
RETURN

ENTER: Input Input Billing Data
Prompt and enter billing time
Clear keyboard buffer
Prompt and enter hourly charge
Clear keyboard buffer
RETURN

ENTER: Calculate Bill
Add 1 to client count
Compute client bill:
     billing time × hourly charge
RETURN

ENTER: Print Detail Line
Print Detail Line
     client name
     billing time
     hourly charge
     client bill
RETURN

ENTER: Calculate Average Bill
Compute average bill:
     total bill/client count
RETURN

ENTER: Print Totals
Print total bill
Print average bill
RETURN

Hierarchy Chart: See Figure 4.9.

Program Flowchart: See Figure 4.10.

```
/*-------------------------------------------------------------
BILLING LOG: Compute and print the daily billing log for Action
Advertising.

Program:   CHAP4C.C
Author:    David M. Collopy
Date:      mm/dd/yy
Project:   Sample program
***********************************************************/

/*---- PREPROCESSING DIRECTIVES ------------------------------*/

#include <stdio.h>
#include <string.h>
#include <graph.h>

/*---- FUNCTION PROTOTYPES -----------------------------------*/

void  PrnHeadings(void);         /* print headings          */
void  ProcessLoop(void);         /* processing loop         */
void  InputName(void);           /* input client name       */
void  InputBillData(void);       /* input billing data      */
float CalcBill(void);            /* calculate client bill   */
void  PrnDetail(float);          /* print detail line       */
float CalcAvrBill(float);        /* calculate average bill  */
void  PrnTotals(float, float);   /* print total line        */

/*---- PROGRAM SETUP -----------------------------------------*/

/*>    R E P O R T   T I T L E S   A N D   H E A D I N G S   <*/

char PT1[] = "    A C T I O N    A D V E R T I S I N G";
char PT2[] = "              Daily Billing Log";
char HL1[] = "             Time Spent     Hourly     Daily";
char HL2[] = "  Account     on Account    Charge     Bill";
char TL1[] = "Total Daily Billing:             $";
char TL2[] = "Average Daily Billing:           $";

/*>    P R O G R A M   V A R I A B L E S                      <*/

char  sName[18];                 /* client name             */
float fTime;                     /* time spent on account   */
float fCharge;                   /* charge for work         */
int   iCount;                    /* number of clients       */
```

FIGURE 4.11   Sample Program CHAP4C: Compute and Print the Daily Billing Log for Action Advertising

```
/*------------------------------------------------------------------
        MAINLINE CONTROL
--------------------------------------------------------------------*/
main()
{
    PrnHeadings();                /* print report headings */
    ProcessLoop();                /* processing loop        */
    return 0;
}


/*------------------------------------------------------------------
        PRINT REPORT HEADINGS
--------------------------------------------------------------------*/
void PrnHeadings(void)
{
    fprintf(stdprn, "\r\f");       /* reset to top of page */
    fprintf(stdprn, PT1);          /* print page title 1   */
    fprintf(stdprn, "\r\n");       /* reset & single space */
    fprintf(stdprn, PT2);          /* print page title 2   */
    fprintf(stdprn, "\r\n\n\n");   /* reset & triple space */
    fprintf(stdprn, HL1);          /* print heading line 1 */
    fprintf(stdprn, "\r\n");       /* reset & single space */
    fprintf(stdprn, HL2);          /* print heading line 2 */
    fprintf(stdprn, "\r\n");       /* reset & single space */
    return;
}


/*------------------------------------------------------------------
        PROCESSING LOOP
--------------------------------------------------------------------*/
void ProcessLoop(void)
{
    float fBill;                  /* client bill          */
    float fTotBill;               /* report total bill    */
    float fAvrBill;               /* report average bill */

    _clearscreen(0);
    InputName();
    while(strcmp(sName, "stop") != 0)
    {
        InputBillData();
        fBill = CalcBill();
        fTotBill = fTotBill + fBill;
        PrnDetail(fBill);
        _clearscreen(0);
        InputName();
```

FIGURE 4.11 *Continued*

```
        }
        fAvrBill = CalcAvrBill(fTotBill);
        PrnTotals(fTotBill, fAvrBill);
        return;
}


/*-------------------------------------------------------------
        INPUT CLIENT NAME
---------------------------------------------------------------*/
void InputName(void)
{
        printf("\n\nEnter client or 'stop' to Quit: ");
        scanf(" %[^\n]", sName);
        fflush(stdin);
        return;
}


/*-------------------------------------------------------------
        INPUT BILLING DATA
---------------------------------------------------------------*/
void InputBillData(void)
{
        printf("   Enter time spent on account: ");
        scanf(" %f", &fTime);
        fflush(stdin);
        printf("            Enter hourly charge: ");
        scanf(" %f", &fCharge);
        fflush(stdin);
        return;
}


/*-------------------------------------------------------------
        CALCULATE BILL
---------------------------------------------------------------*/
float CalcBill(void)
{
        float fBill;

        iCount++;
        fBill = fTime * fCharge;
        return fBill;
}


/*-------------------------------------------------------------
        PRINT DETAIL LINE
---------------------------------------------------------------*/
```

FIGURE 4.11 *Continued*

```
void PrnDetail(float fBill)
{
    fprintf(stdprn, "\r\n%-15s  %4.1f      %6.2f   %7.2f",
        sName, fTime, fCharge, fBill);
    return;
}


/*--------------------------------------------------------------
        CALCULATE AVERAGE BILL
-------------------------------------------------------------*/
float CalcAvrBill(float fTotBill)
{
    float fAvrBill;

    fAvrBill = fTotBill / iCount;
    return fAvrBill;
}


/*--------------------------------------------------------------
        PRINT TOTAL LINES
-------------------------------------------------------------*/
void PrnTotals(float fTotBill, float fAvrBill)
 {
    fprintf(stdprn, "\r\n\n%-35s%7.2f", TL1, fTotBill);
    fprintf(stdprn, "\r\n%-35s%7.2f\r", TL2, fAvrBill);
    return;
}
```

FIGURE 4.11 *Continued*

```
        A C T I O N   A D V E R T I S I N G
              Daily Billing Log

                  Time Spent      Hourly      Daily
        Account   on Account      Charge       Bill

Carson Pontiac        3.0         50.00       150.00
Bright Cleaners       5.1         75.00       382.50
Davis Delivery        1.6         35.00        56.00
Terrace TV            2.4         45.00       108.00
Zenkido Karate        2.9         35.00       101.50

Total Daily Billing:                       $ 798.00
Average Daily Billing:                     $ 159.60
```

FIGURE 4.12 Program Output for CHAP4C

Dissection of Sample Program CHAP4C

Because we have seen most of the code before, we will focus primarily on how the page titles, column headings, and total lines are set up. We will also look at the processing loop.

R E P O R T   T I T L E S   A N D   H E A D I N G S:

```
char PT1[] = "    A C T I O N    A D V E R T I S I N G";
char PT2[] = "            Daily Billing Log";
```

The above statements assign the literal strings to the page titles *PT1* and *PT2*. The lengths of the variables are implicitly determined by the number of characters in the strings.

```
char HL1[] = "            Time Spent    Hourly    Daily";
char HL2[] = "  Account    on Account   Charge     Bill";
```

The above statements assign the literal strings to the heading line variables *HL1* and *HL2*.

```
char TL1[] = "Total Daily Billing:           $";
char TL2[] = "Average Daily Billing:         $";
```

The above statements assign the literal strings to the total line variables *TL1* and *TL2*.

P R O G R A M   V A R I A B L E S:

```
char   sName[18];
float  fTime;
float  fCharge;
int    iCount;
```

The above statements define the global variables required by the program to process the input and to produce the output.

P R I N T   R E P O R T   H E A D I N G S:

```
void PrnHeadings(void)
{
    fprintf(stdprn, "\r\f");
    fprintf(stdprn, PT1);
    fprintf(stdprn, "\r\n");
    fprintf(stdprn, PT2);
    fprintf(stdprn, "\r\n\n\n");
    fprintf(stdprn, HL1);
    fprintf(stdprn, "\r\n");
    fprintf(stdprn, HL2);
    fprintf(stdprn, "\r\n");
    return;
}
```

The above statements print the report titles and column headings on the printer. Look at the horizontal line spacing between the titles and headings. They are separated to make the format of the report clearer to the reader.

Now look at the carriage return (\r) characters. They are combined with the *newline* character to force the printer to start printing the titles and headings at the beginning of the new line.

```
P R O C E S S I N G   L O O P:

void ProcessLoop(void)
{
    float fBill;
    float fTotBill;
    float fAvrBill;

    _clearscreen(0);
    InputName();
```

The statements coded above the *while* loop declare the local variables, clear the screen, and execute the priming input call to read the name of the first client.

```
    while(strcmp(sName, "stop") != 0)
    {
        InputBillData();
        fBill = CalcBill();
        fTotBill = fTotBill + fBill;
        PrnDetail(fBill);
        _clearscreen(0);
        InputName();
    }
```

As long as the client's name is not equal to *"stop,"* control enters the loop and calls the *InputBillData* module to read the client's billing data. The next module call sends control to *CalcBill* to compute the client's bill. The add statement accumulates the total bill, and the call to *PrnDetail* passes the client's bill to the Print Detail Line module. Control then clears the screen and executes the looping input call to read the name of the next client.

```
    fAvrBill = CalcAvrBill(fTotBill);
    PrnTotals(fTotBill, fAvrBill);
    return;
}
```

The statements coded after the loop send control to *CalcAvrBill* and *PrnTotals* modules to compute the average bill and print the total and average lines, respectively. The *return* statement sends control back to mainline.

Notes and Tips

There is clearly an advantage to setting up the report titles and heading lines as shown in the *PROGRAM SETUP* section of sample program CHAP4C. You can actually see what the report will look like before you print it. This approach makes it easy to align the different parts of the report. The detail line is the only output line you will have to spend some time on aligning the data to fit the column headings.

Tutorial CHAP4C

1. The objectives of this tutorial are to
   - set up an output report
   - direct the output to the printer

2. If necessary, open the text editor and enter the sample program as shown in Figure 4.11.

3. Save the source program on your work disk as CHAP4C. Check for keyboarding errors, correct as needed, and save the program.

4. Compile, run, and debug your program until the output matches the results shown in Figure 4.12.

5. When completed, show your work to your instructor.

Quick Quiz

Answer the following questions.

1. The report titles, headings, and total lines are declared in the *PROGRAM SETUP* section of the program. Why are they set up in this manner?

2. Look at the *PrnHeadings* module. Explain what the first three lines do.

3. Do you really need the *iCount++* statement? Explain your answer.

4. Note the *fprintf( )* statement coded in the *PrnDetail* module. How does it work? Be sure to discuss how the following components work together to display the output on the printer: *fprintf( )*, *stdprn*, and \r.

5. Did you encounter any problems or errors when you ran the sample program? If so, what were they and what did you do to correct them?

Summary

1. The strcat() function joins two strings—concatenates one string to another.

2. The strcpy() function copies one string to another.

3. The strcmp() function compares two strings. If they are equal, the function returns a zero. If the first string is less than the second, the function returns a negative value. If the first string is greater than the second, the function returns a positive value.

4. The strlen() function returns the number of characters found in the string argument, excluding the null character.

5. The scanset is used with the scanf() function to input a specific set of characters at the keyboard.

6. The fflush() function clears the file buffer specified by the file argument. This function may also be used to prevent bad data from entering the program.

7. Iteration is the process of repeating a series of statements a specific number of times.

8. A loop represents a logic structure that processes a set of instructions repetitively until a condition is met. The body of a loop represents the section of code that is repeated during the iteration process.

9. Relational operators are used to set up conditions or relational tests that compare two values.

10. The logical operators (&&, ||, and !) are used to implement compound conditions. A compound condition consists of two or more simple relational tests that are connected by the logical operators.

11. The increment and decrement operators are used to modify the value of a counting variable. The operator may be placed either before or after the variable.

12. Each time a *while* statement is encountered, the condition is tested. As long as the test is true, the statements inside the loop are executed. The looping process continues until the ending condition is satisfied.

13. Accumulating totals is a common processing activity used to count or track total sales, tickets sold, employees hired, stock returned, and so on.

14. On the first pass, the *do/while* loop performs the statements inside the loop before testing the condition. Here, the condition is evaluated at the end of the loop to determine whether to continue or to exit the loop.

15. The *for* statement represents a counter-controlled loop that automatically initializes, tests, and modifies the control variable. A *for* loop should be used when the number of iterations is known.

16. A nested loop is a loop within a loop. Nested loops may be constructed with the *while, do/while,* or *for* statements. They may be mixed or matched.

17. The fprintf() function is used to write formatted output to a file. This function requires a file argument, which may be either system- or programmer-defined.

18. When used with the fprintf() function, the *stdprn* file directs the output to the printer.

Programming Projects

For each project, design the logic and write the modular structured program to produce the output. Model your program after the samples presented in the chapter. Verify your output.

Project 4–1 **Charge Account**

Write a program to compute and print a report showing the month-end balance for each customer. Assume an annual finance rate of 18% on the unpaid balance.

Input (keyboard):

For each customer, prompt for and enter the following data:

Customer Last Name	Previous Balance	Payments & Credits	Purchases & Charges
Allen	5000.00	0.00	200.00
Davis	2150.00	150.00	0.00
Fisher	3400.00	400.00	100.00
Navarez	625.00	125.00	74.00
Stiers	820.00	0.00	0.00
Wyatt	1070.00	200.00	45.00

Output (printer):

Print the following customer accounts report:

```
Author                    CUSTOMER ACCOUNTS              Page 01
                             mm/dd/yy


Customer     Previous     Payments     Purchases     Finance     Month-end
```

```
Name          Balance      & Credits     & Charges     Charge      Balance

X-------X     9999.99       999.99        999.99       99.99       9999.99
    :            :             :             :            :            :
    :            :             :             :            :            :
X-------X     9999.99       999.99        999.99       99.99       9999.99

Totals:      99999.99      9999.99       9999.99      999.99      99999.99
```

Processing Requirements:

- Compute the new balance:
  previous balance – payments + purchases.
- Compute the finance charge:
  new balance × (annual rate / 12)
- Compute the month-end balance:
  new balance + finance charge.
- Accumulate totals for previous balance, payments, purchases,
  finance charge, and month-end balance.

Project 4–2   Payroll

Write a program to calculate and print a weekly payroll roster. Assume the current federal income tax (FIT) rate is 15%.

Input (keyboard):

For each employee, prompt for and enter the following payroll data:

Employee	Hours Worked	Hourly Pay Rate
T. Bauer	40	7.50
S. Erickson	38	12.00
S. Howard	40	9.75
D. Miller	40	10.25
B. Rossi	35	8.00
T. York	36	11.00

Output (printer):

Print the following payroll report:

```
Author                 WEEKLY PAYROLL REPORT              Page 01
                            mm/dd/yy


Employee    Hours     Hourly
Name        Worked    Pay Rate    Gross Pay     FIT      Net Pay

X-------X     99       99.99        999.99      99.99      999.99
    :          :          :            :          :          :
    :          :          :            :          :          :
X-------X     99       99.99        999.99      99.99      999.99

                     Totals:        9999.99     999.99     9999.99

                     Average Net Pay:                      9999.99
```

Processing Requirements:

- Compute the gross pay:
  hours × pay rate.
- Compute the federal income tax amount:
  gross pay × FIT rate.
- Compute the net pay:
  gross pay – FIT amount.
- Accumulate employee count.
- Accumulate totals for gross pay, FIT, and net pay.
- Compute the average net pay:
  total net pay / employee count.

Project 4–3   Sales

Write a program to calculate and print a sales report.

Input (keyboard):

For each salesperson, prompt for and enter the following sales data:

Salesperson Name	Total Sales	Cost Of Sales
Lisa Conrad	8120.52	6450.71
Roy Hickle	2245.78	1072.49
Tara Perkins	12710.14	9735.38
Dennis Tian	4567.51	3119.22
Ann Zimmerman	5793.59	4204.45

Output (printer):

Print the following sales report:

```
Author                  SALES REPORT              Page 01
                         mm/dd/yy

Salesperson   Total Sales   Cost Of Sales   Net Profit
----------------------------------------------------------
X--------X      99999.99       9999.99        9999.99
    :              :              :              :
    :              :              :              :
X--------X      99999.99       9999.99        9999.99
                               Total:        99999.99

                               Average:       9999.99
```

Processing Requirements:

- Compute the net profit:
  total sales – cost of sales.
- Accumulate salesperson count.
- Accumulate a total for net profit.
- Compute average net profit:
  total net profit / salesperson count.

Project 4–4   ## Inventory

Write a program to compute and print an inventory profit report.

Input (keyboard):

For each item, prompt for and enter the following inventory data:

Item Number	Description	Quantity On Hand	Unit Cost	Selling Price
1000	Hammers	24	4.75	9.49
2000	Saws	14	7.50	14.99
3000	Drills	10	7.83	15.95
4000	Screwdrivers	36	2.27	4.98
5000	Pliers	12	2.65	5.49

Output (printer):

Print the following inventory profit report:

```
Author          INVENTORY PROFIT REPORT        Page 01
                      mm/dd/yy


Item Number     Description        Quantity    Item Profit
   9999         X----------X          99         999.99
    :               :                  :            :
    :               :                  :            :
   9999         X----------X          99         999.99

                          Total Profit:        9999.99
```

Processing Requirements:

- Compute the total cost:
  quantity × unit cost.
- Compute the total income:
  quantity × selling price.
- Compute the item profit:
  total income – total cost.
- Accumulate a total for item profit.

Project 4–5   ## Personnel

Write a program to compute and print the annual salary report for the personnel department.

Input (keyboard):

For each employee, prompt for and enter the following personnel data:

Employee Number	Employee Name	Department Number	Annual Salary	Percent Increase
1926	Dana Andrews	10	29000.00	0.10
2071	Scott Cooper	14	30250.00	0.12
3550	Todd Feldman	22	24175.00	0.07
4298	Lori Palmer	35	33400.00	0.11
5409	Bob Shields	47	27500.00	0.08
6552	Pam Wolfe	31	31773.00	0.10

Output (printer):

Print the following personnel report:

```
Author               PERSONNEL ANNUAL SALARY REPORT        Page 01
                             mm/dd/yy


---- Employee ----      Dept.    Old       Dollar
Number   Last Name      Number   Salary    Increase    New Salary

 9999    X----------X     99     99999.99  9999.99     99999.99
   :        :             :         :         :           :
   :        :             :         :         :           :
 9999    X----------X     99     99999.99  9999.99     99999.99

                                 Total:   99999.99    999999.99

            Average Dollar Increase:     9999.99
```

Processing Requirements:

- Compute the dollar increase:
  old salary × percent increase.
- Compute the new salary:
  old salary + dollar increase.
- Accumulate employee count.
- Accumulate totals for dollar increase and new salary.
- Compute the average dollar increase:
  total dollar increase / employee count.

Project 4–6   Accounts Payable

Write a program to compute and print an accounts payable report.

Input (keyboard):

For each vendor, prompt for and enter the following data:

Vendor Number	Vendor Name	Invoice Number	Invoice Amount	Discount Rate
217	Metacraft	A1239	2309.12	0.10
349	IntraTell	T9823	670.00	0.09
712	Reylock	F0176	4563.78	0.12
501	Universal	W0105	1200.00	0.09
196	Northland	X2781	3429.34	0.10

Output (printer):

Print the following accounts payable report:

```
Author                  ACCOUNTS PAYABLE              Page 01
                            mm/dd/yy


Vendor                   Invoice   Invoice   Discount   Amount
Number   Vendor Name     Number    Amount    Amount     Due

 999     X---------X     XXXXX     9999.99   999.99     9999.99
```

```
    :          :            :          :          :            :
    :          :            :          :          :            :
   999     X---------X    XXXXX    9999.99    999.99      9999.99

                       Totals:      99999.99   9999.99     99999.99
```

Processing Requirements:

- Compute the discount amount:
  invoice amount × discount rate.
- Compute the amount due:
  invoice amount – discount amount.
- Accumulate totals for invoice amount, discount amount, and amount due.

Project 4–7   Production Cost

Write a program to compute and print a production cost report.

Input (keyboard):

For each item, prompt for and enter the following production data:

Employee Name	Product Number	Units Produced	Unit Cost
Alan Baum	A1234	24	5.50
Marie Fitch	C4510	36	7.94
Lee Hildebrand	R0934	18	6.75
David Mullins	E3371	36	3.79
Nicole Renner	H9733	24	4.25
Erica Tate	Z0182	27	8.10
Terry West	A3235	30	2.95

Output (printer):

Print the following production report:

```
Author            PRODUCTION COST REPORT        Page 01
                       mm/dd/yy

        Product      Units        Unit      Production
        Number       Produced     Cost      Cost

        XXXXX          99          9.99        999.99
          :            :            :            :
          :            :            :            :
        XXXXX          99          9.99        999.99

        Totals:       999         99.99       9999.99
```

Processing Requirements:

- Compute the production cost:
  units produced × unit cost.
- Accumulate totals for units produced, unit cost, and production cost.

5 Branching

Overview

Learning Objectives

After you have read this chapter and completed the exercises, you should be able to

- distinguish between conditional and unconditional branching
- use *if* and *if/else* decision statements to select alternate processing paths
- code nested decisions using the *if* and *if/else* statements
- use the *switch* and *break* statements to code multipath decisions
- understand why programmers avoid the *goto* statement

Selecting Alternate Processing Paths

Decision processing is common to most programming applications. Computers can be programmed to do much more than repeat a series of statements over and over again. In this chapter, we will learn how to code **decision tests** that will be used to select and perform alternate processing tasks.

In C, decisions are made by comparing two values to see if one is equal to, greater than, or less than the other. Based on the outcome, control branches to the appropriate statement or module and performs the processing given there. In other words, the computer can be programmed to select and follow a particular course of action depending on the comparative values of two data items.

Consider, for example, the following segment that determines the sales commission rate.

```
if (iSalesIncome < 5000)
{
    fCommRate = .05;
}
else
{
    fCommRate = .07;
}
```

According to the code, if *iSalesIncome* is less than $5,000, the commission rate is set to 5%. Otherwise, the rate is set to 7%.

Unconditional and Conditional Branching

In programming, there are two types of branch statements: unconditional and conditional. An **unconditional branch** sends control directly to a specific location in the program. In English, for example, the statement "Go to work" tells us unconditionally *what to do*—go to work. Unconditional branches are implemented with the *goto* statement.

On the other hand, a **conditional branch** is taken only if a certain condition is met. Once again, in English, the statement "If it is snowing, wear your boots" tells us conditionally when to wear our boots. Conditional branches are implemented with the *if, if/else,* and *switch* statements.

The if Statement

Format:

```
if (condition)
{
    statements;
}
```

Purpose: To set up a conditional branch. The commands in the body of the *if* statement are executed only if the condition or relation test is true. Otherwise, control skips the statement body and continues with the first command after the *if*. The braces may be omitted when the body contains only one statement.

Examples:

1. ```
   if (iCredits < 45)
   {
       printf("Welcome freshman");
   }
   ```

   If credit hours are less than 45, then print the welcome message.

2. ```
   if (fPayment > fBalance)
   {
       printf("Customer overpaid");
       printf("Credit the account");
   }
   ```

   If *fPayment* is greater than *fBalance,* then print the overpaid and credit messages.

Nested if Statements

Format:

```
if (condition1)
{
    if (condition2)
    {
        statements;
        .....
    }
}
```

Purpose: To set up a multiconditional branch. A **nested** *if* statement consists of at least one *if* inside the branch of another. According to the format, the statement body is executed only if all the conditions are true. Any time a condition is false, control exits and continues with the first command after the nested *if* statement.

Example:

Two-level nested if() statement

```
if (iCredits < 45)
{
```

```
    if (iFemale == 1)
    {
        iFemaleFresh++;
        printf("Welcome lady freshman");
    {
{
```

If credit hours are less than 45 and the student is a female, then add 1 to the female freshmen counter and print the welcome message.

The if/else Statement

Format:

```
if (condition)
{
    true path;
}
else
{
    false path;
}
```

Purpose: To set up a two-way conditional branch. This command performs the statement body of the true path only if the condition is true. Otherwise, control performs the statement body of the false path.

After executing either the true or false path, control skips to the first command after the *if/else* statement. We may omit the braces when the body contains only one statement.

Examples:

1. ```
   if (iCredits < 45)
   {
       printf("Welcome freshman");
   }
   else
   {
       printf("Welcome upperclassman");
   }
   ```

   If credit hours are less than 45, then print `Welcome freshman`. Otherwise, print `Welcome upperclassman`.

2. ```
   if (fPayment > fBalance)
   {
       printf("Customer overpaid");
       printf("Credit the account");
   }
   else
   {
       printf("Thank you for your payment");
   }
   ```

If *fPayment* is greater than *fBalance,* then print the overpaid message. Otherwise, print the thank-you notice.

Nested if/else Statements

Format:

```
if (condition1)
{
    statements;
}
else if (condition2)
{
    statements;
    .....
}
```

Purpose: To set up a multipath conditional branch. A **nested** *if/else* consists of at least one *if/else* inside the false path of another. If a given condition is true, the program executes the statement body of the true path and then skips to the first command after the nested *if/else* statement. For nested *if/else* statements, each *else* is paired with the nearest *if.*

Example:

```
if (iCredits < 45)
{
    printf("Welcome freshman");
}
else if (iCredits < 90)
{
    printf("Welcome sophomore");
}
else if (iCredits < 135)
{
    printf("Welcome junior");
}
else
{
    printf("Welcome senior");
}
```

If a condition is true, the program prints the corresponding welcome message, control exits the nested *if/else* block, and processing continues with the first executable statement after the closing brace. The closing brace is shown at the end of the *if/else* block.

For example, if credit hours equal 120, the program prints the message *Welcome junior* and control skips to the first statement after the closing brace.

Note that credit hours exceeding 134 will automatically produce the message *Welcome senior.* This represents the **default case**. When no other condition applies, the default case is selected. Also note that each *else* is paired with the nearest *if*—the third *else* is paired to the third *if,* the second *else* is paired to the second *if,* and so on.

Checkpoint 5A

1. Distinguish between unconditional and conditional branching.
2. Identify the type of branching (conditional or unconditional) that occurs with the following statements.
   a. if
   b. goto
   c. if/else
3. What will print when the following statements are executed?

```
a. iPurchase = 450;
   if (iPurchase > 500)
   {
       printf("Thank you for your purchase.");
   }
   else
   {
       printf("Thank you.");
   }
b. iPurchase = 20.00;
   iTaxBracket = 1;
   if (iTaxBracket < 2)
   {
       fTax = fPurchase * 0.03;
       printf("Tax = %4.2f", fTax);
   }
c. fPurchase = 50.00;
   iTaxBracket = 3;
   if (iTaxBracket < 2)
   {
       fTax = fPurchase * 0.03;
   }
   else
   {
       fTax = fPurchase * 0.05;
   }
   printf("Tax = %4.2f", fTax);
d. iColor = 4;
   if (iColor < 10)
   {
       if (iColor == 4)
       {
           printf("Color is Red.");
       }
   }
e. iColor = 7;
   if (iColor < 10)
   {
       if (iColor == 4)
```

```
    {
        printf("Color is Red.");
    }
}
```

Sample Program CHAP5A

Beale-Ross Corporation pays its sales staff on commission as follows:

```
        sales range                      commission formula

        0 < sales <= 10,000                  .10 (sales)
   10,000 < sales <= 20,000          1,000 + .07 (sales - 10,000)
   20,000 < sales <= 35,000          1,700 + .05 (sales - 20,000)
   35,000 < sales                    2,450 + .02 (sales - 35,000)
```

Write a program to compute the earned commission for the sales staff, print the monthly sales report, and show the top salesperson for the month. The hierarchy chart for the sample program CHAP5A is shown in Figure 5.1; the flowchart, in Figure 5.2. The code is shown in Figure 5.3; the program output is shown in Figure 5.4.

Input (keyboard):

For each salesperson, prompt for and enter the following sales data:

Salesperson number
Salesperson name
Monthly sales amount

Output (printer):

Print the monthly sales report shown in Figure 5.4.

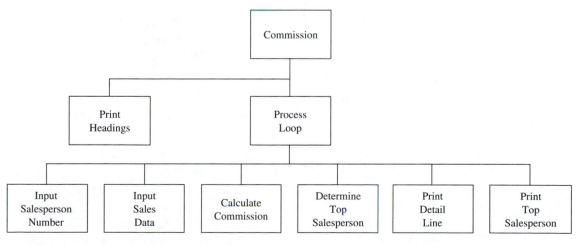

FIGURE 5.1 Hierarchy Chart for CHAP5A

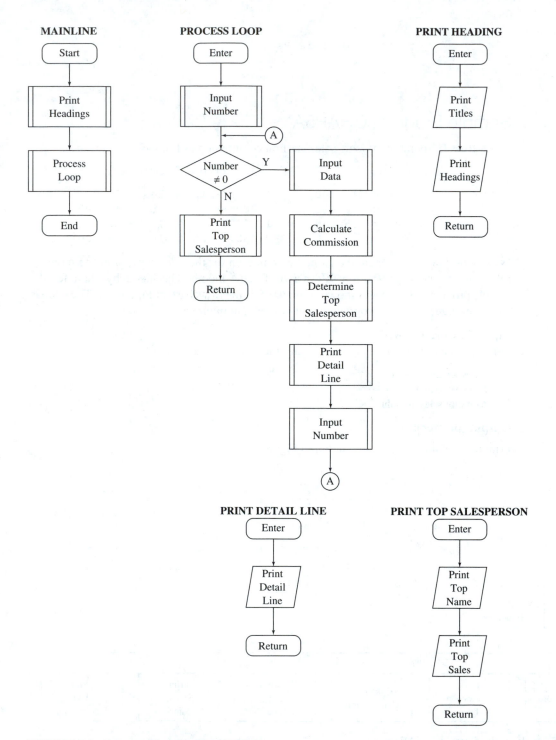

FIGURE 5.2   Program Flowchart for CHAP5A

CALCULATE COMMISSION

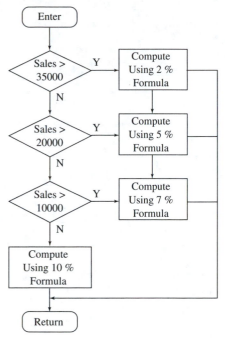

DETERMINE TOP SALESPERSON

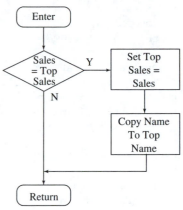

INPUT NUMBER

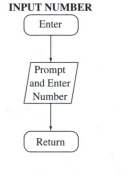

INPUT DATA

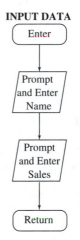

FIGURE 5.2 *Continued*

Processing Requirements:

- Determine the sales commission:
  based on the monthly sales (see the commission schedule).
- Determine the top salesperson and the top sales amount:
  based on the highest monthly sales.
- At the end of the report, print the top salesperson and the top
  sales amount.

```
/*-----------------------------------------------------------
COMMISSION: Compute and print a monthly sales commission report for
the Beale-Ross Corporation.

Program:    CHAP5A.C
Author:     David M. Collopy
Date:       mm/dd/yy
Project:    Sample program
***********************************************************************/

/*---- PREPROCESSING DIRECTIVE ----------------------------------*/

#include <stdio.h>
#include <string.h>
#include <graph.h>


/*---- FUNCTION PROTOTYPES ---------------------------------------*/

void  PrnHeadings(void);        /* print report headings      */
void  ProcessLoop(void);        /* processing loop            */
void  InputNum(void);           /* input salesperson number   */
void  InputOtherData(void);     /* input other sales data     */
float CalcCommis(void);         /* calculate commission       */
void  FindTopSales(void);       /* find top salesperson       */
void  PrnDetail(float);         /* print detail line          */
void  PrnTopSales(void);        /* print top salesperson      */


/*---- PROGRAM SETUP ---------------------------------------------*/

/*>  R E P O R T   T I T L E S   A N D   H E A D I N G S      <*/

char PT1[] = " B E A L E - R O S S   C O R P O R A T I O N  ";
char PT2[] = "             Monthly Sales Report               ";
char HL1[] = "S a l e s p e r s o n      Monthly      Earned  ";
char HL2[] = "Number  Name                  Sales    Commission";
char HL3[] = "------------------------------------------------";
char SL1[] = "  Top Salesperson: ";
char SL2[] = "Top Monthly Sales: ";


/*>  S A L E S   R E C O R D                                  <*/

int   iSalesNum;                /* salesperson number   */
char  sName[21];                /* salesperson name     */
float fSales;                   /* monthly sales        */
```

FIGURE 5.3   Sample Program CHAP5A: Compute and Print the Monthly Sales Report for Beale-Ross Corporation

```
/*>  P R O G R A M   V A R I A B L E S                        <*/

char  sTopName[21];             /* top salesperson     */
float fTopSales = 0.0;          /* top monthly sales   */

/*----------------------------------------------------------------
      MAINLINE CONTROL
----------------------------------------------------------------*/
main()
{
    PrnHeadings();              /* print report headings */
    ProcessLoop();             /* processing loop       */
    return 0;
}


/*----------------------------------------------------------------
      PRINT REPORT HEADINGS
----------------------------------------------------------------*/
void PrnHeadings(void)
{
    fprintf(stdprn, "\f");      /* reset to top of page  */
    fprintf(stdprn, "\r");      /* reset printer         */
    fprintf(stdprn, PT1);       /* print page title 1    */
    fprintf(stdprn, "\r\n");    /* reset & single space  */
    fprintf(stdprn, PT2);       /* print page title 2    */
    fprintf(stdprn, "\r\n\n");  /* reset & double space  */
    fprintf(stdprn, HL1);       /* print heading line 1  */
    fprintf(stdprn, "\r\n");    /* reset & single space  */
    fprintf(stdprn, HL2);       /* print heading line 2  */
    fprintf(stdprn, "\r\n");    /* reset & single space  */
    fprintf(stdprn, HL3);       /* print heading line 3  */
    fprintf(stdprn, "\r");      /* reset printer         */
    return;
}


/*----------------------------------------------------------------
      PROCESS LOOP
----------------------------------------------------------------*/
void ProcessLoop(void)
{
    float fCommission;          /* sales commission     */

    _clearsceen(0);
    InputNum();
    while (iSalesNum != 0)
```

FIGURE 5.3   *Continued*

```
    {
        InputOtherData();
        fCommission = CalcCommis();
        FindTopSales();
        PrnDetail(fCommission);
        _clearscreen(0);
        InputNum();
    }
    PrnTopSales();
    return;
}


/*-----------------------------------------------------------------
          INPUT SALESPERSON NUMBER
-------------------------------------------------------------------*/
void InputNum(void)
{
    printf("\n\nEnter salesperson number or '0' to Quit: ");
    scanf(" %d", &iSalesNum);
    fflush(stdin);
    return;
}


/*-----------------------------------------------------------------
          INPUT OTHER SALES DATA
-------------------------------------------------------------------*/
void InputOtherData(void)
{
    printf("Enter salesperson name: ");
    scanf(" %[^\n]", sName);
    fflush(stdin);
    printf("   Enter monthly sales: ");
    scanf(" %f", &fSales);
    fflush(stdin);
    return;
}


/*-----------------------------------------------------------------
          CALCULATE COMMISSION
-------------------------------------------------------------------*/
float CalcCommis(void)
{
    float fCommission;
```

FIGURE 5.3 *Continued*

```
     if (fSales > 35000.00)
         fCommission = 2450.00 + 0.02 * (fSales - 35000.00);
     else if (fSales > 20000.00)
         fCommission = 1700.00 + 0.05 * (fSales - 20000.00);
     else if (fSales > 10000.00)
         fCommission = 1000.00 + 0.07 * (fSales - 10000.00);
     else
         fCommission = 0.10 * fSales;
     return fCommission;
}


/*-------------------------------------------------------------
       FIND TOP SALESPERSON
-------------------------------------------------------------*/
void FindTopSales(void)
{
    if (fSales > fTopSales)
    {
        fTopSales = fSales;
        strcpy(sTopName, sName);
    }
    return;
}


/*-------------------------------------------------------------
       PRINT DETAIL LINE
-------------------------------------------------------------*/
void PrnDetail(float fCommission)
{
    fprintf(stdprn, "\r\n%4d  %-20s %8.2f    %7.2f",
        iSalesNum, sName, fSales, fCommission);
    return;
}


/*-------------------------------------------------------------
       PRINT TOP SALESPERSON
-------------------------------------------------------------*/
void PrnTopSales(void)
{
    fprintf(stdprn, "\r\n\n\n%s %s", SL1, sTopName);
    fprintf(stdprn, "\r\n%s %8.2f", SL2, fTopSales);
    return;
}
```

FIGURE 5.3   *Continued*

```
┌─────────────────────────────────────────────────────┐
│                                                       │
│     B E A L E - R O S S    C O R P O R A T I O N      │
│              Monthly Sales Report                     │
│                                                       │
│  S a l e s p e r s o n        Monthly      Earned     │
│  Num     Name                  Sales     Commissions   │
│  ---------------------------------------------------  │
│                                                       │
│  1000    Travis Coleman       34000.00     2400.00    │
│  2000    Katrina Lopez        50000.00     2750.00    │
│  3000    Mark Chen            25000.00     1950.00    │
│  4000    Erin Hessler         41200.00     2574.00    │
│  5000    Matt Wright          33170.00     2358.50    │
│                                                       │
│                                                       │
│    Top Salesperson:   Katrina Lopez                   │
│  Top Monthly Sales:   50000.00                        │
│                                                       │
└─────────────────────────────────────────────────────┘
```

FIGURE 5.4   Printer Output for CHAP5A

Pseudocode:

> START: Main
> Call Print Headings
> Call Process Loop
> END
>
> ENTER: Print Headings
> Print 2 page title lines
> Print 3 column heading lines
> RETURN
>
> ENTER: Process Loop
> Clear screen
> Call Input Salesperson Number
> LOOP while salesperson number not = 0
>   Call Input Other Data
>   Call Calculate Commission
>   Call Find Top Salesperson
>   Call Print Detail Line
>   Clear screen
>   Call Input Salesperson Number
> END LOOP
> Call Print Top Sales
> RETURN
>
> ENTER: Input Salesperson Number
> Prompt and enter salesperson number
> Clear keyboard buffer

RETURN

ENTER: Input Other Data
Prompt and enter salesperson name
Clear keyboard buffer
Prompt and enter monthly sales
Clear keyboard buffer
RETURN

ENTER: Calculate Commission
IF monthly sales > 35000
        commission = 2450 + 0.02 × (monthly sales - 35000)
else IF monthly sales > 20000
        commission = 1700 + 0.05 × (monthly sales - 20000)
else IF monthly sales > 10000
        commission = 1000 + 0.07 × (monthly sales - 10000)
else
        commission = 0.10 × monthly sales
END IF
RETURN

ENTER: Find Top Salesperson
IF monthly sales > top sales
        Let top sales = monthly sales
        Let top salesperson = salesperson name
END IF
RETURN

ENTER: Print Detail Line
Prompt salesperson detail line
        salesperson number
        salesperson name
        monthly sales
        commission
RETURN

ENTER: Print Top Sales
Print top salesperson
Print top monthly sales
RETURN

Hierarchy Chart: See Figure 5.1.

Program Flowchart: See Figure 5.2.

Dissection of Sample Program CHAP5A

Walk through the program code shown in Figure 5.3. As usual, the preprocessing directives and the function prototypes are defined at the top of the program. However, the *PROGRAM SETUP* is organized a little differently. It is divided into three sections: one for the report titles and column headings; one for the input sales record; and one for the program variables.

This particular arrangement makes the *PROGRAM SETUP* easier to read. Let's take a closer look at the processing performed by the input and calculation modules.

I N P U T   S A L E S P E R S O N   N U M B E R:

```
void InputNum(void)
{
    printf("\n\nEnter salesperson number or '0' to Quit: ");
    scanf(" %d", &iSalesNum);
    fflush(stdin);
    return;
}
```

The above statements prompt the user to enter the salesperson number. The scanf() picks up the salesperson number, whereas the fflush() removes the enter-keypress and clears the input buffer.

If the buffer is not cleared at this point, the enter-keypress will be assigned to the salesperson's name when control branches to the *InputOtherData* module.

Note: When in doubt, the safest rule to follow is to clear the keyboard buffer after each scanf().

I N P U T   O T H E R   S A L E S   D A T A:

```
void InputOtherData(void)
{
    printf("\n\nEnter salesperson name: ");
    scanf(" %[^\n]", sName);
    fflush(stdin);
```

The above statements prompt for and input the salesperson's name. According to the scanset, the input stream is read up to the enter-keypress \n and stored in the string variable called *sName*. The last statement clears the keyboard buffer.

```
    printf("    Enter monthly sales: ");
    scanf(" %f", &fSales);
    fflush(stdin);
    return;
}
```

The above statements prompt for and input the monthly sales. After clearing the input buffer, control returns to the calling module.

C A L C U L A T E   C O M M I S S I O N:

```
float CalcCommis(void)
{
    float fCommission;

    if (fSales > 35000.00)
        fCommission = 2450.00 + 0.02 * (fSales - 35000.00);
```

```
    else if (fSales > 20000.00)
        fCommission = 1700.00 + 0.05 * (fSales - 20000.00);
    else if (fSales > 10000.00)
        fCommission = 1000.00 + 0.07 * (fSales - 10000.00);
    else
        fCommission = 0.10 * fSales;
    return fCommission;
}
```

The nested *if/else* starts by comparing *fSales* to 35,000.00. If *fSales* exceeds 35,000.00, then the program computes commission according to the formula given and control skips to the *return* statement. Else, control branches to the false path and compares *fSales* to 20,000.00. This process continues until either a match is found or commission is assigned the default value. The last statement returns the earned commission to the calling statement.

F I N D   T O P   S A L E S P E R S O N:

```
void FindTopSales(void)
{
    if (fSales > fTopSales)
    {
        fTopSales = fSales;
        strcpy(sTopName, sName);
    }
    return;
}
```

The above module locates the top salesperson and sale. Since *fTopSales* was initially set to zero, the first comparison automatically assigns *fSales* to *fTopSales*. Thereafter, *fSales* is assigned to *fTopSales* only if it is the greater of the two. Notice that the string copy function assigns *sName* to *sTopName* when *fSales* is greater than *fTopSales*.

Notes and Tips

1. A conditional branch is taken only when the given condition is true.

2. An unconditional branch is take each time the statement is executed by the computer.

3. The *if* and *if/else* decision statements allow the program to make a selection from two processing paths.

4. Nested *if* and *if/else* decision statements allow the program to make a selection from multiple processing paths.

5. Do not put a semicolon after the *if* or *else*. A semicolon placed at either location will produce an error.

6. According to the specifications, commission is based on a sales range. Yet the actual condition tests coded in the program do not specify a range. For example, if sales fall within the range 10,000 < sales <= 20,000, then commission is derived using the formula 1,000 + 0.07 (sales – 10,000). However, the corresponding condition test coded in the program is shown as *if (sales > 10000.00)*. What happened to the range check?

In general, if a set of continuous range checks are given in low to high order, then you may code the tests starting with highest value and check for the greater than condition. Subsequent condition tests are coded in a similar manner. To see how it works, take another look at the condition tests shown in the *CalcCommis* module. This method is easier to remember and simpler to code than the range check.

Tutorial CHAP5A

1. The objectives of this tutorial are to
   - use a nested *if/else* structure
   - find the top salesperson
2. Open the text editor, and enter the sample program as shown in Figure 5.3.
3. Save the source program on your work disk as CHAP5A. Check for coding errors, and make corrections as needed.
4. Compile, run, and debug your program until the output matches the report shown in Figure 5.4.
5. Rewrite the condition statements shown in the *CalcCommis* module as range checks. Save the new version of the program as CHAP5A2. Compile and run the program. Did you get the correct output?
6. When completed, show your work to your instructor.

Quick Quiz

Answer the following questions.

1. Did you have any problems (CHAP5A2) when you changed the condition statements to range checks?
2. Discuss how the nested *if/else* statements are used to determine the correct commission.
3. Explain how the *if* statement coded in *FindTopSales* is able to locate the top salesperson.
4. There are two *fprintf* statements coded in the *PrnTopSales* module. Both have two format specifiers and two arguments. Discuss how the specifiers and arguments work together to produce the output.
5. Did you have any problems or errors when you ran your program? If so, what were they and what did you do to correct them?

The switch and break Statements

Format:

```
switch (expression)
{
     case label1:
```

```
                statement(s);
                break;
        case label2:
                statement(s);
                break;

    .  .  .  .  .


        case labeln:
                statement(s);
                break;
        default:
                statement(s);
                break;
}
```

Purpose: To set up a multipath conditional branch. The *switch* statement allows the program to select one option from a given set of options. First, the integer or character expression is compared to the case labels. Each **label** is unique and identifies a processing option or case. A case may have multiple labels, and the actual number of cases depends mostly on the application at hand.

Second, if a match is found, control performs the statement(s) corresponding to the case. The program executes the statement body of the case until *break* is encountered. The *break* statement marks the end of the case and causes control to exit the *switch* statement.

However, if a match is not found, control performs the statements specified by the *default* case (the case that's left when no other cases apply). Although default is shown at the end, it may be placed anywhere within the *switch* statement.

Example:

```
1. int iChoice;
     .....

    printf("Enter your choice... \n");
    printf("Movie menu: 1-Action, 2-Comedy, 3-Drama\n");
    scanf(" %d", &iChoice);
    switch (iChoice)
    {
        case 1:
            printf("Action movie fan\n");
            break;
        case 2:
            printf("Comedy movie fan\n");
            break;
        case 3:
            printf("Drama movie fan\n");
            break;
        default:
            printf("Invalid choice\n");
            break;
    }
```

The user selects a choice from the menu line. A **menu line** displays the list of options available to the user. For example, if the third option (*iChoice* = 3) is selected, then the message Drama movie fan appears on the screen. Any selection other than 1–3 produces the error message Invalid choice.

2.
```
char iChoice;
    .....

printf("Enter your choice... ");
printf("Movie menu: A/ction, C/omedy, D/rama");
scanf(" %c", &iChoice);
switch (iChoice)
{
    case 'A':
    case 'a':
        printf("Action movie fan\n");
        break;
    case 'C':
    case 'c':
        printf("Comedy movie fan\n");
        break;
    case 'D':
    case 'd':
        printf("Drama movie fan\n");
        break;
    default:
        printf("Invalid choice\n");
        break;
}
```

Here the users enter the letters of their choice. To select a comedy video, they press either *C* or *c*. According to the labels, the selection may be in either uppercase or lowercase. Of course, any selection other than the options given will result in the error message Invalid choice.

The goto and label Statements

Format:

```
goto label;
label: statement;
```

Purpose: To transfer the program control. The *goto* statement causes an unconditional branch to a label within the current module. A **label** is an identifier that is attached to a program statement. The labeled statement may be placed anywhere in the body of the module that the *goto* appears. The *goto* and *label* statements end with a semicolon.

Examples:

1. Clear the screen
```
iCount = 1;
repeat:
    printf("\n");
    iCount++;
    if (iCount < 25)
    {
        goto repeat;
}
```
OUTPUT: a blank screen

As long as *count* is less than 25, the looping printf() pushes the lines upward and off the screen.

2. Loop until score falls below 60 points
```
for (iCount = 1; iCount < 25; iCount++)
{
    printf("Enter score: ");
    scanf(" %d", &iScore)
    if (iScore < 60)
    {
        goto failed;
    }
}
failed:
    printf("\n Since the class did not pass the test,");
    printf("\n a retest will be given on Friday.");
```
OUTPUT: none—unless score is less than 60

Caution: It would be wise to avoid the *goto* statement altogether. Unconditional branching encourages a patchwork (spaghetti code) style of programming that leads to messy code and unreliable performance. A *goto*-riddled program destroys the benefits of top-down design and modular structured programming by making the code harder (if not impossible) to read, understand, and maintain.

Checkpoint 5B

1. Why should we avoid using the *goto* statement?
2. For the following code, what will print when *E* is selected?
```
char cSelection;
.....

printf("Enter your selection...");
printf("Dining Menu: S/ide Dish, E/ntree, D/essert");
scanf(" %c", cSelection);
switch(cSelection)
```

```
    {
        case 'S':
        case 's':
            printf("Bean, Broccoli, Chili, Potato\n");
            break;
        case 'E':
        case 'e':
            printf("Fish, Poultry, Beef, Pork\n");
            break;
        case 'D':
        case 'd':
            printf("Cake, Pie, Ice Cream, Cookie\n");
            break;
        default:
            printf("Invalid choice\n");
            break;
    }
```

3. Using the code given in Exercise 2, what will print when *A* is selected?

4. Using the following code, what will print when *s* is selected? Why?

```
char cSelection;
.....

printf("Enter your selection...");
printf("Dining Menu: S/ide Dish, E/ntree, D/essert");
scanf(" %c", cSelection);
switch(cSelection)
{
    case 'S':
    case 's':
        printf("Bean, Broccoli, Chili, Potato\n");
    case 'E':
    case 'e':
        printf("Fish, Poultry, Beef, Pork\n");
    case 'D':
    case 'd':
        printf("Cake, Pie, Ice Cream, Cookie\n");
    default:
        printf("Invalid choice\n");
}
```

Sample Program CHAP5B

Mayesville wants to offer youth sport programs to the elementary school children. Sue Kesler, director of Parks and Recreations, surveyed the elementary schools to find out what sports activities the children would be interested in playing.

Write a program to tabulate the results of the survey and to print a report showing each sport and the number of children interested in playing. The hierarchy chart for sample program CHAP5B is shown in Figure 5.5; the flowchart, in Figure 5.6. The code is shown in Figure 5.7; the output is shown in Figure 5.8.

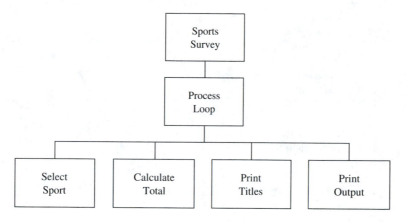

FIGURE 5.5   Hierarchy Chart for CHAP5B

Input (keyboard):
Prompt for and enter choice:

>   1-Baseball, 2-Football, 3-Basketball, 4-Soccer.

Output (printer):
Print the sports survey report shown in Figure 5.8.

Processing Requirements:
Accumulate totals for each sport.

Pseudocode:

>   START: Main
>   Call Process Loop
>   END
>
>   ENTER: Process Loop
>   Clear screen
>   Call Select Sport
>   LOOP while choice not = 0
>   Call Calculate Totals
>   Clear screen
>   Call Select Sport
>   END LOOP
>   Call Print Titles
>   Call Print Survey Report
>   RETURN
>
>   ENTER: Select Sport
>   Prompt and select sport
>   Clear keyboard buffer
>   RETURN
>
>   ENTER: Calculate Totals
>   ON CHOICE add 1 to sport count:

```
        1: baseball
        2: football
        3: basketball
        4: soccer
        otherwise: print error - invalid choice
END ON CHOICE
RETURN

ENTER: Print Titles
Print 2 page title lines
RETURN

ENTER: Print Survey Report
Print totals for:
        baseball
        football
        basketball
        soccer
RETURN
```

Hierarchy Chart: See Figure 5.5.

Program Flowchart: See Figure 5.6.

Dissection of Sample Program CHAP5B

MAINLINE   CONTROL:

```
main()
{
    ProcessLoop();
    return 0;
}
```

The previous statements call the processing loop and perform the statements coded there.

PROCESSING   LOOP:

```
void ProcessLoop(void)
{
    int iChoice;

    _clearscreen(0);
    iChoice = SelectSport();
    while (iChoice != 0)
    {
        CalcTotals(iChoice);
        _clearscreen(0);
        iChoice = SelectSport();
    }
    PrnTitles();
```

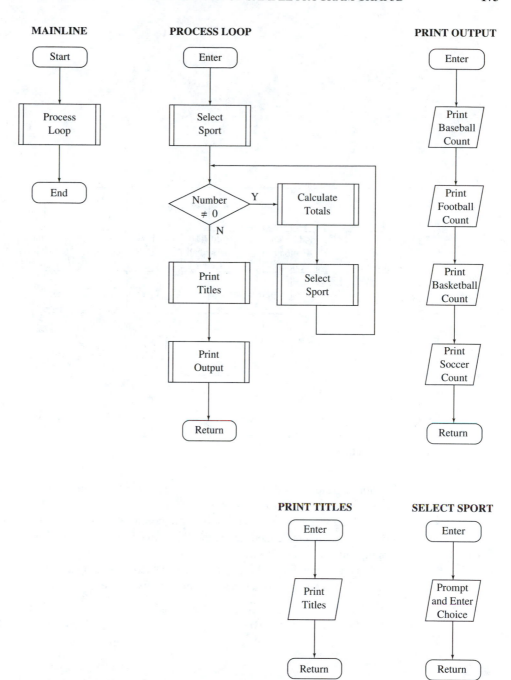

FIGURE 5.6   Program Flowchart for CHAP5B

CALCULATE TOTALS

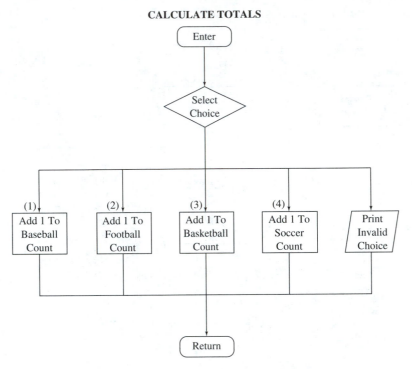

FIGURE 5.6 *Continued*

```
    PrnOutput();
    return;
}
```

The above statements declare a local variable, clear the screen, and call *SelectSport*. Upon a return, the user's choice is assigned to *iChoice*.

As long as the user's response is not 0, control enters the statement body of the *while* loop. The statements coded inside the loop pass *iChoice* to *CalcTotals* module, clear the screen, and call *SelectSport*.

Once the user enters 0 for *iChoice*, control exits the loop and executes calls to the *Prn-Titles* and *PrnOutput* modules, respectively. The *return* sends control back to the *MAINLINE*.

```
S E L E C T    S P O R T S    A C T I V I T Y:
int SelectSport(void)
{
    int iChoice;

    printf("\n\nSelect a sport or '0' to Quit");
    printf("\n1-Baseball, 2-Football, 3-Basketball, 4-Soccer");
    scanf(" %d", &iChoice);
    fflush(stdin);
    return iChoice;
}
```

The above statements prompt the user to either select a sport or enter 0 to quit. After the selection is assigned to *iChoice*, control clears the keyboard buffer and returns *iChoice* to the calling statement in the *PROCESSING LOOP*.

```
CALCULATE  TOTALS:
void CalcTotals(int iChoice)
{
    char cResume;

    switch (iChoice)
    {
        case 1:
            iBaseballCnt++;
            break;
        case 2:
            iFootballCnt++;
            break;
        case 3:
            iBasketballCnt++;
            break;
        case 4:
            iSoccerCnt++;
            break;
        default:
            printf("\nError-invalid choice:");
            printf("\nPress 'c' to continue...");
            scanf(" %c", cResume");
    }
    return;
}
```

The above statements compare the value of the passed argument *iChoice* to the label values. On a match, the program increments the sport count, skips to the end of the *switch* statement, and returns to the *PROCESSING LOOP*. If a match is not found, control branches to *default* and prints the error message.

For the default case, the printf() and scanf() statements are used to hold the screen. This process gives the user time to read the message and to respond.

```
/*-------------------------------------------------------------
SPORTS SURVEY: Tabulate and print the results of a sports survey.

Program:    CHAP5B.C
Author:     David M. Collopy
Date:       mm/dd/yy
Project:    Sample program
*****************************************************************/
```

FIGURE 5.7   Sample Program CHAP5B: Tabulate and Print the Results of a Sports Survey

```
/*---- PREPROCESSING DIRECTIVE --------------------------------*/

#include <stdio.h>
#include <graph.h>

/*---- FUNCTION PROTOTYPES ------------------------------------*/

void   ProcessLoop(void);        /* processing loop        */
int    SelectSport(void);        /* select sport activity  */
void   CalcTotals(int);          /* calculate totals       */
void   PrnTitles(void);          /* print title lines      */
void   PrnOutput(void);          /* print survey report    */


/*---- PROGRAM SETUP ------------------------------------------*/

/*>  R E P O R T   T I T L E S   A N D   H E A D I N G S    <*/

char PT1[] = " MAYESVILLE PARKS AND RECREATIONS DEPARTMENT";
char PT2[] = "              Youth Sports Survey            ";

/*>  P R O G R A M   V A R I A B L E S                      <*/

int iBaseballCnt;              /* baseball count     */
int iFootballCnt;              /* football count     */
int iBasketballCnt;            /* basketball count   */
int iSoccerCnt;                /* soccer count       */


/*-------------------------------------------------------------
        MAINLINE CONTROL
-------------------------------------------------------------*/
main()
{
    ProcessLoop();               /* processing loop       */
    return 0;
}


/*-------------------------------------------------------------
        PROCESSING LOOP
-------------------------------------------------------------*/
void ProcessLoop(void)
{
    int iChoice;

    _clearscreen(0);
    iChoice = SelectSport();
    while (iChoice != 0)
```

FIGURE 5.7 *Continued*

```
      {
          CalcTotals(iChoice);
          _clearscreen(0);
          iChoice = SelectSport();
      }
      PrnTitles();
      PrnOutput();
      return;
}

/*-------------------------------------------------------------
      SELECT SPORTS ACTIVITY
---------------------------------------------------------------*/
int SelectSport(void)
{
    int iChoice;

    printf("\n\nSelect a sport or '0' to Quit");
    printf("\n1-Baseball, 2-Football, 3-Basketball, 4-Soccer: ");
    scanf(" %d", &iChoice);
    fflush(stdin);
    return iChoice;
}

/*-------------------------------------------------------------
      CALCULATE TOTALS
---------------------------------------------------------------*/
void CalcTotals(int iChoice)
{
    char cResume;                        /* resume processing */

    switch (iChoice)
    {
        case 1:
            iBaseballCnt++;
            break;
        case 2:
            iFootballCnt++;
            break;
        case 3:
            iBasketballCnt++;
            break;
        case 4:
            iSoccerCnt++;
            break;
        default:
```

FIGURE 5.7   *Continued*

```
                    printf("\nError--invalid choice:");
                    printf("\nPress 'c' to continue...");
                    scanf(" %c", cResume);
            }
        return;
    }


    /*--------------------------------------------------------------
            PRINT TITLE LINES
    ----------------------------------------------------------------*/
    void PrnTitles(void)
    {
        fprintf(stdprn, "\r\n\n");   /* reset & double space */
        fprintf(stdprn, PT1);        /* print page title 1    */
        fprintf(stdprn, "\r\n");     /* reset & single space */
        fprintf(stdprn, PT2);        /* print page title 2    */
        fprintf(stdprn, "\r\n\n");   /* reset & double space */
        return;
    }


    /*--------------------------------------------------------------
            PRINT SURVEY REPORT
    ----------------------------------------------------------------*/
    void PrnOutput(void)
    {
        fprintf(stdprn, "\r\n\nBaseball:    %4d", iBaseballCnt);
        fprintf(stdprn, "\r\n\nFootball:    %4d", iFootballCnt);
        fprintf(stdprn, "\r\n\nBasketball: %4d", iBasketballCnt);
        fprintf(stdprn, "\r\n\nSoccer:      %4d", iSoccerCnt);
        return;
    }
```

FIGURE 5.7 *Continued*

```
            MAYESVILLE PARKS AND RECREATIONS DEPARTMENT
                        Youth Sports Survey

    Baseball:      153

    Football:      129

    Basketball:    175

    Soccer:        147
```

FIGURE 5.8 Printer Output for CHAP5B

Notes And Tips

1. Do not code a semicolon after the *switch* statement.
2. Do code a colon after each case *label*.
3. Indent the statement body of the *switch/case* structure 4 spaces, and enclose the statement body within braces.
4. For most applications, it would be a wise to establish a *default* case to catch situations that do not fall in the other categories.
5. Avoid the *goto* statement—it destroys the benefits of structured programming.
6. Sample program CHAP5B departs a little from our normal structure—it doesn't print detail lines. It gets the input and based on the user's choice, increments the counter for the corresponding sport. Once the user completes the input task, the program prints a report showing the four totals. Hence, there are no detail lines.

   If you look at the *CalcTotals* module, you'll see the *switch/case* structure in action. A word of warning is in order here. Be sure to match all possible input data to a case label. If you don't, some of the input will dump into the *default* case. Another warning: Don't forget to code the *break* statement at the end of the body of each case. Otherwise, control will drop through the body of the other cases and increment their sport count as well.

Tutorial CHAP5B

1. The objectives of this tutorial are to
   • use the *switch/case* structure
   • understand the purpose of the *break* statement
   • utilize the *default* case
2. Enter the sample program as shown in Figure 5.7.
3. Save the source program on your work disk as CHAP5B.
4. Compile, run, and debug your program until the output looks similar to the report shown in Figure 5.8. Make up your own data, and verify that the output is correct.
5. When completed, show your work to your instructor.

Quick Quiz

Answer the following questions.

1. What is the purpose of the *switch* statement?
2. How, for example, does *iBaseballCnt++* accumulate a total?
3. What does the *break* statement do? Why is *break* coded at the end of each case except for the *default* case?
4. The *default* case displays an error message, stops processing, and waits for the user to enter a *c* to continue. What would happen if the second print statement and the scan were removed from the *default* case and the user entered a choice of 6? Try it and see.
5. Did you have any problems or errors when you ran your program? If so, what were they and what did you do to correct them?

Summary

1. The computer can be programmed to select and follow a particular course of action depending on the comparative values of two data items.

2. An unconditional branch sends control directly to a specific location in the program. On the other hand, a conditional branch is taken only if a given condition is met.

3. The *if* decision performs the statement body only if the condition test is true. Otherwise, control skips to the first command after the *if* statement.

4. A nested *if* consists of at least one *if* inside the branch of another. The statement body is executed only if all conditions are true. Any time a condition is false, control exits the nested *if* statement.

5. The *if/else* decision statement selects one of two options. This function performs the statement body of the true path only if the condition test is true. Otherwise, it performs the statement body of the false path.

6. A nested *if/else* consists of at least one *if* or *if/else* inside the false path of another. If a given condition is true, the program executes the statement body and skips to the first statement after the nested *if/else*.

7. A *goto* statement causes an unconditional jump to a label within the current module. A label is an identifier that is attached to a program statement. Overall, the use of the *goto* statement is considered poor programming.

8. The *switch* statement allows the program to select an option from a given set of options. A case may have more than one label. The *break* statement marks the end of a case and prevents control from falling through the body of the remaining cases.

Programming Projects

For each project, design the logic and write the modular structured program to produce the output. Model your program after the sample programs presented in the chapter. Verify your output.

Project 5–1   Overdue Accounts

Write a program to print a report for customers with account balances that are 90 days overdue.

Input (keyboard):
For each customer, prompt for and enter the following data:

Account Number	Customer Name	Days Overdue	Balance Due
1010	David Ryan	90	400.00
2450	Marie Hill	30	754.00
2730	Rita Fox	90	740.00
3100	Alvin Porter	90	550.00

4080	Corey Adkins	30	233.00
4890	Amy Wyatt	30	700.00
5260	Brian Knox	30	625.00
6350	Susan Cope	90	600.00
7720	Lisa Wilson	60	417.00
8540	Matt Hart	90	900.00
9200	Tori Landis	90	235.00
9630	Pat Rankin	60	342.00

Output (printer):

Print the following overdue accounts report:

```
Author               90-DAY OVERDUE ACCOUNTS              Page 01
                          mm/dd/yy


    Acct Number          Customer Name           Balance Due

        9999            X-----------X              999.99
          :                   :                       :
          :                   :                       :
        9999            X-----------X              999.99


                                  Total:         9999.99


   Number of overdue accounts:  99
   Number of accounts > 500.00: 99
```

Processing Requirements:

- Print a report of all accounts that are 90 days overdue.
- Accumulate a total for balance due.
- Count the number of 90-day overdue accounts.
- Count the number of 90-day overdue accounts with a balance greater than $500.

Project 5–2   Payroll

Write a program to calculate and print a weekly payroll roster. Hours worked over 40 are paid overtime. Assume the current federal income tax (FIT) rate is 15%.

Input (keyboard):

For each employee, prompt for and enter the following payroll data:

Employee Name	Hours Worked	Hourly Pay Rate
Tanya Bauer	40	7.50
Dana Clark	45	14.90
Sara Erickson	38	12.00
Scott Howard	42	9.75
Paul Irwin	48	8.72
Dale Miller	40	10.25
Bret Rossi	35	8.00
Karen Thomas	48	9.00
Tracy York	36	11.00

Output (printer):

Print the following payroll report:

```
Author                  WEEKLY PAYROLL REPORT              Page 01
                              mm/dd/yy


Employee    Hours   Regular   Overtime   Gross
Name        Worked  Pay       Pay        Pay        FIT      Net Pay

X-------X     99    999.99     99.99     999.99     99.99     999.99
    :         :        :          :          :         :          :
    :         :        :          :          :         :          :
X-------X     99    999.99     99.99     999.99     99.99     999.99

          Totals:  9999.99    999.99    9999.99    999.99    9999.99
```

Processing Requirements:

- Compute the regular pay:
  If hours > 40,
    then regular pay = 40 × pay rate
    else regular pay = hours × pay rate.
- Compute the overtime pay:
  If hours > 40,
    then overtime pay = (hours – 40) × 1.5 × pay rate
    else overtime pay = 0.
- Compute the gross pay:
  regular pay + overtime pay.
- Compute the federal income tax amount:
  gross pay × FIT rate.
- Compute the net pay:
  gross pay – FIT amount.
- Accumulate totals for regular pay, overtime pay, gross pay,
  FIT, and net pay.

Project 5–3   Sales Order

Write a program to calculate and print the customers' sales orders. Majestic Music Shop sells CDs at a discount when purchased in quantities. Assume the retail price for a single CD is $14.95 and the following discount schedule is as follows:

Quantity	Discount
2–6	10%
7–12	20%
13–24	30%
25–48	40%
49–up	50%

Input (keyboard):

For each customer, prompt for and enter the number of CDs purchased (or Press '0' to quit). Enter the following purchase quantities: 7, 1, 26, 50, 2, 15, 12, and 24.

Output (screen):
For each customer, print the following sales order:

```
Author          MAJESTIC MUSIC SHOP        mm/dd/yy
                   Sales Order


Enter quantity purchased or '0' to Quit: 99

Discount rate = 0.99

You saved $999.99 on your order.
Please pay the cashier $999.99
```

Processing Requirements:

- Determine the discount rate:
  based on the quantity purchased (see the discount schedule).
- Compute the order total:
  quantity $\times$ 14.95.
- Compute the discount amount:
  order total $\times$ discount rate.
- Compute the bill:
  order total $-$ discount amount.

Project 5–4   Inventory

Write a program to compute and print an inventory reorder report.

Input (keyboard):
For each item, prompt for and enter the following inventory data:

Item Num	Description	Quantity On Hand	Reorder Point	Reorder Quantity	Unit Cost	Selling Price
1000	Hammers	24	12	24	4.75	9.49
2000	Saws	08	16	12	7.50	14.99
3000	Drills	10	12	18	7.83	15.95
4000	Screwdrivers	36	24	12	2.27	4.98
5000	Pliers	12	12	36	2.65	5.49

Output (printer):
Print the following inventory reorder report:

```
Author          INVENTORY REORDER REPORT        Page 01
                     mm/dd/yy


Item                          Quantity   On          Item
Number    Description         On Hand    Order        Cost

 9999     X----------X           99        99        999.99
   :          :                  :         :            :
   :          :                  :         :            :
```

```
9999      X-----------X           99        99       999.99

                                  Total Cost:     9999.99
```

Processing Requirements:

- Determine what items to reorder:
  Order the reorder quantity of an item when the quantity on hand is less than or equal to the reorder point.
- Compute the item cost:
  on order × unit cost.
- Accumulate the total cost.

Project 5–5   Personnel

Write a program to print a salary report of all female employees who are paid over $30,000 a year.

Input (keyboard):

For each employee, prompt for and enter the following personnel data:

Employee Number	Employee Name	Department Number	Sex Code	Annual Salary
1926	Dana Andrews	10	F	29000.00
2071	Scott Cooper	14	M	30250.00
3150	Todd Feldman	22	M	24175.00
3600	Amy Kwon	19	F	36025.00
4100	Derek Lowe	50	M	29120.00
4298	Lori Palmer	35	F	33400.00
5409	Bob Shields	47	M	27500.00
6552	Pam Wolfe	31	F	31773.00

Output (printer):

Print the following personnel report:

```
Author                    SALARY REPORT                  Page 01
                            mm/dd/yy


Employee                              Department      Annual
Number       Employee Name            Number          Salary

 9999        X-----------X                99          99999.99
   :              :                        :              :
   :              :                        :              :
 9999        X-----------X                99          99999.99

                                      Average:        99999.99
```

Processing Requirements:

- Print a report of all female employees who are paid over $30,000 a year.
- Accumulate female count.
- Accumulate a total for annual salary.

- Compute the average annual salary:
  total annual salary / female count.

Project 5–6   Accounts Payable

Write a program to compute and print an accounts payable report. Assume the following discount schedule applies to early payments (in days):

Paid By	Discount
1–10	12%
11–20	10%
21–30	8%
31–45	5%

Input (keyboard):
For each vendor, prompt for and enter the following data:

Vendor Number	Vendor Name	Invoice Number	Invoice Amount	Paid By
217	Metacraft	A1239	2309.12	10
349	IntraTell	T9823	670.00	25
712	Reylock	F0176	4563.78	33
501	Universal	W0105	1200.00	21
196	Northland	X2781	3429.34	45
414	MarxComm	H9205	913.87	18
659	Veston	D1776	5127.63	30

Output (printer):
Print the following accounts payable report:

```
Author                      ACCOUNTS PAYABLE                    Page 01
                               mm/dd/yy


Vendor                      Invoice    Invoice    Discount    Amount
Number    Vendor Name       Number     Amount     Amount      Due

 999      X---------X        XXXX       9999.99     999.99     9999.99
  :           :               :           :           :          :
  :           :               :           :           :          :
 999      X---------X        XXXX       9999.99     999.99     9999.99

              Totals:                  99999.99    9999.99    99999.99
```

Processing Requirements:

- Determine the discount rate:
  Based on early payment (see the discount schedule).
- Compute the discount amount:
  invoice amount × discount rate.
- Compute the amount due:
  invoice amount – discount amount.
- Accumulate totals for invoice amount, discount amount, and amount due.

Project 5–7   Production Bonus

Write a program to compute and print a production bonus report. Assume production workers are paid a bonus according to the number of units they produce over the quota. Use the following bonus pay schedule:

Units Over Quota	Pay Rate Each
1–10	0.60
11–25	0.65
26–45	0.70
46+	0.75

Input (keyboard):

For each item, prompt for and enter the following production data:

Employee Name	Product Number	Quota	Units Produced
Kay Archer	P9511	65	65
Alan Baum	A1234	48	97
Marie Fitch	C4510	60	75
Lee Hildebrand	R0934	50	62
David Mullins	E3371	75	75
Chad Nelson	L8912	40	63
Bill Quinn	S0951	48	56
Nicole Renner	H9733	50	59
Erica Tate	Z0182	65	73
Terry West	A3235	70	116

Output (printer):

Print the following bonus report:

```
Author                    PRODUCTION BONUS REPORT              Page 01
                                 mm/dd/yy


                   Product           Units      Over
Employee Name      Number    Quota   Produced   Quota    Bonus Pay

X----------X       XXXXX        99      999        99      999.99
      :               :          :        :         :         :
      :               :          :        :         :         :
X----------X       XXXXX        99      999        99      999.99

                           Totals:     9999       999     9999.99
```

Processing Requirements:

- Compute the bonus pay:
  Based on units over quota (see the bonus pay schedule).
- Accumulate totals for units produced, units over quota, and bonus pay.

6 Using Menus

Overview

Learning Objectives

After you have read this chapter and completed the exercises, you should be able to

- validate input data and prompt the user to correct data entry errors
- write menu-driven programs that allow the user to select one option from a list of processing options
- design and create user-friendly menus that are easy to read and understand
- implement the menu decision process using nested *if/else* and *switch* statements
- use the getch() statement to halt screen scrolling

Data Validation

Programs that interact with people should be user friendly. A **user-friendly** program is easy to use, tells the user exactly what to do, and catches data entry errors as they enter the system. It is the programmer's responsibility to ensure that the software is user friendly.

The purpose of **data validation** is to check the input data for errors. If the input is invalid, then the output will be invalid. When an error is encountered, the program should alert the user of the error and prompt to reenter it. It would be better to lock the user in the data entry routine until the data is correct than to let bad data enter the system.

Let's consider three simple data validation techniques that we can write at this point. They include range checks, code checks, and cross reference checks.

Range Checks: A **range check** determines if the data is reasonable and lies within a given range of values.

Examples:

1. Check a menu selection to ensure that it is within the range 1–4.

```
printf("\nEnter choice (1 - 4) ===> ");
scanf(" %d", &iChoice);
while (iChoice < 1 || iChoice > 4)
{
    printf("\nERROR...enter valid choice (1 - 4) ===> );
    scanf(" %d", &iChoice);
}
```

2. Check to ensure that no more than 63 (total number of employees) payroll checks were printed.

```
if (iCheckCount > 63)
{
    printf("\nWARNING: The number of checks printed exceeds
        the employee count.");
}
```

Code Checks: A **code check** is used to determine if the data matches a set of predefined codes.

Examples:

1. Compare the size code to ensure that it matches one of the following values: SM, MD, LR.

```
while (strcmp(sSize, "SM") != 0 && strcmp(sSize, "MD") != 0
    && strcmp(sSize, "LR") != 0)
{
    printf("\nERROR...enter valid size codes: SM, MD, LR ");
}
```

2. Check the user's response for the values 0 or 1.

```
if (iResponse == 0 || iResponse == 1)
{
    printf("\n Resonse is OK");
}
else
{
    printf("\n ERROR: Invalid response");
}
```

Cross Reference Checks: A **cross reference check** is used to ensure that the relationship between two or more data items is consistent.

Examples:

1. Check the selling price of an item to ensure that it is greater than the cost.

```
if (fPrice <= fCost)
{
    printf("\nERROR...price should exceed cost ");
}
```

2. Check the size code; if it is *SM* or *MD,* then the only valid color codes are 1, 3, and 8.

```
if (strcmp(sSize, "SM") != 0  && strcmp(sSize, "MD") != 0)
{
    if (iColor == 1 || iColor == 3 || iColor == 8)
    {
        printf("\n Size and color code are OK ");
    }
    else
    {
        printf("\nERROR...either size or color code is wrong");
    }
}
```

Menu-Driven Programs

In Chapter 5, we learned how to use a simple menu line to prompt the user to enter a choice. Whenever there are a variety of options available to the user, it would be simpler to display them on the screen with a menu. A **menu** prints a list of options and prompts the user to enter a choice.

For example, consider the **menu-driven** business processing system in Figure 6.1. At the main menu, the user is asked to select one of the five options. Assume the user selects the second option, "Inventory System." Next, the Inventory System menu appears and asks the user to make a further selection. Assume the user chooses the first option, "Add quantity received." Yet another screen appears and prompts the user to enter the part number and quantity received.

This menu-driven system demonstrates how menus can be used to "walk" the user through a series of menus until the desired processing activity is found. Each menu leads to another until the final selection is made.

First Level
Main Menu:

```
BUSINESS PROCESSING SYSTEMS

   1. Accounting System
   2. Inventory System
   3. Payroll System
   4. Sales Order System
   5. Quit

Enter choice (1-5): 2
```

Second Level
System Menu:

```
INVENTORY SYSTEM

1. Add quantity received
2. Subtract quantity sold
3. Adjust quantity on hand
4. Add new record
5. Delete current record
6. Return

Enter choice (1-6): 1
```

Third Level
Data Entry:

```
INVENTORY SYSTEM
Add Quantity Received

     Enter part number:_____

     Enter quantity: _____

Press 'Y' to continue ('N' to quit):
```

FIGURE 6.1   A Menu-Driven Business Processing System

Guidelines for Creating Menus

There are a few simple guidelines the programmer should follow when designing user-friendly menus. The purpose of the guidelines is to provide a set of standards or procedures that help produce menus that are easy to use.

The following guidelines were used to design the menu-driven systems for the sample program presented in this chapter.

Make the menu easy to read: A menu that is easy to read is also easy to use. When users understand what to do, they are inclined to make fewer errors and feel comfortable with the software.

Center the menu: Center the titles and headings as well as the option list. Organize the contents of the menu from top to bottom, left to right—the normal way a person would read a page in a book.

Keep it simple: Don't clutter the screen with information. Keep the selection process simple. Avoid putting too many options on one screen. If necessary, use two or more screens to show all the options.

Make the choices clear: After reading the menu, it should be obvious to the users what the options are and how to select the one they want. When possible, arrange the options in either numeric or alphabetic order.

Formatting and Printing Menus

Menus may vary in size and layout. Usually, the client has a rough idea of what the menu should look like as well as the options it should contain. However, it may be necessary for the programmer to sit down and work with the client to design the ideal menu.

The menu in Figure 6.2 was designed to be user friendly. Look at the program code for the menu. Notice how the tabs(\t) are used in the printf() statements to format the menu. Each tab moves the cursor to the right a fixed number of spaces. The program code prints the menu and prompts the user to select one of the five numeric options (1–5). Upon choosing an option, scanf() assigns the selection to *iChoice*.

```
void PrnMainMenu(void);
{
    system("cls");
    printf("\n\t\t BUSINESS PROCESSING SYSTEMS");
    printf("\n");
    printf("\n\t\t  Select one:");
    printf("\n\t\t    1. Accounting System");
    printf("\n\t\t    2. Inventory System");
    printf("\n\t\t    3. Payroll System");
    printf("\n\t\t    4. Sales Order System");
    printf("\n\t\t    5. Quit");
    printf("\n");
    printf("\n\t\t  Enter choice (1-5):);
    scanf(" %d", &iChoice);
    fflush(stdin);
    return;
}
```

```
BUSINESS PROCESSING SYSTEMS

Select one:

     1. Accounting System
     2. Inventory System
     3. Payroll System
     4. Sales Order System
     5. Quit

Enter Choice (1-5):
```

FIGURE 6.2   Main Menu Using Numeric Codes

Now look at the menu in Figure 6.2. Note the similarities between the program code and the screen menu.

Menu Selection: Nested if/else Statements

After the user selects an option from the Business Processing Systems menu, the program evaluates the choice and branches to the appropriate processing module. We can implement this decision process with nested *if/else* statements. The program code to evaluate and branch follows.

```
void ProcessLoop(void)
{
    PrnMainMenu();
    while (iChoice != 5)
    {
        if (iChoice == 1)
            PrnAcctMenu();
        else if (iChoice == 2)
            PrnInvMenu();
        else if (iChoice == 3)
            PrnPayrollMenu();
        else
            PrnSalesMenu();
        PrnMainMenu();
    }
    return;
}
```

This module consists of a *while* loop that checks the user's selection and, as long as *iChoice* is not equal to 5 (Quit), transfers control to the respective processing module.

Character Option Codes

By itself, a number bears little (if any) meaning or relationship to its corresponding menu choice, particularly when there are several options available. However, a letter (such as *I*, which stands for Inventory) associates a specific meaning with a menu option. After all, it is easier to remember that *I* stands for the Inventory System than to recall what number *2* means.

Look at the second version of the Business Processing Systems menu in Figure 6.3. Notice that the option codes have been changed to letters.

Now the user is prompted to enter the first letter of the desired option. Hence, the decision process had to be modified to handle non-numeric option codes. This means that the numeric decision tests had to be changed to compare characters. The resulting program code is shown below.

```
void ProcessLoop(void)

{
    PrnMainMenu();
    while (strcmp(iChoice,'Q') != 0)
    {
        if (strcmp(iChoice, 'A') == 0)
            PrnAcctMenu();
        else if (strcmp(iChoice, 'I') == 0)
            PrnInvMenu();
        else if (strcmp(iChoice, 'P') == 0)
            PrnPayrollMenu();
        else
            PrnSalesMenu();
        PrnMainMenu();
    }
    return;
}
```

The above code prompts the user to select the first letter of one of the menu options and then, as long as the choice is not equal to *Q* (Quit), transfers control to the corresponding processing module.

```
BUSINESS PROCESSING SYSTEMS

Select one ( ):

    (A)ccounting System
    (I)nventory System
    (P)ayroll System
    (S)ales Order System
    (Q)uit

Enter letter of choice:
```

FIGURE 6.3   Main Menu Using Character Codes

The getch() Function

Format:

```
identifier = getch();
```

Header File: conio.h

Purpose: To input a single character from the keyboard. As soon as a character is entered on the keyboard, it is passed to the identifier. The getch() function does not display the character on the screen, nor does it wait for the enter-keypress. This means that once the character is keyed, we may not go back and change it. The getch() function requires the *conio.h* header file

Examples:

1. ```
   printf("Enter a grade (A-F) for the midterm and final\n");
   cMidterm = getch();
   cFinal = getch();
   .....
   ```

   At the prompt, the user enters two letter grades, *AB*. The first letter grade, *A,* is assigned to *cMidterm*; the second letter grade, *B,* is assigned to *cFinal*. Neither grade appears on the screen. Immediately after the second keypress, processing continues with the next program statement. Since getch() does not use the keyboard buffer, there is no need to clear it.

2. ```
   printf("\nThe first prize number is: 141959");
   printf("n\nPress ENTER to continue...");
   cWait = getch();
   .....
   ```

   Upon displaying the message on the screen, getch() "holds" the screen and waits for the user to `Press ENTER to continue...` After pressing enter, control continues with the next executable statement in the program.

Checkpoint 6A

1. List three common techniques for validating input data.
2. Identify four guidelines for creating menus.
3. True or false: Letters as well as numbers can be used to make selections from a menu.
4. What does the getch() function do?

Sample Program CHAP6A

Sample program CHAP6A illustrates an application of a menu system that displays the fall, winter, and spring computer science course offerings for Blackmoore University. See Figure 6.4 for the hierarchy chart and Figure 6.5 for the program flowchart. The source code is presented in Figure 6.6. The main menu and the fall quarter display are shown in Figures 6.7a and 6.7b, respectively.

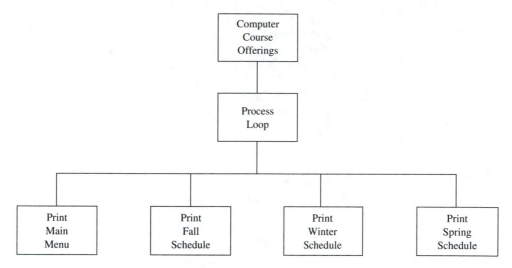

FIGURE 6.4   Hierarchy Chart for CHAP6A

The following specifications apply to sample program CHAP6A:

Menu Choices:

1. Fall quarter
2. Winter quarter
3. Spring quarter
4. Quit

Input (internal):
Code the fall, winter, and spring quarter course offerings inside the program.

Output (screen):

Display the appropriate quarter course offerings (see Figure 6.7b).

Processing Requirements:

- Based on the quarter selected, display the corresponding course offerings on the screen.
- At the bottom of the screen, prompt the user to press enter to continue—return to the main menu.

Pseudocode:

```
START: Main
Call Process Loop
END

ENTER: Process Loop
Call Display Main Menu
LOOP while choice not = 4
```

```
            IF choice = 1
                  Call Display Fall Quarter
            else IF choice = 2
                  Call Display Winter Quarter
            else
                  Call Display Spring Quarter
            END IF
                  Call Display Main Menu
      END LOOP
      RETURN

      ENTER: Display Main Menu
      Clear screen
      Print 2 screen title lines
      Print quarter choices:
            choice 1: Fall quarter
            choice 2: Winter quarter
            choice 3: Spring quarter
            choice 4: Quit
      Prompt and enter choice
      Clear keyboard buffer
      LOOP while choice not = 1 to 4
            Print error - invalid choice
            Prompt and enter choice
            Clear keyboard buffer
      END LOOP
      RETURN

      ENTER: Display Fall Quarter
      Clear screen
      Print 2 screen title lines
      Display fall quarter course offerings
      Hold screen
      RETURN
```

Note: The winter and spring quarters are coded similarly to the fall module.

Hierarchy Chart: See Figure 6.4.

Program Flowchart: See Figure 6.5.

Dissection of Sample Program CHAP6A

```
PROCESSING LOOP:

void ProcessLoop(void)
{
    int iChoice;

    iChoice = PrnMainMenu();
```

```
    while (iChoice != 4)
    {
        if (iChoice == 1)
            PrnFall();
        else if (iChoice == 2)
            PrnWinter();
        else
            PrnSpring();
        iChoice = PrnMainMenu();
    }
    return;
}
```

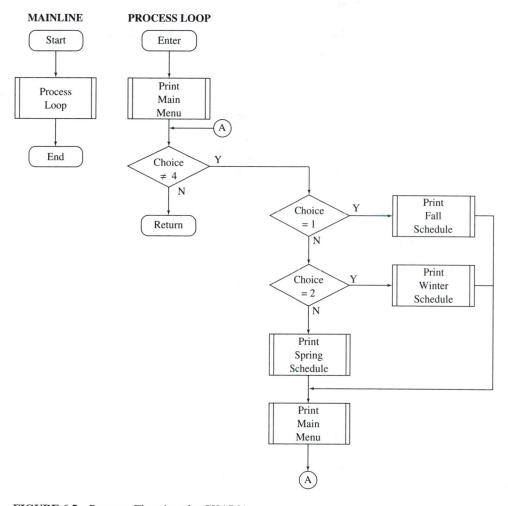

FIGURE 6.5   Program Flowchart for CHAP6A

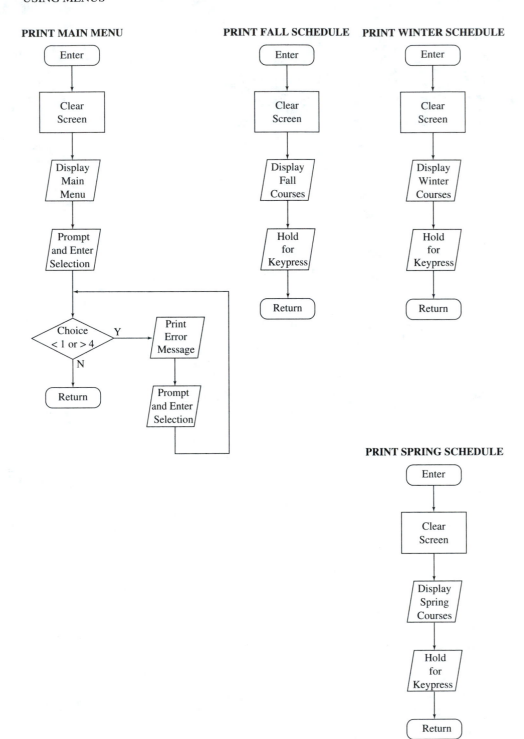

FIGURE 6.5   *Continued*

```
/*------------------------------------------------------------
COURSE OFFERINGS: Menu program to display computer science course
offerings for Blackmoore University.

Program:   CHAP6A.C
Author:    David M. Collopy
Date:      mm/dd/yy
Project:   Sample program
************************************************************/


/*---- PREPROCESSING DIRECTIVES -------------------------------*/

#include <stdio.h>
#include <conio.h>
#include <graph.h>

/*---- FUNCTION PROTOTYPES ------------------------------------*/

int  PrnMainMenu(void);          /* display main menu       */
void ProcessLoop(void);          /* processing loop         */
void PrnFall(void);              /* display fall courses    */
void PrnWinter(void);            /* display winter courses  */
void PrnSpring(void);            /* display spring courses  */

/* ---- PROGRAM SETUP -----------------------------------------*/

/*>  S C R E E N   T I T L E S   A N D   H E A D I N G S    <*/

char PT1[] = "  B L A C K M O O R E    U N I V E R S I T Y";
char PT2[] = "       Computer Science Course Offerings     ";

/*------------------------------------------------------------
      MAINLINE CONTROL
------------------------------------------------------------*/
main()
{
    ProcessLoop();
    return 0;
}


/*------------------------------------------------------------
      PROCESSING LOOP
------------------------------------------------------------*/
void ProcessLoop(void)
{
```

FIGURE 6.6   Sample Program CHAP6A: Menu Selections for Computer Science Course Offerings

```
        int  iChoice;

        iChoice = PrnMainMenu();
        while (iChoice != 4)
        {
            if (iChoice == 1)

                PrnFall();

            else if (iChoice == 2)

                PrnWinter();

            else

                PrnSpring();

            iChoice = PrnMainMenu();
        }
        return;
    }


    /*--------------------------------------------------------------
        DISPLAY MAIN MENU
    ---------------------------------------------------------------*/
    int PrnMainMenu(void)
    {
        int  iChoice;

        _clearscreen(0);
        printf("\n\t%s", PT1);
        printf("\n\t%s", PT2);
        printf("\n\n\t                M A I N   M E N U");
        printf("\n\n\n\t      Select one:");
        printf("\n\n\t          1.  Fall quarter");
        printf("\n\n\t          2.  Winter quarter");
        printf("\n\n\t          3.  Spring quarter");
        printf("\n\n\t          4.  Quit");
        printf("\n\n\n\n\n\t      Enter choice (1 - 4) ===> ");
        scanf(" %d", &iChoice);
        fflush(stdin);
        while (iChoice < 1 || iChoice > 4)
        {
            printf("\nERROR...re-enter choice (1 - 4) ===> ");
            scanf(" %d", &iChoice);
```

FIGURE 6.6 *Continued*

```
            fflush(stdin);
        }
        return iChoice;
}


/*---------------------------------------------------------------
        DISPLAY FALL COURSES
----------------------------------------------------------------*/
void PrnFall(void)
{
    char cWait;

    _clearscreen(0);
    printf("\n\t%s", PT1);
    printf("\n\t%s", PT2);
    printf("\n\n\t                -- Fall Quarter --");
    printf("\n\n\t  CS 101     Computer Literacy");
    printf("\n\n\t  CS 150     Website Development");
    printf("\n\n\t  CS 201     Programming Concepts I");
    printf("\n\n\t  CS 300     Systems Analysis and Design");
    printf("\n\n\n\tPress ENTER to continue...");
    cWait = getch();
    return;
}


/*---------------------------------------------------------------
        DISPLAY WINTER COURSES
----------------------------------------------------------------*/
void PrnWinter(void)
{
    char cWait;

    _clearscreen(0);
    printf("\n\t%s", PT1);
    printf("\n\t%s", PT2);
    printf("\n\n\t                -- Winter Quarter --");
    printf("\n\n\t  CS 101     Computer Literacy");
    printf("\n\n\t  CS 155     Visual Programming");
    printf("\n\n\t  CS 190     Data Communications");
    printf("\n\n\t  CS 202     Programming Concepts II");
    printf("\n\n\t  CS 330     Management Information Systems");
    printf("\n\n\n\tPress ENTER to continue...");
    cWait = getch();
    return;
}
```

FIGURE 6.6   *Continued*

```
/*------------------------------------------------------------
        DISPLAY SPRING COURSES
--------------------------------------------------------------*/
void PrnSpring(void)
{
    char cWait;

    _clearscreen(0);
    printf("\n\t%s", PT1);
    printf("\n\t%s", PT2);
    printf("\n\n\t                -- Spring Quarter --");
    printf("\n\n\t   CS 101      Computer Literacy");
    printf("\n\n\t   CS 210      Website Management");
    printf("\n\n\t   CS 241      Java Programming");
    printf("\n\n\t   CS 260      Networking Systems");
    printf("\n\n\t   CS 340      Database Management Systems");
    printf("\n\n\n\tPress ENTER to continue...");
    cWait = getch();
    return;
}
```

FIGURE 6.6   *Continued*

```
         B L A C K M O O R E    U N I V E R S I T Y
           Computer Science Course Offerings

                   M A I N    M E N U

     Select one:

            1.   Fall quarter

            2.   Winter quarter

            3.   Spring quarter

            4.   Quit


     Enter choice (1 - 4) ===> __
```

FIGURE 6.7a   Main Menu for CHAP6A

```
B L A C K M O O R E   U N I V E R S I T Y
      Computer Science Course Offerings

           -- Fall Quarter --

 CS 101    Computer Literacy

 CS 150    Website Development

 CS 201    Programming Concepts I

 CS 300    Systems Analysis and Design


Press ENTER to continue...
```

FIGURE 6.7b   Fall Course Offerings for CHAP6A

The priming input call transfers control to the main menu and starts the looping process. The user's choice is returned and assigned to *iChoice*. As long as *iChoice* is not equal to 4 (Quit), control enters the body of the loop and calls the appropriate module. The looping input call displays the main menu and continues the looping process.

D I S P L A Y   M A I N   M E N U:

```
int PrnMainMenu(void)
{
    int iChoice;

    _clearscreen(0);
    printf("\n\t%s", PT1);
    printf("\n\t%s", PT2);
    printf("\n\n\t            M A I N   M E N U");
    printf("\n\n\n\t    Select one:");
    printf("\n\n\t         1.  Fall quarter");
    printf("\n\n\t         2.  Winter quarter");
    printf("\n\n\t         3.  Spring quarter");
    printf("\n\n\t         4.  Quit");
    printf("\n\n\n\n\n\t    Enter choice (1 - 4) ===> ");
    scanf(" %d", &iChoice);
    fflush(stdin);
```

The above statements display the main menu. For clarity purposes, the body of the menu is double spaced. Tabs are used to format the menu. The main menu prompts the user to select either a quarter (1–3) or 4 to quit. The scanf() assigns the selection to *iChoice*, and fflush() clears the keyboard buffer.

```
   while (iChoice < 1 || iChoice > 4)
   {
       printf("\nERROR...reenter choice (1 - 4) ===> ");
       scanf(" %d", &iChoice);
       fflush(stdin);
   }
   return;
}
```

The *while* loop performs a range check to ensure that *iChoice* is valid. If it is valid, control returns to the PROCESSING LOOP. If it is not, the user is prompted to reenter a selection 1–4. Control will remain in the *while* loop until the user enters a valid choice.

D I S P L A Y   F A L L   C O U R S E S:

```
void PrnFall(void)
{
    char cWait;

    _clearscreen(0);
    printf("\n\t%s", PT1);
    printf("\n\t%s", PT2);
    printf("\n\n\t              -- Fall Quarter --");
    printf("\n\n\t CS 101    Computer Literacy");
    printf("\n\n\t CS 150    Website Development");
    printf("\n\n\t CS 201    Programming Concepts I");
    printf("\n\n\t CS 300    Systems Analysis and Design");
    printf("\n\n\n\tPress ENTER to continue...");
    cWait = getch();
    return;
}
```

Assuming that *iChoice* is 1, the above statements print the fall quarter course offerings on the screen. Notice that the last two commands "hold" the screen and tell the user what to do to continue. This setup gives the user time to read the course offerings before control returns to the main menu.

The last printf() prompts the user to press ENTER to continue. Upon pressing the enter key, getch() assigns the keypress to *cWait* and control returns to the calling module and redisplays the main menu. This looping process continues until the user selects 4 (Quit).

Notes and Tips

1. The menu should list the available options and allow the user to enter a choice. It is important to keep the menu simple and the choices clear.

2. It is also important to include a range check in the module that displays the main menu (as shown in the sample program). The range check locks the user in the loop until a valid choice is made. Hence, it prevents the user from inputting bad data into the program.

3. Whenever you are displaying information for the user to read, hold the screen. If you don't, the information will flash by so quickly that the user won't get a chance to read it.

Tutorial CHAP6A

1. The objectives of this tutorial are to
   - code a menu-driven program
   - validate user input
   - implement the menu selection routine with a nested *if/else* statement
   - use the getch() function to halt screen scrolling

2. Open the text editor, and enter the sample program as shown in Figure 6.6.

3. Save the source code on your work disk as CHAP6A. Check for coding errors and make corrections as needed.

4. Compile, run, and debug your program until the output matches the screens shown in Figures 6.7a and 6.7b.

5. When completed, show your work to your instructor.

Quick Quiz

Answer the following questions.

1. Will the program accept choices outside the range 1–4? Explain your answer.

2. In what way is the *conio.h* header file related to the variable *cWait*?

3. Look at *PrnMainMenu*. What exactly does the \r do? Explain how the following *while* condition works: (iChoice < 1 || iChoice > 4).

4. Did you have any problems or errors when you ran the sample program? If so, what were they and what did you do to correct them?

5. Change the *while* condition in the *PrnMainMenu* module from an *OR* (||) test to an *AND* (&&) test. Save the program as CHAP6A2. Compile and run. Did you get the correct results?

Menu Selection: The switch Statement

We may also implement the menu decision process with the *switch* statement. The modules that follow demonstrate the evaluate and branch processes for both numeric and character selection codes.

Numeric Selection Codes

```
void ProcessLoop(void)
{
   PrnMainMenu();
   while (iChoice != 5)
   {
      switch(iChoice)
      {
         case 1:
             PrnAcctMenu();
             break;
```

Character Selection Codes

```
void ProcessLoop(void)
{
   PrnMainMenu();
   while (strcmp(cChoice, 'Q') != 0)
   {
      switch(cChoice)
      {
         case 'A':
             PrnAcctMenu();
             break;
```

```
        case 2:                          case 'I':
            PrnInvMenu();                    PrnInvMenu();
            break;                           break;
        case 3:                          case 'P':
            PrnPayrollMenu();                PrnPayrollMenu();
            break;                           break:
      default:                           default:
            PrnSalesMenu();                  PrnSalesMenu();
            break;                           break;
      }                                  }
      PrnMainMenu();                     PrnMainMenu();
    }                                  }
    return;                            return;
}                                    }
```

For either module, the processing loop continues as long as the user's choice is not equal to "Quit." When a selection is made, control branches to the corresponding processing module.

Sample Program CHAP6B

Sample program CHAP6B displays a menu of the daily flights scheduled for Wynfield Metro Airport. When the user selects a destination city, the program displays the departure times for the flights. See Figure 6.8 for the hierarchy chart and Figure 6.9 for the program flowchart. The source code is presented in Figure 6.10. The main menu and the departure times for the flights to New York are shown in Figures 6.11a and 6.11b.

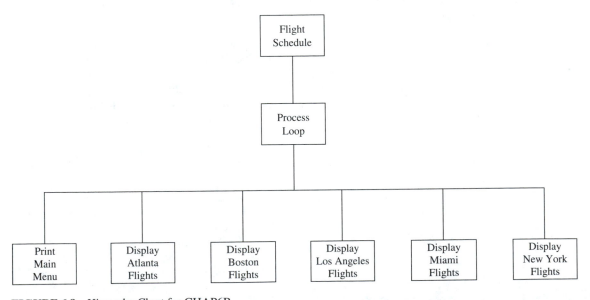

FIGURE 6.8   Hierarchy Chart for CHAP6B

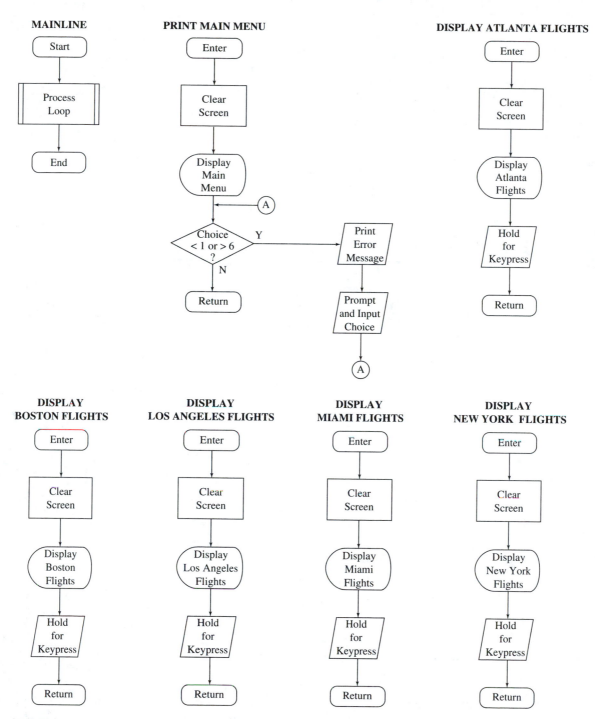

FIGURE 6.9   Program Flowchart for CHAP6B

PROCESS LOOP

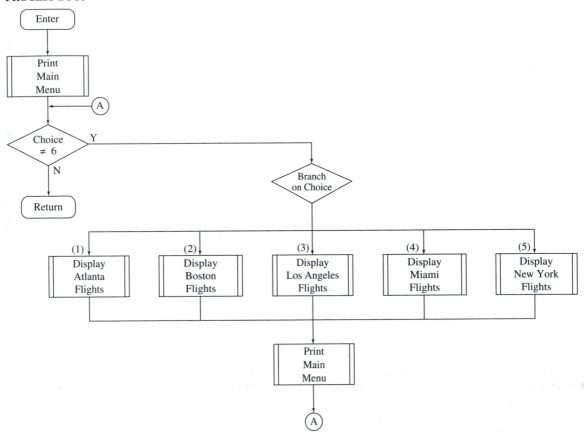

FIGURE 6.9   *Continued*

Menu Choices:

1. Atlanta

2. Boston

3. Los Angeles

4. Miami

5. New York

6. Quit

Input (internal):

Code the daily flight schedule inside the program.

```
/*------------------------------------------------------------
FLIGHT SCHEDULE: Menu program to display the flight schedule for
Wynfield Metro Airport.

Program:    CHAP6B.C
Author:     David M. Collopy
Date:       mm/dd/yy
Project:    Sample program
************************************************************/


/*---- PREPROCESSING DIRECTIVES ------------------------------*/

#include <stdio.h>
#include <conio.h>
#include <graph.h>

/*---- FUNCTION PROTOTYPES -----------------------------------*/

int  PrnMainMenu(void);         /* display main menu          */
void ProcessLoop(void);         /* processing loop            */
void Atlanta(void);             /* display Atlanta flights    */
void Boston(void);              /* display Boston flights     */
void LosAngeles(void);          /* display Los Angeles flights */
void Miami(void);               /* display Miami flights      */
void NewYork(void);             /* display New York flights   */

/*------------------------------------------------------------
      MAINLINE CONTROL
------------------------------------------------------------*/
main()
{
    ProcessLoop();
    return 0;
}


/*------------------------------------------------------------
      PROCESSING LOOP
------------------------------------------------------------*/
void ProcessLoop(void)
{
    int  iChoice;

    iChoice = PrnMainMenu();
    while (iChoice != 6)
    {
        switch (iChoice)
```

FIGURE 6.10   Sample Program CHAP6B: Menu Selections for Wynfield Metro Airport

```
            {
                case 1:
                    Atlanta();
                    break;
                case 2:
                    Boston();
                    break;
                case 3:
                    LosAngeles();
                    break;
                case 4:
                    Miami();
                    break;
                default:
                    NewYork();
                    break;
            }
            iChoice = PrnMainMenu();
        }
        return;
}

/*---------------------------------------------------------------
        DISPLAY MAIN MENU
-----------------------------------------------------------------*/
int PrnMainMenu(void)
{
    int iChoice;

    _clearscreen(0);
    printf("\n\t%s,
        "    W Y N F I E L D   M E T R O   A I R P O R T");
    printf("\n\n\t            M A I N   M E N U");
    printf("\n\n\n\t    Select one:");
    printf("\n\n\t    1.  Atlanta");
    printf("\n\n\t    2.  Boston");
    printf("\n\n\t    3.  Los Angeles");
    printf("\n\n\t    4.  Miami");
    printf("\n\n\t    5.  New York");
    printf("\n\n\t    6.  Quit");
    printf("\n\n\n\n\n\t    Enter choice (1 - 6) ===> ");
    scanf(" %d", &iChoice);
    fflush(stdin);
    while (iChoice < 1 || iChoice > 6)
    {
```

FIGURE 6.10   *Continued*

```
            printf("\nERROR...re-enter choice (1 - 6) ===> ");
            scanf(" %d", &iChoice);
            fflush(stdin);
        }
        return iChoice;
}


/*-------------------------------------------------------------
        DISPLAY ATLANTA FLIGHTS
-------------------------------------------------------------*/
void Atlanta(void)
{
    char cWait;

    _clearscreen(0);
    printf("\n\t%s",
        "   W Y N F I E L D   M E T R O   A I R P O R T");
    printf("\n\n\t    Atlanta Flight Schedule");
    printf("\n\n\t    -------------------------");
    printf("\n\n\t    Flight#   Departure ");
    printf("\n\n\t    101      7:15 p.m.");
    printf("\n\n\t    214      9:20 p.m.");
    printf("\n\n\n\t    Press ENTER to continue...");
    cWait = getch();
    return;
}


/*-------------------------------------------------------------
        DISPLAY BOSTON FLIGHTS
-------------------------------------------------------------*/
void Boston(void)
{
    char cWait;

    _clearscreen(0);
    printf("\n\t%s",
        "   W Y N F I E L D   M E T R O   A I R P O R T");
    printf("\n\n\t    Boston Flight Schedule");
    printf("\n\n\t    -------------------------");
    printf("\n\n\t    Flight#   Departure ");
    printf("\n\n\t    117      5:55 p.m.");
    printf("\n\n\t    201      6:30 p.m.");
    printf("\n\n\n\t    Press ENTER to continue...");
    cWait = getch();
    return;
}
```

FIGURE 6.10   *Continued*

```
    }

    /*--------------------------------------------------------------
          DISPLAY LOS ANGELES FLIGHTS
    ----------------------------------------------------------------*/
    void LosAngeles(void)
    {
        char cWait;

        _clearscreen(0);
        printf("\n\t%s",
            "  W Y N F I E L D   M E T R O   A I R P O R T");
        printf("\n\n\t    Los Angeles Flight Schedule");
        printf("\n\n\t    -------------------------");
        printf("\n\n\t    Flight#   Departure ");
        printf("\n\n\t     122       3:10 p.m.");
        printf("\n\n\t     205       4:30 p.m.");
        printf("\n\n\n\t    Press ENTER to continue...");
        cWait = getch();
        return;
    }

    /*--------------------------------------------------------------
          DISPLAY MIAMI FLIGHTS
    ----------------------------------------------------------------*/
    void Miami(void)
    {
        char cWait;

        _clearscreen(0);
        printf("\n\t%s",
            "  W Y N F I E L D   M E T R O   A I R P O R T");
        printf("\n\n\t    Miami Flight Schedule");
        printf("\n\n\t    -------------------------");
        printf("\n\n\t    Flight#   Departure ");
        printf("\n\n\t     102       1:25 p.m.");
        printf("\n\n\t     204       4:00 p.m.");
        printf("\n\n\n\t    Press ENTER to continue...");
        cWait = getch();
        return;
    }

    /*--------------------------------------------------------------
            DISPLAY NEW YORK FLIGHTS
    ----------------------------------------------------------------*/
    void NewYork(void)
```

FIGURE 6.10 *Continued*

```
{
    char cWait;

    _clearscreen(0);
    printf("\n\t%s",
        "  W Y N F I E L D   M E T R O   A I R P O R T");
    printf("\n\n\t   New York Flight Schedule");
    printf("\n\n\t   -------------------------");
    printf("\n\n\t    Flight#   Departure ");
    printf("\n\n\t     104       2:00 p.m.");
    printf("\n\n\t     119       5:16 p.m.");
    printf("\n\n\t     200       7:20 p.m.");
    printf("\n\n\n\t    Press ENTER to continue...");
    cWait = getch();
    return;
}
```

FIGURE 6.10   *Continued*

```
W Y N F I E L D   M E T R O   A I R P O R T

            M A I N   M E N U



Select one:

    1.  Atlanta

    2.  Boston

    3.  Los Angeles

    4.  Miami

    5.  New York

    6.  Quit



Enter choice (1 - 6) ===> __
```

FIGURE 6.11a   Main Menu for CHAP6B

```
W Y N F I E L D   M E T R O   A I R P O R T

New York Flight Schedule:

----------------------------

Flight#              Departure

   104                 2:00 p.m.

   119                 5:15 p.m.

   200                 7:20 p.m.



Press ENTER to continue...
```

FIGURE 6.11b   New York Flight Schedule for CHAP6B

Output (screen):
Display the appropriate flight schedule (see Figure 6.11b).

Processing Requirements:

- Based on the city selected, display the corresponding flight schedule on the screen.
- At the bottom of the screen, prompt the user to press enter to continue—return to the main menu.

Pseudocode:

START: Main
Call Process Loop
END

ENTER: Process Loop
Call Display Main Menu
LOOP while choice not = 6
    BRANCH on choice:
        1: Call Display Atlanta
        2: Call Display Boston
        3: Call Display Los Angeles
        4: Call Display Miami
        5: Call Display New York
    END BRANCH
    Call Display Main Menu
END LOOP
RETURN

```
ENTER: Display Main Menu
Clear screen
Print screen title line
Display flight choices:
        choice 1: Atlanta
        choice 2: Boston
        choice 3: Los Angeles
        choice 4: Miami
        choice 5: New York
        choice 6: Quit
Prompt and enter choice
Clear keyboard buffer
LOOP while choice not = 1 to 6
        Print error - invalid choice
        Prompt and enter choice
        Clear keyboard buffer
END LOOP
RETURN

ENTER: Display Atlanta Flights
Clear screen
Print screen title line
Display Atlanta flight schedule
Hold screen
RETURN
```

Note: The remaining flights are coded similarly to the Atlanta module.

Hierarchy Chart: See Figure 6.8.

Program Flowchart: See Figure 6.9. Note the flowcharting symbol used to display the main menu and the flight schedules. This symbol is often used to indicate that the output is displayed on the screen. You may also use the standard input/output symbol to specify screen output.

Dissection of Sample Program CHAP6B

With the exception of the *switch* statement, the processing performed by the sample program is similar to that performed by sample program CHAP6A.

```
P R O C E S S I N G    L O O P :

void ProcessLoop(void)
{
    int iChoice;

    iChoice = PrnMainMenu();
    while (iChoice != 6)
    {
        switch (iChoice)
        {
```

```
        case 1:
            Atlanta();
            break;
        case 2:
            Boston();
            break;
        case 3:
            LosAngeles();
            break;
        case 4:
            Miami();
            break;
        default:
            NewYork();
            break;
    }
    iChoice = PrnMainMenu();
  }
  return;
}
```

The above module compares the value of *iChoice* to the case labels. If a match is found, control branches to the module associated with the label. If a match is not found, control defaults to *New York* and displays the New York flight schedule.

At first glance, it may appear that control defaults to *New York* for an invalid choice. This, of course, will not happen because of the range check placed at the end of the *Prn-MainMenu* module. A range check is used to ensure that the input is valid. For a choice outside the range 1–6, the user is prompted to reenter a choice. Control will remain in the *while* loop until a valid selection is entered.

For example, if a 7 is entered at the keyboard, the program prompts the user to reenter the choice. On the other hand, if a 1 is entered, the program displays the flight schedule for *Atlanta*. This looping process continues until the user selects 6 (Quit).

Notes and Tips

In this application, the *break* statements coded in the *switch* structure play an important roll. Once a match is found, the only way to leave the body of the *switch* is to break out. Each *break* statement sends control to the first executable command coded after the closing brace. Without the *break* statements, control would fall through the remaining cases and perform the statement body of each of them.

Tutorial CHAP6B

1. The objectives of this tutorial are to
   - code a user-friendly menu-driven program
   - implement the menu selection routine with the *switch/case* statement

2. Enter the sample program as shown in Figure 6.10.

3. Save the source program on your work disk as CHAP6B.

4. Compile, run, and debug your program until the output looks similar to the screens shown in Figures 6.11a and 6.11b. Save frequently.

5. When completed, show your work to your instructor.

Quick Quiz

Answer the following questions.

1. Line by line discuss the activities performed by the statements shown in the *ProcessLoop* module.

2. Other than keyboarding errors, did you have any problems when you ran your program? If so, what were they and what did you do to correct them?

Summary

1. Interactive programs should be user friendly and catch input errors as they are entered at the keyboard.

2. The purpose of data validation is to check the input for errors. When an error is encountered, the program should prompt the user to reenter the data. Data validation includes range checks, code checks, and cross reference checks.

3. A range check determines if the data is reasonable and lies within a given range of values.

4. Code checking is used to determine if the data matches a given set of codes.

5. A cross reference check is used to ensure that the relationship between two or more data items is consistent.

6. Computer applications that require the user to choose from a variety of options can be easily implemented with menus.

7. A menu displays a list of options and prompts the user to enter a choice. A menu-driven system presents a series of menus that walk the user through the selection process.

8. Menus should be designed to be user friendly, easy to read, and simple to use.

9. Tabs \t are used with printf() statements to format and print menus.

10. The menu selection process may be implemented with either the nested `if/else` or the `switch` statement. Both may use numeric or character codes to represent the menu choices.

11. Character selection codes remind the user of the menu options. They associate meaning with the options and are easier to remember.

12. The getch() function retrieves a character from the keyboard. It neither displays the character on the screen nor waits for the enter-keypress. We may use this function to hold the screen until the user is ready to continue.

Programming Projects

For each project, design the logic and write the modular structured program to produce the output. Model your program after the sample programs presented in the chapter. Verify your output.

Project 6–1   Overdue Accounts

Write a menu program that allows the user to select different processing options for the overdue accounts reporting system.

Menu Choices:

1. 30 days overdue
2. 60 days overdue
3. 90 days overdue
4. Quit

Input (keyboard):

For each customer, prompt for and enter the following data:

Account Number	Customer Name	Days Overdue	Balance Due
1010	David Ryan	90	400.00
2450	Marie Hill	30	754.00
2730	Rita Fox	90	740.00
3100	Alvin Porter	90	550.00
4080	Corey Adkins	30	233.00
4890	Amy Wyatt	30	700.00
5260	Brian Knox	30	625.00
6350	Susan Cope	90	600.00
7720	Lisa Wilson	60	417.00
8540	Matt Hart	90	900.00
9200	Tori Landis	90	235.00
9630	Pat Rankin	60	342.00

Output (printer):

Print the appropriate overdue accounts report:

```
Author          99-DAY OVERDUE ACCOUNTS        Page 01
                     mm/dd/yy


  Acct Number        Customer Name         Balance Due

     9999            X----------X             999.99
       :                 :                      :
       :                 :                      :
     9999            X----------X             999.99

                                    Total:   9999.99

  Number of overdue accounts:  99
```

Processing Requirements:

- Based on the option selected, print the corresponding overdue accounts report.
- Accumulate a total for balance due.
- Count the number of overdue accounts.

Project 6–2   Payroll

Write a menu program that allows the user to select different processing options for the payroll reporting system.

Menu Choices:

1. Hourly employee

2. Salary employee

3. Contract services

4. Other

5. Quit

Input (keyboard):

Prompt for and enter the following payroll data:

ID Number	Employee Name	Pay Code	Gross Pay
1020	Tanya Bauer	3	300.00
3451	Dana Clark	2	670.50
2011	Sara Erickson	1	456.00
8192	Scott Howard	3	409.50
4500	Paul Irwin	4	418.56
5033	Dale Miller	2	410.00
2104	Bret Rossi	1	280.00
7909	Karen Thomas	4	432.00
6100	Tracy York	1	396.00

Output (printer):

Print the appropriate payroll report:

```
Author              PAYROLL REPORT              Page 01
                    (Payroll Type)
                       mm/dd/yy


   ID Number       Employee Name              Gross Pay

     9999          X--------------X             999.99
       :                 :                         :
       :                 :                         :
     9999          X--------------X             999.99

               Total Gross Pay:                9999.99
```

Processing Requirements:

- Write the input record to the payroll report when the pay code matches the processing option selected by the user.

- Include the payroll type on the report:

Options	Print
1	Hourly Employees
2	Salary Employees
3	Contract Services
4	Other

- Accumulate a total for gross pay.

Project 6–3   Sales Staff

Write a menu program that allows the sales manager to list the sales staff by region.

Menu Choices:

1. Northern Region

2. Southern Region

3. Eastern Region

4. Western Region

5. Quit

Input (internal):

Code the sales staff data inside the program. The data shown below represents the sales-person's number, name, and monthly sales, respectively. For each option 1–4, list the sales staff assigned to the region.

Options:

1.	1290	Karen Brown	7541.52
	2100	Bruce Lanning	15675.91
	3455	Nancy Reynolds	8435.75
2.	1657	Megan Andrews	10325.33
	3401	Mike Cruse	6123.81
	5022	Eric Hahn	12805.46
	7178	Linda Mauch	8127.62
	9010	Nikki Stevens	9310.16
3.	2455	Barb Ansel	6578.24
	4339	Gary Kline	16120.00
	6012	Keri Torbett	10451.69
	9120	Adam Yost	7823.45
4.	1042	Linda Arndt	12126.84
	2980	Kelly Fenton	8502.05
	5111	Dave Payton	10452.37
	7008	Nathan Sanders	14934.99
	8541	Beth Valentine	6152.86

Output (printer):

Print the appropriate sales staff report:

```
Author        SALES STAFF BY REGION        Page 01
                    (Region)
```

```
                    mm/dd/yy

Salesperson                             Monthly
Number        Salesperson Name           Sales

 9999         X--------------X          99999.99
   :                :                      :
   :                :                      :
 9999         X--------------X          99999.99
```

Processing Requirements:

- Based on the option selected, print the corresponding sales staff report.
- Include the region on the report:

Options	Print
1	Northern Region
2	Southern Region
3	Eastern Region
4	Western Region

Project 6–4   Inventory

Write a menu program that allows the user to list the status of any item in the inventory.

Menu Choices:

1. Hammers
2. Saws
3. Drills
4. Screwdrivers
5. Pliers
6. Quit

Input (keyboard):
For each item, prompt for and enter the following inventory data:

Item Num	Description	Quantity on Hand	Reorder Point	Reorder Quantity	Unit Cost	Selling Price
1000	Hammers	24	12	24	4.75	9.49
2000	Saws	08	16	12	7.50	14.99
3000	Drills	10	12	18	7.83	15.95
4000	Screwdrivers	36	24	12	2.27	4.98
5000	Pliers	12	12	36	2.65	5.49

Output (printer):
Print the appropriate inventory status report:

```
Author          INVENTORY SYSTEM          mm/dd/yy
                Item Status Report

Item Number: 9999    Description: X------------X
```

```
Quantity On Hand: 99
   Reorder Point: 99
Reorder Quantity: 99

      Unit Cost: $99.99
  Selling Price: $99.99
```

Processing Requirements:

For the item selected, list the current status of the inventory.

Project 6–5   Personnel

Write a menu program that allows the user to list the employees by department.

Menu Choices:

1. Accounting

2. Programming

3. Sales

4. Payroll

5. Maintenance

6. Quit

Input (keyboard):

For each employee, prompt for and enter the following personnel data:

Employee Name	Department	Years of Service	Annual Salary
Dana Andrews	Accounting	2	25124.00
Scott Cooper	Maintenance	4	26400.00
Todd Feldman	Payroll	1	24300.00
Amy Kwon	Sales	5	36049.00
Derek Lowe	Programming	2	26225.00
Lori Palmer	Maintenance	2	22360.00
Bob Shields	Sales	3	30120.00
Pam Wolfe	Programming	6	34725.00

Output (printer):

Print the appropriate personnel report:

```
Author              PERSONNEL REPORT           Page 01
                       mm/dd/yy


Department: X---------X


                    Years Of     Annual
    Employee Name   Service      Salary

    X-----------X      2        99999.99
          :           :            :
          :           :            :
    X-----------X      4        99999.99
```

```
              Total:    999999.99

              Employee count: 99
```

Processing Requirements:

- For the department selected, print the employee name, years of service, and annual salary.
- Accumulate a total for annual salary.
- Count the number of employees in the department.

Project 6–6   Accounts Payable

Write a menu program that allows the user to print the status of any of the vendor accounts listed below.

Menu Choices:

1. Metacraft
2. Reylock
3. Universal
4. Northland
5. Veston
6. Quit

Input (keyboard):

For each vendor, prompt for and enter the following data:

Vendor Number	Vendor Name	Invoice Number	Invoice Amount	Discount Rate
217	Metacraft	A1239	2309.12	0.10
712	Reylock	F0176	4563.78	0.12
501	Universal	W0105	1200.00	0.09
196	Northland	X2781	3429.34	0.10
659	Veston	D1776	5127.63	0.12

Output (printer):

Print the appropriate accounts payable status report:

```
Author                 ACCOUNTS PAYABLE SYSTEM              mm/dd/yy
                           Status Report


Vendor No: 999       Vendor: X---------------X


       Invoice No: XXXXX
  Invoice Amount: $9999.99
 Discount Amount: $ 999.99
     Amount Due: $9999.99
```

Processing Requirements:

- For the vendor selected, print the current status of the vendor account.
- Compute the discount amount:
  invoice amount × discount rate.
- Compute the amount due:
  invoice amount – discount amount.

Project 6–7   Math Practice

Write a menu program that allows the user to practice addition, subtraction, multiplication, and division.

Menu Choices:

1. Addition

2. Subtraction

3. Multiplication

4. Division

5. Quit

Input (keyboard):
Prompt the user to enter two real numbers and the result of the selected operation.

Sample Output (screen):
Assume the user selected the first option (addition)—print the following output:

```
Author              MATH PRACTICE              mm/dd/yy

            ***  A D D I T I O N  ***

    First Number  =  79.3

    Second Number = 123.78

          Sum = 203.08          correct

 Press ENTER to continue...
```

Processing Requirements:
For the option selected, perform the corresponding arithmetic operation. Check the user's result. If it is correct, print the message "correct" next to the result; if it is not correct, print "incorrect" next to the result.

Options	Operations
1	Sum = number1 + number2
2	Difference = number1 – number2
3	Product = number1 × number2
4	Quotient = number1 / number2

7 Text Files

Overview

Learning Objectives

After you have read this chapter and completed the exercises, you should be able to

- use a text editor to enter, edit, and save a data file
- use the *FILE* data type to declare a file pointer variable
- open and close text files using the fopen() and fclose() functions, respectively
- read a file and assign the input data to the program variables using the fscanf() function
- test for the end of file condition using either the feof() function or a trailer record

Files and Records

From Chapter 1, we learned that a program represents a set of instructions that accepts data, processes it, and provides output in the form of information. We also learned that data can be organized into files to facilitate processing by the computer.

By a previous definition, a **file** is a collection of related records that pertain to a specific application. In the example of a company that has a staff of 263 employees, the payroll file would consist of 263 records—one for each employee. Hence, a **record** is a collection of related data fields. For instance, a payroll record would consist of all the fields necessary for computing the paycheck for a given employee.

Furthermore, a **field** is a set of character positions grouped together to form a single unit of information. For the payroll application, a field might include any one of the following items—employee number, name, pay rate, hours worked, and deductions.

Text File

Consider a program that prompts the user to input inventory data until "Quit" is entered. Once a complete record is entered at the keyboard, it is processed by the program. Here the user is interactive with the program. **Interactive** means that the user communicates directly with the program as it executes.

There is, however, another way to input the program data. Instead of keying in one record at a time at the input prompts, we could enter all of the records into a file and save it on disk for later use by the program.

Let's assume that each line in the file represents a record that was previously entered one data item at a time. Therefore, each line consists of a set of constants (numeric and/or string) that make up a complete record. In other words, a text file represents a logically related set of constants that are read and processed by the program.

By definition, a **text file** consists of readable data that can be created with a text editor and saved on disk. Basically, there are two classes of files, **program (source code) files** and **data files**. Both are text files, and both can be read and modified by the programmer with a text editor (such as the one you are currently using to write your C programs).

In this chapter, we will see that text file processing involves the following activities: creating a file, declaring a file pointer variable, opening the file, reading and processing the data stored in the file, and closing the file.

Kelly Antonetz	70	50	100	80	65	85
Robert Cain	100	82	79	73	100	62
Karen Dehaven	81	87	94	85	93	89
Barry Harmon	76	77	80	81	75	92
Katrina Lang	99	100	89	83	94	90
Amanda Mohr	65	67	71	84	88	96
Mike Revell	90	87	78	52	76	89
Woody Synder	76	76	83	85	77	81

FIGURE 7.1   Grades Data File

Creating a Text File

A text file is created by using a text editor to enter, edit, and save data that will be processed by a program. Depending on the C compiler you are using, you may be able to create a text file with your program editor. Your instructor or supervisor will let you know which text editor to use.

Once in the editor, key in one record per line and press the enter key. A record ends with the enter-keypress—the newline character \n. For example, Sample Program CHAP7A reads the grade file in Figure 7.1, processes the data, and prints a six-week grade report. The grades data file was created and saved on disk. Each row in Figure 7.1 represents a record, and each column represents a constant that will be assigned to a program variable. According to Figure 7.1, each record consists of seven constants. When read by the program, the constants are assigned to the program variables *sStudent, iGrade1, iGrade2, iGrade3, iGrade4, iGrade5,* and *iGrade6.*

Notice that the constants are separated by spaces. As you may recall, a blank space serves as delimiter and tells the scan statement that the input consists of multiple substrings or data items. Upon exiting the editor, an **end-of-file marker** is written after the last record. Later, this marker will be used by the program to detect the end of the file.

Although the constants are neatly aligned into columns, this is not necessary as long as they are separated by at least one blank space. Keep this in mind when keying in data for string constants. Since string constants require a fixed number of character positions, at times they may appear to have several spaces at the end of the field when actually they do not.

We will, however, continue to organize the data into columns and adopt this method as a standard. This convention makes it easier for us to read the data and make changes to it as needed.

Declaring a File Pointer Variable: The FILE Data Type

Format:

```
FILE *fileptr;
```

Purpose: To declare a file pointer variable. *FILE* (written in capital letters) is a special data type that identifies a file structure. Notice that the *FILE* argument consists of two items—an asterisk and a variable name. The asterisk indicates that the identifier that follows represents a **file pointer.** Each file pointer must be unique. Later, the file pointer will be used to hold the address of a specific file.

Examples:

1. `FILE *fpInv;`
2. `FILE *fpFileIn, *fpFileOut;`

The first example declares the file pointer variable, *fpInv*. The second, however, declares two file pointer variables, *fpFileIn* and *fpFileOut*. As a standard, append the prefix *fp* to the file pointer variables. This notation reminds you that the variable represents a file pointer.

Checkpoint 7A

1. What is a file? a record? a field?
2. Is it necessary to align the data in a text file into columns? Why or why not?
3. What is the special data type that identifies a file structure?
4. What two items make up the FILE argument?
5. Use the FILE data type to declare a file pointer called fpEmply.

Opening a File: The fopen() Function

Format:

`fileptr = fopen("filename", "mode");`

Header File: stdio.h

Purpose: To open a file. A file must be opened before it can be accessed by the program. According to the format, the first argument refers to the name of the disk file and the second specifies the file **mode**—read, write, or append. The basic file modes are shown in Table 7.1.

When a file is successfully opened, the fopen() function passes the address of the file to the file pointer variable *fileptr*. Otherwise, a zero (the null value) is passed to the file pointer variable. Remember, a file pointer is simply a variable that is used to

TABLE 7.1   Basic File Modes

Open Mode	Meaning
"w"	Write (open new file or overwrite existing file)
"r"	Read (open existing file)
"a"	Append and write (open existing file and add data to the end of file)

READING A RECORD: THE fscanf() FUNCTION

store the address of a specific file. Be sure to code one fopen() function for each file required by the program.

For now, we will open files for *read* only. Later, in the chapters on file processing, we will have the opportunity to use the *write* and *append* modes.

The fopen() function performs the following activities:

1. Checks the disk directory for the file name. If the file is found, returns the address of the file. If the file is not found, returns the null pointer.

2. Sets up an input file buffer—a temporary storage area reserved in memory for holding the input.

3. Sets the file pointer to the beginning of the file and maintains the current position in the file as data is read and processed by the program.

Example:

```
fpInv = fopen("a:txInven.fil", "r");
```

First, the inventory file is opened in *read* mode. This means that data will be read from the "txInven.fil" file stored on the disk in the A drive. Second, the address of the file is passed to the file pointer variable *fpInv*. Hence, it is assumed that the file pointer has been declared prior to executing the fopen().

Note: As a rule, append the prefix *tx* the text file name. The prefix reminds you that the file name represents a text file.

Reading a Record: The fscanf() Function

Format:

```
fscanf(fileptr, "control string", &variable/s);
```

Header File: stdio.h

Purpose: To read a file and assign data to the program variables. The *fileptr* argument points to the address of the file. The control string, enclosed within double quotes, contains the conversion specifiers. We shall normally use the fscanf() function to read a record from the designated file.

This function converts the input to the data types specified by the control string and assigns the results to the variables given by the variable arguments. Since there is no inherent connection between the actual data in the file and the variable names specified by the fscanf() function, it is up to the programmer to maintain a positional relationship and match them accordingly. Otherwise, a mismatch may occur and data may be incorrectly assigned to the variables.

Example:

```
fscanf(fpInv, " %d %s %d %d", &iItemNum, sDescription,
       &iQuant, &iOnOrder);
```

According to the example, data is read from the inventory file and converted to the types given; the results are then assigned to the input variables *iItemNum, sDescription, iQuant,* and *iOnOrder,* respectively.

Testing for the End of File: The feof() Function

Format:

```
feof(fileptr);
```

Header File: stdio.h

Purpose: To test for the end-of-file condition. The argument enclosed within parentheses specifies the name of the file pointer variable. The feof() function prevents the program from reading past the last record. It is commonly used with the *if* or *while* statement to test for the end of a file. If the file pointer is not pointing to the end of the file, the function returns a zero (false). Otherwise, it returns a nonzero value (true), indicating that the pointer is at the end of the file.

Examples:

1. `if (!feof(fpInv))`
        . . . . .
2. `while (!feof(fpInv))`
        . . . . .

Both examples test for the end-of-file condition. If the current position in the file is not equal to the end-of-file marker, then control enters the statement body. Otherwise, control skips to the first command after the *if* or *while* statement.

Closing a File: The fclose() Function

Format:

```
fclose(fileptr);
```

Header File: stdio.h

Purpose: To close a file. A file should be closed prior to exiting the program. For a file opened in *read* mode, the fclose() function releases the input file buffer and closes the file identified by the file pointer argument. For a file opened in *write* mode (used later), the function clears the output file buffer by writing the remaining data to the disk before closing the file.

Examples:

1. `fclose(fpInv);`
2. `fclose(fpFile1, fpFile2, fpFile3);`

In the first example, the fclose() function closes one file. In the second, three files are closed at the same time.

Checkpoint 7B

1. Identify and explain the three basic file modes presented in this chapter.

2. What three activities take place when the fopen() function is executed?

3. Code the fopen() function to open a file on the A drive in read mode. The file is called *txEmploy.fil.* Assign the address of the file to the file pointer variable *fpEmploy.*

4. Code the fscanf() function to read a record from the file. The fields are employee number, employee's last name, pay rate, and hours worked.

5. Code an *if* statement to test for the end of the file.

6. Code the fclose() function to close the file.

Sample Program CHAP7A

Sample program CHAP7A reads a student grade file, processes the data, and prints a six-week grade report. Weekly test scores are totaled and averaged for each student. See Figure 7.2 for the hierarchy chart and Figure 7.3 for the flowchart. The code for sample program CHAP7A is shown in Figure 7.4. The six-week grade report is shown in Figure 7.5.

The following specifications apply:

Input (text file):
For each student record, read and assign data to the following fields. (Field size and type are shown in parentheses.)

1. Student name   (15 char)
2. 1st-week test score   (3 int)
3. 2nd-week test score   (3 int)
4. 3rd-week test score   (3 int)
5. 4th-week test score   (3 int)
6. 5th-week test score   (3 int)
7. 6th-week test score   (3 int)

Text File (txGrades.fil):
Use the data given below to create the grades file. (The numbers shown above the columns correspond to the fields described for the input.)

1	2	3	4	5	6	7
Kelly Antonetz	70	50	100	80	65	85
Robert Cain	100	82	79	73	100	62
Karen Dehaven	81	87	94	85	93	89
Barry Harmon	76	77	80	81	75	92
Katrina Lang	99	100	89	83	94	90
Amanda Mohr	65	67	71	84	88	96
Mike Revell	90	87	78	52	76	89
Woody Synder	76	76	83	85	77	81

Output (screen):
Print the six-week grade report shown in Figure 7.5.

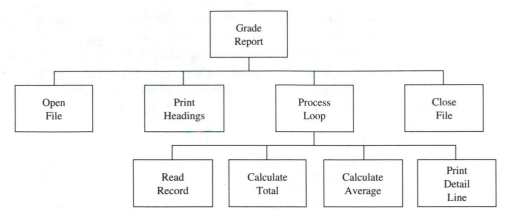

FIGURE 7.2   Hierarchy Chart for CHAP7A

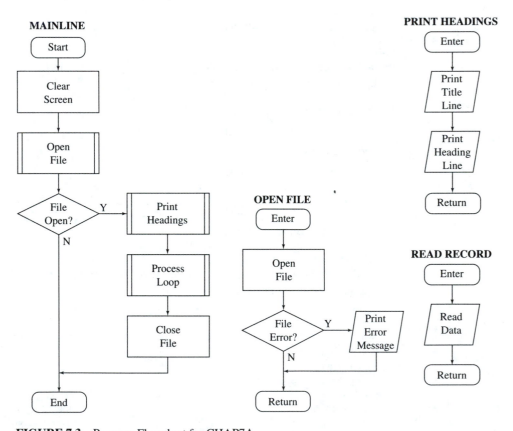

FIGURE 7.3   Program Flowchart for CHAP7A

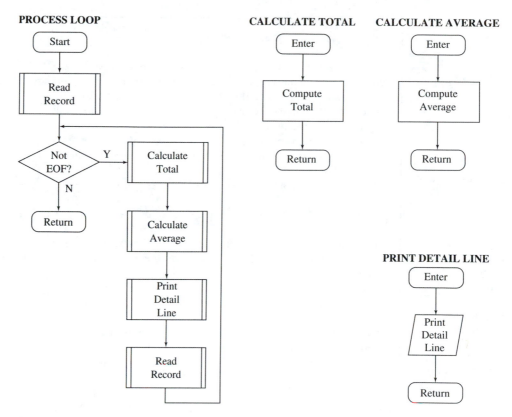

FIGURE 7.3   *Continued*

```
    /*-----------------------------------------------------------------
    GRADE REPORT: Read student grade file, compute six-seek grade average,
    and print a six-week grade report.

    Program:    CHAP7A.C
    Author:     David M. Collopy
    Date:       mm/dd/yy
    Project:    Sample program
    ******************************************************************/


    /*---- PREPROCESSING DIRECTIVES ------------------------------------*/

    #include <stdio.h>
    #include <graph.h>
```

FIGURE 7.4   Sample Program CHAP7A: Compute and Print a Six-Week Grade Report

```
/*---- FUNCTION PROTOTYPES ------------------------------------*/

void  OpenFile(void);           /* open grades file          */
void  PrnHeadings(void);        /* print report headings     */
void  ProcessLoop(void);        /* processing loop           */
void  ReadRecord(void);         /* read grade record         */
float CalcTotal(void);          /* calculate six-week total  */
float CalcAvr(float);           /* calculate six-week average */
void  PrnDetail(float);         /* print grade detail line   */


/*---- PROGRAM SETUP ------------------------------------------*/

/*>  R E P O R T   T I T L E S   A N D   H E A D I N G S      <*/

char PT1[] = "       S I X - W E E K   G R A D E   R E P O R T       ";
char HL1[] = "   Student       T e s t   S c o r e s     Average";
char HL2[] = "--------------------------------------------------";

/*>  G R A D E   R E C O R D                                  <*/

FILE *fpGrade;                  /* file pointer    */
char   sStudent[16];            /* student name    */
int    iGrade1;                 /* 1st week grade */
int    iGrade2;                 /* 2nd week grade */
int    iGrade3;                 /* 3rd week grade */
int    iGrade4;                 /* 4th week grade */
int    iGrade5;                 /* 5th week grade */
int    iGrade6;                 /* 6th week grade */


/*----------------------------------------------------------------
        MAINLINE CONTROL
----------------------------------------------------------------*/
main()
{
    _clearscreen(0);
    OpenFile();
    if (fpGrade != 0)
    {
        PrnHeadings();
        ProcessLoop();
        fclose(fpGrade);
    }
    return 0;
}
```

FIGURE 7.4 *Continued*

```
/*-------------------------------------------------------------------
        OPEN GRADES FILE
-------------------------------------------------------------------*/
void OpenFile(void)
{
    fpGrade = fopen("a:txGrades.fil", "r");
    if (fpGrade == 0)
    {
        printf("\nCannot open grades file for input\n");
    }
    return;
}


/*-------------------------------------------------------------------
        PRINT REPORT HEADINGS
-------------------------------------------------------------------*/
void PrnHeadings(void)
{
    printf(PT1);                    /* print page title 1   */
    printf("\n\n\n");               /* triple space         */
    printf(HL1);                    /* print heading line 1 */
    printf("\n");                   /* single space         */
    printf(HL2);                    /* print heading line 2 */
    printf("\n");                   /* single space         */
    return;
 }


/*-------------------------------------------------------------------
        PROCESSING LOOP
-------------------------------------------------------------------*/
void ProcessLoop(void)
{
    float fGradeTot;               /* six-week grade total   */
    float fGradeAvr;               /* six-week grade average */

    ReadRecord();
    while (!feof(fpGrade))
    {
        fGradeTot = CalcTotal();
        fGradeAvr = CalcAvr(fGradeTot);
        PrnDetail(fGradeAvr);
        ReadRecord();
    }
    return;
}
```

FIGURE 7.4   *Continued*

```
/*-----------------------------------------------------------------
        READ GRADE RECORD
-------------------------------------------------------------------*/
void ReadRecord(void)
{
    fscanf(fpGrade, " %15[^\n] %d %d %d %d %d %d",
        sStudent, &iGrade1, &iGrade2, &iGrade3, &iGrade4,
        &iGrade5, &iGrade6);
    return;
}


/*-----------------------------------------------------------------
        CALCULATE SIX-WEEK TOTAL
-------------------------------------------------------------------*/
float CalcTotal(void)
{
    float fGradeTot;                 /* six-week grade total */

    fGradeTot = iGrade1 + iGrade2 + iGrade3 + iGrade4 +
        iGrade5 + iGrade6;
    return fGradeTot;
}


/*-----------------------------------------------------------------
        CALCULATE SIX-WEEK AVERAGE
-------------------------------------------------------------------*/
float CalcAvr(float fGradeTot)
{
    float fGradeAvr;                 /* six-week grade average */

    fGradeAvr = fGradeTot / 6.0;
    return fGradeAvr;
}


/*-----------------------------------------------------------------
        PRINT GRADE DETAIL LINE
-------------------------------------------------------------------*/
void PrnDetail(float fGradeAvr)
{
    printf("\n %-15s %3d %3d %3d %3d %3d %3d    %6.2f",
        sStudent, iGrade1, iGrade2, iGrade3, iGrade4, iGrade5,
        iGrade6, fGradeAvr);
    return;
}
```

FIGURE 7.4   *Continued*

```
        S I X    W E E K    G R A D E    R E P O R T


    Student          T e s t    S c o r e s      Average
    ---------------------------------------------------------
    Kelly Antonetz   70   50  100   80   65   85    75.00
    Robert Cain     100   82   79   73  100   62    82.67
    Karen Dehaven    81   87   94   85   93   89    88.17
    Barry Harmon     76   77   80   81   75   92    80.17
    Katrina Lang     99  100   89   83   94   90    92.50
    Amanda Mohr      65   67   71   84   88   96    78.50
    Mike Revell      90   87   78   52   76   89    78.67
    Woody Synder     76   76   83   85   77   81    79.67
```

FIGURE 7.5   Screen Output for CHAP7A

Processing Requirements:

- Read the grades file.
- Compute the grade total:
  total = grade1 + grade2 + grade3 + grade4 + grade5 + grade6.
- Compute the average six-week grade:
  average = total / 6.

Pseudocode:

START: Main
Clear screen
Call Open File
IF file opened
     Call Print Headings
     Call Process Loop
     Close file
END IF
END

ENTER: Open File
Open grades file
IF file not opened
    Print cannot open grades file for input
END IF
RETURN

ENTER: Print Headings
Print 1 page title line

Print 2 column heading lines
RETURN

ENTER: Process Loop
Call Read Grade Record
LOOP while not at end of file
      Call Calculate Grade Total
      Call Calculate Grade Average
      Call Print Detail Line
      Call Read Grade Record
END LOOP
RETURN

ENTER: Read Grade Record
Read a record from the file:
    name
    grade1
    grade2
    grade3
    grade4
    grade5
    grade6
RETURN

ENTER: Calculate Grade Total
Compute six-week grade total:
    grade1 + grade2 + grade3 + grade4 + grade5 + grade6
RETURN

ENTER: Calculate Grade Average
Compute six-week grade average:
    grade total / 6
RETURN

ENTER: Print Detail Line
Print student detail line:
    name
    grade1
    grade2
    grade3
    grade4
    grade5
    grade6
    six-week grade average
RETURN

Hierarchy Chart: See Figure 7.2.

Program Flowchart: See Figure 7.3.

Dissection of Sample Program CHAP7A

Let's focus our attention on the file-processing activities performed by sample program CHAP7A and start the dissection by looking at the file pointer declaration and the format of the input grade record.

G R A D E   R E C O R D:

```
FILE *fpGrade;
```

The above statement declares the file pointer variable. The *FILE* * tells the compiler that the identifier that follows represents a file pointer. In this case, *fpGrade* is the file pointer that will be used to hold the address of the grades file. The prefix *fp* is used to remind us that the variable is a *file* pointer.

As a standard, we normally define the format of the input record immediately after declaring the file pointer. Hence, the variable declarations below define the fields belonging to the grades record.

When a record is read from the file, data constants from the file are assigned to the fields defined for the grades record.

```
char  sStudent[16];
```

The above statement defines the character string variable *sStudent* and reserves 16 character positions for the variable—15 for the data and 1 for the null character.

```
int    iGrade1;
int    iGrade2;
int    iGrade3;
int    iGrade4;
int    iGrade5;
int    iGrade6;
```

The above statements define six integer variables. They are used to hold the grades—one for each week in the six-week grading period.

M A I N L I N E   C O N T R O L:

```
main()
{
    _clearscreen(0);
    OpenFile();
    if (fpGrade != 0)
    {
        PrnHeadings();
        ProcessLoop();
        fclose(fpGrade);
    }
    return 0;
}
```

According to the *MAINLINE*, control passes to the print headings and processing modules only if the grades file can be opened. The *OpenFile* module attempts to open the file and sets the file pointer to 0 if the file cannot be opened.

Next, the program tests the value of the file pointer to determine whether to process the body of the *if* statement. If the file pointer is not equal to 0, control passes to the modules in the order shown—*PrnHeadings* and *ProcessLoop*. Otherwise, control skips the body of the *if* statement, returns a 0 to the operating system, and terminates the run.

After processing the grades data, the file is closed. The fclose() function closes the grades file.

```
O P E N    G R A D E S    F I L E :

void OpenFile(void)
{
    fpGrade = fopen("a:txGrades.fil", "r");
    if (fpGrade == 0)
    {
        printf("\nCannot open grades file for input\n");
    }
    return;
}
```

The above statement attempts to open the *txGrades.fil* file in *read (r)* mode. If the file is opened, then the address of the file is returned and assigned to *fpGrade*. On the other hand, if it cannot be opened, then a 0 is returned and assigned to file pointer and the error message `Cannot open grades file for input` is displayed on the screen.

Common open errors include misspelling the file name, forgetting to create the file, and inserting the wrong disk in the drive.

```
P R O C E S S I N G    L O O P :

void ProcessLoop(void)
{
    float fGradeTot;
    float fGradeAvr;

    ReadRecord();
```

The above statements declare the local variables and transfer control to the *ReadRecord* module to read the first record.

```
    while (!feof(fpGrade))
    {
```

The above statement means that as long as the current record position in the grades file is not equal to the end of file marker, control executes the statements in the body of the loop. Otherwise, control skips the statement body of the *while* loop.

```
        fGradeTot = CalcTotal();
        fGradeAvr = CalcAvr(fGradeTot);
        PrnDetail(fGradeAvr);
        ReadRecord();
    }
    return;
}
```

The first statements calls the *CalcTotal* module to compute the grade total and returns the result and assigns it to *fGradeTot*; the second statement passes the grade total to the *CalcAvr* module to compute the grade average and returns the result and assigns it to *fGradeAvr*; the third statement passes the grade average to the *PrnDetail* module to print the student's record; the fourth statement transfers control to the *ReadRecord* module to read the next record from the file.

After all the records in the file have been processed (end of file), control returns to the *MAINLINE.*

R E A D   G R A D E   R E C O R D:

```
void ReadRecord(void)
{
    fscanf(fpGrade, " %15[^\n] %d %d %d %d %d %d",
        sStudent, &iGrade1, &iGrade2, &iGrade3, &iGrade4,
        &iGrade5, &iGrade6);
    return;
}
```

The above statements read a record from the grades file and assign the data to the variables in the order listed—*sStudent, iGrade1, iGrade2, iGrade3, iGrade4, iGrade5,* and *iGrade6.*

The scanset %15[^\n] tells the file scan function to read up to 15 characters (or until the new line character is encountered) and store the resulting string in the first variable *(sStudent)*. After reading a record, control returns to the calling module.

Essentially, the assignment of data from the file to the variable list is based on position. That is, the first constant from the file is assigned to the first variable in the fscanf() list, the second constant is assigned to the second variable, and so on.

Notes and Tips

1. The first letter *(f)* in the function names fopen(), feof(), fscanf(),and fclose() indicates that they manipulate files. Notice that each of these functions requires the file pointer variable.

2. Append the prefix *fp* to the file pointer variable. The prefix makes it easy for you to differentiate a file pointer from a data variable.

3. Append the prefix *tx* to the text file name. The *tx* indicates that the named file represents a text file.

4. Recall that the fopen() function returns either the address of the file or a 0. A 0 means that the file was not found or could not be opened. Therefore, be sure to create the file before you attempt to open it. Also be sure to spell the file name correctly. That is, the name you saved the file under should match the name coded in the open function.

Tutorial CHAP7A

1. The objectives of this tutorial are to
    • enter and save a text file
    • declare a file pointer

- open and close a text file
- read and process the data stored in a text file

2. Open the editor, and enter the text file shown for sample program CHAP7A. Save the file on your disk as *txGrades.fil*.

3. Clear the editor, and enter the sample program as shown in Figure 7.4. Save the source code on your work disk as CHAP7A.

4. Compile, run, and debug the program until your output matches the six-week grade report shown in Figure 7.5.

5. When finished, show your work to your instructor.

Quick Quiz

Answer the following questions.

1. In your own words, explain how the following statement works:
   ```
   fpGrade = fopen("a:txGrades.fil", "r");
   ```

2. Look at the *ReadRecord* module. Explain how the fscanf() function, the file pointer variable, and the text file work together to assign data to the record fields.

3. The *while* statement coded in the *ProcessLoop* uses the feof() function to test for the end of the file. Discuss the method used by the function to detect the end of the file.

4. Did you have any problems or errors when you ran the sample program? If so, what were they and what did you do to correct them?

5. Change the file name in the open function to *txGrades.dat*. Compile and run the program, but don't save it. Did you get any output? Explain your answer.

Text File Processing Steps

Reading a file and assigning data to the program can be as simple as coding the correct fscanf() function. However, there is a relationship among a number of factors that we should clarify at this point.

    Defining a file and reading data involve the following six-step process. Sample Program CHAP7A will be used to illustrate these steps.

Step 1: Create the File
Use a text editor to create the file. Key in one record per line, and press the enter key at the end of each line. After entering all of the data, save the file on your disk.

Step 2: Declare a File Pointer Variable
Declare the file pointer variable. The file pointer declaration

```
FILE *fpGrade;
```

assigns a name (*fpGrade*) to the variable that will be used to hold the address of the grades file.

Step 3: Define the Record Format
Define the input record format. For example, the following record format defines the input fields (data types and names) belonging to the grades record. Recall that the length

assigned to a string variable must be large enough to hold the longest constant and the null character.

```
char    sStudent[16];
int     iGrade1;
int     iGrade2;
int     iGrade3;
int     iGrade4;
int     iGrade5;
int     iGrade6;
```

When data is read from the input file stream, it is assigned to the input fields.

Step 4: Open the File

Before a record can be retrieved from the input file stream, the file must be activated, or opened. The following open statement performs the necessary activities and prepares the *grades.dat* file for the read operation.

```
fpGrade = fopen("a:txGrade.fil", "r");
```

Step 5: Read a Record

In C, the fscanf() function is used to read data from the file and assign it to the program variables. According to the example, data is retrieved from the grades file and is assigned to the input fields *sStudent, iGrade1, iGrade2, iGrade3, iGrade4, iGrade5,* and *iGrade6,* respectively.

```
fscanf(fpGrade, " %15[^\n] %d %d %d %d %d %d", sStudent,
        &iGrade1, &iGrade2, &iGrade3, &iGrade4, &iGrade5,
        &iGrade6);
```

Note that the length specified for a string variable coded in the fscanf() function must be large enough to hold the longest constant.

Step 6: Close the File

After a file has been read and processed, it is closed.

```
fclose(fpGrade);
```

The fclose() function closes the grades file and releases the input file buffer.

Using a Trailer Record

We may use the feof() function to test for the end-of-file condition, or we may use a trailer record. A **trailer record** is a special record that is placed at the end of the file (trails the data) by the programmer. It is not actually processed by the program but is instead used to determine when to stop reading data from the file. As an example, consider the simple inventory file shown in Figure 7.6, which consists of the following data: item number, item description, quantity on hand, and quantity on order. Look at the last record—the trailer record. When the program encounters the trailer record, it stops reading data from the inventory file.

As with the feof() function, the end-of-file test using a trailer record can be implemented with the *if* or *while* statement. The examples below illustrate this process.

```
100  Hammer          10 20
200  Saw             24 00
300  Screwdriver     12 36
400  Pliers          40 00
500  Drill           24 12
600  Wrench          16 05
000  End-Of-File     00 00
```

FIGURE 7.6   File with Trailer Record

Examples:

1. `if (iItemNumber != 0)`

   `. . . . .`

2. `while (iItemNumber != 0)`

   `. . . . .`

Both examples test for the end of file condition by comparing the item number of the input to 0. If the trailer record has not been read, control enters the statement body. Otherwise, control skips to the first command after the *if* or *while* statement.

Checkpoint 7C

1. List and briefly explain the six steps involved in defining a file and reading the input data.

2. What is a trailer record? What is its purpose?

3. Code a *while* statement that checks the input employee number for a trailer record value equal to zero. The *while* statement should continue looping as long as the employee number is not equal to zero.

Sample Program CHAP7B

Sample program CHAP7B reads an inventory file, processes the data, and produces a printed list of the sales activities for the past week. Quantities on hand and on order are totaled, and the results are printed at the end of the report. See Figure 7.7 for the hierarchy chart and Figure 7.8 for the flowchart. The code for the inventory program is presented in Figure 7.9. The output for sample program CHAP7B is shown in Figure 7.10.

The following specifications apply:

Input (text file):
For each inventory record, read and assign data to the following fields. (Field size and type are shown in parentheses.)

1. Item number   (3 int)

2. Item description   (15 char)

3. Quantity on hand   (2 int)

4. Quantity on order   (2 int)

Text File (txInven.fil):

Use the data given below to create the inventory file. (The numbers shown above the columns correspond to the fields described for the input. Note the trailer record.)

1	2	3	4
100	Hammer	10	20
200	Saw	24	00
300	Screwdriver	12	36
400	Pliers	40	00
500	Drill	24	12
600	Wrench	16	05
000	End-Of-File	00	00

Output (printer):

Print the inventory report shown in Figure 7.10.

Processing Requirements:

• Read the inventory file.
• Accumulate the total quantity on hand.
• Accumulate the total quantity on order.

Pseudocode:

```
START: Main
Clear screen
Call Open File
IF file opened
      Call Print Headings
      Call Process Loop
      Close file
END IF
END

ENTER: Open File
Open inventory file
IF file not opened
     Print cannot open inventory file for input
END IF
RETURN

ENTER: Print Headings
Print 2 page title lines
Print 3 column heading lines
RETURN

ENTER: Process Loop
Call Read Inventory Record
LOOP while item number not = 0
```

Call Calculate Total Quantity On Hand
Call Calculate Total Quantity On Order
Call Print Detail Line
Call Read Inventory Record
END LOOP
Call Print Totals
RETURN

ENTER: Read Inventory Record
Read a record from the file:
    item number
    description
    quantity on hand
    quantity on order
RETURN

ENTER: Calculate Total Quantity On Hand
Accumulate total quantity on hand
RETURN

ENTER: Calculate Total Quantity On Order
Accumulate total quantity on order
RETURN

ENTER: Print Detail Line
Print inventory detail line:
    item number
    description
    quantity on hand
    quantity on order
RETURN

ENTER: Print Totals
Print total quantity on hand
Print total quantity on order
RETURN

Hierarchy Chart: See Figure 7.7.

Program Flowchart: See Figure 7.8.

Dissection of Sample Program CHAP7B

Overall, the file-processing activities performed by sample program CHAP7B are similar to those shown for CHAP7A. The only difference is that sample program CHAP7B uses a trailer record and static variables. Therefore, we will look at the *ProcessLoop* and the calculations performed by the *CalcOnHand* and *CalcOnOrder* modules.

```
PROCESSING LOOP:
void ProcessLoop(void)
{
```

```
int iTotOnHand;
int iTotOnOrder;

ReadRecord();
```

The above statements define the local variables and transfer control to *ReadRecord* to get the first record.

```
while (iItemNum != 0)
{
```

In the above statement, as long as the input item number is not equal to 0 (the value specified by the trailer record), control executes the statements in the body of the loop. If the item number is 0, then the file is empty and control skips the statement body of the loop.

```
iTotOnHand = CalcOnHand();
iTotOnOrder = CalcOnOrder();
```

The first statement calls the *CalcOnHand* module to total the items on hand and returns the result and assigns it to *iTotOnHand*; the second statement calls the *CalcOnOrder* module to total the items on order and returns the result and assigns it to *iTotOnOrder*. Once control leaves the *while* loop, *iTotOnHand* and *iTotOnOrder* contain the total items on hand and total items on order, respectively.

```
PrnDetail();
ReadRecord();
}
PrnTotals(iTotOnHand, iTotOnOrder);
return;
}
```

The above statements print a detail line and read the next record from the file. After all the records have been processed *(iItemNum = 0)*, control passes the totals to the *PrnTotals*

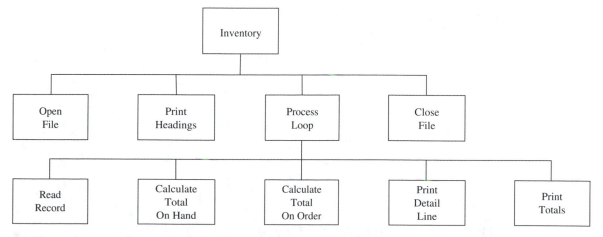

FIGURE 7.7 Hierarchy Chart for CHAP7B

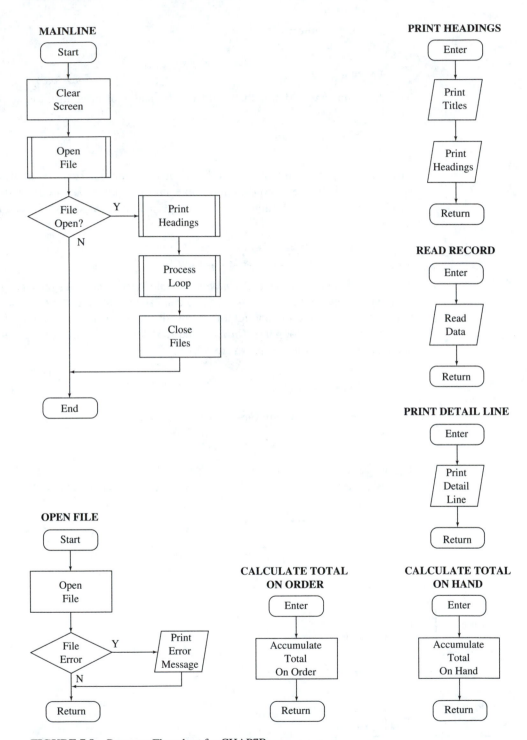

FIGURE 7.8   Program Flowchart for CHAP7B

PROCESS LOOP

PRINT REPORT TOTALS

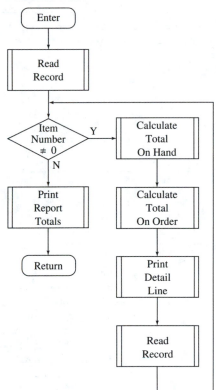

FIGURE 7.8 *Continued*

module to print the total items on hand and the total items on order at the end of the report. Control then returns to the calling module.

```
C A L C U L A T E    T O T A L    O N    H A N D:
int CalcOnHand(void)
{
    static int iTotOnHand;

    iTotOnHand = iTotOnHand + iOnHand;
    return iTotOnHand;
}
```

The first statement declares *iTotOnHand* as a static local variable. A **static local variable** retains its value between calls. As you know, a local variable is initialized each time control enters the module. On the other hand, a static local variable is initialized on the first call and then can be used to accumulate a sum or total on subsequent calls.

The second statement accumulates the total quantity on hand. Each time the module is called, the static variable retains its previous value, thus enabling the statement to maintain a total for the quantity on hand. The last command returns the total stored at *iTotOnHand* to the calling statement.

```
/*-----------------------------------------------------------------
INVENTORY: Read inventory file, compute totals for quantity on hand
and quantity on order, and print an inventory report. A trailer record
is used to mark the end of the file.

Program:   CHAP7B.C
Author:    David M. Collopy
Date:      mm/dd/yy
Project:   Sample program
*********************************************************************/

/*---- PREPROCESSING DIRECTIVES ------------------------------------/

#include <stdio.h>
#include <graph.h>

/*---- FUNCTION PROTOTYPES -----------------------------------------*/

void OpenFile(void);            /* open inventory file         */
void PrnHeadings(void);         /* print report headings       */
void ProcessLoop(void);         /* processing loop             */
void ReadRecord(void);          /* read inventory record       */
int  CalcOnHand(void);          /* calculate total qty on hand */
int  CalcOnOrder(void);         /* calculate total qty on order */
void PrnDetail(void);           /* print inventory detail line */
void PrnTotals(int, int);       /* print report totals         */

/*---- PROGRAM SETUP -----------------------------------------------*/

/*>  R E P O R T   T I T L E S   A N D   H E A D I N G S    <*/

char PT1[] = "             W O R K - L I N E   T O O L S      ";
char PT2[] = "                  Inventory Report               ";
char HL1[] = " Item                        Quantity   Quantity";
char HL2[] = "Number    Item Description    On Hand    On Order";
char HL3[] = "------------------------------------------------";
char TL[]  = "                   Totals: ";


/*>  I N V E N T O R Y   R E C O R D                        <*/

FILE *fpInv;                    /* file pointer      */
int    iItemNum;               /* item number       */
char   sDescription[16];       /* item description  */
int    iOnHand;                /* quantity on hand  */
int    iOnOrder;               /* quantity on order */
```

FIGURE 7.9   Sample Program CHAP7B: This program reads a file, computes totals, and prints a detail line for each inventory record processed.

```
/*-----------------------------------------------------------------
      MAINLINE CONTROL
-----------------------------------------------------------------*/
main()
{
    _clearscreen(0);
    OpenFile();
    if (fpInv != 0)
    {
        PrnHeadings();
        ProcessLoop();
        fclose(fpInv);
    }
    return 0;
}


/*-----------------------------------------------------------------
      OPEN INVENTORY FILE
-----------------------------------------------------------------*/
void OpenFile(void)
{
    fpInv = fopen("a:txInven.fil", "r");
    if (fpInv == 0)
    {
        printf("\nCannot open inventory file for input\n");
    }
    return;
}


/*-----------------------------------------------------------------
      PRINT HEADINGS
-----------------------------------------------------------------*/
void PrnHeadings(void)
{
    printf(PT1);                /* print page title 1   */
    printf("\n");               /* single space         */
    printf(PT2);                /* print page title 2   */
    printf("\n\n");             /* double space         */
    printf(HL1);                /* print heading line 1 */
    printf("\n");               /* single space         */
    printf(HL2);                /* print heading line 2 */
    printf("\n");               /* single space         */
    printf(HL3);                /* print heading line 3 */
    return;
}
```

FIGURE 7.9 *Continued*

```
/*-------------------------------------------------------------------
      PROCESS LOOP
-----------------------------------------------------------------*/
void ProcessLoop(void)
{
    int iTotOnHand;              /* total quantity on hand  */
    int iTotOnOrder;             /* total quantity on order */

    ReadRecord();
    while (iItemNum != 0)
    {
        iTotOnHand = CalcOnHand();
        iTotOnOrder = CalcOnOrder();
        PrnDetail();
        ReadRecord();
    }
    PrnTotals(iTotOnHand, iTotOnOrder);
    return;
}


/*-------------------------------------------------------------------
      READ INVENTORY RECORD
-----------------------------------------------------------------*/
void ReadRecord(void)
{
    fscanf(fpInv, " %d %s %d %d",
        &iItemNum, sDescription, &iOnHand, &iOnOrder);
    return;
}


/*-------------------------------------------------------------------
      CALCULATE TOTAL ON HAND
-----------------------------------------------------------------*/
int CalcOnHand(void)
{
    static int iTotOnHand;       /* total quantity on hand */

    iTotOnHand = iTotOnHand + iOnHand;
    return iTotOnHand;
}



/*-------------------------------------------------------------------
      CALCULATE TOTAL ON ORDER
-----------------------------------------------------------------*/
```

FIGURE 7.9   *Continued*

```
int CalcOnOrder(void)
{
    static int iTotOnOrder;      /* total quantity on order */

    iTotOnOrder = iTotOnOrder + iOnOrder;
    return iTotOnOrder;
}


/*-------------------------------------------------------------------
      PRINT DETAIL LINE
--------------------------------------------------------------------*/
void PrnDetail(void)
{
    printf("\n %3d    %-15s          %2d            %2d",
        iItemNum, sDescription, iOnHand, iOnOrder);
    return;
}


/*-------------------------------------------------------------------
      PRINT REPORT TOTALS
--------------------------------------------------------------------*/
void PrnTotals(int iTotOnHand, int iTotOnOrder)
{
    printf("\n\n  %s%3d         %3d", TL, iTotOnHand, iTotOnOrder);
    return;
}
```

FIGURE 7.9   *Continued*

```
                 W O R K - L I N E   T O O L S
                      Inventory Report

     Item                          Quantity   Quantity
     Number  Item Description      On Hand    On Order
     ------------------------------------------------
       100   Hammer                   10         20
       200   Saw                      24          0
       300   Screwdriver              12         36
       400   Pliers                   40          0
       500   Drill                    24         12
       600   Wrench                   16          5

                      Totals:       126         73
```

FIGURE 7.10   Output Report for CHAP7B

```
CALCULATE   TOTAL   ON   ORDER:
int CalcOnOrder(void)
{
    static int iTotOnOrder;

    iTotOnOrder = iTotOnOrder + iOnOrder;
    return iTotOnOrder;
}
```

The processing activities shown here are similar to those performed by the previous module. The static variable *iTotOnOrder* is used to accumulate the total items on order. The *return* sends control back to the calling statement with the value stored at *iTotOnOrder*.

Notes and Tips

1. When a trailer record is placed at the end of the data file, you can use any one of the input data fields to test for the end-of-file condition. This method allows you to mark and test for the end of the file. Some programmers prefer to control the end-of-file test in this manner rather than to let the feof() function take care of it for them.

2. Whenever you want to preserve the value of a local variable or accumulate a total in a module, code the *static* modifier in front of the variable name. Each time the module is called, the static variables retain their previous values. When used to accumulate a sum, a static variable is initialized once and thereafter maintains a running sum. The thing to remember is that static variables will not be reset to zero on subsequent calls.

Tutorial CHAP7B

1. The objectives of this tutorial are to
   - enter and save a text file
   - read and process the data stored in a text file
   - code static variables to maintain totals
   - use a trailer record to test for the end of a file

2. If necessary, open the editor and enter the inventory file shown in Figure 7.6. Save the data file on your disk as *txInven.fil*.

3. Clear the editor, enter the source code shown in Figure 7.9, and save the program on your work disk as CHAP7B.

4. Compile, run, and debug the program until your output matches the inventory report shown in Figure 7.10.

5. When finished, show your work to your instructor.

Quick Quiz

Answer the following questions.

1. How would the output change if you deleted the *static* modifier from the *iTotOnOrder* variable in the *CalcOnOrder* module?

2. Are there any advantages to using a trailer record for text file applications?

3. Look at the body of the *while* statement coded in the *ProcessLoop*. Why are we returning values to the calling statements when the values are not used inside the loop?

4. Did you have any problems or errors when you ran your program? If so, what were they and what did you do to correct them?

Summary

1. Data is organized into fields, records, and files to facilitate processing by the computer.

2. A text file consists of readable data that can be created with a text editor. Data constants organized into records and stored on disk are read from a file and processed by the program.

3. Text file processing involves the following activities: creating a file, declaring the file pointer variable, opening the file, reading and processing the data in the file, and closing the file.

4. A disk text file is created by using a text editor to enter, edit, and save data for later use by the program. Data is keyed into a file one record at a time. Each record ends with the newline character. The data constants should be organized into columns and separated by at least one blank space.

5. FILE is a special data type that is used to declare a file pointer variable. Each file processed by the program must have a unique file pointer. A file pointer is simply a variable that is used to hold the address of a specific file.

6. The fopen() function opens a file. A file may be opened in read, write, or append mode. When a file is opened, the fopen() function passes the address of the disk file to the file pointer variable. Otherwise, zero (the NULL pointer) is passed to the file pointer.

7. The fscanf() function reads a record from the designated file, converts the data to the types specified by the control string, and assigns the results to the program variables. Since there is no inherent connection between the data in the file and the variable names specified by the fscanf() function, it is up to the programmer to maintain a positional relationship and match them accordingly.

8. In order to prevent the program from reading past the last record, the feof() function is used to test for the end-of-file condition. If the file pointer is not pointing to the end of the file, the feof() function returns a zero (false). Otherwise, it returns a nonzero value (true).

9. All files should be closed prior to exiting the program. The fclose() function clears and releases the file buffer(s) and closes the file(s) identified by the file pointer argument(s).

10. We may use a trailer record to test for the end-of-file condition. A trailer record is a special record that is placed at the end of the file—it trails the data. It is used to signal that the program has reached the end of the file.

Programming Projects

For each project, design the logic and write the modular structured program to produce the output. Model your program after the sample programs presented in the chapter. Verify your output.

Project 7–1 **Overdue Accounts**

Write a program to read an overdue accounts file, and print a report of the customers with account balances that are 90 days overdue.

Input (text file):
For each customer record, read and assign data to the following fields. (Field size and type are shown in parentheses.)

1. Account number   (4 int)
2. Customer name   (15 char)
3. Days overdue   (2 int)
4. Balance due   (6.2 float)

Text File (txOvrdue.fil):
Use the data given below to create the overdue accounts file. (The numbers shown above the columns correspond to the fields described for the input.)

1	2	3	4
1010	David Ryan	90	400.00
2450	Marie Hill	30	754.00
2730	Rita Fox	90	740.00
3100	Alvin Porter	90	550.00
4080	Corey Adkins	30	233.00
4890	Amy Wyatt	30	700.00
5260	Brian Knox	30	625.00
6350	Susan Cope	90	600.00
7720	Lisa Wilson	60	417.00
8540	Matt Hart	90	900.00
9200	Tori Landis	90	235.00
9630	Pat Rankin	60	342.00

Output (printer):
Print the following 90-day overdue accounts report:

```
Author            90-DAY OVERDUE ACCOUNTS            Page 01
                         mm/dd/yy


   Acct Number        Customer Name         Balance Due
```

```
9999           X-----------X          999.99
  :                 :                     :
  :                 :                     :
9999           X-----------X          999.99

                         Total:       9999.99


Number of accounts overdue:  99
Number of accounts > 500.00: 99
```

Processing Requirements:

- Read the overdue accounts file.
- Print a report of all accounts that are 90 days overdue.
- Accumulate a total for balance due.
- Count the number of 90-day overdue accounts.
- Count the number of 90-day overdue accounts that have a balance greater than $500.

Project 7–2   **Payroll**

Write a program to read a payroll file, calculate pay, and print a weekly payroll roster. Hours worked over 40 are paid overtime. Assume the current federal income tax (FIT) rate is 15%.

Input (text file):
For each payroll record, read and assign data to the following fields. (Field size and type are shown in parentheses.)

1. Employee name   (15 char)
2. Hours worked   (2 int)
3. Hourly pay rate   (5.2 float)

Text File (txPayroll.fil):
Use the data given below to create the payroll file. (The numbers shown above the columns correspond to the fields described for the input.)

1	2	3
Tanya Bauer	40	7.50
Dana Clark	45	14.90
Sara Erickson	38	12.00
Scott Howard	42	9.75
Paul Irwin	48	8.72
Dale Miller	40	10.25
Bret Rossi	35	8.00
Karen Thomas	48	9.00
Tracy York	36	11.00

Output (printer):
Print the following weekly payroll report:

```
Author                WEEKLY PAYROLL REPORT              Page 01
                           mm/dd/yy
```

Employee Name	Hours Worked	Regular Pay	Overtime Pay	Gross Pay	FIT	Net Pay
X-------X	99	999.99	99.99	999.99	99.99	999.99
:	:	:	:	:	:	:
:	:	:	:	:	:	:
X-------X	99	999.99	99.99	999.99	99.99	999.99
Totals:		9999.99	999.99	9999.99	999.99	9999.99

Processing Requirements:

- Read the payroll file.
- Compute the regular pay:
  If hours > 40,
      then regular pay = 40 × pay rate
      else regular pay = hours × pay rate.
- Compute the overtime pay:
  If hours > 40,
      then overtime pay = (hours − 40) × 1.5 × pay rate
      else overtime pay = 0.
- Compute the gross pay:
  regular pay + overtime pay.
- Compute the federal income tax amount:
  gross pay × FIT rate.
- Compute the net pay:
  gross pay − FIT amount.
- Accumulate totals for regular pay, overtime pay, gross pay, FIT, and net pay.

Project 7–3   Sales Profit

Write a program to read a sales file, calculate profit per salesperson, and print a sales profit report.

Input (text file):

For each sales record, read and assign data to the following fields. (Field size and type are shown in parentheses.)

1. Salesperson name   (15 char)

2. Total sales   (8.2 float)

3. Cost of sales   (7.2 float)

Text File (txSales.fil):

Use the data given below to create the sales file. (The numbers shown above the columns correspond to the fields described for the input.)

1	2	3
Lisa Conrad	8120.52	6450.71
Roy Hickle	2245.78	1072.49

```
        Tara Perkins        12710.14     9735.38
        Dennis Tian          4567.51     3119.22
        Ann Zimmerman        5793.59     4204.45
```

Output (printer):
Print the following sales profit report:

```
Author                  SALES PROFIT REPORT           Page 01
                            mm/dd/yy


Salesperson     Total Sales    Cost of Sales    Net Profit
------------------------------------------------------------


X--------X       99999.99        9999.99          9999.99
    :               :               :                :
    :               :               :                :
X--------X       99999.99        9999.99          9999.99

                                Total:           99999.99

                                Average:          9999.99
```

Processing Requirements:

- Read the sales file.
- Compute the net profit:
  total sales – cost of sales.
- Count the number of salespeople.
- Accumulate a total for net profit.
- Compute average net profit:
  total net profit / number of salespeople.

Project 7–4   Inventory

Write a program to read an inventory file and print an inventory reorder report.

Input (text file):
For each inventory record, read and assign data to the following fields:

1. Item number   (4 int)
2. Item description   (15 char)
3. Quantity on hand   (2 int)
4. Reorder point   (2 int)
5. Reorder quantity   (2 int)
6. Unit cost   (4.2 float)
7. Selling price   (5.2 float)

Text File (txInven.fil):

Use the data given below to create the inventory file. (The numbers shown above the columns correspond to the fields described for the input.)

1	2	3	4	5	6	7
1000	Hammers	24	12	24	4.75	9.49
2000	Saws	08	16	12	7.50	14.99
3000	Drills	10	12	18	7.83	15.95
4000	Screwdrivers	36	24	12	2.27	4.98
5000	Pliers	12	12	36	2.65	5.49

Output (printer):

Print the following inventory reorder report:

```
Author              INVENTORY REORDER REPORT          Page 01
                          mm/dd/yy


Item                             Quantity   Reorder     Item
Number    Description            On Hand    Quantity    Cost

 9999     X-----------X             99         99      999.99
   :           :                     :          :          :
   :           :                     :          :          :
 9999     X-----------X             99         99      999.99

                                  Total Cost:         9999.99
```

Processing Requirements:

- Read the inventory file.
- Determine what items to reorder:
  Order the reorder quantity of an item when the quantity on hand is less than or equal to the reorder point.
- Compute the item cost:
  reorder quantity × unit cost.
- Accumulate the total cost.

Project 7–5   Personnel

Write a program to read a personnel file and print a salary report of all female employees who are paid over $30,000 a year.

Input (text file):

For each employee record, read and assign data to the following fields. (Field size and type are shown in parentheses.)

1. Employee number   (4 int)
2. Employee name   (15 char)
3. Department number   (2 int)

4. Sex code   (1 char)

5. Annual Salary   (8.2 float)

Text File (txPersnl.fil):

Use the data given below to create the personnel file. (The numbers shown above the columns correspond to the fields described for the record.)

1	2	3	4	5
1926	Dana Andrews	10	F	29000.00
2071	Scott Cooper	14	M	30250.00
3150	Todd Feldman	22	M	24175.00
3600	Amy Kwon	19	F	36025.00
4100	Derek Lowe	50	M	29120.00
4298	Lori Palmer	35	F	33400.00
5409	Bob Shields	47	M	27500.00
6552	Pam Wolfe	31	F	31773.00

Output (printer):

Print the following personnel salary report:

```
Author                PERSONNEL SALARY REPORT            Page 01
                           mm/dd/yy
Employee                                 Department        Annual
Number          Employee Name              Number          Salary

 9999          X------------X                99          99999.99
   :                :                         :              :
   :                :                         :              :
 9999          X-----------X                 99          99999.99

                                         Average:         99999.99
```

Processing Requirements:

- Read the personnel file.
- Print a report of all female employees who are paid over $30,000 a year.
- Accumulate female count.
- Accumulate a total for annual salary.
- Compute the average annual salary:
  total annual salary / female count.

Project 7–6   Accounts Payable

Write a program to read a vendor file, compute amount due, and print an accounts payable report. Assume the following discount schedule applies to early payments:

Paid By (days)	Discount
1 – 10	12%
11 – 20	10%
21 – 30	08%
31 – 45	05%

Input (text file):
For each vendor record, read and assign data to the following fields. (Field size and type are shown in parentheses.)

1. Vendor number   (3 int)
2. Vendor name   (12 char)
3. Invoice number   (5 char)
4. Invoice amount   (7.2 float)
5. Days paid by   (2 int)

Text File (txVendor.fil):
Use the data given below to create the vendor file. The numbers shown above the columns correspond to the fields described for the input.

1	2	3	4	5
217	Metacraft	A1239	2309.12	10
349	IntraTell	T9823	670.00	25
712	Reylock	F0176	4563.78	33
501	Universal	W0105	1200.00	21
196	Northland	X2781	3429.34	45
414	MarxComm	H9205	913.87	18
659	Veston	D1776	5127.63	30

Output (printer):
Print the following accounts payable report:

```
Author                  ACCOUNTS PAYABLE REPORT              Page 01
                              mm/dd/yy

Vendor                      Invoice   Invoice   Discount   Amount
Number   Vendor Name        Number    Amount    Amount     Due

 999     X---------X         XXXXX     9999.99    999.99    9999.99
  :          :                 :          :         :          :
  :          :                 :          :         :          :
 999     X---------X         XXXXX     9999.99    999.99    9999.99

                   Totals:           99999.99   9999.99   99999.99
```

Processing Requirements:

- Read the vendor file.
- Determine the discount rate:
  Based on early payment (see the discount schedule).
- Compute the discount amount:
  invoice amount × discount rate.
- Compute the amount due:
  invoice amount − discount amount.
- Accumulate totals for invoice amount, discount amount, and amount due.

Project 7–7   Production Bonus

Write a program to read a production file, compute bonus pay, and print a bonus pay report. Assume production workers are paid a bonus according to the number of units they produce over the quota. Use the following bonus pay schedule:

units over	1 – 10	pay rate	0.60
quota	11 – 25	each	0.65
	26 – 45		0.70
	46+		0.75

Input (text file):

For each production record, read and assign data to the following fields. (Field size and type are shown in parentheses.)

1. Employee name   (15 char)
2. Product number   (5 char)
3. Production Quota   (2 int)
4. Units Produced   (3 int)

Text File (txProd.fil):

Use the data given below to create the production file. (The numbers shown above the columns correspond to the fields described for the input.)

1	2	3	4
Kay Archer	P9511	65	65
Alan Baum	A1234	48	97
Marie Fitch	C4510	60	75
Lee Hildebrand	R0934	50	62
David Mullins	E3371	75	75
Chad Nelson	L8912	40	63
Bill Quinn	S0951	48	56
Nicole Renner	H9733	50	59
Erica Tate	Z0182	65	73
Terry West	A3235	70	116

Output (printer):

Print the following bonus pay report:

```
Author                    BONUS PAY REPORT                 Page 01
                             mm/dd/yy


                   Product          Units      Over
Employee Name      Number   Quota   Produced   Quota   Bonus Pay

X----------X       XXXXX      99      999        99     999.99
     :              :         :        :          :       :
     :              :         :        :          :       :
X----------X       XXXXX      99      999        99     999.99

                            Totals:   9999       999    9999.99
```

Processing Requirements:

- Read the production file.
- Compute the bonus pay:
  Based on units over quota (see the bonus pay schedule).
- Accumulate totals for units produced, units over quota, and bonus pay.

8 Page and Control Breaks

Learning Objectives

After you have read this chapter and completed the exercises, you should be able to

- use line and page counters to construct page break (multipage report) programs
- explain why control break processing requires that the input data be arranged in control field order
- design and write control break programs
- combine page and control break processing to produce multipage, subtotal reports

Page Break Reports

Computer-generated reports often consist of multipage output. By definition, the term **multi-page** implies that the output consists of two or more pages. Each page of the report should show the title and column headings printed across the top of the page. The body of the report should be printed after the column headings.

Furthermore, we would like to maintain a one-inch margin at the top and bottom and print between 50 and 55 detail lines. Also, when a page is full, we would like the printer to skip to the top of the next page and resume printing.

In other words, a **page break** occurs when the number of lines printed equals the limit established for the page. Accordingly, the printer advances to a new page, prints the title and column headings, and continues with the body of the report.

Page break processing requires the use of a line counter. The purpose of the **line counter** is to keep track of the number of detail lines printed per page. Each time a line is printed, the line counter is incremented and compared to the maximum number of lines allowed per page. If we are also numbering the pages, then we need an additional variable—a page counter. The purpose of the **page counter** is to keep track of the number of pages printed.

To further illustrate the concept of page breaks, let us look at the payroll report shown in Figure 8.1. Assume we are printing 40 lines per page. Once 40 detail lines have been printed, the line counter is set to 0; the page counter is incremented by one; the printer advances to the top of the next page; and the title, page number, and column heading line are printed. The pseudocode version of the page break routine is shown in Figure 8.2.

Given the limit of 40 lines per page, note the page and the line counters shown in Figure 8.2. For each page, the line counter advances from 1 to 40 as the detail lines are printed.

Checkpoint 8A

1. When does a page break occur?
2. What is the purpose of a page counter? a line counter?
3. Write the pseudocode that shows the steps involved in performing a page break.

Sample Program CHAP8A

This program demonstrates page break processing and prints a rental income report for Pernell Properties. Each detail line includes the location, rental agency, property manager, building number, apartment number, and monthly rent. Total monthly income is accumulated and printed at the end of the report. See Figure 8.3 for the hierarchy chart and Figure 8.4 for the flowchart. Sample program CHAP8A is shown in Figure 8.5; the output report is shown in Figures 8.6a and 8.6b.

Input (text file):
For each rent record, read and assign data to the following fields. (Field size and type are shown in parentheses.)

1. Location   (5 char)
2. Agency number   (2 int)

3. Manager number   (3 int)
4. Building number   (2 int)
5. Apartment number   (1 int)
6. Monthly rent   (6.2 float)

```
                    PAYROLL REPORT              Page 1

    ID#    EMPLOYEE NAME        PAYRATE      HOURS WORKED
--------------------------------------------------------
    101    Kami Peyton          12.00            40
     :         :                  :              :
     :         :                  :              :
     :         :                  :              :
     :         :                  :              :
    140    David Kerrington     10.00            39
```

```
                    PAYROLL REPORT              Page 2

    ID#    EMPLOYEE NAME        PAYRATE      HOURS WORKED
--------------------------------------------------------
    141    Kent Broadwell        9.00            37
     :         :                  :              :
     :         :                  :              :
     :         :                  :              :
    165    Elinore McLain       14.00            40
```

FIGURE 8.1   Payroll Report with Page Break

		Counters	
		Page	**Line**
If line count > 40			
Set line count to 0		1	1–40
Add 1 to page number		2	1–40
Advance to the next page		3	1–40
Print titles, page number, and		:	:
column headings		:	:
:		n	1–40

FIGURE 8.2   Page Break Logic

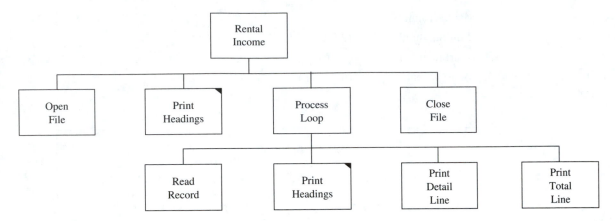

FIGURE 8.3 Hierarchy Chart for CHAP8A. Note: The shaded corners indicate that the symbol represents a module that is called by two or more modules in the program.

Text File (txRent.fil):

Use the data given below to create the rent file. (The numbers shown above the columns correspond to the fields described for the input.)

1	2	3	4	5	6
North	20	201	10	1	400.00
North	20	201	10	2	410.00
North	20	201	10	3	335.00
North	20	201	15	1	375.00
North	20	201	15	2	385.00
North	20	247	17	1	450.00
North	20	247	17	2	450.00
North	43	316	22	1	345.00
North	43	316	22	2	465.00
East	10	237	30	1	410.00
East	10	237	30	2	365.00
East	10	237	30	3	470.00
East	10	237	30	4	345.00
East	10	659	33	1	429.00
East	10	659	33	2	465.00
End	00	000	00	0	000.00 (trailer record)

Output (printer):

Print the page break report shown in Figures 8.6a and 8.6b.

Processing Requirements:

- Read the rent file.
- Print 12 detail lines per page.
- Accumulate a report total for rent.

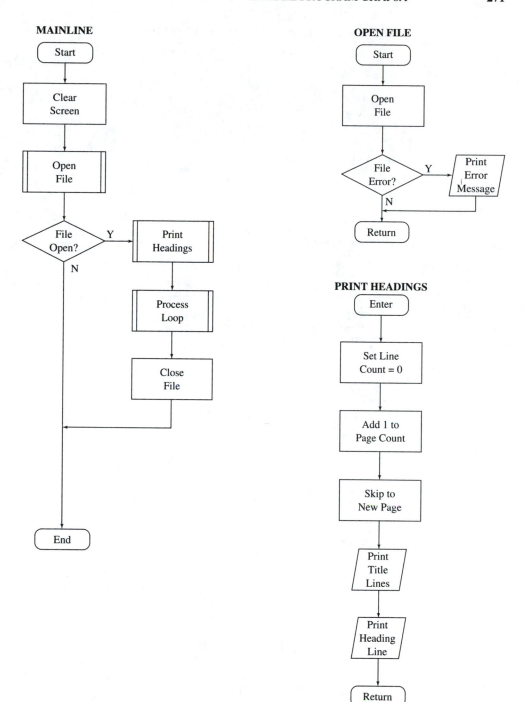

FIGURE 8.4 Program Flowchart for CHAP8A

PRINT TOTAL LINE

READ RECORD

PRINT DETAIL LINE

PROCESS LOOP

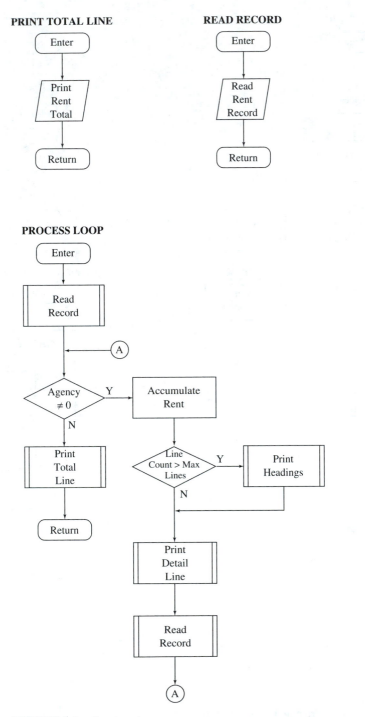

FIGURE 8.4   *Continued*

```
/*--------------------------------------------------------------
RENTAL INCOME: Read rent file and print an income report for Pernell
Properties. This program demonstrates page break processing.

Program:   CHAP8A.C
Author:    David M. Collopy
Date:      mm/dd/yy
Project:   Sample program
*******************************************************************/

/*---- PREPROCESSING DIRECTIVES ----------------------------------*/

#include <stdio.h>
#include <graph.h>
#define IMAXLINES 12

/*---- FUNCTION PROTOTYPES ---------------------------------------*/

void   OpenFile(void);              /* open rent file          */
void   PrnHeadings(void);           /* print report headings   */
void   ProcessLoop(void);           /* processing loop         */
void   ReadRecord(void);            /* read rent record        */
void   PrnDetail(void);             /* print rent detail line  */
void   PrnTotal(float);             /* print total rent        */

/*---- PROGRAM SETUP ---------------------------------------------*/

/*>  R E P O R T   T I T L E S   A N D   H E A D I N G S     <*/

char PT1[] = "P E R N E L L   P R O P E R T I E S      Page ";
char PT2[] = "                  Rental Income                ";
char HL1[] = "LOCATION  AGENCY  MGR  BLDG    APART#     RENT ";
char DTL[] = " %-5s       %2d     %3d   %2d      %d     $%7.2f";
char RTL[] = "                  *****  Report Total: $ %7.2f  ";

/*>  R E N T   R E C O R D                                   <*/

FILE *fpRent;                       /* file pointer            */
char  sLocation[6];                 /* apartment location      */
int   iAgency;                      /* agency ID number        */
int   iMgr;                         /* manager ID number       */
int   iBldg;                        /* building number         */
int   iApart;                       /* apartment number        */
float fRent;                        /* monthly rent income     */
```

FIGURE 8.5 Sample Program CHAP8A: Prints a rental income report for Pernell Properties. Total rent is accumulated and printed at the end of the report.

```
/*>   P R O G R A M   V A R I A B L E S                    <*/

int   iLineCnt = 0;                /* detail line count   */

/*----------------------------------------------------------------
      MAINLINE CONTROL
------------------------------------------------------------------*/
main()
{
    _clearscreen(0);
    OpenFile();
    if (fpRent != 0)
    {
        PrnHeadings();
        ProcessLoop();
        fclose(fpRent);
    }
    return 0;
}


/*----------------------------------------------------------------
      OPEN RENT FILE
------------------------------------------------------------------*/
void OpenFile(void)
{
    fpRent = fopen("a:txRent.fil", "r");
    if (fpRent == 0)
    {
        printf("\nCannot open rent file\n");
    }
    return;
}


/*----------------------------------------------------------------
      PRINT REPORT HEADINGS
------------------------------------------------------------------*/
void PrnHeadings(void)
{
    static int iPageNum;         /* page count               */

    iLineCnt = 0;                /* set line count to 0      */
    iPageNum++;                  /* add 1 to page number     */
    fprintf(stdprn, "\f\r");     /* skip to new page & reset */
```

FIGURE 8.5 *Continued*

```
        fprintf(stdprn, "%s %d",     /* print page title 1      */
            PT1, iPageNum);          /*     & page number       */
        fprintf(stdprn, "\r\n");     /* reset & single space    */
        fprintf(stdprn, PT2);        /* print page title 2      */
        fprintf(stdprn, "\r\n\n");   /* reset & double space    */
        fprintf(stdprn, HL1);        /* print heading line 1    */
        fprintf(stdprn, "\r\n");     /* reset & single space    */
        return;
}


/*------------------------------------------------------------------
        PROCESSING LOOP
--------------------------------------------------------------------*/
void ProcessLoop(void)
{
        float fRptTot;               /* report rent total */

        ReadRecord();
        while (iAgency != 0)
        {
            fRptTot = fRptTot + fRent;
            if (iLineCnt >= IMAXLINES)
                PrnHeadings();
            PrnDetail();
            ReadRecord();
        }
        PrnTotal(fRptTot);
        return;
}


/*------------------------------------------------------------------
        READ RENT RECORD
--------------------------------------------------------------------*/
void ReadRecord(void)
{
        fscanf(fpRent, " %s %d %d %d %d %f",
            sLocation, &iAgency, &iMgr, &iBldg, &iApart, &fRent);
        return;
}


/*------------------------------------------------------------------
        PRINT RENT DETAIL LINE
--------------------------------------------------------------------*/
```

FIGURE 8.5 *Continued*

```
void PrnDetail(void)
{
    fprintf(stdprn, "\r\n");
    fprintf(stdprn, DTL, sLocation, iAgency, iMgr, iBldg, iApart,
            fRent);
    iLineCnt++;
    return;
}


/*-----------------------------------------------------------------
      PRINT TOTAL RENT
-------------------------------------------------------------------*/
void PrnTotal(float fRptTot)
{
    fprintf(stdprn, "\r\n\n");
    fprintf(stdprn, RTL, fRptTot);
    return;
}
```

FIGURE 8.5   *Continued*

```
P E R N E L L    P R O P E R T I E S        Page 1
               Rental Income


LOCATION   AGENCY   MGR   BLDG    APART#       RENT

  North      20     201    10       1       $ 400.00
  North      20     201    10       2       $ 410.00
  North      20     201    10       3       $ 335.00
  North      20     201    15       1       $ 375.00
  North      20     201    15       2       $ 385.00
  North      20     247    17       1       $ 450.00
  North      20     247    17       2       $ 450.00
  North      43     316    22       1       $ 345.00
  North      43     316    22       2       $ 465.00
  East       10     237    30       1       $ 410.00
  East       10     237    30       2       $ 365.00
  East       10     237    30       3       $ 470.00
```

FIGURE 8.6a   Program Output for CHAP8A

```
┌─────────────────────────────────────────────────────────┐
│  P E R N E L L    P R O P E R T I E S      Page 2        │
│                  Rental Income                          │
│                                                         │
│  LOCATION   AGENCY   MGR   BLDG    APART#       RENT     │
│                                                         │
│   East        10     237    30       4      $ 345.00    │
│   East        10     659    33       1      $ 429.00    │
│   East        10     659    33       2      $ 465.00    │
│                                                         │
│                 *****  Report Total:  $ 6099.00         │
│                                                         │
└─────────────────────────────────────────────────────────┘
```

FIGURE 8.6b   Program Output for CHAP8A

Pseudocode:

START: Main
Clear screen
Call Open File
IF file opened
    Call Print Headings
    Call Process Loop
    Close file
END IF
END

ENTER: Open File
Open rent file
IF file not opened
    Print error - cannot open file
END IF
RETURN

ENTER: Print Headings
Set line count to 0
Add 1 to page number
Advance to top of page
Print 2 page title lines and page number
Print 1 column heading lines
RETURN

ENTER: Process Loop
Call Read Rent Record
LOOP while agency not = 0
    Accumulate report rent total
    IF line count > or = 12
        Call Print Headings
    END IF
    Call Print Detail Line

     Call Read Rent Record
  END LOOP
  Call Print Total Rent
  RETURN

  ENTER: Read Rent Record
  Read a record from the file
    apartment location
    agency number
    manager number
    building number
    apartment number
    monthly rent income
  RETURN

  ENTER: Print Detail Line
  Print rent detail line:
    apartment location
    agency number
    manager number
    building number
    apartment number
    monthly rent income
  Add 1 to line count
  RETURN

  ENTER: Print Total Rent
  Print report rent total
  RETURN

Hierarchy Chart: See Figure 8.3.

Program Flowchart: See Figure 8.4.

Dissection of Sample Program CHAP8A

Let's examine the processing performed by sample program CHAP8A, beginning with the *PRINT HEADINGS* module.

```
P R I N T    H E A D I N G S:

void PrnHeadings(void)
{
    static int iPageNum;

    iLineCnt = 0;
    iPageNum++;
    fprintf(stdprn, "\f\r");
    fprintf(stdprn, "%s %d",
        PT1, iPageNum);
```

```
        fprintf(stdprn, "\r\n");
        fprintf(stdprn, PT2);
        fprintf(stdprn, "\r\n\n");
        fprintf(stdprn, HL1);
        fprintf(stdprn, "\r\n");
        return;
}
```

The above statements declare the static local variable to track the page numbers, set line count to 0, and add one to page number. The line numbers run from 1 to 12 per page, and the page numbers run from 1 to *n* (where *n* represents the last page).

The remainder of the statements prints the page titles (with page number) and column headings at the top of the report. Recall that the form-feed character \f forces the printer to advance to the top of a new page and \r resets the carriage return to the first print position on the page.

```
P R O C E S S I N G    L O O P:

void ProcessLoop(void)
{
    int fRptTot;

    ReadRecord();
```

The statements declare a local variable for the total rent and call the *ReadRecord* module; this module retrieves the first record from the rent file.

```
    while (iAgency != 0)
    {
```

In the above statement, as long as the agency number read from the file is not equal to 0 (the value specified by the trailer record), control executes the statements in the body of the loop. If the agency number is 0, then the rent file is empty and control skips to the first executable statement coded after the closing brace of the *while* loop.

```
        fRptTot = fRptTot + fRent;
```

The above statement adds the rent read from the file to the total rent and assigns the sum to *fRptTot*. Here *fRptTot* is used to accumulate the total rent for the report.

```
        if (iLineCnt >= IMAXLINES)
            PrnHeadings();
```

The above statement compares the line counter (*iLineCnt*) to the maximum number of lines (*IMAXLINES*) allowed per page. If the line counter is greater than or equal to the maximum lines, then the program transfers control to the *PrnHeadings* module; this module prints the report titles and column heading. Otherwise, control falls through and continues with the next statement.

```
        PrnDetail();
```

The above statement calls the *PrnDetail* module; this module prints the detail line for the given input record.

```
        ReadRecord();
    }
    PrnTotal(fRptTot);
    return;
}
```

The looping read statement transfers control to the *ReadRecord* module; this module retrieves the next record from the rent file.

When the the trailer record is read, the program calls the *PrnTotal* module; this module prints the total rent at the end of the report. The *return* statement sends control back to the *MAINLINE*, the calling module.

R E A D   R E N T   R E C O R D:

```
void ReadRecord(void)
{
    fscanf(fpRent, " %s %d %d %d %d %f",
        sLocation, &iAgency, &iMgr, &iBldg, &iApart, &fRent);
    return;
}
```

The above statements read a record from the rent file (*fpRent*) and assign the input data to the variables in the order listed—*sLocation, iAgency, iMgr, iBldg, iApart, fRent*.

After reading a record from the file and assigning data to the variables, control returns to the calling module.

P R I N T   R E N T   D E T A I L   L I N E:

```
void PrnDetail(void)
{
    fprintf(stdprn, "\r\n");
    fprintf(stdprn, DTL, sLocation, iAgency, iMgr, iBldg, iApart,
            fRent);
    iLineCnt++;
    return;
}
```

The above statements reset the printer to the beginning of the next line, print the detail line, add one to the line count, and return to the calling module.

Notes and Tips

1. Page break processing always involves two counters—one for page numbers and one for line count. In a way, page break processing resembles a nested loop. Basically, the outside loop increments once for a completed cycle of the inner loop. In sample program CHAP8A, when page number equals 1, the line counter cycles through the count 1 to 12. When page number equals 2, once again the line counter cycles through count 1 to 12, and so on.

2. You may have noticed that a static variable was used for the page number but a global variable was used for the line count. Because page number is completely contained within a single module, it makes sense to define it as a local static variable. On the other hand, line count is manipulated by more than one module. In this particular situation, it would be pointless to make it a local variable and pass and return the count. Since line count is processed in such a straightforward manner, it seems reasonable to define it as a global variable.

3. In the Program Setup section of the sample program, *DTL* is used to describe the detail line. It includes the format specifiers. This shows yet another way to format the output. Note also that *RTL* is used to format the report total line.

Tutorial CHAP8A

1. The objectives of this tutorial are to
   - process the data stored in a text file
   - code a page break application

2. Open the text editor, and enter the sample program exactly as shown in Figure 8.5.

3. Save the source program on your work disk as CHAP8A. Check for coding errors, and make corrections as needed. Save frequently.

4. Compile, run, and debug your program until the output matches the report shown in Figures 8.6a and 8.6b.

5. When completed, show your work to your instructor.

Quick Quiz

Answer the following questions.

1. Briefly explain the processing activities performed during a page break.

2. What does the *RTL* notation stand for?

3. Why is page number a *static* local variable? What characteristics should a variable exhibit before it is declared static?

4. Do you have to increment the page number when the Print Headings module is called the first time? Explain your answer.

5. Did you have any problems with CHAP8A? If so, what were they and what did you do to correct them?

6. Change MAXLINES to 15, but don't save the program. Execute the program and see what the output looks like. Is it what you expected? Explain your answer.

Control Break Reports

Records arranged in either ascending or descending control field order can be processed in a special way to produce a subtotal or a group total. **Subtotal** or **control**

break processing involves grouping related records and then processing them together as a group. A **control field** (such as customer number) is used to detect a change in the group and to determine when to print the subtotal before moving on to the next group. A **subtotal** is part of a report total that is accumulated and printed in relationship to a control group.

Thus, when the control field of the current record equals that of the previous one, the input is added to the subtotal for the related records. On the other hand, when a control break is encountered (the control field changes), the previous subtotal is printed and the input is added to the subtotal for the new control group.

As an example, suppose that in Figure 8.7, the previous and current customer numbers—the control fields—both equal 103. We add the current sales amount to the group subtotal for customer number 103, as shown.

However, a **control break** occurs when the customer number changes from 103 to 104. When the control break is detected, the group subtotal for customer 103 ($6,350.00) is printed. Then the subtotal field is reset to zero in preparation for the next group (104).

After all the data has been processed, the subtotal for the last group (104) is printed along with the report total ($8,650.00).

The pseudocode version of the control break routine is shown in Figure 8.8.

Checkpoint 8B

1. Discuss the purpose of a control field.

2. Explain the concept of control break processing.

3. Why does control break processing require the input data to be arranged in control field order?

4. Write the pseudocode that shows the steps involved in performing a control break.

Sample Program CHAP8B

This program demonstrates application of both page and control break processing by producing a rental income report for Pernell Properties. See Figure 8.9 for the hierarchy chart and Figure 8.10 for the flowchart. Sample program CHAP8B is shown in Figure 8.11; the output report is shown in Figures 8.12a and 8.12b.

Notice that the input is the same as it was for sample program CHAP8A. However, sample program CHAP8B uses the building number as a control field. Note also that the input is arranged in ascending order by building number. This is significant to the operation of the program. Control break processing requires that the control fields be arranged in either ascending or descending order. Otherwise, a break will occur each time the control fields change values.

```
                    CUSTOMER ACCOUNTS

        CUSTOMER NUMBER         SALES AMOUNT
              103               $1,400.00
              103               $1,200.00
              103               $2,000.00
              103               $1,750.00

        Sales subtotal:         $6,350.00

              104               $1,000.00
              104               $1,300.00

        Sales subtotal:         $2,300.00

        * Report total:         $8,650.00
```

FIGURE 8.7   Control Break Processing

```
                          :
    If previous customer not = current customer
       Set previous customer = current customer
       Print customer subtotal
       Add 3 to line count
       Set customer subtotal to zero
                          :
```

FIGURE 8.8   Control Break Logic

Input (text file):

For each rent record, read and assign data to the following fields. (Field size and type are shown in parentheses.)

1. Location   (5 char)

2. Agency number   (2 int)

3. Manager number   (3 int)

4. Building number   (2 int)

5. Apartment number   (1 int)

6. Monthly rent   (6.2 float)

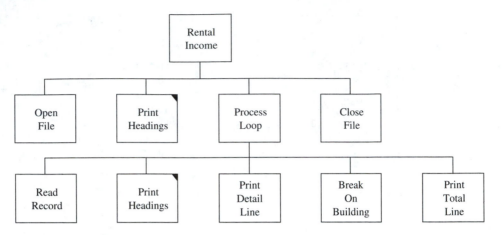

FIGURE 8.9   Hierarchy Chart for CHAP8B

Text File (txRent.fil):

Use the data given below to create the rent file. (The numbers shown above the columns correspond to the fields described for the input.)

1	2	3	4	5	6
North	20	201	10	1	400.00
North	20	201	10	2	410.00
North	20	201	10	3	335.00
North	20	201	15	1	375.00
North	20	201	15	2	385.00
North	20	247	17	1	450.00
North	20	247	17	2	450.00
North	43	316	22	1	345.00
North	43	316	22	2	465.00
East	10	237	30	1	410.00
East	10	237	30	2	365.00
East	10	237	30	3	470.00
East	10	237	30	4	345.00
East	10	659	33	1	429.00
East	10	659	33	2	465.00
End	00	000	00	0	000.00 (trailer record)

Output (printer):

Print the control break report shown in Figure 8.12. Notice the asterisk on the building subtotal line. A single asterisk indicates that the value represents a first-level subtotal. Multilevel totals are covered in Chapter 9.

Processing Requirements:

- Read the rent file.
- Print 21 detail lines per page.
- Subtotal rent by building.
- Accumulate a report total for rent.

Pseudocode:

START: Main
Clear screen
Call Open File
IF file opened
      Call Print Headings
      Call Process Loop
      Close file
END IF
END

ENTER: Open File
Open rent file
IF file not opened
      Print error - cannot open file
END IF
RETURN

ENTER: Print Headings
Set line count to 0
Add 1 to page number
Advance to top of page
Print 2 page title lines and page number
Print 1 column heading lines
RETURN

ENTER: Process Loop
Call Read Rent Record
Save building number
LOOP while agency not = 0
      Accumulate building rent total
      Accumulate report rent total
      IF line count > = 21
            Call Print Headings
      END IF
      Call Print Detail Line
      Call Read Rent Record
      IF new building not = previous building
            Save new building number
            Call Break On Building
      END IF
END LOOP
Call Print Total Rent
RETURN

ENTER: Read Rent Record
Read a record from the file:
      apartment location
      agency ID number
      manager ID number

```
        building number
        apartment number
        monthly rent income
RETURN

ENTER: Print Detail Line
Print rent detail line:
        apartment location
        agency ID number
        manager ID number
        building number
        apartment number
        monthly rent income
Add 1 to line count
RETURN

ENTER: Break On Building
Print building rent total
Add 3 to line count
Set new building rent total to 0
RETURN

ENTER: Print Total Rent
Print report rent total
RETURN
```

Hierarchy Chart: See Figure 8.9.

Program Flowchart: See Figure 8.10.

Dissection of Sample Program CHAP8B

Review the dissection carefully. Notice the similarities between this program and the previous one. In order to implement the subtotal processing, two important things were added to sample program CHAP8B: a control break check and a *Building Control Break* module.

Let's look at the source code and see how it all fits together.

```
P R O C E S S I N G    L O O P :

void ProcessLoop(void)
{
    int   iPrevBldg;
    float fBldgTot = 0.0;
    float fRptTot = 0.0;

    ReadRecord();
```

The above statements define the local variables, set the building subtotal and report total to 0, and transfer control to the *ReadRecord* module. The priming read retrieves the first record from the rent file.

```
    iPrevBldg = iBldg;
```

The above statement saves the building number (control field) for later use. This "sets the stage" for subsequent processing. For example, the first record causes a unique problem because it has no previous building number. By copying the current building number to the previous building number, the program can avoid an untimely break on the first record.

```
    while (iAgency != 0)
    {
```

In the above statement, as long as the agency number is not equal to 0 (the value specified by the trailer record), control enters the statement body of the loop. If the agency number is 0, then the file is empty and control skips to the first executable statement after the *while* loop.

```
        fBldgTot = fBldgTot + fRent;
        fRptTot = fRptTot + fRent;
```

The above statements add the input rent to the building subtotal and the report total; they accumulate the monthly rent for the current building group and the report.

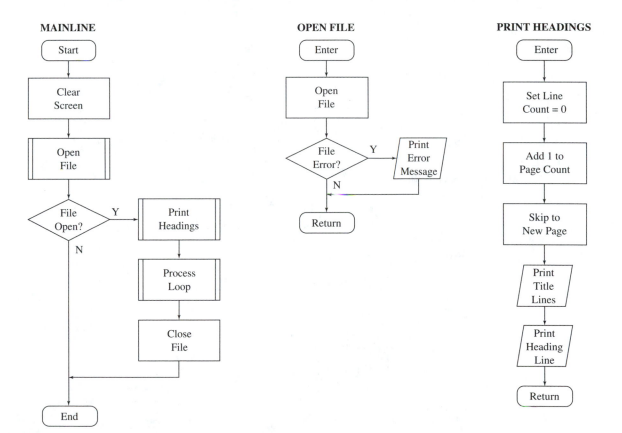

FIGURE 8.10   Program Flowchart for CHAP8B

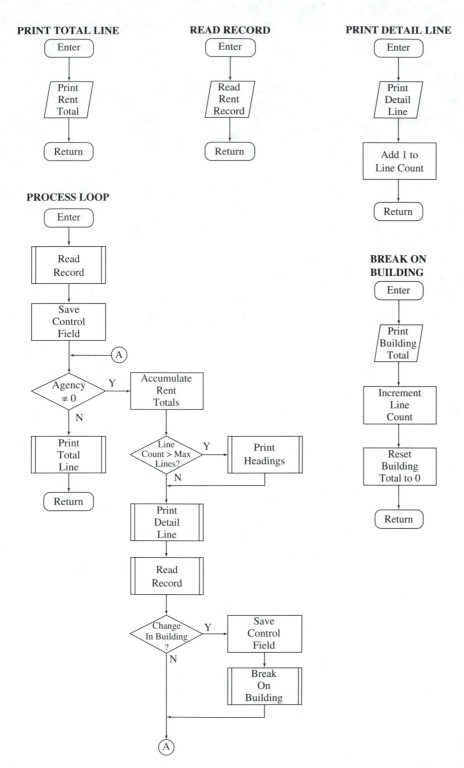

PRINT TOTAL LINE

Enter

Print
Rent
Total

Return

READ RECORD

Enter

Read
Rent
Record

Return

PRINT DETAIL LINE

Enter

Print
Detail
Line

Add 1 to
Line Count

Return

PROCESS LOOP

Enter

Read
Record

Save
Control
Field

(A)

Agency
≠ 0

Y → Accumulate
Rent
Totals

N

Print
Total
Line

Return

Line
Count > Max
Lines?

Y → Print
Headings

N

Print
Detail
Line

Read
Record

Change
In Building
?

Y → Save
Control
Field

Break
On
Building

N

(A)

**BREAK ON
BUILDING**

Enter

Print
Building
Total

Increment
Line
Count

Reset
Building
Total to 0

Return

FIGURE 8.10 *Continued*

288

```
/*----------------------------------------------------------------
RENTAL INCOME: Read rent file and print an income report for Pernell
Properties. This program demonstrates page and control break processing.

Program:   CHAP8B.C
Author:    David M. Collopy
Date:      mm/dd/yy
Project:   Sample program
*************************************************************************/


/*---- PREPROCESSING DIRECTIVES ----------------------------------------*/

#include <stdio.h>
#include <graph.h>
#define IMAXLINES 21


/*---- FUNCTION PROTOTYPES ---------------------------------------------*/

void  OpenFile(void);          /* open rent file          */
void  PrnHeadings(void);       /* print report headings   */
void  ProcessLoop(void);       /* processing loop         */
void  ReadRecord(void);        /* read rent record        */
float BreakOnBldg(float);      /* building control break  */
void  PrnDetail(void);         /* print rent detail line  */
void  PrnTotal(float);         /* print total rent        */


/*---- PROGRAM SETUP ---------------------------------------------------*/

/*>  R E P O R T   T I T L E S   A N D   H E A D I N G S       <*/

char PT1[] = "P E R N E L L   P R O P E R T I E S     Page ";
char PT2[] = "              Rental Income                   ";
char HL1[] = "LOCATION  AGENCY  MGR  BLDG    APART#     RENT ";
char DTL[] = " %-5s      %2d    %3d   %2d      %d     $%7.2f";
char CBL[] = "                     *  Bldg Total:   $ %7.2f  ";
char RTL[] = "                 *****  Report Total: $ %7.2f  ";


/*>  R E N T   R E C O R D                                     <*/

FILE *fpRent;                  /* file pointer            */
char  sLocation[6];            /* apartment location      */
int   iAgency;                 /* agency ID number        */
int   iMgr;                    /* manager ID number       */
int   iBldg;                   /* building number         */
int   iApart;                  /* apartment number        */
```

FIGURE 8.11 Sample Program CHAP8B: Demonstrates subtotal processing for Pernell Properties. Total rent income is accumulated and printed at the end of the report.

```
float fRent;                    /* monthly rent income */

/*>  P R O G R A M   V A R I A B L E S                        <*/

int   iLineCnt = 0;             /* detail line count       */

/*----------------------------------------------------------------------
        MAINLINE CONTROL
----------------------------------------------------------------------*/
main()
{
    _clearscreen(0);
    OpenFile();
    if (fpRent != 0)
    {
        PrnHeadings();
        ProcessLoop();
        fclose(fpRent);
    }
    return 0;
}


/*----------------------------------------------------------------------
        OPEN RENT FILE
----------------------------------------------------------------------*/
void OpenFile(void)
{
    fpRent = fopen("a:txRent.fil", "r");
    if (fpRent == 0)
    {
        printf("\nCannot open rent file\n");
    }
    return;
}


/*----------------------------------------------------------------------
        PRINT HEADINGS
----------------------------------------------------------------------*/
void PrnHeadings(void)
{
    static int iPageNum;         /* page count             */

    iLineCnt = 0;                /* set line count to 0     */
    iPageNum++;                  /* add 1 to page number    */
```

FIGURE 8.11   *Continued*

```
    fprintf(stdprn, "\f\r");      /* skip to new page & reset */
    fprintf(stdprn, "%s %d",      /* print page title 1       */
        PT1, iPageNum);           /*      & page number       */
    fprintf(stdprn, "\r\n");      /* reset & single space     */
    fprintf(stdprn, PT2);         /* print page title 2       */
    fprintf(stdprn, "\r\n\n");    /* reset & double space     */
    fprintf(stdprn, HL1);         /* print heading line 1     */
    fprintf(stdprn, "\r\n");      /* reset & single space     */
    return;
}


/*-----------------------------------------------------------------------
       PROCESSING LOOP
-----------------------------------------------------------------------*/
void ProcessLoop(void)
{
    int    iPrevBldg;              /* previous building number */
    float fBldgTot = 0.0;          /* building rent total      */
    float fRptTot = 0.0;           /* report rent total        */

    ReadRecord();
    iPrevBldg = iBldg;             /* save building number */
    while (iAgency != 0)
    {
        fBldgTot = fBldgTot + fRent;
        fRptTot = fRptTot + fRent;
        if (iLineCnt >= IMAXLINES)
            PrnHeadings();
        PrnDetail();
        ReadRecord();
        if (iBldg != iPrevBldg)
        {
            iPrevBldg = iBldg;
            fBldgTot = BreakOnBldg(fBldgTot);
        }
    }
    PrnTotal(fRptTot);
    return;
}


/*-----------------------------------------------------------------------
       READ RENT RECORD
-----------------------------------------------------------------------*/
void ReadRecord(void)
```

FIGURE 8.11 *Continued*

```
{
    fscanf(fpRent, " %s %d %d %d %d %f",
        sLocation, &iAgency, &iMgr, &iBldg, &iApart, &fRent);
    return;
}


/*-------------------------------------------------------------------
        PRINT RENT DETAIL LINE
--------------------------------------------------------------------*/
void PrnDetail(void)
{
    fprintf(stdprn, "\r\n");
    fprintf(stdprn, DTL, sLocation, iAgency, iMgr, iBldg, iApart, fRent);
    iLineCnt++;
    return;
}


/*-------------------------------------------------------------------
        BUILDING CONTROL BREAK
--------------------------------------------------------------------*/
float BreakOnBldg(float fBldgTot)
{
    fprintf(stdprn, "\r\n\n");
    fprintf(stdprn, CBL, fBldgTot);
    fprintf(stdprn, "\r\n");
    iLineCnt = iLineCnt + 3;
    fBldgTot = 0.0;
    return fBldgTot;
}


/*-------------------------------------------------------------------
        PRINT TOTAL RENT
--------------------------------------------------------------------*/
void PrnTotal(float fRptTot)
{
    fprintf(stdprn, "\r\n\n");
    fprintf(stdprn, RTL, fRptTot);
    return;
}
```

FIGURE 8.11 *Continued*

```
P E R N E L L   P R O P E R T I E S      Page 1
              Rental Income

LOCATION  AGENCY  MGR  BLDG    APART#     RENT

North      20    201   10        1    $  400.00
North      20    201   10        2    $  410.00
North      20    201   10        3    $  335.00

                     *  Bldg Total:   $ 1145.00

North      20    201   15        1    $  375.00
North      20    201   15        2    $  385.00

                     *  Bldg Total:   $  760.00

North      20    247   17        1    $  450.00
North      20    247   17        2    $  450.00

                     *  Bldg Total:   $  900.00

North      43    316   22        1    $  345.00
North      43    316   22        2    $  465.00

                     *  Bldg Total:   $  810.00
```

FIGURE 8.12a   Program Output for CHAP8B

```
P E R N E L L   P R O P E R T I E S      Page 2
              Rental Income

LOCATION  AGENCY  MGR  BLDG    APART#     RENT

East       10    237   30        1    $  410.00
East       10    237   30        2    $  365.00
East       10    237   30        3    $  470.00
East       10    237   30        4    $  345.00

                     *  Bldg Total:   $ 1590.00

East       10    659   33        1    $  429.00
East       10    659   33        2    $  465.00

                     *  Bldg Total:   $  894.00

              *****  Report Total:    $ 6099.00
```

FIGURE 8.12b   Program Output for CHAP8B

```
if (iLineCnt >= IMAXLINES)
    PrnHeadings();
```

The above statement compares line count to the maximum number of lines allowed per page. If line count is greater than or equal to *IMAXLINES*, then control calls *PrnHeadings*; this module prints the report titles and column heading line. Otherwise, control skips the module call and continues with the next command.

```
PrnDetail();
ReadRecord();
```

The above statements call the modules in the order shown. The *PrnDetail* module prints the current detail line, and *ReadRecord* retrieves the next record from the file.

```
if (iBldg != iPrevBldg)
{
    iPrevBldg = iBldg;
    fBldgTot = BreakOnBldg(fBldgTot);
}
```

The *if* statement compares the new and previous building numbers. If they are not equal, the program saves the *new* building number and breaks on the *previous* building. The first statement inside the body of the *if* retains the new building number for later use; this is done to prepare for the next building control group.

The second statement calls and passes the building subtotal to *BreakOnBldg*; this module prints the previous building subtotal (see the Building Control Break module shown below). In brief, 0 is returned and assigned to *fBldgTot*; this resets the new building subtotal to 0.

```
    }
    PrnTotal(fRptTot);
    return;
}
```

The above statements call and pass the total monthly rent to *PrnTotal*; this module prints the total rent at the end of the report.

The *return* statement sends control back to th*e MAINLINE*.

B U I L D I N G   C O N T R O L   B R E A K:

```
float BreakOnBldg(float fBldgTot)
{
    fprintf(stdprn, "\r\n\n");
    fprintf(stdprn, CBL, fBldgTot);
    fprintf(stdprn, "\r\n");
    lineCnt = lineCnt + 3;
```

The above statements reset the printer to the left margin and advance two lines, print the building subtotal, reset the printer to the left margin of the next line, and add three to line count (one for the blank line before, one for the subtotal line, and one for the blank line after).

The *CBL* (Control Break Line) in the second print statement specifies the format of the subtotal line. The *CBL* is defined in the *PROGRAM SETUP* section of the program.

```
    fBldgTot = 0.0;
    return fBldgTot;
}
```

The above statements reset the building subtotal to 0. This is done in preparation for the next building subtotal. Control then returns a 0 to the calling statement.

Notes and Tips

Control breaks can be tricky. If you code the right statements in the right place, you shouldn't have any problems getting them to work. Consequently, it is important to understand what a control break is and how to set up the code to produce the correct output in the proper format. For a single-level control break, use sample program CHAP8B as a guide to construct your programs. Multilevel control breaks are covered in Chapter 9.

Hint: In the processing loop, make sure you save the control field after the priming read call and before you enter the *while* loop. Once inside the loop, the only time you save the control field again is when the new control field does not equal the previous one. A change in value tells you it's time to print the subtotal and to set up for the next control group.

Another thing to watch out for is placement of the control break check. In the sample program, it is coded in the processing loop after the looping read call. But whatever you do, resist the urge to code the control break check right after the page break test. This, of course, will not produce the correct output.

For single-level control breaks, use *CBL* (Control Break Line) to label and format the subtotal. Since subtotals differ from detailed lines, use this notation to identify the control break line. In Chapter 9, we will expand on this notation to include multiple control break lines.

Tutorial CHAP8B

1. The objectives of this tutorial are to
   * process the data stored in a text file
   * code a page and control break application
2. If necessary, open the text editor and enter the sample program as shown in Figure 8.11.
3. Save the source program on your work disk as CHAP8B.
4. Compile, run, and debug your program until the output matches the control break report shown in Figures 8.12a and 8.12b.
5. When completed, show your work to your instructor.

Quick Quiz

Answer the following questions.

1. Briefly explain the processing activities performed during a control break.
2. What does the *CBL* notation stand for?
3. Recall that the line count was used to trigger a page break. In the sample program, what data item was used to force a control break?

4. The body of the *while* statement shown in the Processing Loop accumulates two totals. What are they, and how are the totals used in this application?

5. Why are there two occurrences of the following statement coded in the Processing Loop?

```
iPrevBldg = iBldg;
```

6. Did you have any problems with CHAP8B? If so, what were they and what did you do to correct them?

Summary

1. A page break occurs when the number of lines printed equals the limit established for the page.

2. Line count is used to determine when to perform a page break. Each time a line is printed, line count is incremented and compared to the maximum number of lines allowed per page. If the count equals the limit, then the program performs a page break.

3. Page count is used to keep track of the number of pages printed. Each time a page is printed, page count is incremented.

4. When a page break is encountered, the printer advances to a new page, prints the title and column headings, and continues with the body of the report.

5. A control field is a special field in the input record that is used to arrange the records in either ascending or descending order. The contents of the control field is used by the program to determine when to perform a control break.

6. Records arranged in control field order can be processed to produce a subtotal. A subtotal is part of a total that is accumulated and printed in relationship to a control group.

7. A control break involves grouping related records and processing them together as a single unit.

8. A control break occurs when the contents of the current control field do not match the contents of the previous control field.

9. When a control break is encountered, the previous subtotal is printed and the input is added to the subtotal for the new control group.

10. After the data has been read and processed, the subtotal for the last group is printed along with the report total.

Programming Projects

For each project, design the logic and write the modular structured program to produce the output. Model your program after the sample programs presented in the chapter. Verify your output.

Project 8–1   Payroll-1

Write a page break program to read a payroll file, calculate gross pay, and print a gross pay report. Assume overtime is not computed.

Input (text file):
For each payroll record, read and assign data to the following fields. (Field size and type are shown in parentheses.)

1. Branch number   (1 int)
2. Division number   (2 int)
3. Department number   (3 int)
4. Employee name   (20 char)
5. Hours worked   (2 int)
6. Hourly pay rate   (5.2 float)

Text File (txPayrol.fil):
Use the data given below to create the payroll file. (The numbers shown above the columns correspond to the fields described for the input.)

1	2	3	4	5	6
1	10	100	Tanya Bauer	40	7.50
1	10	100	Diane Dixon	40	9.75
1	10	106	Randy Karns	37	8.55
1	20	112	Dana Clark	45	14.90
1	20	112	Nick Larson	43	7.72
1	20	112	Colleen Norris	40	11.35
1	20	123	Sara Erickson	38	12.00
1	40	117	Scott Howard	42	9.75
2	10	105	Paul Irwin	48	8.72
2	10	105	Cyndi Olson	45	15.10
2	18	144	Dale Miller	40	10.25
3	23	121	Bret Rossi	35	8.00
3	23	121	Karen Thomas	48	9.00
3	23	137	Cheryl Dietz	42	7.50
3	23	137	Neil Kenney	38	7.25
3	34	150	Tracy York	36	11.00
0	00	000	Trailer Record	00	0.00

Output (printer):
Print the following page break report:

```
Author              C O M P A N Y   P A Y R O L L            Page 99

                           Gross Pay Report
                              mm/dd/yy


Branch    Division    Department    Employee Name      Gross Pay
```

```
    9           99          999         X------------ X       999.99
    :           :           :                   :              :
    :           :           :                   :              :
    9           99          999         X------------X        999.99

                                 ****   Report Total:        9999.99
```

Processing Requirements:

- Read the payroll file.
- Print 10 detail lines per page.
- Compute the gross pay:
  hours worked × pay rate.
- Accumulate a report total for gross pay.

Project 8–2   Payroll-2

Modify the program in Project 8–1 to include control break processing. Group and list employee gross pay by department, and print the department subtotal for each group. Print a blank line before and after the subtotal. Be sure to include the blank lines in the line count. Print 28 detail lines per page. Model the logic after sample program CHAP8B.

Print the following control break report:

```
Author               C O M P A N Y    P A Y R O L L          Page 99

                           Gross Pay Report
                             mm/dd/yy

    Branch    Division    Department    Employee Name        Gross Pay

      9          99          999        X------------X         999.99
      :          :           :                 :                 :
      :          :           :                 :                 :
      9          99          999        X------------X         999.99

                                   *   Department Total:       9999.99
                   . . . . .                   . . . . .
                                 ****  Report Total:          99999.99
```

Project 8–3   Sales Analysis-1

Write a page break program to read a sales file, accumulate total customer sales, and print a sales analysis report.

Input (text file):

For each sales record, read and assign data to the following fields. (Field size and type are shown in parentheses.)

1. Region number   (1 int)
2. State code   (2 char)
3. Store number   (3 int)
4. Salesperson number   (3 int)

5. Customer number   (4 int)

6. Sales amount   (6.2 float)

Text File (txSales.fil):

Use the data given below to create the sales file. (The numbers shown above the columns correspond to the fields described for the input.)

1	2	3	4	5	6
1	OH	100	190	1180	380.00
1	OH	100	190	3100	273.00
1	OH	100	225	2510	161.00
1	OH	210	287	5090	492.00
1	IN	198	338	4200	185.00
1	IN	198	412	6100	200.00
1	IN	198	412	9430	300.00
2	KY	279	206	2900	563.00
2	KY	279	490	3000	175.00
2	KY	300	640	3100	100.00
2	KY	313	110	7170	400.00
3	PA	121	720	1200	369.00
3	PA	239	378	2600	349.00
3	PA	239	600	5500	200.00
0	XX	000	000	0000	000.00 (trailer record)

Output (printer):

Print the following page break report:

```
Author              SALES ANALYSIS REPORT           Page 99
                         mm/dd/yy


Region   State   Store   Salesperson   Customer   Sales
------------------------------------------------------------
  9       XX      999        999         9999     999.99
  :        :       :          :            :         :
  :        :       :          :            :         :
  9       XX      999        999         9999     999.99

                       *****  Report Total:       9999.99
```

Processing Requirements:

- Read the sales file.
- Print 10 detail lines per page.
- Accumulate a report total for customer sales.

Project 8–4   Sales Analysis-2

Modify the program in Project 8–3 to include control break processing. Group and list customer sales by salesperson, and print the salesperson subtotal for each group. Print a blank line before and after the subtotal. Be sure to include the blank lines in the line count. Print 30 detail lines per page. Model the logic after sample program CHAP8B.

Print the following control break report:

```
Author                SALES ANALYSIS REPORT              Page 99
                          mm/dd/yy

Region    State   Store   Salesperson   Customer   Sales
------------------------------------------------------------
  9        XX      999        999          9999    999.99
  :         :       :          :             :        :
  :         :       :          :             :        :
  9        XX      999        999          9999    999.99

                              *  Salesperson Total: 9999.99
          . . . . .                      . . . . .
                         *****  Report Total:       9999.99
```

Project 8–5   Inventory-1

Write a page break program to read an inventory file, accumulate total quantity on hand, and print an inventory analysis report.

Input (text file):
For each inventory record, read and assign data to the following fields. (Field size and type are shown in parentheses.)

1. Region number   (1 int)
2. State code   (2 char)
3. Location number   (2 int)
4. Warehouse number   (3 int)
5. Item number   (5 char)
6. Quantity on hand   (2 int)

Text File (txInven.fil):
Use the data given below to create the inventory file. (The numbers shown above the columns correspond to the fields described for the input.)

1	2	3	4	5	6
1	OH	43	101	A7100	24
1	OH	43	101	B0340	12
1	OH	43	101	D0019	35
1	OH	43	340	C1970	48
1	OH	43	340	H0120	16
1	OH	66	220	F3170	96
1	OH	66	220	K8800	24
1	IN	27	125	C5510	12
1	IN	27	125	I1700	36
2	KY	18	107	B1776	24
2	KY	18	107	D0011	30
2	KY	18	130	F0910	36

```
2    KY    18    130    L7650    96
2    KY    18    130    P0150    15
0    XX    00    000    X0000    00    (trailer record)
```

Output (printer):

Print the following page break report:

```
Author            INVENTORY ANALYSIS REPORT              Page 99
                        mm/dd/yy


Region    State    Location    Warehouse    Item#    Quantity

  9         XX        99          999        XXXXX      99
  :         :         :           :          :          :
  :         :         :           :          :          :
  9         XX        99          999        XXXXX      99


                        *****   Report Total:      999
```

Processing Requirements:

- Read the inventory file.
- Print 10 detail lines per page.
- Accumulate a report total for quantity on hand.

Project 8–6   Inventory-2

Modify the program in Project 8–5 to include control break processing. Group and list the quantity on hand by warehouse, and print the warehouse subtotal for each group. Print a blank line before and after the subtotal. Be sure to include the blank lines in the line count. Print 21 detail lines per page. Model the logic after sample program CHAP8B.

Print the following control break report:

```
Author            INVENTORY ANALYSIS REPORT              Page 99
                        mm/dd/yy


Region    State    Location    Warehouse    Item#    Quantity

  9         XX        99          999        XXXXX      99
  :         :         :           :          :          :
  :         :         :           :          :          :
  9         XX        99          999        XXXXX      99


                           *   Warehouse Total:     999
            . . . . .                        . . . .
                        *****   Report Total:       999
```

Project 8–7   Personnel-1

Write a page break program to read a personnel file, count the number of employees, and print a personnel report.

Input (text file):
For each record, read and assign data to the following fields. (Field size and type are shown in parentheses.)

1. Branch number   (1 int)
2. Division number   (2 int)
3. Department number   (3 int)
4. Manager number   (2 int)
5. Supervisor number   (4 int)
6. Employee count   (2 int)

Text File (txPersnl.fil):
Use the data given below to create the personnel file. (The numbers shown above the columns correspond to the fields described for the input.)

1	2	3	4	5	6
1	10	101	20	2010	08
1	10	101	20	2025	12
1	10	101	30	3050	16
1	10	101	30	3055	12
1	10	101	30	3060	10
1	10	120	45	4520	14
1	10	120	45	4530	12
1	20	206	12	1210	07
1	20	206	12	1220	12
2	15	115	22	2210	15
2	15	115	22	2230	12
2	15	210	33	3340	18
2	15	210	33	3360	16
2	15	210	45	4510	10
2	15	210	45	4550	12
2	27	108	26	2630	12
2	27	108	26	2640	16
2	27	108	26	2680	14
0	00	000	00	0000	00 (trailer record)

Output (printer):
Print the following page break report:

```
Author              P E R S O N N E L   R E P O R T              Page 99

                             Employee Count
                               mm/dd/yy

    Branch   Division   Department   Manager   Supervisor   Employees

      9         99         999         99         9999          99
      :          :          :          :           :            :
      :          :          :          :           :            :
```

```
9          99          999      99        9999        99

                    *****  Report Total:          999
```

Processing Requirements:

- Read the personnel file.
- Print 10 detail lines per page.
- Accumulate a report total for employee count.

Project 8–8   Personnel-2

Modify the program in Project 8–7 to include control break processing. Group and list the employee count by manager, and print the manager subtotal for each group. Print a blank line before and after the subtotal. Be sure to include the blank lines in the line count. Print 25 detail lines per page. Model the logic after sample program CHAP8B.

Print the following control break report:

```
Author              P E R S O N N E L   R E P O R T          Page 99

                        Employee Count
                          mm/dd/yy

 Branch  Division  Department  Manager  Supervisor  Employees

   9        99        999        99        9999         99
   :         :         :          :          :           :
   :         :         :          :          :           :
   9        99        999        99        9999         99

                                 *   Manager Total:        99
          . . . . .                          . . . . .
                             *****  Report Total:         999
```

9 Multilevel Control Breaks

Overview

Learning Objectives

After you have read this chapter and completed the exercises, you should be able to

- arrange the input data in multilevel control field order
- design and write multilevel control break programs
- combine page break and control break processing to produce multipage, multilevel subtotal reports

Multilevel Control Break Reports

This chapter expands upon the control break processing techniques introduced in Chapter 8. As you may recall, sample program CHAP8B printed a simple one-level rental income report for Pernell Properties. The program executed a single control break and printed a subtotal line each time the building number (the control field) changed. The format of the income report is shown in Figure 9.1.

Some business applications require reports that contain multilevel control totals or subtotals. Such totals may go two, three, four, or more levels deep; the actual number of levels depends mostly on the application at hand.

In general, a **multilevel control break** consists of two or more subtotals. For example, in Figure 9.1, we could accumulate the rent by manager and building. Or we could accumulate the rent by agency, manager, and building. Actually, there are four levels of totals that we could accumulate for the rent income: location total, agency total, manager total, and building total. Hence, a four-level control break report would show the rent by location, agency, manager, and building.

Chapter 9 presents a structured approach to designing multilevel control break reports. In the sections that follow, we will see how to develop a two-level and a four-level control break program for Pernell Properties. Once you understand the logic behind the approach, you will be able to apply it to other programming applications as well.

Planning a Two-Level Control Break Program

Assume that management wants us to develop a two-level control break program that lists the rent income for Pernell Properties by manager and building. The planning process involves the following steps. First, use a printer spacing chart to design the output; be sure to include the subtotal lines. Second, arrange the data in ascending order by manager and building. Third, develop the logic required to force the program to break when either control field changes value.

```
 P E R N E L L    P R O P E R T I E S        Page 9
                Rental Income


LOCATION   AGENCY   MGR   BLDG    APART#        RENT

  X---X       99    999    99       9       $ 999.99
    :         :      :      :        :           :
    :         :      :      :        :           :
  X---X       99    999    99       9       $ 999.99


                     *  Bldg Total:       $ 9999.99
 . . . . .                      . . . . .
                  *****  Report Total:    $ 9999.99
```

FIGURE 9.1   A One-Level Control Break Report

```
P E R N E L L    P R O P E R T I E S      Page 9
                  Rental Income

LOCATION   AGENCY   MGR   BLDG   APART#     RENT

  X---X      99     999    99      9      $ 999.99
    :         :      :      :       :         :
    :         :      :      :       :         :
  X---X      99     999    99      9      $ 999.99

                      *   Bldg Total:    $ 9999.99
                     **   Mgr Total:     $ 9999.99
      . . . . .              . . . . .
                   *****   Report Total:  $ 9999.99
```

FIGURE 9.2   A Two-Level Control Break Report

Essentially, we want the report to show the rent by manager and building. That is, we want the building subtotal to print when the building number changes, and we want the building and manager subtotals to print when the manager number changes.

A two-level control break (see Figure 9.2) contains a major and a minor control field. For the rental income application, manager number is the major and building number is the minor control field. A break on the **major control field** forces the program to print the minor control total first, followed by the major control total. A break on the **minor control field** forces the program to print only the minor control total. Notice that a two-level control break provides three levels of totals: one for the manager, one for the building, and one for the report. The asterisks shown in Figure 9.2 correspond to the level of the totals; * indicates the first level, ** indicate the second level, and so on. Look at the five asterisks shown next to the report total. This notation indicates that the report total represents the fifth level. This topic will be discussed later in this chapter.

Because a break may occur on the manager or the building number, the program logic must be designed to execute a break on either control field. Here is how it works. According to the logic in Figure 9.3, when a control break is detected for the building number, the program saves the new building number, prints the building subtotal, increments the line counter, and sets the new building subtotal to 0 in preparation for the next building group.

However, when a control break is detected for the manager number, the program saves the new manager and building numbers, prints the building subtotal, increments the line counter, sets the new building subtotal to 0 (for the next *building* group), prints the manager subtotal, increments the line counter, and sets the new manager subtotal to 0 (for the next *manager* group).

The important thing to remember is that when a major control break occurs, the program executes the minor control break first. Hence, for a break on manager, the program must print the building subtotal before it prints the manager subtotal. This must be done this way, because the building subtotal "belongs to," or is part of, the previous manager subtotal.

```
MANAGER CONTROL BREAK DETECTED
Save new manager and building numbers
Call Break On Building
Call Break On Manager

BUILDING CONTROL BREAK DETECTED
Save new building number
Call Break On Building

BREAK ON MANAGER
Print manager rent total, increment line count, and set new
manager rent total to 0

BREAK ON BUILDING
Print building rent total, increment line count, and set new
building rent total to 0
```

FIGURE 9.3   Two-Level Control Break Logic

Checkpoint 9A

1. Explain why it is important to be able to develop multilevel control break programs.

2. List the steps involved in planning a multilevel control break program.

3. How many totals will a two-level control break program produce? a three-level? a four-level? a ten-level?

4. Show the pseudocode logic for the Break on Manager and Break on Building modules.

Sample Program CHAP9A

This program demonstrates application of a two-level control break to produce the rental income report for Pernell Properties. See Figure 9.4 for the hierarchy chart and Figure 9.5 for the flowchart. Sample program CHAP9A is shown in Figure 9.6; the output report is shown in Figure 9.7.

Once again, the input has been arranged in ascending order to facilitate control break processing. Sample program CHAP9A uses the manager number as the major control field and the building number as the minor control field.

The following specifications apply:

Input (text file):
For each record, read and assign data to the following fields. (Field size and type are shown in parentheses.)

1. Location   (5 char)

2. Agency number   (2 int)

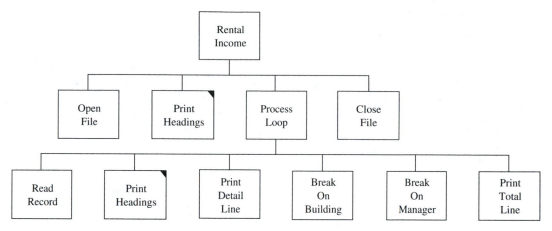

FIGURE 9.4   Hierarchy Chart for CHAP9A

3. Manager number   (3 int)
4. Building number   (2 int)
5. Apartment number   (1 int)
6. Monthly rent   (6.2 float)

Text File (txRent.fil)

Use the data given below to create the rent file. (The numbers shown above the columns correspond to the fields described for the input.)

1	2	3	4	5	6
North	20	201	10	1	400.00
North	20	201	10	2	410.00
North	20	201	10	3	335.00
North	20	201	15	1	375.00
North	20	201	15	2	385.00
North	20	247	17	1	450.00
North	20	247	17	2	450.00
North	43	316	22	1	345.00
North	43	316	22	2	465.00
East	10	237	30	1	410.00
East	10	237	30	2	365.00
East	10	237	30	3	470.00
East	10	237	30	4	345.00
East	10	659	33	1	429.00
East	10	659	33	2	465.00
End	00	000	00	0	000.00 (trailer record)

Output (printer)

Print the two-level control break report shown in Figures 9.7a and 9.7b.

MAINLINE

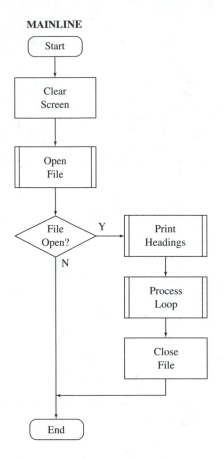

OPEN FILE

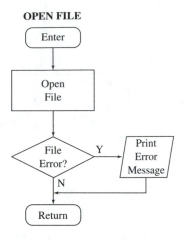

PRINT HEADINGS

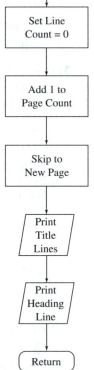

FIGURE 9.5   Program Flowchart for CHAP9A

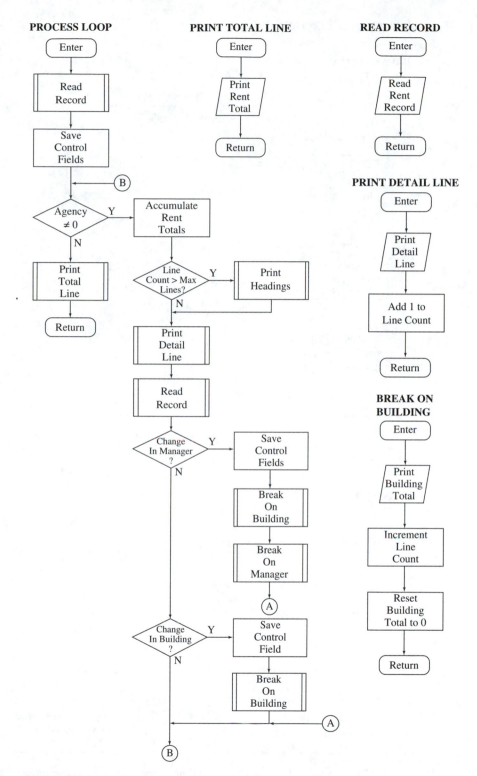

FIGURE 9.5 *Continued*

BREAK ON MANAGER

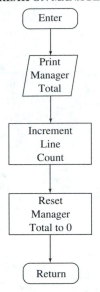

FIGURE 9.5   *Continued*

```
/*--------------------------------------------------------------
RENTAL INCOME: Read rent file and print a two-level control break
report for Pernell Properties.

Program:    CHAP9A.C
Author:     David M. Collopy
Date:       mm/dd/yy
Project:    Sample program
*****************************************************************/


/*---- PREPROCESSING DIRECTIVES ------------------------------*/

#include <stdio.h>
#include <graph.h>
#define IMAXLINES 23


/*---- FUNCTION PROTOTYPES ------------------------------------*/

void  OpenFile(void);               /* open rent file          */
void  PrnHeadings(void);            /* print report headings   */
void  ProcessLoop(void);           /* processing loop         */
```

FIGURE 9.6   Sample Program CHAP9A: Demonstrates a two-level control break report for Pernell Properties.

```
void  ReadRecord(void);          /* read rent record      */
float BreakOnMgr(float);         /* manager control break */
float BreakOnBldg(float);        /* building control break */
void  PrnDetail(void);           /* print rent detail line */
void  PrnTotal(float);           /* print total rent      */

/*---- PROGRAM SETUP -------------------------------------------*/

/*> R E P O R T   T I T L E S   A N D   H E A D I N G S    <*/

char PT1[] = "P E R N E L L   P R O P E R T I E S     Page ";
char PT2[] = "                    Rental Income                ";
char HL1[] = "LOCATION  AGENCY  MGR  BLDG    APART#     RENT ";
char DTL[] = " %-5s      %2d    %3d   %2d       %d       $%7.2f";
char CB1[] = "                     *  Bldg Total:   $ %7.2f   ";
char CB2[] = "                    **  Mgr Total:    $ %7.2f   ";
char RTL[] = "                 *****  Report Total: $ %7.2f   ";

/*> R E N T   R E C O R D                                   <*/

FILE *fpRent;                    /* file pointer          */
char  sLocation[6];              /* apartment location    */
int   iAgency;                   /* agency ID number      */
int   iMgr;                      /* manager ID number     */
int   iBldg;                     /* building number       */
int   iApart;                    /* apartment number      */
float fRent;                     /* monthly rent income   */

/*> P R O G R A M   V A R I A B L E S                       <*/

int   iLineCnt = 0;              /* detail line count     */

/*-------------------------------------------------------------
      MAINLINE CONTROL
-------------------------------------------------------------*/
main()
{
    _clearscreen(0);;
    OpenFile();
    if (fpRent != 0)
    {
        PrnHeadings();
        ProcessLoop();
        fclose(fpRent);
    }
```

FIGURE 9.6 *Continued*

```
        return 0;
    }

/*-------------------------------------------------------------
        OPEN RENT FILE
-----------------------------------------------------------*/
void OpenFile(void)
{
    fpRent = fopen("a:txRent.fil", "r");
    if (fpRent == 0)
    {
        printf("\nCannot open rent file\n");
    }
    return;
}


/*-------------------------------------------------------------
        PRINT REPORT HEADINGS
-----------------------------------------------------------*/
void PrnHeadings(void)
{
    static int iPageNum;         /* page number                 */

    iLineCnt = 0;                /* set line count to 0       */
    iPageNum++;                  /* add 1 to page number      */
    fprintf(stdprn, "\f\r");     /* skip to new page & reset  */
    fprintf(stdprn, "%s %d",     /* print page title 1        */
        PT1, iPageNum);          /*     & page number         */
    fprintf(stdprn, "\r\n");     /* reset & single space      */
    fprintf(stdprn, PT2);        /* print page title 2        */
    fprintf(stdprn, "\r\n\n");   /* reset & double space      */
    fprintf(stdprn, HL1);        /* print heading line 1      */
    fprintf(stdprn, "\r\n");     /* reset & single space      */
    return;
}


/*-------------------------------------------------------------
        PROCESSING LOOP
-----------------------------------------------------------*/
void ProcessLoop(void)
{
    int    iPrevMgr;             /* previous manager number   */
    int    iPrevBldg;            /* previous building number  */
    float  fMgrTot = 0.0;        /* manager rent total        */
    float  fBldgTot = 0.0;       /* building rent total       */
    float  fRptTot = 0.0;        /* report rent total         */
```

FIGURE 9.6 *Continued*

```
        ReadRecord();
        iPrevMgr = iMgr;               /* save manager number    */
        iPrevBldg = iBldg;             /* save building number   */
        while (iAgency != 0)
        {
            fMgrTot = fMgrTot + fRent;
            fBldgTot = fBldgTot + fRent;
            fRptTot = fRptTot + fRent;
            if (iLineCnt >= IMAXLINES)
            {
                PrnHeadings();
            }
            PrnDetail();
            ReadRecord();
            if (iMgr != iPrevMgr)
            {
                iPrevMgr = iMgr;
                iPrevBldg = iBldg;
                fBldgTot = BreakOnBldg(fBldgTot);
                fMgrTot = BreakOnMgr(fMgrTot);
            }
            else if (iBldg != iPrevBldg)
            {
                iPrevBldg = iBldg;
                fBldgTot = BreakOnBldg(fBldgTot);
            }
        }
        PrnTotal(fRptTot);
        return;
}


/*-----------------------------------------------------------
        READ RENT RECORD
-----------------------------------------------------------*/
void ReadRecord(void)
{
    fscanf(fpRent, " %s %d %d %d %d %f",
        sLocation, &iAgency, &iMgr, &iBldg, &iApart, &fRent);
    return;
}


/*-----------------------------------------------------------
        PRINT RENT DETAIL LINE
-----------------------------------------------------------*/
```

FIGURE 9.6 *Continued*

```
void PrnDetail(void)
{
    fprintf(stdprn, "\r\n");
    fprintf(stdprn, DTL, sLocation, iAgency, iMgr, iBldg,
        iApart, fRent);
    iLineCnt++;
    return;
}


/*---------------------------------------------------------------
      MANAGER CONTROL BREAK
-----------------------------------------------------------------*/
float BreakOnMgr(float fMgrTot)
{

    fprintf(stdprn, "\r");
    fprintf(stdprn, CB2, fMgrTot);
    fprintf(stdprn, "\r\n");
    iLineCnt = iLineCnt + 2;
    fMgrTot = 0.0;
    return fMgrTot;
}


/*---------------------------------------------------------------
      BUILDING CONTROL BREAK
-----------------------------------------------------------------*/
float BreakOnBldg(float fBldgTot)
{

    fprintf(stdprn, "\r\n\n");
    fprintf(stdprn, CB1, fBldgTot);
    fprintf(stdprn, "\r\n");
    iLineCnt = iLineCnt + 2;
    fBldgTot = 0.0;
    return fBldgTot;
}


/*---------------------------------------------------------------
      PRINT TOTAL RENT
-----------------------------------------------------------------*/
void PrnTotal(float fRptTot)
{
    fprintf(stdprn, "\r\n\n");
    fprintf(stdprn, RTL, fRptTot);
    return;
}
```

FIGURE 9.6 *Continued*

Processing Requirements:

- Read the rent file.
- Print 23 detail lines per page.
- Subtotal rent by building.
- Subtotal rent by manager.
- Accumulate a report total for the rent.

Pseudocode:

```
START
Clear screen
Call Open file
IF file opened
      Call Print Headings
      Call Process Loop
      Call file
END IF
END
```

```
P E R N E L L   P R O P E R T I E S        Page 1
                 Rental Income


LOCATION  AGENCY  MGR   BLDG    APART#       RENT

North       20    201    10       1      $  400.00
North       20    201    10       2      $  410.00
North       20    201    10       3      $  335.00

                   *  Bldg Total:   $ 1145.00

North       20    201    15       1      $  375.00
North       20    201    15       2      $  385.00

                   *  Bldg Total:   $  760.00
                  **  Mgr Total:    $ 1905.00

North       20    247    17       1      $  450.00
North       20    247    17       2      $  450.00

                   *  Bldg Total:   $  900.00
                  **  Mgr Total:    $  900.00

North       43    316    22       1      $  345.00
North       43    316    22       2      $  465.00

                   *  Bldg Total:   $  810.00
                  **  Mgr Total:    $  810.00
```

FIGURE 9.7a   Program Output for CHAP9A

```
P E R N E L L    P R O P E R T I E S        Page 2
                   Rental Income

LOCATION   AGENCY   MGR   BLDG    APART#      RENT

East         10     237    30       1      $  410.00
East         10     237    30       2      $  365.00
East         10     237    30       3      $  470.00
East         10     237    30       4      $  345.00

                     *   Bldg Total:    $ 1590.00
                    **   Mgr  Total:    $ 1590.00

East         10     659    33       1      $  429.00
East         10     659    33       2      $  465.00

                     *   Bldg Total:    $  894.00
                    **   Mgr  Total:    $  894.00


                 *****   Report Total:  $ 6099.00
```

FIGURE 9.7b   Program Output for CHAP9A

ENTER: Open File
Open rent file
IF file not opened
        Print error - cannot open file
END IF
RETURN

ENTER: Print Headings
Set line counter to 0
Add 1 to page number
Advance to top of page
Print 2 page titles lines and page number
Print 1 column heading line
RETURN

ENTER: Process Loop
Call Read Rent Record
Save manager number
Save building number
LOOP while agency not = 0
        Accumulate manager rent total
        Accumulate building rent total
        Accumulate report rent total
        If line counter > 23
                Call Print Headings

```
            END IF
            Call Print Detail Line
            Call Read Rent Record
            If new manager not = previous manager
                    Save new manager number
                    Save new building number
                    Call Break On Building
                    Call Break On Manager
            else IF new building not = previous building
                    Save new building number
                    Call Break On Building
            END IF
    END LOOP
    Call Print Total Rent
    RETURN

    ENTER: Read Rent Record
    Read a record from the file:
            apartment location
            agency ID number
            manager ID number
            building number
            apartment number
            monthly rent income
    RETURN

    ENTER: Print Detail Line
    Print rent detail line:
            apartment location
            agency ID number
            manager ID number
            building number
            apartment number
            monthly rent income
    Add 1 to line count
    RETURN

    ENTER: Break On Manager
    Print manager rent total
    Add 2 to line count
    Set new manager rent total to 0
    RETURN

    ENTER: Break On Building
    Print building rent total
    Add 2 to line count
    Save new building rent total to 0
    RETURN

    ENTER: Print Total Rent
    Print report rent total
    RETURN
```

Hierarchy Chart: See Figure 9.4.

Program Flowchart: See Figure 9.5.

Dissection of Sample Program CHAP9A

Overall, the logic used for sample program CHAP9A is similar in structure to that shown in sample program CHAP8B. A few modifications were made to include the control break on manager number. For example, the program computes a manager subtotal for rent and checks for a change in manager number—the major control field. When the manager numbers change, the program saves the new control fields, performs a double control break, and prints the building and manager subtotals.

```
P R O C E S S I N G    L O O P:
void ProcessLoop(void)
{
    int    iPrevMgr;
    int    iPrevBldg;
    float fMgrTot = 0.0;
    float fBldgTot = 0.0;
    float fRptTot = 0.0;

    ReadRecord();
```

The above declarations define the local variables; the subtotals and the report total are set to 0. The call statement sends control to *ReadRecord*; this module retrieves the first record from the file.

```
    iPrevMgr = iMgr;
    iPrevBldg = iBldg;
```

The above statements save the major and minor control fields for later use. Recall that this process sets the stage for the control break check coded in the *while* loop. By copying the manager and building numbers to the previous control fields, the program can avoid an untimely break on the first record.

```
    while (iAgency != 0)
    {
```

In the above statement, as long as the agency number is not equal to 0, control enters the body of the loop. Otherwise, the file is empty and control skips to the first executable statement coded after the *while* loop.

```
        fMgrTot = fMgrTot + fRent;
        fBldgTot = fBldgTot + fRent;
        fRptTot = fRptTot + fRent;
```

The above statements add the input rent to the manager and building subtotals and to the report total; they accumulate the monthly rent for the current control groups and the report.

```
        if (iLineCnt >= IMAXLINES)
        {
            PrnHeadings();
        }
```

The above statement compares line count to the maximum number of lines. If line count is greater than or equal to *IMAXLINES*, then control calls the Print Headings module and prints the report titles and column heading. Else, control skips the module call and continues with the next statement.

```
        PrnDetail();
        ReadRecord();
```

The above statements call the modules in the order shown. The *PrnDetail* module prints the current detail line, and *ReadRecord* gets the next record from the file.

```
        if (iMgr != iPrevMgr)
        {
            iPrevMgr = iMgr;
            iPrevBldg = iBldg;
            fBldgTot = BreakOnBldg(fBldgTot);
            fMgrTot = BreakOnMgr(fMgrTot);
        }
```

The *if* statement checks for a break on the major control field. If the new and previous manager numbers are not equal, the program saves the *new* manager and building numbers and breaks on the *previous* building and manager, respectively. The first two statements after the opening brace retain the new manager and building numbers for later use; this is done to prepare for the next manager and building control groups.

The third statement calls and passes the building subtotal to *BreakOnBldg*; this module prints the previous building subtotal, increments line count, and resets the new building subtotal to 0.

The fourth statement calls and passes the manager subtotal to *BreakOnMgr*; this module prints the previous manager subtotal, increments line count, and resets the new manager subtotal to 0.

```
        else if (iBldg != iPrevBldg)
        {
            iPrevBldg = iBldg;
            fBldgTot = BreakOnBldg(fBldgTot);
        }
```

The *else if* statement checks for a break on the minor control field. If the new and previous building numbers are not equal, the program saves the *new* building number and breaks on the *previous* building. The first statement coded after the opening brace retains the new building number for later use; this is done to prepare for the next building control group.

The second statement calls and passes the building subtotal to *BreakOnBldg*; this module prints the previous building subtotal, increments line count, and resets the new building subtotal to 0.

```
    }
    PrnTotal(fRptTot);
    return;
}
```

The above call statement passes the total monthly rent to *PrnTotal*; this module prints the total rent at the end of the report.

The *return* statement sends control back to the *MAINLINE*.

Notes and Tips

The key to coding successful multilevel control breaks can be found in the Processing Loop of the sample program. Take another look at the code shown there. Since you are now dealing with a major and a minor control field, it is important to understand when to break on what field.

Take a look at the second *if* statement coded inside the *while* loop. Notice how the true and false paths are set up.

For the true path, the condition test checks for a change in the manager number. If a change is found, then you have a break on the major control field. Recall that a major control break forces the program to print the minor-level subtotal first, followed by the major-level subtotal.

On the other hand, the false path checks for a change in the building number. If a change is found, then you have a break on the minor control field. A minor control break forces the program to print *only* the minor-level subtotal.

In summary, whenever there is a break on the major control field, the progam must print the minor-level subtotal first, followed by the major-level subtotal. This is an important concept to remember!

One more thing. Did you notice the use of *CB1* and *CB2*? They are declared in the Program Setup section of the sample program. *CB1* (*Control Break 1*) is used to print the minor-level subtotal, and *CB2* (*Control Break 2*) is used to print the major-level subtotal.

Note: In control break applications, it is not unusual to use the words *subtotal* and *total* interchangeably. For example, *manager total* and *manager subtotal* refer to the same thing. Technically speaking, *report total* is the only real total used in sample program CHAP9A. All the others are subtotals.

Tutorial CHAP9A

1. The objectives of this tutorial are to
   - process the data stored in a text file
   - code a multilevel control break program

2. Open the text editor, and enter the sample program shown in Figure 9.6.

3. Save the source code on your work disk as CHAP9A.

4. Compile, run, and debug your program until the output matches the rental report shown in Figures 9.7a and 9.7b.

5. When completed, show your work to your instructor.

Quick Quiz

Answer the following questions.

1. The print lines *CB1*, *CB2*, and *RTL* are declared in the Program Setup section of the program. What do the notations stand for, and how are they used to produce the two-level control break report?

2. Identify two data items that are used to detect the control breaks. Under what conditions do they force the program to execute the control breaks?

3. The second *if* statement coded inside the *Processing Loop* checks for the manager control break before it tests for a change in buildings. Is this really necessary? Or could you check for a change in buildings before you test for a change in managers?

4. Did you have any problems with CHAP9A? If so, what were they and what did you do to correct them?

Planning a Four-Level Control Break Program

Now management would like to see the rent income broken down by location, agency, manager, and building. The format of the report is shown in Figure 9.8. Obviously, the data must be arranged in ascending order by control fields to facilitate processing by the program. That is, the input must be ordered by location. Within each location, the input must be ordered by agency number. Within each agency, the input must be ordered by manager number. And within each manager, the input must be ordered by building number. At first, the logic may seem more complicated than it really is.

Clearly, the program has four control fields: location, agency, manager, and building. Location represents the major control field, agency and manager represent the intermediate, and building represents the minor control field. An **intermediate control field** represents a control field between the major and minor control fields.

```
P E R N E L L   P R O P E R T I E S        Page 9
                Rental Income


LOCATION  AGENCY  MGR  BLDG   APART#        RENT

  X---X      99   999   99      9       $ 999.99
   :         :     :     :      :           :
   :         :     :     :      :           :
  X---X      99   999   99      9       $ 999.99

                    *   Bldg Total:    $ 9999.99
                   **   Mgr Total:     $ 9999.99
                  ***   Agency Total:  $ 9999.99
                 ****   Loc Total:     $ 9999.99


       . . . . .              . . . . .

                *****   Report Total:  $ 9999.99
```

FIGURE 9.8   A Four-Level Control Break Report

Notice that a four-level control break provides five totals, one for each control field and one for the report. Again, the asterisks shown on the report (see Figure 9.8) correspond to the level (1–5) of the totals.

Because a control break may occur at any one of the four levels, the program logic must be designed to print the subtotals from the "inside out." Thus, the minor subtotal (building) must be printed before the intermediate subtotals (manager and agency), and the intermediate subtotals must be printed before the major subtotal (location). This is done this way because the inner subtotals are actually part of the outer subtotals.

In order to see how this works, let's consider a control break on agency number. According to the logic in Figure 9.9, when a control break is detected for the agency number, the program saves the new agency, manager, and building numbers; prints the building subtotal; increments the line counter; sets the new building subtotal to 0 (for the next *building* group); prints the manager subtotal; increments the line counter; sets the new manager subtotal to 0 (for the next *manager* group); and prints the agency subtotal, increments the line counter, and sets the new agency subtotal to 0 (for the next *agency* group).

For a multilevel control break program, it is important to realize that each time a break occurs, the program saves the new control fields and executes the minor control break first. Upon returning from the lower-level control break modules, the program calls and executes the remaining control breaks "inside out."

Checkpoint 9B

1. What is a major control field? an intermediate control field? a minor control field?

2. Explain what it means to design the program logic so the subtotals print from the "inside out."

3. Show the pseudocode logic for the control break checks.

Sample Program CHAP9B

Sample program CHAP9B illustrates application of a four-level control break to produce the rental income report for Pernell Properties. See Figure 9.10 for the hierarchy chart and Figure 9.11 for the flowchart. Sample program CHAP9B is shown in Figure 9.12; the program's output is shown in Figure 9.13.

Sample program CHAP9B uses four control fields—location, agency number, manager number, and building number—to produce the rental income report.

Input (text file):
For each record, read and assign data to the following fields. (Field size and type are shown in parentheses.)

1. Location   (5 char)
2. Agency number   (2 int)

3. Manager number   (3 int)
4. Building number   (2 int)
5. Apartment number   (1 int)
6. Monthly rent   (6.2 float)

```
LOCATION CONTROL BREAK DETECTED
Save new location, agency, manager, and building numbers
Call Break On Building
Call Break On Manager
Call Break On Agency
Call Break On Location

AGENCY CONTROL BREAK DETECTED
Save new agency, manager, and building numbers
Call Break On Building
Call Break On Manager
Call Break On Agency

MANAGER CONTROL BREAK DETECTED
Save new manager and building numbers
Call Break On Building
Call Break On Manager

BUILDING CONTROL BREAK DETECTED
Save new building number
Call Break On Building

BREAK ON LOCATION
Print location rent total, increment line count, and set new
location rent total to 0

BREAK ON AGENCY
Print agency rent total, increment line count, and set new
agency rent total to 0

BREAK ON MANAGER
Print manager rent total, increment line count, and set new
manager rent total to 0

BREAK ON BUILDING
Print building rent total, increment line count, and set new
building rent total to 0
```

FIGURE 9.9   Four-Level Control Break Logic

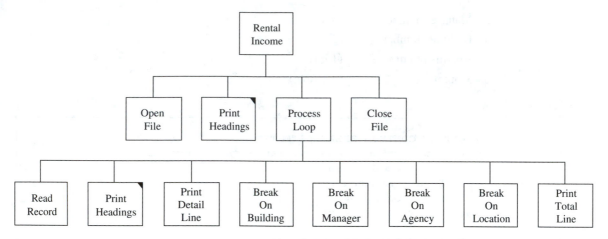

FIGURE 9.10   Hierarchy Chart for CHAP9B

Text File (txRent.fil)

Use the data given below to create the rent file. (The numbers shown above the columns correspond to the fields described for the input.)

1	2	3	4	5	6
North	20	201	10	1	400.00
North	20	201	10	2	410.00
North	20	201	10	3	335.00
North	20	201	15	1	375.00
North	20	201	15	2	385.00
North	20	247	17	1	450.00
North	20	247	17	2	450.00
North	43	316	22	1	345.00
North	43	316	22	2	465.00
East	10	237	30	1	410.00
East	10	237	30	2	365.00
East	10	237	30	3	470.00
East	10	237	30	4	345.00
East	10	659	33	1	429.00
East	10	659	33	2	465.00
End	00	000	00	0	000.00 (trailer record)

Output (printer)

Print the four-level control break report shown in Figures 9.13a and 9.13b.

Processing Requirements:

- Read the rent file.
- Print 26 detail lines per page.
- Subtotal rent by building.
- Subtotal rent by manager.
- Subtotal rent by agency.
- Subtotal rent by location.
- Accumulate a report total for the rent.

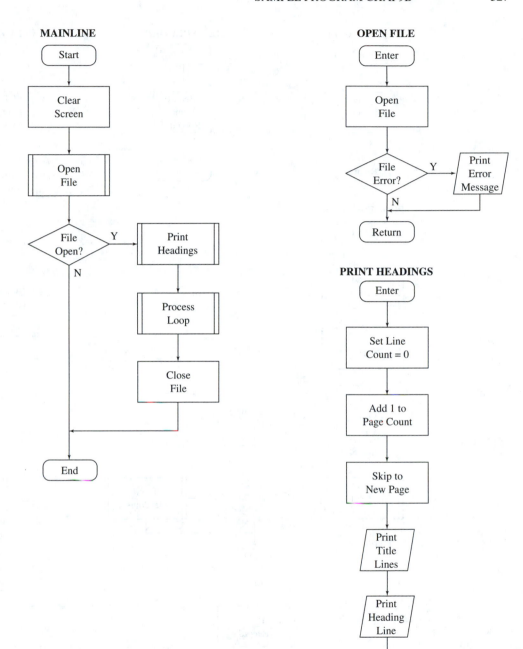

FIGURE 9.11 Program Flowchart for CHAP9B

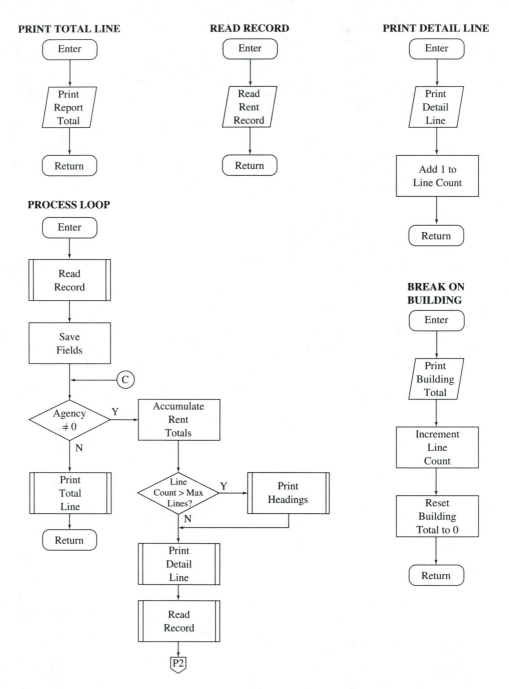

FIGURE 9.11   *Continued*

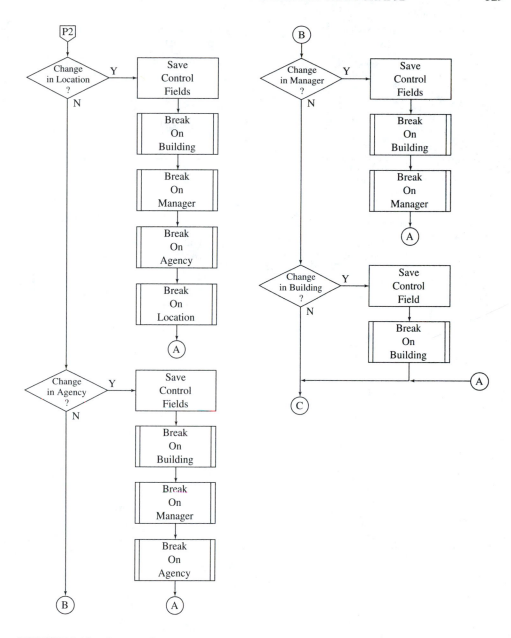

FIGURE 9.11   *Continued*

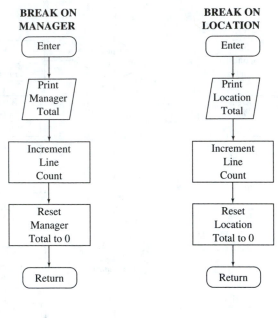

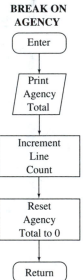

FIGURE 9.11 *Continued*

```
/*-----------------------------------------------------------
RENTAL INCOME: Read rent file and print a four-level control break
report for Pernell Properties.

Program:   CHAP9B.C
Author:    David M. Collopy
Date:      mm/dd/yy
Project:   Sample program
*****************************************************************/

/*---- PREPROCESSING DIRECTIVES -------------------------------*/

#include <stdio.h>
#include <string.h>
#include <graph.h>
#define IMAXLINES 26

/*---- FUNCTION PROTOTYPES -------------------------------------*/

void  OpenFile(void);            /* open rent file         */
void  PrnHeadings(void);         /* print report headings  */
void  ProcessLoop(void);         /* processing loop        */
void  ReadRecord(void);          /* read rent record       */
float BreakOnLoc(float);         /* location control break */
float BreakOnAgency(float);      /* agency control break   */
float BreakOnMgr(float);         /* manager control break  */
float BreakOnBldg(float);        /* building control break */
void  PrnDetail(void);           /* print rent detail line */
void  PrnTotal(float);           /* print total rent       */

/*---- PROGRAM SETUP ------------------------------------------*/

/*> R E P O R T   T I T L E S   A N D   H E A D I N G S    <*/

char PT1[] = "P E R N E L L   P R O P E R T I E S      Page ";
char PT2[] = "                  Rental Income                ";
char HL1[] = "LOCATION  AGENCY  MGR  BLDG    APART#    RENT ";
char DTL[] = " %-5s       %2d     %3d   %2d       %d     $%7.2f";
char CB1[] = "                     *   Bldg Total:   $ %7.2f  ";
char CB2[] = "                    **   Mgr Total:    $ %7.2f  ";
char CB3[] = "                   ***   Agency Total: $ %7.2f  ";
char CB4[] = "                  ****   Loc Total:    $ %7.2f  ";
char RTL[] = "                 *****   Report Total: $ %7.2f  ";

/*> R E N T   R E C O R D                                  <*/
```

FIGURE 9.12 Sample Program CHAP9B: Demonstrates a four-level control break report for Pernell Properties

```
FILE *fpRent;                    /* file pointer      */
char  sLocation[6];              /* apartment location */
int   iAgency;                   /* agency ID number  */
int   iMgr;                      /* manager ID number */
int   iBldg;                     /* building number   */
int   iApart;                    /* apartment number  */
float fRent;                     /* monthly rent income */

/*>  P R O G R A M   V A R I A B L E S                        <*/

int iLineCnt = 0;                /* detail line count  */

/*----------------------------------------------------------------
       MAINLINE CONTROL
-----------------------------------------------------------------*/
main()
{
    _clearscreen(0);
    OpenFile();
    if (fpRent != 0)
    {
        PrnHeadings();
        ProcessLoop();
        fclose(fpRent);
    }
    return 0;
}


/*----------------------------------------------------------------
       OPEN RENT FILE
-----------------------------------------------------------------*/
void OpenFile(void)
{
    fpRent = fopen("a:txRent.fil", "r");
    if (fpRent == 0)
    {
        printf("\nCannot open rent file\n");
    }
    return;
}

/*----------------------------------------------------------------
       PRINT REPORT HEADINGS
-----------------------------------------------------------------*/
void PrnHeadings(void)
```

FIGURE 9.12 *Continued*

```
{
    static int iPageNum;          /* page number              */

    iLineCnt = 0;                 /* set line count to 0      */
    iPageNum++;                   /* add 1 to page number     */
    fprintf(stdprn, "\f\r");      /* skip to new page & reset */
    fprintf(stdprn, "%s %d",      /* print page title 1       */
        PT1, iPageNum);           /*     & page number        */
    fprintf(stdprn, "\r\n");      /* reset & single space     */
    fprintf(stdprn, PT2);         /* print page title 2       */
    fprintf(stdprn, "\r\n\n");    /* reset & double space     */
    fprintf(stdprn, HL1);         /* print heading line 1     */
    fprintf(stdprn, "\r\n");      /* reset & single space     */
    return;
}


/*----------------------------------------------------------------
      PROCESSING LOOP
-----------------------------------------------------------------*/
void ProcessLoop(void)
{
    char   sPrevLoc[6];           /* previous location        */
    int    iPrevAgency;           /* previous agency number   */
    int    iPrevMgr;              /* previous manager number  */
    int    iPrevBldg;             /* previous building number */
    float  fLocTot = 0.0;         /* location rent total      */
    float  fAgencyTot = 0.0;      /* agency rent total        */
    float  fMgrTot = 0.0;         /* manager rent total       */
    float  fBldgTot = 0.0;        /* building rent total      */
    float  fRptTot = 0.0;         /* report rent total        */

    ReadRecord();
    strcpy(sPrevLoc, sLocation);  /* save location            */
    iPrevAgency = iAgency;        /* save agency              */
    iPrevMgr = iMgr;              /* save manager number      */
    iPrevBldg = iBldg;            /* save building number     */
    while (iAgency != 0)
    {
        fLocTot = fLocTot + fRent;
        fAgencyTot = fAgencyTot + fRent;
        fMgrTot = fMgrTot + fRent;
        fBldgTot = fBldgTot + fRent;
        fRptTot = fRptTot + fRent;
        if (iLineCnt >= IMAXLINES)
```

FIGURE 9.12   *Continued*

```
                    PrnHeadings();
            PrnDetail();
            ReadRecord();
            if (strcmp(sLocation, sPrevLoc) != 0)
            {
                strcpy(sPrevLoc, sLocation);
                iPrevAgency = iAgency;
                iPrevMgr = iMgr;
                iPrevBldg = iBldg;
                fBldgTot = BreakOnBldg(fBldgTot);
                fMgrTot = BreakOnMgr(fMgrTot);
                fAgencyTot = BreakOnAgency(fAgencyTot);
                fLocTot = BreakOnLoc(fLocTot);
            }
            else if (iAgency != iPrevAgency)
            {
                iPrevAgency = iAgency;
                iPrevMgr = iMgr;
                iPrevBldg = iBldg;
                fBldgTot = BreakOnBldg(fBldgTot);
                fMgrTot = BreakOnMgr(fMgrTot);
                fAgencyTot = BreakOnAgency(fAgencyTot);
            }
            else if (iMgr != iPrevMgr)
            {
                iPrevMgr = iMgr;
                iPrevBldg = iBldg;
                fBldgTot = BreakOnBldg(fBldgTot);
                fMgrTot = BreakOnMgr(fMgrTot);
            }
            else if (iBldg != iPrevBldg)
            {
                iPrevBldg = iBldg;
                fBldgTot = BreakOnBldg(fBldgTot);
            }
        }
    PrnTotal(fRptTot);
    return;
}

/*------------------------------------------------------------
        READ RENT RECORD
-----------------------------------------------------------*/
```

FIGURE 9.12   *Continued*

```
void ReadRecord(void)
{
    fscanf(fpRent, " %s %d %d %d %d %f",
        sLocation, &iAgency, &iMgr, &iBldg, &iApart, &fRent);
    return;
}


/*-------------------------------------------------------------
        PRINT RENT DETAIL LINE
-------------------------------------------------------------*/
void PrnDetail(void)
{
    fprintf(stdprn, "\r\n");
    fprintf(stdprn, DTL, sLocation, iAgency, iMgr, iBldg,
        iApart, fRent);
    iLineCnt++;
    return;
}


/*-------------------------------------------------------------
        LOCATION CONTROL BREAK
-------------------------------------------------------------*/
float BreakOnLoc(float fLocTot)
{
    fprintf(stdprn, "\r");
    fprintf(stdprn, CB4, fLocTot);
    fprintf(stdprn, "\r\n");
    iLineCnt = iLineCnt + 2;
    fLocTot = 0.0;
    return fLocTot;
}


/*-------------------------------------------------------------
        AGENCY CONTROL BREAK
-------------------------------------------------------------*/
float BreakOnAgency(float fAgencyTot)
{
    fprintf(stdprn, "\r");
    fprintf(stdprn, CB3, fAgencyTot);
    fprintf(stdprn, "\r\n");
    iLineCnt = iLineCnt + 2;
    fAgencyTot = 0.0;
    return fAgencyTot;
}
```

FIGURE 9.12   *Continued*

```
/*-------------------------------------------------------------------
      MANAGER CONTROL BREAK
-----------------------------------------------------------------*/
float BreakOnMgr(float fMgrTot)
{
    fprintf(stdprn, "\r");
    fprintf(stdprn, CB2, fMgrTot);
    fprintf(stdprn, "\r\n");
    iLineCnt = iLineCnt + 2;
    fMgrTot = 0.0;
    return fMgrTot;
}


/*-------------------------------------------------------------------
      BUILDING CONTROL BREAK
-----------------------------------------------------------------*/
float BreakOnBldg(float fBldgTot)
{
    fprintf(stdprn, "\r\n\n");
    fprintf(stdprn, CB1, fBldgTot);
    fprintf(stdprn, "\r\n");
    iLineCnt = iLineCnt + 2;
    fBldgTot = 0.0;
    return fBldgTot;
}


/*-------------------------------------------------------------------
      PRINT TOTAL RENT
-----------------------------------------------------------------*/
void PrnTotal(float fRptTot)
{
    fprintf(stdprn, "\r\n\n");
    fprintf(stdprn, RTL, fRptTot);
    return;
}
```

FIGURE 9.12   *Continued*

Pseudocode:

START: Main
Clear screen
Call Open File
IF file opened
    Call Print Headings
    Call Process Loop
    Close file

```
END IF
END

ENTER: Open File
Open rent file
IF file not opened
      Print error - cannot open file
END IF
RETURN

ENTER. Print Headings
Set line count to 0
Add 1 to page number
```

```
P E R N E L L    P R O P E R T I E S      Page 1
              Rental  Income

LOCATION  AGENCY   MGR   BLDG    APART#       RENT

 North      20    201    10       1       $  400.00
 North      20    201    10       2       $  410.00
 North      20    201    10       3       $  335.00

                   *   Bldg Total:         $ 1145.00

 North      20    201    15       1       $  375.00
 North      20    201    15       2       $  385.00

                   *   Bldg Total:         $  760.00
                  **   Mgr Total:          $ 1905.00

 North      20    247    17       1       $  450.00
 North      20    247    17       2       $  450.00

                   *   Bldg Total:         $  900.00
                  **   Mgr Total:          $  900.00
                 ***   Agency Total:       $ 2805.00

 North      43    316    22       1       $  345.00
 North      43    316    22       2       $  465.00

                   *   Bldg Total:         $  810.00
                  **   Mgr Total:          $  810.00
                 ***   Agency Total:       $  810.00
                ****   Loc Total:          $ 3615.00
```

FIGURE 9.13a   Program Output for CHAP9B

```
P E R N E L L   P R O P E R T I E S      Page 2
                  Rental  Income

LOCATION  AGENCY  MGR   BLDG   APART#      RENT

  East      10    237    30      1     $  410.00
  East      10    237    30      2     $  365.00
  East      10    237    30      3     $  470.00
  East      10    237    30      4     $  345.00

                   *   Bldg  Total:    $ 1590.00
                  **   Mgr   Total:    $ 1590.00


  East      10    659    33      1     $  429.00
  East      10    659    33      2     $  465.00

                   *   Bldg  Total:    $  894.00
                  **   Mgr   Total:    $  894.00
                 ***   Agency Total:   $ 2484.00
                ****   Loc  Total:     $ 2484.00


               *****   Report Total:   $ 6099.00
```

FIGURE 9.13b   Program Output for CHAP9B

Advance to top of page
Print 2 page title lines and page number
Print 1 column heading line
RETURN

ENTER: Process Loop
Call Read Rent Record
Save location
Save agency number
Save manager number
Save building number
LOOP while agency not = 0
    Accumulate location rent total
    Accumulate agency rent total
    Accumulate manager rent total
    Accumulate building rent total
    Accumulate report rent total
    IF line count >= 26
        Call Print Headings
    END IF
    Call Print Detail Line
    Call Read Rent Record

```
            IF new location not = previous location
                    Save new location
                    Save new agency number
                    Save new manager number
                    Save new building number
                    Call Break On Building
                    Call Break On Manager
                    Call Break On Agency
                    Call Break On Location
            else IF new agency not = previous agency
                    Save new agency number
                    Save new manager number
                    Save new building number
                    Call Break On Building
                    Call Break On Manager
                    Call Break On Agency
            else IF new manager not = previous manager
                    Save new manager number
                    Save new building number
                    Call Break On Building
                    Call Break On Manager
            else IF new building not = previous building
                    Save new building number
                    Call Break On Building
            END IF
     END LOOP
     Call Print Total Rent
     RETURN

     ENTER: Read Rent Record
     Read a record from the file:
             apartment location
             agency ID number
             manager ID number
             building number
             apartment number
             monthly rent income
     RETURN

     ENTER: Print Detail Line
     Print rent detail line:
             apartment location
             agency ID number
             manager ID number
             building number
             apartment number
             monthly rent income
     Add 1 to line count
     RETURN

     ENTER: Break On Location
```

```
Print location rent total
Add 2 to line count
Set new location rent total to 0
RETURN

ENTER: Break On Agency
Print agency rent total
Add 2 to line count
Set new agency rent total to 0
RETURN

ENTER: Break On Manager
Print manager rent total
Add 2 to line count
Set new manager rent total to 0
RETURN

ENTER: Break On Building
Print building rent total
Add 2 to line count
Set new building rent total to 0
RETURN

ENTER: Print Total Rent
Print report rent total
RETURN
```

Hierarchy Chart: See Figure 9.10.

Program Flowchart: See Figure 9.11.

Dissection of Sample Program CHAP9B

Although sample programs CHAP9A and CHAP9B are similar in structure, they differ in complexity. The decision-making processes added to the body of the *while* loop are now a little more involved than before. Because of this, we will focus on the activities performed by the Processing Loop.

```
P R O C E S S I N G   L O O P:
void ProcessLoop(void)
{
    char   sPrevLoc[6];
    int    iPrevAgency;
    int    iPrevMgr;
    int    iPrevBldg;
    float  fLocTot = 0.0;
    float  fAgencyTot = 0.0;
    float  fMgrTot = 0.0;
    float  fBldgTot = 0.0;
    float  fRptTot = 0.0;
```

The above declarations define the local variables required by the module. Notice that the subtotals are declared and initialized at the same time.

```
ReadRecord();
strcpy(sPrevLoc, sLocation);
iPrevAgency = iAgency;
iPrevMgr = iMgr;
iPrevBldg = iBldg;
```

The first statement branches to *ReadRecord* and retrieves the first record from the file. The next four statements retain the contents of the control fields for later use. This process sets the stage for the control break checks that appear in the *while* loop.

```
while (iAgency != 0)
{
```

The above statement compares the value stored at *iAgency* to 0. If the condition test is true, control enters the body of the loop. Otherwise, the file is empty and control skips to the first executable statement coded after the *while* loop.

```
fLocTot = fLocTot + fRent;
fAgencyTot = fAgencyTot + fRent;
fMgrTot = fMgrTot + fRent;
fBldgTot = fBldgTot + fRent;
fRptTot = fRptTot + fRent;
```

The above statements add the input rent to the location, agency, manager, and building subtotals and to the report total; they accumulate the monthly rent for the current control groups and the report.

```
if (iLineCnt >= IMAXLINES)
    PrnHeadings();
```

The *if* statement compares line count to *IMAXLINES*. If the outcome is true, control calls the Print Headings module and prints the report titles and column heading. Otherwise, control skips the module call and continue with the next statement.

```
PrnDetail();
ReadRecord();
```

The above statements call the modules in the order shown. The *PrnDetail* module prints the current detail line, and *ReadRecord* gets the next record from the file.

```
if (strcmp(sLocation, sPrevLoc) != 0)
{
    strcpy(sPrevLoc, sLocation);
    iPrevAgency = iAgency;
    iPrevMgr = iMgr;
    iPrevBldg = iBldg;
    fBldgTot = BreakOnBldg(fBldgTot);
    fMgrTot = BreakOnMgr(fMgrTot);
    fAgencyTot = BreakOnAgency(fAgencyTot);
    fLocTot = BreakOnLoc(fLocTot);
}
```

The above block checks for a break on the major control field. If the new and previous locations are not equal, control saves the new control fields and breaks on the previous building, manager, agency, and location, respectively.

Since the previous building, manager, and agency subtotals belong to the previous location, the minor building subtotal must be printed before the intermediate manager and agency subtotals and the intermediate subtotals must be printed before the major location subtotal.

The values returned to the calling statements reset the subtotals to 0 before continuing with the new control groups.

```
else if (iAgency != iPrevAgency)
{
    iPrevAgency = iAgency;
    iPrevMgr = iMgr;
    iPrevBldg = iBldg;
    fBldgTot = BreakOnBldg(fBldgTot);
    fMgrTot = BreakOnMgr(fMgrTot);
    fAgencyTot = BreakOnAgency(fAgencyTot);
}
```

This block checks for a break on an intermediate control field. If the new and previous agencies are not equal, control saves the new agency, manager, and building numbers and breaks on the previous building, manager, and agency, respectively.

Since the previous building and manager subtotals belong to the previous agency, the minor building subtotal must be printed before the intermediate manager subtotal and the intermediate manager subtotal must be printed before the intermediate agency subtotal.

The values returned to the calling statements reset the subtotals to 0 before continuing with the new control groups.

```
else if (iMgr != iPrevMgr)
{
    iPrevMgr = iMgr;
    iPrevBldg = iBldg;
    fBldgTot = BreakOnBldg(fBldgTot);
    fMgrTot = BreakOnMgr(fMgrTot);
}
```

This block also checks for a break on an intermediate control field. If the new and previous manager numbers are not equal, control saves the new manager and building numbers and breaks on the previous building and manager, respectively.

Since the building subtotal belongs to the previous manager, it must be printed before the intermediate manager subtotal.

The values returned to the calling statements reset the subtotals to 0 before continuing with the new control groups.

```
else if (iBldg != iPrevBldg)
{
    iPrevBldg = iBldg;
    fBldgTot = BreakOnBldg(fBldgTot);
}
```

The last *else if* block checks for a break on the minor control field. If the new and previous building numbers are not the same, control saves the new building number and breaks on the previous building.

The value returned to the calling statement resets the building subtotal to 0 before continuing with the new building control group.

```
    }
    PrnTotal(fRptTot);
    return;
}
```

The above call statement passes the report total to the *PrnTotal* module; this module prints the total monthly rent at the end of the report.

The *return* sends control back to the *MAINLINE*.

Notes and Tips

In this chapter, you learned how to construct a two-level and a four-level control break program. Now let's look at what they have in common. Sample program CHAP9A used a two-level nested if statement to check for the control breaks and two control break modules to print the subtotals. Furthermore, sample program CHAP9B used a four-level nested if statement to check for the control breaks and four control break modules to print the subtotals.

So why is this important? It's important because there is pattern developing here. For example, if you are told to construct a six-level control break program, then all you have to do is code a six-level nested if statement to handle the control break checks and six control break modules to print the subtotals. Also, don't forget to save the appropriate control fields and zero out new subtotals as needed.

On another matter, did you notice that the numbers appended to the notation used to specify a control break line (*CB1*, *CB2*, *CB3*, and *CB4*) correspond directly to the number of asterisks (*1*, *2*, *3*, and *4*) displayed on the report? The asterisks are used to emphasize the level of the subtotal. This notation makes it easier for the programmer to identify errors during the debugging phase, particularly when the asterisks are printed out of order.

Tutorial CHAP9B

1. The objectives of this tutorial are to
    *   process the data stored in a text file
    *   code a four-level control break program
2. Open the text editor, and enter the sample program shown in Figure 9.12.
3. Save the source code on your work disk as CHAP9B.
4. Compile, run, and debug your program until the output matches the rental report shown in Figures 9.13a and 9.13b.
5. When completed, show your work to your instructor.

Quick Quiz

Answer the following questions.

1. What relationship is there between the numeric suffixes appended to the print images *CB1*, *CB2*, *CB3*, and *CB4* and the level of the subtotal displayed on the report?

2. Identify four data items that are used to detect the control breaks. Under what conditions do they force the program to execute the control breaks?

3. The nested decision statement coded inside the *Processing Loop* checks for the control breaks. Is it necessary to test for them in the order shown—that is, location before agency, agency before manager, manager before building, and building last?

4. Did you have any problems with CHAP9A? If so, what were they and what did you do to correct them?

Summary

1. Business applications often require reports that contain multilevel control totals or subtotals.

2. Control totals may go two, three, four, or more levels deep; the actual number of levels depends mostly on the application at hand.

3. Designing multilevel reports involves grouping subtotals within subtotals.

4. Planning a multilevel control break involves the following: laying out the report on a printer spacing chart, arranging the data in sequential order by control fields, and developing the logic to force the program to break when the control fields change values.

5. A two-level control break contains a major and a minor control field.

6. A two-level control break program accumulates and prints three levels of totals: one for the major control field, one for the minor, and one for the report.

7. Asterisks are printed next to the total lines to specify the level number of each total. One asterisk indicates the first level, two asterisks indicate the second level, and so on.

8. A four-level control break program has four control fields: one major, two intermediate, and one minor.

9. A four-level control break program provides five totals: one for each control field and one for the report.

10. For a multilevel control break, the program always executes the minor control break first. Then, as the program "backs out" of the other modules one by one, it executes the remaining control breaks "inside out."

Programming Projects

For each project, design the logic and write the modular structured program to produce the output. Model your program after the sample programs presented in the chapter. Verify your output.

Project 9–1   Payroll-1

Write a program to read a payroll file, calculate gross pay, and print a two-level control break report. Assume overtime is not computed.

Input (text file):

For each payroll record, read and assign data to the following fields. (Field size and type are shown in parentheses.)

1. Branch number   (1 int)

2. Division number   (2 int)

3. Department number   (3 int)

4. Employee name   (20 char)

5. Hours worked   (2 int)

6. Hourly pay rate   (5.2 float)

Text File (txPayrol.fil):

Use the data given below to create the payroll file. (The numbers shown above the columns correspond to the fields described for the input.)

1	2	3	4	5	6
1	10	100	Tanya Bauer	40	7.50
1	10	100	Diane Dixon	40	9.75
1	10	106	Randy Karns	37	8.55
1	20	112	Dana Clark	45	14.90
1	20	112	Nick Larson	43	7.72
1	20	112	Colleen Norris	40	11.35
1	20	123	Sara Erickson	38	12.00
1	40	117	Scott Howard	42	9.75
2	10	105	Paul Irwin	48	8.72
2	10	105	Cyndi Olson	45	15.10
2	18	144	Dale Miller	40	10.25
3	23	121	Bret Rossi	35	8.00
3	23	121	Karen Thomas	48	9.00
3	23	137	Cheryl Dietz	42	7.50
3	23	137	Neil Kenney	38	7.25
3	34	150	Tracy York	36	11.00
0	00	000	Trailer Record	00	0.00

Output (printer):

Print the following two-level control break report:

```
Author                C O M P A N Y   P A Y R O L L          Page 99
                          Gross Pay Report
                             mm/dd/yy


Branch    Division    Department    Employee Name      Gross Pay
  9          99          999        X------------X       999.99
  :           :           :              :                 :
  :           :           :              :                 :
```

```
  9          99        999        X------------X       999.99
                                *  Department Total:   9999.99
                               ** Division Total:      9999.99
          . . . . .                          . . . . .
                             ****  Report Total:      99999.99
```

Processing Requirements:

- Read the payroll file.
- Print 31 detail lines per page.
- Compute the gross pay:
  hours worked × pay rate.
- Subtotal gross pay by department.
- Subtotal gross pay by division.
- Accumulate a report total for gross pay.

Project 9–2   Payroll-2

Modify the program in Project 9–1 to include a three-level control break. Group and list employee gross pay by department, division, and branch; print the appropriate subtotal for each group. Print 32 detail lines per page. Model the logic after sample program CHAP9B.

Print the following three-level control break report:

```
Author                  C O M P A N Y   P A Y R O L L            Page 99
                            Gross Pay Report
                              mm/dd/yy


Branch    Division   Department    Employee Name        Gross Pay
  9          99        999        X------------X         999.99
  :          :          :              :                   :
  :          :          :              :                   :
  9          99        999        X------------X         999.99

                                *   Department Total:    9999.99
                               **   Division Total:      9999.99
                              ***   Branch Total:        9999.99
          . . . . .                          . . . . .
                             ****   Report Total:       99999.99
```

Project 9–3   Sales Analysis-1

Write a program to read a sales file, accumulate total customer sales, and print a three-level control break report.

Input (text file):

For each sales record, read and assign data to the following fields. (Field size and type are shown in parentheses.)

1. Region number   (1 int)
2. State code   (2 char)
3. Store number   (3 int)
4. Salesperson number   (3 int)

5. Customer number   (4 int)

6. Sales amount   (6.2 float)

Text File (txSales.fil):

Use the data given below to create the sales file. (The numbers shown above the columns correspond to the fields described for the input.)

1	2	3	4	5	6
1	OH	100	190	1180	380.00
1	OH	100	190	3100	273.00
1	OH	100	225	2510	161.00
1	OH	210	287	5090	492.00
1	IN	198	338	4200	185.00
1	IN	198	412	6100	200.00
1	IN	198	412	9430	300.00
2	KY	279	206	2900	563.00
2	KY	279	490	3000	175.00
2	KY	300	640	3100	100.00
2	KY	313	110	7170	400.00
3	PA	121	720	1200	369.00
3	PA	239	378	2600	349.00
3	PA	239	600	5500	200.00
0	XX	000	000	0000	000.00 (trailer record)

Output (printer):

Print the following three-level control break report:

```
Author              SALES ANALYSIS REPORT              Page 99
                          mm/dd/yy


Region   State   Store   Salesperson   Customer   Sales
--------------------------------------------------------------
  9       XX      999        999         9999     999.99
  :        :       :          :            :        :
  :        :       :          :            :        :
  9       XX      999        999         9999     999.99

                       *   Salesperson Total: 9999.99
                      **   Store Total:        9999.99
                     ***   State Total:        9999.99
           . . . .                      . . . .
                   *****   Report Total:       9999.99
```

Processing Requirements:

- Read the sales file.
- Print 35 detail lines per page.
- Subtotal sales by salesperson.
- Subtotal sales by store.
- Subtotal sales by state.
- Accumulate a report total for sales.

Project 9–4   Sales Analysis-2

Modify the program in Project 9–3 to include a four-level control break. Group and list customer sales by salesperson, store, state, and region; print the appropriate sales subtotal for each group. Print 36 detail lines per page. Model the logic after sample program CHAP9B.

Print the following control break report:

```
Author              SALES ANALYSIS REPORT              Page 99
                         mm/dd/yy


Region    State    Store    Salesperson    Customer    Sales
------------------------------------------------------------
   9       XX       999         999          9999      999.99
   :        :        :           :             :          :
   :        :        :           :             :          :
   9       XX       999         999          9999      999.99

                             *    Salesperson Total: 9999.99
                            **    Store Total:        9999.99
                           ***    State Total:        9999.99
                          ****    Region Total:       9999.99
            . . . . .                     . . . . .
                         *****    Report Total:       9999.99
```

Project 9–5   Inventory-1

Write a program to read an inventory file, accumulate total quantity on hand, and print a three-level control break report.

Input (text file):
For each inventory record, read and assign data to the following fields. (Field size and type are shown in parentheses.)

1. Region number   (1 int)
2. State code   (2 char)
3. Location number   (2 int)
4. Warehouse number   (3 int)
5. Item number   (5 char)
6. Quantity on hand   (2 int)

Text File (txInven.fil):
Use the data given below to create the inventory file. (The numbers shown above the columns correspond to the fields described for the input.)

1	2	3	4	5	6
1	OH	43	101	A7100	24
1	OH	43	101	B0340	12
1	OH	43	101	D0019	35
1	OH	43	340	C1970	48
1	OH	43	340	H0120	16

```
1    OH    66    220    F3170    96
1    OH    66    220    K8800    24
1    IN    27    125    C5510    12
1    IN    27    125    I1700    36
2    KY    18    107    B1776    24
2    KY    18    107    D0011    30
2    KY    18    130    F0910    36
2    KY    18    130    L7650    96
2    KY    18    130    P0150    15
0    XX    00    000    X0000    00    (trailer record)
```

Output (printer):

Print the following three-level control break report:

```
Author              INVENTORY ANALYSIS REPORT              Page 99
                          mm/dd/yy


Region    State    Location    Warehouse    Item#    Quantity
  9        XX         99          999       XXXXX       99
  :         :          :           :          :          :
  :         :          :           :          :          :
  9        XX         99          999       XXXXX       99


                              *    Warehouse Total:    999
                             **    Location Total:     999
                            ***    State Total:        999
              . . . . .                 . . . . .
                          *****    Report Total:       999
```

Processing Requirements:

- Read the inventory file.
- Print 25 detail lines per page.
- Subtotal quantity by warehouse.
- Subtotal quantity by location.
- Subtotal quantity by state.
- Accumulate a report total for quantity on hand.

Project 9–6   Inventory-2

Modify the program in Project 9–5 to include a four-level control break. Group and list the quantity on hand by warehouse, location, state, and region; print the appropriate subtotal for each group. Print 26 detail lines per page. Model the logic after sample program CHAP9B.

Print the following four-level control break report:

```
Author              INVENTORY ANALYSIS REPORT              Page 99
                          mm/dd/yy


Region    State    Location    Warehouse    Item#    Quantity
  9        XX         99          999       XXXXX       99
  :         :          :           :          :          :
  :         :          :           :          :          :
  9        XX         99          999       XXXXX       99
```

```
        *   Warehouse Total:   999
       **   Location Total:    999
      ***   State Total:       999
     ****   Region Total:      999
            .  .  .  .  .
    *****   Report Total:      999
```

Project 9–7   Personnel-1

Write a program to read a personnel file, count the number of employees, and print a two-level control total personnel report.

Input (text file):

For each record, read and assign data to the following fields. (Field size and type are shown in parentheses.)

1. Branch number   (1 int)
2. Division number   (2 int)
3. Department number   (3 int)
4. Manager number   (2 int)
5. Supervisor number   (4 int)
6. Employee count   (2 int)

Text File (txPersnl.fil):

Use the data given below to create the personnel file. (The numbers shown above the columns correspond to the fields described for the input.)

1	2	3	4	5	6
1	10	101	20	2010	08
1	10	101	20	2025	12
1	10	101	30	3050	16
1	10	101	30	3055	12
1	10	101	30	3060	10
1	10	120	45	4520	14
1	10	120	45	4530	12
1	20	206	12	1210	07
1	20	206	12	1220	12
2	15	115	22	2210	15
2	15	115	22	2230	12
2	15	210	33	3340	18
2	15	210	33	3360	16
2	15	210	45	4510	10
2	15	210	45	4550	12
2	27	108	26	2630	12
2	27	108	26	2640	16
2	27	108	26	2680	14
0	00	000	00	0000	00 (trailer record)

Output (printer):

Print the following two-level control break report:

```
Author             P E R S O N N E L    R E P O R T            Page 99
                          Employee Count
                             mm/dd/yy


Branch   Division   Department   Manager   Supervisor   Employees
  9         99         999         99         9999         99
  :          :          :          :           :           :
  :          :          :          :           :           :
  9         99         999         99         9999         99

                              *   Manager Total:         999
                             **   Department Total:      999
             . . . . .                   . . . . .
                           *****  Report Total:          999
```

Processing Requirements:

- Read the personnel file.
- Print 29 detail lines per page.
- Subtotal employee count by manager.
- Subtotal employee count by department.
- Accumulate a report total for employee count.

Project 9–8   Personnel-2

Modify the program in Project 9–7 to include a four-level control break. Group and list the employee count by manager, department, division, and branch; print the appropriate subtotal for each group. Print 32 detail lines per page. Model the logic after sample program CHAP9B.

Print the following four-level control break report:

```
Author             P E R S O N N E L    R E P O R T            Page 99
                          Employee Count
                             mm/dd/yy


Branch   Division   Department   Manager   Supervisor   Employees
  9         99         999         99         9999         99
  :          :          :          :           :           :
  :          :          :          :           :           :
  9         99         999         99         9999         99

                              *   Manager Total:         999
                             **   Department Total:      999
                            ***   Division Total:        999
                           ****   Branch Total:          999
             . . . . .                   . . . . .
                           *****  Report Total:          999
```

10 Arrays and Sorting

Overview

Learning Objectives

After you have read this chapter and completed the exercises, you should be able to

- understand the purpose of arrays and the use of subscripts
- define and load numeric and character arrays
- manipulate and print data stored in arrays
- define and load data into parallel arrays
- search and update data stored in parallel arrays
- sort (rearrange) the elements in an array in ascending and descending order

Arrays

An **array** represents a set of values that is given one name. Each item in the array is called an **element,** and each element has identical data types. Collectively, the elements resemble a list of related objects, such as test scores, close friends, best-selling book titles, paid holidays, top-rated TV shows, and so on.

In this chapter, we will learn how to define two types of arrays: character and numeric. **Character arrays** hold non-numeric or string data, whereas **numeric arrays** hold integer or floating-point values. Integer and floating-point values are stored in separate arrays.

For example, in Figure 10.1, *iQuantity* is an integer array that consists of seven elements and *fMileage* is a floating-point array that consists of five elements. Hence, an **integer array** consists of a set of integers and a **floating-point array** consists of a set of floating-point elements.

Like single variables, array variables (elements) are used to store data in memory. This means that once an array is loaded—values assigned to the elements—the data can be processed repeatedly without requiring the program to reenter it.

```
iQuantity                    fMileage
    12                         78.5
    36                         94.2
    68   ← elements →          86.9
    09                         68.0
    44                         75.3
    51
    87
```

FIGURE 10.1 Numeric Arrays

As an example, assume a series of 36 test scores are loaded into an array. The program could access the scores from the array and print them on the screen. Next, the program could access the scores a second time and compute the class average. Furthermore, the program could access the scores a third time and "curve" them by adding six points to each score before printing them on the printer.

Creating an Array

Arrays are defined by specifying a data type, a name, and a size. Data type refers to the kind of data the array will hold—numeric or character. Name refers to the identifier assigned to the array. And size specifies the number of elements reserved for the array. Size is enclosed within square brackets *[]*.

Both numeric and character data may be stored in arrays.

Numeric Arrays: Numeric data is stored in either integer or floating-point arrays. Declarations that define numeric arrays allocate storage spaces for numeric data items.

Examples of numeric array declarations are as follows:

```
int    iQuantity[7];
float  fMileage[5];
float  fArea[12], fAmountDue[36], int iColorCode[10];
int    iPoints[12],
       iLocation[50],
       iUnits[24];
```

We may define one or more arrays on the same line. Multiple array declarations are separated by commas. We may also list the arrays down the page. Each declaration statement begins with a data type and ends with a semicolon.

The above declarations define the following numeric arrays:

iQuantity	7 elements	(int)
fMileage	5 elements	(float)
fArea	12 elements	(float)
fAmountDue	36 elements	(float)
iColorCode	10 elements	(int)
iPoints	12 elements	(int)
iLocation	50 elements	(int)
iUnits	24 elements	(int)

(The data types are shown in parentheses.)

Character Arrays: String data is stored in character arrays. Declarations that define character arrays allocate storage for string data items. For character arrays, we specify not only the size of the array but also the size of the elements.

Examples of character arrays are:

```
char sDay[7][10];
char sJobTitle[30][20];
char sStudentRank[100][10], sBuilding[5][25];
char sSupplier[40][30],
     sDescription[200][50],
     sMagazine[15][35];
```

Consider the declaration for *sDay*. It reserves enough storage space for seven elements, each of which may hold up to a maximum of nine characters of data. The last position is reserved for the null character.

The above declarations define the following character arrays:

sDay	7 elements	(10)
sJobTitle	30 elements	(20)
sStudentRank	100 elements	(10)
sBuilding	5 elements	(25)
sSupplier	40 elements	(30)
sDescription	200 elements	(50)
sMagazine	15 elements	(35)

(The lengths of the elements are shown in parentheses.)

Checkpoint 10A

1. What is an array? What is an element?

2. Identify two types of arrays, and explain each.

3. What is the benefit of using arrays?

4. What information is specified when creating a numeric array?

5. Using the following definitions, code the statement to define each numeric array.
   a. fAmount   48 elements   (float)
   b. iQtyOnHand   450 elements   (int)
   c. fPrice   25 elements   (float)

6. In addition to data type, array name, and size, what other information is needed to define a character array?

7. Using the following definitions, code the statement to define each character array.
   a. sEmployeeName   268 elements   (20 characters)
   b. sAddress   100 elements   (30 characters)
   c. sSocSecNbr   50 elements   (11 characters)

Subscripts

Since one name applies to the entire array, how can we reference the individual elements? The answer is by using a subscript. Each element can be accessed by appending a subscript to the array name. A **subscript** is an integer value that is used to reference a specific element in the array. Consequently, an element is called a **subscripted variable.** Accordingly, the arrays shown in Figure 10.2 consist of a set of subscripted variables that are numbered from first to last, starting with zero. Zero is always assigned to the first element in the array. This is an important convention to remember—the first subscript is always 0, not 1. Hence the elements stored in the *sDay* array contain the following data: *sDay[0]*: Sunday, *sDay[1]*: Monday, *sDay[2]*: Tuesday, and so on; the elements stored in the *fMileage* array contain the following data: *fMileage[0]*: 78.5, *fMileage[1]*: 94.2, *fMileage[2]*: 86.9, and so on.

```
char sDay[7][10]            float fMileage[5]

sDay[0]   Sunday            fMileage[0]   78.5
sDay[1]   Monday            fMileage[1]   94.2
sDay[2]   Tuesday           fMileage[2]   86.9
sDay[3]   Wednesday         fMileage[3]   68.0
sDay[4]   Thursday          fMileage[4]   75.3
sDay[5]   Friday
sDay[6]   Saturday
```

FIGURE 10.2   Arrays and Subscripts

Another important thing to know about subscripts is that they may not be negative or exceed the size of the array minus one (size − 1). Hence, in Figure 10.2, the only valid subscripts for *sDay* are 0–6. Therefore, a reference to either *sDay[10]* or *sDay[−2]* would cause the compiler to produce an error message indicating that the subscript is out of range.

Subscripts may be expressed as integer constants or variables. Subscripted variables allow the program to access or print the value of a specific element or to perform a variety of arithmetic operations on one or more elements stored in an array.

Constants: An **integer constant** is a whole number that directly references a given element. Any element stored in an array may be directly referenced by specifying its subscripts as an integer constant.

Examples of constant subscripts are as follows:

```
printf("\nGrade = %5.1f", fGrade[0]);

fTotal = fGrade[0] + fGrade[1] + fGrade[2] + fGrade[3];

fGrade[2] = fGrade[2] + 6.0;

strcpy(sDay[2], "TUESDAY");

fMileage[3] = 95.0;
```

Variables: Variable subscripts may be written as either a single variable or as an arithmetic expression. Variable subscripts allow the programmer to tap into the full power of arrays and array processing techniques.

Examples of variable subscripts are as follows:

```
scanf(" %f", &fGrade[iSub]);

printf("\nGrade = %5.1f", fGrade[n]);

fGrade[iSub] = fGrade[iSub] + 6.0;

strcpy(sDay[iIdx], "TUESDAY");

fMileage[iSub+1] = 95.0;
```

Checkpoint 10B

1. What is a subscript?
2. True or false: An element is also referred to as a subscripted variable.
3. What integer subscript is always assigned to the first element in an array?
4. True or false: Subscripts may be negative, and they may exceed the size of the array.
5. What is the purpose of using a variable as a subscript as opposed to using an integer constant?

Loading an Array

Array declarations do not automatically assign data to the elements. It is up to the programmer to decide how to fill the arrays. Essentially, there are three methods of assigning data to an array: (1) initialize the elements when the array is declared, (2) prompt the user to enter the data at the keyboard, and (3) load the data from a file.

Initializing Data: Data may be assigned to an array when it is defined. For character arrays, this is the only time that a string can be directly assigned to an element using the equal sign.

Examples of initializing data are as follows:

```
char  sDay[7][10] = {"Sunday", "Monday", "Tuesday",
                     "Wednesday", "Thursday", "Friday",
                     "Saturday"};

float fMileage[5] = {78.5, 94.2, 86.9, 68.0, 75.3};
```

The first declaration assigns a set of names to the *sDay* array; each element may hold up to nine characters of data. String constants are enclosed within double quotes and are separated by commas. Syntax requires that the set of constants be enclosed within braces *{}*.

Similarly, the second declaration assigns a set of floating-point values to the *fMileage* array. Numeric values are not enclosed within double quotes. Both declarations end with a semicolon.

Interactive Input: Data may be assigned to an array by prompting the user to enter the input at the keyboard. The examples shown below use a counter-controlled loop to prompt for the input. The input is assigned to the elements as it is entered at the keyboard.

```
/*------- LOAD DAY ARRAY -------*/
for (iSub = 0; iSub < 7; iSub++)
{
    printf("\nEnter the day: ");
    scanf(" %s", sDay[iSub]);
}
```

Character arrays do not use the address operator *&*. The identifier name associated with the character array represents an address. Since the address of the array is already known, the address operator is not used.

Although *sDay* has two subscripts, we use only one to load data into the array.

```
/*------- LOAD MILEAGE ARRAY -------*/
for (iSub = 0; iSub < 5; iSub++)
{
    printf("\nEnter the mileage: ");
    scanf(" %f", &fMileage[iSub]);
}
```

File Input: Data can be read from a file and loaded directly into an array. The examples shown below use a conditional loop to read the data from a file. As long as the end-of-file marker has not been read, the input is assigned to the elements as it is read from the file.

```
/*--------- LOAD DAY ARRAY ---------*/
iSub = 0;
while(!feof(fpDay))
{
    fscanf(fpDay, " %s", sDay[iSub]);
    iSub++;
}
```

```
/*---------- LOAD MILEAGE ARRAY ----------*/
iSub = 0;
while(!feof(fpMiles))
{
    fscanf(fpMiles, " %f", &fMileage[iSub]);
    iSub++;
}
```

Printing an Array

Array data is stored in memory. Since the data was assigned directly to the elements, we have no way of knowing for sure what was placed in the array. We cannot see the elements. Therefore, it would be wise to verify the contents of the array. We can do this by reading the array and printing a copy of the elements.

The code shown below prints the contents of the *sDay* and *sMileage* arrays.

```
/*------- PRINT DAY ARRAY -------*/
for (iSub = 0; iSub < 7; iSub++)
{
    printf("\n %-9s", sDay[iSub]);
}
```

```
/*-------- PRINT MILEAGE ARRAY --------*/
for (iSub = 0; iSub < 5; iSub++)
{
    printf("\n %4.1f", fMileage[iSub]);
}
```

Processing an Array

Data stored in an array can be processed much like data stored in a single variable. The only difference is that array variables are subscripted. Other than that, we can perform normal arithmetic operations and logical comparisons, determine high and low values, update elements, compute totals, calculate averages, and so on.

High and Low Values: The first *for* loop locates the high mileage stored in the array, while the second locates the low.

```
float fMileage[5] = {78.5, 94.2, 86.9, 68.0, 75.3};
float fHigh = 0.0;
float fLow = 1000.0;
   . . . . .

/*------- FIND HIGH MILEAGE -------*/
for (iSub = 0; iSub < 5; iSub++)
{
    if (fMileage[iSub] > fHigh)
        fHigh = fMileage[iSub];
}

/*------- FIND LOW MILEAGE -------*/
for (iSub = 0; iSub < 5; iSub++)
{
    if (fMileage[iSub] < fLow)
        fLow = fMileage[iSub];
}
```

Notice that *fHigh* is initialized to 0. This "sets the stage" for subsequent comparisons by forcing the first element into the high position. Inside the loop, the elements are compared one by one to the high value. If an element is greater than the current high value, then it becomes the new high value. See if you can follow the logic for finding the low value.

Totals and Averages: The body of the *for* loop computes a total for the elements stored in the array. Upon exiting the loop, the program computes the average.

```
float fMileage[5] = {78.5, 94.2, 86.9, 68.0, 75.3};
float fTotal = 0.0;
float fAverage;
   . . . . .

/*----- TOTAL AND AVERAGE MILEAGES -----*/
for (iSub = 0; iSub < 5; iSub++)
{
    fTotal = fTotal + fMileage[iSub];
}
fAverage = fTotal/5.0;
```

Parallel Arrays

Parallel arrays consist of two or more single arrays that are related in some way. That is, the elements in one array correspond to the elements in another. Parallel arrays have the

```
              sDriver              fMileage

    (0)    Vicki Cho        (0)    78.5
    (1)    David Nelson     (1)    94.2
    (2)    Karen Sims       (2)    86.9
    (3)    Matt Andrews     (3)    68.0
    (4)    Heather Karr     (4)    75.3
```

FIGURE 10.3   Parallel Arrays

same number of elements defined for each array in the parallel set. Figure 10.3 shows two arrays, *sDriver* and *fMileage*. The names in the first array correspond to the miles driven in the second. Hence, Vicki drove 78.5 miles, David drove 94.2 miles, Karen drove 86.9 miles, Matt drove 68.0 miles, and Heather drove 75.3 miles.

Follow the sample code shown below. The first two modules demonstrate how to load the parallel arrays using interactive and file input. The third module prints the contents of the *sDriver* and *fMileage* arrays.

```c
/*------- LOAD FROM USER INPUT -------*/
for (iSub = 0; iSub < 5; iSub++)
{
    printf("  Enter driver: ");
    scanf(" %20[^\n]", sDriver[iSub]);
    printf("  Enter miles: ");
    scanf(" %f", &fMileage[iSub]);
}


/*------- LOAD FROM FILE INPUT ------*/
for (iSub = 0; iSub < 5; iSub++)
{
    fscanf(fpFile, " %20[^\n] %f",
        sDriver[iSub], &fMileage[iSub]);
}


/*------- PRINT PARALLEL ARRAYS -------*/
for (iSub = 0; iSub < 5; iSub++)
{
    printf("\n %-20s              %4.1f",
        sDriver[iSub], fMileage[iSub]);
}
```

Checkpoint 10C

1. What three methods may be used to load an array with data?

2. Which of the two statements will cause an error? Why?
```c
char sText[5][7] = {"This", "is", "some", "sample", "text."};
sText[2] = "some";
```

3. Why is it good practice to print an array after loading it?

4. What is the difference between processing data stored in arrays and processing data stored in program variables?

5. Explain the concept of parallel arrays.

6. Code the statements to load two parallel arrays with the data shown in the following table. (*Note:* The data will be entered at the keyboard.) Then code the statements to print the arrays to verify that they were loaded correctly. Assume the following definitions:

```
int    iSub;
char   sEmployee[5][20];
float  fHourlyRate[5];
```

Employee	*Hourly Rate*
John Smith	10.75
George Thomas	9.50
Sue Blackstone	9.75
Joan Banner	8.45
Todd Nichols	7.00

Sample Program CHAP10A

Sample program CHAP10A loads employee names and production data into parallel arrays and prints a production report from the data stored in the arrays. See Figure 10.4 for the hierarchy chart and Figure 10.5 for the program flowchart. Sample program CHAP10A is presented in Figure 10.6. Figure 10.7 shows the data entry screen, and Figure 10.8 shows the program's output.

The following specifications apply:

Input (keyboard):
For each employee, prompt for and enter the following data:
    Employee name
    Production output

Output (screen):
Print the production report shown in Figure 10.8.

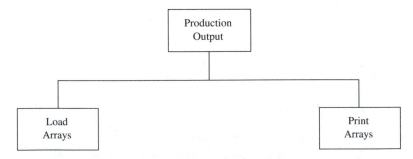

FIGURE 10.4   Hierarchy Chart for CHAP10A

MAINLINE

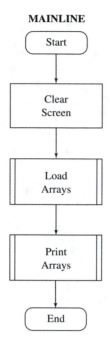

LOAD ARRAYS

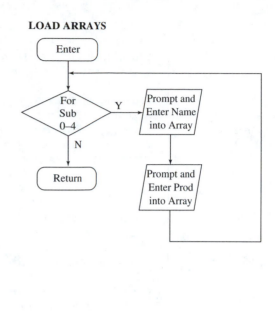

PRINT ARRAYS

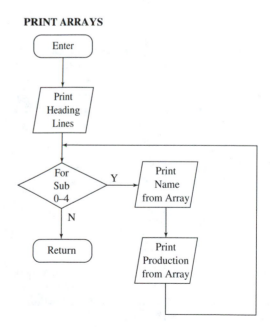

FIGURE 10.5   Program Flowchart for CHAP10A

```
/*-------------------------------------------------------------
PRODUCTION OUTPUT: Load keyboard data into parallel arrays and print
the contents of the arrays.

Program:   CHAP10A.C
Author:    David M. Collopy
Date:      mm/dd/yy
Project:   Sample program
*********************************************************************/

/*---- PREPROCESSING DIRECTIVE ------------------------------------*/

#include <stdio.h>
#include <graph.h>

/*---- FUNCTION PROTOTYPES ----------------------------------------*/

void  LoadArrays(void);        /* load data into arrays       */
void  PrnArrays(void);         /* print data from arrays      */

/*---- PROGRAM SETUP ----------------------------------------------*/

/*>   P R O G R A M    V A R I A B L E S                      <*/

char sName[5][21];             /* 5 element 21 character array */
int  iProd[5];                 /* 5 element integer array      */

/*-------------------------------------------------------------
     MAINLINE CONTROL
-----------------------------------------------------------------*/
main()
{
    _clearscreen(0);
    LoadArrays();
    PrnArrays();
    return 0;
}


/*-------------------------------------------------------------
     LOAD DATA INTO ARRAYS
-----------------------------------------------------------------*/
void LoadArrays(void)
{
    int iSub;                  /* array subscript */
```

FIGURE 10.6   Sample Program CHAP10A: Loads and prints data stored in parallel arrays

```
    for (iSub = 0; iSub < 5; iSub++)
    {
        printf("Enter employee name %d: ", iSub + 1);
        scanf(" %20[^\n]", sName[iSub]);
        fflush(stdin);
        printf("   Enter production %d: ", iSub + 1);
        scanf(" %d", &iProd[iSub]);
        fflush(stdin);
    }
    return;
}


/*-----------------------------------------------------------------
      PRINT DATA FROM ARRAYS
---------------------------------------------------------------------*/
void PrnArrays(void)
{
    int iSub;                      /* array subscript */

    printf("\nEMPLOYEE NAME          PRODUCTION");
    printf("\n-----------------------------");
    for (iSub = 0; iSub < 5; iSub++)
    {
        printf("\n%-20s     %2d", sName[iSub], iProd[iSub]);
    }
    return;
}
```

FIGURE 10.6 *Continued*

```
Enter employee name 1: Melia Sanchez
    Enter production 1: 15
Enter employee name 2: Jason Kimm
    Enter production 2: 16
Enter employee name 3: Nanci Parker
    Enter production 3: 25
Enter employee name 4: Randy Wade
    Enter production 4: 23
Enter employee name 5: Cindy Brown
    Enter production 5: 17
```

FIGURE 10.7 Data Entry Screen for CHAP10A

```
EMPLOYEE NAME              PRODUCTION
------------------------------------
Melia Sanchez                 15
Jason Kimm                    16
Nanci Parker                  25
Randy Wade                    23
Cindy Brown                   17
```

FIGURE 10.8   Program Output for CHAP10A

Processing Requirements:

- Prompt for and enter the employee names and production output.
- Load the input into the name and production arrays, respectively.
- Read and print the contents of the arrays.

Pseudocode:

```
START: Main
Clear screen
Call Load Arrays
Call Print Arrays
END

ENTER: Load Arrays
LOOP for subscript < 5
     Prompt and enter employee name
     Store employee name in name array
     Clear keyboard buffer
     Prompt and enter production output
     Store production output in production array
     Clear keyboard buffer
END LOOP
RETURN

ENTER: Print Arrays
Print 2 column heading lines
LOOP for subscript < 5
     Retrieve data from arrays and print:
          name
          production
END LOOP
RETURN
```

Hierarchy Chart: See Figure 10.4.

Program Flowchart: See Figure 10.5.

Dissection of Sample Program CHAP10A

P R O G R A M   V A R I A B L E S:

```
char  sName[5][21];
```

The above statement defines a five-element character array called *sName* and allocates 20 characters of storage for each name.

```
int   iProd[5];
```

The above statement defines a five-element integer array called *iProd* to hold the production data.

L O A D   D A T A   I N T O   A R R A Y S:

```
void LoadArrays(void)
{
    int iSub;

    for (iSub = 0; iSub < 5; iSub++)
    {
        printf("Enter employee name %d: ", iSub + 1);
        scanf(" %20[^\n]", name[iSub]);
        fflush(stdin);
        printf("   Enter production %d: ", iSub + 1);
        scanf(" %d", &prod[iSub]);
        fflush(stdin);
    }
    return;
}
```

The above statements declare the array subscript. Then as long as the subscript is less than 5, the program prompts the user to enter the employee's name and production data. The first scanf() reads up to 20 characters of input (or until the enter-keypress is encountered) and stores the result in the current *(iSub)* element of the *sName* array. The second scanf() reads the input and stores it in the corresponding element of the *iProd* array. The fflush() clears the keyboard buffer after each scanf().

P R I N T   D A T A   F R O M   A R R A Y S:

```
void PrintArrays(void)
{
    int iSub;

    printf("\nEMPLOYEE NAME           PRODUCTION");
    printf("\n--------------------------------");
```

The above statements define the array subscript and print the column heading lines to describe the output.

```
    for (iSub = 0; iSub < 5; iSub++)
    {
        printf("\n%-20s      %2d", sName[iSub], iProd[iSub]);
```

```
    }
    return;
}
```

In the above statements, as long as the current value of the subscript is less than 5, the printf() function prints the employee's name and the corresponding production output from the arrays. The last brace marks the end of the statement body of the print module.

Notes and Tips

1. Use an array to store a set of related data items in memory. Data stored in memory can be processed repeatedly without reentering it.

2. Character arrays hold string constants, and numeric arrays hold numeric constants. Both require an array size; character arrays also require an element size. Append the prefixes *i, f,* and *s* to integer, float, and character array names, respectively. Terminate each declaration with a semicolon.

3. Although you may declare multiple arrays on the same line or list them down the page, it would be wise to declare only one array on a line. This method eliminates the possibility of (accidentally) coding a semicolon for a comma and makes the array names easier to find during the debugging process.

4. Don't forget to declare the subscript. You need it to locate a specific element in the array. Subscripts are declared like any other program variable.

5. Use parallel arrays to process data stored in multiple arrays that are related on an element-per-element basis.

Tutorial CHAP10A

1. The objectives of this tutorial are to
   - load data into parallel arrays
   - retrieve and print data stored in arrays

2. Read the program specifications for sample program CHAP10A.

3. Log on C, and enter the source code as shown in Figure 10.6. Save the program on your work disk as CHAP10A. Save frequently as you enter the code.

4. Compile, run, and debug your program until the output matches the results shown in Figure 10.8.

5. When completed, show your work to your instructor.

Quick Quiz

Answer the following questions.

1. Explain what the following declarations do:
   ```
   char sName[5][21];
   int  iProd[5];
   ```
   Why does the first declaration have a size and a length?

2. Discuss how the load module uses the *scanf()* function to get the data and place it in the arrays.

3. Study the code shown in the print module. Explain how the program retrieves and prints the contents of the arrays.

4. Did you have any problems or errors when you ran the sample program? If so, what were they and what did you do to correct them?

Array Lookup

At times, it may be necessary to locate (look up) certain data items in an array to either display or update the contents. Hence, **array lookup** is the process of locating data stored in an array. In this section, we will learn how to perform array lookup using direct reference and sequential search. Direct reference uses subscripts to directly locate data, whereas sequential search scans each element until the data is found.

Direct Reference: Direct reference assumes that there is a direct relationship between the user's input and the array subscripts. That is, the input entered at the keyboard is used by the program to access the data stored in the array.

For example, in direct reference, the part number of an inventory item (entered at the keyboard) may be used to directly access the quantity on hand for that item. Similarly, when the user enters a sales number, it may be used as the subscript to update the sales data stored in the array.

Direct reference lookup is illustrated below. Salesperson number is used as a subscript to access the sales data and to add the input to the sales total stored in the array.

```
float fSales[5] = {85.95, 134.72, 57.10, 250.00, 76.43};
int    iNum;
float fAmount;

    . . . . .

/*------------ DIRECT REFERENCE LOOKUP ------------*/
printf("\nEnter salesperson number '-1' to Quit: );
scanf(" %d", &iNum);
while (iNum != -1)
{
    printf("\nEnter sales amount: );
    scanf(" %f", &fAmount);
    fSales[iNum] = fSales[iNum] + fAmount;
    printf("\nEnter salesperson number '-1' to Quit: );
    scanf(" %d", &iNum);
}
```

According to the code, if the user enters the salesperson number 2 and the sales amount 30.00, then the salesperson number is used as the subscript to add the sales amount to the current value stored in the array. Hence, *fSales[2]* = 57.10 + 30.00.

Sequential Search: Sequential search requires, at minimum, two parallel arrays: one for holding the record keys (item number, salesperson number, and so on) and one for holding the corresponding data (quantity on hand, total sales, and so on). **Sequential**

search compares the input—the search key—to each element in the key array until a match is found or the end of the array has been encountered. For a match, the subscript of the key array is used to access the corresponding element stored in the data array.

Sequential search lookup is illustrated below. Assume that the salesperson numbers (100, 200, 300, 400, and 500) are stored in the *iKey* array and that the corresponding sales totals are stored in the *fSales* array. Once the user enters the search key (*iSalesNum*) and the sales income (*fSalesAmt*), the search begins.

```
/*----- SEQUENTIAL SEARCH LOOKUP -----*/
iSub = 0;
iMatch = -1;
while (iSub < 5 && iMatch == -1)
{
    if (iSalesNum == iKey[iSub])
    {
        iMatch = iSub;
    }
    iSub++;
}
```

The variables *iSub* and *iMatch* are set to 0 and –1, respectively. As long as the condition test is true, the search key (*iSalesNum*) is compared to the elements stored in the *iKey* array. If a match is found, *iMatch* is set to *iSub*, the value of the subscript where the search key was found.

```
/*------------- CHECK FOR A MATCH -------------*/
if (iMatch == -1)
{
    printf("\nEmployee not found");
}
else
{
    fSales[iMatch] = fSales[iMatch] + fSalesAmt;
}
```

If *iMatch* equals –1, the message Employee not found is printed. Otherwise, the program uses *iMatch* as the subscript and adds the sales income to the total stored in the *fSales* array.

Checkpoint 10D

1. Define array lookup. Why is it useful?
2. Identify two array lookup or search techniques, and briefly explain each.
3. Code the statements to input data. Then sequentially search the description array until a match is found. Finally, update the *iQtyOnHand* array to add the input data to the current quantity on hand. Assume the following declarations:

```
char sDescription[5][15];
int  iQtyOnHand[5];
char sInputDesc[15];
```

```
int   iNewQty;
int   iSub;
int   iMatch;
```

Note: The user will enter the description into the identifier *sInputDesc*. The user will also enter the update quantity into the identifier *iNewQty*.

element	sDescription
0	Hammer
1	Saw
2	Pliers
3	Screwdriver
4	Wrench

element	iQtyOnHand
0	25
1	13
2	8
3	16
4	22

Sample Program CHAP10B

Sample program CHAP10B allows the user to update the production data stored in parallel arrays. See Figure 10.9 for the hierarchy chart and Figure 10.10 for the program flowchart. The source code is presented in Figure 10.11. Figure 10.12 shows the program's input, and Figure 10.13 displays the output.

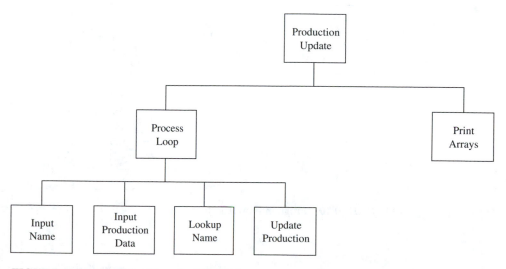

FIGURE 10.9 Hierarchy Chart for CHAP10B

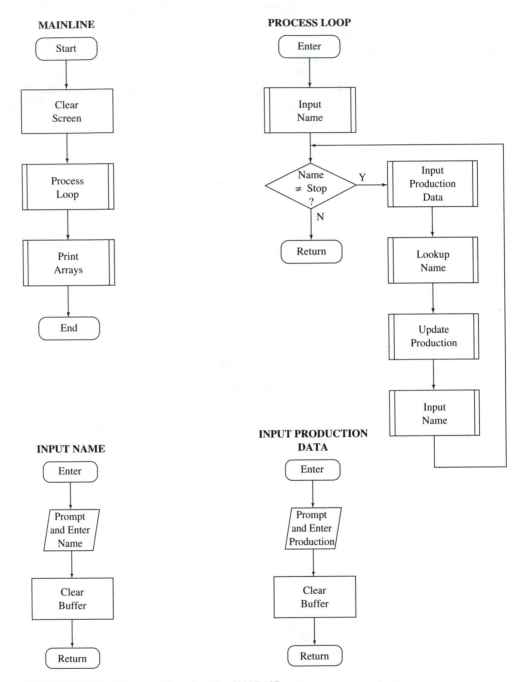

FIGURE 10.10   Program Flowchart for CHAP10B

LOOKUP NAME

```
        ( Enter )
            │
            ▼
    ┌───────────────┐
    │     Sub       │
    │     = 0       │
    └───────────────┘
            │
            ▼
    ┌───────────────┐
    │    Match      │
    │     = –1      │
    └───────────────┘
            │
            ◄──────( A )
            ▼
        ╱─────────╲
       ╱  Sub < 5  ╲      Y
      ╱  and Match   ╲────────►
      ╲    = –1?     ╱
       ╲           ╱
        ╲─────────╱
            │ N
            ▼
      ( Return )
```

```
        ╱─────────╲         ┌───────────────┐
       ╱  Names    ╲    Y   │    Match      │
       ╲  Equal?   ╱───────►│    = Sub      │
        ╲─────────╱         └───────────────┘
            │ N                     │
            ◄──────────────────────┘
            ▼
    ┌───────────────┐
    │    Add 1      │
    │   to Sub      │
    └───────────────┘
            │
            ▼
          ( A )
```

UPDATE PRODUCTION

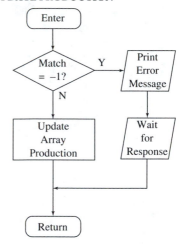

PRINT ARRAYS

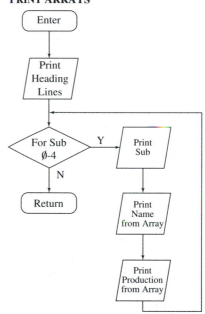

FIGURE 10.10   *Continued*

```
/*----------------------------------------------------------------
PRODUCTION UPDATE: Load parallel arrays and use sequential search to
update the data stored in the arrays.

Program:   CHAP10B.C
Author:    David M. Collopy
Date:      mm/dd/yy
Project:   Sample program
********************************************************************/

/*---- PREPROCESSING DIRECTIVE ------------------------------------*/

#include <stdio.h>
#include <conio.h>
#include <graph.h>

/*---- FUNCTION PROTOTYPES ----------------------------------------*/

void ProcessLoop(void);        /* processing loop              */
void InputName(void);          /* input update name            */
void InputData(void);          /* input update data            */
int  LookUpName(void);         /* lookup employee name         */
void UpdateProd(int);          /* update production data       */
void PrnArrays(void);          /* print data from arrays       */

/*---- PROGRAM SETUP ----------------------------------------------*/

/*>  I N P U T   V A R I A B L E S                           <*/

char sNameIn[21];              /* input employee name          */
int  iProdIn;                  /* input production             */

/*>  P R O G R A M   V A R I A B L E S                       <*/

char sName[5][21] = {"Melia Sanchez", "Jason Kim",
                     "Nanci Parker", "Randy Wade",
                     "Cindy Brown"};

                               /* 5 element 21 character array */

int  iProd[5] = {15, 16, 25, 23, 17};

                               /* 5 element integer array      */
```

FIGURE 10.11   Sample Program CHAP10B: Loads and updates data stored in parallel arrays

```
/*----------------------------------------------------------------
        MAINLINE CONTROL
----------------------------------------------------------------*/
main()
{
    _clearscreen(0);
    ProcessLoop();
    PrnArrays();
    return 0;
}


/*----------------------------------------------------------------
        PROCESSING LOOP
----------------------------------------------------------------*/
void ProcessLoop(void)
{
    int   iMatch;                    /* name match subscript  */

    InputName();
    while (strcmp(sNameIn, "stop") != 0)
    {
        InputData();
        iMatch = LookUpName();
        UpdateProd(iMatch);
        InputName();
    }
    return;
}


/*----------------------------------------------------------------
        INPUT UPDATE NAME
----------------------------------------------------------------*/
void InputName(void)
{
    printf("\nEnter employee name or 'stop' to Quit: ");
    scanf(" %20[^\n]", sNameIn);
    fflush(stdin);
    return;
}


/*----------------------------------------------------------------
        INPUT UPDATE DATA
----------------------------------------------------------------*/
```

FIGURE 10.11   *Continued*

```
void InputData(void)
{
    printf("                    Change production to: ");
    scanf(" %d", &iProdIn);
    fflush(stdin);
    return;
}


/*-----------------------------------------------------------------
        LOOKUP EMPLOYEE NAME
-------------------------------------------------------------------*/
int LookUpName(void)
{
    int   iSub = 0;              /* array subscript      */
    int   iMatch = -1;           /* name match subscript */

    while (iSub < 5 && iMatch == -1)
    {
        if (strcmp(sNameIn, sName[iSub]) == 0)
        {
            iMatch = iSub;       /* name found           */
        }
        iSub++;
    }
    return iMatch;
}


/*-----------------------------------------------------------------
        UPDATE PRODUCTION DATA
-------------------------------------------------------------------*/
void UpdateProd(int iMatch)
{
    char cWait;                  /* wait for enter-keypress     */

    if (iMatch == -1)
    {
        printf("\n** Could not find: %-20s", sNameIn);
        printf("\nPress ENTER to continue...\n");
        cWait = getch();
    }
    else
        iProd[iMatch] = iProdIn;
    return;
}
```

FIGURE 10.11   *Continued*

```
/*-------------------------------------------------------------
        PRINT DATA STORED IN ARRAYS
-----------------------------------------------------------*/
void PrnArrays(void)
{
    int   iSub;                    /* array subscript  */

    printf("\nSUB  EMPLOYEE NAME        PRODUCTION");
    printf("\n----------------------------------");
    for (iSub = 0; iSub < 5; iSub++)
    {
        printf("\n%2d   %-20s     %2d",
            iSub, sName[iSub], iProd[iSub]);
    }
    return;
}
```

FIGURE 10.11 *Continued*

```
Enter employee name or 'stop' to QUIT: Jason Kim
                Change production to: 29

Enter employee name or 'stop' to QUIT: Drew Lanick
                Change production to: 30

Name not found - press ENTER to continue

Enter employee name or 'stop' to QUIT: stop
```

FIGURE 10.12 Program Input for CHAP10B

```
SUB   EMPLOYEE NAME          PRODUCTION
----------------------------------------
 0    Melia Sanchez             15
 1    Jason Kim                 29
 2    Nanci Parker              25
 3    Randy Wade                23
 4    Cindy Brown               17
```

FIGURE 10.13 Program Output for CHAP10B

The following specifications apply:

Input (keyboard):

For each update, prompt for and enter the following data:

> Employee name
> Production output

Output (screen):

Print the output shown in Figure 10.13.

Processing Requirements:

- Define and initialize the name and production arrays.
- Prompt for and enter the employee name and the production update.
- Look up employee name:
  If not found—print "Name not found" and continue.
  If found—update the production array.
- After the updates, print the contents of the arrays.

Pseudocode:

```
START: Main
Clear screen
Call Processing Loop
Call Print Arrays
END

ENTER: Processing Loop
Call Input Employee Name
LOOP while employee name not = stop
        Call Input Production Data
        Call Lookup Name
        Call Update Production Data
        Call Input Employee Name
END LOOP
RETURN

ENTER: Input Employee Name
        Prompt and enter employee name (or stop to quit)
        Clear keyboard buffer
RETURN

ENTER: Input Production Data
        Prompt and enter new value
        Clear keyboard buffer
RETURN

ENTER: Lookup Name
Set subscript to 0
Set match to –1
LOOP while subscript < 5 and match = –1
        IF employee name found in name array
                Set match to subscript
```

```
        END IF
        Add 1 to subscript
END LOOP
RETURN

ENTER: Update Production Data
IF match = -1
        Print could not find employee name
        Hold screen for key press
else
        Change corresponding production data to new value
END IF
RETURN

ENTER: Print Arrays
Print 2 column heading lines
LOOP for subscript < 5
        Retrieve data from arrays and print:
                subscript
                employee name
                production data
END LOOP
RETURN
```

Hierarchy Chart: See Figure 10.9.

Program Flowchart: See Figure 10.10.

Dissection of Sample Program CHAP10B

```
P R O C E S S I N G    L O O P :

void ProcessLoop(void)
{
    int iMatch;

    InputName();
    while (strcmp(sNameIn, "stop") != 0)
    {
        InputData();
        iMatch = LookUpName();
        UpdateProd(iMatch);
        InputName();
    }
    return;
}
```

The above declaration defines the name of the *match* subscript. The priming input call prompts the user for the employee's name. As long as the name is not equal to *stop*, control enters the *while* loop and executes the modules in the order listed.

InputData prompts for the production update data. *LookUpName* searched for the input name in the name array (found or not found, a value is returned and assigned to *iMatch*), and the value stored at *iMatch* is passed to *UpdateProd*. The looping input call prompts for the next name.

I N P U T   U P D A T E   N A M E:

```
void InputName(void)
{
    printf("\nEnter employee name or 'stop' to Quit: ");
    scanf(" %20[^\n]", sNameIn);
    fflush(stdin);
    return;
}
```

The above statements prompt the user to enter the employee name or *stop* to quit. The scanf() reads up to 20 characters (or until the enter-keypress is encountered) and assigns the result to *sNameIn*. The fflush() clears the keyboard buffer.

At the end of the module, control returns to the Processing Loop.

I N P U T   U P D A T E   D A T A:

```
void InputData(void)
{
    printf("                  Change production to: ");
    scanf(" %d", &iProdIn);
    fflush(stdin);
    return;
}
```

The above statements prompt the user to enter the change in production, read the input, convert it to an integer, and assign the result to the *iProdIn*. The fflush() removes the enter-keypress from the keyboard buffer.

After clearing the buffer, control returns to the Processing Loop.

L O O K U P   E M P L O Y E E   N A M E:

```
void LookUpName(void)
{
    iSub = 0;
```

The above statement initializes the array subscript to 0. This forces the program to begin the search with the first element in the name array.

```
    iMatch = -1;
```

The above statement initializes *iMatch* to *–1*. A *–1* tells the program that a match was not found for the employee name. Any value other than *–1* tells the program where the match was found.

```
    while (iSub < 5 && iMatch == -1)
    {
```

In the above statement, as long as the subscript is less than 5 and a match has not been found, control enters the body of the loop.

```
        if (strcmp(sNameIn, sName[iSub]) == 0)
        {
            iMatch = iSub;
        }
```

In the above statements, if the input employee name matches the data stored in the current element, then control assigns the value of the subscript to *iMatch*.

```
        iSub++;
    }
```

The above statement increments the array subscript. One is added to the current value of *iSub*.

```
    return iMatch;
}
```

The above statement returns a value to the calling statement in the Processing Loop. The return value may be either a *–1* (specifying that no match was found) or an integer that indicates where the name was found in the name array.

U P D A T E   P R O D U C T I O N:

```
void UpdateProd(int iMatch)
{
    char cWait;
```

The value (*iMatch*) passed to this module either indicates where the employee name was found or that a match was not found.

```
    if (iMatch == -1)
    {
        printf("\** Could not find: %-20s", sNameIn);
        printf("\nPress ENTER to continue …");
        cWait = getch();
    }
```

In the above statements, if the name was not found, then the printf() function prints the messages on the screen and prompts the user to press the enter key to continue.

```
    else
        iProd[iMatch] = iProdIn;
    return;
}
```

In the above statements, if the employee name was found, then the program assigns the input production to the array element indexed by *iMatch* and control returns to the Processing Loop.

P R I N T   D A T A   S T O R E D   I N   A R R A Y S:

```
void PrintArrays(void)
{
    int iSub;

    printf("\nSUB  EMPLOYEE NAME        PRODUCTION");
    printf("\n-----------------------------------");
```

```
    for (iSub = 0; iSub < 5; iSub++)
    {
        printf("\n%2d     %-20s     %2d",
            iSub, sName[iSub], iProd[iSub]);
    }
    return;
}
```

The above statements declare the array subscript and print the heading lines and the contents of the *sName* and *iProd* arrays. This is done to verify that the updates were correctly applied to the production array.

Notes and Tips

1. Array lookup refers to the process of locating and updating data stored in an array.

2. Direct reference is the simpler of the two methods presented in this chapter. But it only works if there is a direct relationship between the input and the subscripts used to locate the data stored in the array.

3. Sequential search is particularly useful for applications that do not have a direct relationship between the input and the subscripts. It involves at least two arrays—one for the keys and one for the data—and a lookup routine. Essentially, the idea is to locate the input in the key array and use its subscript to access the corresponding element in the data array. The lookup routine is shown in the sample program. Make sure you understand how it works.

Tutorial CHAP10B

1. The objectives of this tutorial are to
   - load data into parallel arrays as they are declared
   - use sequential search to locate and update data stored in an array
   - retrieve and print data stored in arrays

2. Read the program specifications for sample program CHAP10B.

3. Log on C, and enter the source code as shown in Figure 10.11. Save the program on your work disk as CHAP10B. Save frequently.

4. Compile, run, and debug your program until the output matches the production report shown in Figure 10.13.

5. When completed, show your work to your instructor.

Quick Quiz

Answer the following questions.

1. Explain how the data is loaded into the arrays at the same time they are declared.
```
    char sName[5][21] = {"Melia Sanchez", "Jason Kim", "Nanci Parker",
                        "Randy Wade", "Cindy Brown"};
    int  iProd[5] = {15, 16, 25, 23, 17};
```

2. Take a close look at the code shown for the *LookUpName* module, and explain how it works. What happens when the lookup name is not found in the name array?

3. How does the *UpdateProd* module determine if the lookup name was actually found?

4. Did you have any problems or errors when you ran the sample program? If so, what were they and what did you do to correct them?

Sorting

Sorting is the process of arranging data in a given order. The contents of an array may be used to arrange the elements in either ascending or descending order. Usually, data is loaded into an array in the order that it is received. Yet we may want to show a list of names in alphabetic order or a series of numbers in ascending order. Sorting allows us to do this.

Although many sort algorithms have been developed for the computer, we will focus on two relatively simple techniques that are easy to use: the bubble sort and the Shell sort.

The Bubble Sort: For long lists, the bubble sort is not too efficient. It does, however, work quite well for short lists. The **bubble sort** works by repeatedly comparing and exchanging elements until they are arranged in the specified order.

The example below demonstrates the bubble sort. A list of five items is arranged in ascending order. Walk through the steps. Note that it takes, at most, four passes to arrange the list in ascending order. In general, it takes, at most, $n-1$ passes to sort a list of n elements.

BEFORE (unsorted list): 90 20 80 60 10

Pass 1: Compare elements	*Action*
[90 20] 80 60 10	exchange 90 and 20
20 **[90 80]** 60 10	exchange 90 and 80
20 80 **[90 60]** 10	exchange 90 and 60
20 80 60 **[90 10]**	exchange 90 and 10

Pass 2: Compare elements	*Action*
[20 80] 60 10 90	no exchange
20 **[80 60]** 10 90	exchange 80 and 60
20 60 **[80 10]** 90	exchange 80 and 10
20 60 10 **[80 90]**	no exchange

Pass 3: Compare elements	*Action*
[20 60] 10 80 90	no exchange
20 **[60 10]** 80 90	exchange 60 and 10
20 10 **[60 80]** 90	no exchange
20 10 60 **[80 90]**	no exchange

Pass 4: Compare elements	*Action*
[20 10] 60 80 90	exchange 20 and 10
10 **[20 60]** 80 90	no exchange
10 20 **[60 80]** 90	no exchange
10 20 60 **[80 90]**	no exchange

AFTER (sorted list): 10 20 60 80 90

For each pass, the elements enclosed within square brackets *[]* are compared and exchanged only if the first element is greater than the second. During the sort, the low values "ripple" to the left (top) of the list and the high values "ripple" to the right (bottom). Because of this, the bubble sort is also known as the **ripple sort**.

Example:

The bubble sort shown below rearranges an array of five elements in ascending order.

```
iSwap = 1;
while (iSwap == 1)
{
    iSwap = 0;
    for (iSub = 0; iSub < 5; iSub++)
    {
        if (iNum[iSub] > iNum[iSub+1])
        {
            iTemp = iNum[iSub];
            iNum[iSub] = iNum[iSub+1];
            iNum[iSub+1] = iTemp;
            iSwap = 1;
        }
    }
}
```

Dissection: In order to enter the *while* loop, *iSwap* is set to 1. The swap flag is used to determine whether to continue or to terminate the sort. Zero indicates that no exchanges (swaps) were made on the last pass—the sort is complete; 1 indicates that at least one exchange occurred on the last pass—the sort continues.

Inside the *while* loop, the flag is set to 0. This is done in preparation for the next pass. Control now enters the *for* loop. Here, the *if* statement compares adjacent elements and exchanges them only if the first is greater than the second. For an exchange, the flag is reset to 1.

During an exchange, the first element is temporarily copied to *iTemp,* and the second element is assigned to the first. Next, the value stored at *iTemp* is reassigned to the second element. This, of course, completes the exchange.

As long as an exchange is made (*iSwap* = 1), the *while* loop continues to compare and exchange elements. Otherwise, the elements are in order and the sort stops.

The Shell Sort: The Shell sort, developed by Donald Shell, provides a faster and more efficient sort algorithm. For a small list of ten items or so, the execution times for the bubble sort and the Shell sort are comparable. However, for longer lists, the execution times are significantly different. For example, it takes the bubble sort 5 times longer to sort a list of 100 items than it does the Shell sort; it takes about 30 times longer to sort a list of 1,000 items.

Like the bubble sort, the **Shell sort** compares and exchanges elements. However, it compares the elements over a gap. A **gap** is the distance between two elements. The Shell sort works by repeatedly comparing and exchanging elements over a series of gaps until the array is arranged in the specified order.

On the first pass, the gap is computed by dividing the size of the array by two (i.e., iGap = iSize / 2). Subsequent gaps are computed by dividing the previous gap by two (i.e., iGap = iGap / 2) until the length of the gap equals one.

The example below demonstrates how the Shell sort works. Walk through the process as the elements are compared and exchanged over the gaps.

BEFORE (unsorted list):   90 20 80 60 10 70 40 50
Compute the first gap: iGap = iSize / 2 or iGap = 4.

Compare elements	*Action*
90 20 80 60 **10** 70 40 50	exchange 90 and 10
10 **20** 80 60 90 **70** 40 50	no exchange
10 20 **80** 60 90 70 **40** 50	exchange 80 and 40
10 20 40 **60** 90 70 80 **50**	exchange 60 and 50

Compare and exchange elements over the gap until no exchanges are made on a pass.

Compute the next gap: iGap = iGap / 2 or iGap = 2.

Compare elements	*Action*
10 20 **40** 50 90 70 80 60	no exchange
10 **20** 40 **50** 90 70 80 60	no exchange
10 20 **40** 50 **90** 70 80 60	no exchange
10 20 40 **50** 90 **70** 80 60	no exchange
10 20 40 50 **90** 70 **80** 60	exchange 90 and 80
10 20 40 50 80 **70** 90 **60**	exchange 70 and 60

Compare and exchange elements over the gap until no exchanges are made on a pass.

Compute the next gap: iGap = iGap / 2 or iGap = 1.

For iGap = 1, the Shell sort works like the bubble sort.
When no exchanges are made on a pass, the sort is complete.

Example:

The Shell sort shown below rearranges an array of eight elements in ascending order.

```
iSize = 8;
 . . . . .
iGap = iSize / 2;
while (iGap > 0)
```

```
{
    iSwap = 1;
    while (iSwap == 1)
    {
        iSwap = 0;
        for (iSub = 0; iSub < iSize - iGap; iSub++)
        {
            if (iNum[iSub] > iNum[iSub+iGap])
            {
                iTemp = iNum[iSub];
                iNum[iSub] = iNum[iSub+iGap];
                iNum[iSub+iGap] = iTemp;
                iSwap = 1;
            }
        }
    }
    iGap = iGap / 2;
}
```

Dissection: Processing begins by setting the initial *iGap* to *iSize/2*. Basically, the Shell sort consists of a three-level nested loop. The first loop determines whether to continue or to terminate the sort. As long as the gap is greater than 0, *iSwap* is set to 1 and the sort continues.

The second loop determines when to change the gap. As long as *iSwap* equals 1, the flag is reset to 0 (in preparation for the next pass) and control enters the *for* loop to compare elements. But if *iSwap* equals 0, then the elements are in order for the current gap and it is time to exit the second loop and change the gap.

Note that the third loop establishes a sort range of 0 to *iSize–iGap*. This tells the program how many times to compare elements. Here the body of the *for* loop compares the elements and exchanges them only if the first element is greater than the second. For each exchange, the flag is reset to 1.

As long as the gap is greater than 0, the sort continues. Otherwise, the elements are in order and the sort stops.

Checkpoint 10E

1. What is sorting?
2. Identify two sorting methods and briefly explain each.
3. For the Shell sort, how is the gap calculated for:
   a. the first pass?
   b. subsequent passes?
4. Using the Shell sort, code the statements that will arrange the following array values in descending (high-to-low) order.

   ```
   int iList[10] = {30, 80, 68, 42, 79, 90, 43, 51, 25, 100};
   ```

Sample Program CHAP10C

Sample program CHAP10C uses the Shell sort to arrange the random data stored in parallel arrays in ascending order. See Figure 10.14 for the hierarchy chart and Figure 10.15 for the program flowchart. Sample program CHAP10C is presented in Figure 10.16. Figures 10.17 and 10.18 show the program's output.

The following specifications apply:

Input (internal):

Initialize the parallel arrays to the values given below:

Employee number	Employee name	Production
303	Adams	20
400	Wyler	19
510	Brownfield	23
237	Caluci	17
120	Stein	24
101	Nichols	21
100	Perkins	22

Output (screen):

Print the unsorted and sorted production reports shown in Figures 10.17 and 10.18, respectively.

Processing Requirements:

- Create and initialize three parallel arrays—employee number, employee name, and production output. Set the size of each array to 7.
- Print the unsorted data stored in the arrays.
- Sort the arrays, and arrange the elements in ascending order by employee number.
- Print the sorted data stored in the arrays.

Pseudocode:

```
START: Main
Clear screen
Call Print Arrays
Call Sort Arrays
Call Print Arrays
END

ENTER: Print Arrays
Print 2 column heading lines
LOOP for subscript < 7
     Retrieve data from arrays and print:
          employee number
          employee name
          production data
END LOOP
RETURN
```

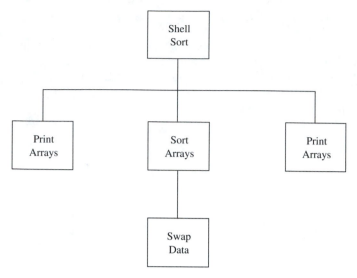

FIGURE 10.14   Hierarchy Chart for CHAP10C

```
ENTER: Sort Arrays
Let gap = array size / 2
LOOP while gap > 0
    Let swap flag = 1
    LOOP while swap flag = 1
        Let swap flag = 0
        LOOP for subscript < array size – gap
            IF employee number 1 > employee number 2
                Call Swap Elements Over Gap
                Let swap flag = 1
            END IF
        END LOOP
    END LOOP
    Let gap = gap / 2
END LOOP
RETURN

ENTER: Swap Elements Over Gap
Let numeric save area = employee number 1
Let employee number 1 = employee number 2
Let employee number 2 = numeric save area
Let string save area = employee name 1
Let employee name 1 = employee name 2
Let employee name 2 = string save area
Let numeric save area = production data 1
Let production data 1 = production data 2
Let production data 2 = numeric save area
RETURN
```

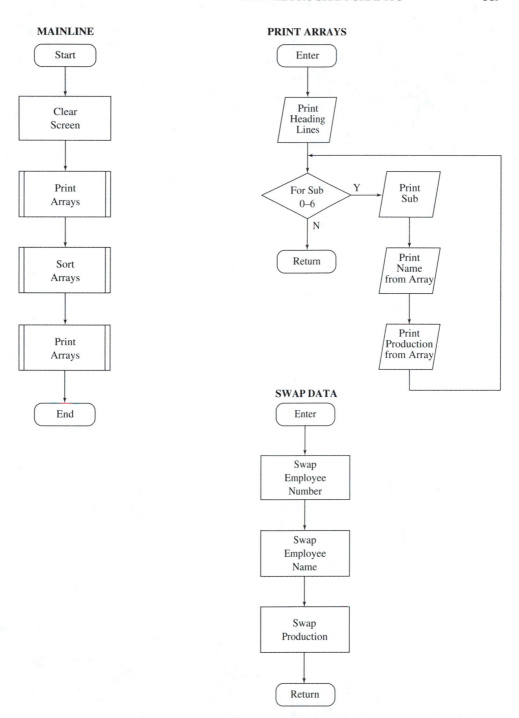

FIGURE 10.15 Program Flowchart for CHAP10C

SORT ARRAYS

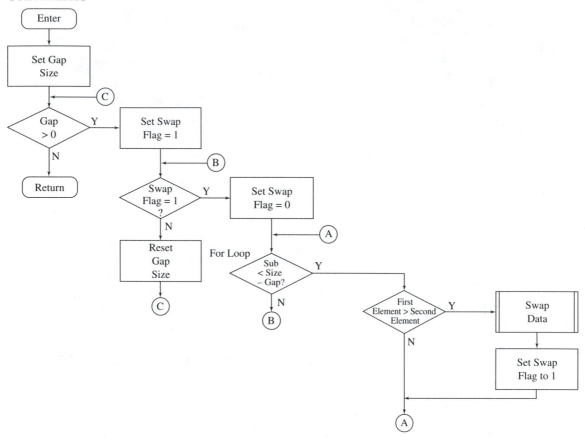

FIGURE 10.15   *Continued*

```
/*-----------------------------------------------------------------
SHELL SORT: Load parallel arrays and use the Shell sort to arrange
the array data in ascending order by employee number.

Program:    CHAP10C.C
Author:     David M. Collopy
Date:       mm/dd/yy
Project:    Sample program
*****************************************************************/

/*---- PREPROCESSING DIRECTIVE ----------------------------------*/

#include <stdio.h>
#include <graph.h>
```

FIGURE 10.16   Sample Program CHAP10C: Application of the Shell Sort

```
/*---- FUNCTION PROTOTYPES --------------------------------------*/

void  PrnArrays(void);          /* print array data */
void  SortArrays(void);         /* sort array data  */
void  SwapData(int);            /* swap elements    */

/*---- PROGRAM SETUP --------------------------------------------*/

/*>  P R O G R A M   V A R I A B L E S                     <*/

int  iSub;                      /* array subscript */

int  iNum[7] = {303, 400, 510, 237, 120, 101, 100};

char sName[7][21] = {"Adams", "Wyler", "Brownfield", "Caluci",
                     "Stein", "Nichols", "Perkins"};

int  iProd[7] = {20, 19, 23, 17, 24, 21, 22};

/*--------------------------------------------------------------
        MAINLINE CONTROL
--------------------------------------------------------------*/
main()
{
    _clearscreen(0);
    PrnArrays();
    SortArrays();
    PrnArrays();
    return 0;
}

/*--------------------------------------------------------------
        PRINT ARRAY DATA
--------------------------------------------------------------*/
void PrnArrays(void)
{
    printf("\n\nEmp#  Employee Name     Production");
    printf("\n----------------------------------");
    for (iSub = 0; iSub < 7; iSub++)
    {
        printf("\n %3d  %-20s  %2d",
            iNum[iSub], sName[iSub], iProd[iSub]);
    }
    return;
}

/*--------------------------------------------------------------
        SORT ARRAY DATA
--------------------------------------------------------------*/
```

FIGURE 10.16 *Continued*

```
void SortArrays(void)
{
    int   iSwap;                     /* swap flag        */
    int   iSize = 7;                 /* array size       */
    int   iGap;                      /* gap size         */

    iGap = iSize / 2;                /* set gap size     */
    while (iGap > 0)
    {
        iSwap = 1;                   /* set flag to yes  */
        while (iSwap == 1)
        {
            iSwap = 0;               /* reset flag to no */
            for (iSub = 0; iSub < iSize-iGap; iSub++)
            {
                if (iNum[iSub] > iNum[iSub+iGap])
                {
                    SwapData(iGap);  /* swap elements    */
                    iSwap = 1;       /* reset flag to yes */
                }
            }
        }
        iGap = iGap / 2;             /* reset gap size   */
    }
    return;
}


/*------------------------------------------------------------------
      SWAP ELEMENTS
-----------------------------------------------------------------*/
void SwapData(int iGap)
{
    int   iTemp;                     /* numeric temporary storage */
    char  sTemp[21];                 /* string temporary storage  */

    iTemp = iNum[iSub];                     /* swap employee number */
    iNum[iSub] = iNum[iSub+iGap];
    iNum[iSub+iGap] = iTemp;
    strcpy(sTemp, sName[iSub]);             /* swap employee name   */
    strcpy(sName[iSub], sName[iSub+ iGap]);
    strcpy(sName[iSub+iGap], sTemp);
    iTemp = iProd[iSub];                    /* swap production data */
    iProd[iSub] = iProd[iSub+iGap];
    iProd[iSub+iGap] = iTemp;
    return;
}
```

FIGURE 10.16 *Continued*

```
Emp#    Employee Name        Production

303   Adams                   20
400   Wyler                   19
510   Brownfield              23
237   Caluci                  17
120   Stein                   24
101   Nichols                 21
100   Perkins                 22
```

FIGURE 10.17   Unsorted Data for CHAP10C

```
Emp#    Employee Name        Production

100       Perkins              22
101       Nichols              21
120       Stein                24
237       Caluci               17
303       Adams                20
400       Wyler                19
510       Brownfield           23
```

FIGURE 10.18   Sorted Output for CHAP10C

Hierarchy Chart: See Figure 10.14.

Program Flowchart: See Figure 10.15.

Dissection of Sample Program CHAP10C

Three arrays are declared and initialized in the *PROGRAM SETUP*.

Sample program CHAP10C prints the arrays twice: once before the sort to show the original order of the elements and once after the sort to verify that all elements were successfully arranged in ascending order.

The heart of the processing takes place in the *SortArrays* module. So let's pick up the program dissection there.

```
S O R T   A R R A Y   D A T A :

void SortArrays(void)
{
```

```
int iSwap;
int iSize = 7;
int iGap;
```

The above statements declare the local variables required by the sort module—a swap flag, an array size, and a gap size.

```
iGap = iSize / 2;
```

The above statement computes the initial gap by dividing the number of elements in the array by 2.

```
while (iGap > 0)
{
    iSwap = 1;
```

In the above statements, as long as the gap is greater than 0, control enters the loop and sets the swap flag to 1. The flag is set to 1 in order to enter the next *while* loop. But when the gap is 0, the sort is finished and control returns to the calling module.

```
while (iSwap == 1)
{
```

In the above statement, as long as the flag equals 1, control enters the loop. Otherwise, control skips the body of the loop and computes the next gap. One indicates that at least one exchange was made on the last pass and that the elements are not yet in order for the current gap.

```
iSwap = 0;
```

The above statement resets the swap flag to 0. Zero represents the initial setting of the flag. This is done in preparation for the next pass.

```
for (iSub = 0; i < iSize-iGap; iSub++)
{
```

The above statement initializes the array subscript to 0 and tests for the ending condition. As long as the subscript is less then *iSize–iGap*, control enters the body of the loop. The expression *iSize–iGap* specifies the number of times to compare the elements.

```
if (iNum[iSub] > iNum[iSub+iGap])
{
    SwapData(iGap);
    iSwap = 1;
}
```

In the above statements, if the first element is greater than the second, then control passes the gap to *SwapData* and sets the swap flag to 1. Otherwise, control skips the body of the *if* statement.

```
        }
    }
    iGap = iGap / 2;
}
```

The above statement calculates the next gap and goes back to the first *while* statement.

```
    return;
}
```

The above statement returns to the calling module.

```
S W A P     E L E M E N T S:

void SwapData(int iGap)
{
    int   iTemp;
    char sTemp[21];
```

The above statements define the local variables required by the module. The temporary holding areas are used to exchange elements when a swap is detected by the program. The first one (*iTemp*) is used to hold the employee number and production output, while the second one (*sTemp*) is used to hold the employee name.

```
    iTemp = iNum[iSub];
```

The above statement copies the first element (the high value) to temporary storage, *iTemp*.

```
    iNum[iSub] = iNum[iSub+iGap];
```

The above statement assigns the second element (the low value) to the first, *iNum[iSub]*.

```
    iNum[iSub+iGap] = iTemp;
```

The above statement assigns the high value stored at *iTemp* to the second element *iNum[iSub+iGap]*. This completes the exchange.

```
    strcpy(sTemp, sName[iSub]);
    strcpy(sName[iSub], sName[iSub+iGap]);
    strcpy(sName[iSub+iGap], sTemp);
```

The above statements exchange the employee names over the current gap.

```
    iTemp = iProd[iSub];
    iProd[iSub] = iProd[iSub+iGap];
    iProd[iSub+iGap] = iTemp;
    return;
}
```

The above statements exchange the employee production over the current gap. The *return* sends control back to the calling statement.

Notes and Tips

1. Sorting is a powerful tool. For some applications, it is absolutely essential that the data be arranged in a given order before the program can process it.

2. Use the bubble sort to arrange a short list of items in either ascending or descending order.

3. Use the Shell sort to arrange a long list of items in either ascending or descending order.

4. Remember, it takes the bubble sort 5 times longer to sort a list of 100 items than it does the Shell sort; it takes the bubble sort about 30 times longer to sort a list of 1,000 items. The Shell sort routine is shown in the sample program. Walk through the code several times to make sure you understand how it works.

Tutorial CHAP10C

1. The objectives of this tutorial are to
   - load data into three parallel arrays as they are declared
   - use the Shell sort to arrange the array data in ascending order by employee number
   - retrieve and print data stored in arrays
2. Read the program specifications for sample program CHAP10C.
3. Log on C, and enter the source code as shown in Figure 10.16. Save the program on your work disk as CHAP10C. Save frequently as you enter the code.
4. Compile, run, and debug your program until the output matches the results shown in Figures 10.17 and 10.18.
5. When completed, show your work to your instructor.

Quick Quiz

Answer the following questions.

1. The *SortArrays* module consist of two *while* loops, a *for* loop, and an *if* statement. Explain how the code works. What role does the swap flag (*iSwap*) play in the sort?
2. The variables *iTemp* and *sTemp* are used in the *SwapData* module to swap data from one location to another in the arrays. Explain how this works.
3. Did you have any problems or errors when you ran the sample program? If so, what were they and what did you do to correct them?

Summary

1. An array represents a set of variables that are given one name. Each item in the array is called an element, and each element has identical data types.
2. Character arrays store non-numeric or string data, and numeric arrays store integer or floating-point values. Integer and floating-point data are stored in separate arrays.
3. Data assigned to an array can be processed repeatedly without requiring the program to reload the array.
4. Arrays are defined by specifying the data type, the name, and the number of elements. For character arrays, the size of the elements is also declared.
5. A subscript is used to uniquely identify or reference a specific element in an array. Subscripts represent integer values that may be expressed as either constants or variables.
6. Subscripts are numbered starting with zero. A subscript may not be negative or exceed the size of the array minus one.

7. Data may be assigned to an array by initializing the elements when the array is declared, prompting the user to enter the data at the keyboard, or reading the data from a file.

8. Data stored in an array can be processed much like data stored in a program variable. We can perform arithmetic operations and logical comparisons, determine high and low values, compute totals, and so on.

9. Parallel arrays consist of two or more single arrays that are processed together. The elements in one array are related (correspond) to the elements in another.

10. Array lookup pertains to the process of locating a specific element stored in an array.

11. Direct reference lookup uses a subscript to directly locate the data stored in the array. This method assumes that there is a direct relationship between user input and the subscripts.

12. Sequential search lookup requires, at minimum, two parallel arrays—one for the record keys and one for the data. This method compares the input, the search key, to each element in the key array.

13. Sorting is the process of rearranging the elements of an array in a specific order.

14. The bubble sort rearranges small lists of items. It works by repeatedly comparing and exchanging elements until the array is arranged in the desired order.

15. The Shell sort rearranges large lists of items. It works by repeatedly comparing and exchanging elements over a series of gaps until the array is arranged in the desired order. A gap is defined as the distance between two elements.

Programming Projects

For each project, design the logic and write the modular structured program to produce the output. Model your program after the sample programs presented in the chapter. Verify your output.

Project 10–1   Overdue Accounts-1

Write a program to read a file, load the input into parallel arrays, and print a report of all customers with account balances 90 days overdue.

Input (text file):
For each customer, read a record and load the data into the following arrays. (Array types are shown in parentheses.)

iAccount	(int)
sName	(char)
iOverdue	(int)
fBalance	(float)

Set the size of each array to 12. Allow for a maximum of 15 characters of data for the elements in the *sName* array.

Text File (txOvrdue.fil):

Create the overdue accounts file from the data given below. Enter the records in the order shown.

Account Number	Customer Name	Days Overdue	Balance Due
4080	Corey Adkins	30	233.00
2730	Rita Fox	90	740.00
7720	Lisa Wilson	60	417.00
3100	Alvin Porter	90	550.00
9630	Pat Rankin	60	342.00
9200	Tori Landis	90	235.00
1010	David Ryan	90	400.00
4890	Amy Wyatt	30	700.00
5260	Brian Knox	30	625.00
2450	Marie Hill	30	754.00
8540	Matt Hart	90	900.00
6350	Susan Cope	90	600.00

Ouput (printer):

Print the following 90-day overdue accounts report:

```
Author              90-DAY OVERDUE ACCOUNTS              Page 01
                          mm/dd/yy


    Acct Number          Customer Name          Amount Due

        9999          X-----------X              999.99
          :                :                       :
          :                :                       :
        9999          X-----------X              999.99

                              Total:            9999.99
```

Processing Requirements:

- Read and load the file input into the arrays.
- Print the unsorted data stored in the arrays.
- Sort the arrays, and arrange the data in ascending order by account number.
- Print the sorted data stored in the arrays.
- Read the arrays, and print a report of all the accounts 90 days overdue.
- Accumulate and print a report total for the amount due.

Project 10–2   Overdue Accounts-2

Modify the program in Project 10–1 to allow the user to update the data stored in the parallel arrays. Prompt for and enter the updates given below. Search for a match on account number (Enter '-1' to quit). If a match is not found, print the message Account not found - press ENTER to continue. Add the lookup and update logic to the program after the arrays are sorted.

Enter the updates in the order shown.

Account Number	Customer Name	Days Overdue	Balance Due
5260	Brian Knox	30	872.00
2459	Marie Hill	90	700.00
6350	Susan Cope	60	610.00
1023	David Ryan	90	435.00
7720	Lisa Wilson	60	495.00
4081	Corey Adkins	30	249.00

Project 10–3 Payroll-1

Write a program to compute and print a weekly payroll roster. Read the data from a file, load the input into parallel arrays, and process the data stored in the arrays. Assume the current federal income tax (FIT) rate is 15% and overtime is not computed.

Input (text file):

For each employee, read a record and load the data into the following arrays. (Array types are shown in parentheses.)

sName	(char)
iHours	(int)
fRate	(float)

Set the size of each array to 9. Allow for a maximum of 15 characters of data for the elements in the sName array.

Text File (txPayrol.fil):

Create the payroll file from the data given below. Enter the records in the order shown.

Employee Name	Hours	Pay Rate
Tracy York	36	11.00
Dale Miller	40	10.25
Sara Erickson	38	12.00
Karen Thomas	48	9.00
Paul Irwin	48	8.72
Dana Clark	45	14.90
Tanya Bauer	40	7.50
Bret Rossi	35	8.00
Scott Howard	42	9.75

Ouput (printer):

Print the following weekly payroll report:

```
Author               WEEKLY PAYROLL REPORT            Page 01
                           mm/dd/yy


Employee   Hours    Pay Rate   Gross Pay    FIT     Net Pay

X-------X    99      99.99       999.99    99.99     999.99
```

```
      :        :        :           :         :         :
      :        :        :           :         :         :
X-------X     99      99.99      999.99     99.99     999.99

           Totals:              9999.99    999.99    9999.99
```

Processing Requirements:
- Read and load the file input into the arrays.
- Print the unsorted data stored in the arrays.
- Sort the arrays, and arrange the data in alphabetic order by employee name.
- Print the sorted data stored in the arrays.
- Compute the gross pay:
  hours × pay rate.
- Compute the federal income tax:
  gross pay × FIT rate.
- Compute the net pay:
  gross pay – FIT.
- Accumulate totals for gross pay, FIT, and net pay.

Project 10–4   Payroll-2

Modify the program in Project 10–3 to allow the user to update the payroll data stored in the parallel arrays. Prompt for and enter the updates given below. Search for a match on employee name (Enter 'Q' to quit). If a match is not found, print the message Name not found - press ENTER to continue. Add the lookup and update logic to the program after the arrays are sorted.

Enter the payroll updates in the order shown.

Employee Name	Hours	Pay Rate
Karen Thomas	44	9.00
Darla Clark	40	10.60
Tracy York	39	11.50
Diane Reeves	38	7.90
Scott Howard	42	10.00
Patsy Ireland	40	8.45

Project 10–5   Sales Profit-1

Write a program to calculate the profit generated by each salesperson, and print a sales profit report. Read the data from a file, load the input into parallel arrays, and process the data stored in the arrays.

Input (text file):
For each sales representative, read a record and load the data into the following arrays. (Array types are shown in parentheses.)

sName	(char)
fSales	(float)
fCost	(float)

Set the size of each array to 5. Allow for a maximum of 15 characters of data for the elements in the *sName* array.

Text File (txSales.fil):

Create the sales file from the data given below. Enter the records in the order shown.

Salesperson	Total Sales	Cost of Sales
Ann Zimmerman	5793.59	4204.45
Tara Perkins	12710.14	9735.38
Dennis Tian	4567.51	3119.22
Roy Hickle	2245.78	1072.49
Lisa Conrad	8120.52	6450.71

Ouput (printer):

Print the following sales profit report:

```
Author                  SALES PROFIT REPORT            Page 01
                            mm/dd/yy


Salesperson    Total Sales   Cost Of Sales   Net Profit
-------------------------------------------------------
X--------X      99999.99        99999.99       99999.99
     :             :               :              :
     :             :               :              :
X--------X      99999.99        99999.99       99999.99

                                Total:        999999.99
```

Processing Requirements:

- Read and load the file input into the arrays.
- Print the unsorted data stored in the arrays.
- Sort the arrays, and arrange the data in alphabetic order by salesperson name.
- Print the sorted data stored in the arrays.
- Compute the net profit:
  total sales – cost of sales.
- Accumulate and print a report total for net profit.

Project 10–6   Sales Profit-2

Modify the program in Project 10–5 to allow the user to update the sales data stored in the parallel arrays. Prompt for and enter the updates given below. Search for a match on salesperson name (Enter `'Q'` to quit). If a match is not found, print the message `Name not found - press ENTER to continue`. Add the lookup and update logic to the program after the arrays are sorted.

Enter the sales updates in the order shown.

Salesperson	Total Sales	Cost of Sales
Tara Perkins	13944.70	10378.59
Lisa Conrad	8001.03	6392.53
Holly Winkler	4316.22	2975.65

Ann Zimmerman	6090.00	4354.64
Roy Hickle	2368.99	1139.16
Barbara Rider	7605.42	4321.28

Project 10–7   Inventory

Write a program to read an inventory file, load the input into parallel arrays, and print an inventory profit report.

Input (text file):

For each inventory item, read a record and load the data into the following arrays. (Array types are shown in parentheses.)

iItemNum	(int)
sDescription	(char)
iQuantity	(int)
fCost	(float)
fPrice	(float)

Set the size of each array to 5. Allow for a maximum of 15 characters of data for the elements in the *sDescription* array.

Text File (txInven.fil):

Create the inventory file from the data given below. Enter the data in the order shown.

Item Number	Description	Quantity on Hand	Unit Cost	Selling Price
4000	Screwdrivers	36	2.27	4.98
3000	Drills	10	7.83	15.95
5000	Pliers	12	2.65	5.49
2000	Saws	08	7.50	14.99
1000	Hammers	24	4.75	9.49

Ouput (printer):

Print the following inventory profit report:

```
Author              INVENTORY PROFIT REPORT           Page 01
                          mm/dd/yy


Item Number     Description         Quantity     Item Profit

   9999         X----------X           99          999.99
    :                :                 :              :
    :                :                 :              :
   9999         X----------X           99          999.99

                          Total Profit:          9999.99
```

Processing Requirements:

• Read and load the file input into the arrays.
• Print the unsorted data stored in the arrays.

- Sort the arrays, and arrange the data in ascending order by item number.
- Print the sorted data stored in the arrays.
- Compute the item cost:
  quantity × unit cost.
- Compute the item income:
  quantity × selling price.
- Compute the item profit:
  item income – item cost.
- Accumulate a report total for the item profit.

Project 10–8   Personnel

Write a program to compute and print the annual salary report for the personnel department. Read the data from a file, load the input into parallel arrays, and process the data stored in the arrays.

Input (text file):

For each employee, read a record and load the data into the following arrays. (Array types are shown in parentheses.)

iEnum	(int)
sName	(char)
iDeptNum	(int)
fSalary	(float)
fIncrease	(float)

Set the size of each array to 8. Allow for a maximum of 15 characters of data for the elements in the *sName* array.

Text File (txPers.fil):

Create the personnel file from the data given below. Enter the data in the order shown.

Employee Number	Employee Name	Department Number	Annual Salary	Percent Increase
5409	Bob Shields	47	27500.00	0.08
2071	Scott Cooper	14	30250.00	0.12
6552	Pam Wolfe	31	31773.00	0.10
4100	Derek Lowe	50	29120.00	0.07
3600	Amy Kwon	19	36025.00	0.09
1926	Dana Andrews	10	29000.00	0.10
4298	Lori Palmer	35	33400.00	0.11
3150	Todd Feldman	22	24175.00	0.07

Ouput (printer):

Print the following personnel report:

```
Author              PERSONNEL ANNUAL SALARY REPORT              Page 01
                              mm/dd/yy
```

Employee Number	Employee Name	Dept. Number	Old Salary	Dollar Increase	New Salary
9999	X-----------X	99	99999.99	9999.99	99999.99
:	:	:	:	:	:
:	:	:	:	:	:
9999	X-----------X	99	99999.99	9999.99	99999.99
			Total:		999999.99

Processing Requirements:

- Read and load the file input into the arrays.
- Print the unsorted data stored in the arrays.
- Sort the arrays, and arrange the data in ascending order by employee number.
- Print the sorted data stored in the arrays.
- Compute the dollar increase:
  old salary × percent increase.
- Compute the new salary:
  old salary + dollar increase.
- Accumulate a report total for annual salary.

Project 10–9   Accounts Payable

Write a program to compute and print an accounts payable report. Read the data from a file, load the input into parallel arrays, and process the data stored in the arrays.

Input (text file):
For each vendor, read a record and load the data to the following arrays. (Array types are shown in parentheses.)

iVnum	(int)
sVendor	(char)
sInvoiceNum	(char)
fInvoiceAmt	(float)
fDiscRate	(float)

Set the size of each array to 7. Allow for a maximum of 12 character positions for the elements in the *sVendor* array and 5 for the eiements in the *sInvoiceNum* array.

Text File (txVendor.fil):
Create the vendor file from the data given below. Enter the records in the order shown.

Vendor Number	Vendor Name	Invoice Number	Invoice Amount	Discount Rate
217	Metacraft	A1239	2309.12	0.10
349	IntraTell	T9823	670.00	0.09
712	Reylock	F0176	4563.78	0.12
501	Universal	W0105	1200.00	0.09

196	Northland	X2781	3429.34	0.10
414	MarxComm	H9205	913.87	0.05
659	Veston	D1776	5127.63	0.08

Ouput (printer):

Print the following accounts payable report:

```
Author                ACCOUNTS PAYABLE REPORT           Page 01
                           mm/dd/yy


Vendor                    Invoice   Invoice   Discount   Amount
Number   Vendor Name      Number    Amount    Amount     Due

  999    X---------X       XXXX     9999.99    999.99    9999.99
   :         :              :          :         :          :
   :         :              :          :         :          :
  999    X---------X       XXXX     9999.99    999.99    9999.99

               Totals:             99999.99   9999.99   99999.99
```

Processing Requirements:

- Read and load the file input into the arrays.
- Print the unsorted data stored in the arrays.
- Sort the arrays, and arrange the data in ascending order by vendor number.
- Print the sorted data stored in the arrays.
- Compute the discount amount:
  invoice amount × discount rate.
- Compute the amount due:
  invoice amount – discount amount.
- Accumulate report totals for the invoice amount, discount amount, and amount due.

Project 10–10 Production Cost

Write a program to compute and print a production cost report. Read the data from a file, load the input into parallel arrays, and process the data stored in the arrays.

Input (text file):

For each production record, read and load the data into the following arrays. (Array types are shown in parentheses.)

sEname	(15 char)
sProduct	(5 char)
iUnits	(3 int)
fCost	(3 float)

Set the size of each array to 10. Allow for a maximum of 15 character positions for the elements in the *sEname* array and 5 for the elements in the *sProduct* array.

Text File (txProd.fil):
Create the production file from the data given below. Enter the data in the order shown.

Employee Name	Product Number	Units Produced	Unit Cost
Kay Archer	P9511	42	2.98
Alan Baum	A1234	24	5.50
Marie Fitch	C4510	36	7.94
Lee Hildebrand	R0934	18	6.75
David Mullins	E3371	36	3.79
Chad Nelson	L8912	20	4.33
Bill Quinn	S0951	48	5.65
Nicole Renner	H9733	24	4.25
Erica Tate	Z0182	27	8.10
Terry West	A3235	30	2.95

Ouput (printer):
Print the following production cost report:

```
Author                  PRODUCTION COST REPORT           Page 01
                            mm/dd/yy


                     Product    Units        Unit      Production
Employee Name        Number     Produced     Cost        Cost

X----------X         XXXXX         99        99.99       999.99
       :               :           :           :           :
       :               :           :           :           :
X----------X         XXXXX         99        99.99       999.99

                     Totals:      999       999.99      9999.99
```

Processing Requirements:

- Read and load the file input into the arrays.
- Print the unsorted data stored in the arrays.
- Sort the arrays, and arrange the data in alphabetic order by employee name.
- Print the sorted data stored in the arrays.
- Compute the production cost:
  units produced × unit cost.
- Accumulate report totals for the units produced, units cost, and production cost.

11 Multidimensional Arrays

Overview

Learning Objectives

After you have read this chapter and completed the exercises, you should be able to

- define and load two-dimensional arrays
- manipulate and print data stored in two-dimensional arrays
- search and update two-dimensional arrays
- understand the purpose and use of multidimensional arrays

Two-Dimensional Arrays

This chapter expands upon the arrays processing techniques introduced in the previous chapter. As you may recall, sample program CHAP10A printed the data stored in two parallel arrays. The output, reproduced in Figure 11.1, consists of a list of employee names and their corresponding production output.

An array that defines a list or a single set of items is called a **one-dimensional array.** All of the arrays presented in Chapter 10 are one-dimensional arrays. The arrays shown in Figure 11.1 represent two one-dimensional arrays—a list of employee names and a list of units produced.

Some data processing applications require that certain data be stored in **two-dimensional arrays**, or **tables**. Consider the example shown in Figure 11.2. The table consists of three

```
EMPLOYEE NAME               PRODUCTION
----------------------------------
Melia Sanchez                   15
Jason Kimm                      16
Nanci Parker                    25
Randy Wade                      23
Cindy Brown                     17
```

FIGURE 11.1   Program Output for CHAP10A

```
                    C o l u m n s

              |  0    1    2    3    4
        R     ---------------------------
        o   0 | 15   17   14   20   19
        w   1 | 16   16   15   17   18
        s   2 | 25   23   24   20   18
```

FIGURE 11.2   Two-Dimensional Production Array

	Columns				
Rows	0	1	2	3	4
0	**15**	**17**	**14**	**20**	**19**
1	**16**	**16**	**15**	**17**	**18**
2	**25**	**23**	**24**	**20**	**18**

FIGURE 11.3 Production Array with Subscripts

rows and five columns. A **row** represents a set of values across the table, whereas a **column** represents a set of values down the table. Hence, row 0 represents the values 15, 17, 14, 20, and 19, whereas column 0 represents the values 15, 16, and 25. The table shown in Figure 11.2 is also called a 3 by 5 or **3 × 5 array**.

Any item stored in a two-dimensional array can be referenced by specifying the appropriate row and column subscript. In general, *iProd[iR][iC]* refers to the data stored in the *prod* array at row *r* and column *c*.

In other words, an element of a two-dimensional array can be directly accessed by coding two subscripts. For example, the data stored in the production array can be referenced accordingly: *iProd[0][0]*: 15, *iProd[0][1]*: 17, *iProd[0][2]*: 14, *iProd[0][3]*: 20, *iProd[0][4]*: 19, *iProd[1][0]*: 16, *iProd[1][1]*: 16, *iProd[1][2]*: 15, and so on.

According to Figure 11.3, the subscripts for the 3 × 5 array are row 0–2, column 0–4. Once again, the subscripts are numbered from first to last starting with 0.

Furthermore, a subscript may not be negative or exceed the size established for either the row or column. Hence, any reference to a subscript outside the row or column range will cause the compiler to produce an error message.

The row and/or column subscripts of a two-dimensional array may be expressed as integer constants or variables.

Creating a Two-Dimensional Array

A two-dimensional array is defined by specifying a data type, a name, and the size of the row and column subscripts. For example, a 3 × 5 array reserves storage space for 15 elements. Similarly, a 10 × 8 array reserves storage for 80 elements.

Examples of two-dimensional array declarations are as follows:

```
int   iQuantity[7][3];
float fMileage[5][4];
float fArea[12][3], fAmountDue[36][2];
int   iPoints[12][16],
      iSamples[10][4];
```

We may, of course, define one or more arrays on the same line. Multiple array declarations are separated by commas. We may also list the arrays down the page. Be sure to end each declaration with a semicolon.

The above declarations define the following arrays:

iQuantity	21 elements	(int)
fMileage	20 elements	(float)
fArea	36 elements	(float)
fAmountDue	72 elements	(float)
iPoints	192 elements	(int)
iSamples	40 elements	(int)

(The data types are shown in parentheses.)

Checkpoint 11A

1. A _____ represents a set of values listed across, or horizontally, in the table, while a _____ represents a set of values listed down, or vertically, in the table.

2. Using the following table, how would you reference the value 8 stored in the *iNum* array?

10	20	30	40	50
5	15	25	35	45
2	4	6	8	12
3	7	9	11	13

3. Can a two-dimensional array be referenced with one subscript?

4. Refer to the table in Question 2. Are the following references valid or invalid? If invalid, explain the problem.
   a. iNum [4][3];
   b. iNum [2][-1];
   c. iNum [0][0];

Loading a Two-Dimensional Array

A two-dimensional array may be loaded by initializing the elements as the array is defined, prompting the user to enter the data at the keyboard or reading the data from a file.

Initializing Data: Data may be assigned to a table as it is declared. This method is frequently used to load an array with data that remains stable or relatively constant over time.

An example of initializing data is as follows:

```
/*----- INITIALIZING DATA -----*/
int iProd[3][5] = {15, 17, 14, 20, 19,
                   16, 16, 15, 17, 18,
                   25, 23, 24, 20, 18};
```

The declaration assigns a set of 15 integer values to the *iProd* array. For convenience, the data is arranged in tabular form. This makes it easier to read and understand.

Interactive Input: Data may be assigned to a table by prompting the user to enter it at the keyboard. Interactive input is used when the data assigned to a table changes frequently over time.

An example of interactive input is as follows:

```
/*---------- INTERACTIVE INPUT ----------*/
int iProd[3][5];

    .  .  .  .  .

for (iRow = 0; iRow < 3; iRow++)
{
    for (iCol = 0; iCol < 5; iCol++)
    {
        printf(" Enter production: ");
        scanf(" %d", &iProd[iRow][iCol]);
    }
}
```

This example uses a nested counter-controlled loop to prompt for the input. As long as *iRow* is less than 3 and *iCol* is less than 5, the input is assigned to the *iProd[iRow][iCol]* element.

Notice that the column subscript advances from 0–4 for each row subscript. Hence, the table is loaded one row at a time.

File Input: Data can be read from a file and loaded into a table. File input saves time by eliminating the data entry step during the program run. This method may be used to load a table with data that remains constant or changes frequently.

An example of file input is as follows:

```
/*------------------ FILE INPUT ------------------*/
int iProd[3][5];

  .  .  .  .  .
while (!feof(fpFile))
{
    for (iRow = 0; iRow < 3; iRow++)
    {
        for (iCol = 0; iCol < 5; iCol++)
        {
            fscanf(fpFile, " %d", &iProd[iRow][iCol]);
        }
    }
}
```

This example uses a nested loop to read data from the file and store it in the table. As long as the end-of-file marker is not encountered, the input is assigned to the *iProd[iRow][iCol]* element.

Printing a Two-Dimensional Array

Once an array has been loaded, it is always a good idea to print the array to verify that the data was correctly loaded. The code shown below prints the contents of a two-dimensional production array.

```
for (iRow = 0; iRow < 3; iRow++)
{
    for (iCol = 0; iCol < 5; iCol++)
    {
        printf("\n %d", iProd[iRow][iCol]);
    }
}
```

Checkpoint 11B

1. What three items are specified when defining a two-dimensional array?
2. Draw the table that is defined with the statement int iStudents[6][2];
3. Load the *iStudent* table (from Question 2) with the following values: 8, 6, 15, 12, 20, 19, 7, 4, 10, 9, 3, and 1. Load the array by initializing the data elements.
4. What other two methods may be used to load a two-dimensional array?
5. Code the statements to print the contents of the *iStudent* array on the screen.

Sample Program CHAP11A

Sample program CHAP11A loads employee name and production into parallel arrays, computes the daily and weekly production totals, and prints an output report from the data stored in the arrays. See Figure 11.4 for the hierarchy chart and Figure 11.5 for the flowchart. Sample program CHAP11A is presented in Figure 11.6. Figures 11.7 and 11.8 show the data entry screen and the weekly production report, respectively.

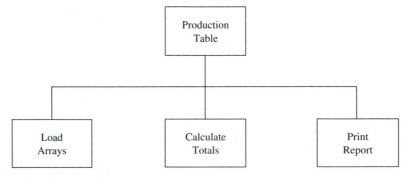

FIGURE 11.4   Hierarchy Chart for CHAP11A

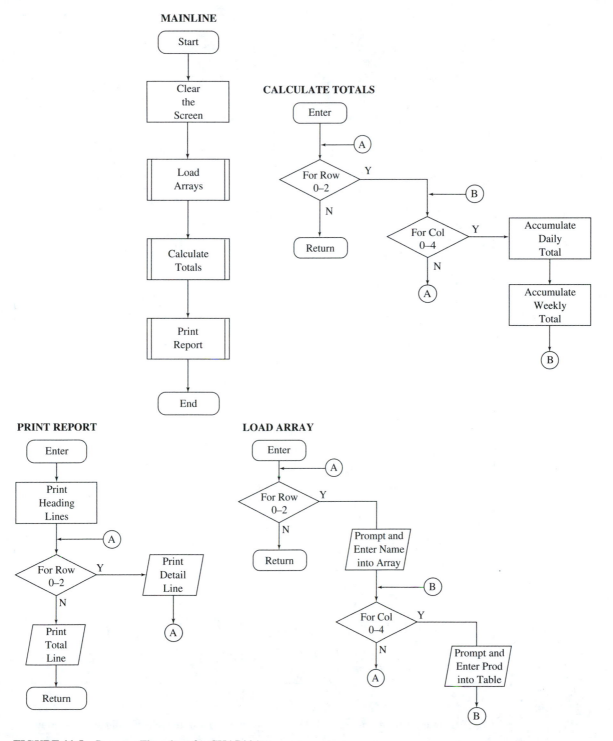

FIGURE 11.5   Program Flowchart for CHAP11A

```
/*-------------------------------------------------------------------
PRODUCTION TABLE: Load production data into a two-dimensional table
and compute the daily and weekly production totals.

Program:    CHAP11A.C
Author:     David M. Collopy
Date:       mm/dd/yy
Project:    Sample program
************************************************************************/

/*---- PREPROCESSING DIRECTIVE --------------------------------------*/

#include <stdio.h>
#include <graph.h>

/*---- FUNCTION PROTOTYPES ------------------------------------------*/

void  LoadArrays(void);         /* load data into arrays       */
void  CalcTotals(void);         /* calculate production totals */
void  PrnReport(void);          /* print production report     */

/*---- PROGRAM SETUP ------------------------------------------------*/

/*>  P R O G R A M   V A R I A B L E S                          <*/

char sName[3][21];      /* 3 element 21 character name array  */
int  iProd[3][5];       /* 3 x 5 production array             */
int  iDayTot[5];        /* 5 element daily production totals  */
int  iWeekTot[3];       /* 3 element weekly production totals */

/*-------------------------------------------------------------------
      MAINLINE CONTROL
-------------------------------------------------------------------*/
main()
{
    _clearscreen(0);
    LoadArrays();
    CalcTotals();
    PrnReport();
    return 0;
}

/*-------------------------------------------------------------------
      LOAD DATA INTO ARRAYS
-------------------------------------------------------------------*/
```

FIGURE 11.6 Sample Program CHAP11A: Processes data stored in a two-dimensional array

```
void LoadArrays(void)
{
    int  iRow;                    /* row subscript    */
    int  iCol;                    /* column subscript */

    for (iRow = 0; iRow < 3; iRow++)
    {
        printf("Enter employee name: ");
        scanf(" %20[^\n]", sName[iRow]);
        fflush(stdin);
        for (iCol = 0; iCol < 5; iCol++)
        {
            printf("   Enter production: ");
            scanf(" %d", &iProd[iRow][iCol]);
            fflush(stdin);
        }
    }
    return;
}


/*------------------------------------------------------------------
       CALCULATE PRODUCTION TOTALS
-------------------------------------------------------------------*/
void CalcTotals(void)
{
    int  iRow;                    /* row subscript    */
    int  iCol;                    /* column subscript */

    for (iRow = 0; iRow < 3; iRow++)
    {
        for (iCol = 0; iCol < 5; iCol++)
        {
            iDayTot[iCol] = iDayTot[iCol] + iProd[iRow][iCol];
            iWeekTot[iRow] = iWeekTot[iRow] + iProd[iRow][iCol];
        }
    }
    return;
}


/*------------------------------------------------------------------
       PRINT PRODUCTION REPORT
-------------------------------------------------------------------*/
void PrnReport(void)
{
    int  iRow;                    /* row subscript    */
```

FIGURE 11.6 *Continued*

```
    int  iCol;                    /* column subscript */

    printf("\n\n   EMPLOYEE NAME       MON TUE WED THR FRI TOTALS");
    printf("\n-------------------------------------------------");
    for (iRow = 0; iRow < 3; iRow++)
    {
        printf("\n   %-20s %2d  %2d  %2d  %2d  %2d  %3d",
            sName[iRow], iProd[iRow][0], iProd[iRow][1], iProd[iRow][2],
            iProd[iRow][3], iProd[iRow][4], iWeekTot[iRow]);
    }
    printf("\n\n            Totals:    %3d %3d %3d %3d %3d",
        iDayTot[0], iDayTot[1], iDayTot[2], iDayTot[3], iDayTot[4]);
    return;
}
```

FIGURE 11.6   *Continued*

```
Enter employee name: Melia Sanchez
    Enter production: 15
    Enter production: 17
    Enter production: 14
    Enter production: 20
    Enter production: 19
Enter employee name: Jason Kimm
    Enter production: 16
            :          :
            :          :
```

FIGURE 11.7   Data Entry Screen for CHAP11A

```
    EMPLOYEE NAME       MON TUE WED THR FRI TOTALS
    -------------------------------------------------
    Melia Sanchez       15  17  14  20  19    85
    Jason Kimm          16  16  15  17  18    82
    Nanci Parker        25  23  24  20  18   110

            Totals:    56  56  53  57  55
```

FIGURE 11.8   Production Output Report for CHAP11A

The following specifications apply:

Input (keyboard):
For each employee, prompt for and enter the following data:

Employee name
Production output

Output (screen):
Print the weekly production report shown in Figure 11.8.

Processing Requirements:

- Prompt for and enter the employee names and the daily production output.
- Load the input into the name and production arrays.
- Compute the daily and weekly production totals.
- Print the weekly production report.

Pseudocode:

START: Main
Clear screen
Call Load Arrays
Call Calculate Totals
Call Print Report
END

ENTER: Load Arrays
LOOP for row < 3
    Prompt for employee name
    Enter employee name into name array
    Clear keyboard buffer
    LOOP for col < 5
        Prompt for production data
        Enter production data into production array
        Clear keyboard buffer
    END LOOP
END LOOP
RETURN

ENTER: Calculate Totals
LOOP for row < 3
    LOOP for col < 5
        Accumulate daily production totals
        Accumulate weekly production totals
    END LOOP
END LOOP
RETURN

ENTER: Print Report
Print 2 column heading lines
LOOP for row < 3

```
                    Print weekly production line:
                            Employee name
                            Monday production
                            Tuesday production
                            Wednesday production
                            Thursday production
                            Friday production
                            Weekly production total
                    END LOOP
                    Print daily production line:
                            Monday total production
                            Tuesday total production
                            Wednesday total production
                            Thursday total production
                            Friday total production
                    RETURN
```

Hierarchy Chart: See Figure 11.4.

Program Flowchart: See Figure 11.5.

Dissection of Sample Program CHAP11A

P R O G R A M   V A R I A B L E S:

```
    char sName[3][20];
```

The above statement defines a three-element character array called *sName* and allocates 20 characters of storage to each name.

```
    int  iProd[3][5];
```

The above statement defines a 3×5 integer array called *iProd*. This declaration allocates storage space for 15 elements.

```
    int  iDayTot[5];
```

The above statement defines a five-element integer array called *iDayTot*. This array will be used to hold the daily production totals for the employees.

```
    int  iWeekTot[3];
```

The above statement defines a three-element integer array called *iWeekTot*. This array will be used to hold the weekly production totals for the employees.

L O A D   D A T A   I N T O   A R R A Y S:

```
void LoadArrays(void)
{
    int  iRow;
    int  iCol;
```

The above statements define the local variables required by the module—the row and column subscripts.

```
for (iRow = 0; iRow < 3; iRow ++)
{
    printf("Enter employee name: ");
    scanf(" %20[^\n]", sName[iRow]);
    fflush(stdin);
    for (iCol = 0; iCol < 5; iCol ++)
    {
        printf("   Enter production: ");
        scanf(" %d", &iProd[iRow][iCol]);
        fflush(stdin);
    }
}
return;
}
```

In the above statements, first, as long as the row subscript is less than 3, the program prompts the user to enter the employee's name (the input is stored in the name array). Second, as long as the column subscript is less than 5, the program prompts the user to enter the daily production output (the input is stored in the production table).

Look at the second *for* loop. Notice that for each increment of the row subscript, the column subscript advances from 0 to 4. This forces the program to prompt the user to enter five days of production work per each employee.

C A L C U L A T E   P R O D U C T I O N   T O T A L S:

```
void CalcTotals(void)
{
    int   iRow;
    int   iCol;

    for (iRow = 0; iRow < 3; iRow++)
    {
        for (iCol = 0; iCol < 5; iCol++)
        {
            iDayTot[iCol] = iDayTot[iCol] + iProd[iRow][iCol];
            iWeekTot[iRow] = iWeekTot[iRow] + iProd[iRow][iCol];
        }
    }
    return;
}
```

The above statements accumulate a daily (column) total for the production output and a weekly production (row) total for each employee. The relationship between the production table and the 2 one-dimensional arrays is illustrated in Figure 11.9.

The process begins by setting the row and column subscripts to 0. Each time the row subscript is incremented, the column subscript advances from 0 to 4. Notice that elements in the *iDayTot* array are computed by adding the column elements in the *iProd* array.

```
iDayTot[iCol] = iDayTot[iCol] + iProd[iRow][iCol];
```

And the elements in the *iWeekTot* array are computed by adding the row elements in the *iProd* array.

`iProd[iR][iC]`   `iWeekTotal[iR]`

15	17	14	20	19
16	16	15	17	18
25	23	24	20	18

85
82
110

`iDayTotal[iC]`

56	56	53	57	55

FIGURE 11.9   Relationship between Production Table and Arrays for CHAP11A

```
        iWeekTot[iRow] = iWeekTot[iRow] + iProd[iRow][iCol];

PRINT   PRODUCTION   REPORT:

void PrintReport(void)
{
    int iRow;
    int iCol;

    printf("\n\n      EMPLOYEE NAME        MON TUE WED THR FRI");
    printf(" TOTALS");
    printf("\n----------------------------------------------");
    printf("-------");
```

The above statements declare the subscripts and print two column heading lines.

```
    for (iRow = 0; iRow < 3; iRow ++)
    {
        printf("\n    %-20s %2d  %2d  %2d  %2d  %2d    %3d",
            sName[iRow], iProd[iRow][0], iProd[iRow][1],
            iProd[iRow][2], iProd[iRow][3], iProd[iRow][4],
            iWeekTot[iRow]);
    }
```

In the above statements, as long as the current value of the row subscript is less than 3, the printf() function prints the employee's name, the production output, and the weekly total. This is accomplished by holding the column subscript constant while incrementing the row subscripts from 0 to 2.

```
    printf("\n\n                    Totals:    %3d %3d %3d %3d %3d",
        iDayTot[0], iDayTot[1], iDayTot[2], iDayTot[3],
        iDayTot[4]);
    return;
}
```

The above statement prints the five-day production totals. The column subscripts are coded as constants in order to print all of the elements at the same time.

Notes and Tips

1. Two-dimensional arrays represent tables of data arranged in row-column format.

2. An element stored in a two-dimensional array can be accessed by specifying its row and column subscripts.

3. Accumulating row and column totals for a two-dimensional array involves a nested loop. Look at the *CalcTotals* module of the sample program. Notice how the body of the inner loop accumulates the row and column totals. Walk through the code several times to see how it works.

4. Students normally have difficulty understanding how the row and column subscripts are used to manipulate the elements of a two-dimensional array. The best way to master this is to go through the code of the sample programs and study the dissections until it becomes clear. Use pencil and paper to track the elements as the program is processing them. It's like shooting hoops; the more you practice, the better you get.

Tutorial CHAP11A

1. The objectives of this tutorial are to
   * load data into multiple arrays
   * accumulate totals using arrays
   * retrieve and print data stored in arrays

2. Read the program specifications for sample program CHAP11A.

3. Log on to your C editor, and enter the source code as shown in Figure 11.6. Save the program on your work disk as CHAP11A. Save frequently as you enter the code.

4. Compile, run, and debug your program until the output matches the results shown in Figure 11.8.

5. When completed, show your work to your instructor.

Quick Quiz

Answer the following questions.

1. What does the following declaration do:
   ```
   int    iProd[3][5];
   ```
   Explain why this program requires four arrays.

2. The load module uses a nested *for* loop to read and load data into the *sName* and *iProd* arrays. Explain how the module is able to load the input into the correct elements of the array and the table.

3. Trace the flow of data through the calculations module. Explain how the program accumulates the row and column totals shown in Figure 11.8.

4. Trace the flow of data through the print module. Explain how the program retrieves and prints the contents of the arrays in the format shown in Figure 11.8.

5. Did you have any problems or errors when you ran the sample program? If so, what were they and what did you do to correct them?

Searching and Updating Tables

From Chapter 10, we know that array lookup is the process of locating data stored in an array. To find a given element in a two-dimensional array, we specify the row and column subscripts. In this section, we will learn how to perform table lookup using direct reference or sequential search.

Direct Reference: Direct reference assumes that there is a direct relationship between the user's input and the subscripts. For a two-dimensional array, the row and column subscripts are entered at the keyboard and are used by the program to access the data stored in the table.

Consider a programming application that records the points scored during a basketball game. The points are recorded at the end of each quarter and stored in a 2×4 table called *iPoints*. According to the code shown below, the team number and quarter are used as the row and column subscripts to access and display the score on the screen.

```
int iPoints[2][4] = {19, 17, 20, 16,
                     14, 18, 19, 15};
int iTeam, iQtr;
 . . . . .

/*------------ DIRECT REFERENCE LOOKUP -------------*/
printf("\nEnter team number 1-2 or '-1' to Quit: ");
scanf(" %d", &iTeam);
while (iTeam != -1)
{
    printf("\nEnter quarter 1-4: ");
    scanf(" %d", &iQtr);
    printf("Score = %d", iPoints[iTeam-1][iQtr-1]);
    printf("\nEnter team number 1-2 or '-1' to Quit: ");
    scanf(" %d", &iTeam);
}
```

For example, if the user enters 2 for the team and 4 for the quarter, then the program displays the score 15 on the screen (*iPoints[iTeam-1][iQtr-1] = iPoints[1][3] = 15*). Remember that the first subscript, row or column, always begins with 0.

Sequential Search: For a two-dimensional array, sequential search requires, at most, two one-dimensional arrays: one for holding the row keys and one for holding the column keys. Sequential search is used when there is no direct relationship between the user's input and one or more of the array subscripts. Consequently, the program compares the input to the elements in the key array until a match is found or the end of the array is encountered. For a match, the subscript of the key array is used to access the corresponding element stored in the two-dimensional table.

In Figure 11.10, assume that the user has entered the team name and the quarter.

```
/*---- SEQUENTIAL SEARCH LOOKUP ----*/
iRow = 0;
iMatch = -1
while (iRow < 2 && iMatch == -1)
{
```

FIGURE 11.10   Relationship between Points Table and Team Array

```
if (strcmp(iTeamIn, iTeam[iRow]) == 0)
{
    iMatch = iRow;
}
iRow++;
}
```

The search begins by setting the variables *iRow* and *iMatch* to 0 and –1, respectively. As long as the *while* condition test is true, the search key *iTeamIn* is compared to the elements stored in the *iTeam* array. If a match is found, *iMatch* is set to *iRow,* the value of the subscript where the team name was found.

```
/*----- CHECK FOR TEAM MATCH -----*/
if (iMatch == -1)
{
    printf("\nTeam not found");
}
else
{
    printf("Score = %d", iPoints[iMatch][iQtr-1]);
}
```

For example, if the user enters Tornados for the team and 2 for the second quarter, then the program displays the score 17 on the screen (*iPoints[0][2-1]* = 17). Of course, if a match is not found, the program prints the message *Team not found* on the screen.

Checkpoint 11C

1. Explain the difference between direct reference and sequential search.

2. Using the following table and direct reference lookup, code the statements to find a specific piece of data in the *fPrice* table. (*Note:* The rows represent the type of item [e.g., blender, toaster, mixer]; the columns represent prices of various models.

27.50	32.45	48.29	54.63
19.12	24.81	36.21	47.40
10.53	21.14	31.16	44.78

3. Using the code segment written in Question 2, if the user enters 2 for the item and 3 for the model, what will print as the price?

4. Using the following arrays and serial search, code the statements to search the item table for a specific household appliance and the price table for the specific model number (e.g., 1, 2, 3, or 4).

		Price		
Item	Model1	Model2	Model3	Model4
Blender	27.50	32.45	48.29	54.63
Toaster	19.12	24.81	36.21	47.40
Mixer	10.53	21.14	31.16	44.78

Sample Program CHAP11B

Sample program CHAP11B updates the data stored in parallel arrays. CHAP11B also computes the daily and weekly production output and prints a simple production report. See Figure 11.11 for the hierarchy chart and Figure 11.12 for the program flowchart. Sample program CHAP11B is presented in Figure 11.13. Figures 11.14 and 11.15 show the data entry screen and the updated production report, resepectively.

The following specifications apply:

Input (keyboard):
For each update, prompt for and enter the following data:
Employee name
Workday
Production update

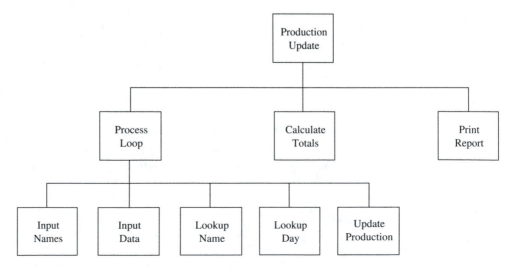

FIGURE 11.11   Hierarchy Chart for CHAP11B

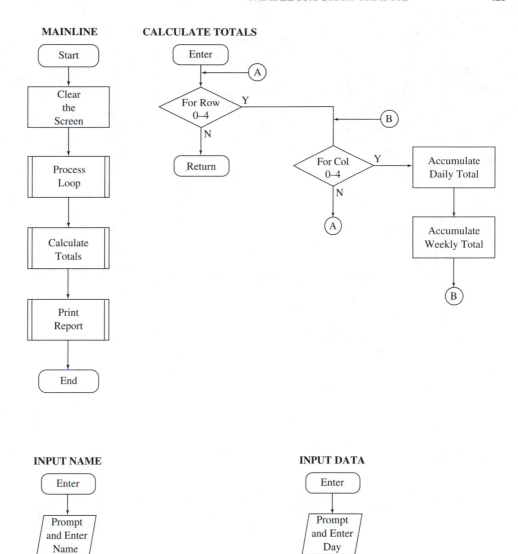

FIGURE 11.12 Program Flowchart for CHAP11B

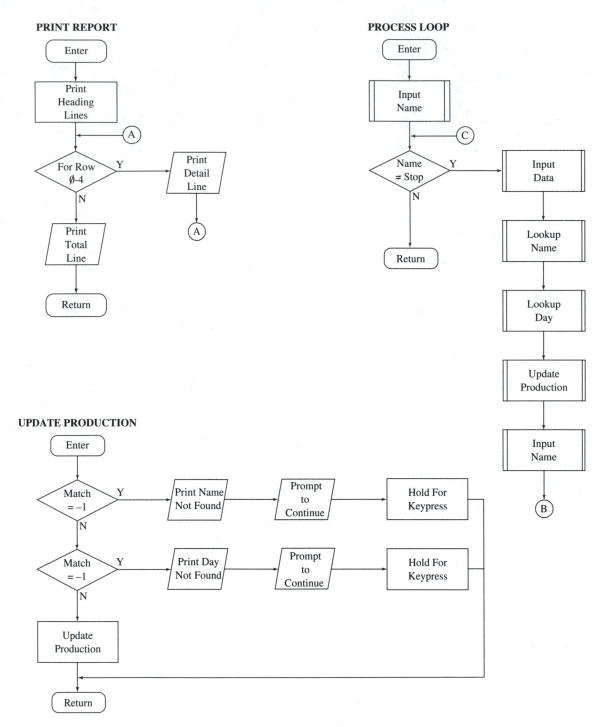

FIGURE 11.12   *Continued*

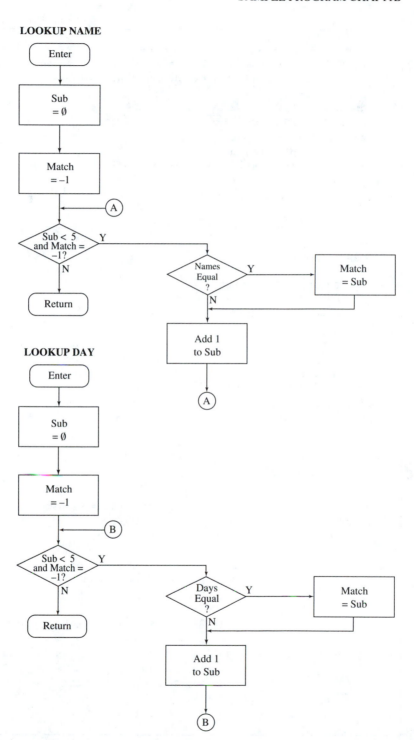

FIGURE 11.12   *Continued*

```
/*-----------------------------------------------------------------
PRODUCTION UPDATE: Load parallel arrays and use sequential search to
update the data stored in a two-dimensional table.

Program:   CHAP11B.C
Author:    David M. Collopy
Date:      mm/dd/yy
Project:   Sample program
*********************************************************************/


/*---- PREPROCESSING DIRECTIVES -----------------------------------*/

#include <stdio.h>
#include <conio.h>
#include <graph.h>


/*---- FUNCTION PROTOTYPES -----------------------------------------*/

void ProcessLoop(void);        /* processing loop          */
void InputName(void);          /* input update name        */
void InputData(void);          /* input update day and data */
int  LookUpName(void);         /* lookup employee name     */
int  LookUpDay(void);          /* lookup production day    */
void UpdateProd(int, int);     /* update production data    */
void CalcTotals(void);         /* calculate production totals */
void PrnReport(void);          /* print production report  */


/*---- PROGRAM SETUP ----------------------------------------------*/

/*>  P R O G R A M   V A R I A B L E S                    <*/

char sNameIn[21];              /* input employee name */
char sDayIn[4];                /* input day           */
int  iProdIn;                  /* input production    */

char sName[5][21] = {"Melia Sanchez", "Jason Kim",
                     "Nanci Parker", "Randy Wade",
                     "Cindy Brown"};

                /* 5 element 21 character name array  */

int  iProd[5][5] = {15, 17, 14, 20, 19,
                    16, 16, 15, 17, 18,
                    25, 23, 24, 20, 18,
                    23, 16, 17, 19, 15,
                    17, 19, 17, 16, 20};
```

FIGURE 11.13   Sample Program CHAP11B: Updates data stored in two-dimensional array

```
                        /* 5 x 5 element production table    */

int   iDayTot[5];    /* 5 element daily production totals  */
int   iWeekTot[5];   /* 5 element weekly production totals */

char sDay[5][4] = {"MON", "TUE", "WED", "THR", "FRI"};

                        /* 5 element 4 character day array    */

/*------------------------------------------------------------------
        MAINLINE CONTROL
-----------------------------------------------------------------*/
main()
{
    _clearscreen(0);
    ProcessLoop();
    CalcTotals();
    PrnReport();
    return 0;
}


/*------------------------------------------------------------------
        PROCESSING LOOP
-----------------------------------------------------------------*/
void ProcessLoop(void)
{
    int   iRow;                  /* row location of match    */
    int   iCol;                  /* column location of match */

    InputName();
    while (strcmp(sNameIn, "stop") != 0)
    {
        InputData();
        iRow = LookUpName();
        iCol = LookUpDay();
        UpdateProd(iRow, iCol);
        InputName();
    }
    return;
}


/*------------------------------------------------------------------
        INPUT UPDATE NAME
-----------------------------------------------------------------*/
void InputName(void)
{
```

FIGURE 11.13   *Continued*

```c
    printf("\nEnter employee name or 'stop' to Quit: ");
    scanf(" %20[^\n]", sNameIn);
    fflush(stdin);
    return;
}


/*------------------------------------------------------------------
        INPUT UPDATE DAY AND DATA
--------------------------------------------------------------------*/
void InputData(void)
{
    printf("  Enter day - MON, TUE, WED, THR, FRI: ");
    scanf(" %[^\n]", sDayIn);
    fflush(stdin);
    printf("              Enter production update: ");
    scanf(" %d", &iProdIn);
    fflush(stdin);
    return;
}


/*------------------------------------------------------------------
        LOOKUP EMPLOYEE NAME
--------------------------------------------------------------------*/
int LookUpName(void)
{
    int iSub = 0;                   /* array subscript      */
    int iMatch = -1;                /* name match subscript */

    while (iSub < 5 && iMatch == -1)
    {
        if (strcmp(sNameIn, sName[iSub]) == 0)
        {
            iMatch = iSub;      /* name found           */
        }
        iSub++;
    }
    return iMatch;
}


/*------------------------------------------------------------------
        LOOKUP PRODUCTION DAY
--------------------------------------------------------------------*/
int LookUpDay(void)
{
    int iSub = 0;                   /* array subscript      */
    int iMatch = -1;                /* day match subscript  */
```

FIGURE 11.13   *Continued*

```
      while (iSub < 5 && iMatch == -1)
      {
          if (strcmp(sDayIn, sDay[iSub]) == 0)
          {
              iMatch = iSub;        /* day found            */
          }
          iSub++;
      }
      return iMatch;
}


/*-------------------------------------------------------------------
      UPDATE PRODUCTION DATA
-------------------------------------------------------------------*/
void UpdateProd(int iRow, int iCol)
{
    char cWait;                   /* wait for enter keypress */

    if (iRow == -1)
    {
        printf("\nNAME NOT FOUND - Press ENTER to continue...\n");
        cWait = getch();
    }
    else if (iCol == -1)
    {
        printf("\nDAY NOT FOUND - Press ENTER to continue...\n");
        cWait = getch();
    }
    else
        iProd[iRow][iCol] = iProd[iRow][iCol] + iProdIn;
    return;
}


/*-------------------------------------------------------------------
      CALCULATE PRODUCTION TOTALS
-------------------------------------------------------------------*/
void CalcTotals(void)
{
    int  iRow;                   /* row subscript    */
    int  iCol;                   /* column subscript */

    for (iRow = 0; iRow < 5; iRow++)
    {
        for (iCol = 0; iCol < 5; iCol++)
        {
            iDayTot[iCol] = iDayTot[iCol] + iProd[iRow][iCol];
```

FIGURE 11.13   *Continued*

```
            iWeekTot[iRow] = iWeekTot[iRow] + iProd[iRow][iCol];
        }
    }
    return;
}


/*----------------------------------------------------------------
        PRINT PRODUCTION REPORT
-------------------------------------------------------------*/
void PrnReport(void)
{
    int   iRow;                      /* row subscript */

    printf("\n\n    EMPLOYEE NAME       MON TUE WED THR FRI TOTALS");
    printf("\n-------------------------------------------------");
    for (iRow = 0; iRow < 5; iRow++)
    {
        printf("\n   %-20s %2d  %2d  %2d  %2d  %2d  %3d",
            sName[iRow], iProd[iRow][0], iProd[iRow][1],
            iProd[iRow][2], iProd[iRow][3], iProd[iRow][4],
            iWeekTot[iRow]);
    }
    printf("\n\n            Totals:    %3d %3d %3d %3d %3d",
        iDayTot[0], iDayTot[1], iDayTot[2], iDayTot[3], iDayTot[4]);
    return;
}
```

FIGURE 11.13 *Continued*

```
Enter employee name or 'stop' to Quit: Tim Mohr
  Enter day - MON, TUE, WED, THR, FRI: TUE
             Enter production update: 7


NAME NOT FOUND - press ENTER to continue...

Enter employee name or 'stop' to Quit: Nanci Parker
  Enter day - MON, TUE, WED, THR, FRI: FRI
             Enter production update: 3


Enter employee name or 'stop' to Quit: quit
```

FIGURE 11.14 Update Prompts for CHAP11B

```
┌─────────────────────────────────────────────────────────────┐
│                                                             │
│     EMPLOYEE NAME          MON TUE WED THR FRI TOTALS       │
│    ----------------------------------------------------     │
│     Melia Sanchez          15  17  14  20  19    85        │
│     Jason Kimm             16  16  15  17  18    82        │
│     Nanci Parker           25  23  24  20  21   113        │
│     Randy Wade             23  16  17  19  15    90        │
│     Cindy Brown            17  19  17  16  20    89        │
│                                                             │
│             Totals:        96  91  87  92  93              │
│                                                             │
└─────────────────────────────────────────────────────────────┘
```

FIGURE 11.15   Updated Production Report for CHAP11B

Output (screen):

Print the weekly production report shown in Figure 11.15.

Processing Requirements:

- Define and initialize the following arrays:

employee names	(5 rows)
production output	(5 × 5 table)
workdays	(5 columns)
daily totals	(5 columns)
weekly totals	(5 rows)

- Prompt for and enter the employee's name, workday, and production update.
- Look up and update data stored in the production array.
- Compute the daily and weekly production totals, and store them in one-dimensional arrays.
- After the updates, print the production output report.

Pseudocode:

```
START: Main
Clear screen
Call Process Loop
Call Calculate Totals
Call Print Report
END

ENTER: Process Loop
Call Input Employee Name
LOOP while employee name not = stop
     Call Input Production Data
     Call Lookup Name
     Call Lookup Day
     Call Update Production Data
     Call Input Employee Name
```

```
END LOOP
RETURN

ENTER: Input Employee Name
     Prompt and enter employee name (or stop to quit)
     Clear keyboard buffer
RETURN

ENTER: Input Production Data
     Prompt and enter update day
     Clear keyboard buffer
     Prompt and enter update production
     Clear keyboard buffer
RETURN

ENTER: Lookup Name
Set subscript to 0
Set match to –1
LOOP while subscript < 5 and match = –1
     IF employee name found in name array
          Set match to subscript
     END IF
     Add 1 to subscript
END LOOP
RETURN

ENTER: Lookup Day
Set subscript to 0
Set match to –1
LOOP while subscript < 5 and match = –1
     IF day found in day array
          Set match to subscript
     END IF
     Add 1 to subscript
END LOOP
RETURN

ENTER: Update Production Data
IF name match = –1
     Print could not find employee name
     Hold screen for keypress
else IF day match = –1
     Print could not find day
     Hold screen for keypress
else
     Add update production to corresponding production data
END IF
RETURN
```

```
        ENTER: Calculate Totals
        LOOP for row < 5
            LOOP for col < 5
                Accumulate daily production totals
                Accumulate weekly production totals
            END LOOP
        END LOOP
        RETURN

        ENTER: Print Report
        Print 2 column heading lines
        LOOP for row < 5
            Print weekly production line:
                Employee name
                Monday production
                Tuesday production
                Wednesday production
                Thursday production
                Friday production
                Week production total
        END LOOP
        Print daily production line:
            Monday total production
            Tuesday total production
            Wednesday total production
            Thursday total production
            Friday total production
        RETURN
```

Hierarchy Chart: See Figure 11.11.

Program Flowchart: See Figure 11.12.

Dissection of Sample Program CHAP11B

Let's begin the program dissection with the activities performed by the processing loop.

```
P R O C E S S I N G    L O O P:

void ProcessLoop(void)
{
    int iRow;
    int iCol;

    InputName();
    while (strcmp(sNameIn, "stop") != 0)
    {
        InputData();
        iRow = LookUpName();
```

```
        iCol = LookUpDay();
        UpdateProd(iRow, iCol);
        InputName();
    }
    return;
}
```

The above statements declare the local variables and transfer control to the InputName module. As long as the input name is not equal to *stop*, control enters the *while* loop and executes the modules in the order listed.

Notice that the calling statements for *LookUpName* and *LookUpDay* receive values that are assigned to *iRow* and *iCol*. Also note that *iRow* and *iCol* are passed to the *UpdateProd* module; the passed values represent the location of the employee's name and update day in the name and day arrays, respectively.

I N P U T   E M P L O Y E E   N A M E:

```
void InputName(void)
{
    printf("\n\nEnter employee name or 'stop' to QUIT: ");
    scanf(" %20[^\n]", sNameIn);
    fflush(stdin);
    return;
}
```

The above statements prompt the user to enter the employee's name or "stop" to quit. The input is assigned to *sNameIn*, and the keyboard buffer is cleared.

I N P U T   U P D A T E   D A Y   A N D   D A T A:

```
void InputData(void)
{
    printf("   Enter day - MON, TUE, WED, THR, FRI: ");
    scanf(" %[^\n]", sDayIn);
    fflush(stdin);
    printf("               Enter production update: ");
    scanf(" %d", &iProdIn);
    fflush(stdin);
    return;
}
```

The above statements prompt the user to enter the workday and production update amount. The workday is assigned to *sDayIn*, and the production update is assigned to *iProdIn*. Once again, the keyboard buffer is cleared after scanf() functions.

L O O K   U P   E M P L O Y E E   N A M E:

```
int LookupName(void)
{
    int iSub = 0;
    int iMatch = 1;
```

```
        while (iSub < 5 && iMatch == -1)
        {
            if (strcmp(sNameIn, sName[iSub]) == 0)
            {
                iMatch = iSub;
            }
            iSub++;
        }
        return iMatch;
}
```

In the above statements, as long as the subscript is less than 5 and a match has not been found, control enters the body of the loop. If the search key (*sNameIn*) matches the employee name stored in the current element of the *sName* array, then the program assigns the value of the subscript (*iSub*) to *iMatch*. Otherwise, the search continues until either the name is found or the end of the array is encountered.

At the end of the module, the integer value stored at *iMatch* is returned to the calling statement, match or no match.

L O O K   U P   P R O D U C T I O N   D A Y:

```
int LookupDay(void)
{
    iSub = 0;
    iMatch = -1;

    while (iSub < 5 && iMatch == -1)
    {
        if (strcmp(sDayIn, sDay[iSub]) == 0)
        {
            iMatch = iSub;
        }
        iSub++;
    }
    return iMatch;
}
```

In the above statements, as long as the subscript is less than 5 and a match has not been found, control enters the body of the loop. If the search key *(sDayIn)* matches the workday stored in the current element of the *sDay* array, then the program assigns the value of the subscript *iSub* to *iMatch*. Otherwise, the search continues until either the workday is found or the end of the array is encountered.

Once again, the value stored at *iMatch* is returned to the calling statement, match or no match.

U P D A T E   P R O D U C T I O N:

```
void UpdateProd(int iRow, int iCol)
{
    char cWait;

    if (iRow == -1)
    {
```

```
            printf("\nNAME NOT FOUND");
            printf(" - press 'ENTER' to continue...");
            cWait = getch();
        }
        else if (iCol == -1)
        {
            printf("\nDAY NOT FOUND");
            printf(" - press 'ENTER' to continue...");
            cWait = getch();
        }
        else
            iProd[iRow][iCol] = iProd[iRow][iCol] + iProdIn;
        return;
}
```

In the above statements, if the employee's name was not found in the *iName* array, then the program prints the name error message and waits for the user to continue. Else, if the workday was not found in the *sDay* array, then the program prints the day error message and waits for the user to continue.

However, if the employee's name and workday are found, then the program adds the production input to the element indexed by the *iRow* and *iCol* subscripts and control returns to the calling module.

C O M P U T E   P R O D U C T I O N   T O T A L S:

```
void ComputeTotals(void)
{
    int iRow;
    int iCol;

    for (iRow = 0; iRow < 5; iRow ++)
    {
        for (iCol = 0; iCol < 5; iCol ++)
        {
            iDayTot[iCol] = iDayTot[iCol] + iProd[iRow][iCol];
            iWeekTot[iRow] = iWeekTot[iRow] + iProd[iRow][iCol];
        }
    }
    return;
}
```

The previous statements accumulate a daily (column) total for the production output and a weekly production (row) total for each employee. The nested loop forces the column subscript to increment from 0 to 4 for each iteration of the row subscript.

P R I N T   P R O D U C T I O N   R E P O R T:

```
void PrintReport(void)
{
    int iRow;

    printf("\n\n      EMPLOYEE NAME        MON TUE WED THR FRI");
```

```
printf(" TOTALS");
printf("\n-----------------------------------------------");
printf("-------");

for (iRow = 0; iRow < 5; iRow ++)
{
    printf("\n    %-20s %2d  %2d  %2d  %2d  %2d    %3d",
        sName[iRow], iProd[iRow][0], iProd[iRow][1],
        iProd[iRow][2], iProd[iRow][3], iProd[iRow][4],
        iWeekTot[iRow]);
}
printf("\n\n                  Totals:    %3d %3d %3d %3d %3d",
    iDayTot[0], iDayTot[1], iDayTot[2], iDayTot[3],
        iDayTot[4]);
return;
}
```

In the above statements, as long as the current value of the row subscript is less than 5, the program prints the employee's name, daily production output, and weekly total. At the end of the report, the program prints the total daily production output.

Notes and Tips

1. Direct reference lookup requires two subscripts (one for the row and one for the column) to locate data stored in a two-dimensional array. Once again, this lookup method only works if there is a direct relationship between the input and the subscripts used to locate the data stored in the array.

2. Sequential search lookup requires three arrays—a one-dimensional array for the row keys, a one-dimensional array for the column keys, and a two-dimensional array (table) for the data. Information entered at the keyboard is used to locate the row and column subscripts to the data stored in the table. The lookup routine is shown in the sample program. Review it several times to make sure you understand how it works.

Tutorial CHAP11B

1. The objectives of this tutorial are to
   • load data into parallel arrays as they are declared
   • use sequential search to locate and update data stored in a table
   • retrieve and print data stored in multiple arrays

2. Read the program specifications for sample program CHAP11B.

3. Log on to C, and enter the source code as shown in Figure 11.13. Save the program on your work disk as CHAP11B. Save frequently.

4. Compile, run, and debug your program until the output matches the updated production report shown in Figure 11.15.

5. When completed, show your work to your instructor.

Quick Quiz

Answer the following questions.

1. Explain how the data loaded into the *sName* array is related to the data loaded into the *iProd* table.

2. The purpose of *LookUpName* and *LookUpDay* is to locate *sNameIn* and *sDayIn* in the *sName* and *iProd* arrays, respectively. Explain how this is accomplished.

3. Two values are passed to the *UpdateProd* module. What are the values used for?

4. Did you have any problems or errors when you ran the sample program? If so, what were they and what did you do to correct them?

Multidimensional Arrays

So far we have seen examples of one- and two-dimensional arrays. Actually, arrays may consist of three, four, or more dimensions; the actual number depends mostly on the application at hand. However, not many applications would go beyond three dimensions.

Consider the basketball score-keeping application presented earlier where the points are recorded at the end of each quarter for team 1 (home) and team 2 (visitors) in a 2×4 array. The two-dimensional array is shown in Figure 11.16.

For the subscripts *iT* and *iQ*, the statement *iPoints[iT][iQ]* represents the points scored by the *t*-team in the *q*-quarter. Hence, *iPoints[1][3]* refers to the points scored by the visitors in the fourth quarter.

Assume that games are played at three different schools; school 1 (Adams), school 2 (Lincoln), and school 3 (Washington). The three-dimensional array is shown in Figure 11.17. For the subscripts *iS*, *iT*, and *iQ*, the statement *iPoints[iS][iT][iQ]* represents the points scored during the game played at *s*-school by the *t*-team in the *q*-quarter. Hence,

```
Quarter    1   2   3   4
           0   1   2   3

Team 1   0 ┌───┬───┬───┬───┐
           │   │   │   │   │
Team 2   1 ├───┼───┼───┼───┤
           │   │   │   │   │
           └───┴───┴───┴───┘
```

FIGURE 11.16   Two-Dimensional Array

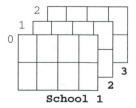

FIGURE 11.17   Three-Dimensional Array

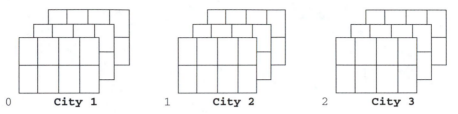

FIGURE 11.18 Four-Dimensional Array

iPoints[2][1][3] refers to the points scored during the game played at Washington High School by the visitors in the fourth quarter.

Furthermore, assume that nine games are played during the week at three high schools located in three different cities; city 1 (Millersburg), city 2 (Rosedale), and city 3 (Westport). The four-dimensional array is shown in Figure 11.18.

For the subscripts *iC, iS, iT,* and *iQ,* the statement *iPoints[iC][iS][iT][iQ]* represents the points scored in *c*-city during the game played at *s*-school by the *t*-team in the *q*-quarter. Hence, *iPoints[0][2][1][3]* refers to the points scored in Millersburg during the game played at Washington High School by the visitors in the fourth quarter.

At first, the concept of multidimensional arrays may seem confusing and somewhat difficult to visualize. However, it may be helpful to think of a two-dimensional array as a table, a three-dimensional array as a sequence of pages, and a four-dimensional array as a group of pages organized into chapters.

For example, look at the array shown in Figure 11.16 as a table, the arrays shown in Figure 11.17 as a sequence of pages (each school represents a page), and the arrays shown in Figure 11.18 as chapters (each city represents a chapter).

Checkpoint 11D

1. Code the statement to dimension the integer array shown in the following illustration.

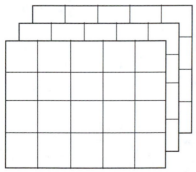

2. The array shown in the illustration in Question 1 is referred to as a _____-dimensional array.

3. Although multidimensional arrays can have several dimensions, for most applications, we seldom go beyond _____ dimensions.

4. A four-dimensional array requires _____ subscripts to locate a specific element stored in the array.

Summary

1. Many data processing applications require that certain data be stored in tables, or two-dimensional arrays.

2. A two-dimensional array consists of a finite number of rows and columns. A row represents a set of values across the table, and a column represents a set of values down the table.

3. A two-dimensional array is defined by specifying a data type, a name, and a size. Size refers to the number of rows and columns reserved for the array. For example, a 5 by 6 array reserves storage space for 30 (5×6) elements.

4. Individual elements stored in a two-dimensional array are referenced by specifying a row and a column subscript. In other words, any element can be accessed by appending two subscripts to the array name.

5. A subscript may not be negative or exceed the size established for either the row or column. Any reference to a subscript outside the row or column range will cause the compiler to produce an error message.

6. The subscripts of a two-dimensional array may be expressed as integer constants or variables.

7. For a two-dimensional array, direct reference lookup requires a row and a column subscript to directly locate the data stored in the table. Direct reference uses the input entered at the keyboard to directly access the data stored in the table.

8. For a two-dimensional array, sequential search requires, at most, two one-dimensional arrays: one for holding the row subscripts and one for holding the column subscripts. Sequential search uses the data entered at the keyboard to search the one-dimensional array(s) to determine the subscript(s) of the data stored in the table.

9. Multidimensional arrays allow the program to store data in two, three, four, or more dimensions.

10. A three-dimensional array requires three subscripts to locate a specific element stored in the array. As a rule, an *n*-dimensional array requires *n* subscripts to locate a given element stored in the array.

Programming Projects

For each project, design the logic and write the modular structured program to produce the output. Model your program after the sample programs presented in the chapter. Verify your output.

Project 11–1   Overdue Accounts-1

Write a program to read a file, load the input into arrays, and print a report of the overdue accounts.

Input (text file):

For each customer, read a record and load the data into to the following arrays. (Array types are shown in parentheses.)

1. name array   (char)
2. 12 × 3 overdue account array   (float)
   columns: 30 days, 60 days, and 90 days

Set the row size of each array to 12. Allow for a maximum of 15 characters of data for the elements in the *sName* array.

Text File (txOvrdue.fil):

Create the overdue accounts file from the data given below. Enter the records in the order shown.

Customer Name	30 Days Overdue	60 Days Overdue	90 Days Overdue
Corey Adkins	233.00	0.00	0.00
Rita Fox	0.00	135.00	740.00
Lisa Wilson	119.00	417.00	0.00
Alvin Porter	100.00	154.00	550.00
Pat Rankin	0.00	342.00	218.00
Tori Landis	0.00	0.00	235.00
David Ryan	100.00	200.00	400.00
Amy Wyatt	700.00	400.00	100.00
Brian Knox	625.00	0.00	0.00
Marie Hill	754.00	122.00	0.00
Matt Hart	136.00	340.00	900.00
Susan Cope	100.00	300.00	600.00

Output (printer):

Print the following overdue accounts report:

```
Author          OVERDUE ACCOUNTS REPORT      Page 01
                      mm/dd/yy


                        30 days   60 days   90 days
Customer Name           Overdue   Overdue   Overdue

X----------X             999.99    999.99    999.99
     :                      :         :         :
     :                      :         :         :
X----------X             999.99    999.99    999.99

            Totals:     9999.99   9999.99   9999.99
```

Processing Requirements:

- Read and load the file into the arrays.
- Read the arrays, and print a report of all the customers with overdue accounts.
- Accumulate totals for the 30-day, 60-day, and 90-day overdue accounts.

Project 11–2   Overdue Accounts-2

Modify the program in Project 11–1 to allow the user to update the data stored in the arrays. Prompt for and enter the updates given below. Search for a match on employee name `Enter 'Q' to quit`. If a match is not found, print the message `Account not found - press ENTER to continue`.

Enter the updates in the order shown.

Customer Name	Days Overdue	Balance Due
Brian Knox	30	872.00
Marie Hill	90	700.00
Susan Cope	60	610.00
David Ryan	90	435.00
Lisa Wilcox	60	495.00
Corey Adkins	30	249.00
Tori Landis	30	112.00

Project 11–3   Payroll-1

Write a program to compute and print a weekly payroll roster. Read the data from a file, load the input into arrays, and process the data stored in the arrays. Do not compute overtime. Assume that the current federal income tax (FIT) rate is 15%.

Input (text file):

For each employee, read a record and load the data into the following arrays. (Array types are shown in parentheses.)

1. name array   (char)
2. 9×2 payroll data array   (float)
   columns: hours and rate

Set the row size of each array to 9. Allow for a maximum of 15 characters of data for the elements in the *sName* array.

Text File (txPayrol.fil):

Create the payroll file from the data given below. Enter the records in the order shown.

Employee Name	Hours	Pay Rate
Tracy York	36.1	11.00
Dale Miller	40.0	10.25
Sara Erickson	38.7	12.00

Karen Thomas	48.0	9.00
Paul Irwin	48.5	8.72
Dana Clark	45.3	14.90
Tanya Bauer	40.0	7.50
Bret Rossi	35.9	8.00
Scott Howard	42.2	9.75

Output (printer):

Print the following weekly payroll report:

```
Author                WEEKLY PAYROLL REPORT           Page 01
                            mm/dd/yy


Employee      Hours      Pay Rate    Gross Pay    FIT      Net Pay

X-------X     99.9        99.99       999.99      99.99     999.99
   :           :            :           :          :          :
   :           :            :           :          :          :
X-------X     99.9        99.99       999.99      99.99     999.99

              Totals:                9999.99     999.99    9999.99
```

Processing Requirements:

- Read and load the file input into the arrays.
- Compute the gross pay:
  hours × pay rate.
- Compute the FIT amount:
  gross pay × FIT rate.
- Compute the net pay:
  gross pay – FIT amount.
- Accumulate totals for gross pay, FIT amount, and net pay.

Project 11–4   Payroll-2

Modify the program in Project 11–3 to allow the user to update the payroll data stored in the arrays. Prompt for and enter the updates given below. Search for a match on employee name `Enter 'Q' to quit`. If a match is not found, print the message `Name not found - press ENTER to continue.`

Enter the payroll updates in the order shown.

Employee Name	Hours	Pay Rate
Karen Thomas	44.1	9.00
Darla Clark	40.0	10.60
Tracy York	39.5	11.50
Diane Reeves	38.3	7.90
Scott Howard	42.2	10.00
Patsy Ireland	40.0	8.45

Project 11–5 Sales Profit-1

Write a program to calculate the profit generated by each salesperson, and print a sales profit report. Read the data from a file, load the input into arrays, and process the data stored in the arrays.

Input (text file):
For each sales representative, read a record and load the data into the following arrays. (Array types are shown in parentheses.)

1. name array (char)

2. 5 × 2 sales data array (float)
   columns: sales and cost

Set the row size of each array to 5. Allow for a maximum of 15 characters of data for the elements in the *sName* array.

Text File (txSales.fil):
Create the sales file from the data given below. Enter the records in the order shown.

Salesperson	Total Sales	Cost of Sales
Ann Zimmerman	5793.59	4204.45
Tara Perkins	12710.14	9735.38
Dennis Tian	4567.51	3119.22
Roy Hickle	2245.78	1072.49
Lisa Conrad	8120.52	6450.71

Output (printer):
Print the following sales profit report:

```
Author              SALES PROFIT REPORT          Page 01
                         mm/dd/yy


Salesperson    Total Sales   Cost Of Sales    Net Profit
--------------------------------------------------------
X--------X      99999.99        9999.99         9999.99
    :              :               :               :
    :              :               :               :
X--------X      99999.99        9999.99         9999.99

                                Total:          99999.99
```

Processing Requirements:

- Read and load the file input into the arrays.
- Compute the net profit:
  total sales – cost of sales.
- Accumulate and print a report total for net profit.

Project 11–6   Sales Profit-2

Modify the program in Project 11–5 to allow the user to update the sales data stored in the arrays. Prompt for and enter the updates given below. Search for a match on salesperson name Enter 'Q' to quit. If a match is not found, print the message Name not found - press ENTER to continue.

Enter the sales updates in the order shown.

Salesperson	Total Sales	Cost of Sales
Tara Perkins	13944.70	10378.59
Lisa Conrad	8001.03	6392.53
Holly Winkler	4316.22	2975.65
Ann Zimmerman	6090.00	4354.64
Roy Hickle	2368.99	1139.16
Barbara Rider	7605.42	4321.28

Project 11–7   Inventory-1

Write a program to read an inventory file, load the input into arrays, and print an inventory profit report.

Input (text file):
For each inventory item, read a record and load the data into the following arrays. (Array types are shown in parentheses.)

1. description array   (char)

2. quantity array   (int)

3. 5×2 cost-price array   (float)
   columns: unit cost and selling price

Set the row size of each array to 5. Allow for a maximum of 15 characters of data for the elements in the *sDescription* array.

Text File (txInven.fil):
Create the inventory file from the data given below. Enter the data in the order shown.

Description	Quantity on Hand	Unit Cost	Selling Price
Screwdrivers	36	2.27	4.98
Drills	10	7.83	15.95
Pliers	12	2.65	5.49
Saws	08	7.50	14.99
Hammers	24	4.75	9.49

Output (printer):
Print the following inventory profit report:

```
Author            INVENTORY PROFIT REPORT          Page 01
                          mm/dd/yy
```

```
Description            Quantity        Item Profit

X----------X              99             999.99
          :                :                :
          :                :                :
X----------X              99             999.99

                    Total Profit:     9999.99
```

Processing Requirements:

- Read and load the file input into the arrays.
- Compute the item cost:
  quantity × unit cost.
- Compute the item income:
  quantity × selling price.
- Compute the item profit:
  item income – item cost.
- Accumulate a report total for the item profit.

Project 11–8   Inventory-2

Modify the program in Project 11–7 to allow the user to update the inventory data stored in the arrays. Prompt for and enter the updates given below. Search for a match on item description `Enter 'Q' to quit`. If a match is not found, print the message `Item not found - press ENTER to continue`.

Enter the inventory updates in the order shown.

Description	Quantity on Hand	Unit Cost	Selling Price
Screwdrivers	48	2.49	5.29
Hatchets	12	4.49	9.99
Pliers	24		
Saws		7.95	
Hammers			9.99

Project 11–9   Proficiency Test-1

Write a program to read data from a file, load the input into arrays, and print a report of the fourth-grade proficiency results for the Hartford County suburban school districts.

Input (text file):
For each school, read a record and load the data into the following arrays. (Array types are shown in parentheses.)

1. school district array   (char)

2. 10 × 4 proficiency array   (int)
   columns: citizenship, math, reading, and writing

Set the row size of each array to 10. Allow for a maximum of 25 characters of data for the elements in the *sDistrict* array.

Text File (txProf.fil):

Create the school file from the data given below. Enter the data in the order shown.

School District	Citizenship	Math	Reading	Writing
Adamsburg	94	85	89	90
Davidson	96	89	91	92
Claymore	93	78	92	91
Hamilton	85	81	86	83
Newland	90	84	88	80
Piketon	92	90	92	93
Reynolds	96	85	95	95
Southford	93	82	89	84
Stockdale	80	75	81	82
Winslow	91	80	90	92

Output (printer):

Print the following proficiency test report:

```
Author                 H A R T F O R D    C O U N T Y        Page 01
                          SUBURBAN SCHOOL DISTRICTS


                       Fourth-Grade Proficiency Results
                                  mm/dd/yy


School District  Citizenship  Math  Reading  Writing  Average

X-----------X        99        99      99       99       99
        :            :         :       :        :        :
        :            :         :       :        :        :
X-----------X        99        99      99       99       99
```

Processing Requirements:

- Read and load the file input into the arrays.
- Compute the proficiency average:
  (citizenship + math + reading + writing) / 4.
- Print the detail line on the report.

Project 11–10   Proficiency Tests-2

Modify the program in Project 11–9 to allow the user to update the data stored in the arrays. Prompt for and enter the updates given below. Search for a match on school district Enter 'Q' to quit. If a match is not found, print the message District not found - press ENTER to continue.

Enter the updates in the order shown.

School District	Citizenship	Math	Reading	Writing
Davis	90	87	89	91
Claymore	95	83	90	90
Newland		80		84
Pike	87	92		
Southford	91	85	90	86
Stockdale		77	85	
Winslow			93	94

12 Sequential Files

Overview

Learning Objectives

After you have read this chapter and completed the exercises, you should be able to

- explain the purpose and use of sequential files
- create a sequential file
- read and print the data stored in a sequential file
- append data to a sequential file

Files, Records, and Keys

As we have seen in previous chapters, data is organized into fields, records, and files to facilitate processing by the computer. A file is a collection of related records that pertain to a specific data processing application—accounts receivable, payroll, sales, inventory, and so on. A record is a collection of related data items or fields that contain information about a single unit in the file—a customer, an employee, a sales rep, an inventory item, and so on. A field is a collection of characters that describe a single unit of data—account number, name, address, zip code, telephone number, and so on.

A special field called a **record key** or **key field** is used to uniquely identify the records in the file. Examples of key fields are account number, social security number, salesperson number, part number, and so on. A key field is used to access records and to arrange the records of a file in a specific order. Because the key field is used to store, retrieve, and access the records in the file, the key field data in each record must be unique.

Sequential File Organization

Sequential file organization stores records on disk or tape in key field order. It offers the advantage of efficient use of storage. For applications that require access to all or most of the records in the file, sequential file organization provides fast and efficient processing and allows the programmer to tap into the real power of file processing—sequential file updating. Chapter 13 presents the fundamentals of updating sequential files.

However, sequential access can be rather time-consuming for applications that require access to only a small number of records at any given time. It can be compared to selecting a song recorded on a cassette tape. The user must manually skip through the other songs until the correct one is found.

For example, in order to access record number 100, the program must first search through all of the records up to record 100. The program actually reads 99 records before it finds the one it is looking for. This, of course, can be a rather lengthy process for a file that contains thousands upon thousands of records.

Creating a Sequential File

Consider an application that requires a sequential file for the courses offered at the regional campus of Blackmoore University. Once administration has decided what information is required for the course offering system, a file is created. Data is collected for each course offered at the regional campus and stored on disk for future reference.

Since each record in the file contains information about one course, we will need some way of organizing the file so that any record can be accessed and processed by the computer. We will use the call number as the key field to uniquely identify each record. Hence, the records in the course file will be stored sequentially in ascending (low to high) order according to the key field—the call number.

Creating a sequential file involves the following process:

1. Declare the file pointer variable.
2. Define the record format—the fields of the record.
3. Open the file in *write* mode.
4. Prompt for and enter the file data.
5. Write the data to the file.
6. Close the file.

This process is illustrated in sample program CHAP12A. The course file is created from the data entered at the keyboard.

Checkpoint 12A

1. Describe the organization of data in order from the smallest unit to the largest unit. Briefly discuss each.
2. Define a record key or key field.
3. Explain the concept of sequential file organization.
4. What are the advantages of sequential file organization?
5. List the six steps involved in creating a sequential file.

Sample Program CHAP12A

Sample program CHAP12A creates a sequential file for the courses offered at the regional campus of Blackmoore University. See Figure 12.1 for the hierarchy chart and Figure 12.2 for the flowchart. Sample program CHAP12A is presented in Figure 12.3. The data is entered by the user in ascending key order (Figure 12.4). The specifications, logic design, and program listing follow.

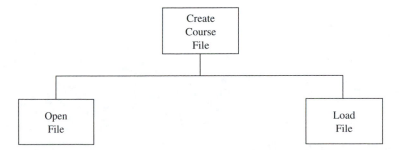

FIGURE 12.1   Hierarchy Chart for CHAP12A

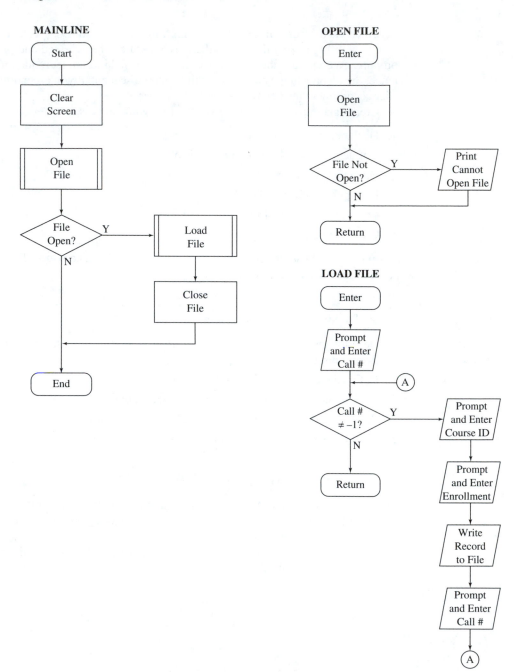

FIGURE 12.2   Program Flowchart for CHAP12A

```
/*---------------------------------------------------------------
CREATE FILE: Create a sequential file to store the courses offered
at the regional campus of Blackmoore University.

Program:    CHAP12A.C
Author:     David M. Collopy
Date:       mm/dd/yy
Project:    Sample program

****************************************************************/

/*---- PREPROCESSING DIRECTIVES --------------------------------*/

#include <stdio.h>
#include <graph.h>

/*---- FUNCTION PROTOTYPES --------------------------------------*/

void OpenFile(void);               /* open course file    */
void LoadFile(void);               /* load data into file */

/*---- PROGRAM SETUP --------------------------------------------*/

/*>  O U T P U T   C O U R S E   R E C O R D           <*/

FILE *fpFO;                        /* course file pointer */
int    iCallNum;                   /* call number         */
char  sCourse[15];                 /* course ID           */
int    iEnroll;                    /* student enrollment  */

/*---------------------------------------------------------------
      MAINLINE CONTROL
----------------------------------------------------------------*/
main()
{
    _clearscreen(0);
    OpenFile();
    if (fpFO != 0)
    {
        LoadFile();
        fclose(fpFO);
    }
    return 0;
}
```

FIGURE 12.3   Sample Program CHAP12A: Creates a sequential disk file from user input

```
/*----------------------------------------------------------------
        OPEN COURSE FILE
----------------------------------------------------------------*/
void OpenFile(void)
{
    fpFO = fopen("a:sqCrs.fil", "w");
    if (fpFO == 0)
    {
        printf("\nCannot open course file for output\n");
    }
    return;
}


/*----------------------------------------------------------------
        LOAD DATA INTO FILE
----------------------------------------------------------------*/
void LoadFile(void)
{
    printf("\nEnter call number or '-1' to Quit: ");
    scanf(" %d", &iCallNum);
    while (iCallNum != -1)
    {
        printf("                      Enter course ID: ");
        scanf(" %s", sCourse);
        printf("            Enter student enrollment: ");
        scanf(" %d", &iEnroll);
        fprintf(fpFO, "%d %s %d\n", iCallNum, sCourse, iEnroll);
        printf("\nEnter call number or '-1' to Quit: ");
        scanf(" %d", &iCallNum);
    }
    return;
}
```

FIGURE 12.3 *Continued*

```
Enter call number or '-1' to Quit: 100
                    Enter course ID: ACCT101
          Enter student enrollment: 24
Enter call number or '-1' to Quit: 200
            :              :
            :              :
```

FIGURE 12.4 Data Entry Screen for CHAP12A

```
100 ACCT101 24
200 BIOL101 19
300 CHEM201 21
400 ENG200 16
500 HIST225 33
600 MGT330 29
```

FIGURE 12.5   Disk File Output for CHAP12A

Input (keyboard):

For each course, prompt for and enter the following data. (Field size and types are shown in parentheses.)

Call number	(3 int)
Course ID	(15 char)
Student enrollment	(2 int)

Output (sqCrs.fil):

The sequential file is shown in Figure 12.5. As a rule, append the prefix *sq* to sequential file names. The prefix reminds you that the identifier represents a sequential file.

Processing Requirements:

- Open the file in *write* mode.
- Prompt for and enter the data.
- Write the data to the file.
- Close the file.

Pseudocode:

```
START: Main
Clear screen
Call Open File
IF file opened
      Call Load File
      Close file
END IF
END

ENTER: Open File
Open course file for write
IF file not opened
      Print cannot open course file for output
END IF
RETURN

ENTER: Load File
```

```
        Prompt and enter call number (or –1 to quit)
        LOOP while call number not = –1
             Prompt and enter course ID
             Prompt and enter student enrollment
             Write the input to the file:
                   call number
                   course ID
                   student enrollment
             Prompt and enter call number (or –1 to quit)
        END LOOP
        RETURN
```

Hierarchy Chart: See Figure 12.1.

Program Flowchart: See Figure 12.2.

Dissection of Sample Program CHAP12A

O U T P U T   C O U R S E   R E C O R D:

```
FILE *fpFO;
int   iCallNum;
char sCourse[15];
int   iEnroll;
```

The above statements declare the file pointer variable and the record fields. The asterisk (and prefix *fp*) indicates that the variable is a file pointer. The *FO* reminds you that the program is writing file ouput—that is, data is written to the course file.

M A I N L I N E   C O N T R O L:

```
main()
{
    _clearscreen(0);
    OpenFile();
```

The above statements clear the screen and branch to open the course file. The *OpenFile* module attempts to open the file for output.

```
    if (fpFO != 0)
    {
        LoadFile();
        fclose(fpFO);
    }
    return 0;
}
```

In the above statements, if the file pointer is not equal to 0, then control branches to *Load-File* and performs the processing activities given there. After the course file is loaded, the file is closed. As you may recall, the close statement clears the output file buffer by writing the remaining data to the file before releasing the buffer and closing the file.

```
OPEN   COURSE   FILE:

void OpenFile(void)
{
    fpFO = fopen("a:sqCrs.fil", "w");
    if (fpFO == 0)
    {
        printf("Cannot open course file for output\n");
    }
    return;
}
```

The above statements open the course file in write mode; the *"w"* indicates that data is written to the file. If the file is opened, the fopen() statement establishes an address for the file and assigns it to the file pointer. However, if the file is not opened, the error message is displayed on the screen.

```
LOAD   DATA   INTO   FILE:

void LoadFile(void)
{
    printf("\nEnter call number or '-1' to quit: ");
    scanf(" %d", &iCallNum);
    while (iCallNum != -1)
    {
        printf("                     Enter course ID: ");
        scanf(" %s", sCourse);
        printf("              Enter student enrollment: ");
        scanf(" %d", &iEnroll);
        fprintf(fpFO, "%d %s %d\n", iCallNum, sCourse, iEnroll);
        printf("\nEnter call number or '-1' to quit: ");
        scanf(" %d", &iCallNum);
    }
    return;
}
```

In the above statements, as long as the call number is not equal to –1, the user enters the course ID and the student enrollment. The fprintf() statement writes the data to the file. Otherwise, control exits the module and returns to the *MAINLINE*.

Notes and Tips

1. Sequential file organization provides fast and efficient processing for applications that require access to all or most of the records stored in the file. Each record in the file has a unique record key that is used for arranging and processing the individual records.

2. A sequential file is created by opening it in *write* mode.

3. Use the file pointer *fpFO* when creating a sequential file. The file pointer reminds you that the program is writing file output.

4. Append the prefix *sq* to the sequential file name to remind you that the identifier represents a sequential file.

Tutorial CHAP12A

1. The objectives of this tutorial are to
   - declare a file pointer and identify the record layout
   - open a file in write mode and test the open status
   - load data into a sequential file

2. Read the program specifications for sample program CHAP12A.

3. Log on to your C editor, and enter the source code as shown in Figure 12.3. Save the program on your work disk as CHAP12A. Save frequently as you enter the code.

4. Compile, run, and debug your program. When completed, show your work to your instructor.

Quick Quiz

Answer the following questions.

1. What does the following declaration do?
   ```
   FILE *fpFO;
   ```

2. What relationship is there between the file pointer and the file open statement?

3. Why is the file pointer included in the following statement?
   ```
   fprintf(fpFO, "%d %s %d\n", iCallNum, sCourse, iEnroll);
   ```

4. Did you have any problems or errors when you ran the sample program? If so, what were they and what did you do to correct them?

Reading and Printing a Sequential File

The course file created in the previous section was stored on disk. Since the records were written directly to the disk, we have no way of knowing for sure what was actually placed there. We didn't see the output. Therefore, it would be wise to look at the file and verify the contents. Although some C compilers allow the programmer to look at the data stored on disk, others do not. In any case, we can look at the data by simply writing a program to read the file and print the records.

Reading and printing a sequential file involves the following process:

1. Declare the file pointer variable.
2. Define the record fields.
3. Open the file in *read* mode.
4. Read the records from the file.
5. Display the records on the screen.
6. Close the file.

This process is illustrated in sample program CHAP12B. The program reads the course file and prints a copy of the records stored on disk.

Checkpoint 12B

1. List the steps necessary to read and print the contents of a sequential file.
2. Code the module to read and print the records stored in a sequential file. The fields are name (15 characters), hourly pay rate (float), and hours worked (integer).

Sample Program CHAP12B

Sample program CHAP12B reads and prints the course file created in sample program CHAP12A. Each record is read from the file and written to the output report. See Figure 12.6 for the hierarchy chart and Figure 12.7 for the flowchart. Sample program CHAP12B is presented in Figure 12.8. Figure 12.9 shows the output.

The following specifications apply:

Input (sqCrs.fil):

For each record, read the following data from the course file. (Field size and type are shown in parentheses.)

Call number	(3 int)
Course ID	(15 char)
Student enrollment	(2 int)

Output (screen):

The output report is shown in Figure 12.9.

Processing Requirements:

- Open the file in *read* mode.
- Read the course file.
- Write the records to the output report.
- Close the file.

Pseudocode:

```
START: Main
Clear screen
Call Open File
IF file opened
      Call Read File
      Close file
END IF
END

ENTER: Open File
Open course file for read
IF file not opened
      Print cannot open course file for input
END IF
RETURN
```

ENTER: Read File
Print 1 heading line
LOOP while not at end of file
    Read course record:
        call number
        course ID
        student enrollment
    Print course detail line:
        call number
        course ID
        student enrollment
END LOOP
RETURN

Hierarchy Chart: See Figure 12.6.

Program Flowchart: See Figure 12.7.

Dissection of Sample Program CHAP12B

```
INPUT   COURSE   RECORD:

FILE *fpFI;
int   iCallNum;
char  sCourse[15];
int   iEnroll;
```

The above statements define the file pointer variable and the record format. The identifier *fpFI* reminds you that data is input from the file.

```
OPEN   COURSE   FILE:

void OpenFile(void)
{
    fpFI = fopen("a:sqCrs.fil", "r");
    if (fpFI == 0)
    {
        printf("Cannot open course file for input\n");
    }
    return;
}
```

The above statements open the course file in read mode; the *"r"* indicates that data is read from the file. If the file is opened, the fopen() statement establishes an address for the file and assigns it to the file pointer. However, if the file is not opened, the error message is displayed on the screen.

```
READ   AND   PRINT   COURSE   FILE:

void ReadFile(void)
```

```
{
    printf("\nCall#  Course ID               Enrollment\n");
```

The above statement prints the report heading line.

```
    while (!feof(fpFI))
    {
```

In the above statement, as long as the current position in the course file is not equal to the end-of-file marker, control executes the statements in the body of the loop. Otherwise, control skips the loop and returns to the *MAINLINE*.

```
        fscanf(fpFI, " %d %s %d", &iCallNum, sCourse, &iEnroll);
```

The above statement reads a record from the file pointed to by *fpFI* and assigns the data to the variables in the order listed—*iCallNum*, *sCourse*, and *iEnroll*.

```
        printf("\n %3d    %-15s               %2d",
            iCallNum, sCourse, iEnroll);
    }
    return;
}
```

The above statements format and print the call number, course ID, and student enrollment. After printing the detail line to the report, control returns to the *while* statement and tests for the end-of-file condition.

Notes and Tips

1. Once a file has been created, open, read, and print the records. It's always nice to know that the data was correctly written to the file before you start processing it.
2. A sequential file is read by opening it in *read* mode.
3. Use the file pointer *fpFI* when opening a sequential file. The file pointer reminds you that the program is reading file input.

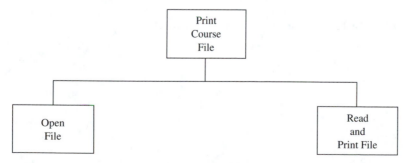

FIGURE 12.6 Hierarchy Chart for CHAP12B

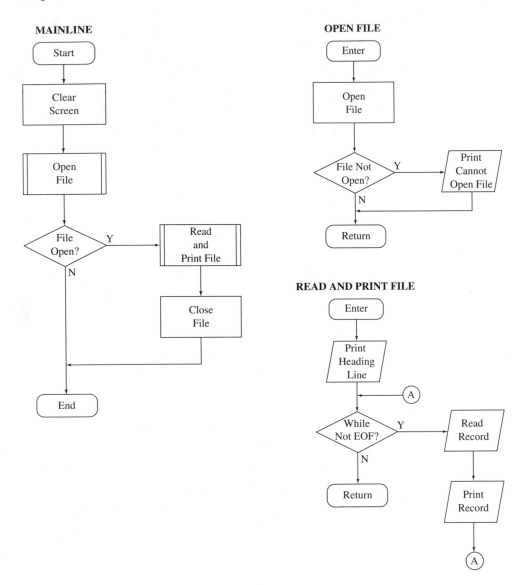

FIGURE 12.7   Program Flowchart for CHAP12B

```
/*--------------------------------------------------------------
PRINT FILE: Read and print the data stored in a sequential file.

Program:    CHAP12B.C
Author:     David M. Collopy
Date:       mm/dd/yy
Project:    Sample program
****************************************************************/

/*---- PREPROCESSING DIRECTIVES --------------------------------*/

#include <stdio.h>
#include <graph.h>

/*---- FUNCTION PROTOTYPES --------------------------------------*/

void  OpenFile(void);              /* open course file          */
void  ReadFile(void);              /* read and print course file */

/*---- PROGRAM SETUP --------------------------------------------*/

/*>  I N P U T    C O U R S E    R E C O R D              <*/

FILE *fpFI;                        /* course file pointer */
int    iCallNum;                   /* call number         */
char  sCourse[15];                 /* course ID           */
int    iEnroll;                    /* student enrollment  */

/*--------------------------------------------------------------
       MAINLINE CONTROL
----------------------------------------------------------------*/
main()
{
    _clearscreen(0);
    OpenFile();
    if (fpFI != 0)
    {
        ReadFile();
        fclose(fpFI);
    }
    return 0;
}
```

FIGURE 12.8 Sample Program CHAP12B: This program reads a sequential disk file and prints the output report

```
/*----------------------------------------------------------------
            OPEN COURSE FILE
---------------------------------------------------------------*/
void OpenFile(void)
{
    fpFI = fopen("a:sqCrs.fil", "r");
    if (fpFI == 0)
    {
        printf("\nCannot open course file for input\n");
    }
    return;
}


/*----------------------------------------------------------------
        READ AND PRINT COURSE FILE
---------------------------------------------------------------*/
void ReadFile(void)
{
    printf("\nCall#  Course ID                Enrollment\n");
    while (!feof(fpFI))
    {
        fscanf(fpFI, " %d %s %d\n", &iCallNum, sCourse, &iEnroll);
        printf("\n %3d    %-14s              %2d",
            iCallNum, sCourse, iEnroll);
    }
    return;
}
```

FIGURE 12.8 *Continued*

```
Call#   Dept-Number#           Enrollment

 100    ACCT101                    24
 200    BIOL101                    19
 300    CHEM201                    21
 400    ENG200                     16
 500    HIST225                    33
 600    MGT330                     29
```

FIGURE 12.9 Screen Output for CHAP12B

Tutorial CHAP12B

1. The objectives of this tutorial are to
   - open a file in read mode
   - read and print the contents of a sequential file
2. Read the program specifications for sample program CHAP12B.
3. Log on to your C editor, and enter the source code as shown in Figure 12.8. Save the program on your work disk as CHAP12B. Save frequently.
4. Compile, run, and debug your program until the results match the screen output shown in Figure 12.9.
5. When completed, show your work to your instructor.

Quick Quiz

Answer the following questions.

1. What two tasks does this open statement do?
   ```
   fpFI = fopen("a:sqCrs.fil", "r");
   ```
2. Identify two situations that would prevent the program from opening a file.
3. Explain how the following condition test works.
   ```
   while(!feof(fpFI))
   ```
4. Why is the file pointer coded in the statement shown below?
   ```
   fscanf(fpFI, " %d %s %d\n", iCallNum, sCourse, iEnroll);
   ```
5. Did you have any problems or errors when you ran the sample program? If so, what were they and what did you do to correct them?

Appending Records to a Sequential File

We can add records to the course file created earlier by specifying the *append* mode for the open statement. For example,

```
fopen("a:sqCrs.fil", "a");
```

opens the course file in *append* mode; `"a"` indicates append. This feature allows the program to add records to the end of a sequential file.

Appending records to a sequential file involves the following process.

1. Declare the file pointer variable.
2. Define the record fields.
3. Open the file in *append* mode.
4. Prompt for and enter the file data.
5. Write the data to the end of the file.
6. Close the file.

This process is illustrated in sample program CHAP12C.

Checkpoint 12C

1. How are records added to the end of a sequential file?

2. Code the statement to open the file called *sqTest.fil* on the A drive in *append* mode.

3. List six steps that are performed when appending records to a sequential file.

Sample Program CHAP12C

Sample program CHAP12C appends records at the end of the course file. See Figure 12.10 for the hierarchy chart and Figure 12.11 for the flowchart. The program code is presented in Figure 12.12, and the disk file output is shown in Figure 12.13.

The following specifications apply:

Input (keyboard):
For each new course, prompt for and enter the following data. (Field size and type are shown in parentheses.)

Call number	(3 int)
Course ID	(15 char)
Student enrollment	(2 int)

Output (sqCrs.fil):
The appended file is shown in Figure 12.13.

Processing Requirements:

- Open the file in *append* mode.
- Prompt for and enter the data.
- Write the new records to the file.
- Close the file.

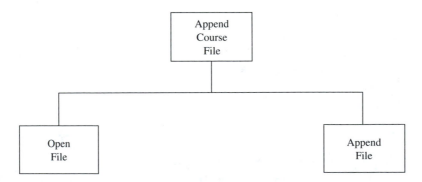

FIGURE 12.10   Hierarchy Chart for CHAP12C

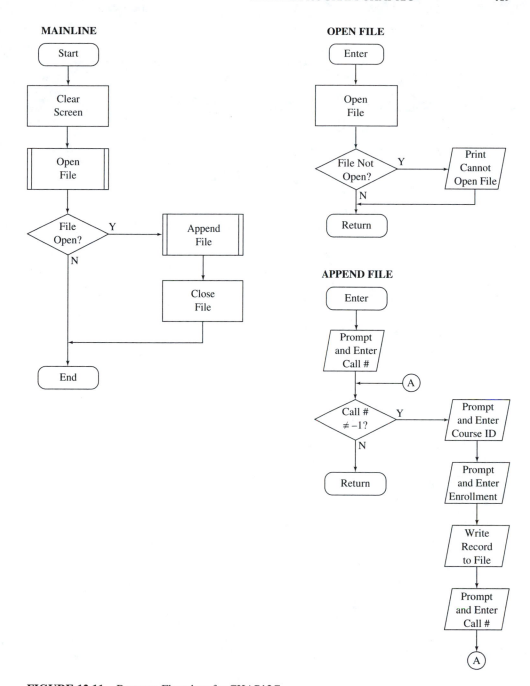

FIGURE 12.11   Program Flowchart for CHAP12C

```
/*----------------------------------------------------------------
CREATE FILE: Append records to the end of the sequential file.

Program:    CHAP12C.C
Author:     David M. Collopy
Date:       mm/dd/yy
Project:    Sample program
******************************************************************/

/*---- PREPROCESSING DIRECTIVES --------------------------------*/

#include <stdio.h>
#include <graph.h>

/*---- FUNCTION PROTOTYPES -------------------------------------*/

void  OpenFile(void);          /* open course file       */
void  AppendFile(void);        /* append records to file */

/*---- PROGRAM SETUP -------------------------------------------*/

/*>  O U T P U T   C O U R S E   R E C O R D            <*/

FILE *fpFO;                    /* course file pointer */
int   iCallNum;               /* call number         */
char  sCourse[15];            /* course ID           */
int   iEnroll;                /* student enrollment  */

/*----------------------------------------------------------------
        MAINLINE CONTROL
----------------------------------------------------------------*/
main()
{
    _clearscreen(0);
    OpenFile();
    if (fpFO != 0)
    {
        AppendFile();
        fclose(fpFO);
    }
    return 0;
}

/*----------------------------------------------------------------
        OPEN COURSE FILE
----------------------------------------------------------------*/
```

FIGURE 12.12   Sample Program CHAP12C: Appends records to the course file

```
void OpenFile(void)
{
    fpFO = fopen("a:sqCrs.fil", "a");
    if (fpFO == 0)
    {
        printf("\nCannot open course file for append\n");
    }
    return;
}


/*----------------------------------------------------------------
      APPEND RECORDS TO FILE
----------------------------------------------------------------*/
void AppendFile(void)
{
    printf("\nEnter call number or '-1' to Quit: ");
    scanf(" %d", &iCallNum);
    while (iCallNum != -1)
    {
        printf("                    Enter course ID: ");
        scanf(" %s", sCourse);
        printf("           Enter student enrollment: ");
        scanf(" %d", &iEnroll);
        fprintf(fpFO, " %d %s %d\n", iCallNum, sCourse, iEnroll);
        printf("\nEnter call number or '-1' to Quit: ");
        scanf(" %d", &iCallNum);
    }
    return;
}
```

FIGURE 12.12 *Continued*

```
100 ACCT101 24
200 BIOL101 19
300 CHEM201 21
400 ENG200 16
500 HIST225 33
600 MGT330 29
700 MATH120 14  ◄─── new records
800 PHYS251 20          appended here
900 SPAN111 12
```

FIGURE 12.13 Disk File Output for CHAP12C

Pseudocode:

```
START: Main
Clear screen
Call Open File
IF file opened
     Call Append File
     Close file
END IF
END

ENTER: Open File
Open course file for append
IF file not opened
     Print cannot open course file for append
END IF
RETURN

ENTER: Append Data
Prompt and enter call number (or -1 to quit)
LOOP while call number not = -1
     Prompt and enter course ID
     Prompt and enter student enrollment
     Write the input to the file:
          call number
          course ID
          student enrollment
     Prompt and enter call number (or -1 to quit)
END LOOP
RETURN
```

Hierarchy Chart: See Figure 12.10.

Program Flowchart: See Figure 12.11.

Dissection of Sample Program CHAP12C

Essentially, the program consists of a three-step process. First, the file pointer variable and the record fields are defined. Second, the open statement specifies *append* mode. Third, the program prompts the user to enter the additional courses and adds them to the end of the file.

The *Append* module is shown below.

```
A P P E N D    R E C O R D S    T O    F I L E:

void AppendFile(void)
{
    printf("\nEnter call number or '-1' to Quit: ");
    scanf(" %d", &iCallNum);
    while (iCallNum != -1)
    {
        printf("                    Enter course ID: ");
```

```
        scanf(" %s", sCourse);
        printf("               Enter student enrollment: ");
        scanf(" %d", &iEnroll);
        fprintf(fpFO, " %d %s %d\n", iCallNum, sCourse, iEnroll);
        printf("\nEnter call number or '-1' to Quit: ");
        scanf(" %d", &iCallNum);
    }
    return;
}
```

In the above statements, as long as the call number is not equal to –1, the user enters the course data and the fprintf() writes the record to the file. Otherwise, control exits the module and returns to the *MAINLINE*.

Notes and Tips

1. The *append* mode allows you to add new records to the end of an existing file. It does not insert the new records in record key order. Chapter 13 shows you how to do that.

2. Did you notice that the code for sample programs CHAP12A and CHAP12C look a lot alike? The only differences are that the second program is opened in append mode and the records are placed at the end of a previously created file.

3. Use the file pointer *fpFO* when appending records to a sequential file. The file pointer reminds you that the program is writing file output.

Tutorial CHAP12C

1. The objectives of this tutorial are to
   • open a sequential file in append mode
   • add new records to the end of a file

2. Read the program specifications for sample program CHAP12C.

3. Log on to your C editor, and enter the source code as shown in Figure 12.12. Save the program on your work disk as CHAP12C. Save frequently.

4. Compile, run, and debug your program. Afterward, load and run sample program CHAP12B to verify that the new records were added to the course file.

5. When completed, show your work to your instructor.

Quick Quiz

Answer the following questions.

1. For sequential files, what does it mean to *append* records to a file?

2. Is there really much difference in the source code shown for sample program CHAP12A and CHAP12C? Explain your answer.

3. Did you have any problems or errors when you ran the sample program? If so, what were they and what did you do to correct them?

Summary

1. Data represents facts that are used to describe a data processing application; data is organized into fields, records, and files.

2. A file is a collection of related records that pertain to a specific data processing application. A record is a collection of related data items or fields that contain information about a single unit in the file. A field is a collection of characters that describe a single unit of data.

3. A key field is used to uniquely identify the records in a file. It is used to access or arrange the records in ascending or descending order.

4. In sequential file organization, the records are stored on disk or tape in key field order.

5. Sequential file organization offers the advantage of efficient use of storage; the records are stored one after another in a specific order.

6. Sequential file organization provides fast and efficient processing for applications that require access to all or most of the records in the file. However, this method can be time-consuming for applications that require access to only a small number of records at any given time.

7. Creating a sequential file involves the following six-step process: (1) declare the file pointer variable, (2) define the record format, (3) open the file in write mode, (4) enter the file data, (5) write the data to the file, and (6) close the file.

8. The contents of a sequential file can be verified by reading the file and copying the records to a report.

9. Records may be added to a sequential file by specifying the *append* mode in the open statement. *Append* attaches the new records to the end of the file.

Programming Projects

For each project, design the logic and write the modular structured program to produce the output. Model your program after the sample programs presented in the chapter. Verify your output.

Project 12–1   Overdue Accounts

Write a program to prompt for the input, and create a sequential file for the overdue accounts. Then read the file and print a report of the customers with account balances 90 days overdue.

Part I: Create the sequential file.

Input (keyboard):
For each customer record, prompt for and enter the following data. (Field size and type are shown in parentheses.)

1. Account number   (4 int)
2. Customer name   (15 char)

3. Days overdue   (2 int)
4. Balance due   (6.2 float)

File Data:

Use the data given below to create the overdue accounts file. (The numbers shown above the columns correspond to the fields described for the input.)

1	2	3	4
1010	David Ryan	90	400.00
2450	Marie Hill	30	754.00
2730	Rita Fox	90	740.00
3100	Alvin Porter	90	550.00
4080	Corey Adkins	30	233.00
4890	Amy Wyatt	30	700.00
5260	Brian Knox	30	625.00
6350	Susan Cope	90	600.00
7720	Lisa Wilson	60	417.00
8540	Matt Hart	90	900.00
9200	Tori Landis	90	235.00
9630	Pat Rankin	60	342.00

Output (sqOvrdue.fil):

Sequential disk file

Processing Requirements:

*   Open the file in *write* mode.
*   Prompt for and enter the data.
*   Write the data to the file.
*   Close the file.

Part II: Read the file, process the data, and print the report.

Input (sqOvrdue.fil):

Sequential disk file

Output (printer):

Print the following 90-day overdue accounts report:

```
Author            90-DAY OVERDUE ACCOUNTS        Page 01
                         mm/dd/yy


 Acct Number        Customer Name           Amount Due

    9999          X-----------X              999.99
      :                 :                      :
      :                 :                      :
    9999          X-----------X              999.99


                              Total:       9999.99
```

Processing Requirements:

- Open the file in *read* mode.
- Read the overdue accounts.
- Print a report of all accounts that are 90 days overdue.
- Accumulate a total for the amount due, and print it at the end of the report.
- Close the file.

Project 12–2   Payroll

Write a program to prompt for the input data, and create a sequential file for the payroll department. Then read the file, calculate pay, and print the weekly payroll roster. Hours worked over 40 are paid overtime. Assume the current federal income tax (FIT) rate is 15%.

Part I: Create the sequential file.

Input (keyboard):
For each payroll record, prompt for and enter the following data. (Field size and type are shown in parentheses.)

1. Employee number   (4 int)

2. Employee name   (15 char)

3. Hours worked   (2 int)

4. Hourly pay rate   (5.2 float)

File Data:
Use the data given below to create the payroll file. The numbers shown above the columns correspond to the fields described for the input.)

1	2	3	4
1000	Tanya Bauer	40	7.50
1200	Dana Clark	45	14.90
1400	Sara Erickson	38	12.00
2000	Scott Howard	42	9.75
3000	Paul Irwin	48	8.72
3100	Dale Miller	40	10.25
3500	Bret Rossi	35	8.00
4000	Karen Thomas	48	9.00
4200	Tracy York	36	11.00

Output (sqPayrol.fil):
Sequential disk file

Processing Requirements:

- Open the file in *write* mode.
- Prompt for and enter the data.
- Write the data to the file.
- Close the file.

Part II: Read the file, process the data, and print the report.

Input (sqPayrol.fil):
Sequential disk file

Output (printer):

Print the following weekly payroll report:

```
Author               WEEKLY PAYROLL REPORT              Page 01
                          mm/dd/yy


             Hours      Hourly    Gross
Enum  Employee   Worked  Pay Rate    Pay         FIT     Net Pay

9999  X--------X   99.9     99.99    999.99    99.99    999.99
         :          :         :         :         :        :
         :          :         :         :         :        :
9999  X--------X   99.9     99.99    999.99    99.99    999.99

                        Totals:    9999.99   999.99   9999.99
```

Processing Requirements:

- Open the file in *read* mode.
- Read the payroll records.
- Compute the regular pay:
  If hours > 40,
      then regular pay = 40 × pay rate
      else regular pay = hours × pay rate.
- Compute the overtime pay:
  If hours > 40,
      then overtime pay = (hours – 40) × 1.5 × pay rate
      else overtime pay = 0.
- Compute the gross pay:
  regular pay + overtime pay.
- Compute the FIT amount:
  gross pay × FIT rate.
- Compute the net pay:
  gross pay – FIT amount.
- Accumulate totals for gross pay, FIT amount, and net pay. Print the totals at the end of the report.
- Close the file.

Project 12–3   Sales Profit

Write a program to prompt for the input, and create a sequential file for the sales department. Then read the file, calculate profit per salesperson, and print a sales profit report.

Part I: Create the sequential file.

Input (keyboard):

For each sales record, prompt for and enter the following data. (Field size and type are shown in parentheses.)

1. Salesperson number   (3 int)
2. Salesperson name   (15 char)

3. Total sales   (8.2 float)
4. Cost of sales   (7.2 float)

File Data:
Use the data given below to create the sales file. (The numbers shown above the columns correspond to the fields described for the input.)

1	2	3	4
100	Lisa Conrad	8120.52	6450.71
300	Roy Hickle	2245.78	1072.49
400	Tara Perkins	12710.14	9735.38
700	Dennis Tian	4567.51	3119.22
900	Ann Zimmerman	5793.59	4204.45

Output (sqSales.fil):
Sequential disk file

Processing Requirements:

- Open the file in *write* mode.
- Prompt for and enter the data.
- Write the data to the file.
- Close the file.

Part II: Read the file, process the data, and print the report.

Input (sqSales.fil):
Sequential disk file

Output (printer):
Print the following sales profit report:

```
Author                    SALES PROFIT REPORT              Page 01
                              mm/dd/yy

                       Total            Cost of         Net
Num    Salesperson     Sales            Sales           Profit
-----------------------------------------------------------------
999    X--------X      99999.99         9999.99         9999.99
 :         :              :                :               :
 :         :              :                :               :
999    X--------X      99999.99         9999.99         9999.99

                                        Total:          99999.99
```

Processing Requirements:

- Open the file in *read* mode.
- Read the sales records.
- Compute the net profit:
  total sales – cost of sales.
- Accumulate a total for the net profit, and print it at the end of the report.
- Close the file.

Project 12–4   Inventory

Write a program to prompt for the input, and create a sequential file for the inventory department. Then read the file and print an inventory reorder report.

Part I: Create the sequential file.

Input (keyboard):
For each inventory record, prompt for and enter the following data. (Field size and type are shown in parentheses.)

1. Item number   (4 int)
2. Item description   (15 char)
3. Quantity on hand   (2 int)
4. Reorder point   (2 int)
5. Reorder quantity   (2 int)
6. Unit cost   (4.2 float)
7. Selling price   (5.2 float)

File Data:
Use the data given below to create the inventory file. (The numbers shown above the columns correspond to the fields described for the input.)

1	2	3	4	5	6	7
1000	Hammers	24	12	24	4.75	9.49
2000	Saws	08	16	12	7.50	14.99
3000	Drills	10	12	18	7.83	15.95
4000	Screwdrivers	36	24	12	2.27	4.98
5000	Pliers	12	12	36	2.65	5.49

Output (sqInven.fil):
Sequential disk file

Processing Requirements:

- Open the file in *write* mode.
- Prompt for and enter the data.
- Write the data to the file.
- Close the file.

Part II: Read the file, process the data, and print the report.

Input (sqInven.fil):
Sequential disk file

Output (printer):
Print the following inventory reorder report:

```
Author              INVENTORY REORDER REPORT          Page 01
                          mm/dd/yy


Item                            Quantity    On        Item
Number    Description           on Hand     Order     Cost
```

```
      9999      X-----------X          99          99          999.99
       :            :                  :           :             :
       :            :                  :           :             :
      9999      X-----------X          99          99          999.99

                                         Total Cost:          9999.99
```

Processing Requirements:

- Open the file in *read* mode.
- Read the inventory records.
- Determine what items to reorder:
  Order the reorder quantity of an item when the quantity on hand is less than or equal to the reorder point.
- Compute the item cost:
  on order × unit cost.
- Accumulate the total cost, and print it at the end of the report.
- Close the file.

Project 12–5   Personnel

Write a program to prompt for the input, and create a sequential file for the personnel department. Then read the file and print a salary report of all female employees who earn over $30,000 a year.

Part I: Create the sequential file.

Input (keyboard):

For each employee record, prompt for and enter the following data. (Field size and type are shown in parentheses.)

1. Employee number   (4 int)
2. Employee name   (15 char)
3. Department number   (2 int)
4. Sex code   (1 char)
5. Annual salary   (8.2 float)

File Data:

Use the data given below to create the personnel file. (The numbers shown above the columns correspond to the fields described for the record.)

1	2	3	4	5
1900	Dana Andrews	10	F	29000.00
2070	Scott Cooper	14	M	30250.00
3150	Todd Feldman	22	M	24175.00
3600	Amy Kwon	19	F	36025.00
4100	Derek Lowe	50	M	29120.00
4290	Lori Palmer	35	F	33400.00
5400	Bob Shields	47	M	27500.00
6500	Pam Wolfe	31	F	31773.00

Output (sqPers.fil):
Sequential disk file

Processing Requirements:

- Open the file in *write* mode.
- Prompt for and enter the data.
- Write the data to the file.
- Close the file.

Part II: Read the file, process the data, and print the report.

Input (sqPers.fil):
Sequential disk file

Output (printer):
Print the following personnel salary report:

```
Author                PERSONNEL  SALARY  REPORT        Page 01
                            mm/dd/yy


Employee                                Department        Annual
Number          Employee Name            Number           Salary

  9999          X------------X              99           99999.99
   :                 :                       :               :
   :                 :                       :               :
  9999          X------------X              99           99999.99

                                        Average:         99999.99
```

Processing Requirements:

- Open the file in *read* mode.
- Read the personnel records.
- Print a report of all female employees who earn over $30,000 a year.
- Accumulate female count.
- Accumulate a total for annual salary.
- Compute the average annual salary, and print it at the end of the report:
  total annual salary / female count.
- Close the file.

Project 12–6   Accounts Payable

Write a program to prompt for the data, and create a sequential file for the accounts payable. Then read the file, compute the amount due, and print an accounts payable report. Assume the following discount schedule applies to early payments:

Paid by (Days)	Discount
1 – 10	12%
11 – 20	10%
21 – 30	8%
31 – 45	5%

Part I: Create the sequential file.

Input (keyboard):

For each vendor record, prompt for and enter the following data. (Field size and type are shown in parentheses.)

1. Vendor number   (3 int)
2. Vendor name   (12 char)
3. Invoice number   (5 char)
4. Invoice amount   (7.2 float)
5. Days paid by   (2 int)

File Data:

Use the data given below to create the vendor file. (The numbers shown above the columns correspond to the fields described for the input.)

1	2	3	4	5
340	IntraTell	T9823	670.00	25
410	MarxComm	H9205	913.87	18
420	Metacraft	A1239	2309.12	10
500	Northland	X2781	3429.34	45
600	Reylock	F0176	4563.78	33
830	Universal	W0105	1200.00	21
950	Veston	D1776	5127.63	30

Output (sqVendor.fil):

Sequential disk file

Processing Requirements:

- Open the file in *write* mode.
- Prompt for and enter the data.
- Write the data to the file.
- Close the file.

Part II: Read the file, process the data, and print the report.

Input (sqVendor.fil):

Sequential disk file

Output (printer):

Print the following accounts payable report:

```
Author                  ACCOUNTS PAYABLE REPORT              Page 01
                              mm/dd/yy


Vendor                   Invoice   Invoice    Discount    Amount
Number   Vendor Name     Number    Amount     Amount      Due

 999     X--------X      XXXXX     9999.99    999.99      9999.99
  :          :             :          :         :           :
  :          :             :          :         :           :
```

```
999     X--------X     XXXXX     9999.99     999.99     9999.99

             Totals:              99999.99    9999.99    99999.99
```

Processing Requirements:

- Open the file in *read* mode.
- Read the vendor records.
- Determine the discount rate:
  based on early payment (see the discount schedule).
- Compute the discount amount:
  invoice amount × discount rate.
- Compute the amount due:
  invoice amount – discount amount.
- Accumulate totals for invoice amount, discount amount, and amount due. Print the totals at the end of the report.
- Close the file.

Project 12–7   Production Output

Write a program to prompt for the input, and create a sequential file for the production output. Then read the file, compute bonus pay, and print a bonus pay report. Assume production workers are paid a bonus according to the number of units produced over the quota. Use the following bonus pay schedule:

Units over Quota	Pay Rate Each
1 – 10	0.60
11 – 25	0.65
26 – 45	0.70
46 +	0.75

Part I: Create the sequential file.

Input (keyboard):

For each production record, prompt for and enter the following data. (Field size and type are shown in parentheses.)

1. Employee number   (3 int)
2. Employee name   (15 char)
3. Product number   (5 char)
4. Production quota   (3 int)
5. Units produced   (3 int)

File Data:

Use the data given below to create the production file. (The numbers shown above the columns correspond to the fields described for the input.)

1	2	3	4	5
110	Kay Archer	P9511	65	65

200	Alan Baum	A1234	48	97
300	Marie Fitch	C4510	60	75
370	Lee Hildebrand	R0934	50	62
430	David Mullins	E3371	75	75
460	Chad Nelson	L8912	40	63
540	Bill Quinn	S0951	48	56
600	Nicole Renner	H9733	50	59
810	Erica Tate	Z0182	65	68
930	Terry West	A3235	70	116

Output (sqProd.fil):
Sequential disk file

Processing Requirements:

- Open the file in *write* mode.
- Prompt for and enter the data.
- Write the data to the file.
- Close the file.

Part II: Read the file, process the data, and print the file.

Input (sqProd.fil):
Sequential disk file

Output (printer):
Print the following bonus pay report:

```
Author                     BONUS PAY REPORT                 Page 01
                              mm/dd/yy


                    Product        Units   Over
Enum    Employee    Number  Quota  Made    Quota   Bonus Pay

999     X---------X  XXXXX    99     99      99      999.99
             :         :      :      :       :         :
             :         :      :      :       :         :
999     X---------X  XXXXX    99     99      99      999.99

                    Totals:   999    999     999     9999.99
```

Processing Requirements:

- Open the file in *read* mode.
- Read the production records.
- Compute the bonus pay:
  based on units over quota (see the bonus pay schedule).
- Accumulate totals for quota, units made, units over quota, and bonus pay. Print the totals at the end of the report.
- Close the file.

13 Updating Sequential Files

Overview

Learning Objectives

After you have read this chapter and completed the exercises, you should be able to

- understand why data files are maintained
- explain the process of updating a sequential file
- create a transaction file and a master file
- use transaction codes to update the master file
- read a transaction file, check for input errors, and update the master file

Sequential File Maintenance

Most organizations require information about their customers, employees, products, services, creditors, and so on. Data processing applications provide this information. Files are created and maintained to reflect the current business situation or financial conditions of the company.

In this book, we learned that data is organized into files to facilitate processing by the computer. There are two major types of files: master files and transaction files. A **master file** contains permanent information about a particular application. A **transaction file** contains temporary information that is used to update the master file. Sequential file maintenance is the process of maintaining information stored in the master file. It consists of the following activities: creating the master and transaction files, updating the master file, and processing the data stored in the master file.

Creating a File

Consider the course scheduling master file *sqCrs.fil* for Blackmoore University created in sample program CHAP12A. This file contains information about the courses offered at the regional campus. As you may recall, the courses were written in the file in ascending key order by call number.

Updating a File

Even though the master file is a permanent repository of information, the data stored in the file must be updated to reflect day-to-day changes. File updating refers to the process of changing the master file to include new information.

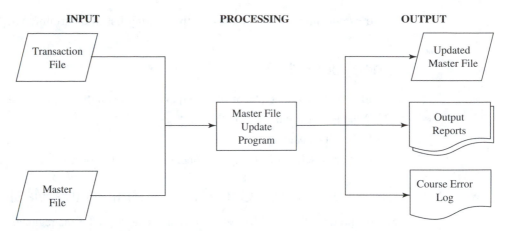

| INPUT | PROCESSING | OUTPUT |

FIGURE 13.1   Sequential File Updating

Once the course master file for Blackmoore University has been created, the records can be maintained to reflect the current course offerings at the regional campus. Periodically, new courses are added, old courses are deleted, and changes are made to existing courses. When a student registers for a course, the enrollment stored in the master file must be adjusted to reflect the change. Similarly, when a new course is offered, a new record must be added to the master file.

For large files that require updates to only a few records at a time, updating can be a rather lengthy process. However, transactions are normally batched (daily, weekly, monthly, and so on) before they are applied to the master file. This, of course, saves both time and resources. Student enrollments, as well as other course-related activities, are batched to form a transaction file that can be used to make changes to the master file.

Once the transactions are arranged (sorted) by call number, they are applied to the old master file to produce the new or updated master file. If errors are detected during the update, they are written to the course error log (Figure 13.1).

Processing a File

When the master file is updated, various reports are produced by the program. Management uses information from the reports to monitor the operation and progress of the business. For example, the course update program could provide the following information about the course registration system:

- student enrollment per course
- closed courses
- income generated per course for a specific quarter
- transactions processed for the current week
- waiting list for closed courses
- male and female enrollment figures

The administration could use this information to monitor the course registration system and to make decisions about opening and closing classes. For instance, the registrar could use the number of students on the waiting list to determine whether to open another session.

Checkpoint 13A

1. Identify two basic types of files, and briefly explain the purpose of each.
2. What is sequential file maintenance?
3. Define file updating.
4. Draw a sketch to illustrate the sequential file update process.

Sample Program CHAP13A (Creating the Master File)

Sample program CHAP13A creates the course master file for the regional campus of Blackmoore University; the logic is similar to that of sample program CHAP12A. See Figure 13.2 for the hierarchy chart and Figure 13.3 for the flowchart. Sample program CHAP13A is presented in Figure 13.4. Figure 13.5 shows the data entry screen, and Figure 13.6 shows the master file output. Notice that the data is entered and written to the file in ascending key order.

The specifications, logic design, and program listing follow.

Input (keyboard):
For each course, prompt for and enter the following data. (Field size and type are shown in parentheses.)

Call number	(3 int)
Course ID	(15 char)
Student enrollment	(2 int)

Output (sqCrsMS.fil):
The master file is shown in Figure 13.6.

Processing Requirements:

- Open the master file in *write* mode.
- Prompt for and enter the master file data.
- Write the input data to the master file.
- After creating the master file, write a trailer record to mark the end of the data stored in the file.

Pseudocode:

```
START: Main
Clear screen
Call Open File
IF file opened
      Call Load File
      Call Close File
END IF
END
```

ENTER: Open File
Open master file for write
IF file not opened
    Print cannot open master file for output
END IF
RETURN

ENTER: Load File
Prompt and enter call number (or –1 to quit)
LOOP while call number not = –1
    Prompt and enter course ID
    Prompt and enter student enrollment
    Write the input to the file:
        call number
        course ID
        student enrollment
    Prompt and enter call number (or –1 to quit)
END LOOP
RETURN

ENTER: Close File
Initialize trailer record:
    Set call number to 999
    Set course ID to END
    Set student enrollment to 0
Write the trailer record to the file
Close file
RETURN

Hierarchy Chart: See Figure 13.2.

Program Flowchart: See Figure 13.3.

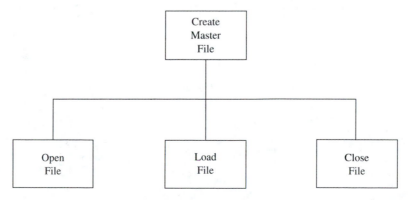

FIGURE 13.2   Hierarchy Chart for CHAP13A

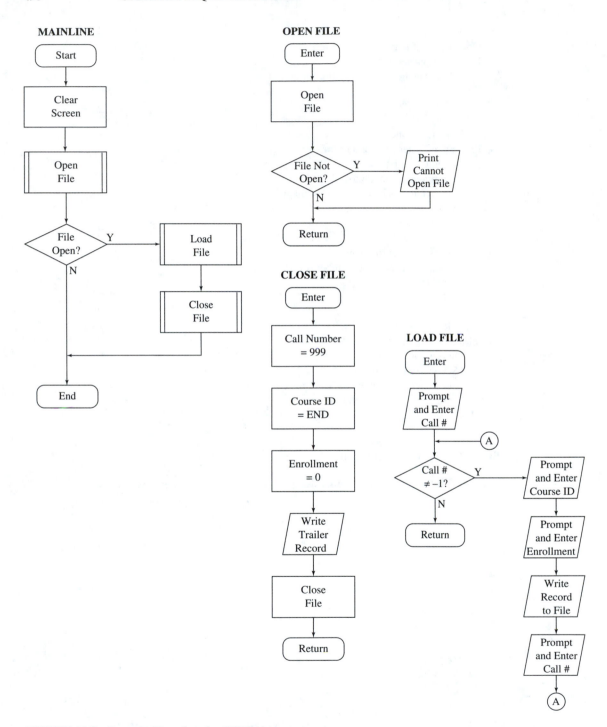

FIGURE 13.3   Program Flowchart for CHAP13A

```
/*----------------------------------------------------------------
CREATE MASTER FILE: Accept keyboard input and create a course master
file.

Program:   CHAP13A.C
Author:    David M. Collopy
Date:      mm/dd/yy
Project:   Sample program
*****************************************************************/

/*---- PREPROCESSING DIRECTIVES ----------------------------------*/

#include <stdio.h>
#include <string.h>
#include <graph.h>

/*---- FUNCTION PROTOTYPES ---------------------------------------*/

void  OpenFile(void);              /* open master file  */
void  LoadFile(void);              /* load master file  */
void  CloseFile(void);             /* close master file */

/*---- PROGRAM SETUP ---------------------------------------------*/

/*>  C O U R S E   M A S T E R   R E C O R D                <*/

FILE *fpMFO;                       /* master file pointer */
int   iCallNum;                    /* call number         */
char  sCourse[15];                 /* course ID           */
int   iEnroll;                     /* student enrollment  */

/*----------------------------------------------------------------
       MAINLINE CONTROL
----------------------------------------------------------------*/
main()
{
    _clearscreen(0);
    OpenFile();
    if (fpMFO != 0)
    {
        LoadFile();
        CloseFile();
    }
    return 0;
}
```

FIGURE 13.4   Sample Program CHAP13A: Creates course master file from user input

```
/*-------------------------------------------------------------------
        OPEN MASTER FILE
-----------------------------------------------------------------*/
void OpenFile(void)
{
    fpMFO = fopen("a:sqCrsMS.fil", "w");
    if (fpMFO == 0)
    {
        printf("\nCannot open master file for output\n");
    }
    return;
}



/*-------------------------------------------------------------------
        LOAD MASTER FILE
-----------------------------------------------------------------*/
void LoadFile(void)
{
    printf("\nEnter call number or '-1' to Quit: ");
    scanf(" %d", &iCallNum);
    while (iCallNum != -1)
    {
        printf("                        Enter course ID: ");
        scanf(" %s", sCourse);
        printf("            Enter student enrollment: ");
        scanf(" %d", &iEnroll);
        fprintf(fpMFO, "%d %s %d\n", iCallNum, sCourse, iEnroll);
        printf("\nEnter call number or '-1' to Quit: ");
        scanf(" %d", &iCallNum);
    }
    return;
}



/*-------------------------------------------------------------------
        CLOSE MASTER FILE
-----------------------------------------------------------------*/
void CloseFile(void)
{
    iCallNum = 999;
    strcpy(sCourse, "END");
    iEnroll = 0;
    fprintf(fpMFO, "%d %s %d\n", iCallNum, sCourse, iEnroll);
    fclose(fpMFO);
    return;
}
```

FIGURE 13.4 *Continued*

```
Enter call number or '-1' to Quit: 100
                  Enter course ID: BIOL101
          Enter student enrollment: 24
Enter call number or '-1' to Quit: 200
               :                 :
               :                 :
```

FIGURE 13.5   Master File Data Entry Screen CHAP13A

```
100 ACCT101 24
200 BIOL101 19
300 CHEM201 21
400 ENG200 16
500 HIST225 33
600 MGT330 29
700 MATH120 14
800 PHYS251 20
900 SPAN111 12
999 END 0          ◄─── trailer record
```

FIGURE 13.6   Master File Output for CHAP13A

Dissection of Sample Program CHAP13A

First, the file pointer and the record fields are declared. The identifier *fpMFO* indicates that data is written (output) to the master file.

Second, the *MAINLINE* clears the screen and branches to the module that opens the master file. If the file can be opened, the program creates the master file from the data entered at the keyboard. But if the file cannot be opened, the program prints an error message and stops the run.

Third, after the data is entered, the program attaches a trailer record to the end of the file. Later, the update program uses the trailer record to control the update process.

C L O S E   M A S T E R   F I L E:

```
void CloseFile(void)
{
    iCallNum = 999;
    strcpy(sCourse, "END");
    iEnroll = 0;
```

The above statements initialize the fields of the trailer record. The constants *999*, *END*, and *0* are assigned to the variables *iCallNum*, *sCourse*, and *iEnroll*, respectively.

```
        fprintf(fpMFO, "%d %s %d\n", iCallNum, sCourse, iEnroll);
        fclose(fpMFO);
        return;
}
```

The above statements format the data and write the trailer record to the master file, then close the file and return to the *MAINLINE*.

Notes and Tips

1. The master file for Blackmoore University contains permanent information about the courses offered at the regional campus.
2. The records are written to the master file in ascending key (call number) order to facilitate the update processing performed later in the chapter.
3. The master file is created by opening it in *write* mode.
4. Use the file pointer *fpMFO* to indicate that the program is writing master file output.

Sample Program CHAP13B (Creating the Transaction File)

Sample program CHAP13B creates a transaction file for the course registration system. See Figure 13.7 for the hierarchy chart and Figure 13.8 for the flowchart. Sample program CHAP13B is presented in Figure 13.9. Figure 13.10 shows the data entry screen, and Figure 13.11 shows the transaction file output. Like the master file, the transaction records are written to the file in ascending order by call number.

The specifications, logic design, and program listing follow.

Input (keyboard):

For each course, prompt for and enter the following data. (Field size and type are shown in parentheses.)

Call number	(3 int)
Course ID	(15 char)
Student enrollment	(2 int)

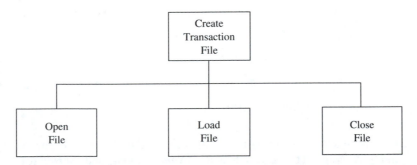

FIGURE 13.7   Hierarchy Chart for CHAP13B

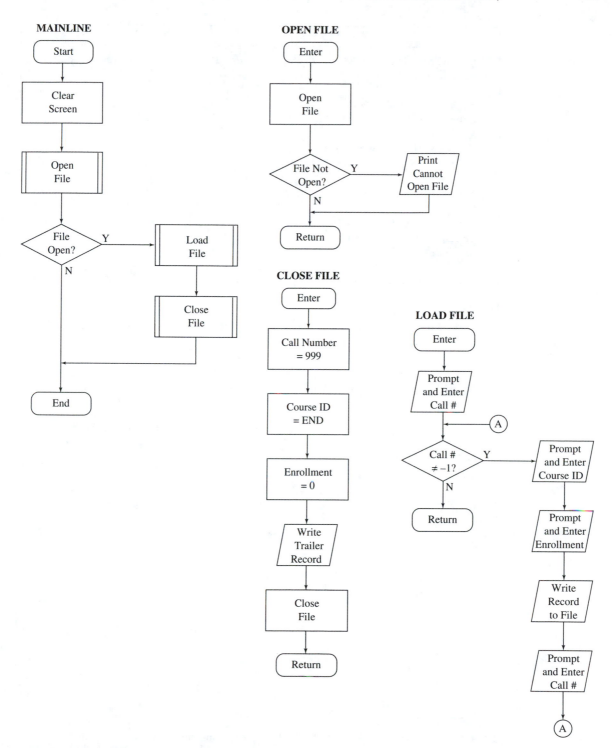

FIGURE 13.8 Program Flowchart for CHAP13B

```
/*----------------------------------------------------------------
CREATE TRANSACTION FILE: Accept keyboard input and create a course
transaction file.

Program:   CHAP13B.C
Author:    David M. Collopy
Date:      mm/dd/yy
Project:   Sample program
******************************************************************/

/*---- PREPROCESSING DIRECTIVES ---------------------------------*/

#include <stdio.h>
#include <string.h>
#include <graph.h>

/*---- FUNCTION PROTOTYPES --------------------------------------*/

void  OpenFile(void);              /* open transaction file  */
void  LoadFile(void);              /* load transaction file  */
void  CloseFile(void);             /* close transaction file */

/*---- PROGRAM SETUP --------------------------------------------*/

/*>  C O U R S E   T R A N S A C T I O N   R E C O R D      <*/

FILE *fpTFO;                       /* transaction file pointer */
int   iCallNum;                    /* call number             */
char  sCourse[15];                 /* course ID               */
int   iEnroll;                     /* student enrollment      */

/*----------------------------------------------------------------
      MAINLINE CONTROL
----------------------------------------------------------------*/
main()
{
    _clearscreen(0);
    OpenFile();
    if (fpTFO != 0)
    {
        LoadFile();
        CloseFile();
    }
    return 0;
}
```

FIGURE 13.9   Sample Program CHAP13B: Creates a transaction file from user input

```c
/*----------------------------------------------------------------
        OPEN TRANSACTION FILE
----------------------------------------------------------------*/
void OpenFile(void)
{
    fpTFO = fopen("a:sqCrsTR.fil", "w");
    if (fpTFO == 0)
    {
        printf("\nCannot open transaction file for ouput\n");
    }
    return;
}


/*----------------------------------------------------------------
        LOAD TRANSACTION FILE
----------------------------------------------------------------*/
void LoadFile(void)
{
    printf("\nEnter call number or '-1' to Quit: ");
    scanf(" %d", &iCallNum);
    while (iCallNum != -1)
    {
        printf("                        Enter course ID: ");
        scanf(" %s", sCourse);
        printf("              Enter student enrollment: ");
        scanf(" %d", &iEnroll);
        fprintf(fpTFO, "%d %s %d\n", iCallNum, sCourse, iEnroll);
        printf("\nEnter call number or '-1' to Quit: ");
        scanf(" %d", &iCallNum);
    }
    return;
}


/*----------------------------------------------------------------
        CLOSE TRANSACTION FILE
----------------------------------------------------------------*/
void CloseFile(void)
{
    iCallNum = 999;
    strcpy(sCourse, "END");
    iEnroll = 0;
    fprintf(fpTFO, "%d %s %d\n", iCallNum, sCourse, iEnroll);
    fclose(fpTFO);
    return;
}
```

FIGURE 13.9 *Continued*

```
Enter call number or '-1' to Quit: 400
                    Enter course ID: ENG200
             Enter student enrollment: 18
Enter call number or '-1' to Quit: 500
            :              :
            :              :
```

FIGURE 13.10   Transaction File Data Entry Screen CHAP13B

```
400  ENG200 18
500  HIST225 37
500  HIST225 42
700  MATH120 20
800  PHYS251 17
850  PSY101 35
999  END 0        ◄── trailer record
```

FIGURE 13.11   Transaction File Output for CHAP13B

Output (sqCrsTR.fil):
The transaction file is shown in Figure 13.11.

Processing Requirements:

- Open the transaction file in *write* mode.
- Prompt for and enter the transaction data.
- Write the input data to the transaction file.
- After creating the file, write a trailer record at the end of the transaction file to indicate the end of the data.

Pseudocode:

```
START: Main
Clear screen
Call Open File
IF file opened
     Call Load File
     Call Close File
END IF
END

ENTER: Open File
Open transaction file for write
```

```
        IF file not opened
                Print cannot open transaction file for ouput
        END IF
        RETURN

        ENTER: Load File
        Prompt and enter call number (or –1 to quit)
        LOOP while call number not = –1
                Prompt and enter course ID
                Prompt and enter student enrollment
                Write the input to the file:
                        call number
                        course ID
                        student enrollment
                Prompt and enter call number (or –1 to quit)
        END LOOP
        RETURN

        ENTER: Close File
        Initialize trailer record:
                Set call number to 999
                Set course ID to END
                Set student enrollment to 0
        Write the trailer record to the file
        Close file
        RETURN
```

Hierarchy Chart: See Figure 13.7.

Program Flowchart: See Figure 13.8.

Dissection of Sample Program CHAP13B

This program is similar to the one used to create the master file. The only difference is that one creates the transaction file and the other creates the master file.

Notes and Tips

1. The transaction file for Blackmoore University contains temporary information that is used to update the course master file. Transactions represent changes that are applied to the master file to keep it up to date.

2. The transaction records are batched (collected over time and arranged in ascending key field order) and written to the transaction file.

3. The transaction file is created by opening it in *write* mode.

4. Use the file pointer *fpTFO* to indicate that the program is writing transaction file output.

Tutorial for CHAP13A and CHAP13B

1. The objectives of this tutorial are to
   - create and load data into the course master file
   - create and load data into the course transaction file

2. Read the program specifications and logic design tools given for sample program CHAP13A and CHAP13B.

3. Log on to your C editor, and enter the source code as shown in Figures 13.4 and 13.9. Save the programs on your work disk as CHAP13A and CHAP13B. Save frequently as you enter the code.

4. Compile, run, and debug your programs. When completed, show your work to your instructor.

Quick Quiz

Answer the following questions.

1. For sequential file processing, why is it necessary to have a master file and a transaction file?

2. Why is it considered good programming practice to open a file and then test to see if the file was actually opened?

3. Look at sample program CHAP13A. Discuss the activities performed by the *Close-File* module.

4. Did you have any problems or errors when you ran the sample programs? If so, what were they and what did you do to correct them?

Updating The Master File: Part I

Sample program CHAP13C does not really update the course master file. Since the update logic is somewhat complex, our goal here is only to construct the top-level control logic and to test it—to see if we can get it to work. We will, for now, ignore the details of how to actually apply the transaction updates to the master file.

The major processing task performed by sample program CHAP13C is as follows: Compare the transaction keys to the master keys and, based on the results of the comparison, print one of the three messages shown in Table 13.1. In other words, we are printing

TABLE 13.1   Update Messages

Compare Keys	Update Messages
iTkey = iMkey	UPDATE MASTER
iTkey < iMkey	ADD NEW MASTER
iTkey > iMkey	WRITE MASTER

messages that correspond to the updates rather than actually performing the updates. It may be helpful to refer to the input files and screen output for sample program CHAP13C (Figures 13.15 and 13.16) as we discuss the update messages.

According to Table 13.1, we want the program to print UPDATE MASTER when the keys are equal. This message implies that the data stored in the current transaction is applied to the current master record. The update logic should allow multiple transactions for any given master record as long as the transactions are grouped together.

We want the program to print ADD NEW MASTER when the master record key is greater than the transaction key. This message implies that the data stored in the transaction is used to create a new master record. That is, the transaction data is written to a new record in the master file.

We want the program to print WRITE MASTER when the transaction key is greater than the master key. This message implies that there is no new data for that record in the transaction file, so either the old master record or the updated master record is written to the new master file.

In the above cases, we are assuming that the records of both files are arranged in ascending order by call number.

Checkpoint 13B

1. What major processing task does sample program CHAP13C perform?
2. If the transaction key is equal to the master key, which message would print?
   a. update master
   b. add new master
   c. write master
3. If the transaction key is greater than the master key, which message would print?
   a. update master
   b. add new master
   c. write master
4. If the transaction key is less than the master key, which message would print?
   a. update master
   b. add new master
   c. write master
5. What happens when a new master record is created?
6. What is implied by the UPDATE MASTER message?

Sample Program CHAP13C

Sample program CHAP13C displays update messages on the screen. The record keys are compared to determine which message to print. See Figure 13.12 for the hierarchy chart and Figure 13.13 for the flowchart. Sample program CHAP13C is presented in Figure 13.14. The input files are shown in Figure 13.15, and the output is shown in Figure 13.16.

The following specifications apply:

Input (disk files):

Transaction file   (sqCrsTR.fil)
Master file   (sqCrsMS.fil)

Output (screen):

The output is shown in Figure 13.16.

Processing Requirements:

- Open the transaction file and master file in *read* mode.
- Read a transaction and a master record.
- Compare the keys to determine the processing, and print the message corresponding to the update.
- Close the files.

Pseudocode:

```
START: Main
Clear screen
Call Open Files
IF files opened
        Call Read Master Record
        Call Read Transaction Record
        LOOP while not at end of files
                Call Check Update Logic
        END LOOP
        Close files
END IF
END


ENTER: Open Files
Open transaction file for read
IF file not opened
        Print cannot open transaction file for input
END IF
Open master file for read
IF file not opened
        Print cannot open master file for input
END IF
RETURN


ENTER: Read Transaction Record
IF not at end of file
        Read transaction record:
                transaction key
                transaction course ID
```

           transaction student enrollment
END IF
RETURN

ENTER: Read Master Record
IF not at end of file
      Read master record:
            master key
            master course ID
            master student enrollment
END IF
RETURN

ENTER: Check Update Logic
IF transaction key = master key
      Print UPDATE MASTER
      Call Read Transaction Record
else IF transaction key < master key
      Print ADD NEW MASTER
      Call Read Transaction Record
else
      Print WRITE MASTER
      Call Read Master Record
END IF
RETURN

Hierarchy Chart: See Figure 13.12.
Program Flowchart: See Figure 13.13.

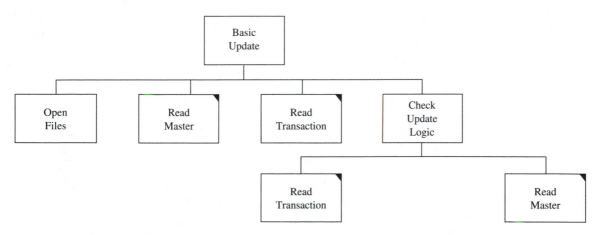

FIGURE 13.12   Hierarchy Chart for CHAP13C

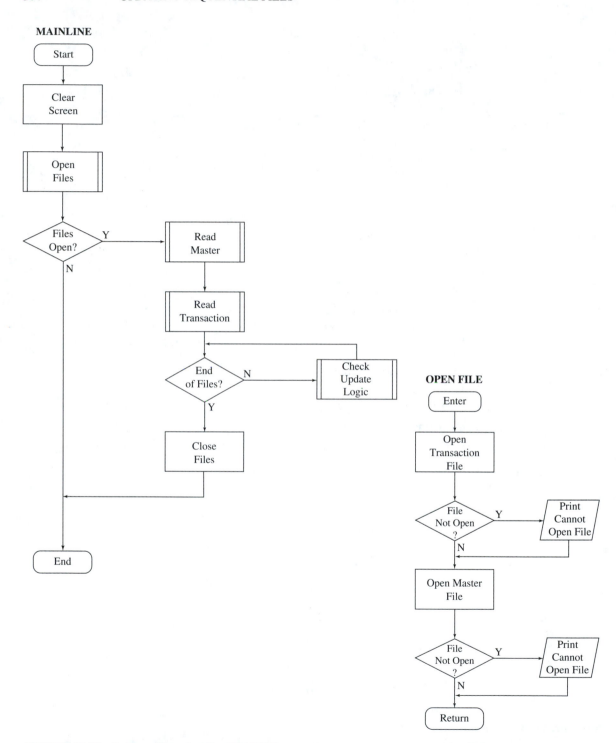

FIGURE 13.13 Program Flowchart for CHAP13C

READ MASTER

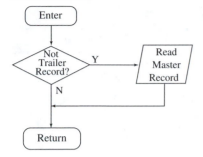

READ TRANSACTION

CHECK UPDATE LOGIC

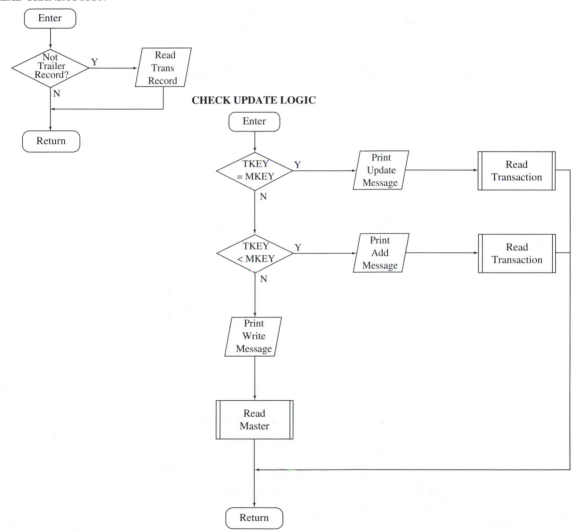

FIGURE 13.13   *Continued*

```
/*----------------------------------------------------------------
BASIC UPDATE LOGIC: Read the master file and the transaction file and
print update messages.

Program:    CHAP13C.C
Author:     David M. Collopy
Date:       mm/dd/yy
Project:    Sample program
*********************************************************************/


/*---- PREPROCESSING DIRECTIVES -----------------------------------*/

#include <stdio.h>
#include <graph.h>


/*---- FUNCTION PROTOTYPES -----------------------------------------*/

void  OpenFiles(void);              /* open the files         */
void  ReadTran(void);               /* read transaction record */
void  ReadMast(void);               /* read master record      */
void  CkUpdLogic(void);             /* check update logic      */


/*---- PROGRAM SETUP -----------------------------------------------*/

/*>   T R A N S A C T I O N   R E C O R D                      <*/

FILE *fpTFI;                        /* transaction file pointer */
int   iTKey;                        /* key: call number         */
char  sTCourse[15];                 /* course ID                */
int   iTEnroll;                     /* student enrollment       */

/*>   M A S T E R   R E C O R D                               <*/

FILE *fpMFI;                        /* master file pointer      */
int   iMKey;                        /* key: call number         */
char  sMCourse[15];                 /* course ID                */
int   iMEnroll;                     /* student enrollment       */

/*>   P R O G R A M   V A R I A B L E S                       <*/

char sUpdMsg[] = " Update Master: Tran key = ";
char sAddMsg[] = "Add New Master: Tran key = ";
char sWrtMsg[] = "  Write Master: Mast key = ";
```

FIGURE 13.14 Sample Program CHAP13C: This programs performs the basic update logic and prints the update messages

```
/*-----------------------------------------------------------------
        MAINLINE CONTROL
-----------------------------------------------------------------*/
main()
{
    _clearscreen(0);
    OpenFiles();
    if (fpMFI != 0 && fpTFI != 0)
    {
        ReadMast();
        ReadTran();
        while ((iTKey != 999 || iMKey != 999))
        {
            CkUpdLogic();
        }
        fclose(fpMFI, fpTFI);
    }
    return 0;
}


/*-----------------------------------------------------------------
        OPEN FILES
-----------------------------------------------------------------*/
void OpenFiles(void)
{
    fpTFI = fopen("a:sqCrsTR.fil", "r");
    if (fpTFI == 0)
    {
        printf("\nCannot open transaction file for input\n");
    }
    fpMFI = fopen("a:sqCrsMS.fil", "r");
    if (fpMFI == 0)
    {
        printf("\nCannot open master file for input\n");
    }
    return;
}


/*-----------------------------------------------------------------
        READ TRANSACTION RECORD
-----------------------------------------------------------------*/
void ReadTran(void)
{
    if (iTKey != 999)
    {
```

FIGURE 13.14   *Continued*

```
            fscanf(fpTFI, " %d %s %d\n", &iTKey, sTCourse, &iTEnroll);
    }
    return;
}


/*----------------------------------------------------------------
      READ MASTER RECORD
------------------------------------------------------------------*/
void ReadMast(void)
{
    if (iMKey != 999)
    {
        fscanf(fpMFI, " %d %s %d\n", &iMKey, sMCourse, &iMEnroll);
    }
    return;
}


/*----------------------------------------------------------------
      CHECK UPDATE LOGIC
------------------------------------------------------------------*/
void CkUpdLogic(void)
{

    if (iTKey == iMKey)
    {
        printf("\n%s%d", sUpdMsg, iTKey);   /* update mast  */
        ReadTran();
    }
    else if (iTKey < iMKey)
    {
        printf("\n%s%d", sAddMsg, iTKey);   /* add new mast */
        ReadTran();
    }
    else
    {
        printf("\n%s%d", sWrtMsg, iMKey);   /* write mast   */
        ReadMast();
    }

    return;
}
```

FIGURE 13.14   *Continued*

```
Transaction File              Master File

400  ENG200  18             100  ACCT101  24
500  HIST225  37            200  BIOL101  19
500  HIST225  42            300  CHEM201  21
700  MATH120  20            400  ENG200   16
800  PHYS251  17            500  HIST225  33
850  PSY101   35            600  MGT330   29
999  END  0                 700  MATH120  14
                            800  PHYS251  20
                            900  SPAN111  12
                            999  END  0
```

FIGURE 13.15   Input Files for CHAP13C

```
    Write Master: Mast key = 100
    Write Master: Mast key = 200
    Write Master: Mast key = 300
   Update Master: Tran key = 400
    Write master: Mast key = 400
   Update Master: Tran key = 500
   Update Master: Tran key = 500
    Write Master: Mast key = 500
    Write Master: Mast key = 600
   Update Master: Tran key = 700
    Write Master: Mast key = 700
   Update Master: Tran key = 800
    Write Master: Mast key = 800
Add New Master: Tran key = 850
    Write Master: Mast key = 900
```

FIGURE 13.16   Screen Output for CHAP13C

Dissection of Sample Program CHAP13C

After clearing the screen and opening the files, the MAINLINE reads the first transaction and the first master record. As long as the transaction key and the master key are not equal to 999 (the end-of-file indicator), control branches to the update module.

Note that if one or both files cannot be opened, the program stops the run.

```
C H E C K    U P D A T E    L O G I C :

void CkUpdLogic(void)
{
```

```
    if (iTKey == iMKey)
    {
        printf("\n%s%d", sUpdMsg, iTKey);
        ReadTran();
    }
```

In the above statements, if the transaction and master keys are equal, the printf() displays the UPDATE MASTER message and the transaction key on the screen and control reads the next transaction. Otherwise, control skips to the next statement.

```
    else if (iTKey < iMKey)
    {
        printf("\n%s%d", sAddMsg, iTKey);
        ReadTran();
    }
```

In the above statements, if the transaction key is less than the master key, the printf() displays the ADD NEW MASTER message and the transaction key on the screen and control reads the next transaction. Otherwise, control skips to the next statement.

```
    else
    {
        printf("\n%s%d", sWrtMsg, iMKey);
        ReadMast();
    }
    return;
}
```

If control reaches this point in the program, then a match was not found for the other two conditions. Then by default, the transaction key is greater than the master key. Hence, the program prints the WRITE MASTER message and the master key and reads the next master record.

The return statement sends control back to the *MAINLINE*.

Notes and Tips

1. Sample program CHAP13C shows the top-level control logic required for the sequential file update. To verify that the logic is working correctly, messages that correspond to the updates are displayed on the screen.

2. If the transaction key = the master key, then the message *UPDATE MASTER* is displayed on the screen. In other words, the program is ready to use the transaction data to update the master record.

3. If the transaction key < the master key, then the message *ADD NEW MASTER* is displayed on the screen. Here the program is ready to add the record stored in the transaction to the master file.

4. If the transaction key > the master key, then the message *WRITE MASTER* is displayed on the screen. At this point, there is no transaction for this record and the program is ready to write the current master record to the new master file.

5. Both the transaction file and the master file are opened in *read* mode.

6. Use the file pointers *fpTFI* and *fpMFI* to indicate that the program is reading transaction file and master file input, respectively.

7. Notice that the read modules shown in the sample program test for the trailer record before a record is read from either file. This is done to prevent the scan function from reading past the end of the file once the trailer record is read. To do so would cause an error. This technique also allows the program to continue with the update even though one of the files is out of data.

Tutorial CHAP13C

1. The objectives of this tutorial are to
   * open and read a master file and a transaction file
   * compare transaction keys to master record keys and print messages that correspond to the update activities.

2. Read the program specifications for sample program CHAP13C.

3. Log on to your C editor, and enter the source code as shown in Figure 13.14. Save the program on your work disk as CHAP13C.

4. Compile, run, and debug your program until the results match the screen output shown in Figure 13.16.

5. When completed, show your work to your instructor.

Quick Quiz

Answer the following questions.

1. Under what circumstances does the following condition test skip the statement body of the *while* loop?
   ```
   while((iTKey != 999 || iMKey != 999))
   ```

2. What situation produces the update message "*Write Master*"?

3. What situation produces the update message "*Add New Master*"?

4. What situation produces the update message "*Update Master*"?

5. Did you have any problems or errors when you ran the sample program? If so, what were they and what did you do to correct them?

Updating The Master File: Part II

Now that we have developed and tested the top-level control logic, we are ready to update the master file. Once again, to avoid becoming entangled in unnecessary details, we will focus only on the update logic and, for the time being, assume that there are no errors in either the transaction file or the master file.

Let's pause briefly to discuss what to do if the program results in an abnormal end (abend). An **abend** occurs when certain logic errors prevent the program from running to completion. Usually, this means that some of the transactions were applied (correctly or incorrectly) to the master file. Once the errors are found and corrected, restart the program. Don't assume that part of the update is correct and that you can continue where the program ended during the last run. It is much safer to correct the errors and rerun the update from the start.

For the next two programs, we will consider six types of updates that will require the use of a special code called a **transaction code** to tell the update logic how to apply the transaction to the master file. These codes are defined as follows:

1- *add students*:   When students register for a course, they must be added to the master record. The transaction enrollment is added to the master record enrollment.

2- *drop students*:   When students drop a course, they must be removed from the master record. The transaction enrollment is subtracted from the master record enrollment.

3- *change enrollment*:   When the student count does not agree with the enrollment shown in the master record, it must be adjusted to reflect the actual count. Hence, the transaction enrollment replaces the enrollment stored in the master record.

4- *change course*:   When the course department or number is incorrect, it must be corrected. The course prefix and number coded in the transaction replaces the course prefix and number stored in the master record.

5- *add master record*:   When new courses are added to the class schedule, they must be added to the master file. New courses are coded as transactions and are inserted into the master file in call number order.

6- *delete master record*:   When courses are deleted from the class schedule, they must be removed from the master file. Old master records are removed by copying only the active courses to the new master file.

Checkpoint 13C

1. What causes an abend?

2. True or false: When an abend occurs, fix the errors and continue processing where the program ended.

3. What special code is used to tell the update logic how to apply a transaction to the master file?

Sample Program CHAP13D

Sample program CHAP13D reads the transaction records and updates the master file. Errors are not considered. See Figure 13.17 for the hierarchy chart and Figure 13.18 for the flowchart. Sample program CHAP13D is presented in Figure 13.19. Figure 13.20 shows the input files, and Figure 13.21 shows the updated (new) master file.

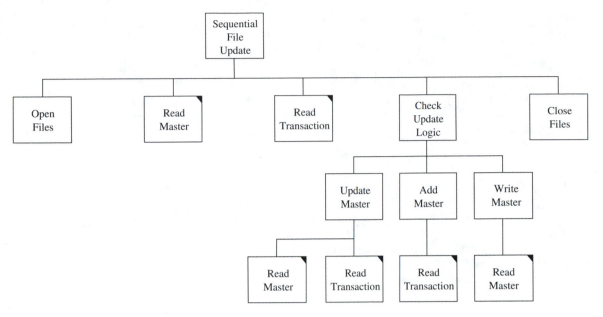

FIGURE 13.17   Hierarchy Chart for CHAP13D

The following specifications apply:

Input (disk files):

Transaction file   (sqCrsTR.fil)
Old master file   (sqCrsMS.fil)

Output (sqCrsNM.fil):
The new master file is shown in Figure 13.21.

Processing Requirements:

- Open the transaction file and old master file in *read* mode.
- Open the new master file in *write* mode.
- Read a transaction and a master record.
- Compare keys and use the transaction code to update the master file.
- Close the files.

Pseudocode:

```
START: Main
Clear screen
Call Open Files
IF files opened
        Call Read Master Record
```

```
            Call Read Transaction Record
            LOOP while not at end of files
                  Call Check Update Logic
            END LOOP
            Call Close Files
      END IF
      END


      ENTER: Open Files
      Open transaction file for read
      IF file not opened
            Print cannot open transaction file for input
      END IF
      Open master file for read
      IF file not opened
            Print cannot open master file for input
      END IF
      Open new master file for write
      IF file not opened
            Print cannot open new master file for output
      END IF
      RETURN


      ENTER: Read Transaction Record
      IF not at end of file
            Read transaction record:
                  transaction key
                  transaction course ID
                  transaction student enrollment
      END IF
      RETURN


      ENTER: Read Master Record
      IF not at end of file
            Read master record:
                  master key
                  master course ID
                  master student enrollment
      END IF
      RETURN


      ENTER: Check Update Logic
      IF transaction key = master key
            Call Update Master Record
      else IF transaction key < master key
            Call Add Master Record
```

else
        Call Write Master Record
END IF
RETURN

ENTER: Update Master Record
IF transaction code = 6
        Call Read Master Record
else IF transaction code = 1
        Add transaction enrollment to master enrollment
else IF transaction code = 2
        Subtract transaction enrollment from master enrollment
else IF transaction code = 3
        Set master enrollment to transaction enrollment
else
        Set master course ID to transaction course ID
END IF
Call Read Transaction Record
RETURN

ENTER: Add Master Record
Set new master key to transaction key
Set new master course ID to transaction course ID
Set new master enrollment to transaction enrollment
Write record to new master file
Call Read Transactions Record
RETURN

ENTER: Write Master Record
Set new master key to master key
Set new master course ID to master course ID
Set new master enrollment to master enrollment
Write record to new master file
Call Read Master Record
RETURN

ENTER: Close Files
Set new master key to 999
Set new master course ID to END
Set new master student enrollment to 0
Write record to the new master file
Close all files
RETURN

Hierarchy Chart: See Figure 13.17.

Program Flowchart: See Figure 13.18.

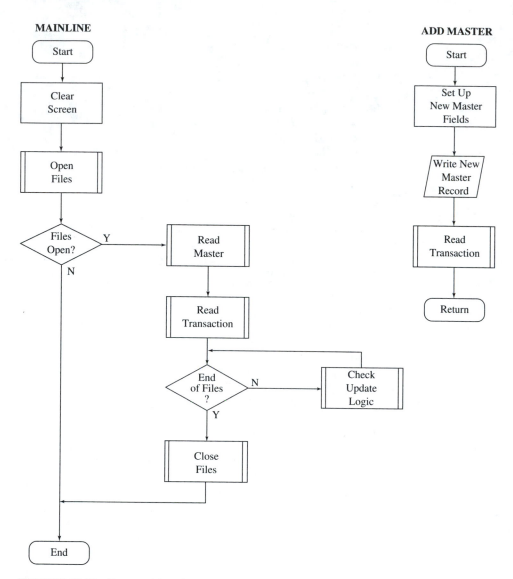

FIGURE 13.18   Program Flowchart for CHAP13D

OPEN FILES

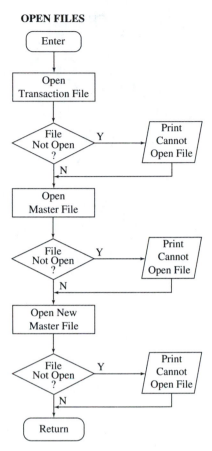

READ MASTER

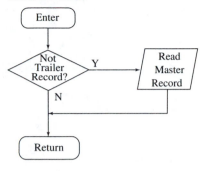

READ TRANSACTION

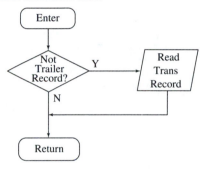

FIGURE 13.18   *Continued*

CHECK UPDATE LOGIC

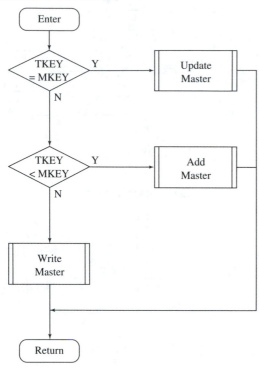

UPDATE MASTER

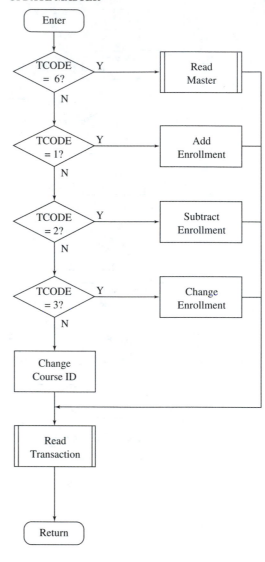

WRITE MASTER

CLOSE FILES

FIGURE 13.18 *Continued*

```
/*------------------------------------------------------------------
SEQUENTIAL FILE UPDATE: Use a transaction file to update the master
file. Errors are not considered.


Program:     CHAP13D.C
Author:      David M. Collopy
Date:        mm/dd/yy
Project:     Sample program
*********************************************************************/


/*---- PREPROCESSING DIRECTIVES ---------------------------------*/


#include <stdio.h>
#include <string.h>
#include <graph.h>


/*---- FUNCTION PROTOTYPES --------------------------------------*/


void   OpenFiles(void);          /* open the files           */
void   ReadTran(void);           /* read transaction record  */
void   ReadMast(void);           /* read master record       */
void   CkUpdLogic(void);         /* check update logic       */
void   UpdMast(void);            /* update master record     */
void   AddMast(void);            /* add master record        */
void   WrtMast(void);            /* write master record      */
void   CloseFiles(void);         /* close files              */


/*---- PROGRAM SETUP --------------------------------------------*/


/*>  T R A N S A C T I O N   R E C O R D                      <*/


FILE *fpTFI;                     /* transaction file pointer */
int   iTKey;                     /* key: call number         */
char  sTCourse[15];              /* course ID                */
int   iTEnroll;                  /* student enrollment       */
int   iTCode;                    /* transaction code         */


/*>  M A S T E R   R E C O R D                                <*/


FILE *fpMFI;                     /* master file pointer      */
int   iMKey;                     /* key: call number         */
char  sMCourse[15];              /* course ID                */
int   iMEnroll;                  /* student enrollment       */


/*>  N E W   M A S T E R   R E C O R D                        <*/
```

FIGURE 13.19 Sample Program CHAP13D: Updates the master file

```
FILE *fpNMFO;                   /* new master file pointer  */
int    iNMKey;                  /* key: call number         */
char   sNMCourse[15];           /* course ID                */
int    iNMEnroll;               /* student enrollment       */


/*----------------------------------------------------------------
        MAINLINE CONTROL
----------------------------------------------------------------*/
main()
{
    _clearscreen(0);
    OpenFiles();
    if (fpMFI != 0 && fpTFI != 0 && fpNMFO != 0)
    {
        ReadMast();
        ReadTran();
        while ((iTKey != 999 || iMKey != 999))
        {
            CkUpdLogic();
        }
        CloseFiles();
    }
    return 0;
}


/*----------------------------------------------------------------
        OPEN FILES
----------------------------------------------------------------*/
void OpenFiles(void)
{
    fpTFI = fopen("a:sqCrsTR.fil", "r");
    if (fpTFI == 0)
    {
        printf("\nCannot open transaction file for input\n");
    }
    fpMFI = fopen("a:sqCrsMS.fil", "r");
    if (fpMFI == 0)
    {
        printf("\nCannot open master file for input\n");
    }
    fpNMFO = fopen("a:sqCrsNM.fil", "w");
    if (fpNMFO == 0)
    {
        printf("\nCannot open new master file for output\n");
    }
```

FIGURE 13.19   *Continued*

```
        return;
}


/*---------------------------------------------------------------
        READ TRANSACTION RECORD
----------------------------------------------------------------*/
void ReadTran(void)
{
    if (iTKey != 999)
    {
        fscanf(fpTFI, " %d %s %d %d\n",
            &iTKey, sTCourse, &iTEnroll, &iTCode);
    }
    return;
}


/*---------------------------------------------------------------
        READ MASTER RECORD
----------------------------------------------------------------*/
void ReadMast(void)
{
    if (iMKey != 999)
    {
        fscanf(fpMFI, " %d %s %d\n",
            &iMKey, sMCourse, &iMEnroll);
    }
    return;
}


/*---------------------------------------------------------------
        CHECK UPDATE LOGIC
----------------------------------------------------------------*/
void CkUpdLogic(void)
{
    if (iTKey == iMKey)
    {
        UpdMast();
    }
    else if (iTKey < iMKey)
    {
        AddMast();
    }
    else
    {
        WrtMast();
```

FIGURE 13.19 *Continued*

```
        }
    return;
}


/*-----------------------------------------------------------------
        UPDATE MASTER RECORD
-----------------------------------------------------------------*/
void UpdMast(void)
{
    if (iTCode == 6)
    {
        ReadMast();
    }
    else if (iTCode == 1)
    {
        iMEnroll = iMEnroll + iTEnroll;
    }
    else if (iTCode == 2)
    {
        iMEnroll = iMEnroll - iTEnroll;
    }
    else if (iTCode == 3)
    {
        iMEnroll = iTEnroll;
    }
    else
    {
        strcpy(sMCourse, sTCourse);
    }
    ReadTran();
    return;
}


/*-----------------------------------------------------------------
        ADD MASTER RECORD
-----------------------------------------------------------------*/
void AddMast(void)
{
    iNMKey = iTKey;
    strcpy(sNMCourse, sTCourse);
    iNMEnroll = iTEnroll;
    fprintf(fpNMFO, "%d %s %d\n",
        iNMKey, sNMCourse, iNMEnroll);
    ReadTran();
    return;
}
```

FIGURE 13.19   *Continued*

```
/*----------------------------------------------------------------
        WRITE MASTER RECORD
----------------------------------------------------------------*/
void WrtMast(void)
{
    iNMKey = iMKey;
    strcpy(sNMCourse, sMCourse);
    iNMEnroll = iMEnroll;
    fprintf(fpNMFO, "%d %s %d\n",
        iNMKey, sNMCourse, iNMEnroll);
    ReadMast();
    return;
}


/*----------------------------------------------------------------
        CLOSE FILES
----------------------------------------------------------------*/
void CloseFiles(void)
{
    iNMKey = 999;
    strcpy(sNMCourse, "END");
    iNMEnroll = 0;
    fprintf(fpNMFO, "%d %s %d\n",
        iNMKey, sNMCourse, iNMEnroll);
    fclose(fpMFI, fpTFI, fpNMFO);
    return;
}
```

FIGURE 13.19   *Continued*

Transaction File				Master File		
300	---	0	6	100	ACCT101	24
400	---	24	1	200	BIOL101	19
500	---	5	2	300	CHEM201	21
500	---	23	3	400	ENG200	16
650	MKT310	15	5	500	HIST225	33
700	MATH114	0	4	600	MGT330	29
800	---	55	3	700	MATH120	14
950	THAR101	17	5	800	PHYS251	20
999	END	0	0	900	SPAN111	12
				999	END 0	

FIGURE 13.20   Input Files for CHAP13D

```
┌─────────────────────────────────┐
│                                 │
│   Updated Master File           │
│                                 │
│   100 ACCT101 24                │
│   200 BIOL101 19                │
│   400 ENG200   40               │
│   500 HIST225 23                │
│   600 MGT330   29               │
│   650 MKT310   15               │
│   700 MATH114 14                │
│   800 PHYS251 55                │
│   900 SPAN111 12                │
│   950 THAR101 17                │
│   999 END       0               │
│                                 │
└─────────────────────────────────┘
```

FIGURE 13.21   New Master File for CHAP13D

Dissection of Sample Program CHAP13D

Notice that several course ID fields in the transaction file are shown with hyphens (Figure 13.20). This means that these fields are empty (not coded). We could have used the null character to accomplish the same thing. It is, however, important to realize that a field cannot be left blank. Something must be coded in each field to satisfy the scanf() when it reads the transactions. Otherwise, the input will be incorrectly assigned to the transaction variables.

After the first transaction and master records are read, the program proceeds to update the master file.

```
C H E C K    U P D A T E    L O G I C:

void CkUpdLogic(void)
{
    if (iTKey == iMKey)
        UpdMast();
```

In the above statement, if the keys are equal, control branches to *UpdMast* and performs the processing activities given there. Otherwise, control skips to the next statement.

```
    else if (iTKey < iMKey)
        AddMast();
```

In the above statement, if the transaction key is less than the master key, control branches to *AddMast* and performs the processing activities given there. Otherwise, control skips to the next statement.

```
    else
        WrtMast();
```

If control reaches this point in the program, then a match was not found for the other two conditions. Hence, the transaction key is greater than the master key, and the program branches to *WrtMast* to perform the processing given there.

```
    return;
}
```

The above statement returns to the *MAINLINE*.

U P D A T E   M A S T E R   R E C O R D:

```
void UpdMast(void)
{
    if (iTCode == 6)
        ReadMast();
```

In the above statement, if the transaction code equals 6, then the module call deletes the current master record by reading the next master record. This action prevents the current master record from being written to the new master file. Otherwise, control skips to the next statement.

```
    else if (iTCode == 1)
        iMEnroll = iMEnroll + iTEnroll;
```

In the above statement, if the transaction code equals 1, then the program adds the transaction enrollment to the master enrollment and stores the result in the current master record. Otherwise, control skips to the next statement.

```
    else if (iTCode == 2)
        iMEnroll = iMEnroll - iTEnroll;
```

In the above statement, if the transaction code equals 2, then the program subtracts the transaction enrollment from the master enrollment and stores the result in the current master record. Otherwise, control skips to the next statement.

```
    else if (iTCode == 3)
        iMEnroll = iTEnroll;
```

In the above statement, if the transaction code equals 3, then the program changes the course enrollment and copies the enrollment stored in the transaction to the master record. Otherwise, control skips to the next statement.

```
    else
        strcpy(sMCourse, sTCourse);
```

In the above statement, by default, the transaction code specifies a course ID change. Therefore, the program copies the course ID stored in the transaction to the master record.

```
    ReadTran();
    return;
}
```

The above statements read the next transaction record and return to the *CHECK UPDATE LOGIC* module.

```
A D D    N E W    M A S T E R    R E C O R D:

void AddMast(void)
{
    iNMKey = iTKey;
    strcpy(sNMCourse, sTCourse);
    iNMEnroll = iTEnroll;
    fprintf(fpMFO, "%d %s %d\n",
        iNMKey, sNMCourse, iNMEnroll);
    ReadTran();
    return;
}
```

The above statements add a new record to the master file, move the data stored in the transaction to the new master record, and write the record to the new master file. Control reads the next transaction and returns to the *CHECK UPDATE LOGIC* module.

```
W R I T E    M A S T E R    R E C O R D:

void WrtMast(void)
{
    iNMKey = iMKey;
    strcpy(sNMCourse, sMCourse);
    iNMEnroll = iMEnroll;
    fprintf(fpMFO, "%d %s %d\n",
        iNMKey, sNMCourse, iNMEnroll);
    ReadMast();
    return;
}
```

The above statements write the old master record to the new master file. The old master record may or may not have been updated previously. In any event, it is written to the new master file.

The return statement sends control back to the *CHECK UPDATE LOGIC* module.

Notes and Tips

1. Sample program CHAP13D uses a transaction code stored in the transaction record to update the master file. The updated file is written to a new master file.

2. If the transaction key = the master key, then use the transaction code to determine what field to update in the master record.

3. If the transaction key < the master key, then add the record stored in the transaction to the master file.

4. If the transaction key > the master key, then write the current master record to the new master file.

5. Because the transaction and master files are input to the program, open them in *read* mode. Because the new master file is output from the program, open it in *write* mode.

6. Use the file pointers *fpTFI* and *fpMFI* to indicate that the program is reading transaction file and master file input, respectively. Use the file pointer *fpNMO* to indicate that the program is writing new master file output.

Tutorial CHAP13D

1. The objectives of this tutorial are to
   • open and read a master file and a transaction file
   • compare transaction keys to the master keys and update the master records
   • create a new master file

2. Read the program specifications and logic design tools for sample program CHAP13D.

3. Log on to your C editor, and enter the source code as shown in Figure 13.19. Save the program on your work disk as CHAP13D. Save frequently.

4. Compile, run, and debug your program. When completed, show your work to your instructor.

Quick Quiz

Answer the following questions.

1. The Program Setup indicates that there are three files. Why do you need three files to complete the updating task?

2. Look at the *if* statement shown in the READ TRANSACTION RECORD module. Why is the program checking for a transaction key equal to *999*?

3. Under what conditions does the program subtract the transaction enrollment from the master enrollment?

4. Notice that the transaction record now includes a transaction code. Could you get by without it? Explain your answer.

5. Did you have any problems or errors when you ran the sample program? If so, what were they and what did you do to correct them?

Updating the Master File: Part III

With sample program CHAP13D, we now have a working model of the update logic. Although errors were not considered, we are now ready to include them in the next program. When an error is detected by the update program, the transaction record is written to a special *error log* for future reference.

Sample program CHAP13E checks for three types of transaction errors: adding master records that already exist, processing unmatched transactions, and processing invalid transaction codes.

Adding Master Records That Already Exist: Any transaction that adds a record to the master file cannot be processed if the record is already in the master file. This error implies that the transaction key may have been coded incorrectly.

Processing Unmatched Transactions: Any transaction key that does not match a master record key (the keys are not equal) cannot be processed by the program. In other words, the transaction is attempting to update a master record that does not exist. This error implies that the transaction key may have been coded incorrectly.

Processing Invalid Transaction Codes: Any transaction record with a transaction code other than 1–6 is invalid. This error implies that the transaction code was coded incorrectly.

Checkpoint 13D

1. Identify three common types of transaction errors.
2. Briefly explain the purpose of an error log report.

Sample Program CHAP13E

Sample program CHAP13E reads the transaction file, checks for errors, and updates the master file. See Figure 13.22 for the hierarchy chart and Figure 13.23 for the flowchart. Sample program CHAP13E is presented in Figure 13.24. Figure 13.25 shows the input files, Figure 13.26 shows the updated (new) master file, and Figure 13.27 shows the course error log.

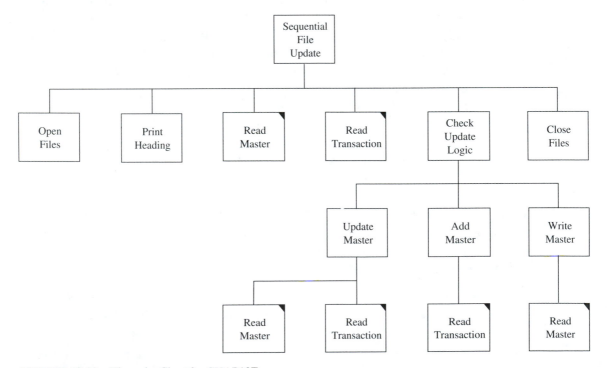

FIGURE 13.22   Hierarchy Chart for CHAP13E

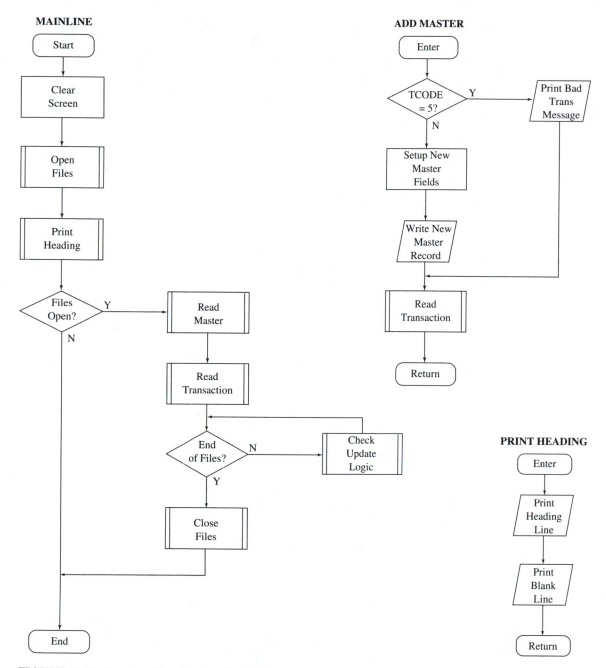

FIGURE 13.23   Program Flowchart for CHAP13E

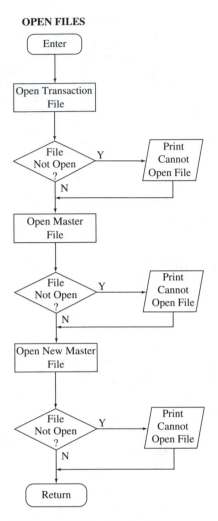

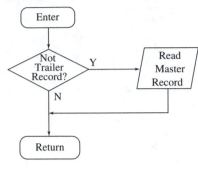

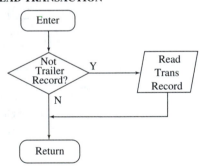

FIGURE 13.23 *Continued*

CHECK UPDATE LOGIC

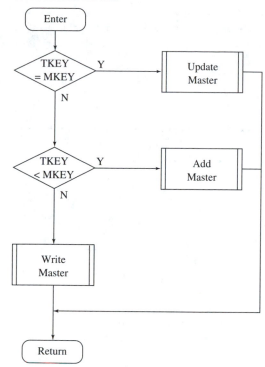

WRITE MASTER   **CLOSE FILES**

UPDATE MASTER

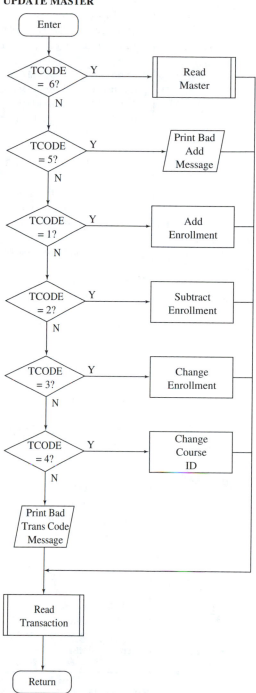

FIGURE 13.23   *Continued*

```
/*------------------------------------------------------------------
SEQUENTIAL FILE UPDATE: Use a transaction file to update the master
file and check for errors.

Program:    CHAP13E.C
Author:     David M. Collopy
Date:       mm/dd/yy
Project:    Sample program
**********************************************************************/


/*---- PREPROCESSING DIRECTIVES ---------------------------------*/

#include <stdio.h>
#include <string.h>
#include <graph.h>


/*---- FUNCTION PROTOTYPES --------------------------------------*/

void   OpenFiles(void);          /* open the files          */
void   PrnHeading(void);         /* print heading line      */
void   ReadTran(void);           /* read transaction record */
void   ReadMast(void);           /* read master record      */
void   CkUpdLogic(void);         /* check update logic      */
void   UpdMast(void);            /* update master record    */
void   AddMast(void);            /* add master record       */
void   WrtMast(void);            /* write master record     */
void   CloseFiles(void);         /* close files             */


/*---- PROGRAM SETUP --------------------------------------------*/

/*>   T R A N S A C T I O N    R E C O R D              <*/

FILE *fpTFI;                     /* transaction file pointer */
int    iTKey;                    /* key: call number         */
char   sTCourse[15];             /* course ID                */
int    iTEnroll;                 /* student enrollment       */
int    iTCode;                   /* transaction code         */

/*>   M A S T E R    R E C O R D                        <*/

FILE *fpMFI;                     /* master file pointer      */
int    iMKey;                    /* key: call number         */
char   sMCourse[15];             /* course ID                */
int    iMEnroll;                 /* student enrollment       */
```

FIGURE 13.24 Sample Program CHAP13E: Reads a transaction file, updates the master file, and checks for errors

```
/*>   N E W   M A S T E R   R E C O R D                    <*/

FILE *fpMFO;                    /* new master file pointer  */
int   iNMKey;                   /* key: call number         */
char  sNMCourse[15];            /* course ID                */
int   iNMEnroll;                /* student enrollment       */

/*>   P R O G R A M   V A R I A B L E S                    <*/

char PT[] = "        C O U R S E   E R R O R   L O G";
char sBadAdd[22]    = "MASTER EXISTS";
char sBadTrn[22]    = "UNMATCHED TRANSACTION";
char sBadTCode[22] = "BAD TRANSACTION CODE";


/*-----------------------------------------------------------------
      MAINLINE CONTROL
-----------------------------------------------------------------*/
main()
{
    _clearscreen(0);
    OpenFiles();
    PrnHeading();
    if (fpMFI != 0 && fpTFI != 0 && fpNMFO != 0)
    {
        ReadMast();
        ReadTran();
        while ((iTKey != 999 || iMKey != 999))
        {
            CkUpdLogic();
        }
        CloseFiles();
    }
    return 0;
}


/*-----------------------------------------------------------------
      OPEN FILES
-----------------------------------------------------------------*/
void OpenFiles(void)
{
    fpTFI = fopen("a:sqCrsTR3.fil", "r");
    if (fpTFI == 0)
    {
        printf("\nCannot open transaction file for input\n");
    }
```

FIGURE 13.24   *Continued*

```
    fpMFI = fopen("a:sqCrsMS.fil", "r");
    if (fpMFI == 0)
    {
        printf("\nCannot open master file for input\n");
    }
    fpNMFO = fopen("a:sqCrsNM.fil", "w");
    if (fpNMFO == 0)
    {
        printf("\nCannot open new master file for output\n");
    }
    return;
}


/*----------------------------------------------------------------
        PRINT HEADING LINE
-------------------------------------------------------------------*/
void PrnHeading(void)
{
    fprintf(stdprn, "\r%s", PT);
    fprintf(stdprn, "\r\n\n");
    return;
}


/*----------------------------------------------------------------
        READ TRANSACTION RECORD
-------------------------------------------------------------------*/
void ReadTran(void)
{
    if (iTKey != 999)
    {
        fscanf(fpTFI, " %d %s %d %d\n",
            &iTKey, sTCourse, &iTEnroll, &iTCode);
    }
    return;
}


/*----------------------------------------------------------------
        READ MASTER RECORD
-------------------------------------------------------------------*/
void ReadMast(void)
{
    if (iMKey != 999)
    {
        fscanf(fpMFI, " %d %s %d\n",
            &iMKey, sMCourse, &iMEnroll);
```

FIGURE 13.24   *Continued*

```
    }
    return;
}


/*----------------------------------------------------------------
        CHECK UPDATE LOGIC
----------------------------------------------------------------*/
void CkUpdLogic(void)
{
    if (iTKey == iMKey)
    {
        UpdMast();                  /* update master record */
    }
    else if (iTKey < iMKey)
    {
        AddMast();                  /* add master record    */
    }
    else
    {
        WrtMast();                  /* write master record  */
    }
    return;
}


/*----------------------------------------------------------------
        UPDATE MASTER RECORD
----------------------------------------------------------------*/
void UpdMast(void)
{

    if (iTCode == 6)
    {
        ReadMast();
    }
    else if (iTCode == 5)
    {
        fprintf(stdprn, "\r\n%3d %-14s %2d %1d  %-21s",
            iTKey, sTCourse, iTEnroll, iTCode, sBadAdd);
    }
    else if (iTCode == 1)
    {
        iMEnroll = iMEnroll + iTEnroll;
    }
    else if (iTCode == 2)
    {
```

FIGURE 13.24   *Continued*

```
            iMEnroll = iMEnroll - iTEnroll;
        }
        else if (iTCode == 3)
        {
            iMEnroll = iTEnroll;
        }
        else if (iTCode == 4)
        {
            strcpy(sMCourse, sTCourse);
        }
        else
        {
            fprintf(stdprn, "\r\n%3d %-14s %2d %1d  %-21s",
                iTKey, sTCourse, iTEnroll, iTCode, sBadTCode);
        }
        ReadTran();
        return;
    }


/*----------------------------------------------------------------
        ADD MASTER RECORD
-----------------------------------------------------------------*/
void AddMast(void)
{
    if (iTCode != 5)
    {
        fprintf(stdprn, "\r\n%3d %-14s %2d %1d  %-21s",
            iTKey, sTCourse, iTEnroll, iTCode, sBadTrn);
    }
    else
    {
        iNMKey = iTKey;
        strcpy(sNMCourse, sTCourse);
        iNMEnroll = iTEnroll;
        fprintf(fpNMFO, "%d %s %d\n",
            iNMKey, sNMCourse, iNMEnroll);
    }
    ReadTran();
    return;
}


/*----------------------------------------------------------------
        WRITE MASTER RECORD
-----------------------------------------------------------------*/
void WrtMast(void)
```

FIGURE 13.24 *Continued*

```
{
    iNMKey = iMKey;
    strcpy(sNMCourse, sMCourse);
    iNMEnroll = iMEnroll;
    fprintf(fpNMFO, "%d %s %d\n",
        iNMKey, sNMCourse, iNMEnroll);
    ReadMast();
    return;
}


/*----------------------------------------------------------------
      CLOSE FILES
-----------------------------------------------------------------*/
void CloseFiles(void)
{
    iNMKey = 999;
    strcpy(sNMCourse, "END");
    iNMEnroll = 0;
    fprintf(fpNMFO, "%d %s %d\n",
        iNMKey, sNMCourse, iNMEnroll);
    fclose(fpMFI, fpTFI, fpNMFO);
    return;
}
```

FIGURE 13.24   *Continued*

```
  Transaction File                     Master File

300 ---        0    6           100 ACCT101 24
400 ---       24    1           200 BIOL101 19
450 ---        0    6           300 CHEM201 21
500 ---        5    2           400 ENG200  16
500 ---       12    7           500 HIST225 33
500 HIST291  35    5           600 MGT330  29
650 MKT310   15    5           700 MATH120 14
700 MATH114   0    4           800 PHYS251 20
800 ---       55    3           900 SPAN111 12
950 THAR101  17    5           999 END 0
970 ---       28    3
999 END        0    0
```

FIGURE 13.25   Input Files for CHAP13E

```
 Updated Master File

   100  ACCT101  24
   200  BIOL101  19
   400  ENG200   40
   500  HIST225  28
   600  MGT330   29
   650  MKT310   15
   700  MATH114  14
   800  PHYS251  55
   900  SPAN111  12
   950  THAR101  17
   999  END       0
```

FIGURE 13.26   Output Master File for CHAP13E

```
        C O U R S E   E R R O R   L O G

   450                  0  6   UNMATCHED TRANSACTION
   500                 12  7   BAD TRANSACTION CODE
   500  HIST291        35  5   MASTER EXISTS
   970                 28  3   UNMATCHED TRANSACTION
```

FIGURE 13.27   Error Log for CHAP13E

The following specifications apply:

Input (disk files):
Transaction file (sqCrsTR.fil)
Old master file (sqCrsMS.fil)

Output (sqCrsNM.fil):
The new master file is shown in Figure 13.26, and the course error log is shown in Figure 13.27.

Processing Requirements:

• Open the transaction file and old master file in *read* mode.
• Open the new master file in *write* mode.
• Read a transaction and a master record.
• Compare keys and use the transaction code to update the master file. (Check the transaction for errors.)
• Close the files.

Pseudocode:

```
START: Main
Clear screen
Call Open Files
Call Print Headings
IF files opened
    Call Read Master Record
    Call Read Transaction Record
    LOOP while not at end of files
        Call Check Update Logic
    END LOOP
    Call Close Files
END IF
END


ENTER: Open Files
Open transaction file for read
IF file not opened
    Print cannot open transaction file for input
END IF
Open master file for read
IF file not opened
    Print cannot open master file for input
END IF
Open new master file for write
IF file not opened
    Print cannot open new master file for output
END IF
RETURN


ENTER: Print Headings
Print 1 title line for error report
RETURN


ENTER: Read Transaction Record
IF not at end of file
    Read transaction record:
        transaction key
        transaction course ID
        transaction student enrollment
END IF
RETURN


ENTER: Read Master Record
IF not at end of file
    Read master record:
        master key
        master course ID
        master student enrollment
END IF
```

RETURN

ENTER: Check Update Logic
IF transaction key = master key
    Call Update Master Record
else IF transaction key < master key
    Call Add Master Record
else
    Call Write Master Record
END IF
RETURN

ENTER: Update Master Record
IF transaction code = 6
    Call Read Master Record
else IF transaction code = 5
    Print error report line:
        transaction key
        transaction course ID
        transaction enrollment
        transaction code
        error message: MASTER EXITS
else IF transaction code = 1
    Add transaction enrollment to master enrollment
else IF transaction code = 2
    Subtract transaction enrollment from master enrollment
else IF transaction code = 3
    Set master enrollment to transaction enrollment
else IF transaction code = 4
    Set master course ID to transaction course ID
else
    Print error report line:
        transaction key
        transaction course ID
        transaction enrollment
        transaction code
        error message: BAD TRANSACTION CODE
END IF
Call Read Transaction Record
RETURN

ENTER: Add Master Record
IF transaction code not = 5
    Print error report line:
        transaction key
        transaction course ID
        transaction enrollment
        transaction code
        error message: UNMATCHED TRANSACTION
else

        Set new master key to transaction key
        Set new master course ID to transaction course ID
        Set new master enrollment to transaction enrollment
        Write record to new master file
END IF
Call Read Transaction Record
RETURN

ENTER: Write Master Record
Set new master key to master key
Set new master course ID to master course ID
Set new master enrollment to master enrollment
Write record to new master file
Call Read Master Record
RETURN

ENTER: Close Files
Set new master key to 999
Set new master course ID to END
Set new master student enrollment to 0
Write record to new master file
Close all files
RETURN

Hierarchy Chart: See Figure 13.22.

Program Flowchart: See Figure 13.23.

Dissection of Sample Program CHAP13E

With the exception of the error checks and the Course Error Log, the logic for sample program CHAP13E is similar to the logic shown for sample program CHAP13D. The update module remains basically the same.

However, two error checks were added to *UPDATE MASTER RECORD: sBadAdd* (bad record addition/master exists—we may not add a record to the master file if it already exists) and *sBadTcode* (bad transaction code—we cannot process transaction codes that fall outside the range of acceptable values).

A third error check was added to *ADD MASTER RECORD: sBadTrn* (bad transaction record/unmatched transaction—we cannot process transactions, other than new record additions, that do not match an existing master record).

When the program detects an error, the transaction record and its corresponding error message are written to the Course Error Log. The code for the *UPDATE MASTER RECORD* follows.

```
U P D A T E    M A S T E R    R E C O R D:

void UpdMast(void)
{
    if (iTCode == 6)
    {
```

```
        ReadMast();
    }
    else if (iTCode == 5)
    {
        fprintf(stdprn, "\r\n%3d %-15s %2d %1d  %-21s",
            iTKey, sTCourse, iTEnroll, iTCode, sBadAdd);
    }
    else if (iTCode == 1)
    {
        iMEnroll = iMEnroll + iTEnroll;
    }
    else if (iTCode == 2)
    {
        iMEnroll = iMEnroll - iTEnroll;
    }
    else if (iTCode == 3)
    {
        iMEnroll = iTEnroll;
    }
    else if (iTCode == 4)
    {
        strcpy(sMCourse, sTCourse);
    }
    else
    {
        fprintf(stdprn, "\r\n%3d %-15s %2d %1d  %-21s",
            iTKey, sTCourse, iTEnroll, iTCode, sBadTcode);
    }
    ReadTran();
    return;
}
```

When the transaction and master keys are equal, control branches to *UPDATE MASTER RECORD* and checks the transaction code to determine what type of update to perform.

If the transaction and the master keys are equal and the transaction code (5) specifies a record addition, the master already exists; so the transaction record and the error message MASTER EXISTS are written to the error log. Control then branches to *ReadTran* and reads the next transaction record.

If the transaction code falls outside the range 1–6, then the transaction record and the error message BAD TRANSACTION CODE are written to the error log. Control then branches to *ReadTran* and reads the next transaction record.

```
A D D    M A S T E R    R E C O R D:

void AddMast(void)
{
    if (iTCode != 5)
    {
        fprintf(stdprn, "\r\n%3d %-15s %2d %1d  %-21s",
            iTKey, sTCourse, iTEnroll, iTCode, sBadTrn);
    }
    else
```

```
    {
        iNMKey = iTKey;
        strcpy(sNMCourse, sTCourse);
        iNMEnroll = iTEnroll;
        fprintf(fpMFO, "%d %s %d\n",
            iNMKey, sNMCourse, iNMEnroll);
    }
    ReadTran();
    return;
}
```

When the transaction key is less than the master key and the transaction code specifies processing other than a new record addition, then we have an unmatched transaction. The transaction record and the error message UNMATCHED TRANSACTION are written to the error log, and the next transaction is read from the transaction file.

Notes and Tips

1. Sample program CHAP13E uses the transaction file to update the master file while checking for processing errors. The updated file is written to a new master file.
2. Do not add a record to the master file if one is already there.
3. Do not process a transaction that does not match a master record.
4. Do not process transactions with an invalid transaction code.

Tutorial CHAP13E

1. The objectives of this tutorial are to
   - open and read a master file and a transaction file
   - compare transaction keys to the master keys and update the master records
   - create a new master file
   - check for errors and write them to an error log
2. Read the program specifications and review the logic design tools for sample program CHAP13E
3. Log on to your C editor, and enter the source code as shown in Figure 13.24. Save the program on your work disk as CHAP13E. Save frequently as you enter the code.
4. Compile, run, and debug your program until the error report matches the results shown in Figure 13.27.
5. When completed, show your work to your instructor.

Quick Quiz

Answer the following questions.

1. Under what conditions does the program add a new record to the master file? Be specific and refer to the program code.

2. Under what conditions does the program print the BAD TRANSACTION CODE message on the error log? Be specific and refer to the program code.

3. Under what conditions does the program print the MASTER EXISTS message on the error log? Be specific and refer to the program code.

4. Under what conditions does the program print the UNMATCHED TRANSACTION message on the error log? Be specific and refer to the program code.

5. Did you have any problems or errors when you ran the sample program? If so, what were they and what did you do to correct them?

Summary

1. Files are created and maintained to reflect the current business and financial conditions of the company.

2. There are two basic types of files: master files and transaction files. A master file contains permanent information about a specific application, whereas a transaction file contains temporary information that is used to update the master file.

3. File maintenance is the process of keeping the master file up to date. It consists of creating the files, updating the master file, and processing the data stored in the master file.

4. Once a need has been identified, a master file is created. Data is collected and organized into records. In turn, the records are organized into a file and stored on disk or tape for future use.

5. File updating refers to the process of updating the master file. New records are added, old records are deleted, and changes are made to the existing records.

6. Transactions are arranged in record key order and are applied to the master file one at a time.

7. Updates to the master file are scheduled on a regular basis. When the file is updated, various reports are produced by the program. Information from the reports is used to monitor the operations of the business.

8. A special code called a transaction code is used to tell the program how to apply the transaction to the master record.

9. The update logic compares the master key to the transaction key and uses the transaction code to apply the data to the master record.

10. When the master key equals the transaction key, either the data stored in the transaction is used to update the master record or the master record is deleted.

11. When the master key is greater than the transaction key, the data stored in the transaction is used to create a new master record.

12. When the transaction key is greater than the master key, the current master record is written to the new master file.

13. An abnormal end (abend) occurs when certain logic errors prevent the program from running to completion. Once the errors have been corrected, the program is executed again.

14. Errors detected during the update run are written to an error log. Information provided by the log is used to correct the transactions.

15. Sequential file update programs should be designed to catch the following errors: adding master records that already exist, processing unmatched transactions, and processing invalid transaction codes.

Programming Projects

For each project, design the logic and write the modular structured program to produce the output. Model your program after the sample programs presented in the chapter. Verify your output.

Project 13–1 Course Schedule

Sample program CHAP13E updates the master file and checks for errors. It does not, however, check for input sequence errors. Include an error check in the read modules to assure that the record keys are in ascending order. Make up four or five additional transaction records and master records, and add them to the input files in out-of-sequence order. When a sequence error is detected, print the record and an error message TRANS OUT OF SEQUENCE or MAST OUT OF SEQUENCE and continue processing.

Project 13–2 Overdue Accounts-1

Update the sequential master file created in Programming Project 12–1. This three-part project creates the transaction file, updates the master file, and prints the overdue accounts report.

Part I: Write a program to create the transaction file for the overdue accounts. For each transaction record, prompt for and enter the data given below. Write the input data to the transaction file.

File Data (sqOvrTR.fil):
Enter the transaction data in the order shown.

Account Number	Customer Name	Days Overdue	Balance Due	Trans Code
1000	Sarah Brooks	60	220.00	4
1010	Ryan Davis			1
2450			700.00	3
2730		30		2
3100				5
4890	Amy Clark			1
4900	Marla Stevens	90	594.00	4
6350		60		2
8540				5
9200			300.00	3
9700	Adam Norris	60	475.00	4

The transaction codes (defined below) specify the type of updates to apply to the master file.

> 1 – change customer name
> 2 – change days overdue
> 3 – change balance due
> 4 – add master record
> 5 – delete master record

Part II: Write a second program to update the master file. Open the transaction file and the master file in *read* mode. Open the new master file in *write* mode. Read a transaction and a master record and compare keys. Use the transaction code to determine the type of update to apply to the master file.

Part III: Upon completing the update, write a third program to read the new master file and print the overdue accounts report shown below. Accumulate a total for amount due, and print the total at the end of the report.

```
Author                    OVERDUE ACCOUNTS              Page 01
                             mm/dd/yy


Acct Number      Customer Name     Days Overdue      Amount Due

   9999          X-----------X          99             999.99
    :                 :                 :                 :
    :                 :                 :                 :
   9999          X-----------X          99             999.99

                                      Total:          9999.99
```

Project 13–3   Overdue Accounts-2

Modify the program in Project 13–2 to include error checks for illegal transaction codes, unmatched transactions, and illegal record additions. Write the errors to an error log. Insert the following transactions into the transaction file. Be sure to insert them in key field (account number) order.

Account Number	Customer Name	Days Overdue	Balance Due	Trans Code
2740		60		2
4080	Corey Adkins	30	233.00	4
5260			652.00	6
5310				5
5700			375.00	3
9630	Pat Rankin	60	342.00	4

Project 13–4   Overdue Accounts-3

Modify the program in Project 13–3 to check for input sequence errors. Test your program by making up four or five additional transaction records and master records. Insert them in the files in out-of-sequence order. Write the sequence errors to the error log.

Project 13–5   Sales Profit-1

Update the sequential master file created in Programming Project 12–3. This three-part project creates the transaction file, updates the master file, and prints the sales profit report.

Part I: Write a program to create the transaction file for the sales department. For each transaction record, prompt for and enter the data given below. Write the input data to the sales transaction file.

File Data (sqSaleTR.fil):
Enter the transaction data in the order shown.

Number	Salesperson	Total Sales	Cost of Sales	Trans Code
200	Allison Dunn	6518.02	4131.78	4
300	Roy Henderson			1
400				5
700			3191.22	3
940	Sean Zorich	7465.92	5641.39	4

The transaction codes (defined below) specify the type of updates to apply to the master file.

    1–change salesperson name
    2–change total sales
    3–change cost of sales
    4–add master record
    5–delete master record

Part II: Write a second program to update the master file. Open the transaction file and the master file in *read* mode. Open the new master file in *write* mode. Read a transaction and a master record and compare keys. Use the transaction code to determine the type of update to apply to the master file.

Part III: Upon completing the update, write a third program to read the new master file and print the sales profit report that follows. Compute net profit (sales – cost), and print the result on the detail line. Accumulate the total net profit, and print the total at the end of the report.

```
Author                SALES PROFIT REPORT              Page 01
                          mm/dd/yy


                      Total       Cost of      Net
Num     Salesperson   Sales       Sales        Profit
--------------------------------------------------------------
999     X---------X   99999.99    9999.99      9999.99
 :          :            :           :            :
 :          :            :           :            :
999     X---------X   99999.99    9999.99      9999.99

                                   Total:      99999.99
```

Project 13–6   Sales Profit-2

Modify the program in Project 13–5 to include error checks for illegal transaction codes, unmatched transactions, and illegal record additions. Write the errors to an error log. Insert the following transactions into the transaction file. Be sure to insert them in key field (salesperson number) order.

Number	Salesperson	Total Sales	Cost of Sales	Trans Code
100				7
250		3974.63		2
340	David Kock			1
490			5591.15	3
900	Ann Zimmerman	5793.59	4204.45	4
960				5

Project 13–7   Sales Profit-3

Modify the program in Project 13–6 to check for input sequence errors. Test your program by making up four or five additional transaction records and master records. Insert them in the files in out-of-sequence order. Write the sequence errors to the error log.

Project 13–8   Inventory-1

Update the sequential master file created in Programming Project 12–4. This three-part project creates the transaction file, updates the master file, and prints the inventory status report.

Part I: Write a program to create the transaction file for the inventory system. For each transaction record, prompt for and enter the data given below. Write the data to the inventory transaction file. Note that the reorder point and reorder quantity are not updated. Hence, they are not included in the transaction.

File Data (sqInvTR.fil):
Enter the transaction data in the order shown.

Item Number	Description	Quantity on Hand	Unit Cost	Trans Code
1000		20		2
1600	Shovels	12	6.29	4
3000				5
4000			2.37	3
4500	Wrenches	18	3.95	4

The transaction codes (defined below) specify the type of update to apply to the master file.

    1-change item description
    2-change quantity on hand
    3-change unit cost
    4-add master record
    5-delete master record

Part II: Write a second program to update the master file. Open the transaction file and the master file in *read* mode. Open the new master file in *write* mode. Read a transaction and a master record and compare keys. Use the transaction code to determine the type of update to apply to the master file.

Part III: Upon completing the update, write a third program to read the new master file and print the inventory status report shown below. Accumulate a total for item cost, and print the total at the end of the report.

```
   Author              INVENTORY STATUS REPORT        Page 01
                             mm/dd/yy


    Item                                  Quantity        Item
   Number          Description            on Hand         Cost

    9999          X----------X               99          999.99
      :                :                      :             :
      :                :                      :             :
    9999          X----------X               99          999.99

                                  Total Cost:            9999.99
```

Project 13–9   Inventory-2

Change the program in Project 13–8 to include error checks for illegal transaction codes, unmatched transactions, and illegal record additions. Write the errors to an error log. Insert the following transactions into the transaction file. Be sure to insert them in key field (item number) order.

Item Number	Description	Quantity on Hand	Unit Cost	Trans Code
1100				5
2000	Saws	08	7.50	4
2400		24		2
3500			3.49	6
4100	Hatchets			1
5000	Pliers	12	2.65	4
5200			4.17	3

Project 13–10   Inventory-3

Modify the program in Project 13–9 to check for input sequence errors. Test your program by making up four or five additional transaction records and master records. Insert them in the files in out-of-sequence order. Write the sequence errors to the error log.

14   Structures and Random Files

Overview

Learning Objectives

After you have read this chapter and completed the exercises, you should be able to

- declare data structures and structure variables
- discuss the advantages of random file organization
- create a random file
- use fseek() to move around in a random file
- print data stored in a random file
- update data stored in a random file

Defining a Structure

Until now, we have been using individual data types *int, char,* and *float* to describe our programming applications. However, some applications can be processed more efficiently if the individual data types are grouped to form a single unit.

For example, consider an inventory application that consists of the following variables: item number (int), description (char), quantity (int), cost (float), and selling price (float). What we would like to do is access a complete item (a record) or any variable (a field) belonging to the record.

C uses structures to group data types. A **structure** is a group item that may hold two or more data types, called **members**. A structure may be processed as a single unit, or the members may be processed individually. In simpler terms, a structure is a **record**, and a member of the structure is a **field**.

It may help to think of a structure as a *template* that describes the format of the data. By itself, the template does not reserve storage for the structure. It isn't until a structure variable is declared that storage is allocated to the members of the structure. In other words, a structure merely tells the program what the data looks like.

A structure must be declared before it can be used by the program. The keyword *struct* is used to define a structure or record template.

Format:

```
struct tag
{
    type member_1;
```

```
        type member_2;
          :   :
        type member_n;
    };
```

Example:

```
struct stInventory
{
    int    iNumber;
    char   sDesc[20];
    int    iQuantity;
    float  fCost;
    float  fPrice;
};
```

In the example, *struct* describes the format of the inventory structure and *tag* gives a name to it. The member definitions describe the fields and their data types. Hence, both the structure and its members have names. For processing purposes, we may reference the entire structure or any member of it. As a standard, use the prefix *st* to indicate that the identifier represents a structure tag.

Defining a Structure Variable

Once a structure has been declared, we may use it to define one or more structure variables. A **structure variable** is a variable that consists of the members described by the data structure. Defining a structure variable reserves storage space for each member of the template. Use the prefix *sv* to indicate that the identifier represents a structure variable.

For example, assume the inventory structure has been defined as shown below. The second *struct* statement defines the structure variable *svItem* and allocates storage space for the following members—*iNumber* (int), *sDesc* (char), *iQuantity* (int), *fCost* (float), and *fPrice* (float).

```
    .  .  .  .  .

struct stInventory
{
    int    iNumber;
    char   sDesc[20];
    int    iQuantity;
    float  fCost;
    float  fPrice;
};

struct stInventory svItem;


    .  .  .  .  .
```

Essentially, a data structure describes what the data looks like and a structure variable assigns a memory location to the members of the data structure.

Assigning Data to a Structure Variable

Data may be assigned to a structure variable either at the time it is declared or by the program during the run.

Initializing Data: A structure variable may be initialized when it is declared. For example, the statements below define the template and initialize the structure variable. The first **struct** statement describes the template, whereas the second *struct* defines the structure variable *svItem* and initializes the members to the values listed.

```
/*  DEFINE THE INVENTORY TEMPLATE   */

    struct stInventory
    {
        int     iNumber;
        char    sDesc[20];
        int     iQuantity;
        float   fCost;
        float   fPrice;
    };

/*  DEFINE THE STRUCTURE VARIABLE   */

    struct stInventory svItem = {0, "", 0, 0.0, 0.0};
```

The values are assigned on a positional basis; the first value is assigned the first member, the second value is assigned the second member, and so on. Consequently, *iNumber* equals 0, *sDesc* holds a Null string, *iQuantity* equals 0, *fCost* equals 0.0, and *fPrice* equals 0.0.

Interactive Input: Data may be assigned to a structure variable by prompting the user to enter the data at the keyboard. The example shown below prompts for the data one field at a time and assigns it to the members as it is entered by the user.

```
    .  .  .  .  .

    struct stInventory
    {
        int     iNumber;
        char    sDesc[20];
        int     iQuantity;
        float   fCost;
        float   fPrice;
    };

    struct stInventory svItem;

    .  .  .  .  .

        printf("     Enter item number: ");
        scanf(" %d", &svItem.iNumber);
        printf(" Enter item description: ");
        scanf(" %s", svItem.iDesc);
```

```
printf(" Enter quantity on hand: ");
scanf(" %d", &svItem.iQuantity);
printf("        Enter item cost: ");
scanf(" %f", &svItem.fCost);
printf("     Enter selling price: ");
scanf(" %f", &svItem.fPrice);
```

. . . . .

Notice that a dot (.), called a dot operator, appears in the scanf() statements. The **dot operator** links the structure variable to the members of the data template. For example, the first scanf() assigns the input to the *iNumber* member of the *svItem* variable. The structure variable is coded on the left side of the dot operator, and the member is coded on the right.

Checkpoint 14A

1. Define the term *structure*.
2. True or false: A structure may be processed as a single unit, or the members may be processed individually.
3. True or false: The following statements assign a memory location to the members of the data structure.
```
struct stPayroll
{
    char    sEmployee[20];
    float   fPayRate;
    int     iHoursWorked;
};
```
4. What is a structure variable?
5. Code the statements to define a structure variable called *svGrossPay* using the *stPayroll* template from Question 3. Then code the statements to assign data to the members by prompting the user to enter data at the keyboard.
6. Explain the purpose and use of a dot operator.

Random File Organization

Random file organization stores data on disk in random order. The word *random* implies that the data may be read or written in any order. Thus, the user may skip around in the file rather than passing through the records sequentially one by one. Unlike sequential files, random files do not require that the records be arranged in key field order.

Random file processing **(direct access)** offers the advantage of fast data retrieval; any record can be accessed in a matter of seconds. For example, if the user wants to view a specific record in the file, the program can go directly to that record and retrieve the data stored there.

Random access can be compared to selecting a song recorded on a CD. When you make a selection, the CD player automatically locates and plays the song for you.

TABLE 14.1   Random File Open Modes

Open Modes	Meaning
`"w+"`	Write and read (open new file or overwrite existing file)
`"r+"`	Read and write (open existing file)
`"a+"`	Append, read, and write (open existing file—add data to end of file)

For applications that require access to a small number of records at any given time, random file organization provides fast and efficient retrieval. However, it can be rather cumbersome and slow for applications that require access to all or most of the records in a large file, particularly if the records must be processed in sequential order.

Opening a Random File

A file must be opened before the program can do anything with it. According to the statement

```
fileptr = fopen("a:rdCrs.fil", "w+");
```

the course file is opened in *write* mode. The *write* mode tells the compiler that data is written to a new file. The `"w+"` indicates that once data is written to the course file it may also be read. The random file open modes are shown in Table 14.1.

When a file is opened, the address of the file is passed to the file pointer. The fopen() function always sets the file pointer to the beginning of the file. Once the file is opened, the position of the file pointer is maintained by the program. Use the prefix *rd* to indicate that the file represents a random file.

Writing a Record: The fwrite() Function

Format:

```
fwrite(&recordptr, size, number, fileptr);
```

Header File: stdio.h

Purpose: To write a record to a random file. The fwrite() consists of four arguments that specify the record pointer, the record length, the number of records to write, and the file pointer.

The *recordptr* specifies the address from which to get the data, and *size* indicates the length of the record in bytes. The *number* argument indicates how many records to write, and *fileptr* specifies the address where the data in the file should be put.

Examples:

1. `fwrite(&svItem, 35, 1, fpOutFile);`
2. `fwrite(&svRecord, sizeof(struct course), 1, fpFile);`

Example 1 writes the 35-byte record stored at the variable called *svItem* to the file pointed to by the pointer called *fpOutFile*. The third argument tells the compiler that one record is written to the file.

Example 2 writes one record to the designated file. Notice that the second argument is determined by the *sizeof* operator. This special operator is used to compute the number of bytes associated with the course structure. For example, if `sizeof(struct course)` equals 17, then the size argument indicates that 17 bytes of data will be written to the file.

Creating a Random File

Let's continue with the course scheduling application introduced in Chapter 12. In order to create a random file, we need to describe the data structure, declare the record variable, and reserve space for the file records. Essentially, we will initialize the structure variable and write empty records to the file. The idea is to prepare the file for storing future data.

Creating a random file involves the following tasks:

1. Declare the file pointer.
2. Define the data structure.
3. Define and initialize the empty record.
4. Open the file in *write w+* mode.
5. Write empty records to the file.
6. Close the file.

This process is illustrated in sample program CHAP14A. The course file is created from the initial values assigned to the empty record variable.

Checkpoint 14B

1. Briefly explain random file organization.
2. True or false: The records of a random file must be arranged in key field order.
3. What is the advantage of random file processing? When is random file processing used?
4. What do the following open modes mean?
   a. `"r+"`
   b. `"a+"`
   c. `"w+"`
5. What statement is used to write a record to a random file?
6. Identify the arguments specified in an *fwrite* statement. Briefly explain each.
7. The special operator used to compute the number of bytes associated with a structure is the _____ operator.
8. List the six steps involved in creating a random file.

Sample Program CHAP14A

Sample program CHAP14A creates a random access file for the courses offered at the regional campus of Blackmoore University. Each record is initialized and written to the file. In the interest of brevity, the file has been set up for 20 records. See Figure 14.1 for the hierarchy chart and Figure 14.2 for the program flowchart. Sample program CHAP14A is presented in Figure 14.3.

The following specifications apply:

Input (internal):

Define the course data structure and the members given below. (Field size and type are shown in parentheses.)

Call number	(3 int)
Course ID	(15 char)
Student enrollment	(2 int)

Output (rdCrs.fil):

The random access file is shown in Figure 14.4.

Processing Requirements:

- Define and initialize the empty record.
- Open the file in *writeplus (w+)* mode.
- Write empty records to the file.
- Close the file.

Pseudocode:

```
START: Main
Clear screen
Call Open File
IF file opened
       Call Create Random File
       Close file
END IF
END


ENTER: Open File
Open random file for write+
IF file not opened
       Print cannot open random file
END IF
RETURN


ENTER: Create Random File
LOOP for record number 1 to 20
       Write empty record to the file
END LOOP
RETURN
```

Hierarchy Chart: See Figure 14.1.

Program Flowchart: See Figure 14.2.

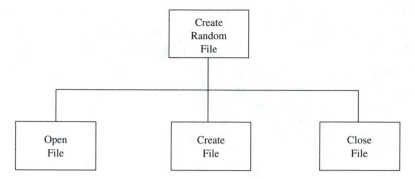

FIGURE 14.1   Hierarchy Chart for CHAP14A

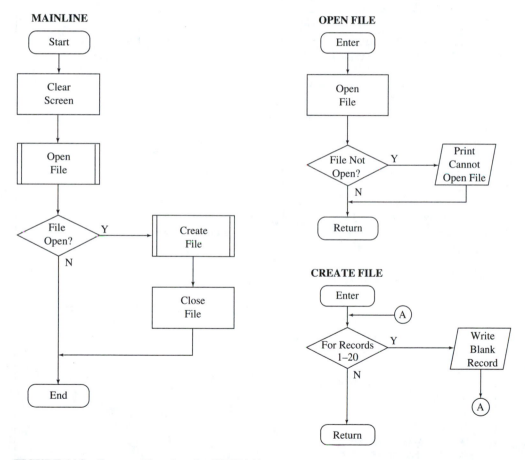

FIGURE 14.2   Program Flowchart for CHAP14A

```
/*------------------------------------------------------------
CREATE RANDOM FILE: Create a ramdom file of 20 empty records.

Program:    CHAP14A.C
Author:     David M. Collopy
Date:       mm/dd/yy
Project:    Sample program
**************************************************************/

/*---- PREPROCESSING DIRECTIVES ----------------------------*/

#include <stdio.h>
#include <graph.h>

/*---- FUNCTION PROTOTYPES ---------------------------------*/

void OpenFile(void);               /* open random file   */
void CreateFile(void);             /* create random file */

/*---- PROGRAM SETUP ---------------------------------------*/

/*>  C O U R S E   R E C O R D                           <*/

FILE *fpRF;                        /* file pointer       */

struct stCrsForm
{
    int  iCallNum;                 /* call number        */
    char sCourse[15];              /* course ID          */
    int  iEnroll;                  /* student enrollment */
};

struct stCrsForm svEmpty = {0, "", 0};

/*------------------------------------------------------------
       MAINLINE CONTROL
------------------------------------------------------------*/
main()
{
    _clearscreen(0);
    OpenFile();
    if (fpRF != 0)
    {
        CreateFile();
        fclose(fpRF);
    }
```

FIGURE 14.3   Sample Program CHAP14A: Creates a random access file

```
        return 0;
}


/*-----------------------------------------------------------
        OPEN RANDOM FILE
----------------------------------------------------------*/
void OpenFile(void)
{
    fpRF = fopen("a:rdCrs.fil", "w+");
    if (fpRF == 0)
    {
        printf("\nCannot open random file\n");
    }
    return;
}


/*-----------------------------------------------------------
        CREATE RANDOM FILE
----------------------------------------------------------*/
void CreateFile(void)
{
    int iRecNum;                    /* record number */

    for (iRecNum = 1; iRecNum <= 20; iRecNum++)
    {
        fwrite(&svEmpty, sizeof(struct stCrsForm), 1, fpRF);
    }
    return;
}
```

FIGURE 14.3 *Continued*

Rec#	Call#	Dept-Course#	Enrollment
1	0	blank	0
2	0	blank	0
3	0	blank	0
		. . . . .	
20	0	blank	0

FIGURE 14.4 File Output for CHAP14A

Dissection of Sample Program CHAP14A

C O U R S E   R E C O R D:

```
FILE *fpRF;
```

The above statement defines the file pointer to the random file. The asterisk (and the prefix *fp*) indicates that variable is a file pointer. The *RF* reminds us that the program will be processing a random file. The variable *fpRF* will be used to hold the address of the course file.

```
struct stCrsForm
{
    int   iCallNum;
    char  sCourse[15];
    int   iEnroll;
};
```

The above statements define the format of the course data structure and give its template the name *stCrsForm*. The prefix *st* is used to remind you that the identifier name represents a structure. The structure describes the members—*iCallNum* (int), *sCourse* (char), and *iEnroll* (int).

This *struct* statement only describes the format of the structure (record); it does not reserve storage space for it.

```
struct stCrsForm svEmpty = {0, "", 0};
```

The above statement defines the empty record, reserves storage space for it, and initializes the data fields; *iCallNum* equals 0, *sCourse* holds a Null string, and *iEnroll* equals 0. The prefix *sv* is used to remind you that the identifier name represents a structure variable.

O P E N   R A N D O M   F I L E:

```
void OpenFile(void)
{
    fpRF = fopen("a:rdCrs.fil", "w+");
    if (fpRF == 0)
    {
        printf("Cannot open random file\n");
    }
    return;
}
```

The above statements open the course file in *write* mode; the *"w+"* indicates that data may be written to and read from the file. If the file is opened, the fopen() function establishes a file address and assigns it to the file pointer *fpRF*. But if the file cannot be opened, the error message is displayed on the screen.

C R E A T E   R A N D O M   F I L E:

```
void CreateFile(void)
```

```
{
    int iRecNum;

    for (iRecNum = 1; iRecNum <= 20; iRecNum++)
    {
        fwrite(&svEmpty, sizeof(struct stCrsForm), 1, fpRF);
    }
    return;
}
```

In the above statements, as long as the value of *iRecNum* is less than or equal to 20, the fwrite() writes the empty record to the file.

Essentially, the output statement writes the record stored at the structure variable (*svEmpty*) to the course file. The size of the record is determined by the *sizeof* operator, which returns the number of bytes associated with *svEmpty*. The third argument specifies that one record is written to the file, and the file pointer (*fpRF*) indicates where to write the record.

Notes and Tips

1. Random file organization provides fast and efficient processing for applications that require access to a small number of records at a time. Records may be written or retrieved in any order.
2. A random file is created by opening it in *write plus* mode.
3. Use the file pointer *fpRF* when creating a random file. The file pointer reminds you that the program is processing (writing to or reading from) a random file.
4. Append the prefix *rd* to the random file name to remind you that the identifier represents a random file.
5. Append the prefix *st* to structure tags and the prefix *sv* to structure variables.
6. Terminate the *structure* and *structure variable* declarations with a semicolon (;).

Tutorial CHAP14A

1. The objectives of this tutorial are to
   • create a random access file
   • initialize the record in the file
2. Read the program specifications and logic design tools given for sample program CHAP14A.
3. Log on to your C editor, and enter the source code as shown in Figure 14.3. Save the programs on your work disk as CHAP14A. Save frequently as you enter the code.
4. Compile, run, and debug your programs. When completed, show your work to your instructor.

Quick Quiz

Answer the following questions.

1. For sample program CHAP14A, what is the name of the structure?

2. List the members of the structure, and explain how the members are related to the structure.

3. Explain the relationship that exists between a structure and its structure variable.

4. What input/output activities does the *write plus* (*w+*) mode permit?

5. In detail, discuss what the following statement does.
   ```
   fwrite(&svEmpty, sizeof(struct stCrsForm), 1, fpRF);
   ```

6. Did you have any problems or errors when you ran the sample programs? If so, what were they and what did you do to correct them?

Moving the File Pointer: The fseek() Function

Format:

```
fseek(fileptr, offset, origin);
```

Header File: stdio.h

Purpose: To move the file position pointer. The fseek() function is used to position the file pointer to a specific location in a random file prior to executing a read or write operation. The statement consists of three arguments that specify the file position pointer, the data offset, and the starting point.

The file position pointer *(fileptr)* refers to the file specified in the fopen(). The **offset** may be a constant, a variable, or an expression that specifies the number of bytes from the starting point. By specifying a plus or minus offset, we may move the file position pointer forward or backward in the file. The **origin** is the starting point in the file. The origin values are shown in Table 14.2.

Examples:

1. `fseek(fpRF, 0, SEEK_SET);`

2. `fseek(fpRF, 17, SEEK_CUR);`

3. `fseek(fpRF, -17, SEEK_CUR);`

4. `fseek(fpRF, 0, SEEK_END);`

TABLE 14.2   Origin Values

Origin	Meaning
SEEK_SET	Seek from the beginning of the file
SEEK_CUR	Seek from the current position
SEEK_END	Seek from the end of the file

The first example sets the file pointer to the beginning of the file. Examples 2 and 3 set the file pointer forward 17 bytes and backward 17 bytes, respectively, from the current position in the file. The last example sets the file pointer to the end of the file.

Writing Data to a Random File

Sample program CHAP14A created a random file of 20 empty records. Now we are ready to load the file with live data. Since we are using random file organization, we may load the data in any order we wish.

Loading a random file involves the following tasks:

1. Declare the file pointer.
2. Define the data structure and the structure variable.
3. Open the file in *read (r+)* mode.
4. Prompt and enter the data.
5. Assign the input to the structure variable.
6. Set the file pointer, and write the data to the file.
7. Close the file.

The load process is illustrated in sample program CHAP14B. Pay close attention to how fseek() and fwrite() are used to set the file pointer and write the input data to the file.

Checkpoint 14C

1. Explain the purpose of the fseek() statement.
2. Identify the arguments that appear in the fseek() statement. Briefly explain each.
3. True or false: It is possible to move the file pointer forward in a file but not backward.
4. Identify the meaning of each origin.
   a. SEEK_SET
   b. SEEK_END
   c. SEEK_CUR
5. List seven tasks involved in writing data to a random access file.

Sample Program CHAP14B

Sample program CHAP14B prompts the user to enter the data at the keyboard and loads the input into the course file. See Figure 14.5 for the hierarchy chart and Figure 14.6 for the program flowchart. Sample program CHAP14B is presented in Figure 14.7, and the data entry screen is shown in Figure 14.8.

The following specifications apply:

Input (disk file and keyboard):

Disk file: Random access file (rdCrs.fil)

Keyboard: For each course record, prompt for and enter the following data. (Field size and type are shown in parentheses.)

Call number	(3 int)
Course ID	(15 char)
Student enrollment	(2 int)

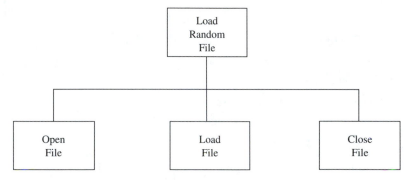

FIGURE 14.5   Hierarchy Chart for CHAP14B

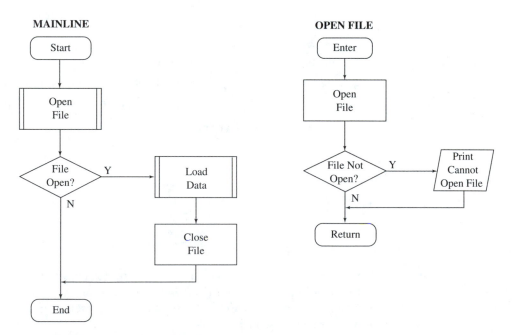

FIGURE 14.6   Program Flowchart for CHAP14B

LOAD DATA

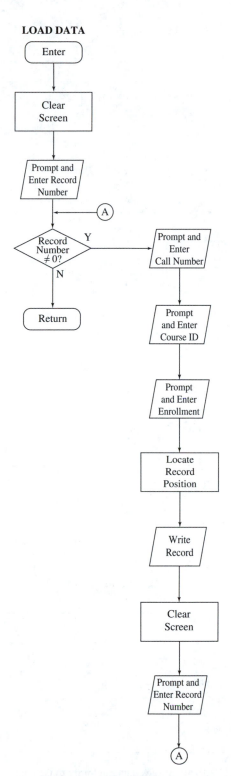

FIGURE 14.6 *Continued*

567

```
/*-----------------------------------------------------------------
LOAD RANDOM FILE: Accept keyboard input and load the data into the
ramdom file.

Program:    CHAP14B.C
Author:     David M. Collopy
Date:       mm/dd/yy
Project:    Sample program


******************************************************************/

/*---- PREPROCESSING DIRECTIVES --------------------------------*/

#include <stdio.h>
#include <graph.h>


/*---- FUNCTION PROTOTYPES --------------------------------------*/

void  OpenFile(void);               /* open random file   */
void  LoadFile(void);               /* load random file   */


/*---- PROGRAM SETUP --------------------------------------------*/

/*>  C O U R S E   R E C O R D                              <*/

FILE *fpRF;                         /* file pointer to random file */

struct stCrsForm
{
    int  iCallNum;                  /* call number        */
    char sCourse[15];               /* course ID          */
    int  iEnroll;                   /* student enrollment */
};

struct stCrsForm svRec;             /* course record      */

/*-----------------------------------------------------------------
      MAINLINE CONTROL
-------------------------------------------------------------*/
main()
{
    OpenFile();
    if (fpRF != 0)
    {
        LoadFile();
```

FIGURE 14.7   Sample Program CHAP14B: Writes data randomly to the course file

```
          fclose(fpRF);
      }
      return 0;
}


/*----------------------------------------------------------------
       OPEN RANDOM FILE
----------------------------------------------------------------*/
void OpenFile(void)
{
    fpRF = fopen("a:rdCrs.fil", "r+");
    if (fpRF == 0)
    {
        printf("\nCannot open random file\n");
    }
    return;
}


/*----------------------------------------------------------------
       LOAD RANDOM FILE
----------------------------------------------------------------*/
void LoadFile(void)
{
    int iRecNum;                   /* record number */

    _clearscreen(0);
    printf("\nEnter Record# 1-20 or '0' to Quit: ");
    scanf(" %d", &iRecNum);
    while (iRecNum != 0)
    {
        printf("                  Enter call number: ");
        scanf(" %d", &svRec.iCallNum);
        printf("                    Enter course ID: ");
        scanf(" %s", svRec.sCourse);
        printf("           Enter student enrollment: ");
        scanf(" %d", &svRec.iEnroll);
        fseek(fpRF, (iRecNum - 1) * sizeof(struct stCrsForm),
            SEEK_SET);
        fwrite(&svRec, sizeof(struct stCrsForm), 1, fpRF);
        _clearscreen(0);
        printf("\nEnter Record# 1-20 or '0' to Quit: ");
        scanf(" %d", &iRecNum);
    }
```

FIGURE 14.7 *Continued*

```
Enter Record# 1 - 20 or '0' to Quit:  ──
                    Enter call number:  ──
                      Enter course ID:  ──
               Enter course enrollment:  ──
```

FIGURE 14.8   Data Entry Screen for CHAP14B

```
Rec#      Call#      Dept-Course#      Enrollment

  1        400          ENG200            16
  2        300          CHEM201           21
  3        600          MGT330            29
  4        200          BIOL101           19
  5          0                             0
  6        500          HIST225           33
  7        900          SPAN111           12
  8        700          MATH120           14
  9        800          PHYS251           20
 10        100          ACCT101           24
                   . . . . .

 20          0                             0
```

FIGURE 14.9   File Output for CHAP14B

Output (rdCrs.fil):
The random access file is shown in Figure 14.9.

Processing Requirements:

- Open the file in *read (r+)* mode.
- Prompt for and enter the data.
- Assign the input to the structure variable.
- Write the structure variable (record) to the file.
- Close the file.

Pseudocode:

```
START: Main
Call Open File
IF file opened
      Call Load Random File
      Close file
END IF
```

```
END

ENTER: Open File
Open random file for read+
IF file not opened
     Print cannot open random file
END IF
RETURN

ENTER: Load Random File
Clear screen
Prompt and enter record number (or 0 to quit)
LOOP while record number not = 0
     Prompt and enter call number
     Prompt and enter course ID
     Prompt and enter student enrollment
     Seek record position
     Write record to the file
     Clear screen
     Prompt and enter record number (or 0 to quit)
END LOOP
RETURN
```

Hierarchy Chart: See Figure 14.5.

Program Flowchart: See Figure 14.6.

Dissection of Sample Program CHAP14B

First, the random file pointer, the course data structure, and the structure variable (record) are defined.

Second, the *MAINLINE* clears the screen and sends control to the module that opens the random file. If the file is opened, the program proceeds to load the input data to the file. But if the file cannot be opened, the program prints an error message and stops the run.

```
L O A D    R A N D O M    F I L E:

void LoadFile(void)
{
    int iRecNum;

    _clearscreen(0);
    printf("\nEnter Record# 1 - 20 or '0' to Quit: ");
    scanf(" %d", &iRecNum);
```

The above statements declare the local variable *iRecNum* and clear the screen, prompt the user to enter a record number 1 through 20 (or 0 to quit), read the record number, convert it to an integer, and assign the result to *iRecNum*.

```
    while (iRecNum != 0)
    {
```

In the above statement, as long as the value of *iRecNum* is not equal to 0, control executes the statements in the body of the loop. Otherwise, control returns to the *MAINLINE*.

```
printf("                    Enter call number: ");
scanf(" %d", &svRec.iCallNum);
printf("                    Enter course ID: ");
scanf(" %s", svRec.sCourse);
printf("              Enter student enrollment: ");
scanf(" %d", &svRec.iEnroll);
```

The above statements prompt the user to enter the course data and assign the input to the structure variable. The printf() prompts for the input, and the scanf() assigns the data to the course record.

```
fseek(fpRF, (iRecNum - 1) * sizeof(struct stCrsForm),
      SEEK_SET);
```

The above statement moves the file position pointer to the position that is offset from the beginning of the file. For example, if the user enters 2 for *iRecNum* and the sizeof operator returns a 23, then, according to the calculation given below, the offset is 23 bytes.

```
(iRecNum - 1) * sizeof(struct stCrsForm) = (2 - 1) * 23 = 23
```

In other words, fseek() moves the file position pointer forward 23 bytes from the beginning of the file. This location represents the address to the second record position in the file.

Notice that 1 was subtracted from *iRecNum*. This causes the file position pointer to move to the beginning of the second record.

```
fwrite(&svRec, sizeof(struct stCrsForm), 1, fpRF);
```

The above statement writes the record stored at the structure variable (*svRec*) to the file. The size of the record is determined by the *sizeof* operator, which returns the number of bytes associated with *svRec*. The third argument specifies that one record is written to the file, and the file pointer (*fpRF*) indicates where to write the record.

```
    _clearscreen(0);
    printf("\nEnter Record# 1 - 20 or '0' to Quit: ");
    scanf(" %d", &iRecNum);
    }
  return;
}
```

The above statements clear the screen and prompt the user to enter a record number 1 through 20 to continue or 0 to quit, read the input, convert it to an integer, and assign the result to *iRecNum*.

Notes and Tips

1. Because the course file has already been created, it is opened in *read plus* mode.

2. Use the *fseek()* function to move the file pointer in a random file. Once a record position has been established, you can write a record to the file. Hence, the procedure is to move the file pointer and write the record.

3. Note that the sample program is using *stCrsForm* for the structure and *svRec* for the structure variable.

4. When referencing a given member of the structure, use the *dot* operator to append the structure variable to the member name.

Tutorial CHAP14B

1. The objectives of this tutorial are to
   - open a random file
   - load course data into a random file

2. Read and study the program specifications and the logic tools given for sample program CHAP14B.

3. Log on to your C editor, and enter the source code as shown in Figure 14.7. Save the program on your work disk as CHAP14B. Save frequently.

4. Compile, run, and debug your program until the input is loaded into the file.

5. When completed, show your work to your instructor.

Quick Quiz

Answer the following questions.

1. Look at the first scanf() statement coded inside the body of the *while* loop. Why is the structure variable appended (using the *dot* operator) to the *iCallNum* member of the *stCrsForm* structure?

2. Discuss the relationship of the fseek() to that of the fwrite().

3. Is it necessary to include the record number in the fseek() statement? Explain your answer.

4. Did you have any problems or errors when you ran the sample program? If so, what were they and what did you do to correct them?

Reading a Record: The fread() Function

Format:

```
fread(&recordptr, size, number, fileptr);
```

Header File: stdio.h

Purpose: To read data from a random file. The fread() function consists of four arguments that specify the record pointer, the record length, the number of records to read, and the file pointer.

The *recordptr* specifies the address where the incoming data should be put, and *size* indicates the length of the record. The *number* argument indicates how many records to read, and *fileptr* specifies the address from which to get the data.

Examples:

1. `fread(&svItem, 35, 1, fpItemMast);`
2. `fread(&svRecord, sizeof(struct stCrsForm), 1, fpFile);`

Example 1 reads 35 bytes of data from the *fpItemMast* file and stores it at the address specified by *svItem*. The number argument indicates that one record is written to the file. Example 2 reads one record from the file, the size of which is determined by the *sizeof* operator, and stores the data in the structure variable called *svRecord*.

Reading and Printing a Random File

The random course file created in sample program CHAP14B was stored on disk. Since the data was written directly to the disk, we have no way of knowing for sure what was actually placed in the file. Hence, it would be wise to look at the file and verify that the data was correctly written to the disk.

Reading and printing a random access file involves the following tasks:

1. Declare the file pointer.
2. Define the data structure and the structure variable.
3. Open the file in *read (r+)* mode.
4. Read a record, and assign the data to the structure variable.
5. Display the record on the screen.
6. Close the file.

This process is illustrated in sample program CHAP14C. The program uses the fread() to read the course file and prints a copy of the records to a report.

Checkpoint 14D

1. Explain the purpose of the fread() statement.
2. Identify the four arguments used in the fread() statement and explain each.
3. Explain how this statement works:
   `fread(&svInv, sizeof(struct stInvForm, 1, fpRF);`
4. Define the account data structure and the members given below. (Field size and type are shown in parentheses.)

Account number	(4 int)
Customer name	(15 char)
Days overdue	(2 int)
Balance due	(6.2 float)

5. Using the statements coded in Question 4, code the module to read and print the contents of the overdue account file. Assume the file contains a maximum of 20 records and the file pointer was defined as `FILE *fpRF;`.

Sample Program CHAP14C

Sample program CHAP14C reads and prints a copy of the random file created in sample program CHAP14B. Each record is read from the disk and written to an output report. See Figure 14.10 for the hierarchy chart and Figure 14.11 for the program flowchart. Sample program CHAP14C is presented in Figure 14.12, and the report output is shown in Figure 14.13. The following specifications apply:

Input (rdCrs.fil):
For each course record, read the following data from the random file. (Field size and type are shown in parentheses.)

Call number	(3 int)
Course ID	(15 char)
Student enrollment	(2 int)

Output (screen):
The output is shown in Figure 14.13.

Processing Requirements:

- Open the file in *read (r+)* mode.
- Read a record into the structure variable.
- Write the nonempty records to the report.
- Close the file.

Pseudocode:

```
START: Main
Clear screen
Call Open File
IF file opened
      Call Read and Print Random File
      Close file
END IF
END

ENTER: Open File
Open random file for read
IF file not opened
      Print cannot open random file
END IF
RETURN

ENTER: Read and Print Random File
Print 2 heading lines
LOOP for record number 1 to 20
      Seek record position
      Read record
      IF call number not = 0
```

                    Print detail line:
                            record number
                            call number
                            course ID
                            student enrollment
            END IF
            END LOOP
            RETURN

Hierarchy Chart: See Figure 14.10.

Program Flowchart: See Figure 14.11.

Dissection of Sample Program CHAP14C

Since the *PROGRAM SETUP*, *MAINLINE*, and *OPEN COURSE FILE* modules are similar to those shown for sample program CHAP14B, we will skip them and begin the dissection with the *READ AND PRINT RANDOM FILE* module.

```
R E A D    A N D    P R I N T    R A N D O M    F I L E:

void ReadFile(void)
{
    printf("\nRec# Call#  Course ID  Enrollment");
    printf("\n--------------------------------");
```

The above statements print the report heading lines.

```
    for (iRecNum = 1; iRecNum <= 20; iRecNum++)
    {
```

In the above statement, as long as the current value of *iRecNum* is less than or equal to 20, control executes the statement body of the *for* loop.

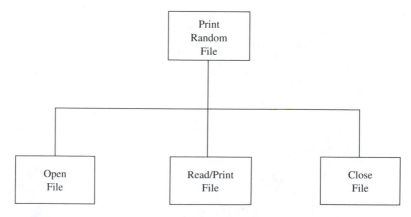

FIGURE 14.10   Hierarchy Chart for CHAP14C

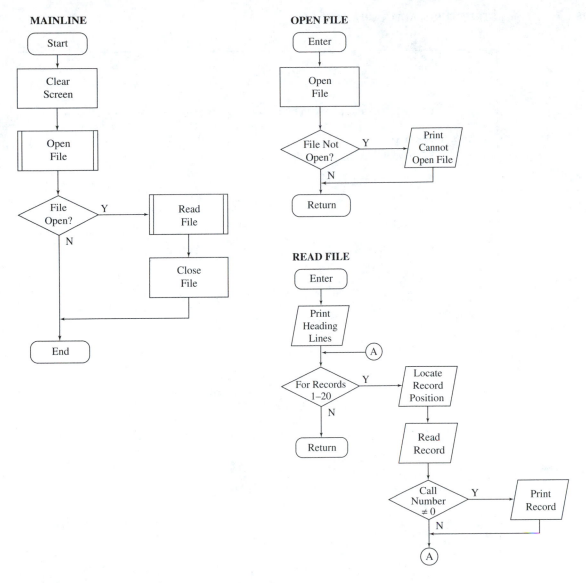

FIGURE 14.11 Program Flowchart for CHAP14C

```
/*-----------------------------------------------------------------
READ RANDOM FILE: Read and print the data stored in the ramdom file.

Program:    CHAP14C.C
Author:     David M. Collopy
Date:       mm/dd/yy
```

FIGURE 14.12 Sample Program CHAP14C: This program reads a random file and copies the course records to the output report.

```
    Project:   Sample program
    **************************************************************/

    /*---- PREPROCESSING DIRECTIVES ---------------------------------*/

    #include <stdio.h>
    #include <graph.h>

    /*---- FUNCTION PROTOTYPES ---------------------------------------*/

    void  OpenFile(void);           /* open random file   */
    void  ReadFile(void);           /* read and print file */

    /*---- PROGRAM SETUP --------------------------------------------*/

    /*> C O U R S E   R E C O R D                             <*/

    FILE *fpRF;                     /* file pointer to random file */

    struct stCrsForm
    {
        int  iCallNum;              /* call number         */
        char sCourse[15];           /* course ID           */
        int  iEnroll;               /* student enrollment */
    };

    struct stCrsForm svRec;         /* course record       */

    /*---------------------------------------------------------------
           MAINLINE CONTROL
    ----------------------------------------------------------------*/
    main()
    {
        system("cls");
        OpenFile();
        if (fpRF != 0)
        {
            ReadFile();
            fclose(fpRF);
        }
        return 0;
    }

    /*---------------------------------------------------------------
           OPEN RANDOM FILE
    ----------------------------------------------------------------*/
    void OpenFile(void)
    {
```

FIGURE 14.12 *Continued*

```
        fpRF = fopen("a:rdCrs.fil", "r+");
        if (fpRF == 0)
        {
            printf("\nCannot open random file\n");
        }
        return;
    }


/*-----------------------------------------------------------------
        READ AND PRINT RANDOM FILE
------------------------------------------------------------------*/
void ReadFile(void)
{
    int iRecNum;                        /* record number */

    printf("\nRec# Call#  Course ID  Enrollment");
    printf("\n-------------------------------");
    for (iRecNum = 1; iRecNum <= 20; iRecNum++)
    {
        fseek(fpRF, (iRecNum - 1) * sizeof(struct stCrsForm),
            SEEK_SET);
        fread(&svRec, sizeof(struct stCrsForm), 1, fpRF);
        if (svRec.iCallNum != 0)
        {
            printf("\n %2d    %3d   %-14s %2d", iRecNum,
                svRec.iCallNum, svRec.sCourse, svRec.iEnroll);
        }
    }
    return;
}
```

FIGURE 14.12 *Continued*

```
Rec# Call#   Dept-Course#  Enrollment
-------------------------------------
  1   400    ENG200           16
  2   300    CHEM201          21
  3   600    MGT330           29
  4   200    BIOL101          19
  6   500    HIST225          33
  7   900    SPAN111          12
  8   700    MATH120          14
  9   800    PHYS251          20
 10   100    ACCT101          24
```

FIGURE 14.13 File Output for CHAP14C: Notice that record numbers 5 and 11–20 are not on the report.

```
fseek(fpRF, (iRecNum - 1) * sizeof(struct stCrsForm),
    SEEK_SET);
```

The above statement moves the file position pointer to the position that is offset from the beginning of the file. For *iRecNum* = 1, fseek() moves the file position pointer to the first record position in the file; for *iRecNum* = 2, fseek() moves the file position pointer to the second record position in the file; and so on.

```
fread(&svRec, sizeof(struct stCrsForm), 1, fpRF);
```

The above statement reads a record from the file referenced by the file pointer and stores the data in the *svRec* structure variable. The record size is determined by the *sizeof* operator. The third argument indicates that one record is read from the file.

```
if (svRec.iCallNum != 0)
{
    printf("\n %2d    %3d    %-14s    %2d", iRecNum,
        svRec.iCallNum, svRec.sCourse, svRec.iEnroll);
}
```

In the above statements, if the value of the call number is not equal to 0, then the printf() prints the record on the report. Any value other than 0 indicates that data is stored in the record.

```
    }
    return;
}
```

After processing the body of the *for* loop, control returns to the *MAINLINE*.

Notes and Tips

1. The purpose of reading and printing the nonempty records to a report is to verify that the file was correctly stored on disk.
2. Use the *fseek()* function to move the file pointer in a random file. Once a record position has been established, use *fread()* to retrieve a record from the file. Now the procedure is to move the file pointer and read the record.

Tutorial CHAP14C

1. The objectives of this tutorial are to
   • open and read a random file
   • write the nonempty records to a report
2. Read the program specifications and review the logic design tools shown for sample program CHAP14C.
3. Log on to your C editor, and enter the source code as given in Figure 14.12. Save the program on your work disk as CHAP14C. Save frequently.

4. Compile, run, and debug your program until the output matches the report shown in Figure 14.13.

5. When completed, show your work to your instructor.

Quick Quiz

Answer the following questions.

1. If you ran your program and the message *"Cannot open random file"* appeared on the screen, what would you do to correct the problem?

2. Why is there an *if* statement coded inside the *for* loop?

3. For a random file, what is a nonempty record?

4. Suppose you had a random file with 200 records, but only 15 had data stored in them. If you printed all the records, what would the output report look like?

5. Did you have any problems or errors when you ran the sample program? If so, what were they and what did you do to correct them?

Updating a Random File

As the enrollment changes, so must the data stored in the course file. From Chapter 13, we know that file updating refers to the process of changing the data stored in a file. From time to time, new courses are added, old courses are deleted, and changes are made to the current courses. The following sample program allows the user to modify the contents of the course file and to maintain the integrity of the data stored there.

Updating a random access file involves the following tasks:

1. Declare the file pointer.

2. Define the data structure and the structure variable.

3. Open the file in *read (r+)* mode.

4. Prompt the user to select the update option (menu).

5. Enter the data and update the file.

6. Close the file.

The update process is illustrated in sample program CHAP14D. The menu-driven program instructs the user to select from a series of available file updating options.

Sample Program CHAP14D

Sample program CHAP14D is menu driven. It accepts data from the keyboard, checks for errors, and updates the course file. See Figure 14.14 for the hierarchy chart and Figure 14.15 for the program flowchart. Sample program CHAP14D is presented in Figure 14.16. The selection menu is shown in Figure 14.17, and the data entry screens are shown in Figures 14.18, 14.19, and 14.20.

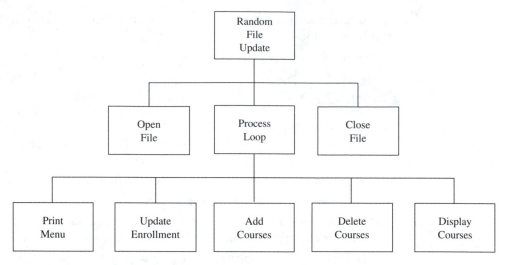

FIGURE 14.14   Hierarchy Chart for CHAP14D

The following specifications apply:

Menu Choices:

1. Update enrollment
2. Add courses
3. Delete courses
4. Display all courses
5. Quit

Input (disk file and keyboard):

Disk file: Random access file (rdCrs.fil)

Keyboard: For options 1–3, prompt for and enter the following data:

Option	Input Data
1	Record number and enrollment count
2	Record number, call number, course ID, and student enrollment
3	Record number

Output (rdCrs.fil):
The updated random file is shown in Figure 14.21.

Processing Requirements:

- Open the file in *read (r+)* mode.
- Display the menu options, and prompt for a selection.
- Perform the processing specified by the option selected. Enter the data transaction, and update the file as needed.
- Close the file.

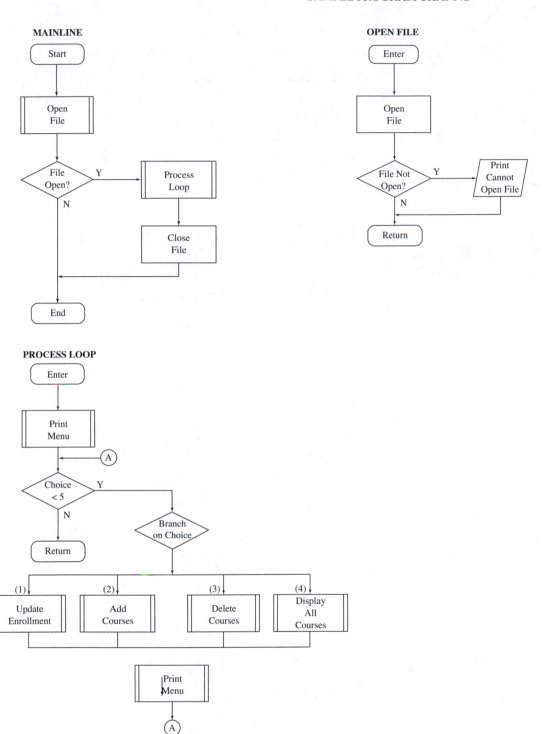

FIGURE 14.15   Program Flowchart for CHAP14D

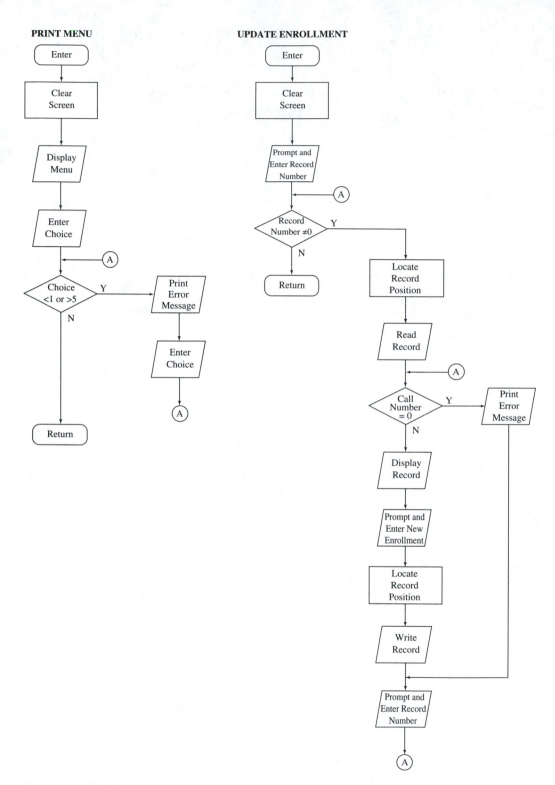

FIGURE 14.15   *Continued*

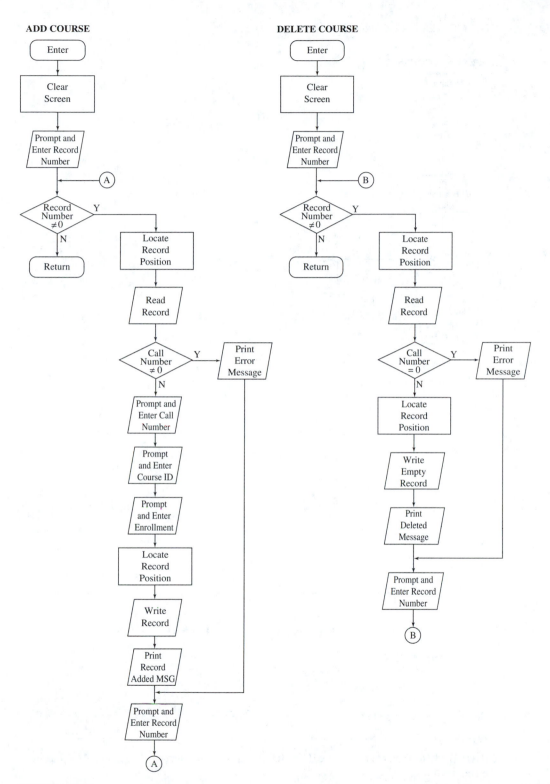

FIGURE 14.15 *Continued*

DISPLAY ALL COURSES

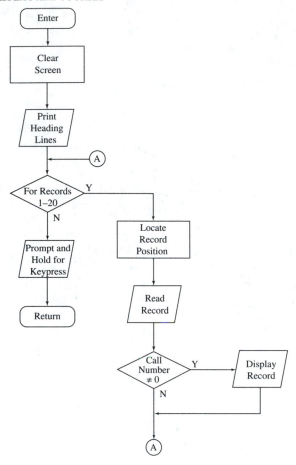

FIGURE 14.15   *Continued*

```
/*---------------------------------------------------------------
UPDATE RANDOM FILE: Randomly access and update the course file.

Program:    CHAP14D.C
Author:     David M. Collopy
Date:       mm/dd/yy
Project:    Sample program
****************************************************************/
```

FIGURE 14.16   Sample Program CHAP14D: Prompts for and accepts data randomly and updates the course file

```
/*---- PREPROCESSING DIRECTIVES ------------------------------*/

#include <stdio.h>
#include <conio.h>
#include <graph.h>

/*---- FUNCTION PROTOTYPES ----------------------------------*/

void  OpenFile(void);           /* open random file    */
void  ProcessLoop(void);        /* processing loop     */
void  UpdEnroll(void);          /* update enrollment   */
void  AddCourses(void);         /* add courses         */
void  DletCourses(void);        /* delete courses      */
void  DisplayAll(void);         /* display all courses */
int   PrnMenu(void);            /* print menu          */

/*---- PROGRAM SETUP ----------------------------------------*/

/*>  C O U R S E   R E C O R D                         <*/

FILE *fpRF;                     /* file pointer to random file */

struct stCrsForm
{
    int  iCallNum;              /* call number        */
    char sCourse[15];           /* course ID          */
    int  iEnroll;               /* student enrollment */
};

struct stCrsForm svRec;
struct stCrsForm svEmpty = {0, "", 0};

/*-----------------------------------------------------------
      MAINLINE CONTROL
-----------------------------------------------------------*/
main()
{
    OpenFile();
    if (fpRF != 0)
    {
        ProcessLoop();
        fclose(fpRF);
    }
    return 0;
}
```

FIGURE 14.16 *Continued*

```c
/*---------------------------------------------------------------
        OPEN RANDOM FILE
-----------------------------------------------------------------*/
void OpenFile(void)
{
    fpRF = fopen("a:rdCrs.fil", "r+");
    if (fpRF == 0)
    {
        printf("\nCannot open random file\n");
    }
    return;
}


/*---------------------------------------------------------------
        PROCESSING LOOP
-----------------------------------------------------------------*/
void ProcessLoop(void)
{
    int iChoice;

    iChoice = PrnMenu();        /* display menu          */
    while (iChoice < 5)
    {
        switch (iChoice)
        {
            case 1:
                UpdEnroll();    /* update enrollment     */
                break;
            case 2:
                AddCourses();   /* add courses           */
                break;
            case 3:
                DletCourses();  /* delete courses        */
                break;
            default:
                DisplayAll();   /* display all courses   */
                break;
        }
        iChoice = PrnMenu();    /* display menu          */
    }
    return;
}


/*---------------------------------------------------------------
        PRINT MENU
-----------------------------------------------------------------*/
```

FIGURE 14.16 *Continued*

```
int PrnMenu(void)
{
    int iChoice;                  /* user choice */

    _clearscreen(0);
    printf("\nCourse Maintenance System\n");
    printf("\nSelect one:\n\n");
    printf("     1.   Update enrollment\n");
    printf("     2.   Add courses\n");
    printf("     3.   Delete courses\n");
    printf("     4.   Display all courses\n");
    printf("     5.   Quit\n");
    printf("\nEnter choice (1 - 5) ===> ");
    scanf(" %d", &iChoice);
    while (iChoice < 1 || iChoice > 5)
    {
        printf("\nERROR...re-enter choice (1 - 5) ===> ");
        scanf(" %d", &iChoice);
    }
    return iChoice;
}


/*-------------------------------------------------------------
        UPDATE ENROLLMENT
-------------------------------------------------------------*/
void UpdEnroll(void)
{
    int iRecNum;

    _clearscreen(0);
    printf("\nUPDATE ENROLLMENT: Enter Rec# 1-20");
    printf(" or 0 to Quit: ");
    scanf(" %d", &iRecNum);
    while (iRecNum != 0)
    {
        fseek(fpRF, (iRecNum - 1) * sizeof(struct stCrsForm),
            SEEK_SET);
        fread(&svRec, sizeof(struct stCrsForm), 1, fpRF);
        if (svRec.iCallNum == 0)
        {
            printf("\nError: Record does not exist\n");
        }
        else
        {
            printf("\n%2d    %3d    %-14s    %2d\n",
```

FIGURE 14.16 *Continued*

```
                    iRecNum, svRec.iCallNum, svRec.sCourse,
                    svRec.iEnroll);
                printf("\nEnter new enrollment: ");
                scanf(" %d", &svRec.iEnroll);
                fseek(fpRF, (iRecNum - 1) * sizeof(struct stCrsForm),
                    SEEK_SET);
                fwrite(&svRec, sizeof(struct stCrsForm), 1, fpRF);
            }
            printf("\nUPDATE ENROLLMENT: Enter Rec# 1-20");
            printf(" or 0 to Quit: ");
            scanf(" %d", &iRecNum);
        }
        return;
    }


    /*---------------------------------------------------------------
          ADD COURSES
    -----------------------------------------------------------*/
    void AddCourses(void)
    {
        int iRecNum;

        _clearscreen(0);
        printf("\nADD COURSE: Enter Rec# 1-20");
        printf(" or 0 to Quit: ");
        scanf(" %d", &iRecNum);
        while (iRecNum != 0)
        {
            fseek(fpRF, (iRecNum - 1) * sizeof(struct stCrsForm),
                SEEK_SET);
            fread(&svRec, sizeof(struct stCrsForm), 1, fpRF);
            if (svRec.iCallNum != 0)
            {
                printf("\nError: Record already exists\n");
            }
            else
            {
                printf("        Enter call number: ");
                scanf(" %d", &svRec.iCallNum);
                printf("          Enter course ID: ");
                scanf(" %s", svRec.sCourse);
                printf("Enter student enrollment: ");
                scanf(" %d", &svRec.iEnroll);
                fseek(fpRF, (iRecNum - 1) * sizeof(struct stCrsForm),
                    SEEK_SET);
```

FIGURE 14.16   *Continued*

```
                    fwrite(&svRec, sizeof(struct stCrsForm), 1, fpRF);
                    printf("\nRecord# %d added to the course file\n",
                        iRecNum);
            }
        printf("\nADD COURSE: Enter Rec# 1-20");
        printf(" or 0 to Quit: ");
        scanf(" %d", &iRecNum);
    }
    return;
}


/*-----------------------------------------------------------------
      DELETE COURSES
-----------------------------------------------------------------*/
void DletCourses(void)
{
    int iRecNum;

    _clearscreen(0);
    printf("\nDELETE COURSE: Enter Rec# 1-20");
    printf(" or 0 to Quit: ");
    scanf(" %d", &iRecNum);
    while (iRecNum != 0)
    {
        fseek(fpRF, (iRecNum - 1) * sizeof(struct stCrsForm),
            SEEK_SET);
        fread(&svRec, sizeof(struct stCrsForm), 1, fpRF);
        if (svRec.iCallNum == 0)
        {
            printf("\nError: Record does not exist\n");
        }
        else
        {
            fseek(fpRF, (iRecNum - 1) * sizeof(struct stCrsForm),
                SEEK_SET);
            fwrite(&svEmpty, sizeof(struct stCrsForm), 1, fpRF);
            printf("\nRecord# %d deleted from the course file\n",
                iRecNum);
        }
        printf("\nDELETE COURSE: Enter Rec# 1-20");
        printf(" or 0 to Quit: ");
        scanf(" %d", &iRecNum);
    }
    return;
}
```

FIGURE 14.16 *Continued*

```
/*------------------------------------------------------------------
        DISPLAY ALL COURSES
----------------------------------------------------------------*/
void DisplayAll(void)
{
    int  iRecNum;               /* record number    */
    char cWait;                 /* wait for keypress */

    _clearscreen(0);
    printf("\nRec# Call#  Course ID  Enrollment");
    printf("\n--------------------------------");
    for (iRecNum = 1; iRecNum <= 20; iRecNum++)
    {
        fseek(fpRF, (iRecNum - 1) * sizeof(struct stCrsForm),
            SEEK_SET);
        fread(&svRec, sizeof(struct sCrsForm), 1, fpRF);
        if (svRec.iCallNum != 0)
        {
            printf("\n %2d    %3d    %-14s %2d",
                iRecNum, svRec.iCallNum, svRec.sCourse,
                svRec.iEnroll);
        }
    }
    printf("\n\nPress ENTER to continue...");
    cWait = getch();
    return;
}
```

FIGURE 14.16 *Continued*

```
Course Maintenance System

Select one:

    1.  Update enrollment
    2.  Add courses
    3.  Delete courses
    4.  Display all courses
    5.  Quit

Enter choice (1 - 5) ===>____
```

FIGURE 14.17 Menu Options for CHAP14D

```
UPDATE ENROLLMENT: Enter Rec# 1 - 20 or 0 to quit: 12

Error: Record does not exist

UPDATE ENROLLMENT: Enter Rec# 1 - 20 or 0 to quit: 8

8    700    MATH120                14

Enter change in enrollment: 21

UPDATE ENROLLMENT: Enter Rec# 1 - 20 or 0 to quit: 0
```

FIGURE 14.18   Choice 1: Update Enrollment

```
ADD COURSE: Enter Rec# 1 - 20 or 0 to quit: 3

Error: Record already exists

ADD COURSE: Enter Rec# 1 - 20 or 0 to quit: 5
            Enter call number: 650
             Enter department: MKT310
             Enter enrollment: 15

Record# 5 added to the course file

ADD COURSE: Enter Rec# 1 - 20 or 0 to quit: 0
```

FIGURE 14.19   Choice 2: Add Courses

```
DELETE COURSE: Enter Rec# 1 - 20 or 0 to quit: 14

Error: Record does not exist

DELETE COURSE: Enter Rec# 1 - 20 or 0 to quit: 7

Record# 7 deleted from the course file

DELETE COURSE: Enter Rec# 1 - 20 or 0 to quit: 0
```

FIGURE 14.20   Choice 3: Delete Courses

```
Rec# Call#  Dept-Course#  Enrollment
------------------------------------
  1    400    ENG200          16
  2    300    CHEM201         21
  3    600    MGT330          29
  4    200    BIOL101         19
  5    650    MKT310          15
  6    500    HIST225         33
  8    700    MATH120         21
  9    800    PHYS251         20
 10    100    ACCT101         24
```

FIGURE 14.21   Choice 4: Display All Courses

Pseudocode:

START: Main
Call Open File
IF file opened
    Call Processing Loop
    Close file
END IF
END

ENTER: Open File
Open random file for read plus
IF file not opened
    Print cannot open random file
END IF
RETURN

ENTER: Processing Loop
Call Print Menu
LOOP while choice < 5
    BRANCH on choice:
        1: Call Update Enrollment
        2: Call Add Courses
        3: Call Delete Courses
        4: Call Display All Courses
    END BRANCH
    Call Print Menu
END LOOP
RETURN

ENTER: Print Menu
Clear screen
Print 1 title line

Print 1 heading line
Display processing choices:
     choice 1: Update enrollment
     choice 2: Add courses
     choice 3: Delete courses
     choice 4: Display all courses
     choice 5: Quit
Prompt and enter choice
LOOP while choice not = 1 to 5
     Prompt (error message) and reenter choice
END LOOP
RETURN

ENTER: Update Enrollment
Clear screen
Prompt and enter record number (or 0 to quit)
LOOP while record number not = 0
    Seek record position
    Read record
    IF call number = 0
       Print error message: RECORD DOES NOT EXIST
    else
       Display record
       Prompt and enter new enrollment
       Seek record position
       Write record
    END IF
    Prompt and enter record number (or 0 to quit)
END LOOP
RETURN

ENTER: Add Courses
Clear screen
Prompt and enter record number (or 0 to quit)
LOOP while record number not = 0
    Seek record position
    Read record
    IF call number not = 0
       Print error message: RECORD ALREADY EXISTS
    else
       Prompt and enter new record
       Seek record position
       Write record
       Print message record was added to file
    END IF
    Prompt and enter record number (or 0 to quit)
END LOOP
RETURN

ENTER: Delete Courses
Clear screen

```
Prompt and enter record number (or 0 to quit)
LOOP while record number not = 0
    Seek record position
    Read record
    IF call number = 0
        Print error message: RECORD DOES NOT EXIST
    else
        Seek record position
        Write empty record
        Print message record was deleted from file
    END IF
    Prompt and enter record number (or 0 to quit)
END LOOP
RETURN

ENTER: Display All Courses
Clear screen
Print 2 title lines
LOOP for record numbers 1 to 20
    Seek record position
    Read record
    IF call number not = 0
        Print detail line:
            record number
            call number
            course ID
            student enrollment
    END IF
END LOOP
Hold screen
RETURN
```

Hierarchy Chart: See Figure 14.14.

Program Flowchart: See Figure 14.15.

Dissection of Sample Program CHAP14D

```
PROCESSING   LOOP:

void ProcessLoop(void)
{
    int iChoice;

    iChoice = PrintMenu();
    while (iChoice < 5)
    {
        switch (iChoice)
        {
            case 1:
                UpdEnroll();
```

```
              break;
          case 2:
              AddCourses();
              break;
          case 3:
              DletCourses();
              break;
          default:
              DisplayAll();
              break;
        }
        iChoice = PrintMenu();
    }
    return;
}
```

The above module displays the menu and compares the user's choice to the case labels. If a match is found, control branches to the module associated with the matching label. If a match is not found, control skips to the *default* case and returns to the *while* statement.

P R I N T   M E N U:

```
void PrintMenu(void)
{
    int iChoice;

    _clearscreen(0);
    printf("\nCourse Maintenance System\n");
    printf("\nSelect one:\n\n");
    printf("      1.   Update enrollment\n");
    printf("      2.   Add courses\n");
    printf("      3.   Delete courses\n");
    printf("      4.   Display all courses\n");
    printf("      5.   Quit\n");
    printf("\nEnter choice (1 - 5) ===> ");
    scanf(" %d", &iChoice);
```

The above statements display the course maintenance menu on the screen. The menu prompts the user to select either a processing option (1–4) or 5 to quit. The scanf() assigns the selection to *iChoice*.

```
    while (iChoice < 1 || iChoice > 5)
    {
        printf("\nERROR...re-enter choice (1 - 5) ===> ");
        scanf(" %d", &iChoice);
    }
    return iChoice;
}
```

The *while* loop performs a range check to ensure that *iChoice* is valid. If the input is valid, control returns *iChoice* to the *PROCESSING LOOP*. Otherwise, the user is instructed to re-enter a valid selection.

U P D A T E   E N R O L L M E N T:

```
void UpdEnroll(void)
{
    int iRecNum;

    _clearscreen(0);
    printf("\nUPDATE ENROLLMENT: Enter Rec# 1 - 20");
    printf(" or 0 to Quit: ");
    scanf(" %d", &iRecNum);
    while (iRecNum != 0)
    {
        fseek(fpRF, (iRecNum - 1) * sizeof(struct stCrsForm),
            SEEK_SET);
        fread(&svRec, sizeof(struct stCrsForm), 1, fpRF);
        if (svRec.iCallNum == 0)
        {
            printf("\nError: Record does not exist\n");
        }
        else
        {
            printf("\n%2d     %3d    %-14s    %2d\n",
                iRecNum, svRec.iCallNum, svRec.sCourse,
                svRec.iEnroll);
            printf("\nEnter new enrollment: ");
            scanf(" %d", &svRec.iEnroll);
            fseek(fpRF, (iRecNum - 1) * sizeof(struct stCrsForm),
                SEEK_SET);
            fwrite(&svRec, sizeof(struct stCrsForm), 1, fpRF);
        }
        printf("\nUPDATE ENROLLMENT: Enter Rec# 1 - 20");
        printf(" or 0 to Quit: ");
        scanf(" %d", &iRecNum);
    }
    return;
}
```

When *iChoice* is 1, control branches to *UpdEnroll* and prompts the user to enter the number of the record that requires an update. If *iRecNum* is not 0, the program reads the record into the structure variable. If *svRec.iCallNum* is 0, then the record does not exist and the error message is displayed on the screen. Control then prompts the user to enter the next record number or 0 to quit.

If *svRec.iCallNum* is not 0, the program displays the record on the screen and prompts the user to enter the new enrollment. The new enrollment is placed in the record, and the record is written back to the file.

A D D   C O U R S E S:

```
void AddCourses(void)
{
```

```
    int iRecNum;

    _clearscreen(0);
    printf("\nADD COURSE: Enter Rec# 1 - 20");
    printf(" or 0 to Quit: ");
    scanf(" %d", &iRecNum);
    while (iRecNum != 0)
    {
        fseek(fpRF, (iRecNum - 1) * sizeof(struct stCrsForm),
            SEEK_SET);
        fread(&svRec, sizeof(struct stCrsForm), 1, fpRF);
        if (svRec.iCallNum != 0)
        {
            printf("\nError: Record already exists");
        }
        else
        {
            printf("        Enter call number: ");
            scanf(" %d", &svRec.iCallNum);
            printf("          Enter course ID: ");
            scanf(" %s", svRec.sCourse);
            printf("Enter student enrollment: ");
            scanf(" %d", &svRec.iEnroll);
            fseek(fpRF, (iRecNum - 1) * sizeof(struct stCrsForm),
                SEEK_SET);
            fwrite(&svRec, sizeof(struct stCrsForm), 1, fpRF);
            printf("\nRecord# %d added to the course file",
                recNum);
        }
        printf("\n\nADD COURSE: Enter Rec# 1 - 20");
        printf(" or 0 to Quit: ");
        scanf(" %d", &iRecNum);
    }
    return;
}
```

When *iChoice* is 2, control branches to *AddCourses* and prompts the user to enter the record number of the record being added to the file. If *iRecNum* is not 0, the program reads the record into the structure variable. If *svRec.iCallNum* is not 0, then the record already exists and the error message is displayed on the screen. Control then prompts the user to enter the next record number or 0 to quit.

If the call number is 0, the program prompts the user to enter the data for the new record. The input is placed in a record, and the record is written to the file.

D E L E T E   C O U R S E S:

```
void DletCourses(void)
{
    int iRecNum;
```

```
    _clearscreen(0);
    printf("\nDELETE COURSE: Enter Rec# 1 - 20");
    printf(" or 0 to Quit: ");
    scanf(" %d", &iRecNum);
    while (iRecNum != 0)
    {
        fseek(fpRF, (iRecNum - 1) * sizeof(struct stCrsForm),
            SEEK_SET);
        fread(&svRec, sizeof(struct stCrsForm), 1, fpRF);
        if (svRec.iCallNum == 0)
        {
            printf("\nError: Record does not exist");
        }
        else
        {
            fseek(fpRF, (iRecNum - 1) * sizeof(struct stCrsForm),
                SEEK_SET);
            fwrite(&svRec, sizeof(struct stCrsForm), 1, fpRF);
            printf("\nRecord# %d deleted from the course file",
                iRecNum);
        }
        printf("\n\nDELETE COURSE: Enter Rec# 1 - 20");
        printf(" or 0 to Quit: ");
        scanf(" %d", &iRecNum);
    }
    return;
}
```

When *iChoice* is 3, control branches to *DletCourse* and prompts the user to enter the record number of the record being deleted from the file. If *iRecNum* is not 0, the program reads the record into the structure variable. If *svRec.iCallNum* is 0, then the record does not exist and the error message is displayed on the screen. Control then prompts the user to enter the next record number or 0 to quit.

If the call number is not 0, the program writes an empty record back to the file. Hence, a record is deleted from the file by writing an empty record in its place.

D I S P L A Y   A L L   C O U R S E S :

```
void DisplayAll(void)
{
    int   iRecNum;
    char  cWait;

    _clearscreen(0);
    printf("\nRec# Call#  Course ID  Enrollment");
    printf("\n-------------------------------");
    for (iRecNum = 1; iRecNum <= 20; iRecNum++)
    {
        fseek(fpRF, (iRecNum - 1) * sizeof(struct stCrsForm),
```

```
        SEEK_SET);
    fread(&svRec, sizeof(struct stCrsForm), 1, fpRF);
    if (svRec.iCallNum != 0)
    {
        printf("\n %2d    %3d    %-14s %2d",
            iRecNum, svRec.iCallNum, svRec.sCourse,
            svRec.iEnroll);
    }
    }
    printf("\n\nPress RETURN to continue...");
    cWait = getch();
    return;
}
```

When *iChoice* is 4, control defaults to *DisplayAll* and prints a report of all the records stored in the course file. If *svRec.iCallNum* does not equal 0, the program prints the record on the report. Any value other than 0 indicates that data is stored in the record.

After reading and printing the contents of the course file, control returns to the *MAINLINE*.

Notes and Tips

1. Sample program CHAP14D uses a menu to update the master file. Changes to the master file include the following: update student enrollment, add new courses offered, delete courses no longer offered, and print a list of all current courses.

2. Do not add a record to the master file if it already exists.

3. Do not delete or update a record that does not exist.

Tutorial CHAP14D

1. The objectives of this tutorial are to
   - open a random file in *read plus* mode
   - display menu options for the processing activities
   - enter transaction data and update a random file
   - check for errors and display them on the screen

2. Read the program specifications and review the logic design tools for sample program CHAP14D.

3. Log on to your C editor, and enter the source code as shown in Figure 14.16. Save the program on your work disk as CHAP14D. Save frequently as you enter the code.

4. Compile, run, and debug your program.

5. When completed, run sample program CHAP14C and compare your output report to the one shown in Figure 14.21.

6. Show your work to your instructor.

Quick Quiz

Answer the following questions.

1. Why is there a range check coded in the *PrnMenu* module?

2. In your own words, describe the processing activities performed by the *UpdEnroll* module. Under what circumstances does the error message *"Record does not exist"* display on the screen?

3. In your own words, describe the processing activities performed by the *AddCourses* module. Under what circumstances does the error message *"Record already exists"* display on the screen?

4. In your own words, describe the processing activities performed by the *DletCourses* module. Under what circumstances does the error message *"Record does not exist"* display on the screen?

5. Did you have any problems or errors when you ran the sample program? If so, what were they and what did you do to correct them?

Summary

1. Structures are used to group multiple data types. A structure is a group item that is made up of two or more related data types.

2. A structure defines a record and its members; a member defines a field.

3. A structure may be processed as a single unit, or the members may be processed individually.

4. The keyword *struct* defines the format of the data, and *tag* assigns a name to the structure. Member definitions define the names of the members and their data types.

5. A structure variable assigns a memory location to the members of the data structure.

6. Data may be assigned to a structure either at the time the structure is declared or by the program during the run.

7. A structure may be initialized by assigning values to the structure variable. The values are assigned on a positional basis to the members—the first value is assigned the first member, the second value is assigned the second member, and so on.

8. Data may be assigned to a structure variable by prompting the user to enter it at the keyboard.

9. The dot operator links the structure variable to the member of the structure. The structure variable is coded on left of the dot operator, and the member name is coded on the right.

10. Random file organization stores data on disk in random order. Random file access allows the user to skip around in the file.

11. Random file processing offers the advantage of fast data retrieval. For example, if the user wants a specific record from the random file, the program can go directly to the record and retrieve the data.

12. Random access can be rather cumbersome and slow for applications that require access to all or most of the records in a large file, particularly if the records must be processed in sequential order.

13. Use fopen() to open a random file. The random access open modes are write and read *(w+),* read and write *(r+),* and append, read, and write *(a+).*

14. The fwrite() function writes data to a random file. The statement consists of four arguments that specify the record pointer, the record length, the number of records to write, and the file pointer.

15. The *sizeof* operator may be used to determine the number of bytes associated with the structure variable.

16. Creating a random file involves the following steps: (1) declare the file pointer, (2) define the data structure, (3) define and initialize the empty record, (4) open the file in *write (w+)* mode, (5) write empty records to the file, and (6) close the file.

17. The fseek() function is used to move the file pointer to a specific location in a random file prior to executing a read or write operation. The statement consists of three arguments that specify the file pointer, the data offset, and the origin.

18. Loading a random file involves the following steps: (1) declare the file pointer, (2) define the data structure and the structure variable, (3) open the file in *read (r+)* mode, (4) prompt and enter the data, (5) assign the input to the structure variable, (6) set the file pointer and write the data to the file, and (7) close the file.

19. The fread() function reads data from a random file. The statement consists of four arguments that specify the structure variable, the record length, the number of records to read, and the file pointer.

20. Reading and printing a random access file involves the following tasks: (1) declare the file pointer, (2) define the data structure and the structure variable, (3) open the file in *read (r+)* mode, (4) read a record and assign the data to the structure variable, (5) print the record, and (6) close the file.

21. Updating a random access file involves the following tasks: (1) declare the file pointer, (2) define the data structure and the structure variable, (3) open the file in *read (r+)* mode, (4) determine the update type, (5) enter the transaction and update the record, and (6) close the file.

Programming Projects

For each project, design the logic and write the modular structured program to produce the output. Model your program after the sample programs presented in the chapter. Verify your output.

Project 14–1   Overdue Accounts-1

Write a program to create a random access file for the overdue accounts. Write a total of 30 empty records to the file.

Input (internal):

Define the account data structure and the members given below. (Field size and type are shown in parentheses.)

Account number	(4 int)
Customer name	(15 char)
Days overdue	(2 int)
Balance due	(6.2 float)

Output (rdOvrdue.fil):

Initialized random access file

Processing Requirements:

- Define and initialize the empty record.
- Open the file in *write (w+)* mode.
- Write empty records to the file.
- Close the file.

Project 14–2   Overdue Accounts-2

Write a program to prompt the user to enter the data at the keyboard, and load the overdue accounts file created in Project 14–1.

Input (disk file and keyboard):

Disk file: Random access file (rdOvrdue.fil)

Keyboard: For each customer record, prompt for and enter the following data. (Field size and type are shown in parentheses.)

1. Account number   (4 int)

2. Customer name   (15 char)

3. Days overdue   (2 int)

4. Balance due   (6.2 float)

File Data (keyboard):

Use the data given below to load the overdue accounts file. (The numbers shown above the columns correspond to the fields described for the input. The record numbers are shown on the left.)

Rec#	1	2	3	4
20	6350	Susan Cope	90	600.00
11	2730	Rita Fox	90	740.00
5	3100	Alvin Porter	90	550.00
27	4080	Corey Adkins	30	233.00
9	5260	Brian Knox	30	625.00
21	7720	Lisa Wilson	60	417.00
26	9200	Tori Landis	90	235.00
17	4890	Amy Wyatt	30	700.00
14	1010	David Ryan	90	400.00
15	9630	Pat Rankin	60	342.00
28	2450	Marie Hill	30	754.00
3	8540	Matt Hart	90	900.00

Output (overdue.fil):
Random access file

Processing Requirements:

- Open the file in *read (r+)* mode.
- Prompt for and enter the data.
- Assign the input to the structure variable.
- Write the structure variable (record) to the file.
- Close the file.

Project 14–3   Overdue Accounts-3

Write a menu program that allows the user to select from several file updating options. Prompt and enter the data, check for errors, and update the overdue accounts file from Project 14–2. Write the input errors to an error log.

Menu Choices:

1. Update accounts
2. Add accounts
3. Delete accounts
4. Display all accounts
5. Quit

Input (disk file and keyboard):

Disk file: Random access file (rdOvrdue.file)

Keyboard: For options 1–3, prompt for and enter the following data:

Option	Input Data
1	Record number, account number, customer name, days overdue, and amount due
2	Record number, account number, customer name, days overdue, and amount due
3	Record number

File Data (keyboard):
Enter the updates in the random order shown. For each, use the menu option to apply the data to the record specified by the record number.

Menu Option	Record Number	Account Number	Customer Name	Days Overdue	Balance Due
delete	2				
update	17	4890	Amy Clark	30	700.00
add	23	1000	Sarah Brooks	60	220.00
delete	3				
update	14	1010	Ryan Davis	90	400.00
add	11	9630	Pat Rankin	60	342.00
add	7	9700	Adam Norris	60	475.00
update	22	6350	Susan Cope	60	600.00
update	28	2450	Marie Hill	30	700.00
delete	5				

add	9	4080	Corey Adkins	30	233.00
update	11	2730	Rita Fox	30	740.00
update	26	9200	Tori Landis	90	300.00
add	18	4900	Marla Stevens	90	594.00
update	25	2740	Tia Marlowe	30	135.00

Output (overdue.fil):
Updated random access file

Processing Requirements:

- Open the file in *read (r+)* mode.
- Display the menu options, and prompt for a selection.
- Enter the data and update the file.
- Close the file.

Project 14–4   Overdue Accounts-4

Write a program to read the updated overdue accounts file in Project 14–3, and print the overdue accounts report shown below. Accumulate a total for amount due, and print the total at the end of the report.

```
Author                      OVERDUE ACCOUNTS                Page 01
                               mm/dd/yy


Acct Number        Customer Name        Days Overdue        Amount Due

    9999           X-----------X             99               999.99
      :                  :                    :                  :
      :                  :                    :                  :
    9999           X-----------X             99               999.99

                                          Total:             9999.99
```

Processing Requirements:

- Open the file in *read (r+)* mode.
- Read the overdue accounts file.
- Print a report of the overdue accounts.
- Accumulate a total for amount due, and print it at the end of the report.
- Close the file.

Project 14–5   Sales Profit-1

Write a program to create a random access file for the sales department. Write a total of 20 empty records to the file.

Input (internal):
Define the sales data structure and the members given below. (Field size and type are shown in parentheses.)

| Salesperson number | (3 int) |
| Salesperson name | (15 char) |

| | Total sales | (8.2 float) |
| | Cost of sales | (7.2 float) |

Output (rdSales.fil):
Initialized random access file

Processing Requirements:

- Define and initialize the empty record.
- Open the file in *write (w+)* mode.
- Write empty records to the file.
- Close the file.

Project 14–6   Sales Profit-2

Write a program to prompt the user to enter the data at the keyboard, and load the sales file created in Project 14–5.

Input (disk file and keyboard):

Disk file: Random access file (rdSales.fil)

Keyboard: For each sales record, prompt for and enter the following data. (Field size and type are shown in parentheses.)

1. Salesperson number   (3 int)

2. Salesperson name   (15 char)

3. Total sales   (8.2 float)

4. Cost of sales   (7.2 float)

File Data (keyboard):
Use the data given below to create the sales file. (The numbers shown above the columns correspond to the fields described for the input. The record numbers are shown on the left.)

Rec#	1	2	3	4
19	400	Tara Perkins	12710.14	9735.38
11	700	Dennis Tian	4567.51	3119.22
5	300	Roy Hickle	2245.78	1072.49
12	100	Lisa Conrad	8120.52	6450.71
7	900	Ann Zimmerman	5793.59	4204.45

Output (sales.fil):
Random access file

Processing Requirements:

- Open the file in *read (r+)* mode.
- Prompt for and enter the data.
- Assign the input to the structure variable.
- Write the structure variable (record) to the file.
- Close the file.

Project 14–7   Sales Profit-3

Write a menu program that allows the user to select from several file processing options. Prompt and enter the data, check for errors, and update the sales file from Project 14–6. Write the input errors to an error log.

Menu Choices:

1. Update sales records
2. Add sales records
3. Delete sales records
4. Display all sales records
5. Quit

Input (disk file and keyboard):

Disk file: Random access file (rdSales.fil)

Keyboard: For options 1–3, prompt for and enter the following data:

Option	Input Data
1	Record number, salesperson number, salesperson name, total sales, and cost of sales
2	Record number, salesperson number, salesperson name, total sales, and cost of sales
3	Record number

File Data (keyboard):

Enter the updates in the random order shown. For each, use the menu option to apply the data to the record specified by the record number.

Menu Option	Record Number	Number	Salesperson Name	Total Sales	Cost of Sales
add	7	900	Ann Zimmerman	5793.59	4204.45
update	4	340	David Kock	4339.16	2124.83
update	5	300	Roy Henderson	2245.78	1072.49
update	16	490	Michael Torres	9634.28	5593.15
add	14	940	Sean Zorich	7465.92	5641.39
update	11	700	Dennis Tian	4567.51	3191.22
update	9	250	Robert Minelli	3974.63	2016.24
delete	19				
add	2	200	Allison Dunn	6518.02	4131.78

Output (sales.fil):

Updated random access file

Processing Requirements:

- Open the file in *read (r+)* mode.
- Display the menu options, and prompt for a selection.
- Enter the data and update the file.
- Close the file.

Project 14–8   Sales Profit-4

Write a program to read the updated sales file (see Project 14–7), and print the sales profit report shown below. Accumulate a total for net profit, and print the total at the end of the report.

```
Author                    SALES PROFIT REPORT              Page 01
                               mm/dd/yy


                          Total           Cost of         Net
Num    Salesperson        Sales           Sales           Profit
-----------------------------------------------------------------
999    X---------X        99999.99        9999.99         9999.99
 :         :                 :               :               :
 :         :                 :               :               :
999    X---------X        99999.99        9999.99         9999.99

                                          Total:          99999.99
```

Processing Requirements:

- Open the file in *read (r+)* mode.
- Read the sales file.
- Print a report of the sales profit.
- Accumulate a total for net profit, and print it at the end of the report.
- Close the file.

15   Indexed Files

Overview

Learning Objectives

After you have read this chapter and completed the exercises, you should be able to

- explain the purpose and use of indexed files
- create and load an indexed file
- read and print data stored in an indexed file
- update data stored in an indexed file

Indexed File Organization

Sequential files store data in key field order. Whether the number of change transactions is large or small, a sequential file update always creates and writes a new master file. To update the 100th record, the program copies the first 99 records to the file, updates the 100th record, and copies the remainder of the records to the file. Obviously, this process is slow and time-consuming.

Although random files store data in random order, they, too, have limitations. For example, random files can waste disk space because empty record positions go unfilled. Additionally, random files store and retrieve data by record number. For many applications, this simply will not work. For example, social security numbers, serial numbers, zip codes, and customer names do not easily equate to a series of record numbers that fall in the range 1 to n.

Indexed files, however, do not impose these restrictions on us. Although more complicated to work, indexed files use a key field to access the data and save disk space. By definition, an **indexed file** is a pseudofile organization method that consists of an array and a random access file. The array holds the record keys, and the random file holds the data. Since the record keys are stored directly in memory and not in a file, they can be read quickly by the program. After the file has been processed, the keys stored in the array are copied to a sequential file for future reference.

Because of the way C accesses files, the process of locating a key stored in an array takes far less time than searching for it in a file. C accesses files through special input/output (I/O) control routines that are part of the computer's operating system access method. Each time a record is read from a file, the program executes the I/O routines to access the data. Overall, the time associated with performing these routines is significantly longer than the time required to locate the key stored in an array.

Once again, consider the course registration system for Blackmoore University. The key array and random access data file are shown in Figure 15.1. Assume the user enters the call number 200. To access the record, the program searches the array and compares the 200—the search key—to each call number stored in the array until a match is found or the end of the array is encountered. For a match, the subscript of the array is used to access the data stored in the random file. Notice that a match is found where subscript equals 3. Hence, the course data is stored in the random access file at record number subscript + 1.

Creating an Indexed File

In the section that follows, we will create an indexed file for the course scheduling application for Blackmoore University. To create the indexed file, we must define a key array and a random data file. Later, we will copy the array to a sequential file for future

	Key Array			Call#	DATA FILE Dept-Course	Enrollment
Sub 0	400		Rec# 1	400	ENG200	16
1	300		2	300	CHEM201	21
2	600		3	600	MGT330	29
►3	200		4	200	BIOL101	19
4	500		5	500	HIST225	33
5	900		6	900	SPAN111	12
6	700		7	700	MATH120	14
7	800		8	800	PHYS251	20
8	100		9	100	ACCT101	24
					. . . .	
19	0		20	0	blank	0

FIGURE 15.1   Indexed File

reference. Our objective is to reserve disk space for the course records and to set up an array to track the record keys.

Creating an indexed file involves the following tasks:

1. Set up the indexed file.
2. Open the files.
3. Set the array to 0.
4. Write empty records to the random file.
5. Copy the array to the sequential file.
6. Close the files.

This process is illustrated in sample program CHAP15A. Both the sequential key file and the random data file are initialized by the program.

Checkpoint 15A

1. True or false: A sequential file update always creates and writes a new master file.
2. True or false: A disadvantage of random files is that they can waste disk space.
3. Briefly define and explain an indexed file.
4. List six steps involved in creating an indexed file.
5. Briefly explain how a record is located using indexed-file organization.

Sample Program CHAP15A

Sample program CHAP15A creates and initializes an indexed file for the courses offered at the regional campus of Blackmoore University. Again, the size of the file has been limited to 20 data records. See Figure 15.2 for the hierarchy chart and Figure 15.3 for the program flowchart. Sample program CHAP15A is presented in Figure 15.4

The following specifications apply:

Input (internal):

Define the course data structure and the members given below. (Field size and type are shown in parentheses.)

Call number	(3 int)
Course ID	(15 char)
Student enrollment	(2 int)

Output (disk files):

Sequential key file	(sqKey.fil)
Random data file	(rdData.fil)

The files are shown in Figure 15.5.

Processing Requirements:

- Define and initialize the empty record.
- Define a sequential key file, a random data file, and a key array.
- Open the sequential key file (w) and the random data file ($w+$).
- Set the elements of the array to 0.
- Write empty records to the random data file.
- After creating the data file, copy the array to the sequential key file.
- Close the files.

Pseudocode:

```
START: Main
Clear screen
Call Open Files
IF files opened
      Call Create Indexed File
      Call Save Record Keys
      Close files
END IF
END


ENTER: Open Files
Open sequential key file for write
IF file not opened
    Print cannot open sequential key file for output
END IF
Open random data file for write
IF file not opened
    Print cannot open random data file
END IF
RETURN
```

ENTER: Create Indexed File
LOOP for record number 1 to 20
    Set key array element to 0
    Write empty record to the data file
END LOOP
RETURN

ENTER: Save Record Keys
LOOP for record number 1 to 20
    Write key array element to key file
END LOOP
RETURN

Hierarchy Chart: See Figure 15.2.

Program Flowchart: See Figure 15.3.

Dissection of Sample Program CHAP15A

K E Y   R E C O R D:

```
FILE *fpKey;
int  iRecKey;
```

The above statements define the file pointer for the sequential key file and the record field *iRecKey*. The key record has one field.

D A T A   R E C O R D:

```
FILE *fpData;
struct stCrsForm
{
    int  iCallNum;
    char sCourse[15];
    int  iEnroll;
};
```

The above statements define the file pointer for the random data file and the format of the course data structure. The structure describes the members—*iCallNum (integer), sCourse (character string)*, and *iEnroll (integer)*.

```
struct stCrsForm svEmpty = {0,"", 0};
```

The above statement declares the empty record and sets *iCallNum* to 0, *sCourse* to Null string, and *iEnroll* to 0.

P R O G R A M   V A R I A B L E S:
```
int  iKeyArray[20];
```

The above statement defines the key array. It reserves storage for 20 call numbers and is used to hold the record keys during the program run.

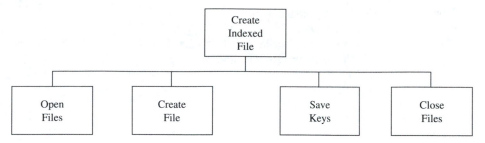

FIGURE 15.2   Hierarchy Chart for CHAP15A

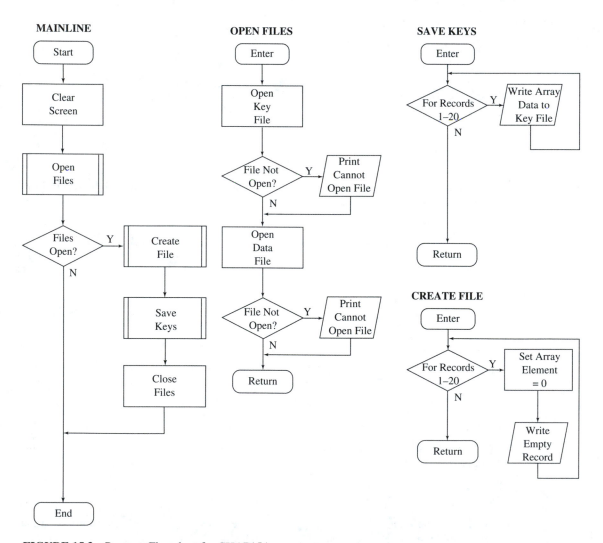

FIGURE 15.3   Program Flowchart for CHAP15A

```
/*------------------------------------------------------------
CREATE INDEXED FILE: Use an array and a random file to create an
indexed file of 20 empty records.

Program:    CHAP15A.C
Author:     David M. Collopy
Date:       mm/dd/yy
Project:    Sample program
*************************************************************/

/*---- PREPROCESSING DIRECTIVES ----------------------------*/

#include <stdio.h>
#include <graph.h>

/*---- FUNCTION PROTOTYPES ---------------------------------*/

void  OpenFiles(void);          /* open program files */
void  CreateFile(void);         /* create random file */
void  SaveKeys(void);           /* save record keys   */

/*---- PROGRAM SETUP ---------------------------------------*/

/*> C O U R S E   I N D E X E D   F I L E          <*/

/*> K E Y   R E C O R D                            <*/

FILE *fpKey;                    /* key file pointer        */
int   iRecKey;                  /* record key-call number  */

/*> D A T A   R E C O R D                          <*/

FILE *fpData;                   /* data file pointer       */

struct stCrsForm
{
    int  iCallNum;              /* call number             */
    char sCourse[15];           /* course ID               */
    int  iEnroll;               /* student enrollment      */
};

struct stCrsForm svEmpty = {0, "", 0};

/*> P R O G R A M   V A R I A B L E S              <*/

int  iKeyArray[20];             /* 20 element key array    */
```

FIGURE 15.4 Sample Program CHAP15A: Creates an index file

```
/*--------------------------------------------------------------
        MAINLINE CONTROL
-----------------------------------------------------------*/
main()
{
    _clearscreen(0);
    OpenFiles();
    if (fpKey != 0 && fpData != 0)
    {
        CreateFile();
        SaveKeys();
        fclose(fpKey, fpData);
    }
    return 0;
}


/*--------------------------------------------------------------
        OPEN PROGRAM FILES
-----------------------------------------------------------*/
void OpenFiles(void)
{
    fpKey = fopen("a:sqKey.fil", "w");
    if (fpKey == 0)
    {
        printf("\nCannot open sequential key file for ouput\n");
    }
    fpData = fopen("a:rdData.fil", "w+");
    if (fpData == 0)
    {
        printf("\nCannot open random data file\n");
    }
    return;
}


/*--------------------------------------------------------------
        CREATE INDEXED FILE
-----------------------------------------------------------*/
void CreateFile(void)
{
    int iRecNum;                    /* record number */

    for (iRecNum = 1; iRecNum <= 20; iRecNum++)
    {
        iKeyArray[iRecNum - 1] = 0;
        fwrite(&svEmpty, sizeof(struct stCrsForm), 1, fpData);
    }
```

FIGURE 15.4 *Continued*

```
    return;
}


/*-------------------------------------------------------------
        SAVE RECORD KEYS
----------------------------------------------------------------*/
void SaveKeys(void)
{
    int iRecNum;                     /* record number */

    for (iRecNum = 1; iRecNum <= 20; iRecNum++)
    {
        fprintf(fpKey, "%d\n", iKeyArray[iRecNum - 1]);
    }
    return;
}
```

FIGURE 15.4   *Continued*

	Key File		Call#	**D A T A F I L E** Dept-Course	Enrollment
Sub 0	0	Rec# 1	0	blank	0
1	0	2	0	blank	0
2	0	3	0	blank	0
			. . . . .		
19	0	20	0	blank	0

FIGURE 15.5   Index File for CHAP15A

```
M A I N L I N E    C O N T R O L:

main()
{
    system("cls");
    OpenFiles();
    if (fpKey != 0 && fpData != 0)
    {
        CreateFile();
        SaveKeys();
        fclose(fpKey, fpData);
    }
    return 0;
}
```

The *MAINLINE* clears the screen and executes the modules in the order listed. The *if* statement determines whether to perform the statements enclosed within the braces. If the sequential and random files are opened, processing continues. Otherwise, the program terminates the run.

```
O P E N    P R O G R A M    F I L E S:

void OpenFiles(void)
{
    fpKey = fopen("a:sqKey.fil", "w");
    if (fpKey == 0)
    {
        printf("\nCannot open sequential key file for output\n");
    }
```

The above statements open the sequential key file in *write* mode. If the file is opened, the address of the file is passed to the file pointer *fpKey*. If the file is not opened, the error message is displayed on the screen.

```
    fpData = fopen("a:rdData.fil", "w+");
    if (fpData == 0)
    {
        printf("\nCannot open random data file\n");
    }
    return;
}
```

The above statements open the random data file in *write plus* mode. If the file is opened, the address of the data file is passed to the file pointer *fpData*. If the file is not opened, the error message is displayed on the screen.

```
C R E A T E    I N D E X    F I L E:

void CreateFile(void)
{
    int iRecNum;

    for (iRecNum = 1; iRecNum <= 20; iRecNum++)
    {
        iKeyArray[iRecNum - 1] = 0;
        fwrite(&svEmpty, sizeof(struct stCrsForm), 1, fpData);
    }
    return;
}
```

In the above statements, as long as *iRecNum* is less than or equal to 20, the module stores a 0 in the key array and writes an empty record to the random file. The expression *iRecNum - 1* specifies the subscript of the corresponding element in the key array. The record number is adjusted to produce the subscript. As you may recall, subscripts are numbered starting with 0.

```
S A V E    R E C O R D    K E Y S:

void SaveKeys(void)
{
    int iRecNum;

    for (iRecNum = 1; iRecNum <= 20; iRecNum++)
    {
        fprintf(fpKey, "%d\n", iKeyArray[iRecNum - 1]);
    }
    return;
}
```

In the above statements, as long as *iRecNum* is less than or equal to 20, the fprintf() copies the call number stored in the key array to the sequential key file. This module saves the course call numbers (record keys) on disk for subsequent processing.

Notes and Tips

1. An indexed file consist of a key array and a random data file.
2. The course records are placed in the data file.
3. The record keys are maintained in a key array and are used to access the records stored in the data file. When coding statements involving the key array, don't forget to use subscripts.
4. Sample program CHAP15A creates a random file of 20 empty records. After the data file is initialized, the key array is copied to a sequential key file for later use.

Tutorial CHAP15A

1. The objectives of this tutorial are to
   • create a 20-record indexed course file
   • initialize the elements in the key array and the records in the random data file
   • copy the contents of the key array to a sequential key file
2. Read the program specifications and logic design tools given for sample program CHAP15A.
3. Log on to your C editor, and enter the source code as shown in Figure 15.4. Save the programs on your work disk as CHAP15A.
4. Compile, run, and debug your programs. When completed, show your work to your instructor.

Quick Quiz

Answer the following questions.

1. Discuss the purpose of the key array.

2. Explain how the statements shown in the *CreateFile* module accomplish the task of initializing the elements in the key array and the records in the data file.

3. Why is it necessary to copy the contents of the key array to a sequential file?

4. Did you have any problems or errors when you ran the sample programs? If so, what were they and what did you do to correct them?

Writing Data to an Indexed File

Now that the indexed file has been created, we are ready to load the file with live data. Since we are using an indexed file, we may enter the data in any order we wish.

Loading an indexed file involves the following tasks:

1. Set up the indexed file.

2. Load the array.

3. Open the files.

4. Prompt and enter the data.

5. Store the keys in the array and write the data to the random file.

6. Copy the array to the sequential file.

7. Close the files.

The load process is illustrated in sample program CHAP15B. Notice how the key array and the sequential file work together to maintain the record keys.

Sample Program CHAP15B

Sample program CHAP15B prompts the user to enter the data at the keyboard and loads the indexed file. The record keys are copied to the sequential file, and the data is written to the random file. See Figure 15.6 for the hierarchy chart and Figure 15.7 for the program flowchart. Sample program CHAP15B is represented in Figure 15.8, and the contents of the indexed file is shown in Figure 15.9.

The following specifications apply:

Input (disk files and keyboard):

Disk files: Sequential key file   (sqKey.fil)
                Random data file   (rdData.fil)

Keyboard: For each course record, prompt for and enter the following data. (Field size and type are shown in parentheses.)

Call number   (3 int)
Course ID   (15 char)
Student enrollment   (2 int)

Output (disk files):

Sequential key file   (sqKey.fil)
Random data file   (rdData.fil)

The files are shown in Figure 15.9.

Processing Requirements:

- Define a sequential key file, a random data file, and a key array.
- Open the sequential key file (*r*), load the array, and close the file.
- Open the sequential key file (*w*) and the random data file (*r+*).
- Prompt for and enter the course data.
- Store the record keys in the array, and write the course data to the random data file.
- After loading the data file, copy the array to the sequential key file.
- Close the files.

Pseudocode:

```
START: Main
Call Set Up Key Array
Call Open Files
IF files opened
      Call Load Array and Data File
      Call Save Record Keys
      Close files
END IF
END


ENTER: Set Up Key Array
Open sequential key file for read
IF file not opened
      Print cannot open sequential key file for input
else
      LOOP for record number 1 to 20
            Read record key from sequential file
            Set array element to record key
      END LOOP
      Close key file
END IF
RETURN


ENTER: Open Files
Open sequential key file for write
IF file not opened
      Print cannot open sequential key file for output
END IF
Open random data file for read plus
IF file not opened
      Print cannot open random data file
END IF
RETURN
```

ENTER: Load Array and Data File
Set record number to 1
Clear screen
Prompt and enter call number (or 0 to quit)
LOOP while record number <= 20 and call number not = 0
    Load call number into key array
    Prompt and enter course ID
    Prompt and enter student enrollment
    Seek record position
    Write record to the random file
    Add 1 to record number
    Clear screen
    Prompt and enter call number (or 0 to quit)
END LOOP
RETURN

ENTER: Save Record Keys
LOOP for record number = 1 to 20
    Write key array element to sequential key file
END LOOP
RETURN

Hierarchy Chart: See Figure 15.6.

Program Flowchart: See Figure 15.7.

Dissection of Sample Program CHAP15B

For the most part, the front end of the program remains the same. Like sample program CHAP15A, the file pointers, the course data structure, the key array, and the record number are defined in the *PROGRAM SETUP*.

This time, however, the structure variable defines the course record:

```
struct stCrsForm svRec;
```

The input data entered by the user is assigned to the course record and is written to the random data file.

Essentially, the *MAINLINE* clears the screen, loads the key array, opens the random file, and prompts the user to enter the input. Afterwards, the program copies the contents of the array to the sequential key file and closes both files.

```
S E T   U P   A R R A Y:

void SetupArray(void)
{
    int iRecNum;

    fpKey = fopen("a:sqKey.fil", "r");
    if (fpKey == 0)
    {
        printf("Cannot open sequential key file for input\n");
```

```
        }
        else
        {
            for (iRecNum = 1; iRecNum <= 20; iRecNum++)
            {
                fscanf(fpKey, " %d", &iRecKey);
                iKeyArray[iRecNum - 1] = iRecKey;
            {
            fclose(fpKey);
        }
        return;
}
```

The above statements open the sequential key file in *read* mode and store the address of the file in the file pointer variable *fpKey*. If the file was not opened, then the printf() displays the error message on the screen. But if the file was opened, then the module loads the course data in the array. As long as *iRecNum* is less than or equal to 20, the statement body of the *for* loop reads a key from the file and stores it in the array. After loading the array, the module closes the file.

O P E N   P R O G R A M   F I L E S:

```
void OpenFiles(void)
{
    fpKey = fopen("a:sqKey.fil", "w");
    if (fpKey == 0)
    {
        printf("Cannot open sequential key file for output\n");
    }
    fpData = fopen("a:rdData.fil", "r+");
    if (fpData == 0)
    {
        printf("Cannot open random key file\n");
    }
    return;
}
```

The above statements open the sequential key file in *write* mode and store the address of the file in the file pointer variable *fpKey*. If the key file was not opened, then the module displays the first error message on the screen. The module opens the random data file in *read plus* mode and stores the address of the file in the file pointer variable *fpData*. If the data file was not opened, then the module displays the second error message on the screen.

L O A D   A R R A Y   &   D A T A   F I L E:

```
void LoadData(void)
{
    int iRecNum = 1;
```

The above statement declares and initializes *iRecNum* to 1.

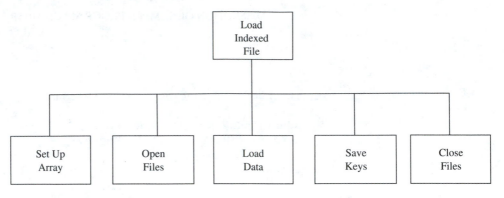

FIGURE 15.6 Hierarchy Chart for CHAP15B

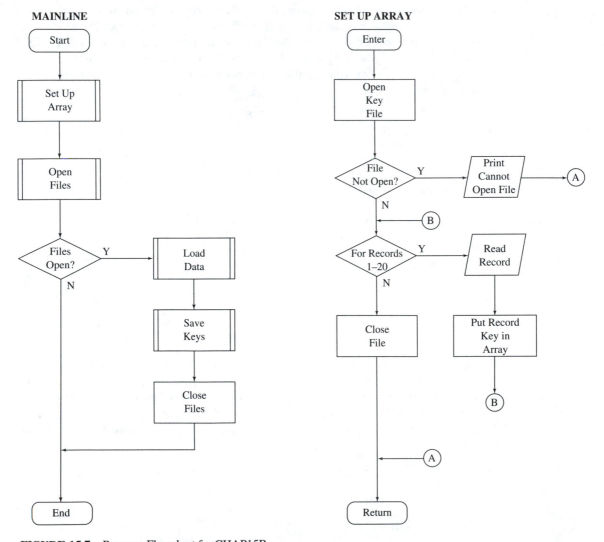

FIGURE 15.7 Program Flowchart for CHAP15B

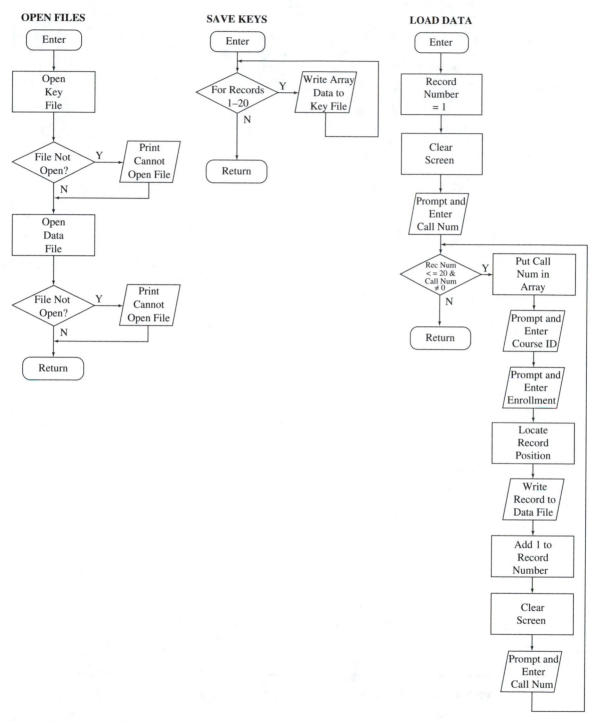

FIGURE 15.7 *Continued*

```
/*-------------------------------------------------------------
LOAD INDEXED FILE: Accept keyboard input and load data into the
indexed file.

Program:   CHAP15B.C
Author:    David M. Collopy
Date:      mm/dd/yy
Project:   Sample program
****************************************************************/

/*---- PREPROCESSING DIRECTIVES ------------------------------*/

#include <stdio.h>
#include <graph.h>

/*---- FUNCTION PROTOTYPES -----------------------------------*/

void SetupArray(void);          /* set up key array       */
void OpenFiles(void);           /* open program files     */
void LoadData(void);            /* load array & data file */
void SaveKeys(void);            /* save record keys       */

/*---- PROGRAM SETUP -----------------------------------------*/

/*>  C O U R S E    I N D E X E D    F I L E           <*/

/*>  K E Y    R E C O R D                              <*/

FILE *fpKey;                    /* key file pointer       */
int   iRecKey;                  /* record key-call number */

/*>  D A T A    R E C O R D                            <*/

FILE *fpData;                   /* data file pointer      */

struct stCrsForm
{
    int  iCallNum;              /* call number            */
    char sCourse[15];           /* course ID              */
    int  iEnroll;               /* student enrollment     */
};
```

FIGURE 15.8 Sample Program CHAP15B: Writes data randomly to an indexed file

```
struct stCrsForm svRec;

/*>   P R O G R A M   V A R I A B L E S                    <*/

int  iKeyArray[20];                /* 20 element key array    */

/*----------------------------------------------------------------
      MAINLINE CONTROL
-----------------------------------------------------------------*/
main()
{
    SetupArray();
    OpenFiles();
    if (fpKey != 0 && fpData != 0)
    {
        LoadData();
        SaveKeys();
        fclose(fpKey, fpData);
    }
    return 0;
}


/*----------------------------------------------------------------
      SET UP ARRAY
-----------------------------------------------------------------*/
void SetupArray(void)
{
    int iRecNum;                  /* record number */

    fpKey = fopen("a:sqKey.fil", "r");
    if (fpKey == 0)
    {
        printf("\nCannot open sequential key file for input\n");
    }
    else
    {
        for (iRecNum = 1; iRecNum <= 20; iRecNum++)
        {
            fscanf(fpKey, " %d", &iRecKey);
            iKeyArray[iRecNum - 1] = iRecKey;
        }
```

FIGURE 15.8   *Continued*

```
            fclose(fpKey);
        }
    return;
}


/*----------------------------------------------------------------
        OPEN PROGRAM FILES
----------------------------------------------------------------*/
void OpenFiles(void)
{
    fpKey = fopen("a:sqKey.fil", "w");
    if (fpKey == 0)
    {
        printf("\nCannot open sequential key file for output\n");
    }
    fpData = fopen("a:rdData.fil", "r+");
    if (fpData == 0)
    {
        printf("\nCannot open random data file\n");
    }
    return;
}


/*----------------------------------------------------------------
        LOAD ARRAY & DATA FILE
----------------------------------------------------------------*/
void LoadData(void)
{
    int iRecNum = 1;              /* record number */

    _clearscreen(0);
    printf("\nEnter call number or '0' to Quit: ");
    scanf(" %d", &svRec.iCallNum);
    while (iRecNum <= 20 && svRec.iCallNum != 0)
    {
        iKeyArray[iRecNum - 1] = svRec.iCallNum;
        printf("\n                  Enter course ID: ");
        scanf(" %s", svRec.sCourse);
        printf("\n        Enter student enrollment: ");
        scanf(" %d", &svRec.iEnroll);
        fseek(fpData, (iRecNum - 1) * sizeof(struct stCrsForm),
```

FIGURE 15.8 *Continued*

```
                SEEK_SET);
          fwrite(&svRec, sizeof(struct stCrsForm), 1, fpData);
          iRecNum++;
          _clearscreen(0);
          printf("\nEnter call number or '0' to Quit: ");
          scanf(" %d", &svRec.iCallNum);
     }
     return;
}




/*-------------------------------------------------------------
     SAVE RECORD KEYS
----------------------------------------------------------------*/
void SaveKeys(void)
{
    int iRecNum;                    /* record number */

    for (iRecNum = 1; iRecNum <= 20; iRecNum++)
    {
        fprintf(fpKey, "%d\n", iKeyArray[iRecNum - 1]);
    }
    return;
}
```

FIGURE 15.8   *Continued*

	Key File				D A T A F I L E	
				Call#	Dept-Course	Enrollment
Sub 0	400		Rec# 1	400	ENG200	16
1	300		2	300	CHEM201	21
2	600		3	600	MGT330	29
3	200		4	200	BIOL101	19
4	500		5	500	HIST225	33
5	900		6	900	SPAN111	12
6	700		7	700	MATH120	14
7	800		8	800	PHYS251	20
8	100		9	100	ACCT101	24
					. . . . .	
19	0		20	0	blank	0

FIGURE 15.9   Index File for CHAP15B

```
        _clearscreen(0);
        printf("\nEnter call number or '0' to Quit: ");
        scanf(" %d", &svRec.iCallNum);
```

The above statements clear the screen and prompt the user to enter the call number or 0 to quit. The scan function gets the input, converts it to an integer, and assigns the result to the *svRec.iCallNum* field of the course record.

```
        while (iRecNum <= 20 && svRec.iCallNum != 0)
        {
```

In the above statement, as long as *iRecNum* is less than or equal to 20 and the *svRec.iCallNum* is not equal to 0, control executes the statement body of the loop.

```
            iKeyArray[iRecNum - 1] = svRec.iCallNum;
```

This statement copies the course call number to the key array. The expression *iRecNum - 1* specifies the subscript and tells the program where to store the call number in the key array.

```
            printf("\n                      Enter course ID: ");
            scanf(" %s", svRec.sCourse);
            printf("\n          Enter student enrollment: ");
            scanf(" %d", &svRec.iEnroll);
```

The above statements prompt the user to enter the course data (department prefix number and enrollment) and assign the input to the fields in the course record.

```
            fseek(fpData, (iRecNum - 1) *
                sizeof(struct stCrsForm), SEEK_SET);
            fwrite(&svRec, sizeof(struct stCrsForm), 1, fpData);
```

The fseek() sets the file pointer to the address location specified by the *offset* expression. The fwrite() writes the data stored in the course record to the current record position in the random data file.

```
            iRecNum++;
            _clearscreen(0);
            printf("\nEnter call number or '0' to Quit: ");
            scanf(" %d", &svRec.iCallNum);
        }
        return;
}
```

The above statements increment *iRecNum*, clear the screen, and prompt the user to enter the call number of the next course. The *while* loop continues until the user enters a 0 to quit. Afterward, the program returns to the *MAINLINE*.

S A V E   R E C O R D   K E Y S :

```
void SaveKeys(void)
{
    int iRecNum;

    for (iRecNum = 1; iRecNum <= 20; iRecNum++)
```

```
    {
        fprintf(fpKey, "%d\n", iKeyArray[iRecNum - 1]);
    }
    return;
}
```

The above module copies the record keys (temporarily stored in the key array) to the sequential key file. This important step saves the record keys for subsequent processing.

Notes and Tips

1. Remember, both the sequential key file and the random file must be initialized prior to executing sample program CHAP15B.

2. The following is done before the file load takes place: Open the sequential key file for input (to place the record keys in the key array), and open the random data file.

3. During the file load, the input key is placed in the key array and the input record is stored in the data file. Once again, the procedure is to move the file pointer and write the record to the random file.

4. After the file load is completed, copy the record keys from the array to the sequential key file. This activity saves the keys on disk for subsequent processing.

Tutorial CHAP15B

1. The objectives of this tutorial are to
   • set up the key array using the sequential key file
   • load input record keys into the key array
   • load input course records into the random data file

2. Read the program specifications and logic design tools shown for sample program CHAP15B.

3. Log on to your C editor, and enter the source code as shown in Figure 15.8. Save the program on your work disk as CHAP15B. Save frequently.

4. Compile, run, and debug your program until the input is loaded into the file.

5. When completed, show your work to your instructor.

Quick Quiz

Answer the following questions.

1. The following code is from the *SetupArray* module. Explain what each statement does.
   ```
   fscanf(fpKey, " %d", &iRecKey);
   iKeyArray[iRecNum - 1] = iRecKey;
   ```

2. Would it have been easier to use a *for* loop to load the data instead of the *while* loop? Explain your answer.

3. At this point in creating the indexed file, how important is it to save the contents of the key array to a sequential key file? What would happen if you did not save the keys?

5. Did you have any problems or errors when you ran the sample program? If so, what were they and what did you do to correct them?

Reading and Printing an Indexed File

The sequential and random files created in sample program CHAP15B were stored on disk. Since the record keys and course data were written directly to the disk, we have no way of knowing for sure what was actually stored in the files. Therefore, it would be a good idea to look at the files and verify that the contents are correct.

Reading and printing an indexed file involves the following tasks:

1. Set up the indexed file.

2. Load the array.

3. Open the files.

4. Read the keys and course data.

5. Write the nonempty records to the report.

6. Close the files.

This process is illustrated in sample program CHAP15C.

Sample Program CHAP15C

Sample program CHAP15C reads and prints a copy of the indexed file created in sample program CHAP15B. The record keys and their corresponding data records are read from the disk and written to the output report. See Figure 15.10 for the hierarchy chart and Figure 15.11 for the program flowchart. Sample program CHAP15C is presented in Figure 15.12, and the output is shown in Figure 15.13.

The following specifications apply:

Input (disk files):
Sequential key file   (sqKey.fil)
Random data file   (rdData.fil)

Output (screen):
The output report is shown in Figure 15.13.

Processing Requirements:

• Define a sequential key file, a random data file, and a key array.
• Open the sequential key file (r), load the array, and close the file.
• Open the random data file in read ($r+$) mode.
• Write the nonempty course records to the report.
• Close the random data file.

Pseudocode:

```
START: Main
Clear screen
Call Set Up Key Array
Call Open File
IF file opened
      Call Read and Print Random File
      Close data file
END IF
END

ENTER: Set Up Key Array
Open sequential key file for read
IF file not opened
      Print cannot open sequential key file for input
else
      LOOP for record numbers 1 to 20
            Read record key from sequential file
            Set array element to record key
      END LOOP
      Close sequential key file
END IF
RETURN

ENTER: Open File
Open random data file for read plus
IF file not opened
      Print cannot open random data file
END IF
RETURN

ENTER: Read and Print Random File
Print 2 heading lines
LOOP for record number 1 to 20
      Seek record position
      Read record from random file
      IF key array element not = 0
            Print detail line:
                  record number
                  key array element
                  call number
                  course ID
                  student enrollment
      END IF
END LOOP
RETURN
```

Hierarchy Chart: See Figure 15.10.

Program Flowchart: See Figure 15.11.

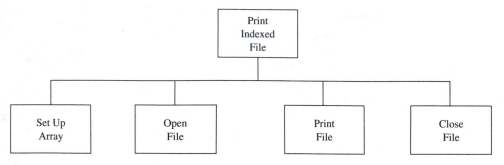

FIGURE 15.10   Hierarchy Chart for CHAP15C

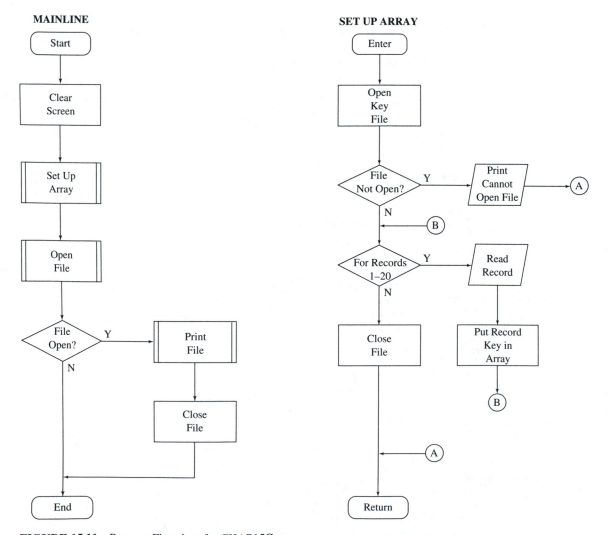

FIGURE 15.11   Program Flowchart for CHAP15C

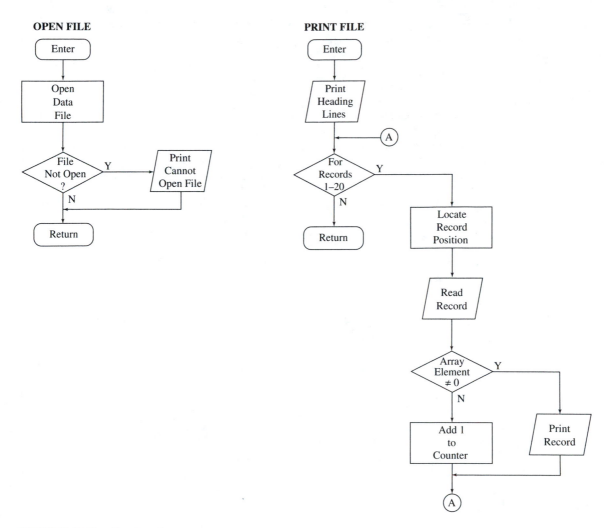

FIGURE 15.11 *Continued*

```
/*-----------------------------------------------------------------
READ INDEXED FILE: Read and print the data stored in an indexed file.


Program:    CHAP15C.C
Author:     David M. Collopy
Date:       mm/dd/yy
Project:    Sample program
******************************************************************/
```

FIGURE 15.12 Sample Program CHAP15C: This program reads an indexed file and copies the records to the output report

```
/*---- PREPROCESSING DIRECTIVES ---------------------------------*/

#include <stdio.h>
#include <graph.h>

/*---- FUNCTION PROTOTYPES -------------------------------------*/

void  SetupArray(void);          /* set up key array       */
void  OpenFile(void);            /* open random data file  */
void  PrnFile(void);             /* print key & course data */

/*---- PROGRAM SETUP -------------------------------------------*/

/*>  C O U R S E   I N D E X E D   F I L E                   <*/

/*>  K E Y   R E C O R D                                     <*/

FILE *fpKey;                     /* key file pointer       */
int   iRecKey;                   /* record key-call number */

/*>  D A T A   R E C O R D                                   <*/

FILE *fpData;                    /* data file pointer      */

struct stCrsForm
{
    int  iCallNum;               /* call number            */
    char sCourse[15];            /* course ID              */
    int  iEnroll;                /* student enrollment     */
};

struct stCrsForm svRec;

/*>  P R O G R A M   V A R I A B L E S                       <*/

int  iKeyArray[20];              /* 20 element key array   */

/*---------------------------------------------------------------
      MAINLINE CONTROL
---------------------------------------------------------------*/
main()
{
    _clearscreen(0);
    SetupArray();
    OpenFile();
```

FIGURE 15.12   *Continued*

```
    if (fpData != 0)
    {
        PrnFile();
        fclose(fpData);
    }
    return 0;
}


/*------------------------------------------------------------------
     SET UP ARRAY
---------------------------------------------------------------------*/
void SetupArray(void)
{
    int iRecNum;                     /* record number */

    fpKey = fopen("a:sqKey.fil", "r");
    if (fpKey == 0)
    {
        printf("\nCannot open sequential key file for input\n");
    }
    else
    {
        for (iRecNum = 1; iRecNum <= 20; iRecNum++)
        {
            fscanf(fpKey, " %d", &iRecKey);
            iKeyArray[iRecNum - 1] = iRecKey;
        }
        fclose(fpKey);
    }
    return;
}


/*------------------------------------------------------------------
     OPEN RANDOM DATA FILE
---------------------------------------------------------------------*/
void OpenFile(void)
{
    fpData = fopen("a:rdData.fil", "r+");
    if (fpData == 0)
    {
        printf("\nCannot open random data file\n");
    }
    return;
}
```

FIGURE 15.12   *Continued*

```
/*--------------------------------------------------------------------
        PRINT KEY & COURSE DATA
-------------------------------------------------------------------*/
void PrnFile(void)
{
    int iRecNum;                    /* record number */

    printf("\nRec# Key  Call#  Course ID  Enrollment");
    printf("\n-----------------------------------");
    for (iRecNum = 1; iRecNum <= 20; iRecNum++)
    {
        fseek(fpData, (iRecNum - 1) * sizeof(struct stCrsForm),
            SEEK_SET);
        fread(&svRec, sizeof(struct stCrsForm), 1, fpData);
        if (iKeyArray[iRecNum - 1] != 0)
        {
            printf("\n %2d  %3d    %3d    %-14s %2d",
                iRecNum, iKeyArray[iRecNum - 1], svRec.iCallNum,
                svRec.sCourse, svRec.iEnroll);
        }
    }
    return;
}
```

FIGURE 15.12   *Continued*

```
Rec#   Key   Call#   Dept-Course#        Enrollment
---------------------------------------------------
  1    400    400    ENG200                  16
  2    300    300    CHEM201                 21
  3    600    600    MGT330                  29
  4    200    200    BIOL101                 19
  5    500    500    HIST225                 33
  6    900    900    SPAN111                 12
  7    700    700    MATH120                 14
  8    800    800    PHYS251                 20
  9    100    100    ACCT101                 24
```

FIGURE 15.13   File Output for CHAP15C

Dissection of Sample Program CHAP15C

```
M A I N L I N E   C O N T R O L:

main()
{
    _clearscreen(0);
    SetupArray();
    OpenFile();
    if (fpData != 0)
    {
        PrnFile();
        fclose(fpData);
    }
    return 0;
}
```

The above statements clear the screen and execute the modules in the order given—
SetupArray, *OpenFile*, and *PrnFile*. After printing the report, the *MAINLINE* closes the
random file.

SetupArray opens the sequential key file, loads the call numbers into the key array,
and closes the file; *OpenFile* opens the random data file. If the data file was opened, control branches to the *PrnFile* module, reads the file, and displays the records on the screen.
But if the data file was not opened, control prints the "cannot open" error message and terminates the program.

```
P R I N T   K E Y   &   C O U R S E   D A T A:

void PrnFile(void)
{
    int iRecNum;

    printf("\nRec# Key  Call#  Dept-Course#    Enrollment");
    printf("\n-------------------------------------------");
```

The above statements display the report heading lines on the screen.

```
    for (iRecNum = 1; iRecNum <= 20; iRecNum++)
    {
```

In the above statement, as long as *iRecNum* is less than or equal to 20, control executes the
statement body of the loop.

```
        fseek(fpData, (iRecNum - 1) * sizeof(struct stCrsForm),
            SEEK_SET);
        fread(&svRec, sizeof(struct stCrsForm), 1, fpData);
```

The above statements set the file pointer to the record position specified by the offset expression, read the record from the random data file, and store the input in the course record.

```
        if (iKeyArray[iRecNum - 1] != 0)
        {
            printf("\n %2d  %3d   %3d   %-14s %2d",
```

```
                iRecNum, iKeyArray[iRecNum - 1], svRec.iCallNum,
                svRec.sCourse, svRec.iEnroll);
        }
    }
    return;
}
```

In the above segment, if the call number stored in the array is not equal to 0, then the printf() prints the record number, array key, and course data on the report. Otherwise, control skips the record and goes back to the for statement.

Control returns to the *MAINLINE* after the file has been printed.

Notes and Tips

1. Make it a habit to read and print the contents of a file once it has been created. Your time is well spent verifying that the file contains the correct data.

2. The output from the file is, at most, 20 records long. Hence, it is relatively easy to display the report on the screen to verify the contents of the file. However, for longer reports, it would be simpler to direct the output to the printer. Then you could go through the hard copy one record at a time (or randomly select a sample) and verify the contents of the file.

Tutorial CHAP15C

1. The objectives of this tutorial are to
   • open and read an indexed file
   • write the nonempty records to a report

2. Read the program specifications and review the logic design tools shown for sample program CHAP15C.

3. Log on to your C editor, and enter the source code as given in Figure 15.12. Modify the report to include a title line that displays your name and "*Contents of the Course Indexed File*" across the top of the page. Save the program on your work disk as CHAP15C. Save frequently.

4. Compile, run, and debug your program until the output matches the report shown in Figure 15.13.

5. When completed, show your work to your instructor.

Quick Quiz

Answer the following questions.

1. Look at the *PrnFile* module. Why is the check for a nonempty record coded after a record is retrieved from the data file? Would it be more efficient to first check the array for a zero key and then retrieve the record if the key is not equal to 0? Try it and see what happens.

2. Modify the print module to display all the records in the data file. What advantages (if any) are there in printing each record of the file?

3. Did you have any problems or errors when you ran the sample program? If so, what were they and what did you do to correct them?

Updating an Indexed File

From time to time, it may be necessary to update the contents of an indexed file in order to keep it current. For our course scheduling system, we would like to delete courses that are no longer offered, add new courses, and change the data for existing courses.

Deleting a Course: A delete is made by locating the call number of the deleted course in the array and changing it to 0. A deleted course is not actually removed from the random file until a new record is written over the old one.

Adding a Course: An add is made by locating the first empty element in the array—call number 0. The new call number is stored in the array, and the course data is written to the corresponding record position in the random file.

Changing an Existing Course: A change is made to an existing course by locating the call number in the array, retrieving the record from the random file, updating the record, and writing it back to the file.

Updating an indexed file involves the following tasks:

1. Set up the indexed file.

2. Load the array.

3. Open the files.

4. Prompt the user to select the update option (menu).

5. Enter the data and update the array and the random file.

6. Copy the array to the sequential file.

7. Close the files.

The update process is illustrated in sample program CHAP15D. The menu program instructs the user to select from a series of available updating options.

Checkpoint 15B

1. Explain how a record is deleted from an indexed file.

2. How is a record added to an indexed file?

3. What is the process for changing a record in an indexed file?

Sample Program CHAP15D

Sample program CHAP15D is menu driven. It accepts data from the keyboard, checks for errors, and updates the course file. See Figure 15.14 for the hierachy chart and Figure

15.15 for the program flowchart. Sample program CHAP15D is presented in Figure 15.16 and the selection menu is shown in Figure 15.17. Screens corresponding to the various menu choices are shown in Figures 15.18 through 15.22.

The following specifications apply:

Menu Choices:

1. Update enrollment
2. Add course
3. Delete course
4. Display all courses
5. Quit

Input (disk files and keyboard):

Disk files: Sequential key file   (sqKey.fil)
              Random data file   (rdData.fil)

Keyboard: For menu options 1–3, prompt for and enter the following data:

Option	*InputData*
1	Call number and enrollment count
2	Call number, course ID, and student enrollment
3	Call number

Output (disk files):

Sequential key file   (sqKey.fil)
Random data file   (rdData.fil)

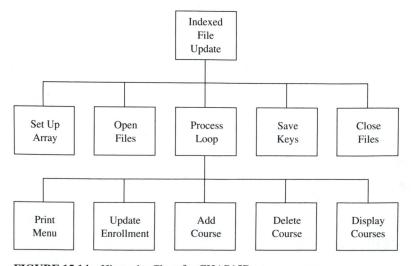

FIGURE 15.14   Hierarchy Chart for CHAP15D

MAINLINE

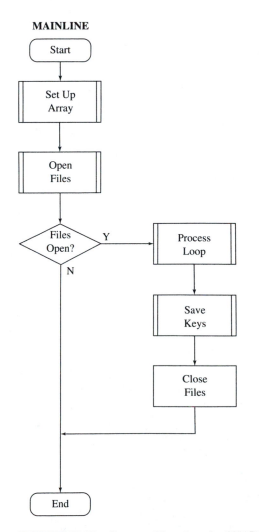

SET UP ARRAY

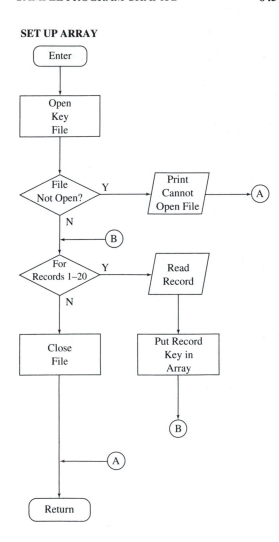

FIGURE 15.15   Program Flowchart for CHAP15D

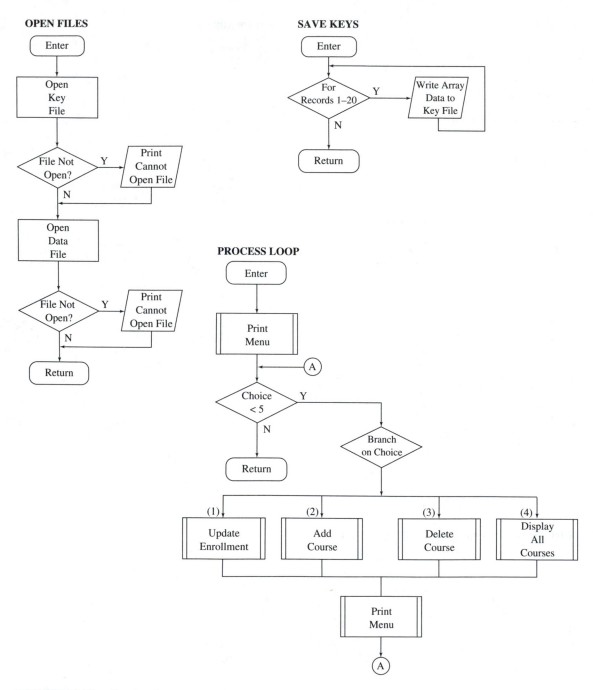

PROCESS LOOP

FIGURE 15.15   *Continued*

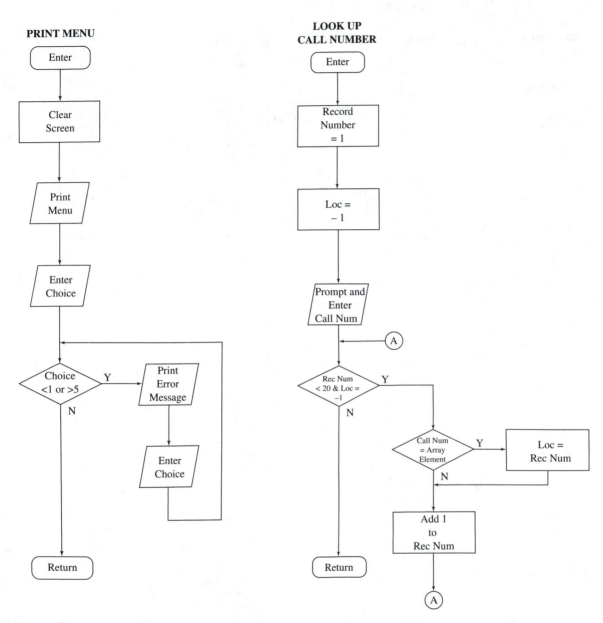

FIGURE 15.15   *Continued*

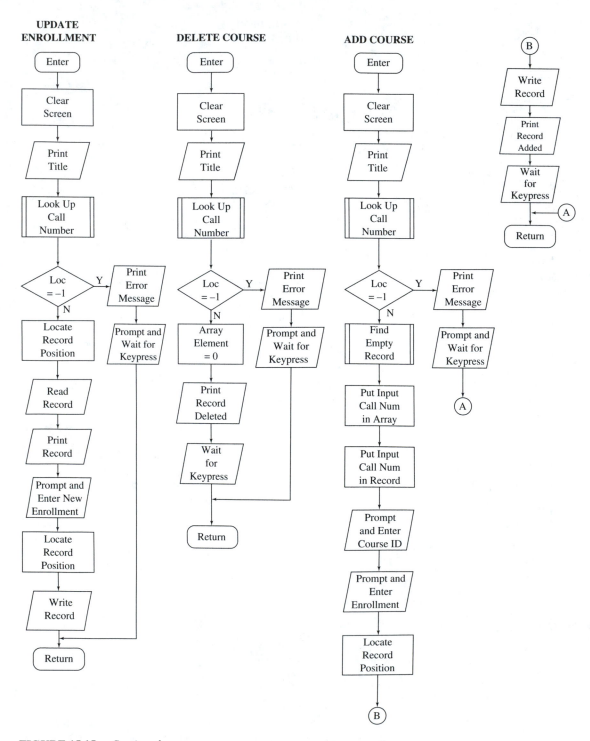

FIGURE 15.15 *Continued*

**FIND EMPTY
RECORD**

**DISPLAY
ALL COURSES**

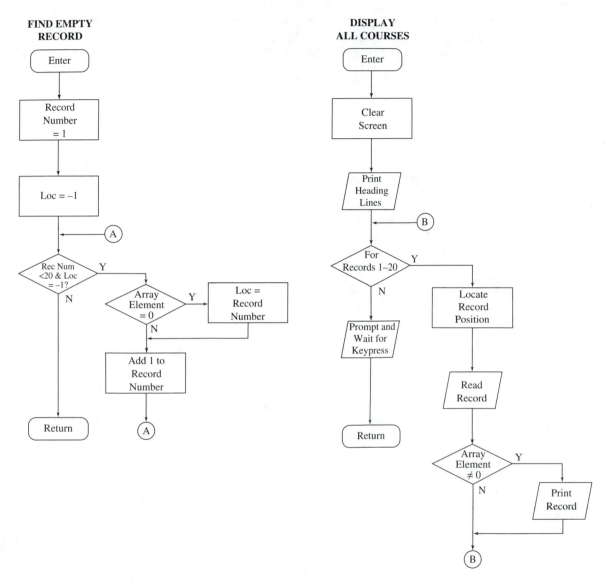

FIGURE 15.15   *Continued*

```
/*---------------------------------------------------------------
UPDATE INDEXED FILE: Randomly access and update the course file.

Program:    CHAP15D.C
Author:     David M. Collopy
```

FIGURE 15.16   Sample Program CHAP15D: Prompts for and accepts data randomly and updates
the indexed file

```
Date:      mm/dd/yy
Project:   Sample program
*******************************************************************/

/*---- PREPROCESSING DIRECTIVES -------------------------------*/

#include <stdio.h>
#include <conio.h>
#include <graph.h>

/*---- FUNCTION PROTOTYPES ------------------------------------*/

void SetupArray(void);          /* set up key array        */
void OpenFiles(void);           /* open program files      */
void ProcessLoop(void);         /* processing loop         */
int  PrnMenu(void);             /* print menu              */
void UpdEnroll(void);           /* update enrollment       */
int  LookUpCallNum(void);       /* look up call number     */
int  FindEmptyRec(void);        /* find empty record       */
void AddCourse(void);           /* add course              */
void DletCourse(void);          /* delete course           */
void DisplayAll(void);          /* display all courses     */
void SaveKeys(void);            /* save record keys        */

/*---- PROGRAM SETUP -----------------------------------------*/

/*> C O U R S E   I N D E X E D   F I L E          <*/

/*> K E Y   R E C O R D                            <*/

FILE *fpKey;                    /* key file pointer        */
int   iRecKey;                  /* record key-call number  */

/*> D A T A   R E C O R D                          <*/

FILE *fpData;                   /* data file pointer       */

struct stCrsForm
{
    int  iCallNum;             /* call number             */
    char sCourse[15];          /* course ID               */
    int  iEnroll;              /* student enrollment      */
};
struct stCrsForm svRec;

/*> P R O G R A M   V A R I A B L E S              <*/

int  iKeyArray[20];            /* 20 element key array    */
```

FIGURE 15.16 *Continued*

```
int  iCallNumIn;                    /* input call number */

/*-------------------------------------------------------------
        MAINLINE CONTROL
---------------------------------------------------------------*/
main()
{
    SetupArray();
    OpenFiles();
    if (fpKey != 0 && fpData != 0)
    {
        ProcessLoop();
        SaveKeys();
        fclose(fpKey, fpData);
    }
    return 0;
}


/*-------------------------------------------------------------
        SET UP ARRAY
---------------------------------------------------------------*/
void SetupArray(void)
{
    int iRecNum;                    /* record number */

    fpKey = fopen("a:sqKey.fil", "r");
    if (fpKey == 0)
    {
        printf("\nCannot open sequential key file for input\n");
    }
    else
    {
        for (iRecNum = 1; iRecNum <= 20; iRecNum++)
        {
            fscanf(fpKey, " %d", &iRecKey);
            iKeyArray[iRecNum - 1] = iRecKey;
        }
        fclose(fpKey);
    }
    return;
}

/*-------------------------------------------------------------
        OPEN PROGRAM FILES
---------------------------------------------------------------*/
void OpenFiles(void)
{
    fpKey = fopen("a:sqKey.fil", "w");
```

FIGURE 15.16 *Continued*

```
    if (fpKey == 0)
    {
        printf("\nCannot open sequential key file for output\n");
    }
    fpData = fopen("a:rdData.fil", "r+");
    if (fpData == 0)
    {
        printf("\nCannot open random data file\n");
    }
    return;
}

/*-------------------------------------------------------------
        PROCESSING LOOP
----------------------------------------------------------------*/
void ProcessLoop(void)
{

    int iChoice;

    iChoice = PrnMenu();          /* display menu          */
    while (iChoice < 5)
    {
        switch (iChoice)
        {
            case 1:
                UpdEnroll();    /* update enrollment   */
                break;
            case 2:
                AddCourse();    /* add course          */
                break;
            case 3:
                DletCourse();   /* delete course       */
                break;
            default:
                DisplayAll();   /* display all courses */
                break;
        }
        iChoice = PrnMenu();    /* display menu          */
    }
    return;
}

/*-------------------------------------------------------------
        PRINT MENU
----------------------------------------------------------------*/
int PrnMenu(void)
{
```

FIGURE 15.16   *Continued*

```
    int iChoice;                        /* user choice */

    _clearscreen(0);
    printf("\nCourse Maintenance System\n");
    printf("\nSelect one:\n\n");
    printf("    1.   Update enrollment\n");
    printf("    2.   Add course\n");
    printf("    3.   Delete course\n");
    printf("    4.   Display all courses\n");
    printf("    5.   Quit\n");
    printf("\nEnter choice (1 - 5) ===> ");
    scanf(" %d", &iChoice);
    while (iChoice < 1 || iChoice > 5)
    {
        printf("\nERROR...re-enter choice (1 - 5) ===> ");
        scanf(" %d", &iChoice);
    }
    return iChoice;
}


/*----------------------------------------------------------------
      UPDATE ENROLLMENT
----------------------------------------------------------------*/
void UpdEnroll(void)
{
    int  iRecNum;                 /* record number           */
    int  iLoc;                    /* location of call number */
    char cWait;                   /* wait for keypress       */

    _clearscreen(0);
    printf("\nUPDATE ENROLLMENT: ");
    iLoc = LookUpCallNum();
    if (iLoc == -1)
    {
        printf("\n\nError: Record does not exist");
        printf(" - press ENTER to continue");
        cWait = getch();
    }
    else
    {
        fseek(fpData, (iLoc - 1) * sizeof(struct stCrsForm),
            SEEK_SET);
        fread(&svRec, sizeof(struct stCrsForm), 1, fpData);
        printf("\n%3d   %-14s   %2d\n", svRec.iCallNum,
            svRec.sCourse, svRec.iEnroll);
        printf("\nEnter new enrollment: ");
        scanf(" %d", &svRec.iEnroll);
        fseek(fpData, (iLoc - 1) * sizeof(struct stCrsForm),
```

FIGURE 15.16 *Continued*

```
                     SEEK_SET);
            fwrite(&svRec, sizeof(struct stCrsForm), 1, fpData);
        }
    return;
}


/*----------------------------------------------------------------
        LOOK UP CALL NUMBER
  --------------------------------------------------------------*/
int LookUpCallNum(void)
{
    int iRecNum = 1;                /* record number */
    int iLoc = -1;                  /* location of call number */

    printf("Enter call number: ");
    scanf(" %d", &iCallNumIn);
    while (iRecNum < 20 && iLoc == -1)
    {
        if (iCallNumIn == iKeyArray[iRecNum - 1])
        {
            iLoc = iRecNum;         /* location found */
        }
        iRecNum++;
    }
    return iLoc;
}


/*----------------------------------------------------------------
          ADD COURSE
  --------------------------------------------------------------*/
void AddCourse(void)
{
    int  iRecNum;                   /* record number */
    int  iLoc;                      /* location of call number */
    char cWait;                     /* wait for keypress */

    _clearscreen(0);
    printf("\nADD COURSE: ");
    iLoc = LookUpCallNum();
    if (iLoc != -1)
    {
        printf("\n\nError: Record already exist");
        printf(" - press ENTER to continue");
        cWait = getch();
    }
    else
    {
        iLoc = FindEmptyRec();
```

FIGURE 15.16   *Continued*

```
            iKeyArray[iLoc - 1] = iCallNumIn;
            svRec.iCallNum = iCallNumIn;
            printf("          Enter course ID: ");
            scanf(" %s", svRec.sCourse);
            printf("Enter student enrollment: ");
            scanf(" %d", &svRec.iEnroll);
            fseek(fpData, (iLoc - 1) * sizeof(struct stCrsForm),
                SEEK_SET);
            fwrite(&svRec, sizeof(struct stCrsForm), 1, fpData);
            printf("\nCall# %3d added - press ENTER to continue\n",
                iCallNumIn);
            cWait = getch();
        }
        return;
}


/*-------------------------------------------------------------
        FIND EMPTY RECORD
-----------------------------------------------------------*/
int FindEmptyRec(void)
{
    int iRecNum = 1;              /* record number */
    int iLoc = -1;               /* location of call number */

    while (iRecNum < 20 && iLoc == -1)
    {
        if (iKeyArray[iRecNum - 1] == 0)
        {
            iLoc = iRecNum;      /* location found */
        }
        iRecNum++;
    }
    return iLoc;
}


/*-------------------------------------------------------------
        DELETE COURSE
-----------------------------------------------------------*/
void DletCourse(void)
{
    int   iLoc;                  /* location of call number */
    char cWait;                  /* wait for keypress */

    _clearscreen(0);
    printf("\nDELETE COURSE: ");
    iLoc = LookUpCallNum();
    if (iLoc == -1)
    {
```

FIGURE 15.16   *Continued*

```
            printf("\n\nError: Record does not exist ");
            printf(" - press ENTER to continue");
            cWait = getch();
        }
        else
        {
            iKeyArray[iLoc - 1] = 0;
            printf("\nRecord deleted - press ENTER to continue\n");
            cWait = getch();
        }
        return;
    }


/*----------------------------------------------------------------
        DISPLAY ALL COURSES
----------------------------------------------------------------*/
void DisplayAll(void)
{
    int iRecNum;                    /* record number     */
    int cWait;                      /* wait for keypress */

    _clearscreen(0);
    printf("\nRec# Key  Call#  Course ID  Enrollment");
    printf("\n-----------------------------------");
    for (iRecNum = 1; iRecNum <= 20; iRecNum++)
    {
        fseek(fpData, (iRecNum - 1) * sizeof(struct stCrsForm),
            SEEK_SET);
        fread(&svRec, sizeof(struct stCrsForm), 1, fpData);
        if (iKeyArray[iRecNum - 1] != 0)
        {
            printf("\n %2d  %3d   %3d   %-14s %2d",
                iRecNum, iKeyArray[iRecNum - 1], svRec.iCallNum,
                svRec.sCourse, svRec.iEnroll);
        }
    }
    printf("\n\nPress ENTER to continue...");
    cWait = getch();
    return;
}


/*----------------------------------------------------------------
        SAVE RECORD KEYS
----------------------------------------------------------------*/
void SaveKeys(void)
{
    int iRecNum;                    /* record number */
```

FIGURE 15.16 *Continued*

```
    for (iRecNum = 1; iRecNum <= 20; iRecNum++)
    {
        fprintf(fpKey, "%d\n", iKeyArray[iRecNum - 1]);
    }
    return;
}
```

FIGURE 15.16　*Continued*

```
Course Maintenance System

Select one:

    1.  Update enrollment
    2.  Add a course
    3.  Delete a course
    4.  Display all courses
    5.  Quit

Enter choice (1 - 5) ===>__
```

FIGURE 15.17　Menu Options for CHAP15D

```
UPDATE ENROLLMENT: Enter call number: 450

Error: Record does not exist - press 'Enter' to continue


UPDATE ENROLLMENT: Enter call number: 700

700    MATH120                 14

Enter new enrollment: 23
```

FIGURE 15.18　Choice 1: Update Enrollment

```
DELETE COURSE: Enter call number: 630

Error: Record does not exist - press 'Enter' to continue


DELETE COURSE: Enter call number: 900

Record deleted - press 'Enter' to continue
```

FIGURE 15.19   Choice 3: Delete a Course

```
Rec#  Key  Call#  Dept-Course#  Enrollment
-------------------------------------------
 1    400   400    ENG200          16
 2    300   300    CHEM201         21
 3    600   600    MGT330          29
 4    200   200    BIOL101         19
 5    500   500    HIST225         33
 7    700   700    MATH120         23
 8    800   800    PHYS251         20
 9    100   100    ACCT101         24
```

FIGURE 15.20   Choice 4: Display All Courses. Note that the sixth record has been deleted.

```
ADD COURSE: Enter call number: 600

Error: Record already exists - press ENTER to continue


ADD COURSE: Enter call number: 310
            Enter department & number: CIS252
            Enter student enrollment: 17

Call# 310 Added - press ENTER to continue
```

FIGURE 15.21   Choice 2: Add a Course

```
Rec#  Key  Call#  Dept-Course#  Enrollment
-------------------------------------------
 1    400   400    ENG200          16
 2    300   300    CHEM201         21
 3    600   600    MGT330          29
 4    200   200    BIOL101         19
 5    500   500    HIST225         33
 6    310   310    CIS252          17
 7    700   700    MATH120         23
 8    800   800    PHYS251         20
 9    100   100    ACCT101         24
```

FIGURE 15.22   Choice 4: Display All Courses. Note that the sixth record now holds the new course.

Processing Requirements:

- Define a sequential key file, a random data file, and a key array.
- Open the sequential key file (*r*), load the array, and close the file.
- Open the sequential key file (*w*) and the random data file (*r+*).
- Display the menu options, and prompt for a selection.
- Enter the data, and update the array and the random data file.
- After updating the file, copy the array to the sequential key file.
- Close the files.

Pseudocode:

START: Main
Call Set Up Key Array
Call Open Files
IF files opened
    Call Processing Loop
    Call Save Record Keys
    Close files
END IF
END

ENTER: Set Up Key Array
Open sequential key file for read
IF file not opened
    Print cannot open sequential key file for input
else
    LOOP for record number 1 to 20
        Read record key from sequential file
        Set array element to record key
    END LOOP
    Close sequential key file
END IF
RETURN

```
ENTER: Open Files
Open sequential key file for write
IF file not opened
    Print cannot open sequential key file for output
END IF
Open random data file for read plus
IF file not opened
    Print cannot open random data file
END IF
RETURN

ENTER: Processing Loop
Call Print Menu
LOOP while choice < 5
    BRANCH on choice:
            1: Call Update Enrollment
            2: Call Add Course
            3: Call Delete Course
            4: Call Display All Courses
    END BRANCH
    Call Print Menu
END LOOP
RETURN

ENTER: Print Menu
Clear screen
Print 1 title line
Print 1 heading line
Display processing choices:
        choice 1: Update enrollment
        choice 2: Add course
        choice 3: Delete course
        choice 4: Display all courses
        choice 5: Quit
Prompt and enter choice
LOOP while choice not = 1 to 5
        Prompt (error message) and reenter choice
END LOOP
RETURN

ENTER: Update Enrollment
Clear screen
Print Update Enrollment title
Call Look Up Call Number
IF input call number not found
    Print error message: RECORD DOES NOT EXIST
    Wait for keypress
else
    Seek record position
    Read record from random file
    Display record on screen
```

```
        Prompt and enter new enrollment
        Seek record position
        Write record to random file
END IF
RETURN


ENTER: Look Up Call Number
Set record number to 1
Set location to –1
Prompt and enter input call number
LOOP while record number < 20 and location = –1
        IF input call number found in key array
            Set location to record number
        END IF
        Add 1 to record number
END LOOP
RETURN


ENTER: Add Course
Clear screen
Print Add Course title
Call Look Up Call Number
IF input call number found
        Print error message: RECORD ALREADY EXISTS
        Wait for keypress
else
        Call Find First Empty Array Element
        Set key array element to input call number
        Set record call number to input call number
        Prompt and enter course ID
        Prompt and enter student enrollment
        Seek record position
        Write record to random file
        Print message record added to file
        Wait for keypress
END IF
RETURN


ENTER: Find First Empty Array Element
Set record number to 1
Set location to –1
LOOP while record number < 20 and location = –1
        IF element in key array = 0
            Set location to record number
        END IF
        Add 1 to record number
END LOOP
RETURN


ENTER: Delete Course
Clear screen
```

```
Print Delete Course title
Call Look Up Call Number
IF input call number not found
    Print error message: RECORD DOES NOT EXIST
    Wait for keypress
else
    Set key array element to 0
    Print message record deleted from file
    Wait for keypress
END IF
RETURN

ENTER: Display All Courses
Clear screen
Print 2 heading lines
LOOP for record number 1 to 20
    Seek record position
    Read record from random file
    IF key array element not = 0
        Print detail line:
            record number
            key array element
            call number
            course ID
            student enrollment
    END IF
END LOOP
Hold screen
RETURN

ENTER: Save Record Keys
LOOP for record number 1 to 20
    Write key array element to sequential key file
END LOOP
RETURN
```

Hierarchy Chart: See Figure 15.14.

Program Flowchart: See Figure 15.15.

Dissection of Sample Program CHAP15D

```
U P D A T E   E N R O L L M E N T:
void UpdEnroll(void)
{
    int   iRecNum;
    int   iLoc;
    char cWait:

    _clearscreen(0);
    printf("\nUPDATE ENROLLMENT: ");
    iLoc = LookUpCallNum();
```

The above statements declare the local variables required by the module, clear the screen, print the title line, and call the lookup module. *LookUpCallNum* prompts for and attempts to locate the input call number. Upon a return, a value is assigned to *iLoc*.

```
if (iLoc == -1)
{
    printf("\n\Error: Record does not exist ");
    printf(" - press ENTER to continue ");
    wait = getch();
}
```

In the following statements, if the lookup call number was not found in the array, then the segment prints the error message and waits for the user to continue.

```
else
{
    fseek(fpData, (iLoc - 1) * sizeof(struct stCrsForm),
        SEEK_SET);
    fread(&svRec, sizeof(struct stCrsForm), 1, fpData);
```

In the above statements, if the call number was found, then the fseek() moves the file pointer to the position in the data file that corresponds to the offset. The fread() gets the data from the random file and stores it in the course record.

```
    printf("\n%3d    %-14s    %2d\n", svRec.iCallNum,
        svRec.sCourse, svRec.iEnroll);
```

The above statement displays the record retrieved from the random data file on the screen. This is done to verify that the correct record has been retrieved by the program.

```
    printf("\nEnter new enrollment: ");
    scanf(" %d", &svRec.iEnroll);
```

The above statements prompt the user to enter the new student enrollment and place the input to the *rec.iEnroll* field of the course record.

```
    fseek(fpData, (iLoc - 1) * sizeof(struct stCrsForm),
        SEEK_SET);
    fwrite(&svRec, sizeof(struct stCrsForm), 1, fpData);
}
return;
}
```

The above statements reset the file pointer to the previous record position in the random file and write the data stored in the course record back to the file. Control then returns to the *PROCESSING LOOP* and displays the menu.

```
L O O K    U P    C A L L    N U M B E R:

int LookUpCallNum(void)
{
    int iRecNum = 1;
    int iLoc = -1;
    printf("Enter call number: ");
    scanf(" %d", &iCallNumIn);
```

The above statements declare and initialize record number and location. This is done in preparation for the call number lookup. Next, the program prompts the user to enter the call number and assigns the input to *iCallNumIn*.

```
    while (iRecNum <= 20 && iLoc == -1)
    {
        if (iCallNumIn == iKeyArray[iRecNum - 1])
        {
            iLoc = iRecNum;
        }
        iRecNum++;
    }
    return iLoc;
}
```

In the above statement, as long as *iRecNum* is less than or equal to 20 and *iLoc* equals –1, control searches the array for the input call number and increments *iRecNum*. If the input call number is found, then the program sets *iLoc* to *iRecNum*. Control exits the loop when either a match is found or the end of the array is encountered and returns *iLoc* to the calling statement.

A D D   A   C O U R S E:

```
void AddCourse(void)
{
    int   iRecNum;
    int   iLoc;
    char  cWait;

    _clearscreen(0);
    printf("\nADD COURSE: ");
    iLoc = LookUpCallNum();
    if (iLoc != -1)
    {
        printf("\n\nRecord already exists ");
        printf(" - press ENTER to continue ");
        cWait = getch();
    }
```

The above statements declare the local variables, clear the screen, print the title line, and branch to input and look up the call number. If the input call number is found in the array, then the body of the *if* statement prints the error message and waits for the user to continue.

```
    else
    {
        iLoc = FindEmptyRec();
        iKeyArray[iLoc - 1] = iCallNumIn;
        svRec.iCallNum = iCallNumIn;
```

The above statements branch and find the first empty element in the array, store the input call number in the array (first empty element), and assign the input call number to the *svRec.iCallNum* field of the course record.

```
        printf("          Enter course ID:   ");
        scanf(" %s", svRec.sCourse);
        printf("Enter student enrollment:   ");
        scanf(" %d", &svRec.iEnroll);
```

The above statements prompt for and enter the course ID and student enrollment and assign them to the *svRec.sCourse* and *svRec.iEnroll* fields, respectively.

```
        fseek(fpData, (iLoc - 1) * sizeof(struct stCrsForm),
            SEEK_SET);
        fwrite(&svRec, sizeof(struct stCrsForm), 1, fpData);
        printf("\nCall# %3d added - press ENTER to continue\n",
            iCallNumIn);
        cWait = getch();
    }
    return;
}
```

The above statements set the file pointer to the record location that corresponds to the array subscript and write the course record to the random data file. The printf() displays the add message, and getch() waits for the user to continue.

F I N D   E M P T Y   R E C O R D:

```
int FindEmptyRec(void)
{
    int iRecNum = 1;
    int iLoc = -1;

    while (iRecNum < 20 && iLoc == -1)
    {
        if (iKeyArray[iRecNum - 1] == 0)
        {
            iLoc = iRecNum;
        }
        iRecNum++;
    }
    return iLoc;
}
```

The above statements declare and initialize record number and location. As long as *iRecNum* is less than 20 and *iLoc* equals −1, control searches the array for the first empty element. If the value stored in the element is 0, then control sets *iLoc* to *iRecNum* and returns *iLoc* to the calling statement.

D E L E T E   C O U R S E:

```
void DletCourse(void)
{
    int    iLoc;
    char   cWait;

    _clearscreen(0);
    printf("\nDELETE COURSE: ");
```

```
        iLoc = LookUpCallNum();
        if (iLoc == -1)
        {
            printf("\n\nRecord does not exist ");
            printf(" - press 'Enter' to continue. ");
            cWait = getch();
        }
        else
        {
            iKeyArray[iLoc - 1] = 0;
            printf("\nRecord deleted - press ENTER to continue\n");
            cWait = getch();
        }
        return;
}
```

The above statements declare the local variables, clear the screen, print the title line, branch to input, and look up the call number. If the call number is not found in the array, the program prints the error message and waits for the user to continue. If the call number is found, the program replaces it with 0, prints the delete message, and waits for the user to continue.

D I S P L A Y   A L L   C O U R S E S:

```
void DisplayAll(void)
{
    int   iRecNum;
    char  cWait;

    _clearscreen(0);
    printf("\nRec# Key  Call#  Course ID#  Enrollment");
    printf("\n--------------------------------------");
    for (iRecNum = 1; iRecNum <= 20; iRecNum++)
    {
        fseek(fpData, (iRecNum - 1) * sizeof(struct stCrsForm),
            SEEK_SET);
        fread(&svRec, sizeof(struct stCrsForm), 1, fpData);
        if (iKeyArray[iRecNum - 1] != 0)
        {
            printf("\n %2d  %3d   %3d   %-14s %2d",
                iRecNum, iKeyArray[iRecNum - 1], svRec.iCallNum,
                svRec.sCourse, svRec.iEnroll);
        }
    }
    printf("\n\nPress ENTER to continue...");
    cWait = getch();
    return;
}
```

The above statements declare the local variables, clear the screen, and print the report heading lines. As long as *iRecNum* is less than or equal to 20, control executes the statements in the body of the loop.

The module seeks and reads a record from the random data file. If the call number stored in the corresponding element of the array is not equal to 0, the body of the *if* statement prints the record number, array key, and course data on the report. Otherwise, control skips the print statement and goes back to the *for* statement.

Notes and Tips

1. Sample program CHAP15D uses a menu to update the master file. Changes to the master file include the following: update student enrollment, add new course, delete old course, and print a list of all current courses.
2. Do not add a record to the master file if one already exists.
3. Do not delete or update a record that does not exist.

Tutorial CHAP15D

1. The objectives of this tutorial are to
   - display menu options for the processing activities
   - enter change data and update an indexed file
   - check for errors and display them on the screen
2. Read the program specifications and review the logic design tools for sample program CHAP15D.
3. Log on to your C editor, and enter the source code as shown in Figure 15.16. Save the program on your work disk as CHAP15D. Save frequently as you enter the code.
4. Compile, run, and debug your program. Use the updates shown in Figures 15.17 through 15.21.
5. When completed, compare your output report to the one shown in Figure 15.22.
6. Show your work to your instructor.

Quick Quiz

Answer the following questions.

1. In your own words, explain the processing activities performed by the *LookUp-CallNum* module.
2. In your own words, explain the processing activities performed by the *FindEmptyRec* module.
3. In your own words, describe the processing activities performed by the *UpdEnroll* module. Under what circumstances does the error message *"Record does not exist"* display on the screen?
4. Describe the processing activities performed by the *AddCourses* module. Under what circumstances does the error message *"Record already exists"* display on the screen?

5. Describe the processing activities performed by the *DletCourses* module. Under what circumstances does the error message *"Record does not exist"* display on the screen?

6. Did you have any problems or errors when you ran the sample program? If so, what were they and what did you do to correct them?

Summary

1. Indexed files store data on disk in random order. Although more complicated to work with, indexed files provide relatively fast access to the information stored on disk.

2. Indexed files use record keys to access the data and save disk space.

3. An indexed file is a pseudofile organization method that consists of a key array and a random access file. The array holds the record keys, and the random file holds the corresponding data.

4. To locate a given record, the program searches the array and compares the search key to the record keys stored in the array. On a match, the program uses the array subscript to access the data stored in the random file.

5. To create an indexed file, the programmer defines a key array and a random data file. The objective is to reserve disk space for the data and to set up an array to track the record keys.

6. Once disk space has been reserved for the records, the data is loaded into the file—the keys are stored in the array, and the records are written to the random file. Later, the array is copied to a sequential file for future reference.

7. After the file has been loaded, the records are read one by one and copied to an output report to verify that the data was correctly loaded into the file.

8. A delete is made by locating the key of the deleted record in the array and changing it to 0. A deleted record is not removed from the random file until a new record is written over the old one.

9. An add is made by locating the first empty element in the array. The new record key is stored in the array, and the data is written to the corresponding record position in the random file.

10. A change is made to an existing record by locating the key in the array, retrieving the corresponding record, updating the data, and writing the record back to the file.

Programming Projects

For each project, design the logic and write the modular structured program to produce the output. Model your program after the sample programs presented in the chapter. Verify your output.

Project 15–1   Overdue Accounts-1

Write a program to create an indexed file for the overdue accounts. Write a total of 30 empty records to the file.

Input (internal):
Define the account data structure and the members given below. (Field size and type are shown in parentheses.)

       Account number   (4 int)
       Customer name   (15 char)
       Days overdue   (2 int)
       Balance due   (6.2 float)

Output (disk files):
Sequential key file   (sqKey.fil)
Random data file   (rdData.fil)

Processing Requirements:

- Define and initialize the empty record.
- Define a sequential key file, a random data file, and a key array.
- Open the sequential key file *(w)* and the random data file *(w+)*.
- Set the elements of the array to 0.
- Write empty records to the random data file.
- After creating the file, copy the array to the sequential key file.
- Close the files.

Project 15–2   Overdue Accounts-2

Write a program to prompt the user to enter the data at the keyboard, and load the indexed file created in Project 15–1.

Input (disk files and keyboard):

Disk files: Sequential key file   (sqKey.fil)
               Random data file   (rdData.fil)

Keyboard: For each customer record, prompt for and enter the following data. (Field size and type are shown in parentheses.)

1. Account number   (4 int)
2. Customer name   (15 char)
3. Days overdue   (2 int)
4. Balance due   (6.2 float)

File Data (keyboard):
Use the data given below to load the indexed file. (The numbers shown above the columns correspond to the fields described for the input.)

1	2	3	4
6350	Susan Cope	90	600.00
2730	Rita Fox	90	740.00
3100	Alvin Porter	90	550.00
4080	Corey Adkins	30	233.00
5260	Brian Knox	30	625.00
7720	Lisa Wilson	60	417.00
9200	Tori Landis	90	235.00

4890	Amy Wyatt	30	700.00
1010	David Ryan	90	400.00
9630	Pat Rankin	60	342.00
2450	Marie Hill	30	754.00
8540	Matt Hart	90	900.00

Output (disk files):

Sequential key file   (sqKey.fil)
Random data file   (rdData.fil)

Processing Requirements:

- Define a sequential key file, a random data file, and an array.
- Open the sequential key file *(r)*, load the array, and close the file.
- Open the sequential key file *(w)* and the random data file *(r+)*.
- Prompt for and enter the data.
- Store the record keys in the array, and write the input to the random data file.
- After loading the file, copy the array to the sequential key file.
- Close the files.

Project 15–3   Overdue Accounts-3

Write a menu program that allows the user to select from several file-updating options. Prompt and enter the data, check for errors, and update the indexed file from Project 15–2. Write the input errors to an error log.

Menu Choices:

1. Update accounts

2. Add accounts

3. Delete accounts

4. Display all accounts

5. Quit

Input (disk files and keyboard):

Disk files: Sequential key file   (sqKey.fil)
                  Random data file   (rdData.fil)

Keyboard: For options 1–3, prompt for and enter the following data:

Option	Input Data
1	Account number, customer name, days overdue, and amount due
2	Account number, customer name, days overdue, and amount due
3	Account number

File Data (keyboard):

Enter the updates in the random order shown. For each, use the menu option to apply the data to the record specified by the account number.

Menu Option	Account Number	Customer Name	Days Overdue	Balance Due
delete	1450			

update	4890	Amy Clark	30	700.00
add	1000	Sarah Brooks	60	220.00
delete	8540			
update	1010	Ryan Davis	90	400.00
add	9630	Pat Rankin	60	342.00
add	9700	Adam Norris	60	475.00
update	6350	Susan Cope	60	600.00
update	2450	Marie Hill	30	700.00
delete	3100			
add	4080	Corey Adkins	30	233.00
update	2730	Rita Fox	30	740.00
update	9200	Tori Landis	90	300.00
add	4900	Marla Stevens	90	594.00
update	2740	Tia Marlowe	30	135.00

Output (disk files):

Sequential key file	(sqKey.fil)
Random data file	(rdData.fil)

Processing Requirements:

- Define a sequential key file, a random data file, and an array.
- Open the sequential key file *(r)*, load the array, and close the file.
- Open the sequential key file *(w)* and the random data file *(r+)*.
- Display the menu options, and prompt for a selection.
- Enter the data, and update the array and the random data file.
- After updating the file, copy the array to the sequential key file.
- Close the files.

Project 15–4   Overdue Accounts-4

Write a program to read the updated indexed file in Project 15–3, and print the overdue accounts report shown below. Accumulate a total for amount due, and print the total at the end of the report.

```
Author                OVERDUE ACCOUNTS              Page 01
                         mm/dd/yy


Acct Number     Customer Name     Days Overdue     Amount Due

   9999         X----------X           99            999.99
    :                :                  :               :
    :                :                  :               :
   9999         X----------X           99            999.99

                                          Total:    9999.99
```

Processing Requirements:

- Define a sequential key file, a random data file, and an array.
- Open the sequential key file *(r)*, load the array, and close the file.
- Open the random data file in *read (r+)* mode.
- Write the nonempty account records to the report.

- Accumulate a total for amount due, and print it at the end of the report.
- Close the random data file.

Project 15–5   Sales Profit-1

Write a program to create an indexed file for the sales department. Write a total of 20 empty records to the file.

Input (internal):

Define the sales data structure and the members given below. (Field size and type are shown in parentheses.)

Salesperson number	(3 int)
Salesperson name	(15 char)
Total sales	(8.2 float)
Cost of sales	(7.2 float)

Output (disk files):

Sequential key file	(sqKey.fil)
Random data file	(rdData.fil)

Processing Requirements:

- Define and initialize the empty record.
- Define a sequential key file, a random data file, and a key array.
- Open the sequential key file *(w)* and the random data file *(w+)*.
- Set the elements in the array to 0.
- Write empty records to the random data file.
- After creating the file, copy the array to the sequential key file.
- Close the files.

Project 15–6   Sales Profit-2

Write a program to prompt the user to enter the data at the keyboard, and load the indexed file created in Project 15–5.

Input (disk files and keyboard):

Disk files: Sequential key file   (sqKey.fil)
           Random data file   (rdData.fil)

Keyboard: For each sales record, prompt for and enter the following data. (Field size and type are shown in parentheses.)

1. Salesperson number (3 int)
2. Salesperson name (15 char)
3. Total sales (8.2 float)
4. Cost of sales (7.2 float)

File Data (keyboard):

Use the data given below to load the indexed file. (The numbers shown above the columns correspond to the fields described for the input.)

1	2	3	4
400	Tara Perkins	12710.14	9735.38
700	Dennis Tian	4567.51	3119.22
300	Roy Hickle	2245.78	1072.49
100	Lisa Conrad	8120.52	6450.71
900	Ann Zimmerman	5793.59	4204.45

Output (disk files):

Sequential key file   (sqKey.fil)
Random data file   (rdData.fil)

Processing Requirements:

- Define a sequential key file, a random data file, and an array.
- Open the sequential key file *(r)*, load the array, and close the file.
- Open the sequential key file *(w)* and the random data file *(r+)*.
- Prompt for and enter the data.
- Store the record keys in the array, and write the sales data to the random data file.
- After loading the file, copy the array to the sequential key file.
- Close the files.

Project 15–7 Sales Profit-3

Write a menu program that allows the user to select from several file-processing options. Prompt and enter the data, check for errors, and update the sales file from Project 15–6. Write the input errors to an error log.

Menu Choices:

1. Update sales records
2. Add sales records
3. Delete sales records
4. Display all sales records
5. Quit

Input (disk files and keyboard):

Disk files: Sequential key file   (sqKey.fil)
                 Random data file   (sqData.fil)

Keyboard: For options 1–3, prompt for and enter the following data:

Option	Input Data
1	Salesperson number, salesperson name, total sales, and cost of sales
2	Salesperson number, salesperson name, total sales, and cost of sales
3	Salesperson number

File Data (keyboard):

Enter the updates in the random order shown. For each, use the menu option to apply the data to the record specified by the salesperson number.

Menu Option	Salesperson Number	Name	Total Sales	Cost of Sales
add	900	Ann Zimmerman	5793.59	4204.45
update	340	David Kock	4339.16	2124.83
update	300	Roy Henderson	2245.78	1072.49
update	490	Michael Torres	9634.28	5593.15
add	940	Sean Zorich	7465.92	5641.39
update	700	Dennis Tian	4567.51	3191.22
update	250	Robert Minelli	3974.63	2016.24
delete	400			
add	200	Allison Dunn	6518.02	4131.78

Output (disk files):

Sequential key file   (sqKey.fil)

Random data file   (rdData.fil)

Processing Requirements:

- Define a sequential key file, a random data file, and a key array.
- Open the sequential key file *(r)*, load the array, and close the file.
- Open the sequential key file *(w)* and the random data file *(r+)*.
- Display the menu options, and prompt for a selection.
- Enter the data, and update the array and the random data file.
- After updating the file, copy the array to the sequential key file.
- Close the files.

Project 15–8   Sales Profit-4

Write a program to read the updated indexed file in Project 15–7, and print the sales profit report shown below. Accumulate a total for net profit, and print the total at the end of the report.

```
Author                    SALES PROFIT REPORT              Page 01
                              mm/dd/yy

                       Total            Cost of          Net
Num    Salesperson     Sales            Sales            Profit
-----------------------------------------------------------------
999    X---------X     99999.99         99999.99         99999.99
 :          :             :                :                :
 :          :             :                :                :
999    X---------X     99999.99         99999.99         99999.99

                                        Total:           999999.99
```

Processing Requirements:

- Define a sequential key file, a random data file, and an array.
- Open the sequential key file *(r)*, load the array, and close the file.
- Open the random data file in *read (r+)* mode.
- Write the nonempty sales records to the output report.
- Accumulate a total for net profit, and print it at the end of the report.
- Close the random data file.

Appendix A
ASCII Table

Dec	Char	
0	NUL	(null)
1	SOH	control char
2	STX	control char
3	ETX	control char
4	EOT	control char
5	ENQ	control char
6	ACK	control char
7	BEL	(bell)
8	BS	control char
9	HT	(tab)
10	LF	(line feed)
11	VT	(home)
12	FF	(form feed)
13	CR	(return)
14	SO	control char
15	SI	control char
16	DLE	control char
17	DC1	control char
18	DC2	control char
19	DC3	control char
20	DC4	control char
21	NAK	control char
22	SYN	control char

Dec	Char	
23	ETB	control char
24	CAN	control char
25	EM	control char
26	SUB	control char
27	ESC	(escape)
28	FS	(cursor right)
29	GS	(cursor left)
30	RS	(cursor up)
31	US	(cursor down)
32	SP	(space)
33	!	
34	"	
35	#	
36	$	
37	%	
38	&	
39	'	
40	(	
41	)	
42	*	
43	+	
44	,	
45	-	

Dec	Char	Dec	Char
46	.	87	W
47	/	88	X
48	0	89	Y
49	1	90	Z
50	2	91	[
51	3	92	\
52	4	93	]
53	5	94	^
54	6	95	—
55	7	96	`
56	8	97	a
57	9	98	b
58	:	99	c
59	;	00	d
60	<	01	e
61	=	02	f
62	>	03	g
63	?	04	h
64	@	05	i
65	A	106	j
66	B	107	k
67	C	108	l
68	D	109	m
69	E	110	n
70	F	111	o
71	G	112	p
72	H	113	q
73	I	114	r
74	J	115	s
75	K	116	t
76	L	117	u
77	M	118	v
78	N	119	w
79	O	120	x
80	P	121	y
81	Q	122	z
82	R	123	{
83	S	124		
84	T	125	}
85	U	126	~
86	V	127	DEL (delete)

Appendix B
Programming Standards

Standards provide uniform guidelines for planning, coding, and testing programs. Programming standards are established by management to improve the quality of its information systems and to increase the productivity of the programmers. The standards below were used to construct the sample programs in this textbook.

General

Plan and design the logic first. Use the hierarchy chart to identify the modules and the relationships among them. Use the logic design (flowchart or pseudocode) to write the program code. Keep the code simple. Write as if you were coding the program for someone else to read and maintain.

Variables

For a single-word variable name, append the data type, capitalize the first letter, and lowercase the remaining letters. For a multiple-word variable name, capitalize the first letter in each word. Each name should be self-documenting. Examples of valid variable names are *iCount*, *fProfit*, *fTopSales*, *sFirstName*, *cChoice*, *fCostOfSales*, and *iQuantOnHand*.

Append one of the following prefixes to the identifier name to specify the type of the data stored at the variable:

Use *f* for float.
Use *d* for double.
Use *i* for integer.
Use *l* for long.
Use *s* for character string.
Use *c* for single character.

Statements

Code one statement (or function) per line. If the statement is too long for one line, break the statement, indent four positions, and continue on the next line. See the following example.

```
printf(stdprn, "\r\n %4d  %-20s %7.2f    %7.2f",
    iSalesNum, sName, fSales, fCommission);
```

Modules

Names: Capitalize the first letter in each word used to create the module name. Each name should be self-documenting. Examples of module names are *PrnHeadings()*, *ProcessLoop()*, *InputNum()*, *CalcCommis()*, *PrnDetail()*, and *PrnTopSales()*.

Order: The *main()* is always first. After *main()*, the modules are arranged in processing order; that is, in the order that they are called and executed by the program.

Braces and Indentation: The statement body of each module is enclosed within braces and indented (aligned) four positions. See the following example.

```
/*----------------------------------------------
            PRINT DETAIL LINE
----------------------------------------------*/
void PrnDetail(void)
{
    printf("\n%4d  %-20s %7.2f    %7.2f",
        iSalesNum, sName, fSales, fCommission);
    return;
}
```

Program Documentation

Program documentation appears at the top of the program and includes the name of the program, the purpose of the program, the program file name, the programmer, and the run date. See the following example.

```
/*-------------------------------------------------------------
PAYROLL ROSTER: Compute and print a weekly payroll roster. Hours
worked over 40 are paid overtime.

Program:    PAYROLL
Author:     David M. Collopy
Date:       mm/dd/yy
Project:    Lab 5, page 151, exercise 5-2
*************************************************************/
```

Preprocessing Directives

Group the preprocessing directives together. See the following example.

```
/*-------- PREPROCESSING DIRECTIVES ------------------------*/

#include <stdio.h>
#include <string.h>
#include <graph.h>
```

Function Prototypes

Group the function prototypes together. Write a brief comment to describe each. See the following example.

```
/*----------- FUNCTION PROTOTYPES ---------------------------*/

void PrnHeadings(void);      /*  print report headings   */
void ProcessLoop(void);      /*  processing loop         */
void InputNum(void);         /*  input salesperson number */
void InputOtherData(void);   /*  input other sales data   */
float CalcCommis(void);      /*  calculate commission     */
void FindTopSales(void);     /*  find top salesperson     */
void PrnDetail(float);       /*  print detail line        */
void PrnTopSales(void);      /*  print top sales          */
```

Program Setup

This section defines the titles and column headings, record formats, and constants and variables required by the program.

Report Titles and Headings: As a standard, the variables (written in capital letters) PT, HL, DL, TL, and SL are used to define the Page Titles, Heading Lines, Detail Lines, Total Lines, and Summary Lines, respectively. See the following example.

```
/*-------- PROGRAM SETUP ------------------------------------*/

/*>  R E P O R T    T I T L E S    A N D    H E A D I N G S     <*/

char PT1[] = " B E A L E - R O S S    C O R P O R A T I O N   ";
char PT2[] = "               Monthly Sales Report              ";
char HL1[] = "S a l e s p e r s o n      Monthly      Earned   ";
char HL2[] = "Number  Name                 Sales    Commissions";
char HL3[] = "-------------------------------------------------";
char SL1[] = "  Top Salesperson: ";
char SL2[] = "Top Monthly Sales: ";
```

Records: Record formats are defined after the report titles and column headings. Write a brief comment to describe each. See the following example.

```
/*>  S A L E S    R E C O R D                              <*/

int   iSalesNum:                /*  salesperson number */
char  sName[21];                /*  salesperson name   */
float fSales;                   /*  monthly sales      */
```

Program Variables: The program constants and variables are defined after the record formats. Write a brief comment to describe each. Follow the example shown below.

```
/*>  P R O G R A M   V A R I A B L E S                        <*/

char  sTopName[21];              /*  top salesperson    */
float fTopSales = 0.0;           /*  top monthly sales  */
```

Loops and Decisions

As a rule, enclose the statement body in braces and indent each statement four positions. Although C does not require braces for a one-statement body, we will continue to use them for clarity. See the following examples.

```
while:      InputData();
            while (iCredits < 45)
            {
                Calculations();
                PrnDetail();
                InputData();
            }
nested      iOuter = 1;
while:      while (iOuter <= 3)
            {
                printf("\nOutside %d", iOuter);
                iInner = 1;
                while (iInner <= 2)
                {
                    printf("\n    Inside %d", iInner);
                    iInner++;
                }
                iOuter++;
            }
do/while: InputID();
            do
            {
                InputOtherData();
                CalcResults();
                PrnDetail();
                InputID();
            }
            while (iStudentID != 0);
nested      iOuter = 1;
do/while: do
            {
                printf("\nOutside %d", iOuter);
                iInner = 1;
                do
                {
```

```
                        printf("\n    Inside %d", iInner);
                        iInner++;
                    }
                    while (iInner <= 2);
                    iOuter++;
                }
                while (iOuter <= 3);
for:            for (iNum = 1; iNum <= 5; iNum++)
                {
                    CalcSquare();
                    CalcSum();
                    PrnDetail();
                }
nested         for (iOuter = 1; iOuter <= 3; iOuter++)
for:            {
                    printf(\nOutside %d", iOuter);
                    for (iInner = 1; iInner <= 2; iInner++)
                    {
                        printf(\n    Inside %d", iInner);
                    }
                }
if:            if (iCredits < 45)
                {
                    printf("Welcome freshman");
                }
nested         if (iCredits < 45)
if:             {
                    if (iFemale == 1)
                    {
                        iFemaleFresh++;
                        printf("Welcome lady freshman");
                    }
                }
if/else:       if (iCredits < 45)
                {
                    printf("Welcome freshman");
                }
                else
                {
                    printf("Welcome upper classman");
                }
nested         if (iCredits < 45)
if/else:        {
                    printf("Welcome freshman");
                 }
                 else if (iCredits < 90)
                 {
                    printf("Welcome sophomore");
                 }
```

```
            else if (iCredits < 135)
            {
                printf("Welcome junior");
            }
            else
            {
                printf("Welcome senior");
            }
switch:    switch (iChoice)
            {
                case 1:
                    printf("Action movie\n");
                    break;
                case 2:
                    printf("Comedy movie\n");
                    break;
                case 3:
                    printf("Drama movie\n");
                    break;
                case 4:
                    printf("Scifi movie\n");
                    break;
                default:
                    printf("Invalid choice\n");
                    break;
            }
```

Files and Structures

File Pointers: Append *fp* to file pointer identifier names. Examples of valid file pointer variables are *fpInv*, *fpOvrdue*, *fpPayroll*, and *fpMFI*.

File Types: Append one of the following prefixes to the file identifier name to specify the file type:

  Use *tx* for text file—example, *txGrades.fil*
  Use *sq* for sequential file—example, *sqCrs.fil*
  Use *rd* for random file—example, *rdData.fil*

Note: Use the file extension *fil* to indicate that the dataset represents a file.

Structures: Append *st* to structure tags and *sv* to structure variables. See the following example.

```
    struct stAcctForm
    {
        int    iAcctNum;
        char   sCustName[30];
        float  fAmtDue;
    };
    struct stAcctForm svAcctRec;
```

Appendix C
Input/Output Functions

Input Functions

Standard Input

getchar():   The getchar() function reads a character from the keyboard.

Example:
```
char cCharIn;
cCharIn = getchar();
```

The first character entered at the keyboard is assigned to *cCharIn*. The getchar() function waits for the enter-keypress before assigning the character to the variable.

gets():   The gets() function reads a string from the keyboard.

Example:
```
char sStringIn[21];
sStringIn = gets();
```

The input stream, up to 20 characters, is assigned to *sStringIn*. The gets() function waits for the enter-keypress before assigning the data to the variable.

scanf():   The scanf() function formats data read from the keyboard.

Example:
```
float fScore;
scanf(" %f", &fScore);
```

The scanf() function reads the input stream, converts it to a floating-point value, and assigns the result to *fScore*.

File Input

fgetc():   The fgetc() function reads a character from a specific file.

Example:
```
FILE *fpFileIn;
char cCharIn;
cCharIn = fgetc(fpFileIn);
```

The fgetc() function reads a character from the file specified by the file pointer argument *fpFileIn* and assigns it to the variable called *cCharIn*.

fgets():   The fgets() function reads a string from a specific file.

Example:
```
FILE *fpFileIn;
char sStringIn[21];
fgets(sStringIn, 20, fpFileIn);
```

The fgets() function reads up to 20 characters of data from the file specified by the file pointer argument fpFileIn and assigns the input to sStringIn.

fscanf():   The fscanf() function uses a format specifier to read data from a specific file.

Example:
```
FILE *fpFileIn;
int   iNumIn;
char sStringIn[21];
fscanf(fpFileIn, " %d %s", &iNumIn, sStringIn);
```

The fscanf() function reads two items from the file, converts the first one to an integer and the second to a string, and assigns the results to *iNumIn* and *sStringIn*, respectively.

Output Functions

Standard Output

putchar():   The putchar() function prints a character on the screen.

Example:
```
char cCharOut = 'A';
putchar(cCharOut);
putchar('B');
```

The first putchar() prints the letter *A* on the screen, whereas the second prints the letter *B*. The complete output is *AB*.

puts():   The puts() function prints a string on the screen.

Example:
```
char sName[] = "Daniel";
puts(sName);
puts(" Webster");
```

The first puts() prints *Daniel* on the screen, and the second prints *Webster*. The complete output is *Daniel Webster*.

printf():   The printf() function displays the output on the screen.

Example:
```
float fScore = 87.4;
printf("Your test score is: %f", fScore);
```

The printf() function prints the message enclosed within double quotes and the score on the screen: *Your test score is: 87.4.*

File Output

fputc():   The fputc() function writes a character to a specific file.

Example:
```
FILE *fpFileOut;
char cCharOut = 'A';
```

```
            fputc(cCharOut, fpFileOut);
```

The fputc() function writes the letter *A* to the file specified by the file pointer argument *fp-FileOut*.

fputs():   The fputs() function writes a string to a specific file.

Example: ```
FILE *fpFileOut;
char sStringOut[] = "Hammers 24";
fputc(sStringOut, fpFileOut);
```

The fputc() function writes the string data to the file specified by the file argument *fp-FileOut*.

**fprintf():**   The fprintf() function writes the output to a specific file.

**Example:**   ```
FILE *fpFileOut;
char sDesc[] = "Hammers";
int  iQuant = 24;
fprintf(fpFileOut, "%s %d\n", sDesc, iQuant);
```

The fprintf() function writes the item description and item quantity to the file specified by the file pointer argument *fpFileOut*.

Note: These functions require the *stdio.h* header file.

Appendix D
Math and Related Functions

The basic math, trigonometric, and logarithmic functions require the *math.h* header file, whereas the random number functions require the *stdio.h* header file.

Basic Math Functions

abs(x):   The abs(x) function returns the absolute value of the integer x. The argument and return value are type *integer*.

Example: `abs(4)   returns 4`
`abs(-4)  returns 4`

fabs(x):   The fabs(x) function returns the absolute value of x. The argument and return value are type *double*.

Example: `fabs(5.63)   returns 5.0`
`fabs(-5.63)  returns 5.0`

ceil(x):   The ceil(x) function returns x raised to the nearest whole number. The argument and return value are type *double*.

Example: `ceil(7.15)   returns 8.0`
`ceil(-7.15)  returns -7.0`

floor(x):   The floor(x) function returns x lowered to the nearest whole number. The argument and the return value are type *double*.

Example: `floor(7.15)   returns 7.0`
`floor(-7.15)  returns -8.0`

pow(x, y):   The pow(x, y) function returns the floating-point value x^y. The arguments x and y and return value are type *double*.

Example: `pow(7.0, 2.0) returns 49.0`

sqrt(x):   The sqrt(x) function returns the square root of *x*. The argument and return value are type *double*.

Example: `sqrt(81.0) returns 9.0`

Trigonometric Functions

sin(x):   The sin(x) function returns the sine of angle *x*. The argument (expressed in radians) and return value are type *double*.

Example: `sin(45.0) returns 0.8509`

cos(x):   The cos(x) function returns the cosine of angle *x*. The argument (expressed in radians) and return value are type *double*.

Example: `cos(10.0) returns -0.8390`

tan(x):   The tan(x) function returns the tangent of angle *x*. The argument (expressed in radians) and return value are type *double*.

Example: `tan(25.0) returns -0.1335`

Logarithmic Functions

exp(x):   The exp(x) function returns the natural logarithm e^x. The argument *x* and return value are type *double*.

Example: `exp(.637) returns 2.8907`

log(x):   The log(x) function returns the natural logarithm of the positive argument *x*. The argument *x* and return value are type *double*.

Example: `log(7.14) returns 4.4874`

log10(x):   The log10(x) function returns the base ten logarithm of the positive argument *x*. The argument *x* and return value are type *double*.

Example: `log10(14.3) returns 2.2505`

Random Number Functions

rand(x):   The rand(x) function returns a random integer in the range 0 to 32767. It returns the same set of integers each time the function is executed.

srand(x):   The srand(x) function seeds the random number generator and changes the set of numbers returned by rand() each time it is executed.

Index